SOME COMMONLY USED SYMBOLS

Symbol	Definition
APV	Adjusted present value
BV	Book value
C_t	Cash flow at time t
CEQ_t	Certainty-equivalent cash flow at time t
DIV_t	Dividend payment at time t
D	Market value of firm's debt
DEP_t	Depreciation in year t
DF_t	Discount factor for cash flow in period t
e	2.718 (base for natural logarithms)
E	Market value of firm's equity
EPS_t	Earnings per share in year t
EX	Exercise price of option
$f_{\$/£}$	Forward rate of exchange between dollars and pounds
g	Growth rate
i_t	Expected inflation in year t
IRR	Internal rate of return
LCF_t	Lease's cash outflow in year t
NPV	Net present value
P_t	Price at time t
PV	Present value
PVGO	Present value of growth opportunities
r_t	Expected rate of return (or cost of capital) in period t. We omit the subscript where the expected return is identical in each period.
$\tilde{r}_t$	Uncertain actual rate of return in period t
r_D	Expected rate of return on firm's debt
r_E	Expected rate of return on firm's equity
r_f	Risk-free interest rate
r_m	Expected rate of return on the market portfolio
$r_\$$	Dollar rate of interest
$s_{SFr/\$}$	Spot rate of exchange between Swiss francs and dollars
t	Time
T_c	Rate of corporate income tax
T_p	Rate of personal income tax
V	Market value of firm: $V = D + E$
y	Yield to maturity
β	Beta: A measure of market risk
δ	Delta: Hedge ratio
ρ_{12}	Rho: Correlation coefficient between investments 1 and 2
σ	Sigma: Standard deviation
σ_{12}	Covariance of investment 1 with investment 2
σ^2	Sigma squared: Variance
Σ	Capital sigma: "The sum of"

Principles *of*
Corporate Finance, Concise Edition

THE MCGRAW-HILL/IRWIN SERIES IN FINANCE, INSURANCE, AND REAL ESTATE

Stephen A. Ross, Franco Modigliani Professor of Finance and Economics, Sloan School of Management, Massachusetts Institute of Technology, Consulting Editor

Financial Management

Adair
Excel Applications for Corporate Finance
First Edition

Block, Hirt, and Danielsen
Foundations of Financial Management
Thirteenth Edition

Brealey, Myers, and Allen
Principles of Corporate Finance
Tenth Edition

Brealey, Myers, and Allen
Principles of Corporate Finance, Concise
Second Edition

Brealey, Myers, and Marcus
Fundamentals of Corporate Finance
Sixth Edition

Brooks
FinGame Online 5.0

Bruner
Case Studies in Finance: Managing for Corporate Value Creation
Sixth Edition

Chew
The New Corporate Finance: Where Theory Meets Practice
Third Edition

Cornett, Adair, and Nofsinger
Finance: Applications and Theory
First Edition

DeMello
Cases in Finance
Second Edition

Grinblatt (editor)
Stephen A. Ross, Mentor: Influence through Generations

Grinblatt and Titman
Financial Markets and Corporate Strategy
Second Edition

Higgins
Analysis for Financial Management
Ninth Edition

Kellison
Theory of Interest
Third Edition

Kester, Ruback, and Tufano
Case Problems in Finance
Twelfth Edition

Ross, Westerfield, and Jaffe
Corporate Finance
Ninth Edition

Ross, Westerfield, Jaffe, and Jordan
Corporate Finance: Core Principles and Applications
Second Edition

Ross, Westerfield, and Jordan
Essentials of Corporate Finance
Seventh Edition

Ross, Westerfield, and Jordan
Fundamentals of Corporate Finance
Ninth Edition

Shefrin
Behavioral Corporate Finance: Decisions That Create Value
First Edition

White
Financial Analysis with an Electronic Calculator
Sixth Edition

Investments

Bodie, Kane, and Marcus
Essentials of Investments
Eighth Edition

Bodie, Kane, and Marcus
Investments
Eighth Edition

Hirt and Block
Fundamentals of Investment Management
Ninth Edition

Hirschey and Nofsinger
Investments: Analysis and Behavior
Second Edition

Jordan and Miller
Fundamentals of Investments: Valuation and Management
Fifth Edition

Stewart, Piros, and Heisler
Running Money: Professional Portfolio Management
First Edition

Sundaram and Das
Derivatives: Principles and Practice
First Edition

Financial Institutions and Markets

Rose and Hudgins
Bank Management and Financial Services
Eighth Edition

Rose and Marquis
Money and Capital Markets: Financial Institutions and Instruments in a Global Marketplace
Tenth Edition

Saunders and Cornett
Financial Institutions Management: A Risk Management Approach
Seventh Edition

Saunders and Cornett
Financial Markets and Institutions
Fourth Edition

International Finance

Eun and Resnick
International Financial Management
Fifth Edition

Kuemmerle
Case Studies in International Entrepreneurship: Managing and Financing Ventures in the Global Economy
First Edition

Robin
International Corporate Finance
First Edition

Real Estate

Brueggeman and Fisher
Real Estate Finance and Investments
Fourteenth Edition

Ling and Archer
Real Estate Principles: A Value Approach
Third Edition

Financial Planning and Insurance

Allen, Melone, Rosenbloom, and Mahoney
Retirement Plans: 401(k)s, IRAs, and Other Deferred Compensation Approaches
Tenth Edition

Altfest
Personal Financial Planning
First Edition

Harrington and Niehaus
Risk Management and Insurance
Second Edition

Kapoor, Dlabay, and Hughes
Focus on Personal Finance: An Active Approach to Help You Develop Successful Financial Skills
Third Edition

Kapoor, Dlabay, and Hughes
Personal Finance
Ninth Edition

Principles *of* Corporate Finance, Concise Edition

SECOND EDITION

Richard A. Brealey
Professor of Finance
London Business School

Stewart C. Myers
Robert C. Merton (1970) Professor of Finance
Sloan School of Management
Massachusetts Institute of Technology

Franklin Allen
Nippon Life Professor of Finance
The Wharton School
University of Pennsylvania

McGraw-Hill Irwin

McGraw-Hill Irwin

PRINCIPLES OF CORPORATE FINANCE, CONCISE EDITION

Published by McGraw-Hill/Irwin, a business unit of The McGraw-Hill Companies, Inc., 1221 Avenue of the Americas, New York, NY, 10020. Copyright © 2011, 2009 by The McGraw-Hill Companies, Inc. All rights reserved. No part of this publication may be reproduced or distributed in any form or by any means, or stored in a database or retrieval system, without the prior written consent of The McGraw-Hill Companies, Inc., including, but not limited to, in any network or other electronic storage or transmission, or broadcast for distance learning.

Some ancillaries, including electronic and print components, may not be available to customers outside the United States.

This book is printed on acid-free paper.

1 2 3 4 5 6 7 8 9 0 RJE/RJE 1 0 9 8 7 6 5 4 3 2 1 0

ISBN 978-0-07-353074-1
MHID 0-07-353074-3

Vice president and editor-in-chief: *Brent Gordon*
Publisher: *Douglas Reiner*
Executive editor: *Michele Janicek*
Director of development: *Ann Torbert*
Development editor II: *Karen L. Fisher*
Vice president and director of marketing: *Robin J. Zwettler*
Marketing director: *Rhonda Seelinger*
Senior marketing manager: *Melissa S. Caughlin*
Vice president of editing, design, and production: *Sesha Bolisetty*
Project manager: *Dana M. Pauley*
Lead production supervisor: *Michael R. McCormick*
Interior designer: *Laurie J. Entringer*
Media project manager: *Suresh Babu, Hurix Systems Pvt. Ltd.*
Typeface: *10/12 Garamond BE Regular*
Compositor: *Laserwords Private Limited*
Printer: *R. R. Donnelley*

Library of Congress Cataloging-in-Publication Data

Brealey, Richard A.
    Principles of corporate finance/Richard A. Brealey, Stewart C. Myers, Franklin Allen.—Concise ed., 2nd ed.
       p. cm.—(The McGraw-Hill/Irwin series in finance, insurance, and real estate)
    Includes index.
    ISBN-13: 978-0-07-353074-1 (alk. paper)
    ISBN-10: 0-07-353074-3 (alk. paper)
    1. Corporations—Finance. I. Myers, Stewart C. II. Allen, Franklin, 1956-III. Title.
HG4026.B6673 2011
658.15—dc22   2010005406

www.mhhe.com

To Our Parents ├─────────────────────────────

About the Authors

▶ Richard A. Brealey

Professor of Finance at the London Business School. He is the former president of the European Finance Association and a former director of the American Finance Association. He is a fellow of the British Academy and has served as a special adviser to the Governor of the Bank of England and director of a number of financial institutions. Other books written by Professor Brealey include *Introduction to Risk and Return from Common Stocks.*

▶ Stewart C. Myers

Robert C. Merton (1970) Professor of Finance at MIT's Sloan School of Management. He is past president of the American Finance Association and a research associate of the National Bureau of Economic Research. His research has focused on financing decisions, valuation methods, the cost of capital, and financial aspects of government regulation of business. Dr. Myers is a director of Entergy Corporation and The Brattle Group, Inc. He is active as a financial consultant.

▶ Franklin Allen

Nippon Life Professor of Finance at the Wharton School of the University of Pennsylvania. He is past president of the American Finance Association, Western Finance Association, and Society for Financial Studies. His research has focused on financial innovation, asset price bubbles, comparing financial systems, and financial crises. He is a scientific adviser at Sveriges Riksbank (Sweden's central bank).

This book describes the theory and practice of corporate finance. We hardly need to explain why financial managers have to master the practical aspects of their job, but we should spell out why down-to-earth managers need to bother with theory.

Managers learn from experience how to cope with routine problems. But the best managers are also able to respond to change. To do so you need more than time-honored rules of thumb; you must understand *why* companies and financial markets behave the way they do. In other words, you need a *theory* of finance.

Does that sound intimidating? It shouldn't. Good theory helps you to grasp what is going on in the world around you. It helps you to ask the right questions when times change and new problems need to be analyzed. It also tells you which things you do *not* need to worry about. Throughout this book we show how managers use financial theory to solve practical problems.

Of course, the theory presented in this book is not perfect and complete—no theory is. There are some famous controversies where financial economists cannot agree. We have not glossed over these disagreements. We set out the arguments for each side and tell you where we stand.

Much of this book is concerned with understanding what financial managers do and why. But we also say what financial managers *should* do to increase company value. Where theory suggests that financial managers are making mistakes, we say so, while admitting that there may be hidden reasons for their actions. In brief, we have tried to be fair but to pull no punches.

This book may be your first view of the world of modern finance theory. If so, you will read first for new ideas, for an understanding of how finance theory translates into practice, and occasionally, we hope, for entertainment. But eventually you will be in a position to make financial decisions, not just study them. At that point you can turn to this book as a reference and guide.

▶ Changes in the Second Edition

We are proud of the success of the first edition of *Principles,* and we have done our best to make the second edition even better.

What is new in the second edition? First, we have rewritten and refreshed several basic chapters. Content remains much the same, but we think that the revised chapters are simpler and flow better. These chapters also contain more **real-world examples**.

- **Chapter 1** is now titled "Goals and Governance of the Firm." We introduce financial management by recent examples of capital investment and financing decisions by several well-known corporations. We explain why value maximization makes sense as a financial objective. Finally, we look at why good governance and incentive systems are needed to encourage managers and employees to work together to increase firm value and to behave ethically.
- **Chapter 2** combines Chapters 2 and 3 from the first edition. It goes directly into how present values are calculated. We think that it is better organized and easier to understand in its new presentation.
- **Chapter 3** introduces bond valuation. The material here has been reordered and simplified. The chapter focuses on default-free bonds, but also includes an introduction to corporate debt and default risk.
- Short-term and long-term financial planning are now combined in **Chapter 19**. We decided that covering financial planning in two chapters was awkward and inefficient. We have also added an Appendix that covers bank loans and other short-term debt, and the possible parking places for any surplus cash.
- **Chapter 18** is now devoted entirely to financial analysis, which should be more convenient to instructors who wish to assign this topic early in their courses. We explain how the financial statements and ratios help to reveal the value, profitability, efficiency, and financial strength of a real company (Lowe's).

The **credit crisis** that started in 2007 dramatically demonstrated the importance of a well-functioning financial system and the problems that occur when it ceases to function properly. Some have suggested that the crisis disproved the lessons of modern finance. On the contrary, we believe that it was a wake-up call—a call to remember basic principles, including the importance of good systems of governance, proper management incentives, sensible capital structures, and effective risk management.

We have added **examples and discussion of the crisis throughout the book**, starting in Chapter 1 with a discussion of agency costs and the importance of good governance. Other chapters have required significant revision as a result of the crisis. These include **Chapter 11**, where the review of market efficiency includes an expanded discussion of asset price bubbles, and the Appendix to **Chapter 19** where we note the effect of the crisis on money-market mutual funds.

The first edition of the comprehensive version of this book appeared in 1981. Basic principles are the same now as then, but the last three decades have also generated important changes in theory and practice. Research in finance has focused less on what financial managers should do, and more on understanding and interpreting what they do in practice. In other words, finance has become more positive and less normative. For example, we now have careful surveys of firms' capital investment practices and payout and financing policies. We review these surveys and look at how they cast light on competing theories.

Many financial decisions seem less clear-cut than they were 20 or 30 years ago. It no longer makes sense to ask whether high payouts are always good or always bad, or whether companies should always borrow less or more. The right answer is, "It depends." Therefore we set out pros and cons of different policies. We ask "What questions should the financial manager ask when setting financial policy?" You will, for example, see this shift in emphasis when we discuss payout decisions in **Chapter 12**.

This edition builds on other changes from earlier editions. We recognize that financial managers work more than ever in an international environment and therefore need to be familiar with international differences in financial management and in financial markets and institutions. Accordingly, we have found more and more opportunities to draw cross-border comparisons or use non-U.S. examples. We hope that this material will both provide a better understanding of the wider financial environment and be useful to our many readers around the world.

As every first-grader knows, it is easier to add than to subtract. To make way for new topics we have needed to make some judicious pruning. We will not tell you where we have cut out material, because we hope that the deletions will be invisible.

▶ Making Learning Easier

Each chapter of the book includes an introductory preview, a summary, and an annotated list of suggested further reading. The list of possible candidates for further reading is now voluminous. Rather than trying to list every important article, we have largely listed survey articles or general books. More specific references have been moved to footnotes.

Each chapter is followed by a set of **basic questions, intermediate questions** on both numerical and conceptual topics, and a few **challenge questions**. Answers to the odd-numbered basic questions appear in an Appendix at the end of the book.

We have added a **Real-Time Data Analysis** section to chapters where it makes sense to do so. This section now houses some of the Web Projects you have seen in the previous edition, along with new Data Analysis problems. These exercises seek to familiarize the reader with some useful Web sites and to explain how to download and process data from the Web. Many of the Data Analysis problems use financial data that the reader can download from **Standard & Poor's Educational Version of Market Insight**, an exclusive partnership with McGraw-Hill.

The book also contains 7 end-of-chapter **mini-cases**. These include specific questions to guide the case analyses. Answers to the mini-cases are available to instructors on the book's Web site.

Spreadsheet programs such as **Excel** are tailor-made for many financial calculations. Several chapters now include boxes that introduce **the most useful financial functions** and provide some short practice questions. We show how to use the Excel function key to locate the function and then enter the data. We think that this approach is much simpler than trying to remember the formula for each function.

Many tables in the text appear as spreadsheets. In these cases an equivalent "live" spreadsheet appears on the book's Web site. Readers can use these live spreadsheets to understand better the calculations behind the table and to see the effects of changing the underlying data. We have also linked end-of-chapter questions to the spreadsheets.

We conclude the book with a glossary of financial terms.

The 19 chapters in this book are divided into 7 parts. Parts 1 to 3 cover valuation and capital investment decisions, and Parts 4 to 6 discuss long-term financing. Part 7 focuses on financial planning and short-term financial decisions.

▶ Acknowledgments

We have a long list of people to thank for their helpful criticism of earlier editions and for assistance in preparing this one. They include Faiza Arshad, Aleijda de Cazenove Balsan, Kedran Garrison, Robert Pindyck, Sara Salem, and Gretchen Slemmons at MIT; Elroy Dimson, Paul Marsh, Mike Staunton, and Stefania Uccheddu at London Business School; Lynda Borucki, Michael Barhum, Marjorie Fischer, Larry Kolbe, Michael Vilbert, Bente Villadsen, and Fiona Wang at The Brattle Group, Inc.; Alex Triantis at the University of Maryland; Adam Kolasinski at the University of Washington; Simon Gervais at Duke University; Michael Chui at The Bank for International Settlements; Pedro Matos at the University of Southern California; Yupana Wiwattanakantang at Hitotsubashi University; Nickolay Gantchev, Tina Horowitz, and Chenying Zhang at the University of Pennsylvania; Julie Wulf at Harvard University; Jinghua Yan at Tykhe Capital; Roger Stein at Moody's Investor Service; Bennett Stewart at EVA Dimensions; and James Matthews at Towers Perrin.

We want to express our appreciation to those instructors whose insightful comments and suggestions were invaluable to us during the revision process:

Neyaz Ahmed *University of Maryland*
Anne Anderson *Lehigh University*
Noyan Arsen *Koc University*
Anders Axvarn *Gothenburg University*
Phil Baird *Duquesne University*
Jan Bartholdy *ASB, Denmark*
Penny Belk *Loughborough University*
Omar Benkato *Ball State University*
Eric Benrud *University of Baltimore*
Peter Berman *University of New Haven*
Tom Boulton *Miami University of Ohio*
Edward Boyer *Temple University*
Alon Brav *Duke University*
Jean Canil *University of Adelaide*
Celtin Ciner *University of North Carolina, Wilmington*
John Cooney *Texas Tech University*
Charles Cuny *Washington University, St. Louis*
John Davenport *Regent University*
Ray DeGennaro *University of Tennessee, Knoxville*
Adri DeRidder *Gotland University*
William Dimovski *Deakin University, Melbourne*
David Ding *Nanyang Technological University*
Robert Dittmar *University of Michigan*
Robert Duvic *University of Texas at Austin*
Alex Edmans *University of Pennsylvania*

Susan Edwards *Grand Valley State University*
Robert Everett *Johns Hopkins University*
Frank Flanegin *Robert Morris University*
Zsuzanna Fluck *Michigan State University*
Connel Fullenkamp *Duke University*
Mark Garmaise *University of California, Los Angeles*
Sharon Garrison *University of Arizona*
Christopher Geczy *University of Pennsylvania*
George Geis *University of Virginia*
Stuart Gillan *University of Delaware*
Felix Goltz *Edhec Business School*
Ning Gong *Melbourne Business School*
Levon Goukasian *Pepperdine University*
Gary Gray *Pennsylvania State University*
C. J. Green *Loughborough University*
Mark Griffiths *Thunderbird, American School of International Management*
Re-Jin Guo *University of Illinois, Chicago*
Ann Hackert *Idaho State University*
Winfried Hallerbach *Erasmus University, Rotterdam*
Milton Harris *University of Chicago*
Mary Hartman *Bentley College*
Glenn Henderson *University of Cincinnati*
Donna Hitscherich *Columbia University*
Ronald Hoffmeister *Arizona State University*
James Howard *University of Maryland, College Park*
George Jabbour *George Washington University*
Ravi Jagannathan *Northwestern University*
Abu Jalal *Suffolk University*
Nancy Jay *Mercer University*
Kathleen Kahle *University of Arizona*
Jarl Kallberg *NYU, Stern School of Business*
Ron Kaniel *Duke University*
Steve Kaplan *University of Chicago*
Arif Khurshed *Manchester Business School*
Ken Kim *University of Wisconsin, Milwaukee*
C. R. Krishnaswamy *Western Michigan University*
George Kutner *Marquette University*
Dirk Laschanzky *University of Iowa*
David Lins *University of Illinois, Urbana*
David Lovatt *University of East Anglia*
Debbie Lucas *Northwestern University*
Brian Lucey *Trinity College, Dublin*
Suren Mansinghka *University of California, Irvine*
Ernst Maug *Mannheim University*
George McCabe *University of Nebraska*
Eric McLaughlin *California State University, Pomona*
Joe Messina *San Francisco State University*
Dag Michalsen *BI, Oslo*
Franklin Michello *Middle Tennessee State University*
Peter Moles *University of Edinburgh*

Katherine Morgan *Columbia University*
Darshana Palkar *Minnesota State University, Mankato*
Claus Parum *Copenhagen Business School*
Dilip Patro *Rutgers University*
John Percival *University of Pennsylvania*
Birsel Pirim *University of Illinois, Urbana*
Latha Ramchand *University of Houston*
Rathin Rathinasamy *Ball State University*
Raghavendra Rau *Purdue University*
Joshua Raugh *University of Chicago*
Charu Reheja *Wake Forest University*
Thomas Rhee *California State University, Long Beach*
Tom Rietz *University of Iowa*
Robert Ritchey *Texas Tech University*
Michael Roberts *University of Pennsylvania*
Mo Rodriguez *Texas Christian University*
John Rozycki *Drake University*
Frank Ryan *San Diego State University*
Marc Schauten *Eramus University*
Brad Scott *Webster University*
Nejat Seyhun *University of Michigan*
Jay Shanken *Emory University*
Chander Shekhar *University of Melbourne*
Hamid Shomali *Golden Gate University*
Richard Simonds *Michigan State University*
Bernell Stone *Brigham Young University*
John Strong *College of William & Mary*
Brian Strope *Rutgers University*
Avanidhar Subrahmanyam *University of California, Los Angeles*
Tim Sullivan *Bentley College*
Shrinivasan Sundaram *Ball State University*
Chu-Sheng Tai *Texas Southern University*
Stephen Todd *Loyola University, Chicago*
Walter Torous *University of California, Los Angeles*
Emery Trahan *Northeastern University*
Ilias Tsiakas *University of Warwick*
Narendar V. Rao *Northeastern University*
David Vang *St. Thomas University*

Steve Venti *Dartmouth College*
Joseph Vu *DePaul University*
John Wald *Rutgers University*
John Wald, *University of Texas-San Antonio*
Chong Wang *Naval Postgraduate School*
Kelly Welch *University of Kansas*
Jill Wetmore *Saginaw Valley State University*
Patrick Wilkie *University of Virginia*
Matt Will *University of Indianapolis*
Art Wilson *George Washington University*
Shee Wong *University of Minnesota, Duluth*
Bob Wood *Tennessee Tech University*
Fei Xie *George Mason University*
Minhua Yang *University of Central Florida*
Chenying Zhang *University of Pennsylvania*

This list is surely incomplete. We know how much we owe to our colleagues at the London Business School, MIT's Sloan School of Management, and the University of Pennsylvania's Wharton School. In many cases, the ideas that appear in this book are as much their ideas as ours.

We would also like to thank all those at McGraw-Hill/Irwin who worked on the book, including Michele Janicek, Executive Editor; Lori Koetters, Managing Editor; Christina Kouvelis, Senior Developmental Editor; Karen Fisher, Developmental Editor II; Melissa Caughlin, Senior Marketing Manager; Jennifer Jelinski, Marketing Specialist; Dana Pauley, Project Manager; Laurie Entringer, Designer; Michael McCormick, Lead Production Supervisor; and Suresh Babu, Media Project Manager.

Finally, we record the continuing thanks due to our wives, Diana, Maureen, and Sally, who were unaware when they married us that they were also marrying the *Principles of Corporate Finance*.

Richard A. Brealey
Stewart C. Myers
Franklin Allen

Guided Tour

Pedagogical Features

▶ Chapter Overview

Each chapter begins with a brief narrative and outline to explain the concepts that will be covered in more depth. Useful Web sites related to material for each Part are provided on the book's Web site at **www.mhhe.com/bma**.

PART 1   **CHAPTER 1**

VALUE

Goals and Governance of the Firm

▶ **This book is** about how corporations make financial decisions. We start by explaining what these decisions are and what they are seeking to accomplish.

Corporations invest in real assets, which generate cash inflows and income. Some of the assets are tangible

of these things, it does cover the concepts that govern good financial decisions, and it shows you how to use the tools of the trade of modern finance.

We start this chapter by looking at a fundamental trade-off. The corporation can either invest in new

---

▶ Finance in Practice Boxes

Relevant news articles from financial publications appear in various chapters throughout the text. Aimed at bringing real-world flavor into the classroom, these boxes provide insight into the business world today.

FINANCE IN PRACTICE

Prediction Markets

▶ Stock markets allow investors to bet on their favorite stocks. Prediction markets allow them to bet on almost anything else. These markets reveal the collective guess of traders on issues as diverse as New York City snowfall, an avian flu outbreak, and the occurrence of a major earthquake.

Prediction markets are conducted on the major futures exchanges and on a number of smaller online exchanges such as Intrade (www.intrade.com) and the Iowa Electronic Markets (www.biz.uiowa.edu/iem). Take the 2008 presidential race as an example. On the Iowa Electronic Markets you could bet that Barack Obama would win by buying one of his contracts. Each Obama contract paid $1 if he won the

and selling, the market price of a contract revealed the collective wisdom of the crowd.

Take a look at the accompanying figure from the Iowa Electronic Markets. It shows the contract prices for the two contenders for the White House between June and November 2008. Following the Republican convention at the start of September, the price of a McCain contract reached a maximum of $.47. From then on the market suggested a steady fall in the probability of a McCain victory.

Participants in prediction markets are putting their money where their mouth is. So the forecasting accuracy of these markets compares favorably with those of major polls. Some businesses have also formed inter-

---

▶ Numbered Examples

New to this edition! Numbered and titled examples are called out within chapters to further illustrate concepts. Students can learn how to solve specific problems step-by-step as well as gain insight into general principles by seeing how they are applied to answer concrete questions and scenarios.

EXAMPLE 2.3 ● Winning Big at the Lottery

When 13 lucky machinists from Ohio pooled their money to buy Powerball lottery tickets, they won a record $295.7 million. (A fourteenth member of the group pulled out at the last minute to put in his own numbers.) We suspect that the winners received unsolicited congratulations, good wishes, and requests for money from dozens of more or less worthy charities. In response, they could fairly point out that the prize wasn't really worth $295.7 million. That sum was to be repaid in 25 annual installments of $11.828 million each. Assuming that the first payment occurred at the end of one year, what was the present value of the prize? The interest rate at the time was 5.9%.

These payments constitute a 25-year annuity. To value this annuity we simply multiply $11.828 million by the 25-year annuity factor:

$$PV = 11.828 \times 25\text{-year annuity factor}$$

$$= 11.828 \times \left[\frac{1}{r} - \frac{1}{r(1+r)^{25}} \right]$$

Excel Treatment

Useful Spreadsheet Functions Boxes

New to this edition! These boxes provide detailed examples of how to use Excel spreadsheets when applying financial concepts. Questions that apply to the spreadsheet follow for additional practice.

USEFUL SPREADSHEET FUNCTIONS

Internal Rate of Return

▶ Spreadsheet programs such as Excel provide built-in functions to solve for internal rates of return. You can find these functions by pressing *fx* on the Excel toolbar. If you then click on the function that you wish to use, Excel will guide you through the inputs that are required. At the bottom left of the function box there is a Help facility with an example of how the function is used.

Here is a list of useful functions for calculating internal rates of return, together with some points to remember when entering data:

- **IRR:** Internal rate of return on a series of regularly spaced cash flows.
- **XIRR:** The same as IRR, but for irregularly spaced flows.

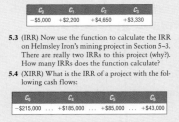

Note the following:

- For these functions, you must enter the addresses of the cells that contain the input values.
- The IRR functions calculate only one IRR even when there are multiple IRRs.

SPREADSHEET QUESTIONS

The following questions provide an opportunity to practice each of the above functions:

5.1 (IRR) Check the IRRs on projects F and G in Section 5–3.

5.2 (IRR) What is the IRR of a project with the following cash flows:

C_0	C_1	C_2	C_3
−$5,000	+$2,200	+$4,650	+$3,330

5.3 (IRR) Now use the function to calculate the IRR on Helmsley Iron's mining project in Section 5–3. There are really two IRRs to this project (why?). How many IRRs does the function calculate?

5.4 (XIRR) What is the IRR of a project with the following cash flows:

C_0	C_4	C_5	C_6
−$215,000 ...	+$185,000 ...	+$85,000 ...	+$43,000

(All other cash flows are 0.)

Excel Exhibits

Select exhibits are set as Excel spreadsheets and have been denoted with an icon. They are also available on the book's Web site at **www.mhhe.com/bma**.

(1)	(2)	(3)	(4)	(5)	(6)	(7)
						Product of
			Deviation	Deviation	Squared	deviations
			from	from average	deviation	from average
	Market	Anchovy Q	average	Anchovy Q	from average	returns
Month	return	return	market return	return	market return	(cols 4 × 5)
1	−8%	−11%	−10	−13	100	130
2	4	8	2	6	4	12
3	12	19	10	17	100	170
4	−6	−13	−8	−15	64	120
5	2	3	0	1	0	0
6	8	6	6	4	36	24
Average	2	2		Total	304	456
			Variance = σ_m^2 = 304/6 = 50.67			
			Covariance = σ_{im} = 456/6 = 76			
			Beta (β) = σ_{im}/σ_m^2 = 76/50.67 = 1.5			

▶ **TABLE 7.7** Calculating the variance of the market returns and the covariance between the returns on the market and those of Anchovy Queen. Beta is the ratio of the variance to the covariance (i.e., $\beta = \sigma_{im}/\sigma_m^2$).

Visit us at
www.mhhe.com/bma

End-of-Chapter Features

▸ Problem Sets

New end-of-chapter problems are included for even more hands-on practice. We have separated the questions by level of difficulty: Basic, Intermediate, and Challenge. Answers to the odd-numbered basic questions are included at the back of the book.

BASIC

1. Suppose a firm uses its company cost of capital to evaluate all projects. Will it underestimate or overestimate the value of high-risk projects?

2. A company is 40% financed by risk-free debt. The interest rate is 10%, the expected market risk premium is 8%, and the beta of the company's common stock is .5. What is the company cost of capital? What is the after-tax WACC, assuming that the company pays tax at a 35% rate?

3. Look back to the top-right panel of Figure 9.2. What proportion of Amazon's returns was explained by market movements? What proportion of risk was diversifiable? How does the diversifiable risk show up in the plot? What is the range of possible errors in the estimated beta?

INTERMEDIATE

11. The total market value of the common stock of the Okefenokee Real Estate Company is $6 million, and the total value of its debt is $4 million. The treasurer estimates that the beta of the stock is currently 1.5 and that the expected risk premium on the market is 6%. The Treasury bill rate is 4%. Assume for simplicity that Okefenokee debt is risk-free and the company does not pay tax.

    a. What is the required return on Okefenokee stock?

    b. Estimate the company cost of capital.

    c. What is the discount rate for an expansion of the company's present business?

    d. Suppose the company wants to diversify into the manufacture of rose-colored spectacles. The beta of unleveraged optical manufacturers is 1.2. Estimate the required return on Okefenokee's new venture.

12. Nero Violins has the following capital structure:

CHALLENGE

23. Suppose you are valuing a future stream of high-risk (high-beta) cash *outflows*. High risk means a high discount rate. But the higher the discount rate, the less the present value. This seems to say that the higher the risk of cash outflows, the less you should worry about them! Can that be right? Should the sign of the cash flow affect the appropriate discount rate? Explain.

24. An oil company executive is considering investing $10 million in one or both of two wells: Well 1 is expected to produce oil worth $3 million a year for 10 years; well 2 is expected to produce $2 million for 15 years. These are *real* (inflation-adjusted) cash flows.

▸ Excel Problems

Most chapters contain problems, denoted by an icon, specifically linked to Excel templates that are available on the book's Web site at **www.mhhe.com/bma**.

15. A 10-year German government bond (Bund) has a face value of €100 and a coupon rate of 5% paid annually. Assume that the interest rate (in euros) is equal to 6% per year. What is the bond's PV?

e**X**cel
Visit us at
www.mhhe.com/bma

16. A 10-year U.S. Treasury bond with a face value of $10,000 pays a coupon of 5.5% (2.75% of face value every six months). The semiannually compounded interest rate is 5.2% (a six-month discount rate of 5.2/2 = 2.6%).

    a. What is the present value of the bond?

    b. Generate a graph or table showing how the bond's present value changes for semiannually compounded interest rates between 1% and 15%.

e**X**cel
Visit us at
www.mhhe.com/bma

Real-Time Data Analysis Section

Featured among select chapters, this section includes Web exercises as well as Standard & Poor's questions. The Web exercises give students the opportunity to explore financial Web sites on their own to gain familiarity and apply chapter concepts. The Standard & Poor's questions directly incorporate the Educational Version of Market Insight, a service based on S&P's renowned Compustat database. These problems provide an easy method of including current, real-world data in the classroom. An access code for this S&P site is provided *free* with the purchase of a new book.

Mini-Cases

To enhance concepts discussed within a chapter, Mini-Cases are included in select chapters so students can apply their knowledge to real-world scenarios.

MINI-CASE • • • • •

Waldo County

Waldo County, the well-known real estate developer, worked long hours, and he expected his staff to do the same. So George Chavez was not surprised to receive a call from the boss just as George was about to leave for a long summer's weekend.

Mr. County's success had been built on a remarkable instinct for a good site. He would exclaim "Location! Location! Location!" at some point in every planning meeting. Yet finance was not his strong suit. On this occasion he wanted George to go over the figures for a new $90 million outlet mall designed to intercept tourists heading downeast toward Maine. "First thing Monday will do just fine," he said as he handed George the file. "I'll be in my house in Bar Harbor if you need me."

George's first task was to draw up a summary of the projected revenues and costs. The results are shown in Table 10.8. Note that the mall's revenues would come from two sources: The company would charge retailers an annual rent for the space they occupied, and in addition it would receive 5% of each store's gross sales.

Construction of the mall was likely to take three years. The construction costs could be depreciated straight-line over 15 years starting in year 3. As in the case of the company's other developments, the mall would be built to the highest specifications and would not need to be rebuilt until year 17. The land was expected to retain its value, but could not be depreciated for tax purposes.

Supplements

In this edition, we have gone to great lengths to ensure that our supplements are equal in quality and authority to the text itself.

FOR THE INSTRUCTOR

The following supplements are available to you via the book's Web site at **www.mhhe.com/bma** and are password protected for security. Print copies are available through your McGraw-Hill/Irwin representative.

Instructor's Manual

The Instructor's Manual was extensively revised and updated by Matthew Will of the University of Indianapolis. It contains an overview of each chapter, teaching tips, learning objectives, challenge areas, key terms, and an annotated outline that provides references to the PowerPoint slides.

Test Bank

The Test Bank, also revised by Matthew Will, has been updated to include hundreds of new multiple-choice and short answer/discussion questions based on the revisions of the authors. The level of difficulty varies, as indicated by the easy, medium, or difficult labels.

Computerized Test Bank

McGraw-Hill's EZ Test is a flexible and easy-to-use electronic testing program. The program allows you to create tests from book-specific items. It accommodates a wide range of question types and you can add your own questions. Multiple versions of the test can be created and any test can be exported for use with course management systems such as WebCT, BlackBoard, or PageOut. EZ Test Online is a new service and gives you a place to easily administer your EZ Test–created exams and quizzes online. The program is available for Windows and Macintosh environments.

PowerPoint Presentation

Matthew Will of the University of Indianapolis prepared the PowerPoint presentation, which contains exhibits, outlines, key points, and summaries in a visually stimulating collection of slides. You can edit, print, or rearrange the slides to fit the needs of your course.

Solutions Manual

The Solutions Manual, carefully revised by George Geis of the University of Virginia, contains solutions to all basic, intermediate, and challenge problems found at the end of each chapter. This supplement can be found on the instructor's side of the Online Learning Center.

Finance Video Series DVD
ISBN 9780073363653
MHID 0073363650

The McGraw-Hill/Irwin Finance Video Series is a complete video library designed to be added points of discussion to your class. You will find examples of how real businesses face hot topics like mergers and acquisitions, going public, time value of money, and careers in finance.

▶ Online Support

ONLINE LEARNING CENTER

www.mhhe.com/bma

Find a wealth of information online! This site contains information about the book and the authors as well as teaching and learning materials for the instructor and student, including:

- **Excel templates**   There are templates for select exhibits ("live" Excel), as well as various end-of-chapter problems that have been set as Excel spreadsheets—all denoted by an icon. They correlate with specific concepts in the text and allow students to work through financial problems and gain experience using spreadsheets. Also refer to the valuable Useful Spreadsheet Functions boxes that are sprinkled throughout the text for some helpful prompts on working in Excel.
- **Online quizzes**   These multiple-choice questions are provided as an additional testing and reinforcement tool for students. Each quiz is organized by chapter to test the specific concepts presented in that particular chapter. Immediate scoring of the quiz occurs upon submission and the correct answers are provided.
- **Standard & Poor's Educational Version of Market Insight**   McGraw-Hill is proud to partner with

Standard & Poor's by offering students access to the educational version of Market Insight. A passcode card is bound into new books, which gives you access to six years of financial data for over 1,000 real companies. Relevant chapters contain end-of-chapter problems that use this data to help students gain a better understanding of practical business situations.

- **Interactive FinSims** This valuable asset consists of multiple simulations of key financial topics. Ideal for students to reinforce concepts and gain additional practice to strengthen skills.

Brief Contents

Contents

xviii

Note: Present value tables are available on the book's Web site, **www.mhhe.com/bma**.

Goals and Governance of the Firm

▶ **This book is** about how corporations make financial decisions. We start by explaining what these decisions are and what they are seeking to accomplish.

Corporations invest in real assets, which generate cash inflows and income. Some of the assets are tangible assets such as plant and machinery; others are intangible assets such as brand names and patents. Corporations finance these assets by borrowing, by retaining and reinvesting cash flow, and by selling additional shares of stock to the corporation's shareholders. Thus the corporation's financial manager faces two broad financial questions: First, what investments should the corporation make? Second, how should it pay for those investments? The investment decision involves spending money; the financing decision involves raising it.

A large corporation may have hundreds of thousands of shareholders. These shareholders differ in many ways, such as their wealth, risk tolerance, and investment horizon. Yet we will see that they usually endorse the same financial goal: They want the financial manager to increase the value of the corporation and its current stock price.

Thus the secret of success in financial management is to increase value. That is easy to say, but not very helpful. Instructing the financial manager to increase value is like advising an investor in the stock market to "buy low, sell high." The problem is how to do it.

There may be a few activities in which one can read a textbook and then just "do it," but financial management is not one of them. That is why finance is worth studying. Who wants to work in a field where there is no room for judgment, experience, creativity, and a pinch of luck? Although this book cannot guarantee any

of these things, it does cover the concepts that govern good financial decisions, and it shows you how to use the tools of the trade of modern finance.

We start this chapter by looking at a fundamental trade-off. The corporation can either invest in new assets or it can give the cash back to the shareholders, who can then invest that cash in the financial markets. Financial managers add value whenever the company can earn a higher return than shareholders can earn for themselves. The shareholders' investment opportunities *outside* the corporation set the standard for investments *inside* the corporation. Financial managers therefore refer to the *opportunity cost* of the capital that shareholders contribute to the firm.

The success of a corporation depends on how well it harnesses all its managers and employees to work to increase value. We therefore take a first look at how good systems of corporate governance, combined with appropriate incentives and compensation packages, encourage everyone to pull together to increase value.

Good governance and appropriate incentives also help block out temptations to increase stock price by illegal or unethical means. Thoughtful shareholders do not want the maximum possible stock price. They want the maximum honest stock price.

This chapter introduces three themes that return again and again, in various forms and circumstances, throughout the book:

1. Maximizing value.
2. The opportunity cost of capital.
3. The crucial importance of incentives and governance.

●●●●●

To carry on business, a corporation needs an almost endless variety of **real assets.** These assets do not drop free from a blue sky; they need to be paid for. To pay for real assets, the corporation sells claims on the assets and on the cash flow that they will generate. These claims are called **financial assets** or **securities.** Take a bank loan as an example. The bank provides the corporation with cash in exchange for a financial asset, which is the corporation's promise to repay the loan with interest. An ordinary bank loan is not a security, however, because it is held by the bank and not sold or traded in financial markets.

Take a corporate bond as a second example. The corporation sells the bond to investors in exchange for the promise to pay interest on the bond and to pay off the bond at its maturity. The bond is a financial asset, and also a security, because it can be held by and traded among many investors in financial markets. Securities include bonds, shares of stock, and a dizzying variety of specialized instruments. We describe bonds in Chapter 3 and stocks in Chapter 4.

This suggests the following definitions:

$$\text{Investment decision} = \text{purchase of real assets}$$
$$\text{Financing decision} = \text{sale of financial assets}$$

But these equations are too simple. The investment decision also involves managing assets already in place and deciding when to shut down and dispose of assets if profits decline. The corporation also has to manage and control the risks of its investments. The financing decision includes not just raising cash today but also meeting obligations to banks, bondholders, and stockholders that contributed financing in the past. For example, the corporation has to repay its debts when they become due. If it cannot do so, it ends up insolvent and bankrupt. Sooner or later the corporation will also want to pay out cash to its shareholders.[1]

Let's go to more specific examples. Table 1.1 lists nine corporations. Four are U.S. corporations. Five are foreign: GlaxoSmithKline's headquarters are in London, LVMH's in Paris,[2] Shell's in The Hague, Toyota's in Nagoya, and Lenovo's in Beijing. We have chosen very large public corporations that you are probably already familiar with. You probably have traveled on a Boeing jet, shopped at Wal-Mart, or used a Wells Fargo ATM, for example.

Investment Decisions

The second column of Table 1.1 shows an important recent investment decision for each corporation. These investment decisions are often referred to as **capital budgeting** or **capital expenditure (CAPEX)** decisions, because most large corporations prepare an annual capital budget listing the major projects approved for investment. Some of the investments in Table 1.1, such as Wal-Mart's new stores or Union Pacific's new locomotives, involve the purchase of tangible assets—assets that you can touch and kick. Corporations also need to invest in intangible assets, however. These include research and development (R&D), advertising, and marketing. For example, GlaxoSmithKline and other major pharmaceutical companies invest billions every year on R&D for new drugs. These companies also invest to market their existing products.

---

[1] We have referred to the corporation's owners as "shareholders" and "stockholders." The two terms mean exactly the same thing and are used interchangeably. Corporations are also referred to casually as "companies," "firms," or "businesses." We also use these terms interchangeably.

[2] LVMH Moët Hennessy Louis Vuitton (usually abbreviated to LVMH) markets perfumes and cosmetics, wines and spirits, watches, and other fashion and luxury goods. And, yes, we know what you are thinking, but LVMH really is short for Moët Hennessy Louis Vuitton.

Company (revenue in billions for 2008)	Recent Investment Decision	Recent Financing Decision
Boeing ($61 billion)	Began production of its 787 Dreamliner aircraft, at a forecasted cost of more than $10 billion.	The cash flow from Boeing's operations allowed it to repay some of its debt and repurchase $2.8 billion of stock.
Royal Dutch Shell ($458 billion)	Invested in a $1.5 billion deepwater oil and gas field in the Gulf of Mexico.	In 2008 returned $13.1 billion of cash to its stockholders by buying back their shares.
Toyota (¥26,289 billion)	In 2008 opened new engineering and safety testing facilities in Michigan.	Returned ¥431 billion to shareholders in the form of dividends.
GlaxoSmithKline (£24 billion)	Spent £3.7 billion in 2008 on research and development of new drugs.	Financed R&D expenditures largely with reinvested cash flow generated by sales of pharmaceutical products.
Wal-Mart ($406 billion)	In 2008 announced plans to invest over a billion dollars in 90 new stores in Brazil.	In 2008 raised $2.5 billion by an issue of 5-year and 30-year bonds.
Union Pacific ($18 billion)	Acquired 315 new locomotives in 2007.	Largely financed its investment in locomotives by long-term leases.
Wells Fargo ($52 billion)	Acquired Wachovia Bank in 2008 for $15.1 billion.	Financed the acquisition by an exchange of shares.
LVMH (€17 billion)	Acquired the Spanish winery Bodega Numanthia Termes.	Issued a six-year bond in 2007, raising 300 million Swiss francs.
Lenovo ($16 billion)	Expanded its chain of retail stores to cover over 2,000 cities.	Borrowed $400 million for 5 years from a group of banks.

▶ **TABLE 1.1** Examples of recent investment and financing decisions by major public corporations.

Today's capital investments generate future returns. Often the returns come in the distant future. Boeing committed over $10 billion to design, test, and manufacture the Dreamliner. It did so because it expects that the plane will generate cash returns for 30 years or more after it first enters commercial service. Those cash returns must recover Boeing's huge initial investment and provide at least an adequate profit on that investment. The longer Boeing must wait for cash to flow back, the greater the profit that it requires. Thus the financial manager must pay attention to the timing of project returns, not just their cumulative amount. In addition, these returns are rarely certain. A new project could be a smashing success or a dismal failure.

Of course, not every investment has such distant payoffs as Boeing's Dreamliner. Some investments have only short-term consequences. For example, with the approach of the Christmas holidays, Wal-Mart spends about $40 billion to stock up its warehouses and retail stores. As the goods are sold over the following months, the company recovers this investment in inventories.

Financial managers do not make major investment decisions in solitary confinement. They may work as part of a team of engineers and managers from manufacturing, marketing, and other business functions. Also, do not think of the financial manager as making billion-dollar investments on a daily basis. Most investment decisions are smaller and simpler, such as the purchase of a truck, machine tool, or computer system. Corporations make thousands of these smaller investment decisions every year. The cumulative amount of small investments can be just as large as that of the occasional big investments, such as those shown in Table 1.1.

Financing Decisions

The third column of Table 1.1 lists a recent financing decision by each corporation. A corporation can raise money (cash) from lenders or from shareholders. If it borrows, the lenders contribute the cash, and the corporation promises to pay back the debt plus a fixed rate of interest. If the shareholders put up the cash, they get no fixed return, but they hold shares of stock and therefore get a fraction of future profits and cash flow. The shareholders are *equity investors*, who contribute *equity financing*. The choice between debt and equity financing is called the **capital structure** decision. *Capital* refers to the firm's sources of long-term financing.

The financing choices available to large corporations seem almost endless. Suppose the firm decides to borrow. Should it borrow from a bank or borrow by issuing bonds that can be traded by investors? Should it borrow for 1 year or 20 years? If it borrows for 20 years, should it reserve the right to pay off the debt early if interest rates fall? Should it borrow in Paris, receiving and promising to repay euros, or should it borrow dollars in New York? As Table 1.1 shows, the French company LVMH borrowed Swiss francs, but it could have borrowed dollars or euros instead.

Corporations raise equity financing in two ways. First, they can issue new shares of stock. The investors who buy the new shares put up cash in exchange for a fraction of the corporation's future cash flow and profits. Second, the corporation can take the cash flow generated by its existing assets and reinvest the cash in new assets. In this case the corporation is reinvesting on behalf of existing stockholders. No new shares are issued.

What happens when a corporation does not reinvest all of the cash flow generated by its existing assets? It may hold the cash in reserve for future investment, or it may pay the cash back to its shareholders. Table 1.1 shows that in 2008 Toyota paid cash dividends of ¥431 billion, equivalent to about $4.3 billion. In the same year Shell paid back $13.1 billion to its stockholders by repurchasing shares. This was in addition to $9.8 billion paid out as cash dividends. The decision to pay dividends or repurchase shares is called the *payout decision*. We cover payout decisions in Chapter 12.

In some ways financing decisions are less important than investment decisions. Financial managers say that "value comes mainly from the asset side of the balance sheet." In fact the most successful corporations sometimes have the simplest financing strategies. Take Microsoft as an example. It is one of the world's most valuable corporations. At the end of 2008, Microsoft shares traded for $19.44 each. There were about 8.9 billion shares outstanding. Therefore Microsoft's overall market value—its *market capitalization* or *market cap*—was $19.44 × 8.9 = $173 billion. Where did this market value come from? It came from Microsoft's product development, from its brand name and worldwide customer base, from its research and development, and from its ability to make profitable future investments. The value did *not* come from sophisticated financing. Microsoft's financing strategy is very simple: It carries no debt to speak of and finances almost all investment by retaining and reinvesting cash flow.

Financing decisions may not add much value, compared with good investment decisions, but they can destroy value if they are stupid or if they are ambushed by bad news. For example, when real estate mogul Sam Zell led a buyout of the *Chicago Tribune* in 2007, the newspaper took on about $8 billion of additional debt. This was not a stupid decision, but it did prove fatal. As advertising revenues fell away in the recession of 2008, the *Tribune* could no longer service its debt. In December 2008 it filed for bankruptcy with assets of $7.6 billion and debts of $12.9 billion.

Business is inherently risky. The financial manager needs to identify the risks and make sure they are managed properly. For example, debt has its advantages, but too much debt can land the company in bankruptcy, as the *Chicago Tribune* discovered. Companies can also be knocked off course by recessions, by changes in commodity prices, interest rates and exchange rates, or by adverse political developments. The financial manager needs to decide whether the firm should protect itself against these risks.

What Is a Corporation?

We have been referring to "corporations." Before going too far or too fast, we offer some basic definitions. Details follow as needed in later chapters.

A **corporation** is a legal entity. In the view of the law, it is a legal *person* that is owned by its shareholders. As a legal person, the corporation can make contracts, carry on a business, borrow or lend money, and sue or be sued. One corporation can make a takeover bid for another and then merge the two businesses. Corporations pay taxes—but cannot vote!

In the U.S., corporations are formed under state law, based on *articles of incorporation* that set out the purpose of the business and how it is to be governed and operated.[3] For example, the articles of incorporation specify the composition and role of the *board of directors*. A corporation's directors choose and advise top management and are required to sign off on some corporate actions, such as mergers and the payment of dividends to shareholders.

A corporation is owned by its shareholders but is legally distinct from them. Therefore the shareholders have **limited liability,** which means that shareholders cannot be held personally responsible for the corporation's debts. When the U.S. financial corporation Lehman Brothers failed in 2008, no one demanded that its stockholders put up more money to cover Lehman's massive debts. Shareholders can lose their entire investment in a corporation, but no more.

Corporations do not have to be prominent, multinational businesses like those listed in Table 1.1. You can organize a local plumbing contractor or barber shop as a corporation if you want to take the trouble.[4] But usually corporations are larger businesses or businesses that aspire to grow.

When a corporation is first established, its shares may be privately held by a small group of investors, perhaps the company's managers and a few backers. In this case the shares are not publicly traded and the company is *closely held.* Eventually, when the firm grows and new shares are issued to raise additional capital, its shares are traded in public markets such as the New York Stock Exchange. Such corporations are known as *public companies.* Most well-known corporations in the U.S. are public companies with widely dispersed shareholdings. In other countries, it is more common for large corporations to remain in private hands, and many public companies may be controlled by just a handful of investors. The latter category includes such well-known names as Fiat, Porsche, Benetton, Bosch, IKEA, and the Swatch Group.

A large public corporation may have hundreds of thousands of shareholders, who own the business but cannot possibly manage or control it directly. This *separation of ownership and control* gives corporations permanence. Even if managers quit or are dismissed and replaced, the corporation survives. Today's stockholders can sell all their shares to new investors without disrupting the operations of the business. Corporations can, in principle, live forever, and in practice they may survive many human lifetimes. One of the oldest corporations is the Hudson's Bay Company, which was formed in 1670 to profit from the fur trade between northern Canada and England. The company still operates as one of Canada's leading retail chains.

The separation of ownership and control can also have a downside, for it can open the door for managers and directors to act in their own interests rather than in the stockholders' interest. We return to this problem later in the chapter.

---

[3] In the U.S., corporations are identified by the label "Corporation," "Incorporated," or "Inc.," as in US Airways Group, Inc. The U.K. identifies public corporations by "plc" (short for "Public Limited Corporation"). French corporations have the suffix "SA" ("Société Anonyme"). The corresponding labels in Germany are "GmbH" ("Gesellschaft mit beschränkter Haftung") or "AG" ("Aktiengesellschaft").

[4] Single individuals doing business on their own behalf are called sole proprietorships. Smaller, local businesses can also be organized as partnerships or professional corporations (PCs).

What do financial managers do for a living? That simple question can be answered in several ways. We can start with financial managers' job titles. Most large corporations have a **chief financial officer (CFO),** who oversees the work of all financial staff. The CFO is deeply involved in financial policy and financial planning and is in constant contact with the chief executive officer (CEO) and other top management. The CFO is the most important financial voice of the corporation, and explains earnings results and forecasts to investors and the media.

Below the CFO are usually a **treasurer** and a **controller.** The treasurer is responsible for short-term cash management, currency trading, financing transactions, and bank relationships. The controller manages the company's internal accounting systems and oversees preparation of its financial statements and tax returns. The largest corporations have dozens of more specialized financial managers, including tax lawyers and accountants, experts in planning and forecasting, and managers responsible for investing the money set aside for employee retirement plans.

Financial decisions are not restricted to financial specialists. Top management must sign off on major investment projects, for example. But the engineer who designs a new production line is also involved, because the design determines the real assets that the corporation holds. The engineer also rejects many designs before proposing what he or she thinks is the best one. Those rejections are also investment decisions, because they amount to decisions *not* to invest in other types of real assets.

In this book we use the term *financial manager* to refer to anyone responsible for an investment or financing decision. Often we use the term collectively for all the managers drawn into such decisions.

Let's go beyond job titles. What is the essential role of the financial manager? Figure 1.1 gives one answer. The figure traces how money flows from investors to the corporation and back to investors again. The flow starts when cash is raised from investors (arrow 1 in the figure). The cash could come from banks or from securities sold to investors in financial markets. The cash is then used to pay for the real assets (investment projects) needed for the corporation's business (arrow 2). Later, as the business operates, the assets generate cash inflows (arrow 3). That cash is either reinvested (arrow 4*a*) or returned to the investors who furnished the money in the first place (arrow 4*b*). Of course, the choice between arrows 4*a* and 4*b* is constrained by the promises made when cash was raised at arrow 1. For example, if the firm borrows money from a bank at arrow 1, it must repay this money plus interest at arrow 4*b*.

▶ FIGURE 1.1

Flow of cash between financial markets and the firm's operations. Key: (1) Cash raised by selling financial assets to investors; (2) cash invested in the firm's operations and used to purchase real assets; (3) cash generated by the firm's operations; (4a) cash reinvested; (4b) cash returned to investors.

You can see examples of arrows *4a* and *4b* in Table 1.1. GlaxoSmithKline financed its drug research and development by reinvesting earnings (arrow *4a*). Shell decided to return cash to shareholders by buying back its stock (arrow *4b*). Shell could have chosen instead to pay the money out as additional cash dividends.

Notice how the financial manager stands between the firm and outside investors. On the one hand, the financial manager helps manage the firm's operations, particularly by helping to make good investment decisions. On the other hand, the financial manager deals with investors—not just with shareholders but also with financial institutions such as banks and with financial markets such as the New York Stock Exchange.

The Investment Trade-off

Now look at Figure 1.2, which sets out the fundamental trade-off for corporate investment decisions. The corporation has a proposed investment project (a real asset). Suppose it has cash on hand sufficient to finance the project. The financial manager is trying to decide whether to invest in the project. If the financial manager decides not to invest, the corporation can pay out the cash to shareholders, say as an extra dividend. (The investment and dividend arrows in Figure 1.2 are arrows 2 and *4b* in Figure 1.1.)

Assume that the financial manager is acting in the interests of the corporation's owners, its stockholders. What do these stockholders want the financial manager to do? The answer depends on the rate of return on the investment project and on the rate of return that the stockholders can earn by investing in financial markets. If the return offered by the investment project is higher than the rate of return that shareholders can get by investing on their own, then the shareholders would vote for the investment project. If the investment project offers a lower return than shareholders can achieve on their own, the shareholders would vote to cancel the project and take the cash instead.

Figure 1.2 could apply to Wal-Mart's decisions to invest in new retail stores, for example. Suppose Wal-Mart has cash set aside to build 10 new stores in 2012. It could go ahead with the new stores, or it could choose to cancel the investment project and instead pay the cash out to its stockholders. If it pays out the cash, the stockholders could then invest for themselves.

Suppose that Wal-Mart's new-stores project is just about as risky as the U.S. stock market and that investment in the stock market offers a 10% expected rate of return. If the new stores offer a superior rate of return, say 20%, then Wal-Mart's stockholders would be

▶ **FIGURE 1.2**

The firm can either keep and reinvest cash or return it to investors. (Arrows represent possible cash flows or transfers.) If cash is reinvested, the opportunity cost is the expected rate of return that shareholders could have obtained by investing in financial assets.

happy to let Wal-Mart keep the cash and invest it in the new stores. If the new stores offer only a 5% return, then the stockholders are better off with the cash and without the new stores; in that case, the financial manager should turn down the investment project.

As long as a corporation's proposed investments offer higher rates of return than its shareholders can earn for themselves in the stock market (or in other financial markets), its shareholders will applaud the investments and its stock price will increase. But if the company earns an inferior return, shareholders boo, stock price falls, and stockholders demand their money back so that they can invest on their own.

In our example, the minimum acceptable rate of return on Wal-Mart's new stores is 10%. This minimum rate of return is called a *hurdle rate* or *cost of capital*. It is really an **opportunity cost of capital,** because it depends on the investment *opportunities* available to investors in financial markets. Whenever a corporation invests cash in a new project, its shareholders lose the opportunity to invest the cash on their own. Corporations increase value by accepting all investment projects that earn more than the opportunity cost of capital.

Notice that the opportunity cost of capital depends on the risk of the proposed investment project. Why? It's not just because shareholders are risk-averse. It's also because shareholders have to trade off risk against return when they invest on their own. The safest investments, such as U.S. government debt, offer low rates of return. Investments with higher expected rates of return—the stock market, for example—are riskier and sometimes deliver painful losses. (The U.S. stock market was down 38% in 2008, for example.) Other investments are riskier still. For example, high-tech growth stocks offer the prospect of higher rates of return, but are even more volatile.

Notice too that the opportunity cost of capital is generally *not* the interest rate that the company pays on a loan from a bank or on a bond. If the company is making a risky investment, the opportunity cost is the expected return that investors can achieve in financial markets at the same level of risk. The expected return on risky securities is normally well above the interest rate on corporate borrowing.

Managers look to the financial markets to measure the opportunity cost of capital for the firm's investment projects. They can observe the opportunity cost of capital for safe investments by looking up current interest rates on safe debt securities. For risky investments, the opportunity cost of capital has to be estimated. We start to tackle this task in Chapter 7.

Estimating the opportunity cost of capital is one of the hardest tasks in financial management, even when the stock, bond, and other financial markets are behaving normally. When these markets are misbehaving, precise estimates of the cost of capital can be temporarily out of the question.

Financial markets in the U.S. and most developed countries work well most of the time but just like the little girl in the poem, "When they are good, they are very good indeed, but when they are bad they are horrid."[5] In 2008 financial markets were horrid. Security prices bounced around like Tigger on stimulants, and for some types of investment the market temporarily disappeared. Financial markets no longer offered a good yardstick for a project's value or the opportunity cost of capital. That was a year in which financial managers really earned their keep.

We give more specific examples of investment decisions and the opportunity cost of capital at the start of the next chapter.

---

[5] The poem is attributed to Longfellow:

> There was a little girl,
> Who had a little curl,
> Right in the middle of her forehead.
> When she was good,
> She was very good indeed,
> But when she was bad she was horrid.

1-3 Goals of the Corporation

Shareholders Want Managers to Maximize Market Value

Wal-Mart has over 300,000 shareholders. There is no way that Wal-Mart's shareholders can be actively involved in management; it would be like trying to run New York City by town meetings. Authority has to be delegated to professional managers. But how can Wal-Mart's managers make decisions that satisfy all the shareholders? No two shareholders are exactly the same. They differ in age, tastes, wealth, time horizon, risk tolerance, and investment strategy. Delegating the operation of the firm to professional managers can work only if the shareholders have a common objective. Fortunately there is a natural financial objective on which almost all shareholders agree: Maximize the current market value of shareholders' investment in the firm.

A smart and effective manager makes decisions that increase the current value of the company's shares and the wealth of its stockholders. This increased wealth can then be put to whatever purposes the shareholders want. They can give their money to charity or spend it in glitzy nightclubs; they can save it or spend it now. Whatever their personal tastes or objectives, they can all do more when their shares are worth more.

Maximizing shareholder wealth is a sensible goal when the shareholders have access to well-functioning financial markets.[6] Financial markets allow them to share risks and transport savings across time. Financial markets give them the flexibility to manage their own savings and investment plans, leaving the corporation's financial managers with only one task: to increase market value.

A corporation's roster of shareholders usually includes both risk-averse and risk-tolerant investors. You might expect the risk-averse to say, "Sure, maximize value, but don't touch too many high-risk projects." Instead, they say, "Risky projects are OK, *provided* that expected profits are more than enough to offset the risks. If this firm ends up too risky for my taste, I'll adjust my investment portfolio to make it safer." For example, the risk-averse shareholders can shift more of their portfolios to safe assets, such as U.S. government bonds. They can also just say good-bye, selling shares of the risky firm and buying shares in a safer one. If the risky investments increase market value, the departing shareholders are better off than if the risky investments were turned down.

A Fundamental Result

The goal of maximizing shareholder value is widely accepted in both theory and practice. It's important to understand why. Let's walk through the argument step by step, assuming that the financial manager should act in the interests of the firm's owners, its stockholders.

1. Each stockholder wants three things:
   a. To be as rich as possible, that is, to maximize his or her current wealth.
   b. To transform that wealth into the most desirable time pattern of consumption either by borrowing to spend now or investing to spend later.
   c. To manage the risk characteristics of that consumption plan.

2. But stockholders do not need the financial manager's help to achieve the best time pattern of consumption. They can do that on their own, provided they have free

---

[6] Here we use "financial markets" as shorthand for the financial sector of the economy. Strictly speaking, we should say "access to well-functioning financial markets and institutions." Many investors deal mostly with financial institutions, for example, banks, insurance companies, or mutual funds. The financial institutions then engage in financial markets, including the stock and bond markets. The institutions act as financial intermediaries on behalf of individual investors.

access to competitive financial markets. They can also choose the risk characteristics of their consumption plan by investing in more- or less-risky securities.

3. How then can the financial manager help the firm's stockholders? There is only one way: by increasing their wealth. That means increasing the market value of the firm and the current price of its shares.

Economists have proved this value-maximization principle with great rigor and generality. After you have absorbed this chapter, take a look at its Appendix, which contains a further example. The example, though simple, illustrates how the principle of value maximization follows from formal economic reasoning.

We have suggested that shareholders want to be richer rather than poorer. But sometimes you hear managers speak as if shareholders have different goals. For example, managers may say that their job is to "maximize profits." That sounds reasonable. After all, don't shareholders want their company to be profitable? But taken literally, profit maximization is not a well-defined financial objective for at least two reasons:

1. Maximize profits? Which year's profits? A corporation may be able to increase current profits by cutting back on outlays for maintenance or staff training, but those outlays may have added long-term value. Shareholders will not welcome higher short-term profits if long-term profits are damaged.

2. A company may be able to increase future profits by cutting this year's dividend and investing the freed-up cash in the firm. That is not in the shareholders' best interest if the company earns less than the opportunity cost of capital.

Should Managers Look After the Interests of Their Shareholders?

We have described managers as the agent of shareholders, who want that agent to maximize their wealth. But perhaps this begs the question, Is it *desirable* for managers to act in the selfish interests of their shareholders? Does a focus on enriching the shareholders mean that managers must act as greedy mercenaries riding roughshod over the weak and helpless?

Most of this book is devoted to financial policies that increase value. None of these policies requires gallops over the weak and helpless. In most instances, there is little conflict between doing well (maximizing value) and doing good. Profitable firms are those with satisfied customers and loyal employees; firms with dissatisfied customers and a disgruntled workforce will probably end up with declining profits and a low stock price.

Most established corporations can add value by building long-term relationships with their customers and establishing a reputation for fair dealing and financial integrity. When something happens to undermine that reputation, the costs can be enormous. Here is an example.

The Market-Timing Scandal   In 2003 the mutual fund industry confronted a market-timing scandal. Market timing exploits the fact that stock markets in different parts of the world close at different times. For example, if there is a strong surge in U.S. stock prices while the Japanese market is closed, it is likely that Japanese prices will increase when markets open in Asia the next day. Traders who can buy mutual funds invested in Japanese stocks while their prices are frozen will be able to make substantial profits. U.S. mutual funds were not supposed to allow such trading, but some did. After it was disclosed that managers at Putnam Investments had allowed market-timing trades for some of its investors, the company was fined $100 million and obliged to pay $10 million in compensation. But the larger cost by far was Putnam's loss of reputation. When the scandal came to light, Putnam suffered huge withdrawals of funds. Putnam mutual funds suffered outflows of $30 billion in just two months. If Putnam's funds charged roughly 1% of invested assets as an annual management fee (about the industry average), this loss of assets cost the company $300 million of revenue per year.

When we say that the objective of the firm is to maximize shareholder wealth, we do not mean that anything goes. The law deters managers from making blatantly dishonest decisions, but most managers are not simply concerned with observing the letter of the law or with keeping to written contracts. In business and finance, as in other day-to-day affairs, there are unwritten rules of behavior. These rules make routine financial transactions feasible, because each party to the transaction has to trust the other to keep to his or her side of the bargain.[7]

Of course trust is sometimes misplaced. Charlatans and swindlers are often able to hide behind booming markets. It is only "when the tide goes out that you learn who's been swimming naked."[8] The tide went out in 2008 and a number of frauds were exposed. One notorious example was the Ponzi scheme run by the New York financier Bernard Madoff.[9] Individuals and institutions put about $65 billion in the scheme before it collapsed in 2008. (It's not clear what Madoff did with all this money, but much of it was apparently paid out to early investors in the scheme to create an impression of superior investment performance.) With hindsight, the investors should not have trusted Madoff or the financial advisers who steered money to Madoff.

Madoff's Ponzi scheme was (we hope) a once-in-a-lifetime event.[10] Most of the money lost by investors in the crisis of '08 was lost honestly. Few investors or investment managers saw the crisis coming. When it arrived, there was little they could do to get out of the way.

Should Firms Be Managed for Shareholders or All Stakeholders?

It is often suggested that companies should be managed on behalf of all *stakeholders*, not just shareholders. Other stakeholders include employees, customers, suppliers, and the communities where the firm's plants and offices are located.

Different countries take very different views on this question. In the U.S., the U.K, and other "Anglo-Saxon" economies, the idea of maximizing shareholder value is widely accepted as the chief financial goal of the firm.

In other countries, workers' interests are put forward much more strongly. In Germany, for example, workers in large companies have the right to elect up to half the directors to the companies' supervisory boards. As a result they have a significant role in the governance of the firm and less attention is paid to the shareholders.[11] In Japan managers usually put the interests of employees and customers on a par with, or even ahead of, the interests of shareholders. For example, Toyota's business philosophy is "to realize stable, long-term growth by working hard to strike a balance between the requirements of people and society, the global environment and the world economy . . . to grow with all of our stakeholders, including our customers, shareholders, employees, and business partners."[12]

---

[7] See L. Guiso, L. Zingales, and P. Sapienza, "Trusting the Stock Market," *Journal of Finance* 63 (December 2008), pp. 2557–600. The authors show that an individual's lack of trust is a significant impediment to participation in the stock market. "Lack of trust" means a subjective fear of being cheated.

[8] The quotation is from Warren Buffett's annual letter to the shareholders of Berkshire Hathaway, March 2008.

[9] Ponzi schemes are named after Charles Ponzi who founded an investment company in 1920 that promised investors unbelievably high returns. He was soon deluged with funds from investors in New England, taking in $1 million during one three-hour period. Ponzi invested only about $30 of the money that he raised, but used part of the cash provided by later investors to pay generous dividends to the original investors. Within months the scheme collapsed and Ponzi started a five-year prison sentence.

[10] Ponzi schemes pop up frequently, but none has approached the scope and duration of Madoff's.

[11] The following quote from the German banker Carl Fürstenberg (1850–1933) offers an extreme version of how shareholders were once regarded by German managers: "Shareholders are stupid and impertinent—stupid because they give their money to somebody else without any effective control over what the person is doing with it and impertinent because they ask for a dividend as a reward for their stupidity." Quoted by M. Hellwig, "On the Economics and Politics of Corporate Finance and Corporate Control," in *Corporate Governance*, ed. X. Vives (Cambridge, U.K.: Cambridge University Press, 2000), p. 109.

[12] Toyota *Annual Report*, 2003, p. 10.

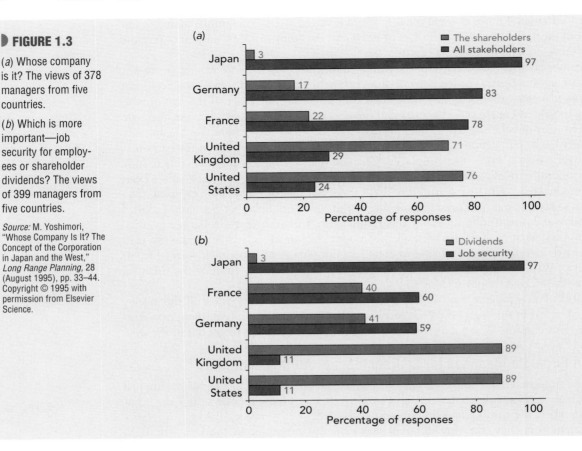

▶ FIGURE 1.3

(*a*) Whose company is it? The views of 378 managers from five countries.

(*b*) Which is more important—job security for employees or shareholder dividends? The views of 399 managers from five countries.

Source: M. Yoshimori, "Whose Company Is It? The Concept of the Corporation in Japan and the West," *Long Range Planning,* 28 (August 1995), pp. 33–44. Copyright © 1995 with permission from Elsevier Science.

Figure 1.3 summarizes the results of interviews with executives from large companies in five countries. Japanese, German, and French executives think that their firms should be run for all stakeholders, while U.S. and U.K. executives say that shareholders come first. When asked about the trade-off between job security and dividends, most U.S. and U.K. executives believe dividends should come first. By contrast, almost all Japanese executives and the majority of German and French executives believe that job security should come first.

As capital markets have become more global, there has been greater pressure for companies in all countries to adopt wealth creation for shareholders as a primary goal. Some German companies, including Daimler and Deutsche Bank, have announced their primary goal as wealth creation for shareholders. In Japan there has been less movement in this direction. For example, the chairman of Toyota has suggested that it would be irresponsible to pursue shareholders' interests. On the other hand, the aggregate market value of Toyota's shares is significantly greater than the market values of GM's and Ford's. So perhaps there is not too much conflict between these goals in practice.

1-4   Agency Problems and Corporate Governance

We have emphasized the *separation of ownership and control* in public corporations. The owners (shareholders) cannot control what the managers do, except indirectly through the board of directors. This separation is necessary but also dangerous. You can see the dangers. Managers may be tempted to buy sumptuous corporate jets or to schedule business meetings at tony resorts. They may shy away from attractive but risky projects because they are worried more about the safety of their jobs than about maximizing shareholder value. They may work just to maximize their own bonuses, and therefore redouble their efforts to make and resell flawed subprime mortgages.

Conflicts between shareholders' and managers' objectives create *agency problems*. Agency problems arise when *agents* work for *principals*. The shareholders are the principals; the managers are their agents. **Agency costs** are incurred when (1) managers do not attempt to maximize firm value and (2) shareholders incur costs to monitor the managers and constrain their actions.

Agency problems can sometimes lead to outrageous behavior. For example, when Dennis Kozlowski, the CEO of Tyco, threw a $2 million 40th birthday bash for his wife, he charged half of the cost to the company. This of course was an extreme conflict of interest, as well as illegal. But more subtle and moderate agency problems arise whenever managers think just a little less hard about spending money when it is not their own.

Pushing Subprime Mortgages: Value Maximization Run Amok, or an Agency Problem?

The economic crisis of 2007–2009[13] started as a *subprime* crisis. "Subprime" refers to mortgage loans made to home buyers with weak credit. Some of these loans were made to naïve buyers who faced severe difficulties in making interest and principal payments. Some loans were made to opportunistic buyers who were willing to gamble that real estate prices would keep increasing. But real estate prices declined sharply, and many of these buyers were forced to default.

Why did many banks and mortgage companies make these loans in the first place? One reason is that they could repackage the loans as mortgage-backed securities and sell them at a profit to other banks and to institutional investors. It's clear with hindsight that buyers of these subprime mortgage-backed securities were in turn naïve and paid too much. When housing prices fell and defaults increased in 2007, the prices of these securities fell drastically. Merrill Lynch wrote off $50 billion of losses on mortgage-backed securities, and the company had to be sold under duress to Bank of America. Other major financial institutions, such as Citigroup and Wachovia Bank, also recorded enormous losses.

Think about the banks and mortgage companies that originated the subprime loans and made a profit by reselling them. With hindsight we see that they were selling defective products that would generate painful losses for their customers. Were these companies really pursuing value maximization? Perhaps they were trying to maximize value and just made a disastrous misjudgment about the course of house prices. But we think it is more likely that the companies were aware that a strategy of originating massive amounts of subprime was likely to end badly. Washington Mutual, one of the most aggressive players in the subprime market, quickly failed when the true risks of the subprime loans were revealed. Washington Mutual's shareholders would surely not have endorsed the company's strategy if they had understood it.

Although there is plenty of blame to pass around in the subprime crisis, some of it must go to the managers who actually promoted and resold the subprime mortgages. Were they acting in shareholders' interests, or were they acting in their own interests, trying to squeeze in one more, fat bonus before the game ended? We think that the managers would have thought much harder about their actions if they had not had a short-term selfish interest in promoting subprime mortgages. If so, the mess was largely an *agency problem*, not value maximization run amok. Agency problems occur when managers do *not* act in shareholders' interests, but in their own interests.

---

[13] We write this chapter in early 2009. We hope that the next edition of this book does *not* refer to the financial crisis of 2007–2010 or 2007–2011.

Agency Problems Are Mitigated by Good Systems of Corporate Governance

A good system of **corporate governance** ensures that the shareholders' pockets are close to the managers' hearts. Here are some of the characteristics of such a system.

Legal and Regulatory Requirements   Managers have a legal duty to act responsibly and in the interests of investors. For example, the U.S. Securities and Exchange Commission (SEC) sets accounting and reporting standards for public companies to ensure consistency and transparency. The SEC also prohibits insider trading, that is, the purchase or sale of shares based on information that is not available to public investors.

Compensation Plans   Managers are spurred on by incentive schemes that produce big returns if shareholders gain but are valueless if they do not. For example, Larry Ellison, CEO of the business software giant Oracle Corporation, received total compensation for 2007 estimated at between $60 and $70 million. Only a small fraction (a mere $1 million) of that amount was salary. A larger amount, a bit more than $6 million, was bonus and incentive pay, and the lion's share was in the form of stock and option grants. Those options will be worthless if Oracle's share price falls below its 2007 level, but will be highly valuable if the price rises. Moreover, as founder of Oracle, Ellison holds over 1 *billion* shares in the firm. No one can say for certain how hard Ellison would have worked with a different compensation package. But one thing is clear: He has a huge personal stake in the success of the firm—and in increasing its market value.

Board of Directors   A company's board of directors is elected by the shareholders and has a duty to represent them. Boards of directors are sometimes portrayed as passive stooges who always champion the incumbent management. But response to past corporate scandals has tipped the balance toward greater independence. The Sarbanes-Oxley Act (commonly known as "SOX") requires that corporations place more independent directors on the board, that is, more directors who are not managers or are not affiliated with management. More than half of all directors are now independent. Boards also now meet in sessions without the CEO present. In addition, institutional shareholders, particularly pension funds and hedge funds, have become more active in monitoring firm performance and proposing changes to corporate governance.

Not surprisingly, more chief executives have been forced out in recent years, among them the CEOs of General Motors, Merrill Lynch, Starbucks, Yahoo!, AIG, Fannie Mae, and Motorola. Boards outside the United States, which traditionally have been more management-friendly, have also become more willing to replace underperforming managers. The list of recent departures includes the heads of Royal Bank of Scotland, UBS, PSA Peugeot Citroen, Lenovo, Samsung, Old Mutual, and Swiss Re.

Monitoring   The company's directors are not the only ones to be scrutinizing management's actions. Managers are also monitored by security analysts, who advise investors to buy, hold, or sell the company's shares, and by banks, which keep an eagle eye on the safety of their loans.

Takeovers   Companies that consistently fail to maximize value are natural targets for takeovers by another company or by corporate raiders. "Raiders" are private investment funds that specialize in buying out and reforming poorly performing companies.

Takeovers are common in industries with slow growth and excess capacity. For example, at the end of the Cold War in 1990, it was clear that the defense industry would have to shrink drastically. A wave of consolidating mergers followed.

Shareholder Pressure If shareholders believe that the corporation is underperforming and that the board of directors is not holding managers to task, they can attempt to elect representatives to the board to make their voices heard. For example, in 2008 billionaire shareholder activist Carl Icahn felt that the directors of Yahoo! were not acting in shareholders' interest when they rejected a bid from Microsoft. He therefore invested $67 million in Yahoo! stock, and muscled himself and two like-minded friends onto the Yahoo! board.

Disgruntled stockholders also take the "Wall Street Walk" by selling out and moving on to other investments. The Wall Street Walk can send a powerful message. If enough shareholders bail out, the stock price tumbles. This damages top management's reputation and compensation. A large part of top managers' paychecks comes from stock options, which pay off if the stock price rises but are worthless if the price falls below a stated threshold. Thus a falling stock price has a direct impact on managers' personal wealth. A rising stock price is good for managers as well as stockholders.

We do not want to leave the impression that corporate life is a series of squabbles and endless micromanagement. It isn't, because practical corporate finance has evolved to reconcile personal and corporate interests—to keep everyone working together to increase the value of the whole pie, not merely the size of each person's slice. Few managers at the top of major U.S. corporations are lazy or inattentive to stockholders' interests. On the contrary, the pressure to perform can be intense. We will return to agency problems and governance many times in the following chapters.

● ● ● ● ●

SUMMARY

Corporations face two principal financial decisions. First, what investments should the corporation make? Second, how should it pay for the investments? The first decision is the investment decision; the second is the financing decision.

The stockholders who own the corporation want its managers to maximize its overall value and the current price of its shares. The stockholders can all agree on the goal of value maximization, so long as financial markets give them the flexibility to manage their own savings and investment plans. Of course, the objective of wealth maximization does not justify unethical behavior. Shareholders do not want the maximum possible stock price. They want the maximum honest share price.

How can financial managers increase the value of the firm? Mostly by making good investment decisions. Financing decisions can also add value, and they can surely destroy value if you screw them up. But it's usually the profitability of corporate investments that separates value winners from the rest of the pack.

Investment decisions force a trade-off. The firm can either invest cash or return it to shareholders, for example, as an extra dividend. When the firm invests cash rather than paying it out, shareholders forgo the opportunity to invest it for themselves in financial markets. The return that they are giving up is therefore called the opportunity cost of capital. If the firm's investments can earn a return higher than the opportunity cost of capital, shareholders cheer and stock price increases. If the firm invests at a return lower than the opportunity cost of capital, shareholders boo and stock price falls.

Managers are not endowed with a special value-maximizing gene. They will consider their own personal interests, which creates a potential conflict of interest with outside shareholders. This conflict is called a principal–agent problem. Any loss of value that results is called an agency cost.

Corporate governance helps to align managers' and shareholders' interests, so that managers pay close attention to the value of the firm. For example, managers are appointed by, and sometimes fired by, the board of directors, who are supposed to represent shareholders. The managers are spurred on by incentive schemes, such as grants of stock options, which pay off big only if the stock price increases. If the company performs poorly, it is more likely to be taken over. The takeover typically brings in a fresh management team.

Remember the following three themes, for you will see them again and again throughout this book:

1. Maximizing value.

2. The opportunity cost of capital.

3. The crucial importance of incentives and governance.

● ● ● ● ●

PROBLEM SETS

BASIC

1. Read the following passage: "Companies usually buy (*a*) assets. These include both tangible assets such as (*b*) and intangible assets such as (*c*). To pay for these assets, they sell (*d*) assets such as (*e*). The decision about which assets to buy is usually termed the (*f*) or (*g*) decision. The decision about how to raise the money is usually termed the (*h*) decision." Now fit each of the following terms into the most appropriate space: *financing, real, bonds, investment, executive airplanes, financial, capital budgeting, brand names.*

2. Which of the following are real assets, and which are financial?

a. A share of stock.

b. A personal IOU.

c. A trademark.

d. A factory.

e. Undeveloped land.

f. The balance in the firm's checking account.

g. An experienced and hardworking sales force.

h. A corporate bond.

3. Vocabulary test. Explain the differences between:

a. Real and financial assets.

b. Capital budgeting and financing decisions.

c. Closely held and public corporations.

d. Limited and unlimited liability.

4. Which of the following statements always apply to corporations?

a. Unlimited liability.

b. Limited life.

c. Ownership can be transferred without affecting operations.

d. Managers can be fired with no effect on ownership.

5. Which of the following statements more accurately describe the treasurer than the controller?

a. Responsible for investing the firm's spare cash.

b. Responsible for arranging any issue of common stock.

c. Responsible for the company's tax affairs.

INTERMEDIATE

6. In most large corporations, ownership and management are separated. What are the main implications of this separation?

7. F&H Corp. continues to invest heavily in a declining industry. Here is an excerpt from a recent speech by F&H's CFO:

   We at F&H have of course noted the complaints of a few spineless investors and uninformed security analysts about the slow growth of profits and dividends. Unlike those confirmed doubters, we have confidence in the long-run demand for mechanical encabulators, despite competing digital products. We are therefore determined to invest to maintain our share of the overall encabulator market. F&H has a rigorous CAPEX approval process, and we are confident of returns around 8% on investment. That's a far better return than F&H earns on its cash holdings.

   The CFO went on to explain that F&H invested excess cash in short-term U.S. government securities, which are almost entirely risk-free but offered only a 4% rate of return.

   a. Is a forecasted 8% return in the encabulator business necessarily better than a 4% safe return on short-term U.S. government securities? Why or why not?

   b. Is F&H's opportunity cost of capital 4%? How in principle should the CFO determine the cost of capital?

8. We can imagine the financial manager doing several things on behalf of the firm's stockholders. For example, the manager might:

   a. Make shareholders as wealthy as possible by investing in real assets.

   b. Modify the firm's investment plan to help shareholders achieve a particular time pattern of consumption.

   c. Choose high- or low-risk assets to match shareholders' risk preferences.

   d. Help balance shareholders' checkbooks.

   But in well-functioning capital markets, shareholders will vote for *only one* of these goals. Which one? Why?

9. Ms. Espinoza is retired and depends on her investments for her income. Mr. Liu is a young executive who wants to save for the future. Both are stockholders in Scaled Composites, LLC, which is building *SpaceShipOne* to take commercial passengers into space. This investment's payoff is many years away. Assume it has a positive net present value for Mr. Liu. Explain why this investment also makes sense for Ms. Espinoza.

10. If a financial institution is caught up in a financial scandal, would you expect its value to fall by more or less than the amount of any fines and settlement payments? Explain.

11. Why might one expect managers to act in shareholders' interests? Give some reasons.

12. Many firms have devised defenses that make it more difficult or costly for other firms to take them over. How might such defenses affect the firm's agency problems? Are managers of firms with formidable takeover defenses more or less likely to act in the shareholders' interests rather than their own? What would you expect to happen to the share price when management proposes to institute such defenses?

APPENDIX • • • • •

Foundations of the Net Present Value Rule

We have suggested that well-functioning financial markets allow different investors to agree on the objective of maximizing value. This idea is sufficiently important that we need to pause and examine it more carefully.

How Financial Markets Reconcile Preferences for Current vs. Future Consumption   Suppose that there are two possible investors with entirely different preferences. Think of A as an ant, who wishes to save for the future, and of G as a grasshopper, who would prefer to spend all his wealth on some ephemeral frolic, taking no heed of tomorrow. Suppose that each has a nest egg of exactly $100,000 in cash. G chooses to spend all of it today, while A prefers to invest it in the financial market. If the interest rate is 10%, A would then have $1.10 \times \$100,000 = \$110,000$ to spend a year from now. Of course, there are many possible intermediate strategies. For example, A or G could choose to split the difference, spending $50,000 now and putting the remaining $50,000 to work at 10% to provide $1.10 \times \$50,000 = \$55,000$ next year. The entire range of possibilities is shown by the green line in Figure 1A.1.

In our example, A used the financial market to postpone consumption. But the market can also be used to bring consumption forward in time. Let's illustrate by assuming that instead of having cash on hand of $100,000, our two friends are due to receive $110,000 each at the end of the year. In this case A will be happy to wait and spend the income when it arrives. G will prefer to borrow against his future income and party it away today. With an interest rate of 10%, G can borrow and spend $\$110,000/1.10 = \$100,000$. Thus the financial market provides a kind of time machine that allows people to separate the timing of their income from that of their spending. Notice that with an interest rate of 10%, A and G are equally happy with cash on hand of $100,000 or an income of $110,000 at the end of the year. They do not care about the timing of the cash flow; they just prefer the cash flow that has the highest value today ($100,000 in our example).

Investing in Real Assets   In practice individuals are not limited to investing in financial markets; they may also acquire plant, machinery, and other real assets. For example, suppose that A and G are offered the opportunity to invest their $100,000 in a new business that a friend is founding. This will produce a one-off surefire payment of $121,000 next year. A would clearly be happy to invest in the business. It will provide her with $121,000 to spend at the end of the year, rather than the $110,000 that she gets by investing her $100,000 in the financial market. But what about G, who wants money now, not in one year's time? He too is happy to invest, as long as he can borrow against the future payoff of the investment project. At an interest rate of 10%, G can borrow $110,000 and so will have an extra $10,000 to spend today. Both A and G are better off investing in their friend's venture. The investment increases their wealth. It moves them up from the green to the maroon line in Figure 1A.1.

A Crucial Assumption   The key condition that allows A and G to agree to invest in the new venture is that both have access to a well-functioning, competitive capital market, in which they can borrow and lend at the same rate. Whenever the corporation's shareholders have equal access to competitive capital markets, the goal of maximizing market value makes sense.

▶ **FIGURE 1A.1**

The green line shows the possible spending patterns for the ant and grasshopper if they invest $100,000 in the capital market. The maroon line shows the possible spending patterns if they invest in their friend's business. Both are better off by investing in the business as long as the grasshopper can borrow against the future income.

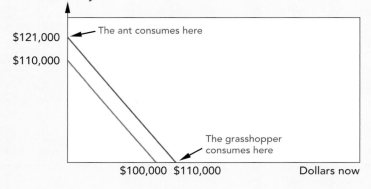

It is easy to see how this rule would be damaged if we did *not* have such a well-functioning capital market. For example, suppose that G could not easily borrow against future income. In that case he might well prefer to spend his cash today rather than invest it in the new venture. If A and G were shareholders in the same enterprise, A would be happy for the firm to invest, while G would be clamoring for higher current dividends.

No one believes unreservedly that capital markets function perfectly. Later in this book we discuss several cases in which differences in taxation, transaction costs, and other imperfections must be taken into account in financial decision making. However, we also discuss research indicating that, in general, capital markets function fairly well. In this case maximizing shareholder value is a sensible corporate objective. But for now, having glimpsed the problems of imperfect markets, we shall, like an economist in a shipwreck, simply *assume* our life jacket and swim safely to shore.

QUESTIONS

1. Look back to the numerical example graphed in Figure 1A.1. Suppose the interest rate is 20%. What would the ant (A) and grasshopper (G) do if they both start with $100,000? Would they invest in their friend's business? Would they borrow or lend? How much and when would each consume?

2. Answer this question by drawing graphs like Figure 1A.1. Casper Milktoast has $200,000 available to support consumption in periods 0 (now) and 1 (next year). He wants to consume *exactly* the same amount in each period. The interest rate is 8%. There is no risk.

   a. How much should he invest, and how much can he consume in each period?

   b. Suppose Casper is given an opportunity to invest up to $200,000 at 10% risk-free. The interest rate stays at 8%. What should he do, and how much can he consume in each period?

How to Calculate Present Values

▶ **A corporation's shareholders** want maximum value and the maximum honest share price. To reach this goal, the company needs to invest in real assets that are worth more than they cost. In this chapter we take the first steps toward understanding how assets are valued and capital investments are made.

There are a few cases in which it is not that difficult to estimate asset values. In real estate, for example, you can hire a professional appraiser to do it for you. Suppose you own a warehouse. The odds are that your appraiser's estimate of its value will be within a few percent of what the building would actually sell for. After all, there is continuous activity in the real estate market, and the appraiser's stock-in-trade is knowledge of the prices at which similar properties have recently changed hands. Thus the problem of valuing real estate is simplified by the existence of an active market in which all kinds of properties are bought and sold.[1] No formal theory of value is needed. We can take the market's word for it.

But we need to go deeper than that. First, it is important to know how asset values are reached in an active market. Even if you can take the appraiser's word for it, it is important to understand *why* that warehouse is worth, say, $2 million and not a higher or lower figure. Second, the market for most corporate assets is pretty thin. Look in the classified advertisements in *The Wall Street Journal:* It is not often that you see a blast furnace for sale.

Companies are always searching for assets that are worth more to them than to others. That warehouse is worth more to you if you can manage it better than others

can. But in that case, the price of similar buildings may not tell you what the warehouse is worth under your management. You need to know how asset values are determined.

In the first section of this chapter we work through a simple numerical example: Should you invest in a new office building in the hope of selling it at a profit next year? You should do so if net present value is positive, that is, if the new building's value today exceeds the investment that is required. A positive net present value implies that the rate of return on your investment is higher than your opportunity cost of capital, that is, higher than you could earn by investing in financial markets.

Next we introduce shortcut formulas for calculating present values. We show how to value an investment that delivers a steady stream of cash flows forever (a *perpetuity*) and one that produces a steady stream for a limited period (an *annuity*). We also look at investments that produce growing cash flows. We illustrate the formulas by applications to some personal financial decisions.

The term *interest rate* sounds straightforward enough, but rates can be quoted in various ways. We conclude the chapter by explaining the difference between the quoted rate and the true or effective interest rate.

By then you will deserve some payoff for the mental investment you'll have made in learning how to calculate present values. Therefore, in the next two chapters we will try out these new tools on bonds and stocks. After that we will tackle capital investment decisions at a practical level of detail.

For simplicity, every problem in this chapter is set out in dollars, but the concepts and calculations are identical in euros, yen, or any other currency.

---

[1] Needless to say, there are some properties that appraisers find nearly impossible to value—for example, nobody knows the potential selling price of the Taj Mahal, the Parthenon, or Windsor Castle.

● ● ● ● ●

2-1 Future Values and Present Values

Calculating Future Values

Money can be invested to earn interest. So, if you are offered the choice between $100 today and $100 next year, you naturally take the money now to get a year's interest. Financial managers make the same point when they say that money has a *time value* or when they quote the most basic principle of finance: *A dollar today is worth more than a dollar tomorrow.*

Suppose you invest $100 in a bank account that pays interest of $r = 7\%$ a year. In the first year you will earn interest of $.07 \times \$100 = \$7$ and the value of your investment will grow to $107:

$$\text{Value of investment after 1 year} = \$100 \times (1 + r) = 100 \times 1.07 = \$107$$

By investing, you give up the opportunity to spend $100 today and you gain the chance to spend $107 next year.

If you leave your money in the bank for a second year, you earn interest of $.07 \times \$107 = \$7.49$ and your investment will grow to $114.49:

$$\text{Value of investment after 2 years} = \$107 \times 1.07 = \$100 \times 1.07^2 = \$114.49$$

Today		Year 2
$100	$\times 1.07^2$	$114.49

Notice that in the second year you earn interest on both your initial investment ($100) and the previous year's interest ($7). Thus your wealth grows at a *compound rate* and the interest that you earn is called **compound interest.**

If you invest your $100 for t years, your investment will continue to grow at a 7% compound rate to $\$100 \times (1.07)^t$. For any interest rate r, the future value of your $100 investment will be

$$\text{Future value of } \$100 = \$100 \times (1 + r)^t$$

The higher the interest rate, the faster your savings will grow. Figure 2.1 shows that a few percentage points added to the interest rate can do wonders for your future wealth. For example, by the end of 20 years $100 invested at 10% will grow to $\$100 \times (1.10)^{20} = \$672.75$. If it is invested at 5%, it will grow to only $\$100 \times (1.05)^{20} = \$265.33$.

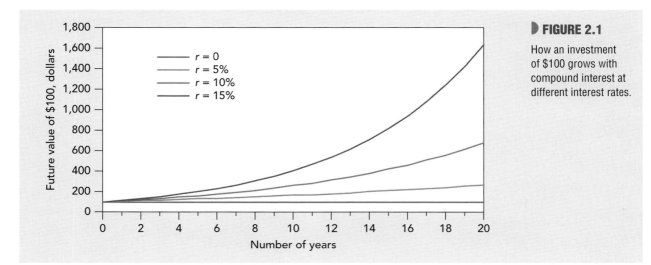

▶ **FIGURE 2.1**

How an investment of $100 grows with compound interest at different interest rates.

Calculating Present Values

We have seen that $100 invested for two years at 7% will grow to a future value of $100 \times 1.07^2 = \$114.49$. Let's turn this around and ask how much you need to invest *today* to produce $114.49 at the end of the second year. In other words, what is the **present value (PV)** of the $114.49 payoff?

You already know that the answer is $100. But, if you didn't know or you forgot, you can just run the future value calculation in reverse and divide the future payoff by $(1.07)^2$:

$$\text{Present value} = \text{PV} = \frac{\$114.49}{(1.07)^2} = \$100$$

Today		Year 2
$100	÷ 1.07²	$114.49

In general, suppose that you will receive a cash flow of C_t dollars at the end of year t. The present value of this future payment is

$$\text{Present value} = \text{PV} = \frac{C_t}{(1+r)^t}$$

You sometimes see this present value formula written differently. Instead of *dividing* the future payment by $(1 + r)^t$, you can equally well *multiply* the payment by $1/(1 + r)^t$. The expression $1/(1 + r)^t$ is called the **discount factor.** It measures the present value of one dollar received in year t. For example, with an interest rate of 7% the two-year discount factor is

$$\text{DF}_2 = 1/(1.07)^2 = .8734$$

Investors are willing to pay $.8734 today for delivery of $1 at the end of two years. If each dollar received in year 2 is worth $.8734 today, then the present value of your payment of $114.49 in year 2 must be

$$\text{Present value} = \text{DF}_2 \times C_2 = .8734 \times 114.49 = \$100$$

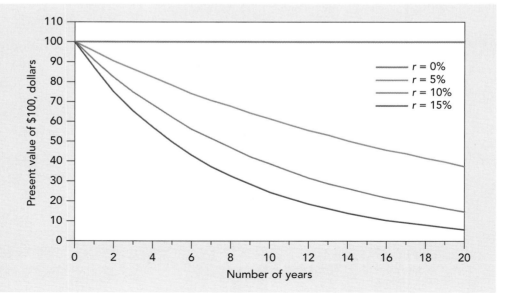

▶ **FIGURE 2.2**

Present value of a future cash flow of $100. Notice that the longer you have to wait for your money, the less it is worth today.

The longer you have to wait for your money, the lower its present value. This is illustrated in Figure 2.2. Notice how small variations in the interest rate can have a powerful effect on the present value of distant cash flows. At an interest rate of 5%, a payment of $100 in year 20 is worth $37.69 today. If the interest rate increases to 10%, the value of the future payment falls by about 60% to $14.86.

Calculating the Present Value of an Investment Opportunity

How do you decide whether an investment opportunity is worth undertaking? Suppose you own a small company that is contemplating construction of an office block. The total cost of buying the land and constructing the building is $370,000, but your real estate adviser forecasts a shortage of office space a year from now and predicts that you will be able sell the building for $420,000. For simplicity, we will assume that this $420,000 is a sure thing.

You should go ahead with the project if the present value (PV) of the cash inflows is greater than the $370,000 investment. Suppose that the rate of interest on U.S. government securities is $r = 5\%$ per year. Then, the present value of your office building is:

$$PV = \frac{420,000}{1.05} = \$400,000$$

The rate of return r is called the **discount rate, hurdle rate,** or **opportunity cost of capital.** It is an opportunity cost because it is the return that is foregone by investing in the project rather than investing in financial markets. In our example the opportunity cost is 5%, because you could earn a safe 5% by investing in U.S. government securities. Present value was found by *discounting* the future cash flows by this opportunity cost.

Suppose that as soon as you have bought the land and paid for the construction, you decide to sell your project. How much could you sell it for? That is an easy question. If the venture will return a surefire $420,000, then your property ought to be worth its PV of $400,000 today. That is what investors would need to pay to get the same future payoff. If you tried to sell it for more than $400,000, there would be no takers, because the property would then offer an expected rate of return lower than the 5% available on government securities. Of course, you could always sell your property for less, but why sell for less than the market will bear? The $400,000 present value is the only feasible price that satisfies both buyer and seller. Therefore, the present value of the property is also its market price.

Net Present Value

The office building is worth $400,000 today, but that does not mean you are $400,000 better off. You invested $370,000, so the **net present value (NPV)** is $30,000. Net present value equals present value minus the required investment:

$$NPV = PV - \text{investment} = 400,000 - 370,000 = \$30,000$$

In other words, your office development is worth more than it costs. It makes a *net* contribution to value and increases your wealth. The formula for calculating the NPV of your project can be written as:

$$NPV = C_0 + C_1/(1 + r)$$

Remember that C_0, the cash flow at time 0 (that is, today) is usually a negative number. In other words, C_0 is an investment and therefore a cash outflow. In our example, $C_0 = -\$370,000$.

When cash flows occur at different points in time, it is often helpful to draw a time line showing the date and value of each cash flow. Figure 2.3 shows a time line for your office development. It sets out the present value calculations assuming that the discount rate r is 5%.

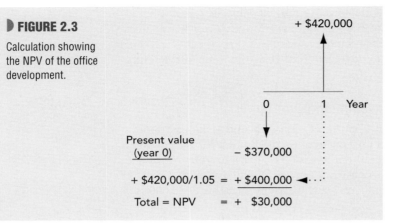

> **FIGURE 2.3**
>
> Calculation showing the NPV of the office development.

+ $420,000

0   1   Year

Present value
(year 0)   − $370,000

+ $420,000/1.05 = + $400,000 ◄····

Total = NPV   = + $30,000

Risk and Present Value

We made one unrealistic assumption in our discussion of the office development: Your real estate adviser cannot be certain about the profitability of an office building. Those future cash flows represent the best forecast, but they are not a sure thing.

If the cash flows are uncertain, your calculation of NPV is wrong. Investors could achieve those cash flows with certainty by buying $400,000 worth of U.S. government securities, so they would not buy your building for that amount. You would have to cut your asking price to attract investors' interest.

Here we can invoke a second basic financial principle: *A safe dollar is worth more than a risky dollar.* Most investors avoid risk when they can do so without sacrificing return. However, the concepts of present value and the opportunity cost of capital still make sense for risky investments. It is still proper to discount the payoff by the rate of return offered by a risk-equivalent investment in financial markets. But we have to think of *expected* payoffs and the *expected* rates of return on other investments.[2]

Not all investments are equally risky. The office development is more risky than a government security but less risky than a start-up biotech venture. Suppose you believe the project is as risky as investment in the stock market and that stocks offer a 12% expected return. Then 12% is the opportunity cost of capital. That is what you are giving up by investing in the office building and *not* investing in equally risky securities.

Now recompute NPV with $r = .12$:

$$PV = \frac{420,000}{1.12} = \$375,000$$

$$NPV = PV - 370,000 = \$5,000$$

The office building still makes a net contribution to value, but the increase in your wealth is smaller than in our first calculation, which assumed that the cash flows from the project were risk-free.

The value of the office building depends, therefore, on the timing of the cash flows and their risk. The $420,000 payoff would be worth just that if you could get it today. If the office building is as risk-free as government securities, the delay in the cash flow reduces value by $20,000 to $400,000. If the building is as risky as investment in the stock market, then the risk further reduces value by $25,000 to $375,000.

Unfortunately, adjusting asset values for both time and risk is often more complicated than our example suggests. Therefore, we take the two effects separately. For the most part, we dodge the problem of risk in Chapters 2 through 6, either by treating all cash flows as if they were known with certainty or by talking about expected cash

---

[2] We define "expected" more carefully in Chapter 9. For now think of expected payoff as a realistic forecast, neither optimistic nor pessimistic. Forecasts of expected payoffs are correct on average.

flows and expected rates of return without worrying how risk is defined or measured. Then in Chapter 7 we turn to the problem of understanding how financial markets cope with risk.

Present Values and Rates of Return

We have decided that constructing the office building is a smart thing to do, since it is worth more than it costs. To discover how much it is worth, we asked how much you would need to invest directly in securities to achieve the same payoff. That is why we discounted the project's future payoff by the rate of return offered by these equivalent-risk securities—the overall stock market in our example.

We can state our decision rule in another way: Your real estate venture is worth undertaking because its rate of return exceeds the opportunity cost of capital. The rate of return is simply the profit as a proportion of the initial outlay:

$$\text{Return} = \frac{\text{profit}}{\text{investment}} = \frac{420,000 - 370,000}{370,000} = .135, \text{ or } 13.5\%$$

The cost of capital is once again the return foregone by *not* investing in financial markets. If the office building is as risky as investing in the stock market, the return foregone is 12%. Since the 13.5% return on the office building exceeds the 12% opportunity cost, you should go ahead with the project.

Here, then, we have two equivalent decision rules for capital investment:[3]

- *Net present value rule.* Accept investments that have positive net present values.
- *Rate of return rule.* Accept investments that offer rates of return in excess of their opportunity costs of capital.[4]

Calculating Present Values When There Are Multiple Cash Flows

One of the nice things about present values is that they are all expressed in current dollars—so you can add them up. In other words, the present value of cash flow (A + B) is equal to the present value of cash flow A plus the present value of cash flow B.

Suppose that you wish to value a stream of cash flows extending over a number of years. Our rule for adding present values tells us that the *total* present value is:

$$PV = \frac{C_1}{(1+r)} + \frac{C_2}{(1+r)^2} + \frac{C_3}{(1+r)^3} + \cdots + \frac{C_T}{(1+r)^T}$$

This is called the **discounted cash flow** (or **DCF**) formula. A shorthand way to write it is

$$PV = \sum_{t=1}^{T} \frac{C_t}{(1+r)^t}$$

where Σ refers to the sum of the series. To find the *net* present value (NPV) we add the (usually negative) initial cash flow:

$$NPV = C_0 + PV = C_0 + \sum_{t=1}^{T} \frac{C_t}{(1+r)^t}$$

---

[3] You might check for yourself that these are equivalent rules. In other words, if the return of $50,000/$370,000 is greater than r, then the net present value − $370,000 + [$420,000/(1 + r)] *must* be greater than 0.

[4] The two rules can conflict when there are cash flows at more than two dates. We address this problem in Chapter 5.

EXAMPLE 2.1 ● Present Values with Multiple Cash Flows

Your real estate adviser has come back with some revised forecasts. He suggests that you rent out the building for two years at $20,000 a year, and predicts that at the end of that time you will be able to sell the building for $400,000. Thus there are now two future cash flows—a cash flow of $C_1 = \$20,000$ at the end of one year and a further cash flow of $C_2 = (20,000 + 400,000) = \$420,000$ at the end of the second year.

The present value of your property development is equal to the present value of C_1 plus the present value of C_2. Figure 2.4 shows that the value of the first year's cash flow is $C_1/(1 + r) = 20,000/1.12 = \$17,900$ and the value of the second year's flow is $C_2/(1 + r)^2 = 420,000/1.12^2 = \$334,800$. Therefore our rule for adding present values tells us that the *total* present value of your investment is

$$PV = \frac{C_1}{1 + r} + \frac{C_2}{(1 + r)^2} = \frac{20,000}{1.12} + \frac{420,000}{1.12^2} = 17,900 + 334,800 = \$352,700$$

Sorry, but your office building is now worth less than it costs. NPV is negative:

$$NPV = \$352,700 - \$370,000 = -\$17,300$$

Perhaps you should revert to the original plan of selling in year 1.

> **FIGURE 2.4**
>
> Calculation showing the NPV of the revised office project.

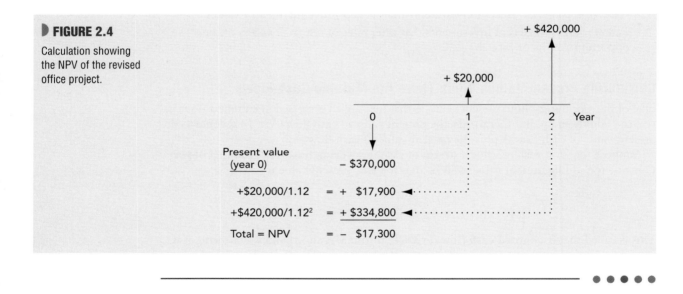

● ● ● ● ●

Your two-period calculations in Example 2.1 required just a few keystrokes on a calculator. Real problems can be much more complicated, so financial managers usually turn to financial calculators especially programmed for present value calculations or to computer spreadsheet programs. A box near the end of the chapter introduces you to some useful Excel functions that can be used to solve discounting problems. In addition, the Web site for this book (**www.mhhe.com/bma**) contains appendixes to help get you started using financial calculators and Excel spreadsheets. It also includes tables that can be used for a variety of discounting problems.

The Opportunity Cost of Capital

By investing in the office building you gave up the opportunity to earn an expected return of 12% in the stock market. The opportunity cost of capital is therefore 12%. When you discount the expected cash flows by the opportunity cost of capital, you are asking how much investors in the financial markets are prepared to pay for a security that produces a similar stream of future cash flows. Your calculations showed that investors would need to pay only $352,700 for an investment that produces cash flows of $20,000 at year 1 and $420,000 at year 2. Therefore, they won't pay any more than that for your office building.

Confusion sometimes sneaks into discussions of the cost of capital. Suppose a banker approaches. "Your company is a fine and safe business with few debts," she says. "My bank will lend you the $370,000 that you need for the office block at 8%." Does this mean that the cost of capital is 8%? If so, the project would be worth doing. At an 8% cost of capital, PV would be $20,000/1.08 + 420,000/1.08^2 = $378,600$ and NPV = $378,600 − $370,000 = + $8,600.

But that can't be right. First, the interest rate on the loan has nothing to do with the risk of the project: It reflects the good health of your existing business. Second, whether you take the loan or not, you still face the choice between the office building and an equally risky investment in the stock market. The stock market investment could generate the same expected payoff as your office building at a lower cost. A financial manager who borrows $370,000 at 8% and invests in an office building is not smart, but stupid, if the company or its shareholders can borrow at 8% and invest the money at an even higher return. That is why the 12% expected return on the stock market is the opportunity cost of capital for your project.

2-2 Looking for Shortcuts—Perpetuities and Annuities

How to Value Perpetuities

Sometimes there are shortcuts that make it easy to calculate present values. Let us look at some examples.

On occasion, the British and the French have been known to disagree and sometimes even to fight wars. At the end of some of these wars the British consolidated the debt they had issued during the war. The securities issued in such cases were called consols. Consols are **perpetuities.** These are bonds that the government is under no obligation to repay but that offer a fixed income for each year to perpetuity. The British government is still paying interest on consols issued all those years ago. The annual rate of return on a perpetuity is equal to the promised annual payment divided by the present value:[5]

$$\text{Return} = \frac{\text{cash flow}}{\text{present value}}$$

$$r = \frac{C}{\text{PV}}$$

---

[5] You can check this by writing down the present value formula

$$\text{PV} = \frac{C}{1+r} + \frac{C}{(1+r)^2} + \frac{C}{(1+r)^3} + \ \cdots$$

Now let $C/(1 + r) = a$ and $1/(1 + r) = x$. Then we have (1) PV = $a(1 + x + x^2 + \cdots)$.
Multiplying both sides by x, we have (2) PV$x = a(x + x^2 + \cdots)$.
Subtracting (2) from (1) gives us PV$(1 − x) = a$. Therefore, substituting for a and x,

$$\text{PV}\left(1 - \frac{1}{1+r}\right) = \frac{C}{1+r}$$

Multiplying both sides by $(1 + r)$ and rearranging gives

$$\text{PV} = \frac{C}{r}$$

We can obviously twist this around and find the present value of a perpetuity given the discount rate r and the cash payment C:

$$PV = \frac{C}{r}$$

The year is 2030. You have been fabulously successful and are now a billionaire many times over. It was fortunate indeed that you took that finance course all those years ago. You have decided to follow in the footsteps of two of your heroes, Bill Gates and Warren Buffet. Malaria is still a scourge and you want to help eradicate it and other infectious diseases by endowing a foundation to combat these diseases. You aim to provide $1 billion a year in perpetuity, starting next year. So, if the interest rate is 10%, you are going to have to write a check today for

$$\text{Present value of perpetuity} = \frac{C}{r} = \frac{\$1 \text{ billion}}{.1} = \$10 \text{ billion}$$

Two warnings about the perpetuity formula. First, at a quick glance you can easily confuse the formula with the present value of a single payment. A payment of $1 at the end of one year has a present value of $1/(1 + r)$. The perpetuity has a value of $1/r$. These are quite different.

Second, the perpetuity formula tells us the value of a regular stream of payments starting one period from now. Thus your $10 billion endowment would provide the foundation with its first payment in one year's time. If you also want to provide an up-front sum, you will need to lay out an extra $1 billion.

Sometimes you may need to calculate the value of a perpetuity that does not start to make payments for several years. For example, suppose that you decide to provide $1 billion a year with the first payment four years from now. We know that in year 3 this endowment will be an ordinary perpetuity with payments starting in one year. So our perpetuity formula tells us that in year 3 the endowment will be worth $1/r = 1/.1 = $10 billion. But it is not worth that much now. To find *today's* value we need to multiply by the three-year discount factor $1/(1 + r)^3 = 1/(1.1)^3 = .751$. Thus, the "delayed" perpetuity is worth $10 billion × .751 = $7.51 billion. The full calculation is

$$PV = \$1 \text{ billion} \times \frac{1}{r} \times \frac{1}{(1+r)^3} = \$1 \text{ billion} \times \frac{1}{.10} \times \frac{1}{(1.10)^3} = \$7.51 \text{ billion}$$

How to Value Annuities

An **annuity** is an asset that pays a fixed sum each year for a specified number of years. The equal-payment house mortgage or installment credit agreement are common examples of annuities. So are interest payments on most bonds, as we see in the next chapter.

Figure 2.5 illustrates a simple trick for valuing annuities. It shows the payments and values of three investments.

Row 1 The investment in the first row provides a perpetual stream of $1 starting at the end of the first year. We have already seen that this perpetuity has a present value of $1/r$.

Row 2 Now look at the investment shown in the second row. It also provides a perpetual stream of $1 payments, but these payments don't start until year 4. This investment is identical to the delayed perpetuity that we have just valued. In year 3, the investment will be an ordinary perpetuity with payments starting in one year and will be worth $1/r$ in year 3. Its value today is, therefore,

$$PV = \frac{1}{r(1 + r)^3}$$

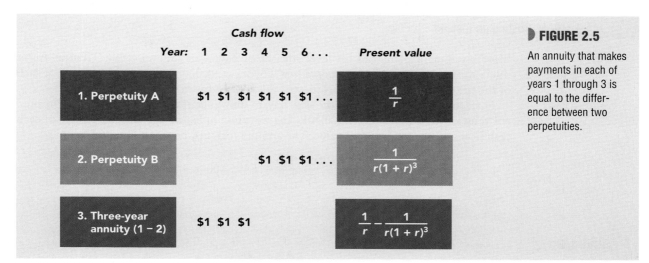

FIGURE 2.5

An annuity that makes payments in each of years 1 through 3 is equal to the difference between two perpetuities.

Row 3 The perpetuities in rows 1 and 2 both provide a cash flow from year 4 onward. The only difference between the two investments is that the first one also provides a cash flow in each of years 1 through 3. In other words, the difference between the two perpetuities is an annuity of three years. Row 3 shows that the present value of this annuity is equal to the value of the row 1 perpetuity less the value of the delayed perpetuity in row 2:[6]

$$\text{PV of 3-year annuity} = \frac{1}{r} - \frac{1}{r(1+r)^3}$$

The general formula for the value of an annuity that pays $1 a year for each of t years starting in year 1 is:

$$\text{Present value of annuity} = \frac{1}{r} - \frac{1}{r(1+r)^t}$$

This expression is generally known as the t-year annuity factor.[7] Remembering formulas is about as difficult as remembering other people's birthdays. But as long as you bear in mind that an annuity is equivalent to the difference between an immediate and a delayed perpetuity, you shouldn't have any difficulty.

---

[6] Again we can work this out from first principles. We need to calculate the sum of the finite geometric series (1) PV = $a(1 + x + x^2 + \cdots + x^{t-1})$, where $a = C/(1 + r)$ and $x = 1/(1 + r)$.

Multiplying both sides by x, we have (2) PV$x = a(x + x^2 + \cdots + x^t)$.

Subtracting (2) from (1) gives us PV$(1 - x) = a(1 - x^t)$.

Therefore, substituting for a and x,

$$\text{PV}\left(1 - \frac{1}{1+r}\right) = C\left[\frac{1}{1+r} - \frac{1}{(1+r)^{t+1}}\right]$$

Multiplying both sides by $(1 + r)$ and rearranging gives

$$\text{PV} = C\left[\frac{1}{r} - \frac{1}{r(1+r)^t}\right]$$

[7] Some people find the following equivalent formula more intuitive:

$$\text{Present value of annuity} = \underbrace{\frac{1}{r}}_{\substack{\text{perpetuity} \\ \text{formula}}} \underbrace{\left[1 - \frac{1}{(1+r)^t}\right]}_{\substack{\$1 \qquad \text{minus } \$1 \\ \text{starting} \quad \text{starting at} \\ \text{next year} \quad t+1}}$$

EXAMPLE 2.2 ● Costing an Installment Plan

Most installment plans call for level streams of payments. Suppose that Tiburon Autos offers an "easy payment" scheme on a new Toyota of $5,000 a year, paid at the end of each of the next five years, with no cash down. What is the car really costing you?

First let us do the calculations the slow way, to show that, if the interest rate is 7%, the present value of these payments is $20,501. The time line in Figure 2.6 shows the value of each cash flow and the total present value. The annuity formula, however, is generally quicker:

$$PV = 5,000\left[\frac{1}{.07} - \frac{1}{.07(1.07)^5}\right] = 5,000 \times 4.100 = \$20,501$$

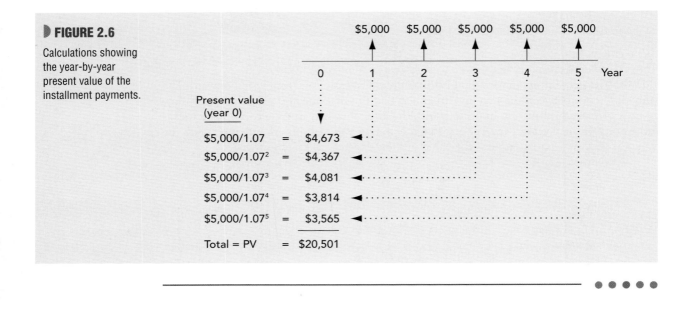

▶ **FIGURE 2.6**

Calculations showing the year-by-year present value of the installment payments.

● ● ● ● ●

EXAMPLE 2.3 ● Winning Big at the Lottery

When 13 lucky machinists from Ohio pooled their money to buy Powerball lottery tickets, they won a record $295.7 million. (A fourteenth member of the group pulled out at the last minute to put in his own numbers.) We suspect that the winners received unsolicited congratulations, good wishes, and requests for money from dozens of more or less worthy charities. In response, they could fairly point out that the prize wasn't really worth $295.7 million. That sum was to be repaid in 25 annual installments of $11.828 million each. Assuming that the first payment occurred at the end of one year, what was the present value of the prize? The interest rate at the time was 5.9%.

These payments constitute a 25-year annuity. To value this annuity we simply multiply $11.828 million by the 25-year annuity factor:

$$PV = 11.828 \times 25\text{-year annuity factor}$$

$$= 11.828 \times \left[\frac{1}{r} - \frac{1}{r(1 + r)^{25}}\right]$$

At an interest rate of 5.9%, the annuity factor is

$$\left[\frac{1}{.059} - \frac{1}{.059(1.059)^{25}}\right] = 12.9057$$

The present value of the cash payments is $11.828 \times 12.9057 = \$152.6$ million, much below the well-trumpeted prize, but still not a bad day's haul.

Lottery operators generally make arrangements for winners with big spending plans to take an equivalent lump sum. In our example the winners could either take the $295.7 million spread over 25 years or receive $152.6 million up front. Both arrangements had the same present value.

● ● ● ● ●

PV Annuities Due

When we used the annuity formula to value the Powerball lottery prize in Example 2.3, we presupposed that the first payment was made at the end of one year. In fact, the first of the 25 yearly payments was made immediately. How does this change the value of the prize?

If we discount each cash flow by one less year, the present value is increased by the multiple $(1 + r)$. In the case of the lottery prize the value becomes $152.6 \times (1 + r) = 152.6 \times 1.059 = \$161.6$ million.

A level stream of payments starting immediately is called an **annuity due.** An annuity due is worth $(1 + r)$ times the value of an ordinary annuity.

Calculating Annual Payments

Annuity problems can be confusing on first acquaintance, but you will find that with practice they are generally straightforward. In Example 2.4, you will need to use the annuity formula to find the amount of the payment given the present value.

EXAMPLE 2.4   ● Finding Mortgage Payments

Suppose that you take out a $250,000 house mortgage from your local savings bank. The bank requires you to repay the mortgage in equal annual installments over the next 30 years. It must therefore set the annual payments so that they have a present value of $250,000. Thus,

$$PV = \text{mortgage payment} \times \text{30-year annuity factor} = \$250,000$$
$$\text{Mortgage payment} = \$250,000/\text{30-year annuity factor}$$

Suppose that the interest rate is 12% a year. Then

$$\text{30-year annuity factor} = \left[\frac{1}{.12} - \frac{1}{.12(1.12)^{30}}\right] = 8.055$$

and

$$\text{Mortgage payment} = 250,000/8.055 = \$31,037$$

● ● ● ● ●

The mortgage loan is an example of an *amortizing loan.* "Amortizing" means that part of the regular payment is used to pay interest on the loan and part is used to reduce the amount of the loan.

Table 2.1 illustrates another amortizing loan. This time it is a four-year loan of $1,000 with an interest rate of 10% and annual payments. The annual payment needed to repay the loan is $315.47. In other words, $1,000 divided by the four-year annuity factor is $315.47. At the end of the first year, the interest charge is 10% of $1,000, or $100. So $100 of the first payment is absorbed by interest, and the remaining $215.47 is used to reduce (or "amortize") the loan balance to $784.53.

Next year, the outstanding balance is lower, so the interest charge is only $78.45. Therefore $315.47 − 78.45 = $237.02 can be applied to amortization. Because the loan is progressively paid off, the fraction of each payment devoted to interest steadily falls over time, while the fraction used to reduce the loan increases. By the end of year 4 the amortization is just enough to reduce the balance of the loan to zero.

Year	Beginning-of-Year Balance	Year-End Interest on Balance	Total Year-End Payment	Amortization of Loan	End-of-Year Balance
1	$1,000.00	$100.00	$315.47	$215.47	$784.53
2	784.53	78.45	315.47	237.02	547.51
3	547.51	54.75	315.47	260.72	286.79
4	286.79	28.68	315.47	286.79	0

▶ **TABLE 2.1**   An example of an amortizing loan. If you borrow $1,000 at an interest rate of 10%, you would need to make an annual payment of $315.47 over four years to repay that loan with interest.

Future Value of an Annuity

Sometimes you need to calculate the *future* value of a level stream of payments.

EXAMPLE 2.5 ● Saving to Buy a Sailboat

Perhaps your ambition is to buy a sailboat; something like a 40-foot Beneteau would fit the bill very well. But that means some serious saving. You estimate that, once you start work, you could save $20,000 a year out of your income and earn a return of 8% on these savings. How much will you be able to spend after five years?

We are looking here at a level stream of cash flows—an annuity. We have seen that there is a shortcut formula to calculate the *present* value of an annuity. So there ought to be a similar formula for calculating the *future value* of a level stream of cash flows.

Think first how much your savings are worth today. You will set aside $20,000 in each of the next five years. The present value of this five-year annuity is therefore equal to

$$PV = \$20,000 \times \text{5-year annuity factor}$$

$$= \$20,000 \times \left[\frac{1}{.08} - \frac{1}{.08(1.08)^5} \right] = \$79,854$$

Now think how much you would have after five years if you invested $79,854 today. Simple! Just multiply by $(1.08)^5$:

$$\text{Value at end of year 5} = \$79,854 \times 1.08^5 = \$117,332$$

You should be able to buy yourself a nice boat for $117,000.

● ● ● ● ●

In Example 2.5 we calculated the future value of an annuity by first calculating its present value and then multiplying by $(1 + r)^t$. The general formula for the future value of a level stream of cash flows of $1 a year for t years is, therefore,

$$\text{Future value of annuity} = \text{present value of annuity of \$1 a year} \times (1 + r)^t$$

$$= \left[\frac{1}{r} - \frac{1}{r(1 + r)^t} \right] \times (1 + r)^t = \frac{(1 + r)^t - 1}{r}$$

2-3 More Shortcuts—Growing Perpetuities and Annuities

Growing Perpetuities

You now know how to value level streams of cash flows, but you often need to value a stream of cash flows that grows at a constant rate. For example, think back to your plans to donate $10 billion to fight malaria and other infectious diseases. Unfortunately, you made no allowance for the growth in salaries and other costs, which will probably average about 4% a year starting in year 1. Therefore, instead of providing $1 billion a year in perpetuity, you must provide $1 billion in year 1, $1.04 \times \$1$ billion in year 2, and so on. If we call the growth rate in costs g, we can write down the present value of this stream of cash flows as follows:

$$\text{PV} = \frac{C_1}{1 + r} + \frac{C_2}{(1 + r)^2} + \frac{C_3}{(1 + r)^3} + \cdots$$

$$= \frac{C_1}{1 + r} + \frac{C_1(1 + g)}{(1 + r)^2} + \frac{C_1(1 + g)^2}{(1 + r)^3} + \cdots$$

Fortunately, there is a simple formula for the sum of this geometric series.[8] If we assume that r is greater than g, our clumsy-looking calculation simplifies to

$$\text{Present value of growing perpetuity} = \frac{C_1}{r - g}$$

Therefore, if you want to provide a perpetual stream of income that keeps pace with the growth rate in costs, the amount that you must set aside today is

$$\text{PV} = \frac{C_1}{r - g} = \frac{\$1 \text{ billion}}{.10 - .04} = \$16.667 \text{ billion}$$

You will meet this perpetual-growth formula again in Chapter 4, where we use it to value the stock of mature, slowly growing companies.

---

[8] We need to calculate the sum of an infinite geometric series PV $= a(1 + x + x^2 + \cdots)$ where $a = C_1/(1 + r)$ and $x = (1 + g)/(1 + r)$. In footnote 5 we showed that the sum of such a series is $a/(1 - x)$. Substituting for a and x in this formula,

$$\text{PV} = \frac{C_1}{r - g}$$

Growing Annuities

You are contemplating membership in the St. Swithin's and Ancient Golf Club. The annual membership dues for the coming year are $5,000, but you can make a single payment of $12,750, which will provide you with membership for the next three years. In each case no payments are due until the end of the first year. Which is the better deal? The answer depends on how rapidly membership fees are likely to increase over the three-year period. For example, suppose that fees are payable at the end of each year and are expected to increase by 6% per annum. The discount rate is 10%.

The problem is to calculate the value of a three-year stream of cash flows that grows at the rate of $g = .06$ each year. Of course, you could calculate each year's cash flow and discount it at 10%. The alternative is to employ the same trick that we used to find the formula for an ordinary annuity. This is illustrated in Figure 2.7. The first row shows the value of a perpetuity that produces a cash flow of $1 in year 1, $1 \times (1 + g)$ in year 2, and so on. It has a present value of

$$PV = \frac{\$1}{(r - g)}$$

The second row shows a similar growing perpetuity that produces its first cash flow of $1 \times (1 + g)^3$ in year 4. It *will* have a present value of $1 \times (1 + g)^3/(r - g)$ in year 3 and therefore has a value today of

$$PV = \frac{\$1}{(r - g)} \times \frac{(1 + g)^3}{(1 + r)^3}$$

The third row in the figure shows that the difference between the two sets of cash flows consists of a three-year stream of cash flows beginning with $1 in year 1 and growing each year at the rate of g. Its value is equal to the difference between our two growing perpetuities:

$$PV = \frac{\$1}{(r - g)} - \frac{\$1}{(r - g)} \times \frac{(1 + g)^3}{(1 + r)^3}$$

In our golf club example, the present value of the three annual membership dues would be:

$$PV = [1/(.10 - .06) - (1.06)^3/(.10 - .06)(1.10)^3] \times \$5,000$$
$$= 2.629 \times \$5,000 = \$13,146$$

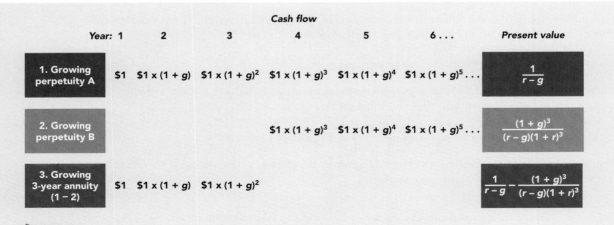

▶ FIGURE 2.7

A three-year stream of cash flows that grows at the rate g is equal to the difference between two growing perpetuities.

				Cash Flow, $				
Year:	**0**	**1**	**2 . . .**	**. . . $t-1$**	**t**	**$t+1$ . . .**	**Present Value**	
Perpetuity		1	1 . . .	1	1	1 . . .	$\dfrac{1}{r}$	
t-period annuity		1	1 . . .	1	1		$\dfrac{1}{r} - \dfrac{1}{r(1+r)^t}$	
t-period annuity due	1	1	1 . . .	1			$(1+r)\left(\dfrac{1}{r} - \dfrac{1}{r(1+r)^t}\right)$	
Growing perpetuity		1	$1 \times (1+g)$ . . .	$1 \times (1+g)^{t-2}$	$1 \times (1+g)^{t-1}$	$1 \times (1+g)^t$ . . .	$\dfrac{1}{r-g}$	
t-period growing annuity		1	$1 \times (1+g)$ . . .	$1 \times (1+g)^{t-2}$	$1 \times (1+g)^{t-1}$		$\dfrac{1}{r-g} - \dfrac{1}{r-g} \times \dfrac{(1+g)^t}{(1+r)^t}$	

▶ **TABLE 2.2** Some useful shortcut formulas.

If you can find the cash, you would be better off paying now for a three-year membership.

Too many formulas are bad for the digestion. So we will stop at this point and spare you any more of them. The formulas discussed so far appear in Table 2.2.

2-4 How Interest Is Paid and Quoted

In our examples we have assumed that cash flows occur only at the end of each year. This is sometimes the case. For example, in France and Germany the government pays interest on its bonds annually. However, in the United States and Britain government bonds pay interest semiannually. So if the interest rate on a U.S. government bond is quoted as 10%, the investor in practice receives interest of 5% every six months.

If the first interest payment is made at the end of six months, you can earn an additional six months' interest on this payment. For example, if you invest $100 in a bond that pays interest of 10% compounded semiannually, your wealth will grow to $1.05 \times \$100 = \$105$ by the end of six months and to $1.05 \times \$105 = \$110.25$ by the end of the year. In other words, an interest rate of 10% compounded semiannually is equivalent to 10.25% compounded annually. The *effective annual interest rate* on the bond is 10.25%.

Let's take another example. Suppose a bank offers you an automobile loan at an **annual percentage rate,** or **APR,** of 12% with interest to be paid monthly. This means that each month you need to pay one-twelfth of the annual rate, that is, $12/12 = 1\%$ a month. Thus the bank is *quoting* a rate of 12%, but the effective annual interest rate on your loan is $1.01^{12} - 1 = .1268$, or 12.68%.[9]

Our examples illustrate that you need to distinguish between the *quoted* annual interest rate and the *effective* annual rate. The quoted annual rate is usually calculated as the total

---

[9] In the U.S., truth-in-lending laws oblige the company to quote an APR that is calculated by multiplying the payment each period by the number of payments in the year. APRs are calculated differently in other countries. For example, in the European Union APRs must be expressed as annually compounded rates, so consumers know the effective interest rate that they are paying.

annual payment divided by the number of payments in the year. When interest is paid once a year, the quoted and effective rates are the same. When interest is paid more frequently, the effective interest rate is higher than the quoted rate.

In general, if you invest \$1 at a rate of r per year compounded m times a year, your investment at the end of the year will be worth $[1 + (r/m)]^m$ and the effective interest rate is $[1 + (r/m)]^m - 1$. In our automobile loan example $r = .12$ and $m = 12$. So the effective annual interest rate was $[1 + .12/12]^{12} - 1 = .1268$, or 12.68%.

Continuous Compounding

Instead of compounding interest monthly or semiannually, the rate could be compounded weekly ($m = 52$) or daily ($m = 365$). In fact there is no limit to how frequently interest could be paid. One can imagine a situation where the payments are spread evenly and continuously throughout the year, so the interest rate is continuously compounded.[10] In this case m is infinite.

It turns out that there are many occasions in finance when continuous compounding is useful. For example, one important application is in option pricing models, such as the Black–Scholes model that we introduce in Chapter 17. These are continuous time models. So you will find that most computer programs for calculating option values ask for the continuously compounded interest rate.

It may seem that a lot of calculations would be needed to find a continuously compounded interest rate. However, think back to your high school algebra. You may recall that as m approaches infinity $[1 + (r/m)]^m$ approaches $(2.718)^r$. The figure 2.718—or e, as it is called—is the base for natural logarithms. Therefore, \$1 invested at a continuously compounded rate of r will grow to $e^r = (2.718)^r$ by the end of the first year. By the end of t years it will grow to $e^{rt} = (2.718)^{rt}$.

Example 1   Suppose you invest \$1 at a continuously compounded rate of 11% ($r = .11$) for one year ($t = 1$). The end-year value is $e^{.11}$, or \$1.116. In other words, investing at 11% a year *continuously* compounded is exactly the same as investing at 11.6% a year *annually* compounded.

Example 2   Suppose you invest \$1 at a continuously compounded rate of 11% ($r = .11$) for two years ($t = 2$). The final value of the investment is $e^{rt} = e^{.22}$, or \$1.246.

Sometimes it may be more reasonable to assume that the cash flows from a project are spread evenly over the year rather than occurring at the year's end. It is easy to adapt our previous formulas to handle this. For example, suppose that we wish to compute the present value of a perpetuity of C dollars a year. We already know that if the payment is made at the end of the year, we divide the payment by the *annually* compounded rate of r:

$$PV = \frac{C}{r}$$

If the same total payment is made in an even stream throughout the year, we use the same formula but substitute the *continuously* compounded rate.

Example 3   Suppose the annually compounded rate is 18.5%. The present value of a \$100 perpetuity, with each cash flow received at the end of the year, is $100/.185 = \$540.54$. If

---

[10] When we talk about *continuous* payments, we are pretending that money can be dispensed in a continuous stream like water out of a faucet. One can never quite do this. For example, instead of paying out \$1 billion every year to combat malaria, you could pay out about \$1 million every 8¾ hours or \$10,000 every 5¼ minutes or \$10 every 3⅙ seconds but you could not pay it out *continuously*. Financial managers *pretend* that payments are continuous rather than hourly, daily, or weekly because (1) it simplifies the calculations and (2) it gives a very close approximation to the NPV of frequent payments.

Discounting Cash Flows

▶ Spreadsheet programs such as Excel provide built-in functions to solve discounted-cash-flow (DCF) problems. You can find these functions by pressing *fx* on the Excel toolbar. If you then click on the function that you wish to use, Excel asks you for the inputs that it needs. At the bottom left of the function box there is a Help facility with an example of how the function is used.

Here is a list of useful functions for DCF problems and some points to remember when entering data:

- **FV:** Future value of single investment or annuity.
- **PV:** Present value of single future cash flow or annuity.
- **RATE:** Interest rate (or rate of return) needed to produce given future value or annuity.
- **NPER:** Number of periods (e.g., years) that it takes an investment to reach a given future value or series of future cash flows.
- **PMT:** Amount of annuity payment with a given present or future value.
- **NPV:** The value of a stream of negative and positive cash flows. (When using this function, note the warning below.)
- **XNPV:** The net present value of a series of unequal cash flows at the date of the first cash flow.
- **EFFECT:** The effective annual interest rate, given the quoted rate (APR) and number of interest payments in a year.

- **NOMINAL:** The quoted interest rate (APR) given the effective annual interest rate.

All the inputs in these functions can be entered directly as numbers or as the addresses of cells that contain the numbers. Three warnings:

1. PV is the amount that needs to be invested today to produce a given future value. It should therefore be entered as a negative number. Entering both PV and FV with the same sign when solving for RATE results in an error message.

2. Always enter the interest or discount rate as a decimal value.

3. Use the NPV function with care. It gives the value of the cash flows one period *before* the first cash flow and not the value at the date of the first cash flow.

SPREADSHEET QUESTIONS

The following questions provide opportunities to practice each of the Excel functions.

2.1 (FV) In 1880 five aboriginal trackers were each promised the equivalent of 100 Australian dollars for helping to capture the notorious outlaw Ned Kelly. One hundred and thirteen years later the granddaughters of two of the trackers claimed that this reward had not been paid. If the interest rate over this period averaged about 4.5%, how much would the A$100 have accumulated to?

2.2 (PV) Your company can lease a truck for $10,000 a year (paid at the end of the year) for six years, or it can buy the truck today for $50,000. At the end of the six years the truck will be worthless. If the interest rate is 6%, what is the present value of the lease payments? Is the lease worthwhile?

2.3 (RATE) Ford Motor stock was one of the victims of the 2008 credit crisis. In June 2007, Ford stock price stood at $9.42. Eighteen months later it was $2.72. What was the annual rate of return over this period to an investor in Ford stock?

2.4 (NPER) An investment adviser has promised to double your money. If the interest rate is 7% a year, how many years will she take to do so?

(*continued on next page*)

(continued)

2.5 (PMT) You need to take out a home mortgage for $200,000. If payments are made annually over 30 years and the interest rate is 8%, what is the amount of the annual payment?

2.6 (XNPV) Your office building requires an initial cash outlay of $370,000. Suppose that you plan to rent it out for three years at $20,000 a year and then sell it for $400,000. If the cost of capital is 12%, what is its net present value?

2.7 (EFFECT) First National Bank pays 6.2% interest compounded annually. Second National Bank pays 6% interest compounded monthly. Which bank offers the higher effective annual interest rate?

2.8 (NOMINAL) What monthly compounded interest rate would Second National Bank need to pay on savings deposits to provide an effective rate of 6.2%?

---

the cash flow is received continuously, we must divide $100 by 17%, because 17% continuously compounded is equivalent to 18.5% annually compounded ($e^{.17} = 1.185$). The present value of the continuous cash flow stream is $100/.17 = 588.24. Investors are prepared to pay more for the continuous cash payments because the cash starts to flow in immediately.

For any other continuous payments, we can always use our formula for valuing annuities. For instance, suppose that you have thought again about your donation and have decided to fund a vaccination program in emerging countries, which will cost $1 billion a year, starting immediately, and spread evenly over 20 years. Previously, we used the annually compounded rate of 10%; now we must use the continuously compounded rate of $r = 9.53\%$ ($e^{.0953} = 1.10$). To cover such an expenditure, then, you need to set aside the following sum:[11]

$$PV = C\left(\frac{1}{r} - \frac{1}{r} \times \frac{1}{e^{rt}}\right)$$

$$= \$1 \text{ billion} \left(\frac{1}{.0953} - \frac{1}{.0953} \times \frac{1}{6.727}\right) = \$1 \text{ billion} \times 8.932 = \$8.932 \text{ billion}$$

If you look back at our earlier discussion of annuities, you will notice that the present value of $1 billion paid at the *end* of each of the 20 years was $8.514 billion. Therefore, it costs you $418 million—or 5%—more to provide a continuous payment stream.

Often in finance we need only a ballpark estimate of present value. An error of 5% in a present value calculation may be perfectly acceptable. In such cases it doesn't usually matter whether we assume that cash flows occur at the end of the year or in a continuous stream. At other times precision matters, and we do need to worry about the exact frequency of the cash flows.

---

[11] Remember that an annuity is simply the difference between a perpetuity received today and a perpetuity received in year t. A continuous stream of C dollars a year in perpetuity is worth C/r, where r is the continuously compounded rate. Our annuity, then, is worth

$$PV = \frac{C}{r} - \text{present value of } \frac{C}{r} \text{ received in year } t$$

Since r is the continuously compounded rate, C/r received in year t is worth $(C/r) \times (1/e^{rt})$ today. Our annuity formula is therefore

$$PV = \frac{C}{r} - \frac{C}{r} \times \frac{1}{e^{rt}}$$

sometimes written as

$$\frac{C}{r}(1 - e)^{-rt}$$

Firms can best help their shareholders by accepting all projects that are worth more than they cost. In other words, they need to seek out projects with positive net present values. To find net present value we first calculate present value. Just discount future cash flows by an appropriate rate r, usually called the *discount rate, hurdle rate,* or *opportunity cost of capital:*

$$\text{Present value (PV)} = \frac{C_1}{(1 + r)} + \frac{C_2}{(1 + r)^2} + \frac{C_3}{(1 + r)^3} + \cdots$$

Net present value is present value plus any immediate cash flow:

$$\text{Net present value (NPV)} = C_0 + \text{PV}$$

Remember that C_0 is negative if the immediate cash flow is an investment, that is, if it is a cash outflow.

The discount rate r is determined by rates of return prevailing in capital markets. If the future cash flow is absolutely safe, then the discount rate is the interest rate on safe securities such as U.S. government debt. If the future cash flow is uncertain, then the expected cash flow should be discounted at the expected rate of return offered by equivalent-risk securities. (We talk more about risk and the cost of capital in Chapters 7 to 9.)

Cash flows are discounted for two simple reasons: because (1) a dollar today is worth more than a dollar tomorrow and (2) a safe dollar is worth more than a risky one. Formulas for PV and NPV are numerical expressions of these ideas.

Financial markets, including the bond and stock markets, are the markets where safe and risky future cash flows are traded and valued. That is why we look to rates of return prevailing in the financial markets to determine how much to discount for time and risk. By calculating the present value of an asset, we are estimating how much people will pay for it if they have the alternative of investing in the capital markets.

You can always work out any present value using the basic formula, but shortcut formulas can reduce the tedium. We showed how to value an investment that makes a level stream of cash flows forever (a *perpetuity*) and one that produces a level stream for a limited period (an *annuity*). We also showed how to value investments that produce growing streams of cash flows.

When someone offers to lend you a dollar at a quoted interest rate, you should always check how frequently the interest is to be paid. For example, suppose that a $100 loan requires six-month payments of $3. The total yearly interest payment is $6 and the interest will be quoted as a rate of 6% compounded semiannually. The equivalent *annually compounded rate* is $(1.03)^2 - 1 = .061$, or 6.1%. Sometimes it is convenient to assume that interest is paid evenly over the year, so that interest is quoted as a continuously compounded rate.

BASIC

1. At an interest rate of 12%, the six-year discount factor is .507. How many dollars is $.507 worth in six years if invested at 12%?

2. If the PV of $139 is $125, what is the discount factor?

3. If the cost of capital is 9%, what is the PV of $374 paid in year 9?

4. A project produces a cash flow of $432 in year 1, $137 in year 2, and $797 in year 3. If the cost of capital is 15%, what is the project's PV?

5. If you invest $100 at an interest rate of 15%, how much will you have at the end of eight years?

6. An investment costs $1,548 and pays $138 in perpetuity. If the interest rate is 9%, what is the NPV?

7. A common stock will pay a cash dividend of $4 next year. After that, the dividends are expected to increase indefinitely at 4% per year. If the discount rate is 14%, what is the PV of the stream of dividend payments?

8. The interest rate is 10%.
   a. What is the PV of an asset that pays $1 a year in perpetuity?
   b. The value of an asset that appreciates at 10% per annum approximately doubles in seven years. What is the approximate PV of an asset that pays $1 a year in perpetuity beginning in year 8?
   c. What is the approximate PV of an asset that pays $1 a year for each of the next seven years?
   d. A piece of land produces an income that grows by 5% per annum. If the first year's income is $10,000, what is the value of the land?

9. a. The cost of a new automobile is $10,000. If the interest rate is 5%, how much would you have to set aside now to provide this sum in five years?
   b. You have to pay $12,000 a year in school fees at the end of each of the next six years. If the interest rate is 8%, how much do you need to set aside today to cover these bills?
   c. You have invested $60,476 at 8%. After paying the above school fees, how much would remain at the end of the six years?

10. The continuously compounded interest rate is 12%.
    a. You invest $1,000 at this rate. What is the investment worth after five years?
    b. What is the PV of $5 million to be received in eight years?
    c. What is the PV of a continuous stream of cash flows, amounting to $2,000 per year, starting immediately and continuing for 15 years?

11. You are quoted an interest rate of 6% on an investment of $10 million. What is the value of your investment after four years if interest is compounded:
    a. Annually?
    b. Monthly? or
    c. Continuously?

INTERMEDIATE

12. What is the PV of $100 received in:
    a. Year 10 (at a discount rate of 1%)?
    b. Year 10 (at a discount rate of 13%)?
    c. Year 15 (at a discount rate of 25%)?
    d. Each of years 1 through 3 (at a discount rate of 12%)?

13. a. If the one-year discount factor is .905, what is the one-year interest rate?
    b. If the two-year interest rate is 10.5%, what is the two-year discount factor?
    c. Given these one- and two-year discount factors, calculate the two-year annuity factor.
    d. If the PV of $10 a year for three years is $24.65, what is the three-year annuity factor?
    e. From your answers to (c) and (d), calculate the three-year discount factor.

14. A factory costs $800,000. You reckon that it will produce an inflow after operating costs of $170,000 a year for 10 years. If the opportunity cost of capital is 14%, what is the net present value of the factory? What will the factory be worth at the end of five years?

15. A machine costs $380,000 and is expected to produce the following cash flows:

Year	1	2	3	4	5	6	7	8	9	10
Cash flow ($000s)	50	57	75	80	85	92	92	80	68	50

If the cost of capital is 12%, what is the machine's NPV?

16. Mike Polanski is 30 years of age and his salary next year will be $40,000. Mike forecasts that his salary will increase at a steady rate of 5% per annum until his retirement at age 60.

    a. If the discount rate is 8%, what is the PV of these future salary payments?

    b. If Mike saves 5% of his salary each year and invests these savings at an interest rate of 8%, how much will he have saved by age 60?

    c. If Mike plans to spend these savings in even amounts over the subsequent 20 years, how much can he spend each year?

17. A factory costs $400,000. It will produce an inflow after operating costs of $100,000 in year 1, $200,000 in year 2, and $300,000 in year 3. The opportunity cost of capital is 12%. Calculate the NPV.

18. Halcyon Lines is considering the purchase of a new bulk carrier for $8 million. The forecasted revenues are $5 million a year and operating costs are $4 million. A major refit costing $2 million will be required after both the fifth and tenth years. After 15 years, the ship is expected to be sold for scrap at $1.5 million. If the discount rate is 8%, what is the ship's NPV?

Visit us at
www.mhhe.com/bma

19. As winner of a breakfast cereal competition, you can choose one of the following prizes:

    a. $100,000 now.

    b. $180,000 at the end of five years.

    c. $11,400 a year forever.

    d. $19,000 for each of 10 years.

    e. $6,500 next year and increasing thereafter by 5% a year forever.

    If the interest rate is 12%, which is the most valuable prize?

20. Siegfried Basset is 65 years of age and has a life expectancy of 12 more years. He wishes to invest $20,000 in an annuity that will make a level payment at the end of each year until his death. If the interest rate is 8%, what income can Mr. Basset expect to receive each year?

21. David and Helen Zhang are saving to buy a boat at the end of five years. If the boat costs $20,000 and they can earn 10% a year on their savings, how much do they need to put aside at the end of years 1 through 5?

22. Kangaroo Autos is offering free credit on a new $10,000 car. You pay $1,000 down and then $300 a month for the next 30 months. Turtle Motors next door does not offer free credit but will give you $1,000 off the list price. If the rate of interest is 10% a year (about .83% a month), which company is offering the better deal?

23. Recalculate the NPV of the office building venture in Section 2-1 at interest rates of 5, 10, and 15%. Plot the points on a graph with NPV on the vertical axis and the discount rates on the horizontal axis. At what discount rate (approximately) would the project have zero NPV? Check your answer.

24. If the interest rate is 7%, what is the value of the following three investments?

    a. An investment that offers you $100 a year in perpetuity with the payment at the *end* of each year.

    b. A similar investment with the payment at the *beginning* of each year.

    c. A similar investment with the payment spread evenly over each year.

25. Refer back to Sections 2-2-2-4. If the rate of interest is 8% rather than 10%, how much would you need to set aside to provide each of the following?

    a. $1 billion at the end of each year in perpetuity.

    b. A perpetuity that pays $1 billion at the end of the first year and that grows at 4% a year.

    c. $1 billion at the end of each year for 20 years.

    d. $1 billion a year spread evenly over 20 years.

26. How much will you have at the end of 20 years if you invest $100 today at 15% *annually* compounded? How much will you have if you invest at 15% *continuously* compounded?

27. You have just read an advertisement stating, "Pay us $100 a year for 10 years and we will pay you $100 a year thereafter in perpetuity." If this is a fair deal, what is the rate of interest?

28. Which would you prefer?

a. An investment paying interest of 12% compounded annually.

b. An investment paying interest of 11.7% compounded semiannually.

c. An investment paying 11.5% compounded continuously.

Work out the value of each of these investments after 1, 5, and 20 years.

29. A leasing contract calls for an immediate payment of $100,000 and nine subsequent $100,000 semiannual payments at six-month intervals. What is the PV of these payments if the *annual* discount rate is 8%?

30. Several years ago *The Wall Street Journal* reported that the winner of the Massachusetts State Lottery prize had the misfortune to be both bankrupt and in prison for fraud. The prize was $9,420,713, to be paid in 19 equal annual installments. (There were 20 installments, but the winner had already received the first payment.) The bankruptcy court judge ruled that the prize should be sold off to the highest bidder and the proceeds used to pay off the creditors.

a. If the interest rate was 8%, how much would you have been prepared to bid for the prize?

b. Enhance Reinsurance Company was reported to have offered $4.2 million. Use Excel to find the return that the company was looking for.

31. A mortgage requires you to pay $70,000 at the end of each of the next eight years. The interest rate is 8%.

a. What is the present value of these payments?

b. Calculate for each year the loan balance that remains outstanding, the interest payment on the loan, and the reduction in the loan balance.

32. You estimate that, by the time you retire in 35 years, you will have accumulated savings of $2 million. If the interest rate is 8% and you live 15 years after retirement, what annual level of expenditure will those savings support?

Unfortunately, inflation will eat into the value of your retirement income. Assume a 4% inflation rate and work out a spending program for your retirement that will allow you to increase your expenditure in line with inflation.

33. The *annually* compounded discount rate is 5.5%. You are asked to calculate the present value of a 12-year annuity with payments of $50,000 per year. Calculate PV for each of the following cases.

a. The annuity payments arrive at one-year intervals. The first payment arrives one year from now.

b. The first payment arrives in six months. Following payments arrive at one-year intervals (i.e., at 18 months, 30 months, etc.).

34. Dear Financial Adviser,

My spouse and I are each 62 and hope to retire in three years. After retirement we will receive $7,500 per month after taxes from our employers' pension plans and $1,500 per month after taxes from Social Security. Unfortunately our monthly living expenses are $15,000. Our social obligations preclude further economies.

We have $1,000,000 invested in a high-grade, tax-free municipal-bond mutual fund. The return on the fund is 3.5% per year. We plan to make annual withdrawals from the mutual fund to cover the difference between our pension and Social Security income and our living expenses. How many years before we run out of money?

Sincerely,

Luxury Challenged

Marblehead, MA

You can assume that the withdrawals (one per year) will sit in a checking account (no interest). The couple will use the account to cover the monthly shortfalls.

35. Your firm's geologists have discovered a small oil field in New York's Westchester County. The field is forecasted to produce a cash flow of $C_1 = \$2$ million in the first year. You estimate that you could earn an expected return of $r = 12\%$ from investing in stocks with a similar degree of risk to your oil field. Therefore, 12% is the opportunity cost of capital.

What is the present value? The answer, of course, depends on what happens to the cash flows after the first year. Calculate present value for the following cases:

a. The cash flows are forecasted to continue forever, with no expected growth or decline.

b. The cash flows are forecasted to continue for 20 years only, with no expected growth or decline during that period.

c. The cash flows are forecasted to continue forever, increasing by 3% per year because of inflation.

d. The cash flows are forecasted to continue for 20 years only, increasing by 3% per year because of inflation.

CHALLENGE

36. Here are two useful rules of thumb. The "Rule of 72" says that with discrete compounding the time it takes for an investment to double in value is roughly 72/interest rate (in percent). The "Rule of 69" says that with continuous compounding the time that it takes to double is exactly 69.3/interest rate (in percent).

a. If the annually compounded interest rate is 12%, use the Rule of 72 to calculate roughly how long it takes before your money doubles. Now work it out exactly.

b. Can you prove the Rule of 69?

37. Use Excel to construct your own set of annuity tables showing the annuity factor for a selection of interest rates and years.

38. You own an oil pipeline that will generate a $2 million cash return over the coming year. The pipeline's operating costs are negligible, and it is expected to last for a very long time. Unfortunately, the volume of oil shipped is declining, and cash flows are expected to decline by 4% per year. The discount rate is 10%.

a. What is the PV of the pipeline's cash flows if its cash flows are assumed to last forever?

b. What is the PV of the cash flows if the pipeline is scrapped after 20 years?

eXcel

Visit us at
www.mhhe.com/bma

● ● ● ● ●

**REAL-TIME
DATA ANALYSIS**

There are dozens of Web sites that provide calculators to help with personal financial decisions. Two good examples are **www.smartmoney.com** and **finance.yahoo.com**. (*Note:* for both calculators the annual rate of interest is quoted as 12 times the monthly rate.)

1. **Amortizing loans** Suppose that you take out a 30-year mortgage loan of $200,000 at an interest rate of 10%.

a. What is your total monthly payment?

b. How much of the first month's payment goes to reduce the size of the loan?

c. How much of the payment after two years goes to reduce the size of the loan?

You can check your answers by logging on to the personal finance page of **www.smartmoney .com** and using the mortgage calculator.

2. **Retirement planning** You need to have accumulated savings of $2 million by the time that you retire in 20 years. You currently have savings of $200,000. How much do you need to save each year to meet your goal? Find the savings calculator on **finance.yahoo.com** to check your answer.

3. In 2006 the State of Indiana sold a 75-year concession to operate and maintain the East-West Toll Road. Before doing so, it commissioned a consulting report that estimated the value of the concession. You can access this report at **www.in.gov/ifa/ files/TollRoadFinancialAnalysis.pdf**. Download the spreadsheet of the forecasted cash flows from the toll road from this book's Web site at **www.mhhe.com/bma** to answer the following questions. (*Note:* Cash flows are reported only for each 10-year block. Except where more information is available, we have arbitrarily assumed cash flows are spread evenly during those 10 years.)

   a. Calculate the present value of the concession using a discount rate of 6%. (*Note:* Your figure will differ slightly from that in the consultant's report because we do not have exact cash flow forecasts for each year.)

   b. The consultant chose this discount rate because it was the interest rate that the state paid on its bonds. Do you think that this was the correct criterion? Why or why not?

   c. How does the value of the concession change if you use a higher discount rate?

VALUE

Valuing Bonds

▶ **Investment in new** plant and equipment requires money—often a lot of money. Sometimes firms can retain and accumulate earnings to cover the cost of investment, but often they need to raise extra cash from investors. If they choose not to sell additional shares of common stock, the cash has to come from borrowing. If cash is needed for only a short while, firms may borrow from a bank. If they need cash for long-term investments, they generally issue bonds, which are simply long-term loans.

Companies are not the only bond issuers. Municipalities also raise money by selling bonds. So do national governments. There is always some risk that a company or municipality will not be able to come up with the cash to repay its bonds, but investors in government bonds can generally be confident that the promised payments will be made in full and on time.

We start our analysis of the bond market by looking at the valuation of government bonds and at the interest rate that the government pays when it borrows. Do not confuse this interest rate with the cost of capital for a corporation. The projects that companies undertake are almost invariably risky, and investors demand higher prospective returns from these projects than from safe government bonds. (In Chapter 7 we start to look at the additional returns that investors demand from risky assets.)

The markets for government bonds are huge. At the end of February 2009, investors held $6.6 trillion of U.S. government securities, and U.S. government agencies held $4.3 trillion more. The bond markets are also sophisticated. Bond traders make massive trades motivated by tiny price discrepancies. This book is not for professional bond traders, but if you are to be involved in managing the company's debt, you will have to get beyond the simple mechanics of bond valuation. Financial managers need to understand the bond pages in the financial press and know what bond dealers mean when they quote spot rates or yields to maturity. They realize why short-term rates are usually lower (but sometimes higher) than long-term rates and why the longest-term bond prices are most sensitive to fluctuations in interest rates. They can distinguish real (inflation-adjusted) interest rates and nominal (money) rates and anticipate how future inflation can affect interest rates. We cover all these topics in this chapter.

Companies can't borrow at the same low interest rates as governments. The interest rates on government bonds are benchmarks for all interest rates, however. When government interest rates go up or down, corporate rates follow more or less proportionally. Therefore, financial managers had better understand how the government rates are determined and what happens when they change.

Corporate bonds are more complex securities than government bonds. A corporation may not be able to come up with the money to pay its debts, so investors have to worry about default risk. Corporate bonds are also less liquid than government bonds: They are not as easy to buy or sell, particularly in large quantities or on short notice. Some corporate bonds give the borrower an option to repay early; others can be exchanged for the company's common stock. All of these complications affect the "spread" of corporate bond rates over interest rates on government bonds of similar maturities.

•••••

If you own a bond, you are entitled to a fixed set of cash payoffs. Every year until the bond matures, you collect regular interest payments. At maturity, when you get the final interest payment, you also get back the **face value** of the bond, which is called the bond's **principal.**

A Short Trip to Paris to Value a Government Bond

Why are we going to Paris, apart from the cafés, restaurants, and sophisticated nightlife? Because we want to start with the simplest type of bond, one that makes payments just once a year.

French government bonds, known as OATs (short for Obligations Assimilables du Trésor), pay interest and principal in euros (€). Suppose that in December 2008 you decide to buy €100 face value of the 8.5% OAT maturing in December 2012. Each December until the bond matures you are entitled to an interest payment of $.085 \times 100 = €8.50$. This amount is the bond's **coupon.**[1] When the bond matures in 2012, the government pays you the final €8.50 interest, plus the principal payment of the €100 face value. Your first coupon payment is in one year's time, in December 2009. So the cash payments from the bond are as follows:

Cash Payments (€)			
2009	**2010**	**2011**	**2012**
€8.50	€8.50	€8.50	€108.50

What is the present value of these payments? It depends on the opportunity cost of capital, which in this case equals the rate of return offered by other government debt issues denominated in euros. In December 2008, other medium-term French government bonds offered a return of about 3.0%. That is what you were giving up when you bought the 8.5% OATs. Therefore, to value the 8.5% OATs, you must discount the cash flows at 3.0%:

$$PV = \frac{8.50}{1.03} + \frac{8.50}{1.03^2} + \frac{8.50}{1.03^3} + \frac{108.50}{1.03^4} = €120.44$$

Bond prices are usually expressed as a percentage of face value. Thus the price of your 8.5% OAT was quoted as 120.44%.

You may have noticed a shortcut way to value this bond. Your OAT amounts to a package of two investments. The first investment gets the four annual coupon payments of €8.50 each. The second gets the €100 face value at maturity. You can use the annuity formula from Chapter 2 to value the coupon payments and then add on the present value of the final payment.

$$PV(bond) = PV(\text{annuity of coupon payments}) + PV(\text{final payment of principal})$$

$$= (\text{coupon} \times \text{4-year annuity factor}) + (\text{final payment} \times \text{discount factor})$$

$$= 8.50 \left[\frac{1}{.03} - \frac{1}{.03(1.03)^4} \right] + \frac{100}{(1.03)^4} = 31.59 + 88.85 = €120.44$$

---

[1] Bonds used to come with coupons attached, which had to be clipped off and presented to the issuer to obtain the interest payments. This is still the case with *bearer bonds,* where the only evidence of indebtedness is the bond itself. In many parts of the world bearer bonds are still issued and are popular with investors who would rather remain anonymous. The alternative is *registered bonds,* where the identity of the bond's owner is recorded and the coupon payments are sent automatically. OATs are registered bonds.

Thus the bond can be valued as a package of an annuity (the coupon payments) and a single, final payment (the repayment of principal).[2]

We just used the 3% interest rate to calculate the present value of the OAT. Now we turn the valuation around: If the price of the OAT is 120.44%, what is the interest rate? What return do investors get if they buy the bond? To answer this question, you need to find the value of the variable y that solves the following equation:

$$120.44 = \frac{8.50}{1+y} + \frac{8.50}{(1+y)^2} + \frac{8.50}{(1+y)^3} + \frac{108.50}{(1+y)^4}$$

The rate of return y is called the bond's **yield to maturity.** In this case, we already know that the present value of the bond is €120.44 at a 3% discount rate, so the yield to maturity must be 3.0%. If you buy the bond at 120.44% and hold it to maturity, you will earn a return of 3.0% per year.

Why is the yield to maturity less than the 8.5% coupon payment? Because you are paying €120.44 for a bond with a face value of only €100. You lose the difference of €20.44 if you hold the bond to maturity. On the other hand, you get four annual cash payments of €8.50. (The immediate, *current yield* on your investment is 8.50/120.44 = .071, or 7.1%.) The yield to maturity blends the return from the coupon payments with the declining value of the bond over its remaining life.

The only general procedure for calculating the yield to maturity is trial and error. You guess at an interest rate and calculate the present value of the bond's payments. If the present value is greater than the actual price, your discount rate must have been too low, and you need to try a higher rate. The more practical solution is to use a spreadsheet program or a specially programmed calculator to calculate the yield. At the end of this chapter, you will find a box which lists the Excel function for calculating yield to maturity plus several other useful functions for bond analysts.

Back to the United States: Semiannual Coupons and Bond Prices

Just like the French government, the U.S. Treasury raises money by regular auctions of new bond issues. Some of these issues do not mature for 20 or 30 years; others, known as *notes*, mature in 10 years or less. The Treasury also issues short-term debt maturing in a year or less. These short-term securities are known as *Treasury bills*. Treasury bonds, notes, and bills are traded in the *fixed-income market*.

Let's look at an example of a U.S. government note. In 2007 the Treasury issued 4.875% notes maturing in 2012. These notes are called "the 4.875s of 2012." Treasury bonds and notes have face values of $1,000, so if you own the 4.875s of 2012, the Treasury will give you back $1,000 at maturity. You can also look forward to a regular coupon but, in contrast to our French bond, coupons on Treasury bonds and notes are paid *semiannually*.[3] Thus, the 4.875s of 2012 provide a coupon payment of 4.875/2 = 2.4375% of face value every six months.

You can't buy Treasury bonds, notes, or bills on the stock exchange. They are traded by a network of bond dealers, who quote prices at which they are prepared to buy and sell. For example, suppose that in 2009 you decide to buy the 4.875s of 2012. You phone a broker who checks the current price on her screen. If you are happy to go ahead with the purchase, your broker contacts a bond dealer and the trade is done.

The prices at which you can buy or sell Treasury notes and bonds are shown each day in the financial press and on the Web. Figure 3.1 is taken from the *The Wall Street Journal*'s

---

[2] You could also value a three-year annuity of €8.50 plus a final payment of €108.50.

[3] The frequency of interest payments varies from country to country. For example, most euro bonds pay interest annually, while most bonds in the U.K., Canada, and Japan pay interest semiannually.

▶ **FIGURE 3.1**

Sample Treasury
bond quotes from *The
Wall Street Journal,*
February 2009.

*Source: The Wall Street
Journal* Web site,
www.wsj.com.

Maturity	Coupon	Bid	Asked	Chg	Asked Yield
2010 Feb 15	4.750	104:00	104:01	unch.	0.6651
2011 Feb 15	5.000	108:16	108:18	+5	0.6727
2012 Feb 15	**4.875**	**110:24**	**110:25**	**+14**	**1.2006**
2013 Feb 15	3.875	109:27	109:29	+24	1.3229
2014 Feb 15	4.000	111.19	111:21	+30	1.5664
2015 Feb 15	4.000	111:20	111:23	+34	1.9227
2016 Feb 15	4.500	115:03	115:04	+59	1.9856
2017 Feb 15	4.625	115:20	115:21	+65	2.4555
2018 Feb 15	3.500	107:14	107:15	+64	2.5646
2019 Feb 15	2.750	100:23	100:25	+63	2.6622
2020 Feb 15	8.500	147:19	147:21	+83	3.2976

Web page and shows the prices of a small sample of Treasury bonds. Look at the entry for our 4.875s of February 2012. The **asked price** of 110:25 is the price you need to pay to buy the note from a dealer. This price is quoted in 32nds rather than decimals. Thus a price of 110:25 means that each bond costs 110 + 25/32, or 110.78125% of face value. The face value of the note is $1,000, so each note costs $1,107.8125.[4]

The **bid price** is the price investors receive if they sell to a dealer. The dealer earns her living by charging a *spread* between the bid and the asked price. Notice that the spread for the 4.875s of 2012 is only 1/32, or about .03% of the note's value.

The next column in Figure 3.1 shows the change in price since the previous day. The price of the 4.875% notes has risen by 14/32, an unusually large move for a single day. Finally, the column "Asked Yield" shows the **asked yield to maturity.** Because interest is semiannual, yields on U.S. bonds are usually quoted as semiannually compounded yields. Thus, if you buy the 4.875% note at the asked price and hold it to maturity, you earn a semiannually compounded return of 1.2006%. This means that every six months you earn a return of 1.2006/2 = .6003%.

You can now repeat the present value calculations that we did for the French government bond. You just need to recognize that bonds in the U.S. have a face value of $1,000, that their coupons are paid semiannually, and that the quoted yield is a semiannually compounded rate.

Here are the cash payments from the 4.875s of 2012:

Cash Payments ($)					
Aug. 2009	**Feb. 2010**	**Aug. 2010**	**Feb. 2011**	**Aug. 2011**	**Feb. 2012**
$24.375	$24.375	$24.375	$24.375	$24.375	$1,024.375

---

[4] The quoted bond price is known as the *flat* (or *clean*) price. The price that the bond buyer actually pays (sometimes called the *full* or *dirty price*) is equal to the flat price *plus* the interest that the seller has already earned on the bond since the last interest payment. The precise method for calculating this *accrued interest* varies from one type of bond to another. We use the flat price to calculate the yield.

If investors demand a semiannual return of .6003%, then the present value of these cash flows is

$$PV = \frac{24.375}{1.006003} + \frac{24.375}{1.006003^2} + \frac{24.375}{1.006003^3} + \frac{24.375}{1.006003^4} + \frac{24.375}{1.006003^5} + \frac{1024.375}{1.006003^6} = \$1107.95$$

Each note is worth $1,107.95, or 110.795% of face value.

Again we could turn the valuation around: Given the price, what's the yield to maturity? Try it, and you'll find (no surprise) that the yield to maturity is $y = .006003$. This is the semiannual rate of return that you can earn over the six remaining half-year periods until the note matures. Take care to remember that the yield is *reported* as an annual rate, calculated as $2 \times .006003 = .012006$, or 1.2006%. If you see a reported yield to maturity of $R\%$, you have to remember to use $y = R/2\%$ as the semiannual rate for discounting cash flows received every six months.

3-2 How Bond Prices Vary with Interest Rates

Figure 3.2 plots the yield to maturity on 10-year U.S. Treasury bonds[5] from 1900 to 2008. Notice how much the rate fluctuates. For example, interest rates climbed sharply after 1979 when Paul Volcker, the new chairman of the Fed, instituted a policy of tight money to rein in inflation. Within two years the interest rate on 10-year government bonds rose from 9% to a midyear peak of 15.8%. Contrast this with 2008, when investors fled to the safety of U.S. government bonds. By the end of that year long-term Treasury bonds offered a measly 2.2% rate of interest.

As interest rates change, so do bond prices. For example, suppose that investors demanded a semiannual return of 4% on the 4.875s of 2012, rather than the .6003% return we used above. In that case the price would be

$$PV = \frac{24.375}{1.04} + \frac{24.375}{1.04^2} + \frac{24.375}{1.04^3} + \frac{24.375}{1.04^4} + \frac{24.375}{1.04^5} + \frac{1024.375}{1.04^6} = \$918.09$$

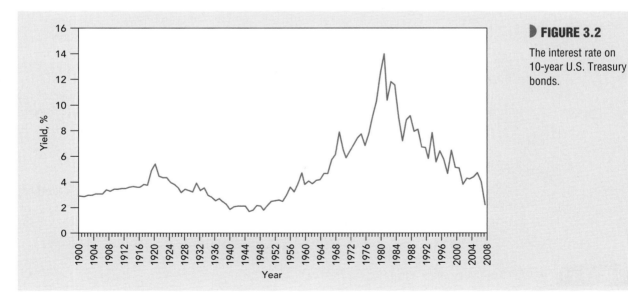

FIGURE 3.2

The interest rate on 10-year U.S. Treasury bonds.

---

[5] From this point forward, we will just say "bonds," and not distinguish notes from bonds unless we are referring to a specific security. Note also that bonds with long maturities end up with short maturities when they approach the final payment date. Thus you will encounter 30-year bonds trading 20 years later at the same prices as new 10-year notes (assuming equal coupons).

▶ **FIGURE 3.3**

Plot of bond prices as a function of the interest rate. The price of long-term bonds is more sensitive to changes in the interest rate than is the price of short-term bonds.

eXcel

Visit us at
www.mhhe.com/bma

The higher interest rate results in a lower price.

Bond prices and interest rates *must* move in opposite directions. The yield to maturity, our measure of the interest rate on a bond, is *defined* as the discount rate that explains the bond price. When bond prices fall, interest rates (that is, yields to maturity) must rise. When interest rates rise, bond prices must fall. We recall a hapless TV pundit who intoned, "The recent decline in long-term interest rates suggests that long-term bond prices may rise over the next week or two." Of course the bond prices had already gone up. We are confident that you won't make the pundit's mistake.

The solid green line in Figure 3.3 shows the value of our 4.875% note for different interest rates. As the yield to maturity falls, the bond price increases. When the annual yield is equal to the note's annual coupon rate (4.875%), the note sells for exactly its face value. When the yield is higher than 4.875%, the note sells at a discount to face value. When the yield is lower than 4.875%, the note sells at a premium.

Bond investors cross their fingers that market interest rates will fall, so that the price of their securities will rise. If they are unlucky and interest rates jump up, the value of their investment declines.

A change in interest rates has only a modest impact on the value of near-term cash flows but a much greater impact on the value of distant cash flows. Thus the price of long-term bonds is affected more by changing interest rates than the price of short-term bonds. For example, compare the two curves in Figure 3.3. The green line shows how the price of the three-year 4.875% note varies with the interest rate. The brown line shows how the price of a 30-year 4.875% bond varies. You can see that the 30-year bond is much more sensitive to interest rate fluctuations than the three-year note.

Duration and Volatility

Changes in interest rates have a greater impact on the prices of long-term bonds than on those of short-term bonds. But what do we mean by "long-term" and "short-term"? A coupon bond that matures in year 30 makes payments in *each* of years 1 through 30. It's misleading to describe the bond as a 30-year bond; the average time to each cash payment is less than 30 years.

EXAMPLE 3.1   ● Which Is the Longest-Term Bond?

A strip is a special type of Treasury bond that repays principal at maturity, but makes no coupon payments along the way. Strips are also called *zero-coupon* bonds. (We cover strips in more detail in the next section.)

Consider a strip maturing in February 2015 and two coupon bonds maturing on the same date. Table 3.1 calculates the prices of these three Treasuries, assuming a yield to maturity of 2% per year. Take a look at the time pattern of each bond's cash payments and review how the prices are calculated.

Which of the three Treasuries is the longest-term investment? They have the same final maturity, of course, February 2015. But the *timing* of the bonds' cash payments is not the same. The two coupon bonds deliver cash payments earlier than the strip, so the strip has the longest effective maturity. The *average* maturity of the 4s is in turn longer than that of the 11 1/4s, because the 4s deliver relatively more of their cash flows at maturity, when the face value is paid off. The 11 1/4s have the shortest average maturity, because a greater fraction of this bond's cash payments comes as coupons rather than the final payment of face value.

	Price (%)		Cash Payments %		
Bond	Feb. 2009	Aug. 2009	Feb. 2010. . .	. . . Aug. 2014	Feb. 2015
Strip for Feb. 2015	88.74	0	0 . . .	. . . 0	100.00
4s of Feb. 2015	111.26	2.00	2.00 . . .	. . . 2.00	102.00
11 1/4s of Feb. 2015	152.05	5.625	5.625 . . .	. . . 5.625	105.625

▶ **TABLE 3.1** A comparison of the cash flows and prices of three Treasuries in February 2009, assuming a yield to maturity of 2%.

Note: All three securities mature in February 2015.

● ● ● ● ●

Investors and financial managers calculate a bond's average maturity by its **duration.** They keep track of duration because it measures the exposure of the bond's price to fluctuations in interest rates. Duration is often called *Macaulay duration* after its inventor.

Duration is the weighted average of the times when the bond's cash payments are received. The times are the future years 1, 2, 3, etc., extending to the final maturity date, which we call T. The weight for each year is the present value of the cash flow received at that time divided by the total present value of the bond.

$$\text{Duration} = \frac{1 \times \text{PV}(C_1)}{\text{PV}} + \frac{2 \times \text{PV}(C_2)}{\text{PV}} + \frac{3 \times \text{PV}(C_3)}{\text{PV}} + \cdots + \frac{T \times \text{PV}(C_T)}{\text{PV}}$$

Table 3.2 shows how to compute duration for the French OATs maturing in 2012. First, we value each of the three annual coupon payments of €8.50 and the final payment of coupon plus face value of €108.50. Of course the present values of these payments add up to the bond price of €120.44. Then we calculate the fraction of the price accounted for by each cash flow and multiply each fraction by the year of the cash flow. The results sum across to a duration of 3.60 years.

Year (t)	1	2	3	4	
Cash payment (C_t)	€8.50	€8.50	€8.50	€108.50	
PV(C_t) at 3%	€8.25	€8.01	€7.78	€96.40	PV = €120.44
Fraction of total value [PV(C_t)/PV]	0.069	0.067	0.065	0.800	
Year × fraction of total value [t × PV(C_t)/PV]	0.069	0.133	0.194	3.202	Total = duration = 3.60

▶ **TABLE 3.2**   Calculating duration for the French OATs maturing in 2012. The yield to maturity is 3% per year.

Table 3.3 shows the same calculation for the 11¼% U.S. Treasury bond maturing in February 2015. The present value of each cash payment is calculated using a 2% yield to maturity. Again we calculate the fraction of the price accounted for by each cash flow and multiply each fraction by the year. The calculations look more formidable than in Table 3.2, but only because the final maturity date is 2016 rather than 2012 and coupons are paid semiannually. Thus in Table 3.3 we have to track 12 dates rather than 4. The duration of the 11 1/4s equals 4.83 years.

We leave it to you to calculate durations for the other two bonds in Table 3.1. You will find that duration increases to 5.43 years for the 4s of 2015. The duration of the strip is six years exactly, the same as its maturity. Because there are no coupons, 100% of the strip's value comes from payment of principal in year 6.

We mentioned that investors and financial managers track duration because it measures how bond prices change when interest rates change. For this purpose it's best to use *modified duration* or *volatility*, which is just duration divided by one plus the yield to maturity:

$$\text{Modified duration} = \text{volatility (\%)} = \frac{\text{duration}}{1 + \text{yield}}$$

Date	Aug. 2009	Feb. 2010	Aug. 2010	Feb. 2011	. . .	Aug. 2013	Feb. 2014	Aug. 2014	Feb. 2015	
Year (t)	0.5	1.0	1.5	2.0	. . .	4.5	5.0	5.5	6.0	
Cash payment (C_t)	5.63	5.63	5.63	5.63	. . .	5.63	5.63	5.63	105.625	
PV(C_t) at 2%	5.57	5.51	5.46	5.41	. . .	5.14	5.09	5.04	93.74	PV = 152.05
Fraction of total value [PV(C_t)/PV]	0.0366	0.0363	0.0359	0.0355	. . .	0.0338	0.0335	0.0332	0.6165	
Year × fraction of total value [t × PV(C_t)/PV]	0.0183	0.0363	0.0539	0.0711	. . .	0.1522	0.1674	0.1824	3.6988	Total = duration = 4.83
Duration (years) = 4.83										

▶ **TABLE 3.3**   Calculating the duration of the 11¼% Treasuries of 2015. The yield to maturity is 2%.

Modified duration measures the percentage change in bond price for a 1 percentage-point change in yield.[6] Let's try out this formula for the OAT bond in Table 3.2. The bond's modified duration is duration/(1 + yield) = 3.60/1.03 = 3.49%. This means that a 1% change in the yield to maturity should change the bond price by 3.49%.

Let's check that prediction. Suppose the yield to maturity either increases or declines by .5%:

Yield to Maturity	Price	Change (%)
3.5%	118.37	− 1.767
3.0	120.44	—
2.5	122.57	+ 1.726

The total difference between price at 2.5% and 3.5% is 1.767 + 1.726 = 3.49%. Thus a 1% change in interest rates means a 3.49% change in bond price, just as predicted.

The modified duration for the 11¼% U.S. Treasury in Table 3.3 is 4.83/1.02 = 4.74%. In other words, a 1% change in yield to maturity results in a 4.74% change in the bond's price. Modified durations for the other bonds in Table 3.1 are larger, which means more exposure of price to changes in interest rates. For example, the modified duration of the strip is 6/1.02 = 5.88%.

You can see why duration (or modified duration) is a handy measure of interest-rate risk. For example, investment managers regularly monitor the duration of their bond portfolios to ensure that they are not running undue risk.[7]

3-3 The Term Structure of Interest Rates

When we explained in Chapter 2 how to calculate present values, we used the same discount rate to calculate the value of each period's cash flow. A single yield to maturity y can also be used to discount all future cash payments from a bond. For many purposes, using a single discount rate is a perfectly acceptable approximation, but there are also occasions when you need to recognize that short-term interest rates are different from long-term rates.

The relationship between short- and long-term interest rates is called the **term structure of interest rates.** Look for example at Figure 3.4 on page 54, which shows the term structure in two different years. Notice that in the later year the term structure sloped downward; long-term interest rates were lower than short-term rates. In the earlier year the pattern was reversed and long-term bonds offered a much higher interest rate than short-term bonds. You now need to learn how to measure the term structure and understand why long- and short-term rates differ.

Consider a simple loan that pays $1 at the end of one year. To find the present value of this loan you need to discount the cash flow by the one-year rate of interest rate, r_1:

$$PV = 1/(1 + r_1)$$

---

[6] In other words, the derivative of the bond price with respect to a change in yield to maturity is $dPV/dy = -$ duration/$(1 + y) = -$ modified duration.

[7] The portfolio duration is a weighted average of the durations of the bonds in the portfolio. The weight for each bond is the fraction of the portfolio invested in that bond. Note that, as time passes and interest rates change, the portfolio manager needs to recalculate duration.

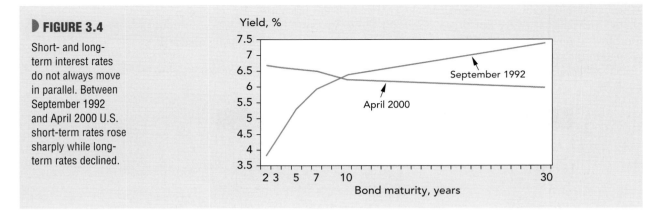

▶ **FIGURE 3.4**

Short- and long-
term interest rates
do not always move
in parallel. Between
September 1992
and April 2000 U.S.
short-term rates rose
sharply while long-
term rates declined.

This rate, r_1, is called the one-year **spot rate.** To find the present value of a loan that pays $1 at the end of two years, you need to discount by the two-year spot rate, r_2:

$$PV = 1/(1 + r_2)^2$$

The first year's cash flow is discounted at today's one-year spot rate and the second year's flow is discounted at today's two-year spot rate. The series of spot rates $r_1, r_2, \ldots, r_t, \ldots$ traces out the term structure of interest rates.

Now suppose you have to value $1 paid at the end of years 1 *and* 2. If the spot rates are different, say $r_1 = 3\%$ and $r_2 = 4\%$, then we need two discount rates to calculate present value:

$$PV = \frac{1}{1.03} + \frac{1}{1.04^2} = 1.895$$

Once we know that PV = 1.895, we can go on to calculate a single discount rate that would give the right answer. That is, we could calculate the yield to maturity by solving for y in the following equation:

$$PV = 1.895 = \frac{1}{(1 + y)} + \frac{1}{(1 + y)^2}$$

This gives a yield to maturity of 3.66%. Once we have the yield, we could use it to value other two-year annuities. But we can't get the yield to maturity until we know the price. The price is determined by the spot interest rates for dates 1 and 2. Spot rates come first. Yields to maturity come later, after bond prices are set. That is why professionals identify spot interest rates and discount each cash flow at the spot rate for the date when the cash flow is received.

Spot Rates, Bond Prices, and the Law of One Price

The *law of one price* states that the same commodity must sell at the same price in a well-functioning market. Therefore, all safe cash payments delivered on the same date must be discounted at the same spot rate.

Table 3.4 illustrates how the law of one price applies to government bonds. It lists four government bonds, which we assume make annual coupon payments. We have put at the top the shortest-duration bond, the 8% coupon bond maturing in year 2, and we've put at the bottom the longest-duration bond, the 4-year strip. Of course the strip pays off only at maturity.

	Year (t)				Bond Price (PV)	Yield to Maturity (y, %)
	1	**2**	**3**	**4**		
Spot rates	.035	.04	.042	.044		
Discount factors	.9662	.9246	.8839	.8418		
Bond A (8% coupon):						
Payment (C_t)	$80	1,080				
PV(C_t)	$77.29	998.52			$1,075.82	3.98
Bond B (11% coupon):						
Payment (C_t)	$110	110	1,110			
PV(C_t)	$106.28	101.70	981.11		$1,189.10	4.16
Bond C (6% coupon):						
Payment (C_t)	$60	60	60	1,060		
PV(C_t)	$57.97	55.47	53.03	892.29	$1,058.76	4.37
Bond D (strip):						
Payment (C_t)				$1,000		
PV(C_t)				$841.78	$841.78	4.40

▶ **TABLE 3.4**   The law of one price applied to government bonds.

eXcel

Visit us at
www.mhhe.com/bma

Spot rates and discount factors are given at the top of each column. The law of one price says that investors place the same value on a risk-free dollar regardless of whether it is provided by bond A, B, C, or D. You can check that the law holds in the table.

Each bond is priced by adding the present values of each of its cash flows. Once total PV is calculated, we have the bond price. Only then can the yield to maturity be calculated.

Notice how the yield to maturity increases as bond maturity increases. The yields increase with maturity because the term structure of spot rates is upward-sloping. Yields to maturity are complex averages of spot rates.

Financial managers who want a quick, summary measure of interest rates bypass spot interest rates and look in the financial press at yields to maturity. They may refer to the *yield curve*, which plots yields to maturity, instead of referring to the term structure, which plots spot rates. They may use the yield to maturity on one bond to value another bond with roughly the same coupon and maturity. They may speak with a broad brush and say, "Ampersand Bank will charge us 6% on a three-year loan," referring to a 6% yield to maturity.

Throughout this book, we too use the yield to maturity to summarize the return required by bond investors. But you also need to understand the measure's limitations when spot rates are not equal.

Measuring the Term Structure

You can think of the spot rate, r_t, as the rate of interest on a bond that makes a single payment at time t. Such simple bonds do exist—we have already seen examples. They are known as **stripped bonds,** or **strips.** On request the U.S. Treasury will split a normal coupon bond into a package of mini-bonds, each of which makes just one cash payment. Our 4.875% notes of 2012 could be exchanged for six semiannual coupon strips, each paying

$24.375, and a principal strip paying $1,000. In February 2009 this package of coupon strips would have cost $143.83 and the principal strip would have cost $964.42, making a total cost of $1,108.25, just a few cents more than it cost to buy one 4.875% note. That should be no surprise. Because the two investments provide identical cash payments, they must sell for very close to the same price.

We can use the prices of strips to measure the term structure of interest rates. For example, in February 2009 a 10-year strip cost $714.18. In return, investors could look forward to a single payment of $1,000 in February 2019. Thus investors were prepared to pay $.71418 for the promise of $1 at the end of 10 years. The 10-year discount factor was $DF_{10} = 1/(1 + r_{10})^{10} = .71418$, and the 10-year spot rate was $r_{10} = (1/.71418)^{.10} - 1 = .0342$, or 3.42%. In Figure 3.5 we use the prices of strips with different maturities to plot the term structure of spot rates from 1 to 10 years. You can see that in 2009 investors required a somewhat higher interest rate for lending for 10 years rather than for 1.

Why the Discount Factor Declines As Futurity Increases— and a Digression on Money Machines

In Chapter 2 we saw that the longer you have to wait for your money, the less its present value is. In other words, the two-year discount factor $DF_2 = 1/(1 + r_2)^2$ is less than the one-year discount factor $DF_1 = (1 + r_1)$. But is this *necessarily* the case when there can be a different spot interest rate for each period?

Suppose that the one-year spot rate of interest is $r_1 = 20\%$, and the two-year spot rate is $r_2 = 7\%$. In this case the one-year discount factor is $DF_1 = 1/1.20 = .833$ and the two-year discount factor is $DF_2 = 1/1.07^2 = .873$. Apparently a dollar received the day after tomorrow is *not* necessarily worth less than a dollar received tomorrow.

But there is something wrong with this example. Anyone who could borrow and invest at these interest rates could become a millionaire overnight. Let us see how such a "money machine" would work. Suppose the first person to spot the opportunity is

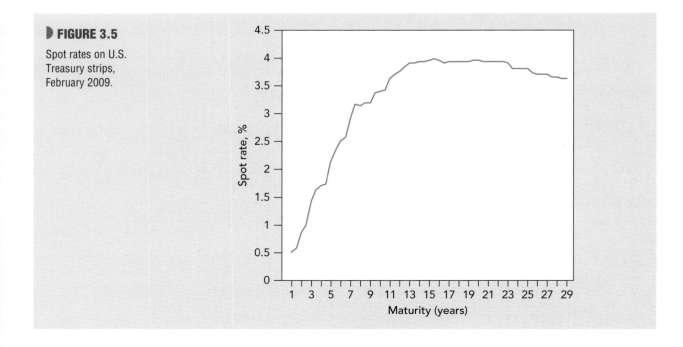

▶ **FIGURE 3.5**

Spot rates on U.S. Treasury strips, February 2009.

Hermione Kraft. Ms. Kraft first buys a one-year Treasury strip for .833 × $1,000 = $833. Now she notices that there is a way to earn an *immediate* surefire profit on this investment. She reasons as follows. Next year the strip will pay off $1,000 that can be reinvested for a further year. Although she does not know what interest rates will be at that time, she does know that she can always put the money in a checking account and be certain of having $1,000 at the end of year 2. Her next step, therefore, is to go to her bank and borrow the present value of this $1,000. At 7% interest the present value is $PV = 1000/(1.07)^2 = \$873$.

So Ms. Kraft borrows $873, invests $830, and walks away with a profit of $43. If that does not sound like very much, notice that by borrowing more and investing more she can make much larger profits. For example, if she borrows $21,778,584 and invests $20,778,584, she would become a millionaire.[8]

Of course this story is completely fanciful. Such an opportunity would not last long in well-functioning capital markets. Any bank that allowed you to borrow for two years at 7% when the one-year interest rate was 20% would soon be wiped out by a rush of small investors hoping to become millionaires and a rush of millionaires hoping to become billionaires. There are, however, two lessons to our story. The first is that a dollar tomorrow *cannot* be worth less than a dollar the day after tomorrow. In other words, the value of a dollar received at the end of one year (DF_1) cannot be less than the value of a dollar received at the end of two years (DF_2). There must be some extra gain from lending for two periods rather than one: $(1 + r_2)^2$ cannot be less than $1 + r_1$.

Our second lesson is a more general one and can be summed up by this precept: "There is no such thing as a surefire money machine." The technical term for money machine is **arbitrage.** In well-functioning markets, where the costs of buying and selling are low, arbitrage opportunities are eliminated almost instantaneously by investors who try to take advantage of them.

Later in the book we invoke the *absence* of arbitrage opportunities to prove several useful properties about security prices. That is, we make statements like, "The prices of securities X and Y must be in the following relationship—otherwise there would be potential arbitrage profits and capital markets would not be in equilibrium."

3-4 Explaining the Term Structure

The term structure that we showed in Figure 3.5 was upward-sloping. Long-term rates of interest in February 2009 were more than 3.5%; short-term rates were 1% or less. Why then didn't everyone rush to buy long-term bonds? Who were the (foolish?) investors who put their money into the short end of the term structure?

Suppose that you held a portfolio of one-year U.S. Treasuries in February 2009. Here are three possible reasons why you might decide to hold on to them, despite their low rate of return:

1. You believe that short-term interest rates will be higher in the future.
2. You worry about the greater exposure of long-term bonds to changes in interest rates.
3. You worry about the risk of higher future inflation.

We review each of these reasons now.

---

[8] We exaggerate Ms. Kraft's profits. There are always costs to financial transactions, though they may be very small. For example, Ms. Kraft could use her investment in the one-year strip as security for the bank loan, but the bank would need to charge more than 7% on the loan to cover its costs.

Expectations Theory of the Term Structure

Recall that you own a portfolio of one-year Treasuries. A year from now, when the Treasuries mature, you can reinvest the proceeds for another one-year period and enjoy whatever interest rate the bond market offers then. The interest rate for the second year may be high enough to offset the first year's low return. You often see an upward-sloping term structure when future interest rates are expected to rise.

EXAMPLE 3.2   ● Expectations and the Term Structure

Suppose that the one-year interest rate, r_1, is 5%, and the two-year rate, r_2, is 7%. If you invest $100 for one year, your investment grows to $100 \times 1.05 = \$105$; if you invest for two years, it grows to $100 \times 1.07^2 = \$114.49$. The *extra* return that you earn for that second year is $1.07^2/1.05 - 1 = .090$, or 9.0%.[9]

Would you be happy to earn that extra 9% for investing for two years rather than one? The answer depends on how you expect interest rates to change over the coming year. If you are confident that in 12 months' time one-year bonds will yield more than 9.0%, you would do better to invest in a one-year bond and, when that matured, reinvest the cash for the next year at the higher rate. If you forecast that the future one-year rate is exactly 9.0%, then you will be indifferent between buying a two-year bond or investing for one year and then rolling the investment forward at next year's short-term interest rate.

If everyone is thinking as you just did, then the two-year interest rate has to adjust so that everyone is equally happy to invest for one year or two. Thus the two-year rate will incorporate both today's one-year rate and the consensus forecast of next year's one-year rate.

● ● ● ● ●

We have just illustrated (in Example 3.2) the **expectations theory** of the term structure. It states that in equilibrium investment in a series of short-maturity bonds must offer the same expected return as an investment in a single long-maturity bond. Only if that is the case would investors be prepared to hold both short- and long-maturity bonds.

The expectations theory implies that the *only* reason for an upward-sloping term structure is that investors expect short-term interest rates to rise; the *only* reason for a declining term structure is that investors expect short-term rates to fall.

If short-term interest rates are significantly lower than long-term rates, it is tempting to borrow short-term rather than long-term. The expectations theory implies that such naïve strategies won't work. If short-term rates are lower than long-term rates, then investors must be expecting interest rates to rise. When the term structure is upward-sloping, you are likely to make money by borrowing short only if investors are *overestimating* future increases in interest rates.

Even at a casual glance the expectations theory does not seem to be the complete explanation of term structure. For example, if we look back over the period 1900–2008, we find that the return on long-term U.S. Treasury bonds was on average 1.5 percentage points higher than the return on short-term Treasury bills. Perhaps short-term interest rates stayed lower than investors expected, but it seems more likely that investors wanted some extra return for holding long bonds and that on average they got it. If so, the expectations theory is only a first step.

These days the expectations theory has few strict adherents. Nevertheless, most economists believe that expectations about future interest rates have an important effect on the term structure. For example, you will hear market commentators remark that the six-month interest rate is higher than the three-month rate and conclude that the market is expecting the

---

[9] The extra return for lending for one more year is termed the *forward rate of interest*. In our example the forward rate is 9.0%. In Ms. Kraft's arbitrage example, the forward interest rate was negative. In real life, forward interest rates can't be negative. At the lowest they are zero.

Federal Reserve Board to raise interest rates. There is good evidence for this type of reasoning. Suppose that every month from 1950 to 2008 you used the extra return from lending for six months rather than three to predict the likely change in interest rates. You would have found on average that the steeper the term structure, the more that interest rates subsequently rose. So it looks as if the expectations theory has some truth to it even if it is not the whole truth.

Introducing Risk

What does the expectations theory leave out? The most obvious answer is "risk." If you are confident about the future level of interest rates, you will simply choose the strategy that offers the highest return. But, if you are not sure of your forecasts, you may well opt for a less risky strategy even if it means giving up some return.

Remember that the prices of long-duration bonds are more volatile than prices of short-duration bonds. A sharp increase in interest rates can knock 30% or 40% off the price of long-term bonds.

For some investors, this extra volatility of long-duration bonds may not be a concern. For example, pension funds and life insurance companies have fixed long-term liabilities, and may prefer to lock in future returns by investing in long-term bonds. However, the volatility of long-term bonds *does* create extra risk for investors who do not have such long-term obligations. These investors will be prepared to hold long bonds only if they offer the compensation of a higher return. In this case the term structure will be upward-sloping more often than not. Of course, if interest rates are expected to fall, the term structure could be downward-sloping and still reward investors for lending long. But the additional reward for risk offered by long bonds would result in a less dramatic downward slope.

Inflation and Term Structure

Suppose you are saving for your retirement 20 years from now. Which of the following strategies is more risky? Invest in a succession of one-year Treasuries, rolled over annually, or invest once in 20-year strips? The answer depends on how confident you are about future inflation.

If you buy the 20-year strips, you know exactly how much money you will have at year 20, but you don't know what that money will buy. Inflation may seem benign now, but who knows what it will be in 10 or 15 years? This uncertainty about inflation may make it uncomfortably risky for you to lock in one 20-year interest rate by buying the strips. This was a problem facing investors in 2009, when no one could be sure whether the country was facing the prospect of prolonged deflation or whether the high levels of government borrowing would prompt rapid inflation.

You can reduce exposure to inflation risk by investing short-term and rolling over the investment. You do not know future short-term interest rates, but you do know that future interest rates will adapt to inflation. If inflation takes off, you will probably be able to roll over your investment at higher interest rates.

If inflation is an important source of risk for long-term investors, borrowers must offer some extra incentive if they want investors to lend long. That is why we often see a steeply upward-sloping term structure when inflation is particularly uncertain.

3-5 Real and Nominal Rates of Interest

It is now time to review more carefully the relation between inflation and interest rates. Suppose you invest $1,000 in a one-year bond that makes a single payment of $1,100 at the end of the year. Your cash flow is certain, but the government makes no promises about what that money will buy. If the prices of goods and services increase by more than 10%, you will lose ground in terms of purchasing power.

Several indexes are used to track the general level of prices. The best known is the Consumer Price Index (CPI), which measures the number of dollars that it takes to pay for a typical family's purchases. The change in the CPI from one year to the next measures the rate of inflation.

Figure 3.6 shows the rate of inflation in the U.S. since 1900. Inflation touched a peak at the end of World War I, when it reached 21%. However, this figure pales into insignificance compared with the hyperinflation in Zimbabwe in 2008. Prices there rose so fast that a Z$50 trillion bill was barely enough to buy a loaf of bread.

Prices can fall as well as rise. The U.S. experienced severe *deflation* in the Great Depression, when prices fell by 24% in three years. More recently, consumer prices in Hong Kong fell by nearly 15% in the six years from 1999 to 2004.

The *average* U.S. inflation rate from 1900 to 2008 was 3.1%. As you can see from Figure 3.7, among major economies the U.S. has been almost top of the class in holding inflation in check. Countries torn by war have generally experienced much higher

▶ **FIGURE 3.6**

Annual rates of inflation in the United States from 1900–2008.

Source: E. Dimson, P. R. Marsh, and M. Staunton, *Triumph of the Optimists: 101 Years of Investment Returns* (Princeton, NJ: Princeton University Press, 2002), with updates provided by the authors.

▶ **FIGURE 3.7**

Average rates of inflation in 17 countries from 1900–2008.

Source: E. Dimson, P. R. Marsh, and M. Staunton, *Triumph of the Optimists: 101 Years of Investment Returns* (Princeton, NJ: Princeton University Press, 2002), with updates provided by the authors.

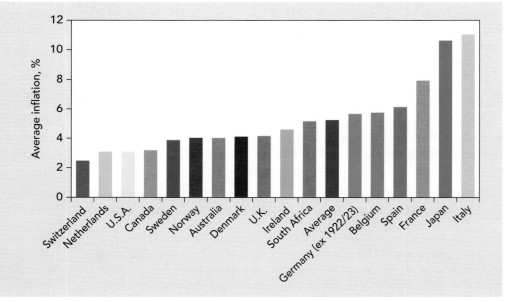

inflation. For example, in Italy and Japan, inflation since 1900 has averaged about 11% a year.

Economists and financial managers refer to current, or *nominal,* dollars versus constant, or *real,* dollars. For example, the nominal cash flow from your one-year bond is $1,100. But if prices rise over the year by 6%, then each dollar will buy you 6% less next year than it does today. So at the end of the year $1,100 has the same purchasing power as 1,100/1.06 = $1,037.74 today. The nominal payoff on the bond is $1,100, but the real payoff is only $1,037.74.

The formula for converting nominal cash flows in a future period *t* to real cash flows today is

$$\text{Real cash flow at date } t = \frac{\text{nominal cash flow at date } t}{(1 + \text{inflation rate})^t}$$

For example, suppose you invest in a 20-year Treasury strip, but inflation over the 20 years averages 6% per year. The strip pays $1,000 in year 20, but the real value of that payoff is only $1,000/1.06^{20} = $311.80. In this example, the purchasing power of $1 today declines to just over $.31 after 20 years.

These examples show you how to get from nominal to real cash flows. The journey from nominal to real interest rates is similar. When a bond dealer says that your bond yields 10%, she is quoting a nominal interest rate. That rate tells you how rapidly your money will grow, say over one year:

Invest Current Dollars	Receive Dollars in Year 1	Result
$1,000 →	$1,100	10% *nominal* rate of return

However, with an expected inflation rate of 6%, you are only 3.774% better off at the end of the year than at the start:

Invest Current Dollars	Expected Real Value of Dollars in Year 1	Result
$1,000 →	$1,037.74 (= 1,100/1.06)	3.774% expected *real* rate of return

Thus, we could say, "The bond offers a 10% nominal rate of return," or "It offers a 3.774% expected real rate of return."

The formula for calculating the real rate of return is:

$$1 + r_{\text{real}} = (1 + r_{\text{nominal}})/(1 + \text{inflation rate})$$

In our example, $1 + r_{\text{real}} = 1.10/1.06 = 1.03774$.[10]

Indexed Bonds and the Real Rate of Interest

Most bonds are like our U.S. Treasury bonds; they promise you a fixed *nominal* rate of interest. The *real* interest rate that you receive is uncertain and depends on inflation. If the inflation rate turns out to be higher than you expected, the real return on your bonds will be lower.

---

[10] A common rule of thumb states that $r_{\text{real}} = r_{\text{nominal}} - $ inflation rate. In our example this gives $r_{\text{real}} = .10 - .06 = .04$, or 4%. This is not a bad approximation to the true real interest rate of 3.774%. But when inflation is high, it pays to use the full formula.

You *can* nail down a real return, however. You do so by buying an *indexed bond* that makes cash payments linked to inflation. Indexed bonds have been around in many other countries for decades, but they were almost unknown in the United States until 1997, when the U.S. Treasury began to issue inflation-indexed bonds known as TIPS (Treasury Inflation-Protected Securities).[11]

The real cash flows on TIPS are fixed, but the nominal cash flows (interest and principal) increase as the CPI increases.[12] For example, suppose that the U.S. Treasury issues 3% 20-year TIPS at a price equal to its face value of $1,000. If during the first year the CPI rises by 10%, then the coupon payment on the bond increases by 10% from $30 to 30 × 1.10 = $33. The amount that you will be paid at maturity also increases to $1,000 × 1.10 = $1,100. The purchasing power of the coupon and face value remain constant at $33/1.10 = $30 and $1,100/1.10 = $1,000. Thus, an investor who buys the bond at the issue price earns a real interest rate of 3%.

Long-term TIPS offered a yield of about 1.7% in February 2009. This is a *real* yield to maturity. It measures the extra goods and services your investment will allow you to buy. The 1.7% yield on TIPS was about 1.0% less than the nominal yield on ordinary Treasury bonds. If the annual inflation rate turns out to be higher than 1.0%, investors will earn a higher return by holding long-term TIPS; if the inflation rate turns out to be less than 1.0%, they would have been better off with nominal bonds.

What Determines the Real Rate of Interest?

The real rate of interest depends on people's willingness to save (the supply of capital)[13] and the opportunities for productive investment by governments and businesses (the demand for capital). For example, suppose that investment opportunities generally improve. Firms have more good projects, so they are willing to invest more than previously at the current real interest rate. Therefore, the rate has to rise to induce individuals to save the additional amount that firms want to invest.[14] Conversely, if investment opportunities deteriorate, there will be a fall in the real interest rate.

Thus the real rate of interest depends on the balance of saving and investment in the overall economy.[15] A high aggregate willingness to save may be associated with high aggregate wealth (because wealthy people usually save more), an uneven distribution of wealth (an even distribution would mean fewer rich people who do most of the saving), and a high proportion of middle-aged people (the young don't need to save and the old don't want to—"You can't take it with you"). A high propensity to invest may be associated with a high level of industrial activity or major technological advances.

Real interest rates do change but they do so gradually. We can see this by looking at the U.K., where the government has issued indexed bonds since 1982. The green line in

---

[11] Indexed bonds were not completely unknown in the United States before 1997. For example, in 1780 American Revolutionary soldiers were compensated with indexed bonds that paid the value of "five bushels of corn, 68 pounds and four-seventh parts of a pound of beef, ten pounds of sheep's wool, and sixteen pounds of sole leather."

[12] The reverse happens if there is deflation. In this case the coupon payment and principal amount are adjusted downward. However, the U.S. government guarantees that when the bond matures it will not pay less than its original face value.

[13] Some of this saving is done indirectly. For example, if you hold 100 shares of IBM stock, and IBM retains and reinvests earnings of $1.00 a share, IBM is saving $100 on your behalf. The government may also oblige you to save by raising taxes to invest in roads, hospitals, etc.

[14] We assume that investors save more as interest rates rise. It doesn't have to be that way. Suppose that 20 years hence you will need $50,000 in today's dollars for your children's college tuition. How much will you have to set aside today to cover this obligation? The answer is the present value of a real expenditure of $50,000 after 20 years, or $50,000/(1 + \text{real interest rate})^{20}$. The higher the real interest rate, the lower the present value and the less you have to set aside.

[15] Short- and medium-term real interest rates are also affected by the monetary policy of central banks. For example, sometimes central banks keep short-term nominal interest rates low despite significant inflation. The resulting real rates can be negative. Nominal interest rates cannot be negative, however, because investors can simply hold cash. Cash always pays zero interest, which is better than negative interest.

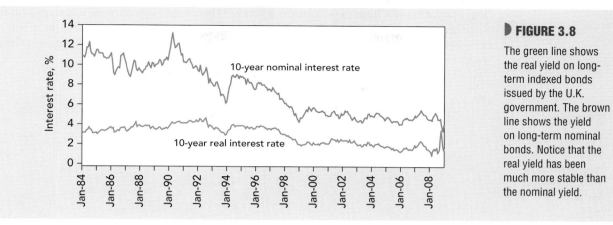

▶ **FIGURE 3.8**

The green line shows the real yield on long-term indexed bonds issued by the U.K. government. The brown line shows the yield on long-term nominal bonds. Notice that the real yield has been much more stable than the nominal yield.

Figure 3.8 shows that the real yield to maturity on these bonds has fluctuated within a relatively narrow range, while the yield on nominal government bonds (the brown line) has declined dramatically.

Inflation and Nominal Interest Rates

How does the inflation outlook affect the nominal rate of interest? Here is how economist Irving Fisher answered the question. Suppose that consumers are equally happy with 100 apples today or 103 apples in a year's time. In this case the real or "apple" interest rate is 3%. If the price of apples is constant at (say) $1 each, then we will be equally happy to receive $100 today or $103 at the end of the year. That extra $3 will allow us to buy 3% more apples at the end of the year than we could buy today.

But suppose now that the apple price is expected to increase by 5% to $1.05 each. In that case we would *not* be happy to give up $100 today for the promise of $103 next year. To buy 103 apples in a year's time, we will need to receive 1.05 × $103 = $108.15. In other words, the nominal rate of interest must increase by the expected rate of inflation to 8.15%.

This is Fisher's theory: A change in the expected inflation rate causes the same proportionate change in the *nominal* interest rate; it has no effect on the required real interest rate. The formula relating the nominal interest rate and expected inflation is

$$1 + r_{\text{nominal}} = (1 + r_{\text{real}})(1 + i)$$

where r_{real} is the real interest rate that consumers require and i is the expected inflation rate. In our example, the prospect of inflation causes $1 + r_{\text{nominal}}$ to rise to 1.03 × 1.05 = 1.0815.

Not all economists would agree with Fisher that the real rate of interest is unaffected by the inflation rate. For example, if changes in prices are associated with changes in the level of industrial activity, then in inflationary conditions I might want more or less than 103 apples in a year's time to compensate me for the loss of 100 today.

We wish we could show you the past behavior of interest rates and *expected* inflation. Instead we have done the next best thing and plotted in Figure 3.9 the return on Treasury bills (short-term government debt) against *actual* inflation for the U.K., the U.S., and Germany. Notice that since 1953 the return on Treasury bills has generally been a little above the rate of inflation. Investors in each country earned an average real return of between 1% and 2% during this period.

Look now at the relationship between the rate of inflation and the Treasury bill rate. Figure 3.9 shows that investors have for the most part demanded a higher rate of interest when inflation was high. So it looks as if Fisher's theory provides a useful rule of thumb for financial managers. If the expected inflation rate changes, it is a good bet that there will be a corresponding change in the interest rate. In other words, a strategy of rolling over short-term investments affords some protection against uncertain inflation.

▶ **FIGURE 3.9**

The return on Treasury bills and the rate of inflation in the U.K., the U.S., and Germany, 1953–2008.

Source: E. Dimson, P. R. Marsh, and M. Staunton, *Triumph of the Optimists: 101 Years of Investment Returns* (Princeton, NJ: Princeton University Press, 2002), with updates provided by the authors.

3-6 Corporate Bonds and the Risk of Default

Our focus so far has been on U.S. Treasury bonds. But the federal government is not the only issuer of bonds. State and local governments borrow by selling bonds.[16] So do corporations. Many foreign governments and corporations also borrow in the U.S. At the same time U.S. corporations may borrow dollars or other currencies by issuing their bonds in other countries. For example, they may issue dollar bonds in London that are then sold to investors throughout the world.

National governments don't go bankrupt—they just print more money. But they can't print money of other countries.[17] Therefore, when a foreign government borrows dollars, investors worry that in some future crisis the government may not be able to come up with enough dollars to repay the debt. This worry shows up in bond prices and yields to maturity. For example, in 2008 a collapse in the Ukrainian exchange rate raised the cost of servicing the country's foreign debts. Despite a bailout from the International Monetary Fund, bondholders worried that the Ukrainian government would not be able to service the dollar bonds that it had issued. By early 2009, the promised yield on Ukrainian government debt had climbed to 25 percentage points above the yield on U.S. Treasuries.

Corporations that get into financial distress may also be forced to default on their bonds. Thus the payments promised to corporate bondholders represent a best-case scenario: The firm will never pay more than the promised cash flows, but in hard times it may pay less.

The safety of most corporate bonds can be judged from bond ratings provided by Moody's, Standard & Poor's (S&P), and Fitch. Table 3.5 lists the possible bond ratings in declining order of quality. For example, the bonds that receive the highest Moody's rating are known as Aaa (or "triple A") bonds. Then come Aa (double A), A, Baa bonds, and so on. Bonds rated Baa and above are called **investment grade,** while those with a rating of Ba or below are referred to as *speculative grade, high-yield,* or **junk bonds.**

It is rare for highly rated bonds to default. However, when an investment-grade bond does go under, the shock waves are felt in all major financial centers. For example, in May 2001 World-Com sold $11.8 billion of bonds with an investment-grade rating. About one year later, WorldCom filed for bankruptcy, and its bondholders lost more than 80% of their investment. For those bondholders, the agencies that had assigned investment-grade ratings were not the flavor of the month.

Moody's	Standard & Poor's and Fitch
Aaa	AAA
Aa	AA
A	A
Baa	BBB
Ba	BB
B	B
Caa	CCC
Ca	CC
C	C

▶ **TABLE 3.5** Key to bond ratings. The highest-quality bonds rated Baa/BBB or above are investment grade. Lower-rated bonds are called high-yield, or junk, bonds.

---

[16] These *municipal bonds* enjoy a special tax advantage, because investors are exempt from federal income tax on the coupon payments on state and local government bonds. As a result, investors accept lower pretax yields on "munis."

[17] The U.S. government can print dollars and the Japanese government can print yen. But governments in the Eurozone don't even have the luxury of being able to print their own currency. For example, during the 2008 credit crisis, investors worried that the Greek government would not be able to service its euro debts. At one point Greek bonds yielded 3% more than equivalent German government bonds.

As you would expect, yields on corporate bonds vary with the bond rating. Figure 3.10 shows the yield spread of corporate bonds against U.S. Treasuries. Notice how spreads widen as safety falls off.

The credit crunch that began in 2008 saw a dramatic widening in yield spreads. Look at Table 3.6, which shows the prices and yields in December 2008 for a sample of corporate bonds ranked by Standard & Poor's rating. The yield on General Motors bonds exceeded 50%. That may seem like a mouth-watering rate of return, but investors foresaw that GM was likely to go bankrupt and that bond investors would not get their money back.

The yields to maturity reported in Table 3.6 depend on the probability of default, the amount recovered by the bondholder in the event of default, and also on *liquidity*. Corporate bonds are less liquid than Treasuries: They are more difficult and expensive to trade, particularly in large quantities or on short notice. Many investors value liquidity and will demand a higher interest rate on a less liquid bond. Lack of liquidity accounts for some of the spread between yields on corporate and Treasury bonds.

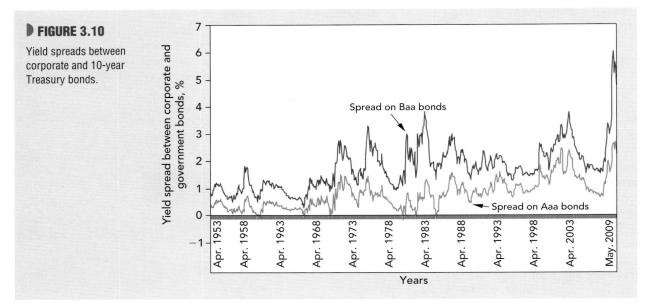

▶ FIGURE 3.10

Yield spreads between corporate and 10-year Treasury bonds.

Issuer	Coupon	Maturity	S&P Rating	Price, % of Face Value	Yield to Maturity
Pfizer	4.65%	2018	AAA	104.00%	4.12%
Wal-Mart	6.75	2023	AA	111.45	5.60
DuPont	6	2018	A	101.97	5.73
ConAgra	9.75	2021	BBB	111.00	8.30
Woolworth	8.50	2022	BB	93.99	9.30
Eastman Kodak	9.20	2021	B	70.00	14.46
General Motors	8.8	2021	CCC	16.66	56.78

▶ TABLE 3.6   Prices and yields of a sample of corporate bonds, December 2008.

Source: Bond transactions reported on FINRA's TRACE service: http://cxa.marketwatch.com/finra/BondCenter.

Valuing Bonds

Spreadsheet programs such as Excel provide built-in functions to solve for a variety of bond valuation problems. You can find these functions by pressing *fx* on the Excel toolbar. If you then click on the function that you wish to use, Excel will ask you for the inputs that it needs. At the bottom left of the function box there is a Help facility with an example of how the function is used.

Here is a list of useful functions for valuing bonds, together with some points to remember when entering data:

- **PRICE:** The price of a bond given its yield to maturity.
- **YLD:** The yield to maturity of a bond given its price.
- **DURATION:** The duration of a bond.
- **MDURATION:** The modified duration (or volatility) of a bond.

Notes:

- You can enter all the inputs in these functions directly as numbers or as the addresses of cells that contain the numbers.

- You must enter the yield and coupon as decimal values, for example, for 3% you would enter .03.
- Settlement is the date that payment for the security is made. Maturity is the maturity date. You can enter these dates directly using the Excel date function, for example, you would enter 15 Feb 2009 as DATE(2009,02,15). Alternatively, you can enter these dates in a cell and then enter the cell address in the function.
- In the functions for PRICE and YLD you need to scroll down in the function box to enter the frequency of coupon payments. Enter 1 for annual payments or 2 for semiannual.
- The functions for PRICE and YLD ask for an entry for "basis." We suggest you leave this blank. (See the Help facility for an explanation.)

SPREADSHEET QUESTIONS

The following questions provide an opportunity to practice each of these functions.

3.1 (PRICE) In February 2009, Treasury 8.5s of 2020 yielded 3.2976% (see Figure 3.1). What was their price? If the yield rose to 4%, what would happen to the price?

3.2 (YLD) On the same day Treasury 3.5s of 2018 were priced at 107:15 (see Figure 3.1). What was their yield to maturity? Suppose that the price was 110:00. What would happen to the yield?

3.3 (DURATION) What was the duration of the Treasury 8.5s? How would duration change if the yield rose to 4%? Can you explain why?

3.4 (MDURATION) What was the modified duration of the Treasury 8.5s? How would modified duration differ if the coupon were only 7.5%?

Corporate Bonds Come in Many Forms

Most corporate bonds are similar to the government bonds that we have analyzed in this chapter. In other words, they promise to make a fixed nominal coupon payment for each year until maturity, at which point they also promise to repay the face value. However, you will find that corporate bonds offer far greater variety than governments. Here are just two examples.

Floating-Rate Bonds   Some corporate bonds are *floating rate*. They make coupon payments that are tied to some measure of current market rates. The rate might be reset once a year to the current short-term Treasury rate plus a spread of 2%, for example. So if the Treasury bill rate at the start of the year is 6%, the bond's coupon rate over the next year is set at 8%. This arrangement means that the bond's coupon rate always approximates current market interest rates.

Convertible Bonds   If you buy a convertible bond, you can choose later to exchange it for a specified number of shares of common stock. For example, a convertible bond that is issued at a face value of $1,000 may be convertible into 50 shares of the firm's stock. Because convertible bonds offer the opportunity to participate in any price appreciation of the company's stock, convertibles can be issued at lower coupon rates than plain-vanilla bonds.

• • • • •

SUMMARY   Bonds are simply long-term loans. If you own a bond, you are entitled to a regular interest (or *coupon*) payment and at maturity you get back the bond's face value (or *principal*). In the U.S., coupons are normally paid every six months, but in other countries they may be paid annually.

The value of any bond is equal to its cash payments discounted at the spot rates of interest. For example, the present value of a 10-year bond with a 5% coupon paid annually equals

$$PV(\% \text{ of face value}) = \frac{5}{(1+r_1)} + \frac{5}{(1+r_2)^2} + \cdots + \frac{105}{(1+r_{10})^{10}}$$

This calculation uses a different spot rate of interest for each period. A plot of spot rates by maturity shows the term structure of interest rates.

Spot interest rates are most conveniently calculated from the prices of strips, which are bonds that make a single payment of face value at maturity, with zero coupons along the way. The price of a strip maturing in a future date t reveals the discount factor and spot rate for cash flows at that date. All other safe cash payments on that date are valued at that same spot rate.

Investors and financial managers use the yield to maturity on a bond to summarize its prospective return. To calculate the yield to maturity on the 10-year 5s, you need to solve for y in the following equation:

$$PV(\% \text{ of face value}) = \frac{5}{(1+y)} + \frac{5}{(1+y)^2} + \cdots + \frac{105}{(1+y)^{10}}$$

The yield to maturity discounts all cash payments at the same rate, even if spot rates differ. Notice that the yield to maturity for a bond can't be calculated until you know the bond's price or present value.

A bond's maturity tells you the date of its final payment, but it is also useful to know the *average* time to each payment. This is called the bond's *duration*. Duration is important because there is a direct relationship between the duration of a bond and the exposure of its price to changes in interest rates. A change in interest rates has a greater effect on the price of long-duration bonds.

The term structure of interest rates is upward-sloping more often than not. This means that long-term spot rates are higher than short-term spot rates. But it does *not* mean that investing long is more profitable than investing short. The *expectations theory* of the term structure tells us that bonds are priced so that an investor who holds a succession of short bonds can expect the same return as another investor who holds a long bond. The expectations theory predicts an upward-sloping term structure only when future short-term interest rates are expected to rise.

The expectations theory cannot be a complete explanation of term structure if investors are worried about risk. Long bonds may be a safe haven for investors with long-term fixed liabilities. But other investors may not like the extra volatility of long-term bonds or may be concerned that a sudden burst of inflation may largely wipe out the real value of these bonds. These investors will be prepared to hold long-term bonds only if they offer the compensation of a higher rate of interest.

Bonds promise fixed nominal cash payments, but the *real* interest rate that they provide depends on inflation. The best-known theory about the effect of inflation on interest rates was suggested by Irving Fisher. He argued that the nominal, or money, rate of interest is equal to the required real rate plus the expected rate of inflation. If the expected inflation rate increases by 1%, so too will the money rate of interest. During the past 50 years Fisher's simple theory has not done a bad job of explaining changes in short-term interest rates.

When you buy a U.S. Treasury bond, you can be confident that you will get your money back. When you lend to a company, you face the risk that it will go belly-up and will not be able to repay its bonds. Defaults are rare for companies with investment-grade bond ratings, but investors worry nevertheless. Companies need to compensate investors for default risk by promising to pay higher rates of interest.

● ● ● ● ●

FURTHER READING

A good general text on debt markets is:

S. Sundaresan, *Fixed Income Markets and Their Derivatives,* 3rd ed. (San Diego, CA: Academic Press, 2009).

Schaefer's paper is a good review of duration and how it is used to hedge fixed liabilities:

A.M. Schaefer, "Immunisation and Duration: A Review of Theory, Performance and Application," in *The Revolution in Corporate Finance,* ed. J. M. Stern and D. H. Chew, Jr. (Oxford: Basil Blackwell, 1986).

● ● ● ● ●

PROBLEM SETS

BASIC

1. A 10-year bond is issued with a face value of $1,000, paying interest of $60 a year. If market yields increase shortly after the T-bond is issued, what happens to the bond's:
   a. Coupon rate?
   b. Price?
   c. Yield to maturity?
2. The following statements are true. Explain why.
   a. If a bond's coupon rate is higher than its yield to maturity, then the bond will sell for more than face value.
   b. If a bond's coupon rate is lower than its yield to maturity, then the bond's price will increase over its remaining maturity.

3. In February 2009 Treasury 6s of 2026 offered a semiannually compounded yield of 3.5965%. Recognizing that coupons are paid semiannually, calculate the bond's price.

4. Here are the prices of three bonds with 10-year maturities:

Bond Coupon (%)	Price (%)
2	81.62
4	98.39
8	133.42

If coupons are paid annually, which bond offered the highest yield to maturity?
Which had the lowest? Which bonds had the longest and shortest durations?

5. Construct some simple examples to illustrate your answers to the following:

   a. If interest rates rise, do bond prices rise or fall?

   b. If the bond yield is greater than the coupon, is the price of the bond greater or less than 100?

   c. If the price of a bond exceeds 100, is the yield greater or less than the coupon?

   d. Do high-coupon bonds sell at higher or lower prices than low-coupon bonds?

   e. If interest rates change, does the price of high-coupon bonds change proportionately more than that of low-coupon bonds?

6. Which comes first in the market for U.S. Treasury bonds:

   a. Spot interest rates or yields to maturity?

   b. Bond prices or yields to maturity?

7. Look again at Table 3.4. Suppose that spot interest rates all change to 4%—a "flat" term structure of interest rates.

   a. What is the new yield to maturity for each bond in the table?

   b. Recalculate the price of bond A.

8. a. What is the formula for the value of a two-year, 5% bond in terms of spot rates?

   b. What is the formula for its value in terms of yield to maturity?

   c. If the two-year spot rate is higher than the one-year rate, is the yield to maturity greater or less than the two-year spot rate?

9. The following table shows the prices of a sample of U.S. Treasury strips in August 2009. Each strip makes a single payment of $1,000 at maturity.

   a. Calculate the annually compounded, spot interest rate for each year.

   b. Is the term structure upward- or downward-sloping, or flat?

   c. Would you expect the yield on a coupon bond maturing in August 2013 to be higher or lower than the yield on the 2013 strip?

Maturity	Price (%)
August 2010	99.423
August 2011	97.546
August 2012	94.510
August 2013	90.524

10. a. An 8%, five-year bond yields 6%. If the yield remains unchanged, what will be its price one year hence? Assume annual coupon payments.

    b. What is the total return to an investor who held the bond over this year?

    c. What can you deduce about the relationship between the bond return over a particular period and the yields to maturity at the start and end of that period?

11. True or false? Explain.

   a. Longer-maturity bonds necessarily have longer durations.

   b. The longer a bond's duration, the lower its volatility.

   c. Other things equal, the lower the bond coupon, the higher its volatility.

   d. If interest rates rise, bond durations rise also.

12. Calculate the durations and volatilities of securities A, B, and C. Their cash flows are shown below. The interest rate is 8%.

	Period 1	Period 2	Period 3
A	40	40	40
B	20	20	120
C	10	10	110

13. The one-year spot interest rate is $r_1 = 5\%$ and the two-year rate is $r_2 = 6\%$. If the expectations theory is correct, what is the expected one-year interest rate in one year's time?

14. The two-year interest rate is 10% and the expected annual inflation rate is 5%.

   a. What is the expected real interest rate?

   b. If the expected rate of inflation suddenly rises to 7%, what does Fisher's theory say about how the real interest rate will change? What about the nominal rate?

INTERMEDIATE

15. A 10-year German government bond (Bund) has a face value of €100 and a coupon rate of 5% paid annually. Assume that the interest rate (in euros) is equal to 6% per year. What is the bond's PV?

16. A 10-year U.S. Treasury bond with a face value of $10,000 pays a coupon of 5.5% (2.75% of face value every six months). The semiannually compounded interest rate is 5.2% (a six-month discount rate of 5.2/2 = 2.6%).

   a. What is the present value of the bond?

   b. Generate a graph or table showing how the bond's present value changes for semiannually compounded interest rates between 1% and 15%.

17. A six-year government bond makes annual coupon payments of 5% and offers a yield of 3% annually compounded. Suppose that one year later the bond still yields 3%. What return has the bondholder earned over the 12-month period? Now suppose that the bond yields 2% at the end of the year. What return would the bondholder earn in this case?

18. A 6% six-year bond yields 12% and a 10% six-year bond yields 8%. Calculate the six-year spot rate. Assume annual coupon payments. (*Hint:* What would be your cash flows if you bought 1.2 10% bonds?)

19. Is the yield on high-coupon bonds more likely to be higher than that on low-coupon bonds when the term structure is upward-sloping or when it is downward-sloping? Explain.

20. You have estimated spot rates as follows:
$r_1 = 5.00\%, r_2 = 5.40\%, r_3 = 5.70\%, r_4 = 5.90\%, r_5 = 6.00\%$.

   a. What are the discount factors for each date (that is, the present value of $1 paid in year t)?

   b. Calculate the PV of the following bonds assuming annual coupons: (i) 5%, two-year bond; (ii) 5%, five-year bond; and (iii) 10%, five-year bond.

   c. Explain intuitively why the yield to maturity on the 10% bond is less than that on the 5% bond.

   d. What should be the yield to maturity on a five-year zero-coupon bond?

   e. Show that the correct yield to maturity on a five-year annuity is 5.75%.

   f. Explain intuitively why the yield on the five-year bonds described in part (c) must lie between the yield on a five-year zero-coupon bond and a five-year annuity.

21. Calculate durations and modified durations for the 4% coupon bond and the strip in Table 3.1. The answers for the strip will be easy. For the 4% bond, you can follow the procedure set out in Table 3.3 for the 11¼% coupon bonds. Confirm that modified duration predicts the impact of a 1% change in interest rates on the bond prices.

22. Find the "live" spreadsheet for Table 3.3 on this book's Web site, **www.mhhe.com/bma**. Show how duration and volatility change if (a) the bond's coupon is 8% of face value and (b) the bond's yield is 6%. Explain your finding.

23. The formula for the duration of a perpetual bond that makes an equal payment each year in perpetuity is $(1 + \text{yield})/\text{yield}$. If each bond yields 5%, which has the longer duration—a perpetual bond or a 15-year zero-coupon bond? What if the yield is 10%?

24. Look up prices of 10 U.S. Treasury bonds with different coupons and different maturities. Calculate how their prices would change if their yields to maturity increased by 1 percentage point. Are long- or short-term bonds most affected by the change in yields? Are high- or low-coupon bonds most affected?

25. Look again at Table 3.4. Suppose the spot interest rates change to the following *downward-sloping* term structure: $r_1 = 4.6\%$, $r_2 = 4.4\%$, $r_3 = 4.2\%$, and $r_4 = 4.0\%$. Recalculate discount factors, bond prices, and yields to maturity for each of the bonds listed in the table.

26. Look at the spot interest rates shown in Problem 25. Suppose that someone told you that the five-year spot interest rate was 2.5%. Why would you not believe him? How could you make money if he was right? What is the minimum sensible value for the five-year spot rate?

27. Look again at the spot interest rates shown in Problem 25. What can you deduce about the one-year spot interest rate in three years if:

    a. The expectations theory of term structure is right?

    b. Investing in long-term bonds carries additional risks?

28. Suppose that you buy a two-year 8% bond at its face value.

    a. What will be your nominal return over the two years if inflation is 3% in the first year and 5% in the second? What will be your real return?

    b. Now suppose that the bond is a TIPS. What will be your real and nominal returns?

29. A bond's credit rating provides a guide to its price. As we write this in Spring 2009, Aaa bonds yield 5.41% and Baa bonds yield 8.47%. If some bad news causes a 10% five-year bond to be unexpectedly downrated from Aaa to Baa, what would be the effect on the bond price? (Assume annual coupons.)

CHALLENGE

30. Write a spreadsheet program to construct a series of bond tables that show the present value of a bond given the coupon rate, maturity, and yield to maturity. Assume that coupon payments are semiannual and yields are compounded semiannually.

31. Find the arbitrage opportunity (opportunities?). Assume for simplicity that coupons are paid annually. In each case the face value of the bond is $1,000.

Bond	Maturity (years)	Coupon ($)	Price ($)
A	3	0	751.30
B	4	50	842.30
C	4	120	1,065.28
D	4	100	980.57
E	3	140	1,120.12
F	3	70	1,001.62
G	2	0	834.00

32. The duration of a bond that makes an equal payment each year in perpetuity is (1 + yield)/ yield. Prove it.

33. What is the duration of a common stock whose dividends are expected to grow at a constant rate in perpetuity?

34. a. What spot and forward rates are embedded in the following Treasury bonds? The price of one-year strips is 93.46%. Assume for simplicity that bonds make only annual payments. (*Hint:* Can you devise a mixture of long and short positions in these bonds that gives a cash payoff only in year 2? In year 3?)

Visit us at
www.mhhe.com/bma

Maturity (years)	Coupon (%)	Price (%)
4	2	94.92
8	3	103.64

b. A three-year bond with a 4% coupon is selling at 95.00%. Is there a profit opportunity here? If so, how would you take advantage of it?

35. Look one more time at Table 3.4.

a. Suppose you knew the bond prices but not the spot interest rates. Explain how you would calculate the spot rates. (*Hint:* You have four unknown spot rates, so you need four equations.)

b. Suppose that you could buy bond C in large quantities at $1,040 rather than at its equilibrium price of $1,058.76. Show how you could make a zillion dollars without taking on any risk.

1. The Web sites of *The Wall Street Journal* (**www.wsj.com**) and the *Financial Times* (**www.ft.com**) are wonderful sources of market data. You should become familiar with them. Use **www.wsj .com** to answer the following questions:

a. Find the prices of coupon strips. Use these prices to plot the term structure. If the expectations theory is correct, what is the expected one-year interest rate three years hence?

b. Find a three- or four-year bond and construct a package of coupon and principal strips that provides the same cash flows. The law of one price predicts that the cost of the package should be very close to that of the bond. Is it?

c. Find a long-term Treasury bond with a low coupon and calculate its duration. Now find another bond with a similar maturity and a higher coupon. Which has the longer duration?

d. Look up the yields on 10-year nominal Treasury bonds and on TIPS. If you are confident that inflation will average 2% a year, which bond will provide the higher real return?

2. Log on to **www.smartmoney.com** and find the Living Yield Curve, which shows a picture of the yield curve. How does today's yield curve compare with yield curves in the past? Do short-term interest rates move more than long rates?

**REAL-TIME
DATA ANALYSIS**

4 CHAPTER ● ● ● ● ●

The Value of Common Stocks

▶ **We should warn** you that being a financial expert has its occupational hazards. One is being cornered at cocktail parties by people who are eager to explain their system for making creamy profits by investing in common stocks. One of the few good things about a financial crisis is that these bores tend to disappear, at least temporarily.

We may exaggerate the perils of the trade. The point is that there is no easy way to ensure superior investment performance. Later in the book we show that in well-functioning capital markets it is impossible to predict changes in security prices. Therefore, in this chapter, when we use the concept of present value to price common stocks, we are not promising you a key to investment success; we simply believe that the idea can help you to understand why some investments are priced higher than others.

Why should you care? If you want to know the value of a firm's stock, why can't you look up the stock price in the newspaper? Unfortunately, that is not always possible. For example, you may be the founder of a successful business. You currently own all the shares but are thinking of going public by selling off shares to other investors. You and your advisers need to estimate the price at which those shares can be sold.

There is also another, deeper reason why managers need to understand how shares are valued. If a firm acts in its shareholders' interest, it should accept those investments that increase the value of their stake in the firm. But in order to do this, it is necessary to understand what determines the shares' value.

We begin with a look at how stocks are traded. Then we explain the basic principles of share valuation and the use of discounted-cash-flow (DCF) models to estimate expected rates of return.

These principles lead us to the fundamental difference between growth and income stocks. A growth stock doesn't just grow; its future investments are also expected to earn rates of return that are higher than the cost of capital. It's the *combination* of growth and superior returns that generates high price–earnings ratios for growth stocks. We explain why price–earnings ratios may differ for growth and income stocks. Finally we show how DCF models can be extended to value entire businesses rather than individual shares.

Still another warning: Everybody knows that common stocks are risky and that some are more risky than others. Therefore, investors will not commit funds to stocks unless the expected rates of return are commensurate with the risks. But we say next to nothing in this chapter about the linkages between risk and expected return. A more careful treatment of risk starts in Chapter 7.

● ● ● ● ●

4-1 How Common Stocks Are Traded

General Electric (GE) has about 10.6 billion shares outstanding and at last count these shares were owned by about 600,000 shareholders. They included large pension funds and insurance companies that each own several million shares, as well as individuals who own a handful of shares. If you owned one GE share, you would own .00000001% of the company and have a claim on the same tiny fraction of GE's profits. Of course, the more shares you own, the larger your "share" of the company.

If GE wishes to raise new capital, it can do so either by borrowing or by selling new shares to investors. Sales of shares to raise new capital are said to occur in the *primary market*. However, such sales occur relatively infrequently and most trades in GE take place on the stock exchange, where investors buy and sell existing GE shares. Stock exchanges are really markets for secondhand shares, but they prefer to describe themselves as *secondary markets*, which sounds more important.

The two principal stock exchanges in the United States are the New York Stock Exchange and Nasdaq. Both compete vigorously for business and just as vigorously tout the advantages of their trading systems. The volume of business that they handle is immense. For example, on an average day the NYSE trades around 2.8 billion shares in some 2,800 companies.

In addition to the NYSE and Nasdaq, there are a number of computer networks called *electronic communication networks* (*ECN*s) that connect traders with each other. Large U.S. companies may also arrange for their shares to be traded on foreign exchanges, such as the London exchange or the Euronext exchange in Paris. At the same time many foreign companies are listed on the U.S. exchanges. For example, the NYSE trades shares in Toyota, Royal Dutch Shell, Canadian Pacific, Tata Motors, Nokia, Brasil Telecom, China Eastern Airlines, and more than 400 other companies.

Suppose that Ms. Jones, a longtime GE shareholder, no longer wishes to hold her shares in the company. She can sell them via the NYSE to Mr. Brown, who wants to increase his stake in the firm. The transaction merely transfers partial ownership of the firm from one investor to another. No new shares are created, and GE will neither care nor know that the trade has taken place.

Ms. Jones and Mr. Brown do not trade the GE shares themselves. Instead, their orders must go through a brokerage firm. Ms. Jones, who is anxious to sell, might give her broker a *market order* to sell stock at the best available price. On the other hand, Mr. Brown might state a price limit at which he is willing to buy GE stock. If his *limit order* cannot be executed immediately, it is recorded in the exchange's limit order book until it can be executed.

When they transact on the NYSE, Brown and Jones are participating in a huge auction market in which the exchange's designated market makers match up the orders of thousands of investors. Most major exchanges around the world, such as the Tokyo Stock Exchange, the London Stock Exchange, and the Deutsche Börse, are also auction markets, but the auctioneer in these cases is a computer.[1] This means that there is no stock exchange floor to show on the evening news and no one needs to ring a bell to start trading.

Nasdaq is not an auction market. All trades on Nasdaq take place between the investor and one of a group of professional dealers who are prepared to buy and sell stock. Dealer markets are relatively rare for trading equities but are common for many other financial instruments. For example, most bonds are traded in dealer markets.

---

[1] Trades are still made face to face on the floor of the NYSE, but computerized trading is expanding rapidly. In 2006 the NYSE merged with Archipelago, an electronic trading system, and transformed itself into a public corporation. The following year it merged with Euronext, an electronic trading system in Europe and changed its name to NYSE Euronext.

The prices at which stocks trade are summarized in the daily press. Here, for example, is how *The Wall Street Journal*'s Web site (**www.wsj.com**) recorded a day's trading in GE in March 2009:

52-week				
Hi	Lo	Volume	Closing Price	Net Change
38.52	5.93	216,297,410	9.62	0.05

You can see that on this day investors traded a total of 216 million shares of GE stock. By the close of the day the stock traded at $9.62 a share, up $0.05 from the day before. Since there were 10.6 billion shares of GE outstanding, investors were placing a total value on the stock of $102 billion.

Buying stocks is a risky occupation. GE's stock price had peaked at about $60 in 2001. By March 2009, an unfortunate investor who had bought in at $60 would have lost 84% of his or her investment. Of course, you don't come across such people at cocktail parties; they either keep quiet or aren't invited.

Most of the trading on the NYSE and Nasdaq is in ordinary common stocks, but other securities are traded also. For example, investors can choose from hundreds of *exchange-traded funds* (ETFs), which are portfolios of stocks that can be bought or sold in a single trade. These include SPDRs (Standard & Poor's Depository Receipts or "spiders"), which are portfolios tracking several Standard & Poor's stock market indexes, including the benchmark S&P 500. You can buy DIAMONDS, which track the Dow Jones Industrial Average; QUBES or QQQQs, which track the Nasdaq 100 index, as well as ETFs that track specific industries or commodities. You can also buy shares in closed-end mutual funds[2] that invest in portfolios of securities. These include country funds, for example, the Mexico and Chile funds, that invest in portfolios of stocks in specific countries.

4-2 How Common Stocks Are Valued

Finding the value of GE stock may sound like a simple problem. Each quarter, the company publishes a balance sheet, which lists the value of the firm's assets and liabilities. At the end of 2008 the book value of all GE's assets—plant and machinery, inventories of materials, cash in the bank, and so on—was $798 billion. GE's liabilities—money that it owes the banks, taxes that are due to be paid, and the like—amounted to $693 billion. The difference between the value of the assets and the liabilities was $105 billion. This was the book value of GE's equity.

Book value is a reassuringly definite number. Each year KPMG, one of America's largest accounting firms, gives its opinion that GE's financial statements present fairly in all material respects the company's financial position, in conformity with U.S. generally accepted accounting principles (commonly called GAAP). However, the book value of GE's assets measures their original (or "historical") cost less an allowance for depreciation. This may not be a good guide to what those assets are worth today. When GE raised money to invest in various projects, it judged that those projects were worth *more* than they cost. If it was right, its shares should sell for more than their book value.

---

[2] *Closed-end* mutual funds issue shares that are traded on stock exchanges. *Open-end* funds are not traded on exchanges. Investors in open-end funds transact directly with the fund. The fund issues new shares to investors and redeems shares from investors who want to withdraw money from the fund.

Valuation by Comparables

When financial analysts need to value a business, they often start by identifying a sample of similar firms. They then examine how much investors in these companies are prepared to pay for each dollar of assets or earnings. This is often called *valuation by comparables*. Look, for example, at Table 4.1. The first column of numbers shows for some well-known companies the ratio of the market value of the equity to its book value. Notice that market value is generally higher than book value. There are two exceptions; GE's stock was worth exactly book value while Dow Chemical stock was selling for much less than book.

The second column of numbers shows the market-to-book ratio for competing firms. For example, you can see from the first row of the table that the stock of the typical large pharmaceutical firm sells for three times its book value. Therefore, if you did not have a market price for the stock of Johnson & Johnson (J&J), you might estimate that it would also sell at three times book value. This would give you a stock price of $46, a bit lower than the actual market price of $52.

An alternative would be to look at how much investors in other pharmaceutical stocks are prepared to pay for each dollar of earnings. The first row of Table 4.1 shows that the typical price–earnings (*P/E*) ratio for these stocks is 10.9. If you assumed that Johnson & Johnson should sell at a similar multiple of earnings, you would get a value for the stock of just under $50, only a shade lower than the actual price in March 2009.

Valuation by comparables worked well for Johnson & Johnson, but that is not the case for all the companies shown in Table 4.1. For example, if you had naïvely assumed that Amazon stock would sell at similar ratios to comparable dot.com stocks, you would have been out by a wide margin. Both the market-to-book ratio and the price–earnings ratio can vary considerably from stock to stock even for firms that are in the same line of business. To understand why this is so, we need to dig deeper and look at what determines a stock's market value.

	Market-to-Book-Value Ratio		Price–Earnings Ratio	
	Company	**Competitors***	**Company**	**Competitors***
Johnson & Johnson	3.4	3.0	11.3	10.9
PepsiCo	6.4	3.0	15.6	12.9
Campbell Soup	9.0	4.6	8.8	11.3
Wal-Mart	3.0	2.1	14.6	13.4
Exxon Mobil	2.9	1.2	7.6	5.3
Dow Chemical	0.5	3.0	12.5	10.6
Dell Computer	4.5	3.7	7.9	11.1
Amazon	11.2	2.7	46.9	22.2
McDonald's	4.4	3.1	14.1	13.6
American Electric Power	1.1	1.1	8.1	11.0
GE	1.0	1.7	4.6	8.8

▶ **TABLE 4.1**   Market-to-book-value ratios and price–earnings ratios for selected companies and their principal competitors, March 2009.

* Figures are median ratios for competing companies.

The Determinants of Stock Prices

Think back to Chapter 2, where we described how to value future cash flows. The discounted-cash-flow (DCF) formula for the present value of a stock is just the same as it is for the present value of any other asset. We just discount the cash flows by the return that can be earned in the capital market on securities of comparable risk. Shareholders receive cash from the company in the form of a stream of dividends. So

$$PV(stock) = PV(expected\ future\ dividends)$$

At first sight this statement may seem surprising. When investors buy stocks, they usually expect to receive a dividend, but they also hope to make a capital gain. Why does our formula for present value say nothing about capital gains? As we now explain, there is no inconsistency.

Today's Price

The cash payoff to owners of common stocks comes in two forms: (1) cash dividends and (2) capital gains or losses. Suppose that the current price of a share is P_0, that the expected price at the end of a year is P_1, and that the expected dividend per share is DIV_1. The rate of return that investors expect from this share over the next year is defined as the expected dividend per share DIV_1 plus the expected price appreciation per share $P_1 - P_0$, all divided by the price at the start of the year P_0:

$$Expected\ return = r = \frac{DIV_1 + P_1 - P_0}{P_0}$$

Suppose Fledgling Electronics stock is selling for $100 a share ($P_0 = 100$). Investors expect a $5 cash dividend over the next year ($DIV_1 = 5$). They also expect the stock to sell for $110 a year hence ($P_1 = 110$). Then the expected return to the stockholders is 15%:

$$r = \frac{5 + 110 - 100}{100} = .15,\ or\ 15\%$$

On the other hand, if you are given investors' forecasts of dividend and price and the expected return offered by other equally risky stocks, you can predict today's price:

$$Price = P_0 = \frac{DIV_1 + P_1}{1 + r}$$

For Fledgling Electronics $DIV_1 = 5$ and $P_1 = 110$. If r, the expected return for Fledgling is 15%, then today's price should be $100:

$$P_0 = \frac{5 + 110}{1.15} = \$100$$

What exactly is the discount rate, r, in this calculation? It's called the **market capitalization rate** or **cost of equity capital**, which are just alternative names for the opportunity cost of capital, defined as the expected return on other securities with the same risks as Fledgling shares.

Many stocks will be safer than Fledgling, and many riskier. But among the thousands of traded stocks there will be a group with essentially the same risks. Call this group Fledgling's *risk class*. Then all stocks in this risk class have to be priced to offer the same expected rate of return.

Let's suppose that the other securities in Fledgling's risk class all offer the same 15% expected return. Then $100 per share has to be the right price for Fledgling stock. In fact it is the only possible price. What if Fledgling's price were above $P_0 = \$100$? In this case investors would shift their capital to the other securities and in the process would force down the price of Fledgling stock. If P_0 were less than $100, the process would reverse.

Investors would rush to buy, forcing the price up to $100. Therefore at each point in time *all securities in an equivalent risk class are priced to offer the same expected return.* This is a condition for equilibrium in well-functioning capital markets. It is also common sense.

But What Determines Next Year's Price?

We have managed to explain today's stock price P_0 in terms of the dividend DIV_1 and the expected price next year P_1. Future stock prices are not easy things to forecast directly. But think about what determines next year's price. If our price formula holds now, it ought to hold then as well:

$$P_1 = \frac{DIV_2 + P_2}{1 + r}$$

That is, a year from now investors will be looking out at dividends in year 2 and price at the end of year 2. Thus we can forecast P_1 by forecasting DIV_2 and P_2, and we can express P_0 in terms of DIV_1, DIV_2, and P_2:

$$P_0 = \frac{1}{1 + r}(DIV_1 + P_1) = \frac{1}{1 + r}\left(DIV_1 + \frac{DIV_2 + P_2}{1 + r}\right) = \frac{DIV_1}{1 + r} + \frac{DIV_2 + P_2}{(1 + r)^2}$$

Take Fledgling Electronics. A plausible explanation for why investors expect its stock price to rise by the end of the first year is that they expect higher dividends and still more capital gains in the second. For example, suppose that they are looking today for dividends of $5.50 in year 2 and a subsequent price of $121. That implies a price at the end of year 1 of

$$P_1 = \frac{5.50 + 121}{1.15} = \$110$$

Today's price can then be computed either from our original formula

$$P_0 = \frac{DIV_1 + P_1}{1 + r} = \frac{5.00 + 110}{1.15} = \$100$$

or from our expanded formula

$$P_0 = \frac{DIV_1}{1 + r} + \frac{DIV_2 + P_2}{(1 + r)^2} = \frac{5.00}{1.15} + \frac{5.50 + 121}{(1.15)^2} = \$100$$

We have succeeded in relating today's price to the forecasted dividends for two years (DIV_1 and DIV_2) plus the forecasted price at the end of the *second* year (P_2). You will not be surprised to learn that we could go on to replace P_2 by $(DIV_3 + P_3)/(1 + r)$ and relate today's price to the forecasted dividends for three years (DIV_1, DIV_2, and DIV_3) plus the forecasted price at the end of the *third* year (P_3). In fact we can look as far out into the future as we like, removing Ps as we go. Let us call this final period H. This gives us a general stock price formula:

$$P_0 = \frac{DIV_1}{1 + r} + \frac{DIV_2}{(1 + r)^2} + \cdots + \frac{DIV_H + P_H}{(1 + r)^H}$$

$$= \sum_{t=1}^{H} \frac{DIV_t}{(1 + r)^t} + \frac{P_H}{(1 + r)^H}$$

The expression $\sum_{t=1}^{H}$ indicates the sum of the discounted dividends from year 1 to year H.

Table 4.2 continues the Fledgling Electronics example for various time horizons, assuming that the dividends are expected to increase at a steady 10% compound rate. The expected price P_t increases at the same rate each year. Each line in the table represents an application

	Expected Future Values		**Present Values**		
Horizon Period (H)	**Dividend (DIV_t)**	**Price (P_t)**	**Cumulative Dividends**	**Future Price**	**Total**
0	—	100	—	—	100
1	5.00	110	4.35	95.65	100
2	5.50	121	8.51	91.49	100
3	6.05	133.10	12.48	87.52	100
4	6.66	146.41	16.29	83.71	100
10	11.79	259.37	35.89	64.11	100
20	30.58	672.75	58.89	41.11	100
50	533.59	11,739.09	89.17	10.83	100
100	62,639.15	1,378,061.23	98.83	1.17	100

▶ **TABLE 4.2**   Applying the stock valuation formula to Fledgling Electronics.

Assumptions:
1. Dividends increase at 10% per year, compounded.
2. Capitalization rate is 15%.

of our general formula for a different value of H. Figure 4.1 is a graph of the table. Each column shows the present value of the dividends up to the time horizon and the present value of the price at the horizon. As the horizon recedes, the dividend stream accounts for an increasing proportion of present value, but the *total* present value of dividends plus terminal price always equals $100.

How far out could we look? In principle, the horizon period H could be infinitely distant. Common stocks do not expire of old age. Barring such corporate hazards as bankruptcy or acquisition, they are immortal. As H approaches infinity, the present value of the terminal price ought to approach zero, as it does in the final column of Figure 4.1. We can, therefore, forget about the terminal price entirely and express today's price as the present value of a perpetual stream of cash dividends. This is usually written as

$$P_0 = \sum_{t=1}^{\infty} \frac{\text{DIV}_t}{(1 + r)^t}$$

where ∞ indicates infinity.

This discounted-cash-flow (DCF) formula for the present value of a stock is just the same as it is for the present value of any other asset. We just discount the cash flows—in this case the dividend stream—by the return that can be earned in the capital market on securities of equivalent risk. Some find the DCF formula implausible because it seems to ignore capital gains. But we know that the formula was *derived* from the assumption that price in any period is determined by expected dividends *and* capital gains over the next period.

Notice that it is *not* correct to say that the value of a share is equal to the sum of the discounted stream of earnings per share. Earnings are generally larger than dividends because part of those earnings is reinvested in new plant, equipment, and working capital. Discounting earnings would recognize the rewards of that investment (a higher *future* dividend) but not the sacrifice (a lower dividend *today*). The correct formulation states that share value is equal to the discounted stream of dividends per share.

FIGURE 4.1

As your horizon recedes, the present value of the future price (shaded area) declines but the present value of the stream of dividends (unshaded area) increases. The total present value (future price and dividends) remains the same.

These days many growth companies do not pay dividends. Any cash that is not plowed back into the company is used to buy back stock. Take Cisco, for example. Cisco has never paid a dividend. Yet it is a successful company with a market capitalization of $100 billion. How can this be consistent with the dividend discount model?

If it were the case that Cisco's shareholders could *never* look forward to receiving a cash dividend or being bought out by another company,[3] then it would indeed be difficult to explain the price of the stock. But sometime in the future profitable investment opportunities for Cisco are likely to become less plentiful, releasing cash that can be paid out as dividends. It is this prospect that accounts for the $100 billion that shareholders are prepared to pay for the company.

4-3 Estimating the Cost of Equity Capital

In Chapter 2 we encountered some simplified versions of the basic present value formula. Let us see whether they offer any insights into stock values. Suppose, for example, that we forecast a constant growth rate for a company's dividends. This does not preclude year-to-year deviations from the trend: It means only that *expected* dividends grow at a constant rate. Such an investment would be just another example of the growing perpetuity that we valued in Chapter 2. To find its present value we must divide the first year's cash payment by the difference between the discount rate and the growth rate:

$$P_0 = \frac{\text{DIV}_1}{r - g}$$

Remember that we can use this formula only when g, the anticipated growth rate, is less than r, the discount rate. As g approaches r, the stock price becomes infinite. Obviously r must be greater than g if growth really is perpetual.

---

[3] If Cisco were taken over, any cash payment to Cisco's shareholders would be equivalent to a bumper dividend.

Our growing perpetuity formula explains P_0 in terms of next year's expected dividend DIV_1, the projected growth trend g, and the expected rate of return on other securities of comparable risk r. Alternatively, the formula can be turned around to obtain an estimate of r from DIV_1, P_0, and g:

$$r = \frac{DIV_1}{P_0} + g$$

The expected return equals the **dividend yield** (DIV_1/P_0) plus the expected rate of growth in dividends (g).

These two formulas are much easier to work with than the general statement that "price equals the present value of expected future dividends."[4] Here is a practical example.

Using the DCF Model to Set Gas and Electricity Prices

In the United States the prices charged by local electric and gas utilities are regulated by state commissions. The regulators try to keep consumer prices down but are supposed to allow the utilities to earn a fair rate of return. But what is fair? It is usually interpreted as r, the market capitalization rate for the firm's common stock. In other words the fair rate of return on equity for a public utility ought to be the cost of equity, that is, the rate offered by securities that have the same risk as the utility's common stock.[5]

Small variations in estimates of this return can have large effects on the prices charged to the customers and on the firm's profits. So both utilities and regulators work hard to estimate the cost of equity accurately. They've noticed that utilities are mature, stable companies that are tailor-made for application of the constant-growth DCF formula.[6]

Suppose you wished to estimate the cost of equity for Northwest Natural Gas, a local natural gas distribution company. Its stock was selling for $42.45 per share at the start of 2009. Dividend payments for the next year were expected to be $1.68 a share. Thus it was a simple matter to calculate the first half of the DCF formula:

$$\text{Dividend yield} = \frac{DIV_1}{P_0} = \frac{1.68}{42.45} = .040, \text{ or } 4.0\%$$

The hard part is estimating g, the expected rate of dividend growth. One option is to consult the views of security analysts who study the prospects for each company. Analysts are rarely prepared to stick their necks out by forecasting dividends to kingdom come, but they often forecast growth rates over the next five years, and these estimates may provide an indication of the expected long-run growth path. In the case of Northwest, analysts in 2009 were forecasting an annual growth of 6.1%.[7] This, together with the dividend yield, gave an estimate of the cost of equity capital:

$$r = \frac{DIV_1}{P_0} + g = .040 + .061 = .101, \text{ or } 10.1$$

---

[4] These formulas were first developed in 1938 by Williams and were rediscovered by Gordon and Shapiro. See J. B. Williams, *The Theory of Investment Value* (Cambridge, MA: Harvard University Press, 1938); and M. J. Gordon and E. Shapiro, "Capital Equipment Analysis: The Required Rate of Profit," *Management Science* 3 (October 1956), pp. 102–110.

[5] This is the accepted interpretation of the U.S. Supreme Court's directive in 1944 that "the returns to the equity owner [of a regulated business] should be commensurate with returns on investments in other enterprises having corresponding risks." *Federal Power Commission v. Hope Natural Gas Company*, 302 U.S. 591 at 603.

[6] There are many exceptions to this statement. For example, Pacific Gas & Electric (PG&E), which serves northern California, used to be a mature, stable company until the California energy crisis of 2000 sent wholesale electric prices sky-high. PG&E was not allowed to pass these price increases on to retail customers. The company lost more than $3.5 billion in 2000 and was forced to declare bankruptcy in 2001. PG&E emerged from bankruptcy in 2004, but we may have to wait a while before it is again a suitable subject for the constant-growth DCF formula.

[7] In this calculation we're assuming that earnings and dividends are forecasted to grow forever at the same rate g. We show how to relax this assumption later in this chapter. The growth rate was based on the average earnings growth forecasted by Value Line and IBES. IBES compiles and averages forecasts made by security analysts. Value Line publishes its own analysts' forecasts.

An alternative approach to estimating long-run growth starts with the **payout ratio,** the ratio of dividends to earnings per share (EPS). For Northwest, this was forecasted at 60%. In other words, each year the company was plowing back into the business about 40% of earnings per share:

$$\text{Plowback ratio} = 1 - \text{payout ratio} = 1 - \frac{\text{DIV}}{\text{EPS}} = 1 - .60 = .40$$

Also, Northwest's ratio of earnings per share to book equity per share was about 11%. This is its **return on equity,** or **ROE:**

$$\text{Return on equity} = \text{ROE} = \frac{\text{EPS}}{\text{book equity per share}} = .11$$

If Northwest earns 11% of book equity and reinvests 40% of income, then book equity will increase by $.40 \times .11 = .044$, or 4.4%. Earnings and dividends per share will also increase by 4.4%:

$$\text{Dividend growth rate} = g = \text{plowback ratio} \times \text{ROE} = .40 \times .11 = .044$$

That gives a second estimate of the market capitalization rate:

$$r = \frac{\text{DIV}_1}{P_0} + g = .040 + .044 = .084, \text{ or } 8.4\%$$

Although these estimates of Northwest's cost of equity seem reasonable, there are obvious dangers in analyzing any single firm's stock with the constant-growth DCF formula. First, the underlying assumption of regular future growth is at best an approximation. Second, even if it is an acceptable approximation, errors inevitably creep into the estimate of g.

Remember, Northwest's cost of equity is not its personal property. In well-functioning capital markets investors capitalize the dividends of all securities in Northwest's risk class at exactly the same rate. But any estimate of r for a single common stock is "noisy" and subject to error. Good practice does not put too much weight on single-company estimates of the cost of equity. It collects samples of similar companies, estimates r for each, and takes an average. The average gives a more reliable benchmark for decision making.

The next-to-last column of Table 4.3, on page 84, gives DCF cost-of-equity estimates for Northwest and seven other gas distribution companies. These are all stable, mature companies for which the constant-growth DCF formula *ought* to work. Notice the variation in the cost-of-equity estimates. Some of the variation may reflect differences in the risk, but some is just noise. The average estimate is 10.2%.

Table 4.4, on page 84, gives another example of DCF cost-of-equity estimates, this time for U.S. railroads in 2009.

Estimates of this kind are only as good as the long-term forecasts on which they are based. For example, several studies have observed that security analysts are subject to behavioral biases and their forecasts tend to be over-optimistic. If so, such DCF estimates of the cost of equity should be regarded as upper estimates of the true figure.

Dangers Lurk in Constant-Growth Formulas

The simple constant-growth DCF formula is an extremely useful rule of thumb, but no more than that. Naïve trust in the formula has led many financial analysts to silly conclusions.

We have stressed the difficulty of estimating r by analysis of one stock only. Try to use a large sample of equivalent-risk securities. Even that may not work, but at least it gives the analyst a fighting chance, because the inevitable errors in estimating r for a single security tend to balance out across a broad sample.

Company	Dividend Yield	Long-Term Growth Rate	DCF Cost of Equity	Multistage DCF Cost of Equity*
AGL Resources Inc.	6.8%	5.0%	11.8%	11.9%
Laclede Group Inc.	4.2	2.2	6.4	8.6
Nicor	6.1	5.2	11.3	11.2
Northwest Natural Gas Co.	4.0	6.1	10.1	9.2
Piedmont Natural Gas Co.	4.6	6.9	11.5	10.1
South Jersey Industries Inc.	3.7	7.4	11.1	9.2
Southwest Gas Corp.	4.7	6.6	11.3	10.1
WGL Holdings Inc.	4.6	3.5	8.0	9.2
		Average:	10.2%	9.9%

▶ **TABLE 4.3**   Cost-of-equity estimates for local gas distribution companies at the start of 2009. The long-term growth rate is based on security analysts' forecasts. In the multistage DCF model, growth after five years is assumed to adjust gradually to the estimated long-term growth rate of Gross Domestic Product (GDP).

* Long-term GDP growth forecasted at 4.9%.
Source: The Brattle Group, Inc.

Company	Dividend Yield	Long-Term Growth Rate	DCF Cost of Equity	Multistage DCF Cost of Equity*
Burlington Northern Santa Fe	2.2%	11.0%	13.2%	7.9%
CSX	2.4	14.9	17.3	8.9
Norfolk Southern	3.4	12.1	15.5	9.7
Union Pacific	2.1	12.2	14.2	7.9
		Average:	15.1%	8.6%

▶ **TABLE 4.4**   Cost-of-equity estimates for U.S. railroads mid-2009. The long-term growth rate is based on security analysts' forecasts. In the multistage DCF model, growth after five years is assumed to adjust gradually to the estimated long-term growth rate of Gross Domestic Product (GDP).

* Long-term GDP growth forecasted at 4.9%.
Source: The Brattle Group, Inc.

In addition, resist the temptation to apply the formula to firms having high current rates of growth. Such growth can rarely be sustained indefinitely, but the constant-growth DCF formula assumes it can. This erroneous assumption leads to an overestimate of r.

DCF Valuation with Varying Growth Rates   Consider Growth-Tech, Inc., a firm with $DIV_1 = \$.50$ and $P_0 = \$50$. The firm has plowed back 80% of earnings and has had a return on equity (ROE) of 25%. This means that *in the past*

Dividend growth rate = plowback ratio × ROE = .80 × .25 = .20

The temptation is to assume that the future long-term growth rate g also equals .20. This would imply

$$r = \frac{.50}{50.00} + .20 = .21$$

But this is silly. No firm can continue growing at 20% per year forever, except possibly under extreme inflationary conditions. Eventually, profitability will fall and the firm will respond by investing less.

In real life the return on equity will decline gradually over time, but for simplicity let's assume it suddenly drops to 16% at year 3 and the firm responds by plowing back only 50% of earnings. Then g drops to $.50 \times .16 = .08$.

Table 4.5 shows what's going on. Growth-Tech starts year 1 with book equity of $10.00 per share. It earns $2.50, pays out 50 cents as dividends, and plows back $2. Thus it starts year 2 with book equity of $10 + 2 = 12. After another year at the same ROE and payout, it starts year 3 with equity of $14.40. However, ROE drops to .16, and the firm earns only $2.30. Dividends go up to $1.15, because the payout ratio increases, but the firm has only $1.15 to plow back. Therefore subsequent growth in earnings and dividends drops to 8%.

Now we can use our general DCF formula:

$$P_0 = \frac{DIV_1}{1+r} + \frac{DIV_2}{(1+r)^2} + \frac{DIV_3 + P_3}{(1+r)^3}$$

Investors in year 3 will view Growth-Tech as offering 8% per year dividend growth. So we can use the constant-growth formula to calculate P_3:

$$P_3 = \frac{DIV_4}{r - .08}$$

$$P_0 = \frac{DIV_1}{1+r} + \frac{DIV_2}{(1+r)^2} + \frac{DIV_3}{(1+r)^3} + \frac{1}{(1+r)^3} \times \frac{DIV_4}{r - .08}$$

$$= \frac{.50}{1+r} + \frac{.60}{(1+r)^2} + \frac{1.15}{(1+r)^3} + \frac{1}{(1+r)^3} \times \frac{1.24}{r - .08}$$

We have to use trial and error to find the value of r that makes P_0 equal $50. It turns out that the r implicit in these more realistic forecasts is approximately .099, quite a difference from our "constant-growth" estimate of .21.

	Year			
	1	2	3	4
Book equity	10.00	12.00	14.40	15.55
Earnings per share, EPS	2.50	3.00	2.30	2.49
Return on equity, ROE	.25	.25	.16	.16
Payout ratio	.20	.20	.50	.50
Dividends per share, DIV	.50	.60	1.15	1.24
Growth rate of dividends (%)	—	20	92	8

▶ **TABLE 4.5** Forecasted earnings and dividends for Growth-Tech. Note the changes in year 3: ROE and earnings drop, but payout ratio increases, causing a big jump in dividends. However, subsequent growth in earnings and dividends falls to 8% per year. Note that the increase in equity equals the earnings not paid out as dividends.

Our present value calculations for Growth-Tech used a *two-stage* DCF valuation model. In the first stage (years 1 and 2), Growth-Tech is highly profitable (ROE = 25%), and it plows back 80% of earnings. Book equity, earnings, and dividends increase by 20% per year. In the second stage, starting in year 3, profitability and plowback decline, and earnings settle into long-term growth at 8%. Dividends jump up to $1.15 in year 3, and then also grow at 8%.

Growth rates can vary for many reasons. Sometimes growth is high in the short run not because the firm is unusually profitable, but because it is recovering from an episode of *low* profitability. Table 4.6 displays projected earnings and dividends for Phoenix Corp., which is gradually regaining financial health after a near meltdown. The company's equity is growing at a moderate 4%. ROE in year 1 is only 4%, however, so Phoenix has to reinvest all its earnings, leaving no cash for dividends. As profitability increases in years 2 and 3, an increasing dividend can be paid. Finally, starting in year 4, Phoenix settles into steady-state growth, with equity, earnings, and dividends all increasing at 4% per year.

Assume the cost of equity is 10%. Then Phoenix shares should be worth $9.13 per share:

$$P_0 = \underbrace{\frac{0}{1.1} + \frac{.31}{(1.1)^2} + \frac{.65}{(1.1)^3}}_{\text{PV (first-stage dividends)}} + \underbrace{\frac{1}{(1.1)^3} \times \frac{.67}{(.10 - .04)}}_{\text{PV (second-stage dividends)}} = \$9.13$$

You could go on to valuation models with three or more stages. For example, the far right columns of Tables 4.3 and 4.4 present multistage DCF estimates of the cost of equity for our local gas distribution companies and railroads. In this case the long-term growth rates reported in the table do not continue forever. After five years, each company's growth rate gradually adjusts to an estimated long-term growth rate for Gross Domestic Product (GDP). The resulting cost-of-equity estimates for the gas distribution companies are fairly similar to the estimates from the simple, perpetual-growth model. The estimates for the railroads are substantially different.

We must leave you with two more warnings about DCF formulas for valuing common stocks or estimating the cost of equity. First, it's almost always worthwhile to lay out a simple spreadsheet, like Table 4.5 or 4.6, to ensure that your dividend projections are consistent with the company's earnings and required investments. Second, be careful about using DCF valuation formulas to test whether the market is correct in its assessment of a stock's value. If your estimate of the value is different from that of the market, it is probably because you have used poor dividend forecasts. Remember what we said at the beginning of this chapter about simple ways of making money on the stock market: there aren't any.

	Year			
	1	**2**	**3**	**4**
Book equity at start of year	10.00	10.40	10.82	11.25
Earnings per share, EPS	.40	.73	1.08	1.12
Return on equity, ROE	.04	.07	.10	.10
Dividends per share, DIV	0	.31	.65	.67
Growth rate of dividends (%)	—	—	110	4

▶ **TABLE 4.6**   Forecasted earnings and dividends for Phoenix Corp. The company can initiate and increase dividends as profitability (ROE) recovers. Note that the increase in book equity equals the earnings not paid out as dividends.

4-4 The Link Between Stock Price and Earnings per Share

Investors separate *growth stocks* from *income stocks*. They buy growth stocks primarily for the expectation of capital gains, and they are interested in the future growth of earnings rather than in next year's dividends. They buy income stocks primarily for the cash dividends. Let us see whether these distinctions make sense.

Imagine first the case of a company that does not grow at all. It does not plow back any earnings and simply produces a constant stream of dividends. Its stock would resemble the perpetual bond described in Chapter 2. Remember that the return on a perpetuity is equal to the yearly cash flow divided by the present value. So the expected return on our share would be equal to the yearly dividend divided by the share price (i.e., the dividend yield). Since all the earnings are paid out as dividends, the expected return is also equal to the earnings per share divided by the share price (i.e., the earnings–price ratio). For example, if the dividend is $10 a share and the stock price is $100, we have

$$\text{Expected return} = \text{dividend yield} = \text{earnings–price ratio}$$

$$= \frac{\text{DIV}_1}{P_0} \qquad = \frac{\text{EPS}_1}{P_0}$$

$$= \frac{10.00}{100} \qquad = .10$$

The price equals

$$P_0 = \frac{\text{DIV}_1}{r} = \frac{\text{EPS}_1}{r} = \frac{10.00}{.10} = 100$$

The expected return for *growing* firms can also equal the earnings–price ratio. The key is whether earnings are reinvested to provide a return equal to the market capitalization rate. For example, suppose our monotonous company suddenly hears of an opportunity to invest $10 a share next year. This would mean no dividend at $t = 1$. However, the company expects that in each subsequent year the project would earn $1 per share, and therefore the dividend could be increased to $11 a share.

Let us assume that this investment opportunity has about the same risk as the existing business. Then we can discount its cash flow at the 10% rate to find its net present value at year 1:

$$\text{Net present value per share at year 1} = -10 + \frac{1}{.10} = 0$$

Thus the investment opportunity will make no contribution to the company's value. Its prospective return is equal to the opportunity cost of capital.

What effect will the decision to undertake the project have on the company's share price? Clearly none. The reduction in value caused by the nil dividend in year 1 is exactly offset by the increase in value caused by the extra dividends in later years. Therefore, once again the market capitalization rate equals the earnings–price ratio:

$$r = \frac{\text{EPS}_1}{P_0} = \frac{10}{100} = .10$$

Table 4.7, on page 88, repeats our example for different assumptions about the cash flow generated by the new project. Note that the earnings–price ratio, measured in terms of EPS_1, next year's expected earnings, equals the market capitalization rate (r) *only* when the new project's NPV = 0. This is an extremely important point—managers frequently make poor financial decisions because they confuse earnings–price ratios with the market capitalization rate.

Project Rate of Return	Incremental Cash Flow, C	Project NPV in Year 1[a]	Project's Impact on Share Price in Year 0[b]	Share Price in Year 0, P_0	$\dfrac{EPS_1}{P_0}$	r
.05	$ .50	−$ 5.00	−$4.55	$ 95.45	.105	.10
.10	1.00	0	0	100.00	.10	.10
.15	1.50	+ 5.00	+ 4.55	104.55	.096	.10
.20	2.00	+ 10.00	+ 9.09	109.09	.092	.10

▶ **TABLE 4.7**   Effect on stock price of investing an additional $10 in year 1 at different rates of return. Notice that the earnings–price ratio overestimates r when the project has negative NPV and underestimates it when the project has positive NPV.

[a] Project costs $10.00 ($EPS_1$). NPV $= -10 + C/r$, where $r = .10$.
[b] NPV is calculated at year 1. To find the impact on P_0, discount for one year at $r = .10$.

In general, we can think of stock price as the capitalized value of average earnings under a no-growth policy, plus **PVGO**, the **net present value of growth opportunities:**

$$P_0 = \frac{EPS_1}{r} + PVGO$$

The earnings–price ratio, therefore, equals

$$\frac{EPS}{P_0} = r\left(1 - \frac{PVGO}{P_0}\right)$$

It will underestimate r if PVGO is positive and overestimate it if PVGO is negative. The latter case is less likely, since firms are rarely forced to take projects with negative net present values.

Calculating the Present Value of Growth Opportunities for Fledgling Electronics

In our last example both dividends and earnings were expected to grow, but this growth made no net contribution to the stock price. The stock was in this sense an "income stock." Be careful not to equate firm performance with the growth in earnings per share. A company that reinvests earnings at below the market capitalization rate r may increase earnings but will certainly reduce the share value.

Now let us turn to that well-known growth stock, Fledgling Electronics. You may remember that Fledgling's market capitalization rate, r, is 15%. The company is expected to pay a dividend of $5 in the first year, and thereafter the dividend is predicted to increase indefinitely by 10% a year. We can use the simplified constant-growth formula to work out Fledgling's price:

$$P_0 = \frac{DIV_1}{r - g} = \frac{5}{.15 - .10} = \$100$$

Suppose that Fledgling has earnings per share of $EPS_1 = \$8.33$. Its payout ratio is then

$$\text{Payout ratio} = \frac{DIV_1}{EPS_1} = \frac{5.00}{8.33} = .6$$

In other words, the company is plowing back $1 - .6$, or 40% of earnings. Suppose also that Fledgling's ratio of earnings to book equity is ROE $= .25$. This explains the growth rate of 10%:

$$\text{Growth rate} = g = \text{plowback ratio} \times \text{ROE} = .4 \times .25 = .10$$

The capitalized value of Fledgling's earnings per share if it had a no-growth policy would be

$$\frac{\text{EPS}_1}{r} = \frac{8.33}{.15} = \$55.56$$

But we know that the value of Fledgling stock is $100. The difference of $44.44 must be the amount that investors are paying for growth opportunities. Let's see if we can explain that figure.

Each year Fledgling plows back 40% of its earnings into new assets. In the first year Fledgling invests $3.33 at a permanent 25% return on equity. Thus the cash generated by this investment is $.25 \times 3.33 = \$.83$ per year starting at $t = 2$. The net present value of the investment as of $t = 1$ is

$$\text{NPV}_1 = -3.33 + \frac{.83}{.15} = \$2.22$$

Everything is the same in year 2 except that Fledgling will invest $3.67, 10% more than in year 1 (remember $g = .10$). Therefore at $t = 2$ an investment is made with a net present value of

$$\text{NPV}_2 = -3.67 + \frac{.83 \times 1.10}{.15} = \$2.44$$

Thus the payoff to the owners of Fledgling Electronics stock can be represented as the sum of (1) a level stream of earnings, which could be paid out as cash dividends if the firm did not grow, and (2) a set of tickets, one for each future year, representing the opportunity to make investments having positive NPVs. We know that the first component of the value of the share is

$$\text{Present value of level stream of earnings} = \frac{\text{EPS}_1}{r} = \frac{8.33}{.15} = \$55.56$$

The first ticket is worth $2.22 in $t = 1$, the second is worth $2.22 \times 1.10 = \$2.44$ in $t = 2$, the third is worth $2.44 \times 1.10 = \$2.69$ in $t = 3$. These are the forecasted cash values of the tickets. We know how to value a stream of future cash values that grows at 10% per year: Use the constant-growth DCF formula, replacing the forecasted dividends with forecasted ticket values:

$$\text{Present value of growth opportunities} = \text{PVGO} = \frac{\text{NPV}_1}{r - g} = \frac{2.22}{.15 - .10} = \$44.44$$

Now everything checks:

$$\text{Share price} = \text{present value of level stream of earnings}$$
$$+ \text{ present value of growth opportunities}$$
$$= \frac{\text{EPS}_1}{r} + \text{PVGO}$$
$$= \$55.56 + \$44.44$$
$$= \$100$$

Why is Fledgling Electronics a growth stock? Not because it is expanding at 10% per year. It is a growth stock because the net present value of its future investments accounts for a significant fraction (about 44%) of the stock's price.

Today's stock price reflects investor expectations about the earning power of the firm's current and *future* assets. Take Google, for example. All its earnings are plowed back into new investments and the stock sells at 26 times current earnings of $13.31 a share. Suppose that the earnings from Google's existing business are expected to stay constant in real terms. In this case the value of the business is equal to the real earnings divided by an estimated 7.4% real cost of equity:

$$\text{PV assets in place} = 13.31/.074 = \$180$$

But, as we write this, Google's stock price is $344. So it looks as if investors are valuing Google's future investment opportunities at 344 − 180 = $164. Google is a growth stock because roughly 50% of the stock price comes from the value that investors place on its future investment opportunities.

<h2>4-5 Valuing a Business by Discounted Cash Flow</h2>

Investors routinely buy and sell shares of common stock. Companies frequently buy and sell entire businesses or major stakes in businesses. For example, in 2009 *The New York Times* announced that it had retained Goldman Sachs to explore the possible sale of its interest in the Boston Red Sox baseball team. You can be sure that *The New York Times*, Goldman Sachs, and potential purchasers all burned a lot of midnight oil to estimate the value of the business.

Do the discounted-cash-flow formulas we presented in this chapter work for entire businesses as well as for shares of common stock? Sure: It doesn't matter whether you forecast dividends per share or the total free cash flow of a business. Value today always equals future cash flow discounted at the opportunity cost of capital.

Valuing the Concatenator Business

Rumor has it that Establishment Industries is interested in buying your company's concatenator manufacturing operation. Your company is willing to sell if it can get the full value of this rapidly growing business. The problem is to figure out what its true present value is.

Table 4.8 gives a forecast of **free cash flow** (FCF) for the concatenator business. Free cash flow is the amount of cash that a firm can pay out to investors after paying for all investments necessary for growth. As we will see, free cash flow can be negative for rapidly growing businesses.

Table 4.8 is similar to Table 4.5, which forecasted earnings and dividends per share for Growth-Tech, based on assumptions about Growth-Tech's equity per share, return on equity,

	Year									
	1	2	3	4	5	6	7	8	9	10
Asset value	10.00	12.00	14.40	17.28	20.74	23.43	26.47	28.05	29.73	31.51
Earnings	1.20	1.44	1.73	2.07	2.49	2.81	3.18	3.36	3.57	3.78
Net investment	2.00	2.40	2.88	3.46	2.69	3.04	1.59	1.68	1.78	1.89
Free cash flow	−.80	−.96	−1.15	−1.39	−.20	−.23	1.59	1.68	1.79	1.89
Earnings growth from previous period (%)	20	20	20	20	20	13	13	6	6	6

▶ **TABLE 4.8**   Forecasts of free cash flow, in $ millions, for the Concatenator Manufacturing Division. Rapid expansion in years 1–6 means that free cash flow is negative, because required additional investment outstrips earnings. Free cash flow turns positive when growth slows down after year 6.

Notes:
1. Starting asset value is $10 million. Assets required for the business grow initially at 20% per year, then at 13%, and finally at 6%.
2. Profitability (earnings/asset values) is constant at 12%.
3. Free cash flow equals earnings minus net investment. Net investment equals total capital expenditures less depreciation. Note that earnings are also calculated net of depreciation.

and the growth of its business. For the concatenator business, we also have assumptions about assets, profitability—in this case, after-tax operating earnings relative to assets—and growth. Growth starts out at a rapid 20% per year, then falls in two steps to a moderate 6% rate for the long run. The growth rate determines the net additional investment required to expand assets, and the profitability rate determines the earnings thrown off by the business.[8]

Free cash flow, the next to last line in Table 4.8, is equal to the firm's earnings less any new investment expenditures. Free cash flow is negative in years 1 through 6. The concatenator business is paying a negative dividend to the parent company; it is absorbing more cash than it is throwing off.

Is that a bad sign? Not really: The business is running a cash deficit not because it is unprofitable, but because it is growing so fast. Rapid growth is good news, not bad, so long as the business is earning more than the opportunity cost of capital. Your company, or Establishment Industries, will be happy to invest an extra $800,000 in the concatenator business next year, so long as the business offers a superior rate of return.

Valuation Format

The value of a business is usually computed as the discounted value of free cash flows out to a *valuation horizon (H)*, plus the forecasted value of the business at the horizon, also discounted back to present value. That is,

$$\text{PV} = \underbrace{\frac{\text{FCF}_1}{1 + r} + \frac{\text{FCF}_2}{(1 + r)^2} + \cdots + \frac{\text{FCF}_H}{(1 + r)^H}}_{\text{PV(free cash flow)}} + \underbrace{\frac{\text{PV}_H}{(1 + r)^H}}_{\text{PV(horizon value)}}$$

Of course, the concatenator business will continue after the horizon, but it's not practical to forecast free cash flow year by year to infinity. PV_H stands in for free cash flow in periods $H + 1, H + 2$, etc.

Valuation horizons are often chosen arbitrarily. Sometimes the boss tells everybody to use 10 years because that's a round number. We will try year 6, because growth of the concatenator business seems to settle down to a long-run trend after year 7.

Estimating Horizon Value

There are several common formulas or rules of thumb for estimating horizon value. First, let us try the constant-growth DCF formula. This requires free cash flow for year 7, which we have from Table 4.8; a long-run growth rate, which appears to be 6%; and a discount rate, which some high-priced consultant has told us is 10%. Therefore,

$$\text{PV (horizon value)} = \frac{1}{(1.1)^6}\left(\frac{1.59}{.10 - .06}\right) = 22.4$$

The present value of the near-term free cash flows is

$$\text{PV(cash flows)} = -\frac{.80}{1.1} - \frac{.96}{(1.1)^2} - \frac{1.15}{(1.1)^3} - \frac{1.39}{(1.1)^4} - \frac{.20}{(1.1)^5} - \frac{.23}{(1.1)^6}$$
$$= -3.6$$

and, therefore, the present value of the business is

$$\begin{aligned}
\text{PV(business)} &= \text{PV(free cash flow)} + \text{PV(horizon value)} \\
&= -3.6 \qquad\qquad\quad + 22.4 \\
&= \$18.8 \text{ million}
\end{aligned}$$

---

[8] Table 4.8 shows *net* investment, which is total investment less depreciation. We are assuming that investment for replacement of existing assets is covered by depreciation and that net investment is devoted to growth.

Now, are we done? Well, the mechanics of this calculation are perfect. But doesn't it make you just a little nervous to find that 119% of the value of the business rests on the horizon value? Moreover, a little checking shows that the horizon value can change dramatically in response to apparently minor changes in assumptions. For example, if the long-run growth rate is 8% rather than 6%, the value of the business increases from $18.8 to $26.3 million.[9]

In other words, it's easy for a discounted-cash-flow business valuation to be mechanically perfect and practically wrong. Smart financial managers try to check their results by calculating horizon value in different ways.

Horizon Value Based on P/E Ratios   Suppose you can observe stock prices for mature manufacturing companies whose scale, risk, and growth prospects today roughly match those projected for the concatenator business in year 6. Suppose further that these companies tend to sell at price–earnings ratios of about 11. Then you could reasonably guess that the price–earnings ratio of a mature concatenator operation will likewise be 11. That implies:

$$PV(\text{horizon value}) = \frac{1}{(1.1)^6}(11 \times 3.18) = 19.7$$

$$PV(\text{business}) = -3.6 + 19.7 = \$16.1 \text{ million}$$

Horizon Value Based on Market–Book Ratios   Suppose also that the market–book ratios of the sample of mature manufacturing companies tend to cluster around 1.4. If the concatenator business market–book ratio is 1.4 in year 6,

$$PV(\text{horizon value}) = \frac{1}{(1.1)^6}(1.4 \times 23.43) = 18.5$$

$$PV(\text{business}) = -3.6 + 18.5 = \$14.9 \text{ million}$$

It's easy to poke holes in these last two calculations. Book value, for example, is often a poor measure of the true value of a company's assets. It can fall far behind actual asset values when there is rapid inflation, and it often entirely misses important intangible assets, such as your patents for concatenator design. Earnings may also be biased by inflation and a long list of arbitrary accounting choices. Finally, you never know when you have found a sample of truly similar companies.

But remember, the purpose of discounted cash flow is to estimate market value—to estimate what investors would pay for a stock or business. When you can *observe* what they actually pay for similar companies, that's valuable evidence. Try to figure out a way to use it. One way to use it is through valuation by comparables, based on price–earnings or market–book ratios. Valuation rules of thumb, artfully employed, sometimes beat a complex discounted-cash-flow calculation hands down.

A Further Reality Check

Here is another approach to valuing a business. It is based on what you have learned about price–earnings ratios and the present value of growth opportunities.

Suppose the valuation horizon is set not by looking for the first year of stable growth, but by asking when the industry is likely to settle into competitive equilibrium. You might go to the operating manager most familiar with the concatenator business and ask:

---

[9] If long-run growth is 8% rather than 6%, an extra 2% of period-7 assets will have to be plowed back into the concatenator business. This reduces free cash flow by $.53 million to $1.06 million. So,

$$PV(\text{horizon value}) = \frac{1}{(1.1)^6}\left(\frac{1.06}{.10 - .08}\right) = \$29.9$$

$$PV(\text{business}) = -3.6 + 29.9 = \$26.3 \text{ million}$$

Sooner or later you and your competitors will be on an equal footing when it comes to major new investments. You may still be earning a superior return on your core business, but you will find that introductions of new products or attempts to expand sales of existing products trigger intense resistance from competitors who are just about as smart and efficient as you are. Give a realistic assessment of when that time will come.

"That time" is the horizon after which PVGO, the net present value of subsequent growth opportunities, is zero. After all, PVGO is positive only when investments can be expected to earn more than the cost of capital. When your competition catches up, that happy prospect disappears.

We know that present value in any period equals the capitalized value of next period's earnings, plus PVGO:

$$PV_t = \frac{\text{earnings}_{t+1}}{r} + PVGO$$

But what if PVGO = 0? At the horizon period H, then,

$$PV_H = \frac{\text{earnings}_{H+1}}{r}$$

In other words, when the competition catches up, the price–earnings ratio equals $1/r$, because PVGO disappears.[10]

Suppose that competition is expected to catch up in period 9. Then we can calculate the horizon value at period 8 as the present value of a level stream of earnings starting in period 9 and continuing indefinitely. The resulting value for the concatenator business is:[11]

$$PV(\text{horizon value}) = \frac{1}{(1+r)^8} \left(\frac{\text{earnings in period 9}}{r} \right)$$

$$= \frac{1}{(1.1)^8} \left(\frac{3.57}{.10} \right)$$

$$= \$16.7 \text{ million}$$

$$PV(\text{business}) = -2.0 + 16.7 = \$14.7 \text{ million}$$

We now have four estimates of what Establishment Industries ought to pay for the concatenator business. The estimates reflect four different methods of estimating horizon value. There is no best method, although in many cases we put most weight on the last method, which sets the horizon date at the point when management expects PVGO to disappear. The last method forces managers to remember that sooner or later competition catches up.

Our calculated values for the concatenator business range from $14.7 to $18.8 million, a difference of about $4 million. The width of the range may be disquieting, but it is not unusual. Discounted-cash-flow formulas only estimate market value, and the estimates change as forecasts and assumptions change. Managers cannot know market value for sure until an actual transaction takes place.

---

[10] In other words, we can calculate horizon value *as if* earnings will not grow after the horizon date, because growth will add no value. But what does "no growth" mean? Suppose that the concatenator business maintains its assets and earnings in real (inflation-adjusted) terms. Then nominal earnings will grow at the inflation rate. This takes us back to the constant-growth formula: Earnings in period H + 1 should be valued by dividing by r − g, where g in this case equals the inflation rate.

We have simplified the concatenator example. In real-life valuations, with big bucks involved, be careful to track growth from inflation as well as growth from investment. For guidance see M. Bradley and G. Jarrell, "Expected Inflation and the Constant-Growth Valuation Model," *Journal of Applied Corporate Finance* 20 (Spring 2008), pp. 66–78.

[11] Three additional points about this calculation: First, the PV of free cash flow before the horizon improves to −$2.0 million because inflows in years 7 and 8 are now included. Second, if competition really catches up by year 9, then the earnings shown for year 10 in Table 4.8 are too high, since they include a 12% return on the investment in year 9. Competition would allow only the 10% cost of capital. Third, we assume earnings in year 9 of $3.57, 12% on assets of $29.73. But competition might force down the rate of return on existing assets in addition to returns on new investment. That is, earnings in year 9 could be only $2.97 (10% of $29.73). Problem 26 explores these possibilities.

SUMMARY

In this chapter we have used our newfound knowledge of present values to examine the market price of common stocks. The value of a stock is equal to the stream of cash payments discounted at the rate of return that investors expect to receive on other securities with equivalent risks.

Common stocks do not have a fixed maturity; their cash payments consist of an indefinite stream of dividends. Therefore, the present value of a common stock is

$$PV = \sum_{t=1}^{\infty} \frac{DIV_t}{(1+r)^t}$$

However, we did not just *assume* that investors purchase common stocks solely for dividends. In fact, we began with the assumption that investors have relatively short horizons and invest for both dividends and capital gains. Our fundamental valuation formula is, therefore,

$$P_0 = \frac{DIV_1 + P_1}{1+r}$$

This is a condition of market equilibrium. If it did not hold, the share would be overpriced or underpriced, and investors would rush to sell or buy it. The flood of sellers or buyers would force the price to adjust so that the fundamental valuation formula holds.

We also made use of the formula for a growing perpetuity presented in Chapter 2. If dividends are expected to grow forever at a constant rate of g, then

$$P_0 = \frac{DIV_1}{r-g}$$

It is often helpful to twist this formula around and use it to estimate the market capitalization rate r, given P_0 and estimates of DIV_1 and g:

$$r = \frac{DIV_1}{P_0} + g$$

Remember, however, that this formula rests on a *very* strict assumption: constant dividend growth in perpetuity. This may be an acceptable assumption for mature, low-risk firms, but for many firms, near-term growth is unsustainably high. In that case, you may wish to use a *two-stage* DCF formula, where near-term dividends are forecasted and valued, and the constant-growth DCF formula is used to forecast the value of the shares at the start of the long run. The near-term dividends and the future share value are then discounted to present value.

The general DCF formula can be transformed into a statement about earnings and growth opportunities:

$$P_0 = \frac{EPS_1}{r} + PVGO$$

The ratio EPS_1/r is the capitalized value of the earnings per share that the firm would generate under a no-growth policy. PVGO is the net present value of the investments that the firm will make in order to grow. A growth stock is one for which PVGO is large relative to the capitalized value of EPS. Most growth stocks are stocks of rapidly expanding firms, but expansion alone does not create a high PVGO. What matters is the profitability of the new investments.

The same formulas that we used to value common shares can also be used to value entire businesses. In that case, we discount not dividends per share but the entire free cash flow generated by the business. Usually a two-stage DCF model is deployed. Free cash flows are forecasted out to a horizon and discounted to present value. Then a horizon value is forecasted, discounted, and added to the value of the free cash flows. The sum is the value of the business.

Valuing a business is simple in principle but not so easy in practice. Forecasting reasonable horizon values is particularly difficult. The usual assumption is moderate long-run growth after the horizon, which allows use of the growing-perpetuity DCF formula at the horizon. Horizon values can also be calculated by assuming "normal" price–earnings or market-to-book ratios at the horizon date.

In earlier chapters you should have acquired—we hope painlessly—a knowledge of the basic principles of valuing assets and a facility with the mechanics of discounting. Now you know something of how common stocks are valued and market capitalization rates estimated. In Chapter 5 we can begin to apply all this knowledge in a more specific analysis of capital budgeting decisions.

For a comprehensive review of company valuation, see:

T. Koller, M. Goedhart, and D. Wessels, *Valuation: Measuring and Managing the Value of Companies,* 4th ed. (New York: Wiley, 2005).

Leibowitz and Kogelman call PVGO the "franchise factor." They analyze it in detail in:

M.L. Leibowitz and S. Kogelman, "Inside the P/E Ratio: The Franchise Factor," *Financial Analysts Journal* 46 (November–December 1990), pp. 17–35.

FURTHER READING

PROBLEM SETS

BASIC

1. True or false?
   a. All stocks in an equivalent-risk class are priced to offer the same expected rate of return.
   b. The value of a share equals the PV of future dividends per share.

2. Respond briefly to the following statement:

   "You say stock price equals the present value of future dividends? That's crazy! All the investors I know are looking for capital gains."

3. Company X is expected to pay an end-of-year dividend of $5 a share. After the dividend its stock is expected to sell at $110. If the market capitalization rate is 8%, what is the current stock price?

4. Company Y does not plow back any earnings and is expected to produce a level dividend stream of $5 a share. If the current stock price is $40, what is the market capitalization rate?

5. Company Z's earnings and dividends per share are expected to grow indefinitely by 5% a year. If next year's dividend is $10 and the market capitalization rate is 8%, what is the current stock price?

6. Company Z-prime is like Z in all respects save one: Its growth will stop after year 4. In year 5 and afterward, it will pay out all earnings as dividends. What is Z-prime's stock price? Assume next year's EPS is $15.

7. If company Z (see Problem 5) were to distribute all its earnings, it could maintain a level dividend stream of $15 a share. How much is the market actually paying per share for growth opportunities?

8. Consider three investors:
   a. Mr. Single invests for one year.
   b. Ms. Double invests for two years.
   c. Mrs. Triple invests for three years.

Assume each invests in company Z (see Problem 5). Show that each expects to earn a rate of return of 8% per year.

9. True or false? Explain.

a. The value of a share equals the discounted stream of future earnings per share.

b. The value of a share equals the PV of earnings per share assuming the firm does not grow, plus the NPV of future growth opportunities.

10. Under what conditions does r, a stock's market capitalization rate, equal its earnings–price ratio EPS_1/P_0?

11. What do financial managers mean by "free cash flow"? How is free cash flow calculated? Briefly explain.

12. What is meant by the "horizon value" of a business? How can it be estimated?

13. Suppose the horizon date is set at a time when the firm will run out of positive-NPV investment opportunities. How would you calculate the horizon value? (*Hint:* What is the P/EPS ratio when PVGO = 0?)

INTERMEDIATE

14. Look in a recent issue of *The Wall Street Journal* at "NYSE-Composite Transactions."

a. What is the latest price of IBM stock?

b. What are the annual dividend payment and the dividend yield on IBM stock?

c. What would the yield be if IBM changed its yearly dividend to $1.50?

d. What is the P/E on IBM stock?

e. Use the P/E to calculate IBM's earnings per share.

f. Is IBM's P/E higher or lower than that of Exxon Mobil?

g. What are the possible reasons for the difference in P/E?

15. Rework Table 4.2 under the assumption that the dividend on Fledgling Electronics is $10 next year and that it is expected to grow by 5% a year. The capitalization rate is 15%.

16. Consider the following three stocks:

a. Stock A is expected to provide a dividend of $10 a share forever.

b. Stock B is expected to pay a dividend of $5 next year. Thereafter, dividend growth is expected to be 4% a year forever.

c. Stock C is expected to pay a dividend of $5 next year. Thereafter, dividend growth is expected to be 20% a year for five years (i.e., until year 6) and zero thereafter.

If the market capitalization rate for each stock is 10%, which stock is the most valuable? What if the capitalization rate is 7%?

17. Pharmecology is about to pay a dividend of $1.35 per share. It's a mature company, but future EPS and dividends are expected to grow with inflation, which is forecasted at 2.75% per year.

a. What is Pharmecology's current stock price? The nominal cost of capital is 9.5%.

b. Redo part (a) using forecasted real dividends and a real discount rate.

18. Company Q's current return on equity (ROE) is 14%. It pays out one-half of earnings as cash dividends (payout ratio = .5). Current book value per share is $50. Book value per share will grow as Q reinvests earnings.

Assume that the ROE and payout ratio stay constant for the next four years. After that, competition forces ROE down to 11.5% and the payout ratio increases to 0.8. The cost of capital is 11.5%.

a. What are Q's EPS and dividends next year? How will EPS and dividends grow in years 2, 3, 4, 5, and subsequent years?

b. What is Q's stock worth per share? How does that value depend on the payout ratio and growth rate after year 4?

Visit us at
www.mhhe.com/bma

19. Mexican Motors stock sells for 200 pesos per share and next year's dividend is 8.5 pesos. Security analysts are forecasting earnings growth of 7.5% per year for the next five years.

    a. Assume that earnings and dividends are expected to grow at 7.5% in perpetuity. What rate of return are investors expecting?

    b. Mexican Motors has generally earned about 12% on book equity (ROE = .12) and paid out 50% of earnings as dividends. Suppose it maintains the same ROE and payout ratio in the long-run future. What is the implication for g? For r? Should you revise your answer to part (a) of this question?

20. Phoenix Corp. faltered in the recent recession but has recovered since. EPS and dividends have grown rapidly since 2017.

	2017	2018	2019	2020	2021
EPS($)	.75	2.00	2.50	2.60	2.65
Dividends($)	0	1.00	2.00	2.30	2.65
Dividend growth(%)	—	—	100	15	15

The figures for 2020 and 2021 are of course forecasts. Phoenix's stock price today in 2019 is $21.75. Phoenix's recovery will be complete in 2021, and there will be *no further growth* in EPS or dividends.

   A security analyst forecasts *next year's* rate of return on Phoenix stock as follows:

$$r = \frac{DIV}{P} + g = \frac{2.30}{21.75} + .15 = .256, \text{ about } 26\%$$

What's wrong with the security analyst's forecast? What is the actual expected rate of return over the next year?

21. Each of the following formulas for determining shareholders' required rate of return can be right or wrong depending on the circumstances:

    a. $r = \dfrac{DIV_1}{P_0} + g$

    b. $r = \dfrac{EPS_1}{P_0}$

    For each formula construct a *simple* numerical example showing that the formula can give wrong answers and explain why the error occurs. Then construct another simple numerical example for which the formula gives the right answer.

22. Alpha Corp.'s earnings and dividends are growing at 15% per year. Beta Corp.'s earnings and dividends are growing at 8% per year. The companies' assets, earnings, and dividends per share are now (at date 0) exactly the same. Yet PVGO accounts for a greater fraction of Beta Corp.'s stock price. How is this possible? (*Hint:* There is more than one possible explanation.)

23. Look again at the financial forecasts for Growth-Tech given in Table 4.5. This time assume you *know* that the opportunity cost of capital is $r = .12$ (discard the .099 figure calculated in the text). Assume you do *not* know Growth-Tech's stock value. Otherwise follow the assumptions given in the text.

    a. Calculate the value of Growth-Tech stock.

    b. What part of that value reflects the discounted value of P_3, the price forecasted for year 3?

    c. What part of P_3 reflects the present value of growth opportunities (PVGO) after year 3?

    d. Suppose that competition will catch up with Growth-Tech by year 4, so that it can earn only its cost of capital on any investments made in year 4 or subsequently. What is Growth-Tech stock worth now under this assumption? (Make additional assumptions if necessary.)

24. Compost Science, Inc. (CSI), is in the business of converting Boston's sewage sludge into fertilizer. The business is not in itself very profitable. However, to induce CSI to remain in business, the Metropolitan District Commission (MDC) has agreed to pay whatever amount is necessary to yield CSI a 10% book return on equity. At the end of the year CSI is expected to pay a $4 dividend. It has been reinvesting 40% of earnings and growing at 4% a year.

    a. Suppose CSI continues on this growth trend. What is the expected long-run rate of return from purchasing the stock at $100? What part of the $100 price is attributable to the present value of growth opportunities?

    b. Now the MDC announces a plan for CSI to treat Cambridge sewage. CSI's plant will, therefore, be expanded gradually over five years. This means that CSI will have to reinvest 80% of its earnings for five years. Starting in year 6, however, it will again be able to pay out 60% of earnings. What will CSI's stock price be once this announcement is made and its consequences for CSI are known?

25. Permian Partners (PP) produces from aging oil fields in west Texas. Production is 1.8 million barrels per year in 2009, but production is declining at 7% per year for the foreseeable future. Costs of production, transportation, and administration add up to $25 per barrel. The average oil price was $65 per barrel in 2009.

    PP has 7 million shares outstanding. The cost of capital is 9%. All of PP's net income is distributed as dividends. For simplicity, assume that the company will stay in business forever and that costs per barrel are constant at $25. Also, ignore taxes.

    a. What is the PV of a PP share? Assume that oil prices are expected to fall to $60 per barrel in 2010, $55 per barrel in 2011, and $50 per barrel in 2012. After 2012, assume a long-term trend of oil-price increases at 5% per year.

    b. What is PP's EPS/P ratio and why is it not equal to the 9% cost of capital?

26. Construct a new version of Table 4.8, assuming that competition drives down profitability (on existing assets as well as new investment) to 11.5% in year 6, 11% in year 7, 10.5% in year 8, and 8% in year 9 and all later years. What is the value of the concatenator business?

CHALLENGE

27. The constant-growth DCF formula:

$$P_0 = \frac{\text{DIV}_1}{r - g}$$

    is sometimes written as:

$$P_0 = \frac{\text{ROE}(1 - b)\text{BVPS}}{r - b\text{ROE}}$$

    where BVPS is book equity value per share, b is the plowback ratio, and ROE is the ratio of earnings per share to BVPS. Use this equation to show how the price-to-book ratio varies as ROE changes. What is price-to-book when ROE $= r$?

28. Portfolio managers are frequently paid a proportion of the funds under management. Suppose you manage a $100 million equity portfolio offering a dividend yield (DIV_1/P_0) of 5%. Dividends and portfolio value are expected to grow at a constant rate. Your annual fee for managing this portfolio is .5% of portfolio value and is calculated at the end of each year. Assuming that you will continue to manage the portfolio from now to eternity, what is the present value of the management contract? How would the contract value change if you invested in stocks with a 4% yield?

29. Suppose the concatenator division, which we valued based on Table 4.8, is spun off as an independent company, Concatco, with 1 million shares of common stock outstanding. What would each share sell for? Before answering, notice the negative free cash flows for

years 1 to 6. The PV of these cash flows is −$3.6 million. Assume that this shortfall will have to be financed by additional shares issued in the near future. Also assume for simplicity that the $3.6 million earns interest at 10% and is sufficient to cover the negative free cash flows in Table 4.8. Concatco will pay no dividends in years 1 to 6, but will pay out all free cash flow starting in year 7.

Now calculate the value of each of the 1 million existing Concatco shares. Briefly explain your answer. *Hints:* Suppose the existing stockholders, who own 1 million shares, buy newly issued shares to cover the $3.6 million financing requirement. In other words, the $3.6 million comes directly out of existing stockholders' wallets. What's the value per share? Now suppose instead that the $3.6 million comes from new investors, who buy shares at a fair price. Does your answer change?

● ● ● ● ●

REAL-TIME DATA ANALYSIS

The major stock exchanges have wonderful Web sites. Look at both the NYSE site (**www.nyse.com**) and the Nasdaq site (**www.nasdaq.com**). You will find plenty of material on their trading systems, and you can also access quotes and other data.

1. Go to **www.nyse.com**. Find *NYSE MarkeTrac* and click on the DJIA ticker tape, which shows trades for the stocks in the Dow Jones Industrial Averages. Stop the tape at GE. What are the latest price, dividend yield, and P/E ratio?

Use data from the Standard & Poor's Market Insight Database at www.mhhe.com/edumarketinsight **or from** finance.yahoo.com **to answer the following questions.**

2. Look up General Mills, Inc., and Kellogg Co. The companies' ticker symbols are GIS and K.

   a. What are the current dividend yield and price–earnings ratio (P/E) for each company? How do the yields and P/Es compare with the average for the food industry and for the stock market as a whole? (The stock market is represented by the S&P 500 index.)

   b. What are the growth rates of earnings per share (EPS) and dividends for each company over the last five years? Do these growth rates appear to reflect a steady trend that could be projected for the long-run future?

   c. Would you be confident in applying the constant-growth DCF valuation model to these companies' stocks? Why or why not?

STANDARD &POOR'S

3. Look up Intel (INTC), Dell Computer (DELL), Dow Chemical (DOW), Harley-Davidson (HOG), and Pfizer, Inc. (PFE). Look at "Financial Highlights" and "Company Profile" for each company. You will note wide differences in these companies' price–earnings ratios. What are the possible explanations for these differences? Which would you classify as growth (high-PVGO) stocks and which as income stocks?

STANDARD &POOR'S

MINI-CASE ● ● ● ● ●

Reeby Sports

In 2001, George Reeby founded a small mail-order company selling high-quality sports equipment. Since those early days Reeby Sports has grown steadily and been consistently profitable. The company has issued 2 million shares, all of which are owned by George Reeby and his five children.

For some months George has been wondering whether the time has come to take the company public. This would allow him to cash in on part of his investment and would make it easier for the firm to raise capital should it wish to expand in the future.

But how much are the shares worth? George's first instinct is to look at the firm's balance sheet, which shows that the book value of the equity is $26.34 million, or $13.17 per share. A share price of $13.17 would put the stock on a P/E ratio of 6.6. That is quite a bit lower than the 13.1 P/E ratio of Reeby's larger rival, Molly Sports.

George suspects that book value is not necessarily a good guide to a share's market value. He thinks of his daughter Jenny, who works in an investment bank. She would undoubtedly know what the shares are worth. He decides to phone her after she finishes work that evening at 9 o'clock or before she starts the next day at 6.00 a.m.

Before phoning, George jots down some basic data on the company's profitability. After recovering from its early losses, the company has earned a return that is higher than its estimated 10% cost of capital. George is fairly confident that the company could continue to grow fairly steadily for the next six to eight years. In fact he feels that the company's growth has been somewhat held back in the last few years by the demands from two of the children for the company to make large dividend payments. Perhaps, if the company went public, it could hold back on dividends and plow more money back into the business.

There are some clouds on the horizon. Competition is increasing and only that morning Molly Sports announced plans to form a mail-order division. George is worried that beyond the next six or so years it might become difficult to find worthwhile investment opportunities.

George realizes that Jenny will need to know much more about the prospects for the business before she can put a final figure on the value of Reeby Sports, but he hopes that the information is sufficient for her to give a preliminary indication of the value of the shares.

	2002	2003	2004	2005	2006	2007	2008	2009	2010	2011E
Earnings per share ($)	−2.10	−0.70	0.23	0.81	1.10	1.30	1.52	1.64	2.00	2.03
Dividend ($)	0.00	0.00	0.00	0.20	0.20	0.30	0.30	0.60	0.60	0.80
Book value per share ($)	9.80	7.70	7.00	7.61	8.51	9.51	10.73	11.77	13.17	14.40
ROE (%)	−27.10	−7.1	3.0	11.6	14.5	15.3	16.0	15.3	17.0	15.4

QUESTIONS

1. Help Jenny to forecast dividend payments for Reeby Sports and to estimate the value of the stock. You do not need to provide a single figure. For example, you may wish to calculate two figures, one on the assumption that the opportunity for further profitable investment is reduced in year 6 and another on the assumption that it is reduced in year 8.

2. How much of your estimate of the value of Reeby's stock comes from the present value of growth opportunities?

Net Present Value and Other Investment Criteria

▶ **A company's shareholders** prefer to be rich rather than poor. Therefore, they want the firm to invest in every project that is worth more than it costs. The difference between a project's value and its cost is its *net present value (NPV)*. Companies can best help their shareholders by investing in all projects with a positive NPV and rejecting those with a negative NPV.

We start this chapter with a review of the net present value rule. We then turn to some other measures that companies may look at when making investment decisions. The first two of these measures, the project's payback period and its book rate of return, are little better than rules of thumb, easy to calculate and easy to communicate. Although there is a place for rules of thumb in this world, an engineer needs something more accurate when designing a 100-story building, and a financial manager needs more than a rule of thumb when making a substantial capital investment decision.

Instead of calculating a project's NPV, companies often compare the expected rate of return from investing in the project with the return that shareholders could earn on equivalent-risk investments in the capital market. The company accepts those projects that provide a higher return than shareholders could earn for themselves. If used correctly, this rate of return rule should always identify projects that increase firm value. However, we shall see that the rule sets several traps for the unwary.

We conclude the chapter by showing how to cope with situations when the firm has only limited capital. This raises two problems. One is computational. In simple cases we just choose those projects that give the highest NPV per dollar invested, but more elaborate techniques are sometimes needed to sort through the possible alternatives. The other problem is to decide whether capital rationing really exists and whether it invalidates the net present value rule. Guess what? NPV, properly interpreted, wins out in the end.

•••••

5-1 A Review of the Basics

Vegetron's chief financial officer (CFO) is wondering how to analyze a proposed $1 million investment in a new venture called project X. He asks what you think.

Your response should be as follows: "First, forecast the cash flows generated by project X over its economic life. Second, determine the appropriate opportunity cost of capital (r). This should reflect both the time value of money and the risk involved in project X. Third, use this opportunity cost of capital to discount the project's future cash flows. The sum of the discounted cash flows is called present value (PV). Fourth, calculate *net* present value (NPV) by subtracting the $1 million investment from PV. If we call the cash flows C_0, C_1, and so on, then

$$\text{NPV} = C_0 + \frac{C_1}{1+r} + \frac{C_2}{(1+r)^2} + \cdots$$

101

"We should invest in project X if its NPV is greater than zero."

However, Vegetron's CFO is unmoved by your sagacity. He asks why NPV is so important.

Your reply: "Let us look at what is best for Vegetron stockholders. They want you to make their Vegetron shares as valuable as possible.

"Right now Vegetron's total market value (price per share times the number of shares outstanding) is $10 million. That includes $1 million cash we can invest in project X. The value of Vegetron's other assets and opportunities must therefore be $9 million. We have to decide whether it is better to keep the $1 million cash and reject project X or to spend the cash and accept the project. Let us call the value of the new project PV. Then the choice is as follows:

	Market Value ($ millions)	
Asset	**Reject Project X**	**Accept Project X**
Cash	1	0
Other assets	9	9
Project X	0	PV
	10	9 + PV

"Clearly project X is worthwhile if its present value, PV, is greater than $1 million, that is, if net present value is positive."

CFO: "How do I know that the PV of project X will actually show up in Vegetron's market value?"

Your reply: "Suppose we set up a new, independent firm X, whose only asset is project X. What would be the market value of firm X?

"Investors would forecast the dividends that firm X would pay and discount those dividends by the expected rate of return of securities having similar risks. We know that stock prices are equal to the present value of forecasted dividends.

"Since project X is the only asset, the dividend payments we would expect firm X to pay are exactly the cash flows we have forecasted for project X. Moreover, the rate investors would use to discount firm X's dividends is exactly the rate we should use to discount project X's cash flows.

"I agree that firm X is entirely hypothetical. But if project X is accepted, investors holding Vegetron stock will really hold a portfolio of project X and the firm's other assets. We know the other assets are worth $9 million considered as a separate venture. Since asset values add up, we can easily figure out the portfolio value once we calculate the value of project X as a separate venture.

"By calculating the present value of project X, we are replicating the process by which the common stock of firm X would be valued in capital markets."

CFO: "The one thing I don't understand is where the discount rate comes from."

Your reply: "I agree that the discount rate is difficult to measure precisely. But it is easy to see what we are *trying* to measure. The discount rate is the opportunity cost of investing in the project rather than in the capital market. In other words, instead of accepting a project, the firm can always return the cash to the shareholders and let them invest it in financial assets.

"You can see the trade-off (Figure 5.1). The opportunity cost of taking the project is the return shareholders could have earned had they invested the funds on their own. When we discount the project's cash flows by the expected rate of return on financial assets, we are measuring how much investors would be prepared to pay for your project."

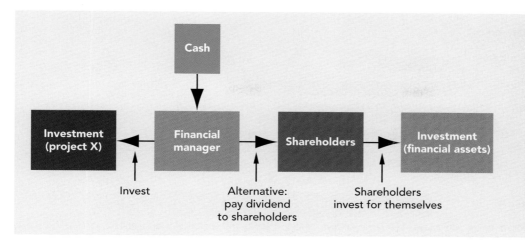

▶ **FIGURE 5.1**

The firm can either keep and reinvest cash or return it to investors. (Arrows represent possible cash flows or transfers.) If cash is reinvested, the opportunity cost is the expected rate of return that shareholders could have obtained by investing in financial assets.

"But which financial assets?" Vegetron's CFO queries. "The fact that investors expect only 12% on IBM stock does not mean that we should purchase Fly-by-Night Electronics if it offers 13%."

Your reply: "The opportunity-cost concept makes sense only if assets of equivalent risk are compared. In general, you should identify financial assets that have the same risk as your project, estimate the expected rate of return on these assets, and use this rate as the opportunity cost."

Net Present Value's Competitors

When you advised the CFO to calculate the project's NPV, you were in good company. These days 75% of firms always, or almost always, calculate net present value when deciding on investment projects. However, as you can see from Figure 5.2 on page 104, NPV is not the only investment criterion that companies use, and firms often look at more than one measure of a project's attractiveness.

About three-quarters of firms calculate the project's internal rate of return (or IRR); that is roughly the same proportion as use NPV. The IRR rule is a close relative of NPV and, when used properly, it will give the same answer. You therefore need to understand the IRR rule and how to take care when using it.

A large part of this chapter is concerned with explaining the IRR rule, but first we look at two other measures of a project's attractiveness—the project's payback and its book rate of return. As we will explain, both measures have obvious defects. Few companies rely on them to make their investment decisions, but they do use them as supplementary measures that may help to distinguish the marginal project from the no-brainer.

Later in the chapter we also come across one further investment measure, the profitability index. Figure 5.2 shows that it is not often used, but you will find that there are circumstances in which this measure has some special advantages.

Three Points to Remember about NPV

As we look at these alternative criteria, it is worth keeping in mind the following key features of the net present value rule. First, the NPV rule recognizes that *a dollar today is worth more than a dollar tomorrow*, because the dollar today can be invested to start earning interest immediately. Any investment rule that does not recognize the *time value of money* cannot be sensible. Second, net present value depends solely on the *forecasted cash flows*

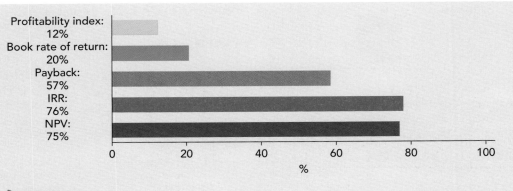

FIGURE 5.2

Survey evidence on the percentage of CFOs who always, or almost always, use a particular technique for evaluating investment projects.

Source: Reprinted from J. R. Graham and C. R. Harvey, "The Theory and Practice of Finance: Evidence from the Field," *Journal of Financial Economics* 61 (2001), pp. 187–243, © 2001 with permission from Elsevier Science.

from the project and the *opportunity cost of capital.* Any investment rule that is affected by the manager's tastes, the company's choice of accounting method, the profitability of the company's existing business, or the profitability of other independent projects will lead to inferior decisions. Third, *because present values are all measured in today's dollars, you can add them up.* Therefore, if you have two projects A and B, the net present value of the combined investment is

$$NPV(A + B) = NPV(A) + NPV(B)$$

This adding-up property has important implications. Suppose project B has a negative NPV. If you tack it onto project A, the joint project (A + B) must have a lower NPV than A on its own. Therefore, you are unlikely to be misled into accepting a poor project (B) just because it is packaged with a good one (A). As we shall see, the alternative measures do not have this property. If you are not careful, you may be tricked into deciding that a package of a good and a bad project is better than the good project on its own.

NPV Depends on Cash Flow, Not on Book Returns

Net present value depends only on the project's cash flows and the opportunity cost of capital. But when companies report to shareholders, they do not simply show the cash flows. They also report book—that is, accounting—income and book assets.

Financial managers sometimes use these numbers to calculate a book (or accounting) rate of return on a proposed investment. In other words, they look at the prospective book income as a proportion of the book value of the assets that the firm is proposing to acquire:

$$\text{Book rate of return} = \frac{\text{book income}}{\text{book assets}}$$

Cash flows and book income are often very different. For example, the accountant labels some cash outflows as *capital investments* and others as *operating expenses.* The operating expenses are, of course, deducted immediately from each year's income. The capital expenditures are put on the firm's balance sheet and then depreciated. The annual depreciation charge is deducted from each year's income. Thus the book rate of return depends on which items the accountant treats as capital investments and how rapidly they are depreciated.[1]

Now the merits of an investment project do not depend on how accountants classify the cash flows[2] and few companies these days make investment decisions just on the basis of the book rate of return. But managers know that the company's shareholders pay considerable attention to book measures of profitability and naturally they think (and worry) about how major projects would affect the company's book return. Those projects that would reduce the company's book return may be scrutinized more carefully by senior management.

You can see the dangers here. The company's book rate of return may not be a good measure of true profitability. It is also an *average* across all of the firm's activities. The average profitability of past investments is not usually the right hurdle for new investments. Think of a firm that has been exceptionally lucky and successful. Say its average book return is 24%, double shareholders' 12% opportunity cost of capital. Should it demand that all *new* investments offer 24% or better? Clearly not: That would mean passing up many positive-NPV opportunities with rates of return between 12 and 24%.

We will come back to the book rate of return in Chapter 18, when we look more closely at accounting measures of financial performance.

5-2 Payback

We suspect that you have often heard conversations that go something like this: "We are spending $6 a week, or around $300 a year, at the laundromat. If we bought a washing machine for $800, it would pay for itself within three years. That's well worth it." You have just encountered the payback rule.

A project's **payback period** is found by counting the number of years it takes before the cumulative cash flow equals the initial investment. For the washing machine the payback period was just under three years. The **payback *rule*** states that a project should be accepted if its payback period is less than some specified cutoff period. For example, if the cutoff period is four years, the washing machine makes the grade; if the cutoff is two years, it doesn't.

EXAMPLE 5.1   ● The Payback Rule

Consider the following three projects:

Cash Flows ($)						
Project	C_0	C_1	C_2	C_3	Payback Period (years)	NPV at 10%
A	−2,000	500	500	5,000	3	+2,624
B	−2,000	500	1,800	0	2	−58
C	−2,000	1,800	500	0	2	+50

---

[1] This chapter's mini-case contains simple illustrations of how book rates of return are calculated and of the difference between accounting income and project cash flow. Read the case if you wish to refresh your understanding of these topics. Better still, do the case calculations.

[2] Of course, the depreciation method used for tax purposes does have cash consequences that should be taken into account in calculating NPV. We cover depreciation and taxes in the next chapter.

Project A involves an initial investment of $2,000 ($C_0 = -2,000$) followed by cash inflows during the next three years. Suppose the opportunity cost of capital is 10%. Then project A has an NPV of +$2,624:

$$NPV(A) = -2,000 + \frac{500}{1.10} + \frac{500}{1.10^2} + \frac{5,000}{1.10^3} = +\$2,624$$

Project B also requires an initial investment of $2,000 but produces a cash inflow of $500 in year 1 and $1,800 in year 2. At a 10% opportunity cost of capital project B has an NPV of −$58:

$$NPV(B) = -2,000 + \frac{500}{1.10} + \frac{1,800}{1.10^2} = -\$58$$

The third project, C, involves the same initial outlay as the other two projects but its first-period cash flow is larger. It has an NPV of +$50.

$$NPV(C) = -2,000 + \frac{1,800}{1.10} + \frac{500}{1.10^2} = +\$50$$

The net present value rule tells us to accept projects A and C but to reject project B.

Now look at how rapidly each project pays back its initial investment. With project A you take three years to recover the $2,000 investment; with projects B and C you take only two years. If the firm used the *payback rule* with a cutoff period of two years, it would accept only projects B and C; if it used the payback rule with a cutoff period of three or more years, it would accept all three projects. Therefore, regardless of the choice of cutoff period, the payback rule gives different answers from the net present value rule.

• • • • •

You can see why payback can give misleading answers as illustrated in Example 5.1:

1. *The payback rule ignores all cash flows after the cutoff date.* If the cutoff date is two years, the payback rule rejects project A regardless of the size of the cash inflow in year 3.

2. *The payback rule gives equal weight to all cash flows before the cutoff date.* The payback rule says that projects B and C are equally attractive, but because C's cash inflows occur earlier, C has the higher net present value at any discount rate.

In order to use the payback rule, a firm has to decide on an appropriate cutoff date. If it uses the same cutoff regardless of project life, it will tend to accept many poor short-lived projects and reject many good long-lived ones.

We have had little good to say about the payback rule. So why do many companies continue to use it? Senior managers don't truly believe that all cash flows after the payback period are irrelevant. We suggest three explanations. First, payback may be used because it is the simplest way to *communicate* an idea of project profitability. Investment decisions require discussion and negotiation between people from all parts of the firm, and it is important to have a measure that everyone can understand. Second, managers of larger corporations may opt for projects with short paybacks because they believe that quicker profits mean quicker promotion. That takes us back to Chapter 1 where we discussed the need to align the objectives of managers with those of shareholders. Finally, owners of family firms with limited access to capital may worry about their future ability to raise capital. These worries may lead them to favor rapid payback projects even though a longer-term venture may have a higher NPV.

Discounted Payback

Occasionally companies discount the cash flows before they compute the payback period. The discounted cash flows for our three projects are as follows:

		Discounted Cash Flows ($)				
Project	C_0	C_1	C_2	C_3	**Discounted Payback Period (years)**	**NPV at 20%**
A	$-2,000$	$500/1.10 =$ 455	$500/1.10^2 =$ 413	$5,000/1.10^3 =$ 3,757	3	$+2,624$
B	$-2,000$	$500/1.10 =$ 455	$1,800/1.10^2 =$ 1,488		—	-58
C	$-2,000$	$1,800/1.10 =$ 1,636	$500/1.10^2 =$ 413		2	$+50$

The *discounted payback rule* asks, How many years does the project have to last in order for it to make sense in terms of net present value? You can see that the value of the cash inflows from project B never exceeds the initial outlay and would always be rejected under the discounted payback rule. Thus the discounted payback rule will never accept a negative-NPV project. On the other hand, it still takes no account of cash flows after the cutoff date, so that good long-term projects such as A continue to risk rejection.

Rather than automatically rejecting any project with a long discounted payback period, many managers simply use the measure as a warning signal. These managers don't unthinkingly reject a project with a long discounted-payback period. Instead they check that the proposer is not unduly optimistic about the project's ability to generate cash flows into the distant future. They satisfy themselves that the equipment has a long life and that competitors will not enter the market and eat into the project's cash flows.

5-3 Internal (or Discounted-Cash-Flow) Rate of Return

Whereas payback and return on book are ad hoc measures, internal rate of return has a much more respectable ancestry and is recommended in many finance texts. If, therefore, we dwell more on its deficiencies, it is not because they are more numerous but because they are less obvious.

In Chapter 2 we noted that the net present value rule could also be expressed in terms of rate of return, which would lead to the following rule: "Accept investment opportunities offering rates of return in excess of their opportunity costs of capital." That statement, properly interpreted, is absolutely correct. However, interpretation is not always easy for long-lived investment projects.

There is no ambiguity in defining the true rate of return of an investment that generates a single payoff after one period:

$$\text{Rate of return} = \frac{\text{payoff}}{\text{investment}} - 1$$

Alternatively, we could write down the NPV of the investment and find the discount rate that makes NPV = 0.

$$\text{NPV} = C_0 + \frac{C_1}{1 + \text{discount rate}} = 0$$

implies

$$\text{Discount rate} = \frac{C_1}{-C_0} - 1$$

Of course C_1 is the payoff and $-C_0$ is the required investment, and so our two equations say exactly the same thing. *The discount rate that makes NPV = 0 is also the rate of return.*

How do we calculate return when the project produces cash flows in several periods? Answer: We use the same definition that we just developed for one-period projects—*the project rate of return is the discount rate that gives a zero NPV.* This discount rate is known as the **discounted-cash-flow (DCF) rate of return** or **internal rate of return (IRR).** The internal rate of return is used frequently in finance. It can be a handy measure, but, as we shall see, it can also be a misleading measure. You should, therefore, know how to calculate it and how to use it properly.

Calculating the IRR

The internal rate of return is defined as the rate of discount that makes NPV = 0. So to find the IRR for an investment project lasting T years, we must solve for IRR in the following expression:

$$\text{NPV} = C_0 + \frac{C_1}{1 + \text{IRR}} + \frac{C_2}{(1 + \text{IRR})^2} + \cdots + \frac{C_T}{(1 + \text{IRR})^T} = 0$$

Actual calculation of IRR usually involves trial and error. For example, consider a project that produces the following flows:

Cash Flows ($)		
C_0	C_1	C_2
$-4,000$	$+2,000$	$+4,000$

The internal rate of return is IRR in the equation

$$\text{NPV} = -4,000 + \frac{2,000}{1 + \text{IRR}} + \frac{4,000}{(1 + \text{IRR})^2} = 0$$

Let us arbitrarily try a zero discount rate. In this case NPV is not zero but $+\$2,000$:

$$\text{NPV} = -4,000 + \frac{2,000}{1.0} + \frac{4,000}{(1.0)^2} = +\$2,000$$

The NPV is positive; therefore, the IRR must be greater than zero. The next step might be to try a discount rate of 50%. In this case net present value is $-\$889$:

$$\text{NPV} = -4,000 + \frac{2,000}{1.50} + \frac{4,000}{(1.50)^2} = -\$889$$

The NPV is negative; therefore, the IRR must be less than 50%. In Figure 5.3 we have plotted the net present values implied by a range of discount rates. From this we can see that a discount rate of 28% gives the desired net present value of zero. Therefore IRR is 28%.

The easiest way to calculate IRR, if you have to do it by hand, is to plot three or four combinations of NPV and discount rate on a graph like Figure 5.3, connect the points with a smooth line, and read off the discount rate at which NPV = 0. It is of course quicker and more accurate to use a computer spreadsheet or a specially programmed calculator, and in practice this is what financial managers do. The Useful Spreadsheet Functions box near the end of the chapter presents Excel functions for doing so.

Some people confuse the internal rate of return and the opportunity cost of capital because both appear as discount rates in the NPV formula. The internal rate of return is a *profitability measure* that depends solely on the amount and timing of the project cash flows. The opportunity cost of capital is a *standard of profitability* that we use to calculate how much the project is worth. The opportunity cost of capital is established in capital markets. It is the expected rate of return offered by other assets with the same risk as the project being evaluated.

Net present value, dollars

IRR = 28%

Discount rate, %

▶ FIGURE 5.3

This project costs $4,000 and then produces cash inflows of $2,000 in year 1 and $4,000 in year 2. Its internal rate of return (IRR) is 28%, the rate of discount at which NPV is zero.

The IRR Rule

The internal rate of return rule is to accept an investment project if the opportunity cost of capital is less than the internal rate of return. You can see the reasoning behind this idea if you look again at Figure 5.3. If the opportunity cost of capital is less than the 28% IRR, then the project has a *positive* NPV when discounted at the opportunity cost of capital. If it is equal to the IRR, the project has a *zero* NPV. And if it is greater than the IRR, the project has a *negative* NPV. Therefore, when we compare the opportunity cost of capital with the IRR on our project, we are effectively asking whether our project has a positive NPV. This is true not only for our example. The rule will give the same answer as the net present value rule *whenever the NPV of a project is a smoothly declining function of the discount rate*.

Many firms use internal rate of return as a criterion in preference to net present value. We think that this is a pity. Although, properly stated, the two criteria are formally equivalent, the internal rate of return rule contains several pitfalls.

Pitfall 1—Lending or Borrowing?

Not all cash-flow streams have NPVs that decline as the discount rate increases. Consider the following projects A and B:

| | Cash Flows ($) | | | |
Project	C_0	C_1	IRR	NPV at 10%
A	−1,000	+1,500	+50%	+364
B	+1,000	−1,500	+50%	−364

Each project has an IRR of 50%. (In other words, $-1{,}000 + 1{,}500/1.50 = 0$ *and* $+1{,}000 - 1{,}500/1.50 = 0$.)

Does this mean that they are equally attractive? Clearly not, for in the case of A, where we are initially paying out $1,000, we are *lending* money at 50%; in the case of B, where we are initially receiving $1,000, we are *borrowing* money at 50%. When we lend money, we want a *high* rate of return; when we borrow money, we want a *low* rate of return.

If you plot a graph like Figure 5.3 for project B, you will find that NPV increases as the discount rate increases. Obviously the internal rate of return rule, as we stated it above, won't work in this case; we have to look for an IRR *less* than the opportunity cost of capital.

Pitfall 2—Multiple Rates of Return

Helmsley Iron is proposing to develop a new strip mine in Western Australia. The mine involves an initial investment of A$3 billion and is expected to produce a cash inflow of A$1 billion a year for the next nine years. At the end of that time the company will incur A$6.5 billion of cleanup costs. Thus the cash flows from the project are:

Cash Flows (A$ billions)				
C_0	C_1	. . .	C_9	C_{10}
−3	1		1	−6.5

Helmsley calculates the project's IRR and its NPV as follows:

IRR (%)	NPV at 10%
+3.50 *and* 19.54	$A253 million

Note that there are *two* discount rates that make NPV = 0. That is, *each* of the following statements holds:

$$NPV = -3 + \frac{1}{1.035} + \frac{1}{1.035^2} + \cdots + \frac{1}{1.035^9} - \frac{6.5}{1.035^{10}} = 0$$

$$NPV = -3 + \frac{1}{1.1954} + \frac{1}{1.1954^2} + \cdots + \frac{1}{1.1954^9} - \frac{6.5}{1.1954^{10}} = 0$$

In other words, the investment has an IRR of both 3.50 *and* 19.54%. Figure 5.4 shows how this comes about. As the discount rate increases, NPV initially rises and then declines. The reason for this is the double change in the sign of the cash-flow stream. There can be as many internal rates of return for a project as there are changes in the sign of the cash flows.[3]

Decommissioning and clean-up costs can sometimes be huge. Phillips Petroleum has estimated that it will need to spend $1 billion to remove its Norwegian offshore oil platforms. It can cost over $300 million to decommission a nuclear power plant. These are obvious instances where cash flows go from positive to negative, but you can probably think of a number of other cases where the company needs to plan for later expenditures. Ships periodically need to go into dry dock for a refit, hotels may receive a major face-lift, machine parts may need replacement, and so on.

Whenever the cash-flow stream is expected to change sign more than once, the company typically sees more than one IRR.

As if this is not difficult enough, there are also cases in which *no* internal rate of return exists. For example, project C has a positive net present value at all discount rates:

	Cash Flows ($)				
Project	C_0	C_1	C_2	IRR (%)	NPV at 10%
C	+1,000	−3,000	+2,500	None	+339

---

[3] By Descartes's "rule of signs" there can be as many different solutions to a polynomial as there are changes of sign.

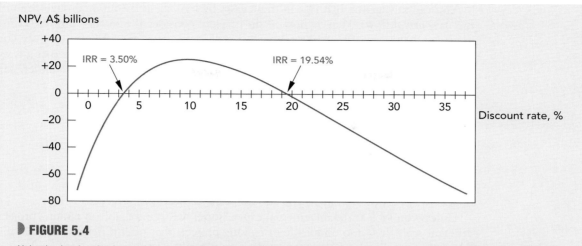

▶ FIGURE 5.4

Helmsley Iron's mine has two internal rates of return. NPV = 0 when the discount rate is +3.50% *and* when it is +19.54%.

A number of adaptations of the IRR rule have been devised for such cases. Not only are they inadequate, but they also are unnecessary, for the simple solution is to use net present value.[4]

Pitfall 3—Mutually Exclusive Projects

Firms often have to choose from among several alternative ways of doing the same job or using the same facility. In other words, they need to choose from among **mutually exclusive projects.** Here too the IRR rule can be misleading.

Consider projects D and E:

Project	C_0	C_1	IRR (%)	NPV at 10%
	Cash Flows ($)			
D	−10,000	+20,000	100	+ 8,182
E	−20,000	+35,000	75	+11,818

Perhaps project D is a manually controlled machine tool and project E is the same tool with the addition of computer control. Both are good investments, but E has the higher NPV and is, therefore, better. However, the IRR rule seems to indicate that, if you have to choose, you should go for D since it has the higher IRR. If you follow the IRR rule, you have the satisfaction of earning a 100% rate of return; if you follow the NPV rule, you are $11,818 richer.

---

[4] Companies sometimes get around the problem of multiple rates of return by discounting the later cash flows back at the cost of capital until there remains only one change in the sign of the cash flows. A *modified internal rate of return* (MIRR) can then be calculated on this revised series. In our example, the MIRR is calculated as follows:

1. Calculate the present value in year 5 of all the subsequent cash flows:
$$\text{PV in year 5} - 1/1.1 + 1/1.1^2 + 1/1.1^3 + +1/1.1^4 - 6.5/1.1^5 = -.866$$

2. Add to the year 5 cash flow the present value of subsequent cash flows:
$$C_5 + \text{PV(subsequent cash flows)} = 1 - .866 = .134$$

3. Since there is now only one change in the sign of the cash flows, the revised series has a unique rate of return, which is 13.7%:
$$\text{NPV} = 1/1.137 + 1/1.137^2 + 1/1.137^3 + 1/1.137^4 + .134/1.137^5 = 0$$

Since the MIRR of 13.7% is greater than the cost of capital (and the initial cash flow is negative), the project has a positive NPV when valued at the cost of capital.

Of course, it would be much easier in such cases to abandon the IRR rule and just calculate project NPV.

You can salvage the IRR rule in these cases by looking at the internal rate of return on the *incremental* flows. Here is how to do it: First, consider the smaller project (D in our example). It has an IRR of 100%, which is well in excess of the 10% opportunity cost of capital. You know, therefore, that D is acceptable. You now ask yourself whether it is worth making the additional $10,000 investment in E. The incremental flows from undertaking E rather than D are as follows:

Cash Flows ($)				
Project	C_0	C_1	IRR (%)	NPV at 10%
E − D	−10,000	+15,000	50	+3,636

The IRR on the incremental investment is 50%, which is also well in excess of the 10% opportunity cost of capital. So you should prefer project E to project D.[5]

Unless you look at the incremental expenditure, IRR is unreliable in ranking projects of different scale. It is also unreliable in ranking projects that offer different patterns of cash flow over time. For example, suppose the firm can take project F *or* project G but not both (ignore H for the moment):

Cash Flows ($)								
Project	C_0	C_1	C_2	C_3	C_4	C_5	Etc.	IRR (%)	NPV at 10%
F	−9,000	+6,000	+5,000	+4,000	0	0	. . .	33	3,592
G	−9,000	+1,800	+1,800	+1,800	+1,800	+1,800	. . .	20	9,000
H		−6,000	+1,200	+1,200	+1,200	+1,200	. . .	20	6,000

Project F has a higher IRR, but project G, which is a perpetuity, has the higher NPV. Figure 5.5 shows why the two rules give different answers. The green line gives the net present value of project F at different rates of discount. Since a discount rate of 33% produces a net present value of zero, this is the internal rate of return for project F. Similarly, the brown line shows the net present value of project G at different discount rates. The IRR of project G is 20%. (We assume project G's cash flows continue indefinitely.) Note, however, that project G has a higher NPV as long as the opportunity cost of capital is less than 15.6%.

The reason that IRR is misleading is that the total cash inflow of project G is larger but tends to occur later. Therefore, when the discount rate is low, G has the higher NPV; when the discount rate is high, F has the higher NPV. (You can see from Figure 5.5 that the two projects have the *same* NPV when the discount rate is 15.6%.) The internal rates of return on the two projects tell us that at a discount rate of 20% G has a zero NPV (IRR = 20%) and F has a positive NPV. Thus if the opportunity cost of capital were 20%, investors would place a higher value on the shorter-lived project F. But in our example the opportunity cost of capital is not 20% but 10%. So investors will

▶ FIGURE 5.5

The IRR of project F exceeds that of project G, but the NPV of project F is higher *only* if the discount rate is greater than 15.6%.

pay a relatively high price for the longer-lived project. At a 10% cost of capital, an investment in G has an NPV of $9,000 and an investment in F has an NPV of only $3,592.[6]

This is a favorite example of ours. We have gotten many businesspeople's reaction to it. When asked to choose between F and G, many choose F. The reason seems to be the rapid payback generated by project F. In other words, they believe that if they take F, they will also be able to take a later project like H (note that H can be financed using the cash flows from F), whereas if they take G, they won't have money enough for H. In other words they implicitly assume that it is a *shortage of capital* that forces the choice between F and G. When this implicit assumption is brought out, they usually admit that G is better if there is no capital shortage.

But the introduction of capital constraints raises two further questions. The first stems from the fact that most of the executives preferring F to G work for firms that would have no difficulty raising more capital. Why would a manager at IBM, say, choose F on the grounds of limited capital? IBM can raise plenty of capital and can take project H regardless of whether F or G is chosen; therefore H should not affect the choice between F and G. The answer seems to be that large firms usually impose capital budgets on divisions and subdivisions as a part of the firm's planning and control system. Since the system is complicated and cumbersome, the budgets are not easily altered, and so they are perceived as real constraints by middle management.

The second question is this. If there is a capital constraint, either real or self-imposed, should IRR be used to rank projects? The answer is no. The problem in this case is to find the package of investment projects that satisfies the capital constraint and has the largest net present value. The IRR rule will not identify this package. As we will show in the next section, the only practical and general way to do so is to use the technique of linear programming.

When we have to choose between projects F and G, it is easiest to compare the net present values. But if your heart is set on the IRR rule, you can use it as long as you look at the internal rate of return on the incremental flows. The procedure is exactly the same as we showed above. First, you check that project F has a satisfactory IRR. Then you look at the return on the incremental cash flows from G.

	Cash Flows ($)								
Project	C_0	C_1	C_2	C_3	C_4	C_5	Etc.	IRR (%)	NPV at 10%
G − F	0	−4,200	−3,200	−2,200	+1,800	+1,800	. . .	15.6	+5,408

The IRR on the incremental cash flows from G is 15.6%. Since this is greater than the opportunity cost of capital, you should undertake G rather than F.[7]

Pitfall 4—What Happens When There Is More than One Opportunity Cost of Capital?

We have simplified our discussion of capital budgeting by assuming that the opportunity cost of capital is the same for all the cash flows, C_1, C_2, C_3, etc. Remember our most general formula for calculating net present value:

$$NPV = C_0 + \frac{C_1}{1 + r_1} + \frac{C_2}{(1 + r_2)^2} + \frac{C_3}{(1 + r_3)^3} + \cdots$$

---

[6] It is often suggested that the choice between the net present value rule and the internal rate of return rule should depend on the probable reinvestment rate. This is wrong. The prospective return on another *independent* investment should *never* be allowed to influence the investment decision.

[7] Because F and G had the same 10% cost of capital, we could choose between the two projects by asking whether the IRR on the incremental cash flows was greater or less than 10%. But suppose that F and G had different risks and therefore different costs of capital. In that case there would be no simple yardstick for assessing whether the IRR on the incremental cash flows was adequate.

In other words, we discount C_1 at the opportunity cost of capital for one year, C_2 at the opportunity cost of capital for two years, and so on. The IRR rule tells us to accept a project if the IRR is greater than the opportunity cost of capital. But what do we do when we have several opportunity costs? Do we compare IRR with r_1, r_2, r_3, . . .? Actually we would have to compute a complex weighted average of these rates to obtain a number comparable to IRR.

What does this mean for capital budgeting? It means trouble for the IRR rule whenever there is more than one opportunity cost of capital. Many firms use the IRR, thereby implicitly assuming that there is no difference between short-term and long-term discount rates. They do this for the same reason that we have so far finessed the issue: simplicity.[8]

The Verdict on IRR

We have given four examples of things that can go wrong with IRR. We spent much less space on payback or return on book. Does this mean that IRR is worse than the other two measures? Quite the contrary. There is little point in dwelling on the deficiencies of payback or return on book. They are clearly ad hoc measures that often lead to silly conclusions. The IRR rule has a much more respectable ancestry. It is less easy to use than NPV, but, used properly, it gives the same answer.

Nowadays few large corporations use the payback period or return on book as their primary measure of project attractiveness. Most use discounted cash flow or "DCF," and for many companies DCF means IRR, not NPV. For "normal" investment projects with an initial cash outflow followed by a series of cash inflows, there is no difficulty in using the internal rate of return to make a simple accept/reject decision. However, we think that financial managers need to worry more about Pitfall 3. Financial managers never see all possible projects. Most projects are proposed by operating managers. A company that instructs nonfinancial managers to look first at project IRRs prompts a search for those projects with the highest IRRs rather than the highest NPVs. It also encourages managers to *modify* projects so that their IRRs are higher. Where do you typically find the highest IRRs? In short-lived projects requiring little up-front investment. Such projects may not add much to the value of the firm.

We don't know why so many companies pay such close attention to the internal rate of return, but we suspect that it may reflect the fact that management does not trust the forecasts it receives. Suppose that two plant managers approach you with proposals for two new investments. Both have a positive NPV of $1,400 at the company's 8% cost of capital, but you nevertheless decide to accept project A and reject B. Are you being irrational?

The cash flows for the two projects and their NPVs are set out in the following table. You can see that, although both proposals have the same NPV, project A involves an investment of $9,000, while B requires an investment of $9 million. Investing $9,000 to make $1,400 is clearly an attractive proposition, and this shows up in A's IRR of nearly 16%. Investing $9 million to make $1,400 might also be worth doing if you could be *sure* of the plant manager's forecasts, but there is almost no room for error in project B. You could spend time and money checking the cash-flow forecasts, but is it really worth the effort? Most managers would look at the IRR and decide that, if the cost of capital is 8%, a project that offers a return of 8.01% is not worth the worrying time.

Alternatively, management may conclude that project A is a clear winner that is worth undertaking right away, but in the case of project B it may make sense to wait and see

---

[8] In Chapter 9 we look at some other cases in which it would be misleading to use the same discount rate for both short-term and long-term cash flows.

whether the decision looks more clear-cut in a year's time.[9] Management postpones the decision on projects such as B by setting a hurdle rate for the IRR that is higher than the cost of capital.

	Cash Flows ($ thousands)					
Project	C_0	C_1	C_2	C_3	NPV at 8%	IRR (%)
A	−9.0	2.9	4.0	5.4	1.4	15.58
B	−9,000	2,560	3,540	4,530	1.4	8.01

5-4 Choosing Capital Investments When Resources Are Limited

Our entire discussion of methods of capital budgeting has rested on the proposition that the wealth of a firm's shareholders is highest if the firm accepts *every* project that has a positive net present value. Suppose, however, that there are limitations on the investment program that prevent the company from undertaking all such projects. Economists call this *capital rationing.* When capital is rationed, we need a method of selecting the package of projects that is within the company's resources yet gives the highest possible net present value.

An Easy Problem in Capital Rationing

Let us start with a simple example. The opportunity cost of capital is 10%, and our company has the following opportunities:

	Cash Flows ($ millions)			
Project	C_0	C_1	C_2	NPV at 10%
A	−10	+30	+5	21
B	−5	+5	+20	16
C	−5	+5	+15	12

All three projects are attractive, but suppose that the firm is limited to spending $10 million. In that case, it can invest *either* in project A *or* in projects B and C, but it cannot invest in all three. Although individually B and C have lower net present values than project A, when taken together they have the higher net present value. Here we cannot choose between projects solely on the basis of net present values. When funds are limited, we need to concentrate on getting the biggest bang for our buck. In other words, we must pick the projects that offer the highest net present value per dollar of initial outlay. This ratio is known as the **profitability index:**[10]

$$\text{Profitability index} = \frac{\text{net present value}}{\text{investment}}$$

---

[9] In Chapter 10 we discuss briefly when it may pay a company to delay undertaking a positive-NPV project. When projects are "deep-in-the-money" (project A), it generally pays to invest right away and capture the cash flows. However, in the case of projects that are close-to-the money (project B) it makes more sense to wait and see.

[10] If a project requires outlays in two or more periods, the denominator should be the present value of the outlays. A few companies do not discount the benefits or costs before calculating the profitability index. The less said about these companies, the better.

For our three projects the profitability index is calculated as follows:[11]

Project	Investment ($ millions)	NPV ($ millions)	Profitability Index
A	10	21	2.1
B	5	16	3.2
C	5	12	2.4

Project B has the highest profitability index and C has the next highest. Therefore, if our budget limit is $10 million, we should accept these two projects.[12]

Unfortunately, there are some limitations to this simple ranking method. One of the most serious is that it breaks down whenever more than one resource is rationed.[13] For example, suppose that the firm can raise only $10 million for investment in *each* of years 0 and 1 and that the menu of possible projects is expanded to include an investment next year in project D:

Project	Cash Flows ($ millions)			NPV at 10%	Profitability Index
	C_0	C_1	C_2		
A	−10	+30	+5	21	2.1
B	−5	+5	+20	16	3.2
C	−5	+5	+15	12	2.4
D	0	−40	+60	13	0.4

One strategy is to accept projects B and C; however, if we do this, we cannot also accept D, which costs more than our budget limit for period 1. An alternative is to accept project A in period 0. Although this has a lower net present value than the combination of B and C, it provides a $30 million positive cash flow in period 1. When this is added to the $10 million budget, we can also afford to undertake D next year. A and D have *lower* profitability indexes than B and C, but they have a *higher* total net present value.

The reason that ranking on the profitability index fails in this example is that resources are constrained in each of two periods. In fact, this ranking method is inadequate whenever there is *any* other constraint on the choice of projects. This means that it cannot cope with cases in which two projects are mutually exclusive or in which one project is dependent on another.

For example, suppose that you have a long menu of possible projects starting this year and next. There is a limit on how much you can invest in each year. Perhaps also you can't undertake both project alpha and beta (they both require the same piece of land), and you can't invest in project gamma unless you invest in delta (gamma is simply an add-on to

---

[11] Sometimes the profitability index is defined as the ratio of the present value to initial outlay, that is, as PV/investment. This measure is also known as the *benefit–cost ratio*. To calculate the benefit–cost ratio, simply add 1.0 to each profitability index. Project rankings are unchanged.

[12] If a project has a positive profitability index, it must also have a positive NPV. Therefore, firms sometimes use the profitability index to select projects when capital is *not* limited. However, like the IRR, the profitability index can be misleading when used to choose between mutually exclusive projects. For example, suppose you were forced to choose between (1) investing $100 in a project whose payoffs have a present value of $200 or (2) investing $1 million in a project whose payoffs have a present value of $1.5 million. The first investment has the higher profitability index; the second makes you richer.

[13] It may also break down if it causes some money to be left over. It might be better to spend all the available funds even if this involves accepting a project with a slightly lower profitability index.

delta). You need to find the package of projects that satisfies all these constraints and gives the highest NPV.

One way to tackle such a problem is to work through all possible combinations of projects. For each combination you first check whether the projects satisfy the constraints and then calculate the net present value. But it is smarter to recognize that linear programming (LP) techniques are specially designed to search through such possible combinations.[14]

Uses of Capital Rationing Models

Linear programming models seem tailor-made for solving capital budgeting problems when resources are limited. Why then are they not universally accepted either in theory or in practice? One reason is that these models can turn out to be very complex. Second, as with any sophisticated long-range planning tool, there is the general problem of getting good data. It is just not worth applying costly, sophisticated methods to poor data. Furthermore, these models are based on the assumption that all future investment opportunities are known. In reality, the discovery of investment ideas is an unfolding process.

Our most serious misgivings center on the basic assumption that capital is limited. When we come to discuss company financing, we shall see that most large corporations do not face capital rationing and can raise large sums of money on fair terms. Why then do many company presidents tell their subordinates that capital is limited? If they are right, the capital market is seriously imperfect. What then are they doing maximizing NPV?[15] We might be tempted to suppose that if capital is not rationed, they do not *need* to use linear programming and, if it is rationed, then surely they *ought* not to use it. But that would be too quick a judgment. Let us look at this problem more deliberately.

Soft Rationing   Many firms' capital constraints are "soft." They reflect no imperfections in capital markets. Instead they are provisional limits adopted by management as an aid to financial control.

Some ambitious divisional managers habitually overstate their investment opportunities. Rather than trying to distinguish which projects really are worthwhile, headquarters may find it simpler to impose an upper limit on divisional expenditures and thereby force the divisions to set their own priorities. In such instances budget limits are a rough but effective way of dealing with biased cash-flow forecasts. In other cases management may believe that very rapid corporate growth could impose intolerable strains on management and the organization. Since it is difficult to quantify such constraints explicitly, the budget limit may be used as a proxy.

Because such budget limits have nothing to do with any inefficiency in the capital market, there is no contradiction in using an LP model in the division to maximize net present value subject to the budget constraint. On the other hand, there is not much point in elaborate selection procedures if the cash-flow forecasts of the division are seriously biased.

Even if capital is not rationed, other resources may be. The availability of management time, skilled labor, or even other capital equipment often constitutes an important constraint on a company's growth.

---

[14] On our Web site at **www.mhhe.com/bma** we show how linear programming can be used to select from the four projects in our earlier example.

[15] Don't forget that in Chapter 1 we had to assume perfect capital markets to derive the NPV rule.

USEFUL SPREADSHEET FUNCTIONS

• • • • •

Internal Rate of Return

▶ Spreadsheet programs such as Excel provide built-in functions to solve for internal rates of return. You can find these functions by pressing *fx* on the Excel toolbar. If you then click on the function that you wish to use, Excel will guide you through the inputs that are required. At the bottom left of the function box there is a Help facility with an example of how the function is used.

Here is a list of useful functions for calculating internal rates of return, together with some points to remember when entering data:

- **IRR:** Internal rate of return on a series of regularly spaced cash flows.

- **XIRR:** The same as IRR, but for irregularly spaced flows.

Note the following:

- For these functions, you must enter the addresses of the cells that contain the input values.
- The IRR functions calculate only one IRR even when there are multiple IRRs.

SPREADSHEET QUESTIONS

The following questions provide an opportunity to practice each of the above functions:

5.1 (IRR) Check the IRRs on projects F and G in Section 5–3.

5.2 (IRR) What is the IRR of a project with the following cash flows:

C_0	C_1	C_2	C_3
−$5,000	+$2,200	+$4,650	+$3,330

5.3 (IRR) Now use the function to calculate the IRR on Helmsley Iron's mining project in Section 5–3. There are really two IRRs to this project (why?). How many IRRs does the function calculate?

5.4 (XIRR) What is the IRR of a project with the following cash flows:

C_0	C_4	C_5	C_6
−$215,000 ...	+$185,000 ...	+$85,000 ...	+$43,000

(All other cash flows are 0.)

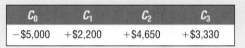

Hard Rationing   Soft rationing should never cost the firm anything. If capital constraints become tight enough to hurt—in the sense that projects with significant positive NPVs are passed up—then the firm raises more money and loosens the constraint. But what if it *can't* raise more money—what if it faces *hard* rationing?

Hard rationing implies market imperfections, but that does not necessarily mean we have to throw away net present value as a criterion for capital budgeting. It depends on the nature of the imperfection.

Arizona Aquaculture, Inc. (AAI), borrows as much as the banks will lend it, yet it still has good investment opportunities. This is not hard rationing so long as AAI can issue stock. But perhaps it can't. Perhaps the founder and majority shareholder vetoes the idea from fear of losing control of the firm. Perhaps a stock issue would bring costly red tape or legal complications.[16]

This does not invalidate the NPV rule. AAI's *shareholders* can borrow or lend, sell their shares, or buy more. They have free access to security markets. The type of portfolio they hold is independent of AAI's financing or investment decisions. The only way AAI can help its shareholders is to make them richer. Thus AAI should invest its available cash in the package of projects having the largest aggregate net present value.

A barrier between the firm and capital markets does not undermine net present value so long as the barrier is the *only* market imperfection. The important thing is that the firm's *shareholders* have free access to well-functioning capital markets.

The net present value rule *is* undermined when imperfections restrict shareholders' portfolio choice. Suppose that Nevada Aquaculture, Inc. (NAI), is solely owned by its founder, Alexander Turbot. Mr. Turbot has no cash or credit remaining, but he is convinced that expansion of his operation is a high-NPV investment. He has tried to sell stock but has found that prospective investors, skeptical of prospects for fish farming in the desert, offer him much less than he thinks his firm is worth. For Mr. Turbot capital markets hardly exist. It makes little sense for him to discount prospective cash flows at a market opportunity cost of capital.

---

[16] A majority owner who is "locked in" and has much personal wealth tied up in AAI may be effectively cut off from capital markets. The NPV rule may not make sense to such an owner, though it will to the other shareholders.

● ● ● ● ●

SUMMARY

If you are going to persuade your company to use the net present value rule, you must be prepared to explain why other rules may *not* lead to correct decisions. That is why we have examined three alternative investment criteria in this chapter.

Some firms look at the book rate of return on the project. In this case the company decides which cash payments are capital expenditures and picks the appropriate rate to depreciate these expenditures. It then calculates the ratio of book income to the book value of the investment. Few companies nowadays base their investment decision simply on the book rate of return, but shareholders pay attention to book measures of firm profitability and some managers therefore look with a jaundiced eye on projects that would damage the company's book rate of return.

Some companies use the payback method to make investment decisions. In other words, they accept only those projects that recover their initial investment within some specified period. Payback is an ad hoc rule. It ignores the timing of cash flows within the payback period, and it ignores subsequent cash flows entirely. It therefore takes no account of the opportunity cost of capital.

The internal rate of return (IRR) is defined as the rate of discount at which a project would have zero NPV. It is a handy measure and widely used in finance; you should therefore know how to calculate it. The IRR rule states that companies should accept any investment offering an IRR in excess of the opportunity cost of capital. The IRR rule is, like net present value, a technique based on discounted cash flows. It will therefore give the correct answer if properly used. The problem is that it is easily misapplied. There are four things to look out for:

1. *Lending or borrowing?* If a project offers positive cash flows followed by negative flows, NPV can *rise* as the discount rate is increased. You should accept such projects if their IRR is *less* than the opportunity cost of capital.

2. *Multiple rates of return.* If there is more than one change in the sign of the cash flows, the project may have several IRRs or no IRR at all.

3. *Mutually exclusive projects.* The IRR rule may give the wrong ranking of mutually exclusive projects that differ in economic life or in scale of required investment. If you insist on using IRR to rank mutually exclusive projects, you must examine the IRR on each incremental investment.

4. *The cost of capital for near-term cash flows may be different from the cost for distant cash flows.* The IRR rule requires you to compare the project's IRR with the opportunity cost of capital. But sometimes there is an opportunity cost of capital for one-year cash flows, a different cost of capital for two-year cash flows, and so on. In these cases there is no simple yardstick for evaluating the IRR of a project.

In developing the NPV rule, we assumed that the company can maximize shareholder wealth by accepting every project that is worth more than it costs. But, if capital is strictly limited, then it may not be possible to take every project with a positive NPV. If capital is rationed in only one period, then the firm should follow a simple rule: Calculate each project's profitability index, which is the project's net present value per dollar of investment. Then pick the projects with the highest profitability indexes until you run out of capital. Unfortunately, this procedure fails when capital is rationed in more than one period or when there are other constraints on project choice. The only general solution is linear programming.

Hard capital rationing always reflects a market imperfection—a barrier between the firm and capital markets. If that barrier also implies that the firm's shareholders lack free access to a well-functioning capital market, the very foundations of net present value crumble. Fortunately, hard rationing is rare for corporations in the United States. Many firms do use soft capital rationing, however. That is, they set up self-imposed limits as a means of financial planning and control.

● ● ● ● ●

FURTHER READING

For a survey of capital budgeting procedures, see:

J. Graham and C. Harvey, "How CFOs Make Capital Budgeting and Capital Structure Decisions," *Journal of Applied Corporate Finance* 15 (Spring 2002), pp. 8–23.

● ● ● ● ●

PROBLEM SETS

BASIC

1. a. What is the payback period on each of the following projects?

Project	C_0	C_1	C_2	C_3	C_4
			Cash Flows ($)		
A	−5,000	+1,000	+1,000	+3,000	0
B	−1,000	0	+1,000	+2,000	+3,000
C	−5,000	+1,000	+1,000	+3,000	+5,000

b. Given that you wish to use the payback rule with a cutoff period of two years, which projects would you accept?

c. If you use a cutoff period of three years, which projects would you accept?

d. If the opportunity cost of capital is 10%, which projects have positive NPVs?

e. "If a firm uses a single cutoff period for all projects, it is likely to accept too many short-lived projects." True or false?

f. If the firm uses the discounted-payback rule, will it accept any negative-NPV projects? Will it turn down positive-NPV projects? Explain.

2. Write down the equation defining a project's internal rate of return (IRR). In practice how is IRR calculated?

3. a. Calculate the net present value of the following project for discount rates of 0, 50, and 100%:

Cash Flows ($)		
C_0	C_1	C_2
−6,750	+4,500	+18,000

b. What is the IRR of the project?

4. You have the chance to participate in a project that produces the following cash flows:

Cash Flows ($)		
C_0	C_1	C_2
+5,000	+4,000	−11,000

The internal rate of return is 13%. If the opportunity cost of capital is 10%, would you accept the offer?

5. Consider a project with the following cash flows:

C_0	C_1	C_2
−100	+200	−75

a. How many internal rates of return does this project have?

b. Which of the following numbers is the project IRR?

(i) −50%; (ii) −12%; (iii) +5%; (iv) +50%

c. The opportunity cost of capital is 20%. Is this an attractive project? Briefly explain.

6. Consider projects Alpha and Beta:

Cash Flows ($)				
Project	C_0	C_1	C_2	IRR (%)
Alpha	−400,000	+241,000	+293,000	21
Beta	−200,000	+131,000	+172,000	31

The opportunity cost of capital is 8%.

Suppose you can undertake Alpha or Beta, but not both. Use the IRR rule to make the choice. (*Hint:* What's the incremental investment in Alpha?)

7. Suppose you have the following investment opportunities, but only $90,000 available for investment. Which projects should you take?

Project	NPV	Investment ($)
1	5,000	10,000
2	5,000	5,000
3	10,000	90,000
4	15,000	60,000
5	15,000	75,000
6	3,000	15,000

INTERMEDIATE

8. Consider the following projects:

Project			Cash Flows ($)			
	C_0	C_1	C_2	C_3	C_4	C_5
A	−1,000	+1,000	0	0	0	0
B	−2,000	+1,000	+1,000	+4,000	+1,000	+1,000
C	−3,000	+1,000	+1,000	0	+1,000	+1,000

a. If the opportunity cost of capital is 10%, which projects have a positive NPV?

b. Calculate the payback period for each project.

c. Which project(s) would a firm using the payback rule accept if the cutoff period were three years?

d. Calculate the discounted payback period for each project.

e. Which project(s) would a firm using the discounted payback rule accept if the cutoff period were three years?

9. Respond to the following comments:

a. "I like the IRR rule. I can use it to rank projects without having to specify a discount rate."

b. "I like the payback rule. As long as the minimum payback period is short, the rule makes sure that the company takes no borderline projects. That reduces risk."

Visit us at
www.mhhe.com/bma

10. Calculate the IRR (or IRRs) for the following project:

C_0	C_1	C_2	C_3
−3,000	+3,500	+4,000	−4,000

For what range of discount rates does the project have positive NPV?

11. Consider the following two mutually exclusive projects:

Project		Cash Flows ($)		
	C_0	C_1	C_2	C_3
A	−100	+60	+60	0
B	−100	0	0	+140

a. Calculate the NPV of each project for discount rates of 0, 10, and 20%. Plot these on a graph with NPV on the vertical axis and discount rate on the horizontal axis.

b. What is the approximate IRR for each project?

c. In what circumstances should the company accept project A?

d. Calculate the NPV of the incremental investment (B − A) for discount rates of 0, 10, and 20%. Plot these on your graph. Show that the circumstances in which you would accept A are also those in which the IRR on the incremental investment is less than the opportunity cost of capital.

12. Mr. Cyrus Clops, the president of Giant Enterprises, has to make a choice between two possible investments:

	Cash Flows ($ thousands)			
Project	C_0	C_1	C_2	IRR (%)
A	−400	+250	+300	23
B	−200	+140	+179	36

The opportunity cost of capital is 9%. Mr. Clops is tempted to take B, which has the higher IRR.

a. Explain to Mr. Clops why this is not the correct procedure.

b. Show him how to adapt the IRR rule to choose the best project.

c. Show him that this project also has the higher NPV.

13. The Titanic Shipbuilding Company has a noncancelable contract to build a small cargo vessel. Construction involves a cash outlay of $250,000 at the end of each of the next two years. At the end of the third year the company will receive payment of $650,000. The company can speed up construction by working an extra shift. In this case there will be a cash outlay of $550,000 at the end of the first year followed by a cash payment of $650,000 at the end of the second year. Use the IRR rule to show the (approximate) range of opportunity costs of capital at which the company should work the extra shift.

Visit us at
www.mhhe.com/bma

14. Look again at projects D and E in Section 5–3. Assume that the projects are mutually exclusive and that the opportunity cost of capital is 10%.

a. Calculate the profitability index for each project.

b. Show how the profitability-index rule can be used to select the superior project.

15. Borghia Pharmaceuticals has $1 million allocated for capital expenditures. Which of the following projects should the company accept to stay within the $1 million budget? How much does the budget limit cost the company in terms of its market value? The opportunity cost of capital for each project is 11%.

Project	Investment ($ thousands)	NPV ($ thousands)	IRR (%)
1	300	66	17.2
2	200	−4	10.7
3	250	43	16.6
4	100	14	12.1
5	100	7	11.8
6	350	63	18.0
7	400	48	13.5

CHALLENGE

16. Some people believe firmly, even passionately, that ranking projects on IRR is OK if each project's cash flows can be reinvested at the project's IRR. They also say that the NPV rule "assumes that cash flows are reinvested at the opportunity cost of capital." Think carefully about these statements. Are they true? Are they helpful?

17. Look again at the project cash flows in Problem 10. Calculate the modified IRR as defined in Footnote 4 in Section 5–3. Assume the cost of capital is 12%.

Now try the following variation on the MIRR concept. Figure out the fraction x such that x times C_1 and C_2 has the same present value as (minus) C_3.

$$xC_1 + \frac{xC_2}{1.12} = -\frac{C_3}{1.12^2}$$

Define the modified project IRR as the solution of

$$C_0 + \frac{(1-x)C_1}{1+\text{IRR}} + \frac{(1-x)C_2}{(1+\text{IRR})^2} = 0$$

Now you have two MIRRs. Which is more meaningful? If you can't decide, what do you conclude about the usefulness of MIRRs?

18. Consider the following capital rationing problem:

Project	C_0	C_1	C_2	NPV
W	−10,000	−10,000	0	+6,700
X	0	−20,000	+5,000	+9,000
Y	−10,000	+5,000	+5,000	+0
Z	−15,000	+5,000	+4,000	−1,500
Financing available	20,000	20,000	20,000	

Set up this problem as a linear program and solve it.

You can allow partial investments, that is, $0 \leq x \leq 1$. Calculate and interpret the shadow prices[17] on the capital constraints.

MINI-CASE ● ● ● ● ●

Vegetron's CFO Calls Again

(The first episode of this story was presented in Section 5–1.)

Later that afternoon, Vegetron's CFO bursts into your office in a state of anxious confusion. The problem, he explains, is a last-minute proposal for a change in the design of the fermentation tanks that Vegetron will build to extract hydrated zirconium from a stockpile of powdered ore. The CFO has brought a printout (Table 5.1) of the forecasted revenues, costs, income, and book rates of return for the standard, low-temperature design. Vegetron's engineers have just proposed an alternative high-temperature design that will extract most of the hydrated zirconium over a shorter period, five instead of seven years. The forecasts for the high-temperature method are given in Table 5.2 on page 126.[18]

---

[17] A shadow price is the marginal change in the objective for a marginal change in the constraint.

[18] For simplicity we have ignored taxes. There will be plenty about taxes in Chapter 6.

CFO: Why do these engineers always have a bright idea at the last minute? But you've got to admit the high-temperature process looks good. We'll get a faster payback, and the rate of return beats Vegetron's 9% cost of capital in every year except the first. Let's see, income is $30,000 per year. Average investment is half the $400,000 capital outlay, or $200,000, so the average rate of return is 30,000/200,000, or 15%—a lot better than the 9% hurdle rate. The average rate of return for the low-temperature process is not that good, only 28,000/200,000, or 14%. Of course we might get a higher rate of return for the low-temperature proposal if we depreciated the investment faster—do you think we should try that?

You: Let's not fixate on book accounting numbers. Book income is not the same as cash flow to Vegetron or its investors. Book rates of return don't measure the true rate of return.

CFO: But people use accounting numbers all the time. We have to publish them in our annual report to investors.

You: Accounting numbers have many valid uses, but they're not a sound basis for capital investment decisions. Accounting changes can have big effects on book income or rate of return, even when cash flows are unchanged.

　　Here's an example. Suppose the accountant depreciates the capital investment for the low-temperature process over six years rather than seven. Then income for years 1 to 6 goes down, because depreciation is higher. Income for year 7 goes up because the depreciation for that year becomes zero. But there is no effect on year-to-year cash flows, because depreciation is not a cash outlay. It is simply the accountant's device for spreading out the "recovery" of the up-front capital outlay over the life of the project.

CFO: So how do we get cash flows?

You: In these cases it's easy. Depreciation is the only noncash entry in your spreadsheets (Tables 5.1 and 5.2), so we can just leave it out of the calculation. Cash flow equals revenue minus operating costs. For the high-temperature process, annual cash flow is:

$$\text{Cash flow} = \text{revenue} - \text{operating cost} = 180 - 70 = 110, \text{ or } \$110,000$$

CFO: In effect you're adding back depreciation, because depreciation is a noncash accounting expense.

You: Right. You could also do it that way:

$$\text{Cash flow} = \text{net income} + \text{depreciation} = 30 + 80 = 110, \text{ or } \$110,000$$

CFO: Of course. I remember all this now, but book returns seem important when someone shoves them in front of your nose.

	Year						
	1	**2**	**3**	**4**	**5**	**6**	**7**
1. Revenue	140	140	140	140	140	140	140
2. Operating costs	55	55	55	55	55	55	55
3. Depreciation*	57	57	57	57	57	57	57
4. Net income	28	28	28	28	28	28	28
5. Start-of-year book value†	400	343	286	229	171	114	57
6. Book rate of return (4 ÷ 5)	7%	8.2%	9.8%	12.2%	16.4%	24.6%	49.1%

▶ **TABLE 5.1**　Income statement and book rates of return for low-temperature extraction of hydrated zirconium ($ thousands).

* Rounded. Straight-line depreciation over seven years is 400/7 = 57.14, or $57,140 per year.
† Capital investment is $400,000 in year 0.

	Year				
	1	**2**	**3**	**4**	**5**
1. Revenue	180	180	180	180	180
2. Operating costs	70	70	70	70	70
3. Depreciation*	80	80	80	80	80
4. Net income	30	30	30	30	30
5. Start-of-year book value†	400	320	240	160	80
6. Book rate of return (4 ÷ 5)	7.5%	9.4%	12.5%	18.75%	37.5%

▶ **TABLE 5.2**   Income statement and book rates of return for high-temperature extraction of hydrated zirconium ($ thousands).

* Straight-line depreciation over five years is 400/5 = 80, or $80,000 per year.
† Capital investment is $400,000 in year 0.

You: It's not clear which project is better. The high-temperature process appears to be less efficient. It has higher operating costs and generates less total revenue over the life of the project, but of course it generates more cash flow in years 1 to 5.

CFO: Maybe the processes are equally good from a financial point of view. If so we'll stick with the low-temperature process rather than switching at the last minute.

You: We'll have to lay out the cash flows and calculate NPV for each process.

CFO: OK, do that. I'll be back in a half hour—and I also want to see each project's true, DCF rate of return.

QUESTIONS

1. Are the book rates of return reported in Tables 5.1 and 5.2 useful inputs for the capital investment decision?

2. Calculate NPV and IRR for each process. What is your recommendation? Be ready to explain to the CFO.

VALUE

Making Investment Decisions with the Net Present Value Rule

▶ **In late 2003** Boeing announced its intention to produce and market the 787 Dreamliner. The decision committed Boeing and its partners to a $10 billion capital investment, involving 3 million square feet of additional facilities. If the technical glitches that have delayed production can be sorted out, it looks as if Boeing will earn a good return on this investment. As we write this in August 2009, Boeing has booked orders for 865 Dreamliners, making it one of the most successful aircraft launches in history.

How does a company, such as Boeing, decide to go ahead with the launch of a new airliner? We know the answer in principle. The company needs to forecast the project's cash flows and discount them at the opportunity cost of capital to arrive at the project's NPV. A project with a positive NPV increases shareholder value.

But those cash flow forecasts do not arrive on a silver platter. First, the company's managers need answers to a number of basic questions. How soon can the company get the plane into production? How many planes are likely to be sold each year and at what price? How much does the firm need to invest in new production facilities, and what is the likely production cost? How long will the model stay in production, and what happens to the plant and equipment at the end of that time?

These predictions need to be checked for completeness and accuracy, and then pulled together to produce a single set of cash-flow forecasts. That requires careful tracking of taxes, changes in working capital, inflation, and the end-of-project salvage values of plant, property, and equipment. The financial manager must also ferret out hidden cash flows and take care to reject accounting entries that look like cash flows but truly are not.

Our first task in this chapter is to look at how to develop a set of project cash flows. We will then work through a realistic and comprehensive example of a capital investment analysis.

We conclude the chapter by looking at how the financial manager should apply the present value rule when choosing between investment in plant and equipment with different economic lives. For example, suppose you must decide between machine Y with a 5-year useful life and Z with a 10-year life. The present value of Y's lifetime investment and operating costs is naturally less than Z's because Z will last twice as long. Does that necessarily make Y the better choice? Of course not. You will find that, when you are faced with this type of problem, the trick is to transform the present value of the cash flow into an *equivalent annual* flow, that is, the total cash per year from buying and operating the asset.

● ● ● ● ●

Many projects require a heavy initial outlay on new production facilities. But often the largest investments involve the acquisition of intangible assets. Consider, for example, the expenditure by major banks on information technology. These projects can soak up hundreds of millions of dollars. Yet much of the expenditure goes to intangibles such as system design, programming, testing, and training. Think also of the huge expenditure by pharmaceutical companies on research and development (R&D). Pfizer, one of the largest pharmaceutical companies, spent $7.9 billion on R&D in 2008. The R&D cost of bringing *one* new prescription drug to market has been estimated at $800 million.

Expenditures on intangible assets such as IT and R&D are investments just like expenditures on new plant and equipment. In each case the company is spending money today in the expectation that it will generate a stream of future profits. Ideally, firms should apply the same criteria to all capital investments, regardless of whether they involve a tangible or intangible asset.

We have seen that an investment in any asset creates wealth if the discounted value of the future cash flows exceeds the up-front cost. But up to this point we have glossed over the problem of *what* to discount. When you are faced with this problem, you should stick to three general rules:

1. Only cash flow is relevant.
2. Always estimate cash flows on an incremental basis.
3. Treat inflation consistently.

We discuss each of these rules in turn.

Rule 1: Only Cash Flow Is Relevant

The first and most important point: Net present value depends on future cash flows. Cash flow is the simplest possible concept; it is just the difference between cash received and cash paid out. Many people nevertheless confuse cash flow with accounting income.

Income statements are intended to show how well the company is performing. Therefore, accountants *start* with "dollars in" and "dollars out," but to obtain accounting income they adjust these inputs in two ways. First, they try to show profit as it is *earned* rather than when the company and its customers get around to paying their bills. Second, they sort cash outflows into two categories: current expenses and capital expenses. They deduct current expenses when calculating income but do not deduct capital expenses. There is a good reason for this. If the firm lays out a large amount of money on a big capital project, you do not conclude that the firm is performing poorly, even though a lot of cash is going out the door. Therefore, the accountant does not deduct capital expenditure when calculating the year's income but, instead, depreciates it over several years.

As a result of these adjustments, income includes some cash flows and excludes others, and it is reduced by depreciation charges, which are not cash flows at all. It is not always easy to translate the customary accounting data back into actual dollars—dollars you can buy beer with. If you are in doubt about what is a cash flow, simply count the dollars coming in and take away the dollars going out. Don't assume without checking that you can find cash flow by routine manipulations of accounting data.

Always estimate cash flows on an after-tax basis. Some firms do not deduct tax payments. They try to offset this mistake by discounting the cash flows before taxes at a rate higher than the opportunity cost of capital. Unfortunately, there is no reliable formula for making such adjustments to the discount rate.

You should also make sure that cash flows are recorded *only when they occur* and not when work is undertaken or a liability is incurred. For example, taxes should be discounted from their actual payment date, not from the time when the tax liability is recorded in the firm's books.

Rule 2: Always Estimate Cash Flows on an Incremental Basis

The value of a project depends on *all* the additional cash flows that follow from project acceptance. Here are some things to watch for when you are deciding which cash flows to include:

Do Not Confuse Average with Incremental Payoffs   Most managers naturally hesitate to throw good money after bad. For example, they are reluctant to invest more money in a losing division. But occasionally you will encounter turnaround opportunities in which the *incremental* NPV from investing in a loser is strongly positive.

Conversely, it does not always make sense to throw good money after good. A division with an outstanding past profitability record may have run out of good opportunities. You would not pay a large sum for a 20-year-old horse, sentiment aside, regardless of how many races that horse had won or how many champions it had sired.

Here is another example illustrating the difference between average and incremental returns: Suppose that a railroad bridge is in urgent need of repair. With the bridge the railroad can continue to operate; without the bridge it can't. In this case the payoff from the repair work consists of all the benefits of operating the railroad. The incremental NPV of such an investment may be enormous. Of course, these benefits should be net of all other costs and all subsequent repairs; otherwise the company may be misled into rebuilding an unprofitable railroad piece by piece.

Include All Incidental Effects   It is important to consider a project's effects on the remainder of the firm's business. For example, suppose Sony proposes to launch PlayStation 4, a new version of its video game console. Demand for the new product will almost certainly cut into sales of Sony's existing consoles. This incidental effect needs to be factored into the incremental cash flows. Of course, Sony may reason that it needs to go ahead with the new product because its existing product line is likely to come under increasing threat from competitors. So, even if it decides not to produce the new PlayStation, there is no guarantee that sales of the existing consoles will continue at their present level. Sooner or later they will decline.

Sometimes a new project will *help* the firm's existing business. Suppose that you are the financial manager of an airline that is considering opening a new short-haul route from Peoria, Illinois, to Chicago's O'Hare Airport. When considered in isolation, the new route may have a negative NPV. But once you allow for the additional business that the new route brings to your other traffic out of O'Hare, it may be a very worthwhile investment.

Forecast Sales Today and Recognize After-Sales Cash Flows to Come Later   Financial managers should forecast all incremental cash flows generated by an investment. Sometimes these incremental cash flows last for decades. When GE commits to the design and production of a new jet engine, the cash inflows come first from the sale of engines and then from service and spare parts. A jet engine will be in use for 30 years. Over that period revenues from service and spare parts will be roughly seven times the engine's purchase price. GE's revenue in 2008 from commercial engine services was $6.8 billion versus $5.2 billion from commercial engine sales.[1]

Many manufacturing companies depend on the revenues that come *after* their products are sold. The consulting firm Accenture estimates that services and parts typically account for about 25% of revenues and 50% of profits for industrial companies.

---

[1] P. Glader, "GE's Focus on Services Faces Test," *The Wall Street Journal*, March 3, 2009, p. B1. The following estimate from Accenture also comes from this article.

Do Not Forget Working Capital Requirements   **Net working capital** (often referred to simply as *working capital*) is the difference between a company's short-term assets and liabilities. The principal short-term assets are accounts receivable (customers' unpaid bills) and inventories of raw materials and finished goods. The principal short-term liabilities are accounts payable (bills that *you* have not paid). Most projects entail an additional investment in working capital. This investment should, therefore, be recognized in your cash-flow forecasts. By the same token, when the project comes to an end, you can usually recover some of the investment. This is treated as a cash inflow. We supply a numerical example of working-capital investment later in this chapter.

Include Opportunity Costs   The cost of a resource may be relevant to the investment decision even when no cash changes hands. For example, suppose a new manufacturing operation uses land that could otherwise be sold for $100,000. This resource is not free: It has an opportunity cost, which is the cash it could generate for the company if the project were rejected and the resource were sold or put to some other productive use.

   This example prompts us to warn you against judging projects on the basis of "before versus after." The proper comparison is "with or without." A manager comparing before versus after might not assign any value to the land because the firm owns it both before and after:

Before	Take Project	After	Cash Flow, Before versus After
Firm owns land	→	Firm still owns land	0

The proper comparison, with or without, is as follows:

With	Take Project	After	Cash Flow, with Project
Firm owns land	→	Firm still owns land	0

Without	Do Not Take Project	After	Cash Flow, without Project
	→	Firm sells land for $100,000	$100,000

Comparing the two possible "afters," we see that the firm gives up $100,000 by undertaking the project. This reasoning still holds if the land will not be sold but is worth $100,000 to the firm in some other use.

   Sometimes opportunity costs may be very difficult to estimate; however, where the resource can be freely traded, its opportunity cost is simply equal to the market price. Why? It cannot be otherwise. If the value of a parcel of land to the firm is less than its market price, the firm will sell it. On the other hand, the opportunity cost of using land in a particular project cannot exceed the cost of buying an equivalent parcel to replace it.

Forget Sunk Costs   Sunk costs are like spilled milk: They are past and irreversible outflows. Because sunk costs are bygones, they cannot be affected by the decision to accept or reject the project, and so they should be ignored.

   For example, when Lockheed sought a federal guarantee for a bank loan to continue development of the TriStar airplane, the company and its supporters argued it would be foolish to abandon a project on which nearly $1 billion had already been spent. Some of Lockheed's critics countered that it would be equally foolish to continue with a project that offered no prospect of a satisfactory return on that $1 billion. Both groups were guilty of the *sunk-cost fallacy;* the $1 billion was irrecoverable and, therefore, irrelevant.

Beware of Allocated Overhead Costs   We have already mentioned that the accountant's objective is not always the same as the investment analyst's. A case in point is the allocation of overhead costs. Overheads include such items as supervisory salaries, rent, heat, and light. These overheads may not be related to any particular project, but they have to be paid for somehow. Therefore, when the accountant assigns costs to the firm's projects, a charge for overhead is usually made. Now our principle of incremental cash flows says that in investment appraisal we should include only the *extra* expenses that would result from the project. A project may generate extra overhead expenses; then again, it may not. We should be cautious about assuming that the accountant's allocation of overheads represents the true extra expenses that would be incurred.

Remember Salvage Value   When the project comes to an end, you may be able to sell the plant and equipment or redeploy the assets elsewhere in the business. If the equipment is sold, you must pay tax on the difference between the sale price and the book value of the asset. The salvage value (net of any taxes) represents a positive cash flow to the firm.

Some projects have significant shut-down costs, in which case the final cash flows may be *negative*. For example, the mining company, FCX, has earmarked over $430 million to cover the future reclamation and closure costs of its New Mexico mines.

Rule 3: Treat Inflation Consistently

As we pointed out in Chapter 3, interest rates are usually quoted in *nominal* rather than *real* terms. For example, if you buy an 8% Treasury bond, the government promises to pay you $80 interest each year, but it does not promise what that $80 will buy. Investors take inflation into account when they decide what is an acceptable rate of interest.

If the discount rate is stated in nominal terms, then consistency requires that cash flows should also be estimated in nominal terms, taking account of trends in selling price, labor and materials costs, etc. This calls for more than simply applying a single assumed inflation rate to all components of cash flow. Labor costs per hour of work, for example, normally increase at a faster rate than the consumer price index because of improvements in productivity. Tax savings from depreciation do *not* increase with inflation; they are constant in nominal terms because tax law in the United States allows only the original cost of assets to be depreciated.

Of course, there is nothing wrong with discounting real cash flows at a real discount rate. In fact this is standard procedure in countries with high and volatile inflation. Here is a simple example showing that real and nominal discounting, properly applied, always give the same present value.

Suppose your firm usually forecasts cash flows in nominal terms and discounts at a 15% nominal rate. In this particular case, however, you are given project cash flows in real terms, that is, current dollars:

Real Cash Flows ($ thousands)			
C_0	C_1	C_2	C_3
−100	+35	+50	+30

It would be inconsistent to discount these real cash flows at the 15% nominal rate. You have two alternatives: Either restate the cash flows in nominal terms and discount at 15%, or restate the discount rate in real terms and use it to discount the real cash flows.

Assume that inflation is projected at 10% a year. Then the cash flow for year 1, which is $35,000 in current dollars, will be $35,000 \times 1.10 = \$38,500$ in year-1 dollars. Similarly the cash flow for year 2 will be 50,000 × (1.10)^2 = $60,500 in year-2 dollars, and so on. If we discount these nominal cash flows at the 15% nominal discount rate, we have

$$NPV = -100 + \frac{38.5}{1.15} + \frac{60.5}{(1.15)^2} + \frac{39.9}{(1.15)^3} = 5.5, \text{ or } \$5,500$$

Instead of converting the cash-flow forecasts into nominal terms, we could convert the discount rate into real terms by using the following relationship:

$$\text{Real discount rate} = \frac{1 + \text{nominal discount rate}}{1 + \text{inflation rate}} - 1$$

In our example this gives

$$\text{Real discount rate} = \frac{1.15}{1.10} - 1 = .045, \text{ or } 4.5\%$$

If we now discount the real cash flows by the real discount rate, we have an NPV of $5,500, just as before:

$$NPV = -100 + \frac{35}{1.045} + \frac{50}{(1.045)^2} + \frac{30}{(1.045)^3} = 5.5, \text{ or } \$5,500$$

The message of all this is quite simple. Discount nominal cash flows at a nominal discount rate. Discount real cash flows at a real rate. *Never* mix real cash flows with nominal discount rates or nominal flows with real rates.

6-2 Example—IM&C's Fertilizer Project

As the newly appointed financial manager of International Mulch and Compost Company (IM&C), you are about to analyze a proposal for marketing guano as a garden fertilizer. (IM&C's planned advertising campaign features a rustic gentleman who steps out of a vegetable patch singing, "All my troubles have guano way.")[2]

You are given the forecasts shown in Table 6.1.[3] The project requires an investment of $10 million in plant and machinery (line 1). This machinery can be dismantled and sold for net proceeds estimated at $1.949 million in year 7 (line 1, column 7). This amount is your forecast of the plant's *salvage value.*

Whoever prepared Table 6.1 depreciated the capital investment over six years to an arbitrary salvage value of $500,000, which is less than your forecast of salvage value. *Straight-line depreciation* was assumed. Under this method annual depreciation equals a constant proportion of the initial investment less salvage value ($9.5 million). If we call the depreciable life T, then the straight-line depreciation in year t is

Depreciation in year $t = 1/T \times$ depreciable amount $= 1/6 \times 9.5 = \$1.583$ million

Lines 6 through 12 in Table 6.1 show a simplified income statement for the guano project.[4] This will be our starting point for estimating cash flow. All the entries in the table are nominal amounts. In other words, IM&C's managers have taken into account the likely effect of inflation on prices and costs.

---

[2] Sorry.

[3] "Live" Excel versions of Tables 6.1, 6.2, 6.4, 6.5, and 6.6 are available on the book's Web site, www.mhhe.com/bma.

[4] We have departed from the usual income-statement format by separating depreciation from costs of goods sold.

Table 6.2 derives cash-flow forecasts from the investment and income data given in Table 6.1. The project's net cash flow is the sum of three elements:

$$\text{Net cash flow} = \text{cash flow from capital investment and disposal}$$
$$+ \text{cash flow from changes in working capital}$$
$$+ \text{operating cash flow}$$

		Period							
		0	1	2	3	4	5	6	7
1	Capital investment	10,000							−1,949[a]
2	Accumulated depreciation		1,583	3,167	4,750	6,333	7,917	9,500	0
3	Year-end book value	10,000	8,417	6,833	5,250	3,667	2,083	500	0
4	Working capital		550	1,289	3,261	4,890	3,583	2,002	0
5	Total book value (3 + 4)		8,967	8,122	8,511	8,557	5,666	2,502	0
6	Sales		523	12,887	32,610	48,901	35,834	19,717	
7	Cost of goods sold[b]		837	7,729	19,552	29,345	21,492	11,830	
8	Other costs[c]	4,000	2,200	1,210	1,331	1,464	1,611	1,772	
9	Depreciation		1,583	1,583	1,583	1,583	1,583	1,583	0
10	Pretax profit (6 − 7 − 8 − 9)	−4,000	−4,097	2,365	10,144	16,509	11,148	4,532	1,449[d]
11	Tax at 35%	−1,400	−1,434	828	3,550	5,778	3,902	1,586	507
12	Profit after tax (10 − 11)	−2,600	−2,663	1,537	6,593	10,731	7,246	2,946	942

▶ **TABLE 6.1** IM&C's guano project—projections ($ thousands) reflecting inflation and assuming straight-line depreciation.

Visit us at
www.mhhe.com/bma

[a] Salvage value.
[b] We have departed from the usual income-statement format by *not* including depreciation in cost of goods sold. Instead, we break out depreciation separately (see line 9).
[c] Start-up costs in years 0 and 1, and general and administrative costs in years 1 to 6.
[d] The difference between the salvage value and the ending book value of $500 is a taxable profit.

		Period							
		0	1	2	3	4	5	6	7
1	Capital investment and disposal	−10,000	0	0	0	0	0	0	1,442[a]
2	Change in working capital		−550	−739	−1,972	−1,629	1,307	1,581	2,002
3	Sales	0	523	12,887	32,610	48,901	35,834	19,717	0
4	Cost of goods sold	0	837	7,729	19,552	29,345	21,492	11,830	0
5	Other costs	4,000	2,200	1,210	1,331	1,464	1,611	1,772	0
6	Tax	−1,400	−1,434	828	3,550	5,778	3,902	1,586	
7	Operating cash flow (3 − 4 − 5 − 6)	−2,600	−1,080	3,120	8,177	12,314	8,829	4,529	
8	Net cash flow (1 + 2 + 7)	−12,600	−1,630	2,381	6,205	10,685	10,136	6,110	3,444
9	Present value at 20%	−12,600	−1,358	1,654	3,591	5,153	4,074	2,046	961
10	Net present value =	+3,520	(sum of 9)						

▶ **TABLE 6.2** IM&C's guano project—initial cash-flow analysis assuming straight-line depreciation ($ thousands).

Visit us at
www.mhhe.com/bma

[a] Salvage value of $1,949 less tax of $507 on the difference between salvage value and ending book value.

Each of these items is shown in the table. Row 1 shows the initial capital investment and the estimated salvage value of the equipment when the project comes to an end. If, as you expect, the salvage value is higher than the depreciated value of the machinery, you will have to pay tax on the difference. So the salvage value in row 1 is shown after payment of this tax. Row 2 of the table shows the changes in working capital, and the remaining rows calculate the project's operating cash flows.

Notice that in calculating the operating cash flows we did not deduct depreciation. Depreciation is an accounting entry. It affects the tax that the company pays, but the firm does not send anyone a check for depreciation. The operating cash flow is simply the dollars coming in less the dollars going out:[5]

$$\text{Operating cash flow} = \text{revenues} - \text{cash expenses} - \text{taxes}$$

For example, in year 6 of the guano project:

$$\text{Operating cash flow} = 19,717 - (11,830 + 1,772) - 1,586 = 4,529$$

IM&C estimates the nominal opportunity cost of capital for projects of this type as 20%. When all cash flows are added up and discounted, the guano project is seen to offer a net present value of about $3.5 million:

$$\text{NPV} = -12,600 - \frac{1,630}{1.20} + \frac{2,381}{(1.20)^2} + \frac{6,205}{(1.20)^3} + \frac{10,685}{(1.20)^4} + \frac{10,136}{(1.20)^5}$$

$$+ \frac{6,110}{(1.20)^6} + \frac{3,444}{(1.20)^7} = +3,520, \text{ or } \$3,520,000$$

Separating Investment and Financing Decisions

Our analysis of the guano project takes no notice of how that project is financed. It may be that IM&C will decide to finance partly by debt, but if it does we will not subtract the debt proceeds from the required investment, nor will we recognize interest and principal payments as cash outflows. We analyze the project as if it were all-equity-financed, treating all cash outflows as coming from stockholders and all cash inflows as going to them.

We approach the problem in this way so that we can separate the analysis of the investment decision from the financing decision. But this does not mean that the financing decision can be ignored. We explain in Chapter 15 how to recognize the effect of financing choices on project values.

Investments in Working Capital

Now here is an important point. You can see from line 2 of Table 6.2 that working capital increases in the early and middle years of the project. What is working capital, you may ask, and why does it increase?

Working capital summarizes the net investment in short-term assets associated with a firm, business, or project. Its most important components are *inventory, accounts receivable,*

[5] There are several alternative ways to calculate operating cash flow. For example, you can add depreciation back to the after-tax profit:

$$\text{Operating cash flow} = \text{after-tax profit} + \text{depreciation}$$

Thus, in year 6 of the guano project:

$$\text{Operating cash flow} = 2,946 + 1,583 = 4,529$$

Another alternative is to calculate after-tax profit assuming *no* depreciation, and then to add back the tax saving provided by the depreciation allowance:

$$\text{Operating cash flow} = (\text{revenues} - \text{expenses}) \times (1 - \text{tax rate}) + (\text{depreciation} \times \text{tax rate})$$

Thus, in year 6 of the guano project:

$$\text{Operating cash flow} = (19,717 - 11,830 - 1,772) \times (1 - .35) + (1,583 \times .35) = 4,529$$

and *accounts payable*. The guano project's requirements for working capital in year 2 might be as follows:

$$\text{Working capital} = \text{inventory} + \text{accounts receivable} - \text{accounts payable}$$
$$\$1,289 = 635 \qquad\quad + 1,030 \qquad\qquad\quad - 376$$

Why does working capital increase? There are several possibilities:

1. Sales recorded on the income statement overstate actual cash receipts from guano shipments because sales are increasing and customers are slow to pay their bills. Therefore, accounts receivable increase.

2. It takes several months for processed guano to age properly. Thus, as projected sales increase, larger inventories have to be held in the aging sheds.

3. An offsetting effect occurs if payments for materials and services used in guano production are delayed. In this case accounts payable will increase.

The additional investment in working capital from year 2 to 3 might be

$$\begin{matrix} \text{Additional} & & & & \text{increase in} & & \text{increase in} \\ \text{investment in} & = & \text{increase in} & + & \text{accounts} & - & \text{accounts} \\ \text{working capital} & & \text{inventory} & & \text{receivable} & & \text{payable} \\ \$1,972 & = & 972 & + & 1,500 & - & 500 \end{matrix}$$

A more detailed cash-flow forecast for year 3 would look like Table 6.3.

Working capital is one of the most common sources of confusion in estimating project cash flows. Here are the most common mistakes:

1. *Forgetting about working capital entirely.* We hope you never fall into that trap.

2. *Forgetting that working capital may change during the life of the project.* Imagine that you sell $100,000 of goods one year and that customers pay six months late. You will therefore have $50,000 of unpaid bills. Now you increase prices by 10%, so revenues increase to $110,000. If customers continue to pay six months late, unpaid bills increase to $55,000, and therefore you need to make an *additional* investment in working capital of $5,000.

3. *Forgetting that working capital is recovered at the end of the project.* When the project comes to an end, inventories are run down, any unpaid bills are paid off (you hope), and you recover your investment in working capital. This generates a cash *inflow*.

There is an alternative to worrying about changes in working capital. You can estimate cash flow directly by counting the dollars coming in from customers and deducting the dollars

Cash Flows		Data from Forecasted Income Statement		Working-Capital Changes
Cash inflow	=	Sales	−	Increase in accounts receivable
$31,110	=	32,610	−	1,500
Cash outflow	=	Cost of goods sold, other costs, and taxes	+	Increase in inventory net of increase in accounts payable
$24,905	=	(19,552 + 1,331 + 3,550)	+	(972 − 500)

Net cash flow = cash inflow − cash outflow
$6,205 = 31,110 − 24,905

▶ **TABLE 6.3**   Details of cash-flow forecast for IM&C's guano project in year 3 ($ thousands).

going out to suppliers. You would also deduct all cash spent on production, including cash spent for goods held in inventory. In other words,

1. If you replace each year's sales with that year's cash payments received from customers, you don't have to worry about accounts receivable.
2. If you replace cost of goods sold with cash payments for labor, materials, and other costs of production, you don't have to keep track of inventory or accounts payable.

However, you would still have to construct a projected income statement to estimate taxes.

A Further Note on Depreciation

Depreciation is a noncash expense; it is important only because it reduces taxable income. It provides an annual *tax shield* equal to the product of depreciation and the marginal tax rate:

$$\text{Tax shield} = \text{depreciation} \times \text{tax rate}$$
$$= 1{,}583 \times .35 = 554, \text{ or } \$554{,}000$$

The present value of the tax shields ($554,000 for six years) is $1,842,000 at a 20% discount rate.

Now if IM&C could just get those tax shields sooner, they would be worth more, right? Fortunately tax law allows corporations to do just that: It allows *accelerated depreciation.*

The current rules for tax depreciation in the United States were set by the Tax Reform Act of 1986, which established a Modified Accelerated Cost Recovery System (MACRS). Table 6.4 summarizes the tax depreciation schedules. Note that there are six schedules, one for each recovery period class. Most industrial equipment falls into the five- and seven-year classes. To keep things simple, we assume that all the guano project's investment goes into five-year assets. Thus, IM&C can write off 20% of its depreciable investment in year 1, as soon as the assets are placed in service, then 32% of depreciable investment in year 2, and so on. Here are the tax shields for the guano project:

	Year					
	1	**2**	**3**	**4**	**5**	**6**
Tax depreciation (MACRS percentage × depreciable investment)	2,000	3,200	1,920	1,152	1,152	576
Tax shield (tax depreciation × tax rate, $T_c = .35$)	700	1,120	672	403	403	202

The present value of these tax shields is $2,174,000, about $331,000 higher than under the straight-line method.

Table 6.5 recalculates the guano project's impact on IM&C's future tax bills, and Table 6.6 shows revised after-tax cash flows and present value. This time we have incorporated realistic assumptions about taxes as well as inflation. We arrive at a higher NPV than in Table 6.2, because that table ignored the additional present value of accelerated depreciation.

There is one possible additional problem lurking in the woodwork behind Table 6.5: In the United States there is an *alternative minimum tax,* which can limit or defer the tax shields of accelerated depreciation or other *tax preference* items. We don't want to get into the mechanics of the alternative minimum tax, but make a mental note not to sign off on a capital budgeting analysis without checking whether your company is subject to the alternative minimum tax.

Tax Depreciation Schedules by Recovery-Period Class						
Year(s)	3-year	5-year	7-year	10-year	15-year	20-year
1	33.33	20.00	14.29	10.00	5.00	3.75
2	44.45	32.00	24.49	18.00	9.50	7.22
3	14.81	19.20	17.49	14.40	8.55	6.68
4	7.41	11.52	12.49	11.52	7.70	6.18
5		11.52	8.93	9.22	6.93	5.71
6		5.76	8.92	7.37	6.23	5.28
7			8.93	6.55	5.90	4.89
8			4.46	6.55	5.90	4.52
9				6.56	5.91	4.46
10				6.55	5.90	4.46
11				3.28	5.91	4.46
12					5.90	4.46
13					5.91	4.46
14					5.90	4.46
15					5.91	4.46
16					2.95	4.46
17-20						4.46
21						2.23

▶ **TABLE 6.4**   Tax depreciation allowed under the modified accelerated cost recovery system (MACRS) (figures in percent of depreciable investment).

Notes:

1. Tax depreciation is lower in the first and last years because assets are assumed to be in service for only six months.

2. Real property is depreciated straight-line over 27.5 years for residential property and 39 years for nonresidential property.

Visit us at www.mhhe.com/bma

		Period							
		0	1	2	3	4	5	6	7
1	Sales[a]		523	12,887	32,610	48,901	35,834	19,717	
2	Cost of goods sold[a]		837	7,729	19,552	29,345	21,492	11,830	
3	Other costs[a]	4,000	2,200	1,210	1,331	1,464	1,611	1,772	
4	Tax depreciation		2,000	3,200	1,920	1,152	1,152	576	
5	Pretax profit (1 − 2 − 3 − 4)	−4,000	−4,514	748	9,807	16,940	11,579	5,539	1,949[b]
6	Tax at 35%[c]	−1,400	−1,580	262	3,432	5,929	4,053	1,939	682

▶ **TABLE 6.5**   Tax payments on IM&C's guano project ($ thousands).

Visit us at www.mhhe.com/bma

[a] From Table 6.1.
[b] Salvage value is zero, for tax purposes, after all tax depreciation has been taken. Thus, IM&C will have to pay tax on the full salvage value of $1,949.
[c] A negative tax payment means a cash *inflow*, assuming IM&C can use the tax loss on its guano project to shield income from other projects.

A Final Comment on Taxes

All large U.S. corporations keep two separate sets of books, one for stockholders and one for the Internal Revenue Service. It is common to use straight-line depreciation on the stockholder books and accelerated depreciation on the tax books. The IRS doesn't object to this, and it makes the firm's reported earnings higher than if accelerated depreciation were used everywhere. There are many other differences between tax books and shareholder books.[6]

---

[6] This separation of tax accounts from shareholder accounts is not found worldwide. In Japan, for example, taxes reported to shareholders must equal taxes paid to the government; ditto for France and many other European countries.

		Period							
		0	1	2	3	4	5	6	7
1	Capital investment and disposal	−10,000	0	0	0	0	0	0	1,949
2	Change in working capital		−550	−739	−1,972	−1,629	1,307	1,581	2,002
3	Sales[a]	0	523	12,887	32,610	48,901	35,834	19,717	0
4	Cost of goods sold[a]	0	837	7,729	19,552	29,345	21,492	11,830	0
5	Other costs[a]	4,000	2,200	1,210	1,331	1,464	1,611	1,772	0
6	Tax[b]	−1,400	−1,580	262	3,432	5,929	4,053	1,939	682
7	Operating cash flow (3 − 4 − 5 − 6)	−2,600	−934	3,686	8,295	12,163	8,678	4,176	−682
8	Net cash flow (1 + 2 + 7)	−12,600	−1,484	2,947	6,323	10,534	9,985	5,757	3,269
9	Present value at 20%	−12,600	−1,237	2,047	3,659	5,080	4,013	1,928	912
10	Net present value =	3,802	(sum of 9)						

▶ **TABLE 6.6** IM&C's guano project—revised cash-flow analysis ($ thousands).

Visit us at
www.mhhe.com/bma

[a] From Table 6.1.
[b] From Table 6.5.

The financial analyst must be careful to remember which set of books he or she is looking at. In capital budgeting only the tax books are relevant, but to an outside analyst only the shareholder books are available.

Project Analysis

Let us review. Several pages ago, you embarked on an analysis of IM&C's guano project. You started with a simplified statement of assets and income for the project that you used to develop a series of cash-flow forecasts. Then you remembered accelerated depreciation and had to recalculate cash flows and NPV.

You were lucky to get away with just two NPV calculations. In real situations, it often takes several tries to purge all inconsistencies and mistakes. Then you may want to analyze some alternatives. For example, should you go for a larger or smaller project? Would it be better to market the fertilizer through wholesalers or directly to the consumer? Should you build 90,000-square-foot aging sheds for the guano in northern South Dakota rather than the planned 100,000-square-foot sheds in southern North Dakota? In each case your choice should be the one offering the highest NPV. Sometimes the alternatives are not immediately obvious. For example, perhaps the plan calls for two costly high-speed packing lines. But, if demand for guano is seasonal, it may pay to install just one high-speed line to cope with the base demand and two slower but cheaper lines simply to cope with the summer rush. You won't know the answer until you have compared NPVs.

You will also need to ask some "what if" questions. How would NPV be affected if inflation rages out of control? What if technical problems delay start-up? What if gardeners prefer chemical fertilizers to your natural product? Managers employ a variety of techniques to develop a better understanding of how such unpleasant surprises could damage NPV. For example, they might undertake a *sensitivity analysis,* in which they look at how far the project could be knocked off course by bad news about one of the variables. Or they might construct different *scenarios* and estimate the effect of each on NPV. Another technique, known as *break-even analysis,* is to explore how far sales could fall short of forecast before the project went into the red.

In Chapter 10 we practice using each of these "what if" techniques. You will find that project analysis is much more than one or two NPV calculations.[7]

Calculating NPV in Other Countries and Currencies

Our guano project was undertaken in the United States by a U.S. company. But the principles of capital investment are the same worldwide. For example, suppose that you are the financial manager of the German company, K.G.R. Ökologische Naturdüngemittel GmbH (KGR), that is faced with a similar opportunity to make a €10 million investment in Germany. What changes?

1. KGR must also produce a set of cash-flow forecasts, but in this case the project cash flows are stated in euros, the Eurozone currency.

2. In developing these forecasts, the company needs to recognize that prices and costs will be influenced by the German inflation rate.

3. Profits from KGR's project are liable to the German rate of corporate tax.

4. KGR must use the German system of depreciation allowances. In common with many other countries, Germany allows firms to choose between two methods of depreciation—the straight-line system and the declining-balance system. KGR opts for the declining-balance method and writes off 30% of the depreciated value of the equipment each year (the maximum allowed under current German tax rules). Thus, in the first year KGR writes off .30 × 10 = €3 million and the written-down value of the equipment falls to 10 − 3 = €7 million. In year 2, KGR writes off .30 × 7 = €2.1 million and the written-down value is further reduced to 7 − 2.1 = €4.9 million. In year 4 KGR observes that depreciation would be higher if it could switch to straight-line depreciation and write off the balance of €3.43 million over the remaining three years of the equipment's life. Fortunately, German tax law allows it to do this. Therefore, KGR's depreciation allowance each year is calculated as follows:

	Year					
	1	**2**	**3**	**4**	**5**	**6**
Written-down value, start of year (€ millions)	10	7	4.9	3.43	2.29	1.14
Depreciation (€ millions)	.3 × 10 = 3	.3 × 7 = 2.1	.3 × 4.9 = 1.47	3.43/3 = 1.14	3.43/3 = 1.14	3.43/3 = 1.14
Written-down value, end of year (€ millions)	10 − 3 = 7	7 − 2.1 = 4.9	4.9 − 1.47 = 3.43	3.43 − 1.14 = 2.29	2.29 − 1.14 = 1.14	1.14 − 1.14 = 0

Notice that KGR's depreciation deduction declines for the first few years and then flattens out. That is also the case with the U.S. MACRS system of depreciation. In fact, MACRS is just another example of the declining-balance method with a later switch to straight-line.

---

[7] In the meantime you might like to get ahead of the game by viewing the live spreadsheets for the guano project and seeing how NPV would change with a shortfall in sales or an unexpected rise in costs on the book's Web site, **www.mhhe.com/bma.**

6-3 Investment Timing

The fact that a project has a positive NPV does not mean that it is best undertaken now. It might be even more valuable if undertaken in the future.

The question of optimal timing is not difficult when the cash flows are certain. You must first examine alternative start dates (t) for the investment and calculate the net *future* value at each of these dates. Then, to find which of the alternatives would add most to the firm's *current* value, you must discount these net future values back to the present:

$$\text{Net present value of investment if undertaken at date } t = \frac{\text{Net future value at date } t}{(1 + r)^t}$$

For example, suppose you own a large tract of inaccessible timber. To harvest it, you have to invest a substantial amount in access roads and other facilities. The longer you wait, the higher the investment required. On the other hand, lumber prices will rise as you wait, and the trees will keep growing, although at a gradually decreasing rate.

Let us suppose that the net present value of the harvest at different *future* dates is as follows:

	Year of Harvest					
	0	**1**	**2**	**3**	**4**	**5**
Net *future* value ($ thousands)	50	64.4	77.5	89.4	100	109.4
Change in value from previous year (%)		+28.8	+20.3	+15.4	+11.9	+9.4

As you can see, the longer you defer cutting the timber, the more money you will make. However, your concern is with the date that maximizes the net *present* value of your investment, that is, its contribution to the value of your firm *today*. You therefore need to discount the net future value of the harvest back to the present. Suppose the appropriate discount rate is 10%. Then, if you harvest the timber in year 1, it has a net *present* value of $58,500:

$$\text{NPV if harvested in year 1} = \frac{64.4}{1.10} = 58.5, \text{ or } \$58,500$$

The net present value for other harvest dates is as follows:

	Year of Harvest					
	0	**1**	**2**	**3**	**4**	**5**
Net present value ($ thousands)	50	58.5	64.0	67.2	68.3	67.9

The optimal point to harvest the timber is year 4 because this is the point that maximizes NPV.

Notice that before year 4 the net future value of the timber increases by more than 10% a year: The gain in value is greater than the cost of the capital tied up in the project. After year 4 the gain in value is still positive but less than the cost of capital. So delaying the harvest further just reduces shareholder wealth.[8]

The investment-timing problem is much more complicated when you are unsure about future cash flows. We return to the problem of investment timing under uncertainty in Chapter 10.

6-4 Equivalent Annual Cash Flows

When you calculate NPV, you transform future, year-by-year cash flows into a lump-sum value expressed in today's dollars (or euros, or other relevant currency). But sometimes it's helpful to reverse the calculation, transforming an investment today into an equivalent stream of future cash flows. Consider the following example.

Investing to Produce Reformulated Gasoline at California Refineries

In the early 1990s, the California Air Resources Board (CARB) started planning its "Phase 2" requirements for reformulated gasoline (RFG). RFG is gasoline blended to tight specifications designed to reduce pollution from motor vehicles. CARB consulted with refiners, environmentalists, and other interested parties to design these specifications.

As the outline for the Phase 2 requirements emerged, refiners realized that substantial capital investments would be required to upgrade California refineries. What might these investments mean for the retail price of gasoline? A refiner might ask: "Suppose my company invests $400 million to upgrade our refinery to meet Phase 2. How much extra revenue would we need every year to recover that cost?" Let's see if we can help the refiner out.

Assume $400 million of capital investment and a real (inflation-adjusted) cost of capital of 7%. The new equipment lasts for 25 years, and does not change raw-material and operating costs.

How much additional revenue does it take to cover the $400 million investment? The answer is simple: Just find the 25-year annuity payment with a present value equal to $400 million.

$$\text{PV of annuity} = \text{annuity payment} \times \text{25-year annuity factor}$$

At a 7% cost of capital, the 25-year annuity factor is 11.65.

$$\$400 \text{ million} = \text{annuity payment} \times 11.65$$
$$\text{Annuity payment} = \$34.3 \text{ million per year}[9]$$

---

[8] Our timber-cutting example conveys the right idea about investment timing, but it misses an important practical point: The sooner you cut the first crop of trees, the sooner the second crop can start growing. Thus, the value of the second crop depends on when you cut the first. The more complex and realistic problem can be solved in one of two ways:

1. Find the cutting dates that maximize the present value of a series of harvests, taking into account the different growth rates of young and old trees.

2. Repeat our calculations, counting the future market value of cut-over land as part of the payoff to the first harvest. The value of cut-over land includes the present value of all subsequent harvests.

The second solution is far simpler if you can figure out what cut-over land will be worth.

[9] For simplicity we have ignored taxes. Taxes would enter this calculation in two ways. First, the $400 million investment would generate depreciation tax shields. The easiest way to handle these tax shields is to calculate their PV and subtract it from the initial outlay. For example, if the PV of depreciation tax shields is $83 million, equivalent annual cost would be calculated on an after-tax investment base of $400 − 83 = $317 million. Second, our annuity payment is after-tax. To actually achieve after-tax revenues of, say, $34.3 million, the refiner would have to achieve pretax revenue sufficient to pay tax and have $34.3 million left over. If the tax rate is 35%, the required pretax revenue is 34.3/(1 − .35) = $52.8 million. Note how the after-tax figure is "grossed up" by dividing by one minus the tax rate.

This annuity is called an **equivalent annual cash flow.** It is the annual cash flow sufficient to recover a capital investment, including the cost of capital for that investment, over the investment's economic life. In our example the refiner would need to generate an extra $34.3 million for each of the next 25 years to recover the initial investment of $400 million.

Equivalent annual cash flows are handy—and sometimes essential—tools of finance. Here is a further example.

Choosing between Long- and Short-Lived Equipment

Suppose the firm is forced to choose between two machines, A and B. The two machines are designed differently but have identical capacity and do exactly the same job. Machine A costs $15,000 and will last three years. It costs $5,000 per year to run. Machine B is an economy model costing only $10,000, but it will last only two years and costs $6,000 per year to run. These are real cash flows: The costs are forecasted in dollars of constant purchasing power.

Because the two machines produce exactly the same product, the only way to choose between them is on the basis of cost. Suppose we compute the present value of cost:

Machine	C_0	C_1	C_2	C_3	PV at 6% ($ thousands)
	Costs ($ thousands)				
A	+15	+5	+5	+5	28.37
B	+10	+6	+6		21.00

Should we take machine B, the one with the lower present value of costs? Not necessarily, because B will have to be replaced a year earlier than A. In other words, the timing of a future investment decision depends on today's choice of A or B.

So, a machine with total PV(costs) of $21,000 spread over three years (0, 1, and 2) is not necessarily better than a competing machine with PV(costs) of $28,370 spread over four years (0 through 3). We have to convert total PV(costs) to a cost per year, that is, to an equivalent annual cost. For machine A, the annual cost turns out to be 10.61, or $10,610 per year:

Machine	C_0	C_1	C_2	C_3	PV at 6% ($ thousands)
	Costs ($ thousands)				
Machine A	+15	+5	+5	+5	28.37
Equivalent annual cost		+10.61	+10.61	+10.61	28.37

We calculated the equivalent annual cost by finding the three-year annuity with the same present value as A's lifetime costs.

$$\text{PV of annuity} = \text{PV of A's costs} = 28.37$$
$$= \text{annuity payment} \times \text{3-year annuity factor}$$

The annuity factor is 2.673 for three years and a 6% real cost of capital, so

$$\text{Annuity payment} = \frac{28.37}{2.673} = 10.61$$

A similar calculation for machine B gives:

	C_0	C_1	C_2	PV at 6% ($ thousands)
	Costs ($ thousands)			
Machine B	+10	+6	+6	21.00
Equivalent annual cost		+11.45	+11.45	21.00

Machine A is better, because its equivalent annual cost is less ($10,610 versus $11,450 for machine B).

You can think of the equivalent annual cost of machine A or B as an annual rental charge. Suppose the financial manager is asked to *rent* machine A to the plant manager actually in charge of production. There will be three equal rental payments starting in year 1. The three payments must recover both the original cost of machine A in year 0 and the cost of running it in years 1 to 3. Therefore the financial manager has to make sure that the rental payments are worth $28,370, the total PV(costs) of machine A. You can see that the financial manager would calculate a fair rental payment equal to machine A's equivalent annual cost.

Our rule for choosing between plant and equipment with different economic lives is, therefore, to select the asset with the lowest fair rental charge, that is, the lowest equivalent annual cost.

Equivalent Annual Cash Flow and Inflation

The equivalent annual costs we just calculated are *real* annuities based on forecasted *real* costs and a 6% *real* discount rate. We could, of course, restate the annuities in nominal terms. Suppose the expected inflation rate is 5%; we multiply the first cash flow of the annuity by 1.05, the second by $(1.05)^2 = 1.1025$, and so on.

		C_0	C_1	C_2	C_3
A	Real annuity		10.61	10.61	10.61
	Nominal cash flow		11.14	11.70	12.28
B	Real annuity		11.45	11.45	
	Nominal cash flow		12.02	12.62	

Note that B is still inferior to A. Of course the present values of the nominal and real cash flows are identical. Just remember to discount the real annuity at the real rate and the equivalent nominal cash flows at the consistent nominal rate.[10]

When you use equivalent annual costs simply for comparison of costs per period, as we did for machines A and B, we strongly recommend doing the calculations in real terms.[11] But if you actually rent out the machine to the plant manager, or anyone else, be careful to specify that the rental payments be "indexed" to inflation. If inflation runs on at 5% per year and rental payments do not increase proportionally, then the real value of the rental payments must decline and will not cover the full cost of buying and operating the machine.

Equivalent Annual Cash Flow and Technological Change

So far we have the following simple rule: Two or more streams of cash outflows with different lengths or time patterns can be compared by converting their present values to equivalent annual cash flows. Just remember to do the calculations in real terms.

Now any rule this simple cannot be completely general. For example, when we evaluated machine A versus machine B, we implicitly assumed that their fair rental charges would *continue* at $10,610 versus $11,450. This will be so only if the *real* costs of buying and operating the machines stay the same.

---

[10] The nominal discount rate is

$$r_{nominal} = (1 + r_{real})(1 + \text{inflation rate}) - 1$$
$$= (1.06)(1.05) - 1 = .113, \text{ or } 11.3\%$$

Discounting the nominal annuities at this rate gives the same present values as discounting the real annuities at 6%.

[11] Do *not* calculate equivalent annual cash flows as level *nominal* annuities. This procedure can give incorrect rankings of true equivalent annual flows at high inflation rates. See Challenge Question 32 at the end of this chapter for an example.

Suppose that this is not the case. Suppose that thanks to technological improvements new machines each year cost 20% less in real terms to buy and operate. In this case future owners of brand-new, lower-cost machines will be able to cut their rental cost by 20%, and owners of old machines will be forced to match this reduction. Thus, we now need to ask: If the real level of rents declines by 20% a year, how much will it cost to rent each machine?

If the rent for year 1 is $rent_1$, rent for year 2 is $rent_2 = .8 \times rent_1$. $Rent_3$ is $.8 \times rent_2$, or $.64 \times rent_1$. The owner of each machine must set the rents sufficiently high to recover the present value of the costs. In the case of machine A,

$$\text{PV of renting machine A} = \frac{rent_1}{1.06} + \frac{rent_2}{(1.06)^2} + \frac{rent_3}{(1.06)^3} = 28.37$$

$$= \frac{rent_1}{1.06} + \frac{.8(rent_1)}{(1.06)^2} + \frac{.64(rent_1)}{(1.06)^3} = 28.37$$

$$rent_1 = 12.94, \text{ or } \$12,940$$

For machine B,

$$\text{PV of renting machine B} = \frac{rent_1}{1.06} + \frac{.8(rent_1)}{(1.06)^2} = 21.00$$

$$rent_1 = 12.69, \text{ or } \$12,690$$

The merits of the two machines are now reversed. Once we recognize that technology is expected to reduce the real costs of new machines, then it pays to buy the shorter-lived machine B rather than become locked into an aging technology with machine A in year 3.

You can imagine other complications. Perhaps machine C will arrive in year 1 with an even lower equivalent annual cost. You would then need to consider scrapping or selling machine B at year 1 (more on this decision below). The financial manager could not choose between machines A and B in year 0 without taking a detailed look at what each machine could be replaced with.

Comparing equivalent annual cash flow should never be a mechanical exercise; always think about the assumptions that are implicit in the comparison. Finally, remember why equivalent annual cash flows are necessary in the first place. The reason is that A and B will be replaced at different future dates. The choice between them therefore affects future investment decisions. If subsequent decisions are not affected by the initial choice (for example, because neither machine will be replaced), then we do *not need to take future decisions into account.*[12]

Equivalent Annual Cash Flow and Taxes   We have not mentioned taxes. But you surely realized that machine A's and B's lifetime costs should be calculated after-tax, recognizing that operating costs are tax-deductible and that capital investment generates depreciation tax shields.

Deciding When to Replace an Existing Machine

The previous example took the life of each machine as fixed. In practice the point at which equipment is replaced reflects economic considerations rather than total physical collapse. *We* must decide when to replace. The machine will rarely decide for us.

Here is a common problem. You are operating an elderly machine that is expected to produce a net cash *inflow* of $4,000 in the coming year and $4,000 next year. After that it

---

[12] However, if neither machine will be replaced, then we have to consider the extra revenue generated by machine A in its third year, when it will be operating but B will not.

will give up the ghost. You can replace it now with a new machine, which costs $15,000 but is much more efficient and will provide a cash inflow of $8,000 a year for three years. You want to know whether you should replace your equipment now or wait a year.

We can calculate the NPV of the new machine and also its *equivalent annual cash flow*, that is, the three-year annuity that has the same net present value:

Cash Flows ($ thousands)				
	C_0	C_1	C_2	C_3	NPV at 6% ($ thousands)
New machine	− 15	+8	+8	+8	6.38
Equivalent annual cash flow		+2.387	+2.387	+2.387	6.38

In other words, the cash flows of the new machine are equivalent to an annuity of $2,387 per year. So we can equally well ask at what point we would want to replace our old machine with a new one producing $2,387 a year. When the question is put this way, the answer is obvious. As long as your old machine can generate a cash flow of $4,000 a year, who wants to put in its place a new one that generates only $2,387 a year?

It is a simple matter to incorporate salvage values into this calculation. Suppose that the current salvage value is $8,000 and next year's value is $7,000. Let us see where you come out next year if you wait and then sell. On one hand, you gain $7,000, but you lose today's salvage value *plus* a year's return on that money. That is, 8,000 × 1.06 = $8,480. Your net loss is 8,480 − 7,000 = $1,480, which only partly offsets the operating gain. You should not replace yet.

Remember that the logic of such comparisons requires that the new machine be the best of the available alternatives and that it in turn be replaced at the optimal point.

Cost of Excess Capacity Any firm with a centralized information system (computer servers, storage, software, and telecommunication links) encounters many proposals for using it. Recently installed systems tend to have excess capacity, and since the immediate marginal costs of using them seem to be negligible, management often encourages new uses. Sooner or later, however, the load on a system increases to the point at which management must either terminate the uses it originally encouraged or invest in another system several years earlier than it had planned. Such problems can be avoided if a proper charge is made for the use of spare capacity.

Suppose we have a new investment project that requires heavy use of an existing information system. The effect of adopting the project is to bring the purchase date of a new, more capable system forward from year 4 to year 3. This new system has a life of five years, and at a discount rate of 6% the present value of the cost of buying and operating it is $500,000.

We begin by converting the $500,000 present value of the cost of the new system to an equivalent annual cost of $118,700 for each of five years.[13] Of course, when the new system in turn wears out, we will replace it with another. So we face the prospect of future information-system expenses of $118,700 a year. If we undertake the new project, the series of expenses begins in year 4; if we do not undertake it, the series begins in year 5. The new project, therefore, results in an *additional* cost of $118,700 in year 4. This has a present value of $118,700/(1.06)^4$, or about $94,000. This cost is properly charged against the new project. When we recognize it, the NPV of the project may prove to be negative. If so, we still need to check whether it is worthwhile undertaking the project now and abandoning it later, when the excess capacity of the present system disappears.

---

[13] The present value of $118,700 a year for five years discounted at 6% is $500,000.

● ● ● ● ●

SUMMARY

By now present value calculations should be a matter of routine. However, forecasting project cash flows will never be routine. Here is a checklist that will help you to avoid mistakes:

1. Discount cash flows, not profits.
   a. Remember that depreciation is not a cash flow (though it may affect tax payments).
   b. Concentrate on cash flows after taxes. Stay alert for differences between tax depreciation and depreciation used in reports to shareholders.
   c. Exclude debt interest or the cost of repaying a loan from the project cash flows. This enables you to separate the investment from the financing decision.
   d. Remember the investment in working capital. As sales increase, the firm may need to make additional investments in working capital, and as the project comes to an end, it will recover those investments.
   e. Beware of allocated overhead charges for heat, light, and so on. These may not reflect the incremental costs of the project.

2. Estimate the project's *incremental* cash flows—that is, the difference between the cash flows with the project and those without the project.
   a. Include all indirect effects of the project, such as its impact on the sales of the firm's other products.
   b. Forget sunk costs.
   c. Include *opportunity costs,* such as the value of land that you would otherwise sell.

3. Treat inflation consistently.
   a. If cash flows are forecasted in nominal terms, use a nominal discount rate.
   b. Discount real cash flows at a real rate.

These principles of valuing capital investments are the same worldwide, but inputs and assumptions vary by country and currency. For example, cash flows from a project in Germany would be in euros, not dollars, and would be forecasted after German taxes.

When we assessed the guano project, we transformed the series of future cash flows into a single measure of their present value. Sometimes it is useful to reverse this calculation and to convert the present value into a stream of annual cash flows. For example, when choosing between two machines with unequal lives, you need to compare equivalent annual cash flows. Remember, though, to calculate equivalent annual cash flows in real terms and adjust for technological change if necessary.

● ● ● ● ●

PROBLEM SETS

BASIC

1. Which of the following should be treated as incremental cash flows when deciding whether to invest in a new manufacturing plant? The site is already owned by the company, but existing buildings would need to be demolished.
   a. The market value of the site and existing buildings.
   b. Demolition costs and site clearance.
   c. The cost of a new access road put in last year.
   d. Lost earnings on other products due to executive time spent on the new facility.
   e. A proportion of the cost of leasing the president's jet airplane.

   f. Future depreciation of the new plant.

   g. The reduction in the corporation's tax bill resulting from tax depreciation of the new plant.

   h. The initial investment in inventories of raw materials.

   i. Money already spent on engineering design of the new plant.

2. Mr. Art Deco will be paid $100,000 one year hence. This is a nominal flow, which he discounts at an 8% nominal discount rate:

$$PV = \frac{100,000}{1.08} = \$92,593$$

The inflation rate is 4%.

    Calculate the PV of Mr. Deco's payment using the equivalent *real* cash flow and *real* discount rate. (You should get exactly the same answer as he did.)

3. True or false?

   a. A project's depreciation tax shields depend on the actual future rate of inflation.

   b. Project cash flows should take account of interest paid on any borrowing undertaken to finance the project.

   c. In the U.S., income reported to the tax authorities must equal income reported to shareholders.

   d. Accelerated depreciation reduces near-term project cash flows and therefore reduces project NPV.

4. How does the PV of depreciation tax shields vary across the recovery-period classes shown in Table 6.4? Give a general answer; then check it by calculating the PVs of depreciation tax shields in the five-year and seven-year classes. The tax rate is 35% and the discount rate is 10%.

5. The following table tracks the main components of working capital over the life of a four-year project.

	2010	2011	2012	2013	2014
Accounts receivable	0	150,000	225,000	190,000	0
Inventory	75,000	130,000	130,000	95,000	0
Accounts payable	25,000	50,000	50,000	35,000	0

Calculate net working capital and the cash inflows and outflows due to investment in working capital.

6. When appraising mutually exclusive investments in plant and equipment, financial managers calculate the investments' equivalent annual costs and rank the investments on this basis. Why is this necessary? Why not just compare the investments' NPVs? Explain briefly.

7. Air conditioning for a college dormitory will cost $1.5 million to install and $200,000 per year to operate. The system should last 25 years. The real cost of capital is 5%, and the college pays no taxes. What is the equivalent annual cost?

8. Machines A and B are mutually exclusive and are expected to produce the following real cash flows:

	Cash Flows ($ thousands)			
Machine	C_0	C_1	C_2	C_3
A	−100	+110	+121	
B	−120	+110	+121	+133

The real opportunity cost of capital is 10%.

a.   Calculate the NPV of each machine.

b.   Calculate the equivalent annual cash flow from each machine.

c.   Which machine should you buy?

9.   Machine C was purchased five years ago for $200,000 and produces an annual real cash flow of $80,000. It has no salvage value but is expected to last another five years. The company can replace machine C with machine B (see Problem 8) *either* now *or* at the end of five years. Which should it do?

INTERMEDIATE

10.   Restate the net cash flows in Table 6.6 in real terms. Discount the restated cash flows at a real discount rate. Assume a 20% *nominal* rate and 10% expected inflation. NPV should be unchanged at +3,802, or $3,802,000.

11.   CSC is evaluating a new project to produce encapsulators. The initial investment in plant and equipment is $500,000. Sales of encapsulators in year 1 are forecasted at $200,000 and costs at $100,000. Both are expected to increase by 10% a year in line with inflation. Profits are taxed at 35%. Working capital in each year consists of inventories of raw materials and is forecasted at 20% of sales in the following year.

The project will last five years and the equipment at the end of this period will have no further value. For tax purposes the equipment can be depreciated straight-line over these five years. If the nominal discount rate is 15%, show that the net present value of the project is the same whether calculated using real cash flows or nominal flows.

12.   In 1898 Simon North announced plans to construct a funeral home on land he owned and rented out as a storage area for railway carts. (A local newspaper commended Mr. North for not putting the cart before the hearse.) Rental income from the site barely covered real estate taxes, but the site was valued at $45,000. However, Mr. North had refused several offers for the land and planned to continue renting it out if for some reason the funeral home was not built. Therefore he did not include the value of the land as an outlay in his NPV analysis of the funeral home. Was this the correct procedure? Explain.

13.   Each of the following statements is true. Explain why they are consistent.

a.   When a company introduces a new product, or expands production of an existing product, investment in net working capital is usually an important cash outflow.

b.   Forecasting changes in net working capital is not necessary if the timing of *all* cash inflows and outflows is carefully specified.

14.   Ms. T. Potts, the treasurer of Ideal China, has a problem. The company has just ordered a new kiln for $400,000. Of this sum, $50,000 is described by the supplier as an installation cost. Ms. Potts does not know whether the Internal Revenue Service (IRS) will permit the company to treat this cost as a tax-deductible current expense or as a capital investment. In the latter case, the company could depreciate the $50,000 using the five-year MACRS tax depreciation schedule. How will the IRS's decision affect the after-tax cost of the kiln? The tax rate is 35% and the opportunity cost of capital is 5%.

15.   After spending $3 million on research, Better Mousetraps has developed a new trap. The project requires an initial investment in plant and equipment of $6 million. This investment will be depreciated straight-line over five years to a value of zero, but, when the project comes to an end in five years, the equipment can in fact be sold for $500,000. The firm believes that working capital at each date must be maintained at 10% of next year's forecasted sales. Production costs are estimated at $1.50 per trap and the traps will be sold for $4 each. (There are no marketing expenses.) Sales forecasts are given in the following table. The firm pays tax at 35% and the required return on the project is 12%. What is the NPV?

Year:	0	1	2	3	4	5
Sales (millions of traps)	0	.5	.6	1.0	1.0	.6

16. A project requires an initial investment of $100,000 and is expected to produce a cash inflow before tax of $26,000 per year for five years. Company A has substantial accumulated tax losses and is unlikely to pay taxes in the foreseeable future. Company B pays corporate taxes at a rate of 35% and can depreciate the investment for tax purposes using the five-year MACRS tax depreciation schedule. Suppose the opportunity cost of capital is 8%. Ignore inflation.

a. Calculate project NPV for each company.

b. What is the IRR of the after-tax cash flows for each company? What does comparison of the IRRs suggest is the effective corporate tax rate?

17. Go to the "live" Excel spreadsheet versions of Tables 6.1, 6.5, and 6.6 at **www.mhhe.com/bma** and answer the following questions.

a. How does the guano project's NPV change if IM&C is forced to use the seven-year MACRS tax depreciation schedule?

b. New engineering estimates raise the possibility that capital investment will be more than $10 million, perhaps as much as $15 million. On the other hand, you believe that the 20% cost of capital is unrealistically high and that the true cost of capital is about 11%. Is the project still attractive under these alternative assumptions?

c. Continue with the assumed $15 million capital investment and the 11% cost of capital. What if sales, cost of goods sold, and net working capital are each 10% higher in every year? Recalculate NPV. (*Note:* Enter the revised sales, cost, and working-capital forecasts in the spreadsheet for Table 6.1.)

18. A widget manufacturer currently produces 200,000 units a year. It buys widget lids from an outside supplier at a price of $2 a lid. The plant manager believes that it would be cheaper to make these lids rather than buy them. Direct production costs are estimated to be only $1.50 a lid. The necessary machinery would cost $150,000 and would last 10 years. This investment could be written off for tax purposes using the seven-year tax depreciation schedule. The plant manager estimates that the operation would require additional working capital of $30,000 but argues that this sum can be ignored since it is recoverable at the end of the 10 years. If the company pays tax at a rate of 35% and the opportunity cost of capital is 15%, would you support the plant manager's proposal? State clearly any additional assumptions that you need to make.

19. Reliable Electric is considering a proposal to manufacture a new type of industrial electric motor which would replace most of its existing product line. A research breakthrough has given Reliable a two-year lead on its competitors. The project proposal is summarized in Table 6.7.

a. Read the notes to the table carefully. Which entries make sense? Which do not? Why or why not?

b. What additional information would you need to construct a version of Table 6.7 that makes sense?

c. Construct such a table and recalculate NPV. Make additional assumptions as necessary.

20. Marsha Jones has bought a used Mercedes horse transporter for her Connecticut estate. It cost $35,000. The object is to save on horse transporter rentals.

Marsha had been renting a transporter every other week for $200 per day plus $1.00 per mile. Most of the trips are 80 or 100 miles in total. Marsha usually gives the driver a $40 tip. With the new transporter she will only have to pay for diesel fuel and maintenance, at about $.45 per mile. Insurance costs for Marsha's transporter are $1,200 per year.

The transporter will probably be worth $15,000 (in real terms) after eight years, when Marsha's horse Nike will be ready to retire. Is the transporter a positive-NPV investment? Assume a nominal discount rate of 9% and a 3% forecasted inflation rate. Marsha's transporter is a personal outlay, not a business or financial investment, so taxes can be ignored.

	2009	2010	2011	2012–2019
1. Capital expenditure	−10,400			
2. Research and development	−2,000			
3. Working capital	−4,000			
4. Revenue		8,000	16,000	40,000
5. Operating costs		−4,000	−8,000	−20,000
6. Overhead		−800	−1,600	−4,000
7. Depreciation		−1,040	−1,040	−1,040
8. Interest		−2,160	−2,160	−2,160
9. Income	−2,000	0	3,200	12,800
10. Tax	0	0	420	4,480
11. Net cash flow	−16,400	0	2,780	8,320
12. Net present value = +13,932				

▶ **TABLE 6.7**   Cash flows and present value of Reliable Electric's proposed investment ($ thousands). See Problem 19.

Notes:

1. *Capital expenditure:* $8 million for new machinery and $2.4 million for a warehouse extension. The full cost of the extension has been charged to this project, although only about half of the space is currently needed. Since the new machinery will be housed in an existing factory building, no charge has been made for land and building.
2. *Research and development:* $1.82 million spent in 2008. This figure was corrected for 10% inflation from the time of expenditure to date. Thus 1.82 × 1.1 = $2 million.
3. *Working capital:* Initial investment in inventories.
4. *Revenue:* These figures assume sales of 2,000 motors in 2010, 4,000 in 2011, and 10,000 per year from 2012 through 2019. The initial unit price of $4,000 is forecasted to remain constant in real terms.
5. *Operating costs:* These include all direct and indirect costs. Indirect costs (heat, light, power, fringe benefits, etc.) are assumed to be 200% of direct labor costs. Operating costs per unit are forecasted to remain constant in real terms at $2,000.
6. *Overhead:* Marketing and administrative costs, assumed equal to 10% of revenue.
7. *Depreciation:* Straight-line for 10 years.
8. *Interest:* Charged on capital expenditure and working capital at Reliable's current borrowing rate of 15%.
9. *Income:* Revenue less the sum of research and development, operating costs, overhead, depreciation, and interest.
10. *Tax:* 35% of income. However, income is negative in 2009. This loss is carried forward and deducted from taxable income in 2011.
11. *Net cash flow:* Assumed equal to income less tax.
12. *Net present value:* NPV of net cash flow at a 15% discount rate.

Visit us at
www.mhhe.com/bma

21. United Pigpen is considering a proposal to manufacture high-protein hog feed. The project would make use of an existing warehouse, which is currently rented out to a neighboring firm. The next year's rental charge on the warehouse is $100,000, and thereafter the rent is expected to grow in line with inflation at 4% a year. In addition to using the warehouse, the proposal envisages an investment in plant and equipment of $1.2 million. This could be depreciated for tax purposes straight-line over 10 years. However, Pigpen expects to terminate the project at the end of eight years and to resell the plant and equipment in year 8 for $400,000. Finally, the project requires an initial investment in working capital of $350,000. Thereafter, working capital is forecasted to be 10% of sales in each of years 1 through 7.

Year 1 sales of hog feed are expected to be $4.2 million, and thereafter sales are forecasted to grow by 5% a year, slightly faster than the inflation rate. Manufacturing costs are expected to be 90% of sales, and profits are subject to tax at 35%. The cost of capital is 12%. What is the NPV of Pigpen's project?

Visit us at
www.mhhe.com/bma

22. Hindustan Motors has been producing its Ambassador car in India since 1948. As the company's Web site explains, the Ambassador's "dependability, spaciousness and comfort factor have made it the most preferred car for generations of Indians." Hindustan is now considering producing the car in China. This will involve an initial investment of RMB 4

billion.[14] The plant will start production after one year. It is expected to last for five years and have a salvage value at the end of this period of RMB 500 million in real terms. The plant will produce 100,000 cars a year. The firm anticipates that in the first year it will be able to sell each car for RMB 65,000, and thereafter the price is expected to increase by 4% a year. Raw materials for each car are forecasted to cost RMB 18,000 in the first year, and these costs are predicted to increase by 3% annually. Total labor costs for the plant are expected to be RMB 1.1 billion in the first year and thereafter will increase by 7% a year. The land on which the plant is built can be rented for five years at a fixed cost of RMB 300 million a year payable at the *beginning* of each year. Hindustan's discount rate for this type of project is 12% (nominal). The expected rate of inflation is 5%. The plant can be depreciated straight-line over the five-year period and profits will be taxed at 25%. Assume all cash flows occur at the end of each year except where otherwise stated. What is the NPV of the plant?

23. In the International Mulch and Compost example (Section 6–2), we assumed that losses on the project could be used to offset taxable profits elsewhere in the corporation. Suppose that the losses had to be carried forward and offset against future taxable profits from the project. How would the project NPV change? What is the value of the company's ability to use the tax deductions immediately?

24. As a result of improvements in product engineering, United Automation is able to sell one of its two milling machines. Both machines perform the same function but differ in age. The newer machine could be sold today for $50,000. Its operating costs are $20,000 a year, but in five years the machine will require a $20,000 overhaul. Thereafter operating costs will be $30,000 until the machine is finally sold in year 10 for $5,000.

    The older machine could be sold today for $25,000. If it is kept, it will need an immediate $20,000 overhaul. Thereafter operating costs will be $30,000 a year until the machine is finally sold in year 5 for $5,000.

    Both machines are fully depreciated for tax purposes. The company pays tax at 35%. Cash flows have been forecasted in real terms. The real cost of capital is 12%. Which machine should United Automation sell? Explain the assumptions underlying your answer.

25. Low-energy lightbulbs cost $3.50, have a life of nine years, and use about $1.60 of electricity a year. Conventional lightbulbs cost only $.50, but last only about a year and use about $6.60 of energy. If the real discount rate is 5%, what is the equivalent annual cost of the two products?

26. Hayden Inc. has a number of copiers that were bought four years ago for $20,000. Currently maintenance costs $2,000 a year, but the maintenance agreement expires at the end of two years and thereafter the annual maintenance charge will rise to $8,000. The machines have a current resale value of $8,000, but at the end of year 2 their value will have fallen to $3,500. By the end of year 6 the machines will be valueless and would be scrapped.

    Hayden is considering replacing the copiers with new machines that would do essentially the same job. These machines cost $25,000, and the company can take out an eight-year maintenance contract for $1,000 a year. The machines will have no value by the end of the eight years and will be scrapped.

    Both machines are depreciated by using seven-year MACRS, and the tax rate is 35%. Assume for simplicity that the inflation rate is zero. The real cost of capital is 7%. When should Hayden replace its copiers?

27. Return to the start of Section 6–4, where we calculated the equivalent annual cost of producing reformulated gasoline in California. Capital investment was $400 million. Suppose this amount can be depreciated for tax purposes on the 10-year MACRS schedule from Table 6.4. The marginal tax rate, including California taxes, is 39%, the cost of

capital is 7%, and there is no inflation. The refinery improvements have an economic life of 25 years.

a. Calculate the after-tax equivalent annual cost. (*Hint:* It's easiest to use the PV of depreciation tax shields as an offset to the initial investment).

b. How much extra would retail gasoline customers have to pay to cover this equivalent annual cost? (*Note:* Extra income from higher retail prices would be taxed.)

Visit us at
www.mhhe.com/bma

28. The Borstal Company has to choose between two machines that do the same job but have different lives. The two machines have the following costs:

Year	Machine A	Machine B
0	$40,000	$50,000
1	10,000	8,000
2	10,000	8,000
3	10,000 + replace	8,000
4		8,000 + replace

These costs are expressed in real terms.

a. Suppose you are Borstal's financial manager. If you had to buy one or the other machine and rent it to the production manager for that machine's economic life, what annual rental payment would you have to charge? Assume a 6% real discount rate and ignore taxes.

b. Which machine should Borstal buy?

c. Usually the rental payments you derived in part (a) are just hypothetical—a way of calculating and interpreting equivalent annual cost. Suppose you actually do buy one of the machines and rent it to the production manager. How much would you actually have to charge in each future year if there is steady 8% per year inflation? (*Note:* The rental payments calculated in part (a) are real cash flows. You would have to mark up those payments to cover inflation.)

Visit us at
www.mhhe.com/bma

29. Look again at your calculations for Problem 28 above. Suppose that technological change is expected to reduce costs by 10% per year. There will be new machines in year 1 that cost 10% less to buy and operate than A and B. In year 2 there will be a second crop of new machines incorporating a further 10% reduction, and so on. How does this change the equivalent annual costs of machines A and B?

30. The president's executive jet is not fully utilized. You judge that its use by other officers would increase direct operating costs by only $20,000 a year and would save $100,000 a year in airline bills. On the other hand, you believe that with the increased use the company will need to replace the jet at the end of three years rather than four. A new jet costs $1.1 million and (at its current low rate of use) has a life of six years. Assume that the company does not pay taxes. All cash flows are forecasted in real terms. The real opportunity cost of capital is 8%. Should you try to persuade the president to allow other officers to use the plane?

CHALLENGE

31. One measure of the effective tax rate is the difference between the IRRs of pretax and after-tax cash flows, divided by the pretax IRR. Consider, for example, an investment I generating a perpetual stream of pretax cash flows C. The pretax IRR is C/I, and the after-tax IRR is $C(1 - T_C)/I$, where T_C is the statutory tax rate. The effective rate, call it T_E, is

$$T_E = \frac{C/I - C(1 - T_C)/I}{C/I} = T_C$$

In this case the effective rate equals the statutory rate.

a. Calculate T_E for the guano project in Section 6–2.

b. How does the effective rate depend on the tax depreciation schedule? On the inflation rate?

c. Consider a project where all of the up-front investment is treated as an expense for tax purposes. For example, R&D and marketing outlays are always expensed in the United States. They create no tax depreciation. What is the effective tax rate for such a project?

32. We warned that equivalent annual costs should be calculated in real terms. We did not fully explain why. This problem will show you.

   Look back to the cash flows for machines A and B (in "Choosing between Long- and Short-Lived Equipment"). The present values of purchase and operating costs are 28.37 (over three years for A) and 21.00 (over two years for B). The real discount rate is 6% and the inflation rate is 5%.

a. Calculate the three- and two-year *level nominal* annuities which have present values of 28.37 and 21.00. Explain why these annuities are *not* realistic estimates of equivalent annual costs. (*Hint:* In real life machinery rentals increase with inflation.)

b. Suppose the inflation rate increases to 25%. The real interest rate stays at 6%. Recalculate the level nominal annuities. Note that the *ranking* of machines A and B appears to change. Why?

33. In December 2005 Mid-American Energy brought online one of the largest wind farms in the world. It cost an estimated $386 million and the 257 turbines have a total capacity of 360.5 megawatts (mW). Wind speeds fluctuate and most wind farms are expected to operate at an average of only 35% of their rated capacity. In this case, at an electricity price of $55 per megawatt-hour (mWh), the project will produce revenues in the first year of $60.8 million (i.e., .35 × 8,760 hours × 360.5 mW × $55 per mWh). A reasonable estimate of maintenance and other costs is about $18.9 million in the first year of operation. Thereafter, revenues and costs should increase with inflation by around 3% a year.

   Conventional power stations can be depreciated using 20-year MACRS, and their profits are taxed at 35%. Suppose that the project will last 20 years and the cost of capital is 12%. To encourage renewable energy sources, the government offers several tax breaks for wind farms.

a. How large a tax break (if any) was needed to make Mid-American's investment a positive-NPV venture?

b. Some wind farm operators assume a capacity factor of 30% rather than 35%. How would this lower capacity factor alter project NPV?

MINI-CASES ●●●●●

New Economy Transport (A)

The New Economy Transport Company (NETCO) was formed in 1955 to carry cargo and passengers between ports in the Pacific Northwest and Alaska. By 2008 its fleet had grown to four vessels, including a small dry-cargo vessel, the *Vital Spark*.

   The *Vital Spark* is 25 years old and badly in need of an overhaul. Peter Handy, the finance director, has just been presented with a proposal that would require the following expenditures:

Overhaul engine and generators	$340,000
Replace radar and other electronic equipment	75,000
Repairs to hull and superstructure	310,000
Painting and other repairs	95,000
	$820,000

Mr. Handy believes that all these outlays could be depreciated for tax purposes in the seven-year MACRS class.

NETCO's chief engineer, McPhail, estimates the postoverhaul operating costs as follows:

Fuel	$ 450,000
Labor and benefits	480,000
Maintenance	141,000
Other	110,000
	$1,181,000

These costs generally increase with inflation, which is forecasted at 2.5% a year.

The *Vital Spark* is carried on NETCO's books at a net depreciated value of only $100,000, but could probably be sold "as is," along with an extensive inventory of spare parts, for $200,000. The book value of the spare parts inventory is $40,000. Sale of the *Vital Spark* would generate an immediate tax liability on the difference between sale price and book value.

The chief engineer also suggests installation of a brand-new engine and control system, which would cost an extra $600,000.[15] This additional equipment would not substantially improve the *Vital Spark*'s performance, but would result in the following reduced annual fuel, labor, and maintenance costs:

Fuel	$ 400,000
Labor and benefits	405,000
Maintenance	105,000
Other	110,000
	$1,020,000

Overhaul of the *Vital Spark* would take it out of service for several months. The overhauled vessel would resume commercial service next year. Based on past experience, Mr. Handy believes that it would generate revenues of about $1.4 million next year, increasing with inflation thereafter.

But the *Vital Spark* cannot continue forever. Even if overhauled, its useful life is probably no more than 10 years, 12 years at the most. Its salvage value when finally taken out of service will be trivial.

NETCO is a conservatively financed firm in a mature business. It normally evaluates capital investments using an 11% cost of capital. This is a nominal, not a real, rate. NETCO's tax rate is 35%.

QUESTION

1. Calculate the NPV of the proposed overhaul of the *Vital Spark*, with and without the new engine and control system. To do the calculation, you will have to prepare a spreadsheet table showing all costs after taxes over the vessel's remaining economic life. Take special care with your assumptions about depreciation tax shields and inflation.

New Economy Transport (B)

There is no question that the *Vital Spark* needs an overhaul soon. However, Mr. Handy feels it unwise to proceed without also considering the purchase of a new vessel. Cohn and Doyle, Inc., a Wisconsin shipyard, has approached NETCO with a design incorporating a Kort nozzle, extensively automated navigation and power control systems, and much more

---

[15] This additional outlay would also qualify for tax depreciation in the seven-year MACRS class.

comfortable accommodations for the crew. Estimated annual operating costs of the new vessel are:

Fuel	$380,000
Labor and benefits	330,000
Maintenance	70,000
Other	105,000
	$885,000

The crew would require additional training to handle the new vessel's more complex and sophisticated equipment. Training would probably cost $50,000 next year.

The estimated operating costs for the new vessel assume that it would be operated in the same way as the *Vital Spark*. However, the new vessel should be able to handle a larger load on some routes, which could generate additional revenues, net of additional out-of-pocket costs, of as much as $100,000 per year. Moreover, a new vessel would have a useful service life of 20 years or more.

Cohn and Doyle offered the new vessel for a fixed price of $3,000,000, payable half immediately and half on delivery next year.

Mr. Handy stepped out on the foredeck of the *Vital Spark* as she chugged down the Cook Inlet. "A rusty old tub," he muttered, "but she's never let us down. I'll bet we could keep her going until next year while Cohn and Doyle are building her replacement. We could use up the spare parts to keep her going. We might even be able to sell or scrap her for book value when her replacement arrives.

"But how do I compare the NPV of a new ship with the old *Vital Spark?* Sure, I could run a 20-year NPV spreadsheet, but I don't have a clue how the replacement will be used in 2023 or 2028. Maybe I could compare the overall *cost* of overhauling and operating the *Vital Spark* to the cost of buying and operating the proposed replacement."

QUESTIONS

1. Calculate and compare the equivalent annual costs of (a) overhauling and operating the *Vital Spark* for 12 more years, and (b) buying and operating the proposed replacement vessel for 20 years. What should Mr. Handy do if the replacement's annual costs are the same or lower?

2. Suppose the replacement's equivalent annual costs are higher than the *Vital Spark*'s. What additional information should Mr. Handy seek in this case?

7 CHAPTER ● ● ● ● ●

Introduction to Risk and Return

▶ **We have managed** to go through six chapters without directly addressing the problem of risk, but now the jig is up. We can no longer be satisfied with vague statements like "The opportunity cost of capital depends on the risk of the project." We need to know how risk is defined, what the links are between risk and the opportunity cost of capital, and how the financial manager can cope with risk in practical situations.

In this chapter we concentrate on the first of these issues and leave the other two to Chapters 8 and 9. We start by summarizing more than 100 years of evidence on rates of return in capital markets. Then we take a first look at investment risks and show how they can be reduced by portfolio diversification. We introduce you to beta, the standard risk measure for individual securities.

The themes of this chapter, then, are portfolio risk, security risk, and diversification. For the most part, we take the view of the individual investor. But at the end of the chapter we turn the problem around and ask whether diversification makes sense as a corporate objective.

● ● ● ● ●

7-1 Over a Century of Capital Market History in One Easy Lesson

Financial analysts are blessed with an enormous quantity of data. There are comprehensive databases of the prices of U.S. stocks, bonds, options, and commodities, as well as huge amounts of data for securities in other countries. We focus on a study by Dimson, Marsh, and Staunton that measures the historical performance of three portfolios of U.S. securities:[1]

1. A portfolio of Treasury bills, that is, U.S. government debt securities maturing in less than one year.[2]
2. A portfolio of U.S. government bonds.
3. A portfolio of U.S. common stocks.

These investments offer different degrees of risk. Treasury bills are about as safe an investment as you can make. There is no risk of default, and their short maturity means that the prices of Treasury bills are relatively stable. In fact, an investor who wishes to lend money for, say, three months can achieve a perfectly certain payoff by purchasing a Treasury bill maturing in three months. However, the investor cannot lock in a *real* rate of return: There is still some uncertainty about inflation.

---

[1] See E. Dimson, P. R. Marsh, and M. Staunton, *Triumph of the Optimists: 101 Years of Investment Returns* (Princeton, NJ: Princeton University Press, 2002).

[2] Treasury bills were not issued before 1919. Before that date the interest rate used is the commercial paper rate.

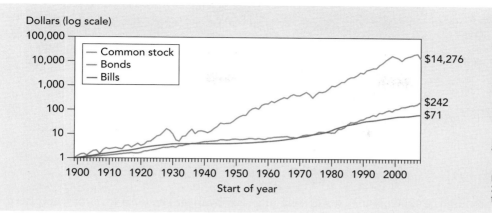

Dollars (log scale)

FIGURE 7.1

How an investment of $1 at the start of 1900 would have grown by the end of 2008, assuming reinvestment of all dividend and interest payments.

Source: E. Dimson, P. R. Marsh, and M. Staunton, *Triumph of the Optimists: 101 Years of Investment Returns* (Princeton, NJ: Princeton University Press, 2002), with updates provided by the authors.

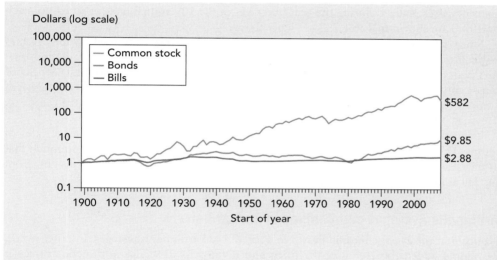

Dollars (log scale)

FIGURE 7.2

How an investment of $1 at the start of 1900 would have grown in real terms by the end of 2008, assuming reinvestment of all dividend and interest payments. Compare this plot with Figure 7.1, and note how inflation has eroded the purchasing power of returns to investors.

Source: E. Dimson, P. R. Marsh, and M. Staunton, *Triumph of the Optimists: 101 Years of Investment Returns* (Princeton, NJ: Princeton University Press, 2002), with updates provided by the authors.

By switching to long-term government bonds, the investor acquires an asset whose price fluctuates as interest rates vary. (Bond prices fall when interest rates rise and rise when interest rates fall.) An investor who shifts from bonds to common stocks shares in all the ups and downs of the issuing companies.

Figure 7.1 shows how your money would have grown if you had invested $1 at the start of 1900 and reinvested all dividend or interest income in each of the three portfolios.[3] Figure 7.2 is identical except that it depicts the growth in the *real* value of the portfolio. We focus here on nominal values.

Investment performance coincides with our intuitive risk ranking. A dollar invested in the safest investment, Treasury bills, would have grown to $71 by the end of 2008, barely enough to keep up with inflation. An investment in long-term Treasury bonds would have

---

[3] Portfolio values are plotted on a log scale. If they were not, the ending values for the common stock portfolio would run off the top of the page.

► **TABLE 7.1** Average rates of return on U.S. Treasury bills, government bonds, and common stocks, 1900–2008 (figures in % per year).

Source: E. Dimson, P. R. Marsh, and M. Staunton, *Triumph of the Optimists: 101 Years of Investment Returns* (Princeton, NJ: Princeton University Press, 2002), with updates provided by the authors.

	Average Annual Rate of Return		
	Nominal	Real	Average Risk Premium (Extra Return versus Treasury Bills)
Treasury bills	4.0	1.1	0
Government bonds	5.5	2.6	1.5
Common stocks	11.1	8.0	7.1

produced $242. Common stocks were in a class by themselves. An investor who placed a dollar in the stocks of large U.S. firms would have received $14,276.

We can also calculate the rate of return from these portfolios for each year from 1900 to 2008. This rate of return reflects both cash receipts—dividends or interest—and the capital gains or losses realized during the year. Averages of the 109 annual rates of return for each portfolio are shown in Table 7.1.

Since 1900 Treasury bills have provided the lowest average return—4.0% per year in *nominal* terms and 1.1% in *real* terms. In other words, the average rate of inflation over this period was about 3% per year. Common stocks were again the winners. Stocks of major corporations provided an average nominal return of 11.1%. By taking on the risk of common stocks, investors earned a *risk premium* of 11.1 − 4.0 = 7.1% over the return on Treasury bills.

You may ask why we look back over such a long period to measure average rates of return. The reason is that annual rates of return for common stocks fluctuate so much that averages taken over short periods are meaningless. Our only hope of gaining insights from historical rates of return is to look at a very long period.[4]

Arithmetic Averages and Compound Annual Returns

Notice that the average returns shown in Table 7.1 are arithmetic averages. In other words, we simply added the 109 annual returns and divided by 109. The arithmetic average is higher than the compound annual return over the period. The 109-year compound annual return for common stocks was 9.2%.[5]

The proper uses of arithmetic and compound rates of return from past investments are often misunderstood. Therefore, we call a brief time-out for a clarifying example.

Suppose that the price of Big Oil's common stock is $100. There is an equal chance that at the end of the year the stock will be worth $90, $110, or $130. Therefore, the return could be −10%, +10%, or +30% (we assume that Big Oil does not pay a dividend). The *expected* return is $1/3 \, (−10 + 10 + 30) = +10\%$.

---

[4] We cannot be sure that this period is truly representative and that the average is not distorted by a few unusually high or low returns. The reliability of an estimate of the average is usually measured by its *standard error*. For example, the standard error of our estimate of the average risk premium on common stocks is 1.9%. There is a 95% chance that the *true* average is within plus or minus 2 standard errors of the 7.1% estimate. In other words, if you said that the true average was between 3.3 and 10.9%, you would have a 95% chance of being right. *Technical note:* The standard error of the average is equal to the standard deviation divided by the square root of the number of observations. In our case the standard deviation is 20.2%, and therefore the standard error is $20.2/\sqrt{109} = 1.9\%$.

[5] This was calculated from $(1 + r)^{109} = 14{,}276$, which implies $r = .092$. *Technical note:* For lognormally distributed returns the annual compound return is equal to the arithmetic average return minus half the variance. For example, the annual standard deviation of returns on the U.S. market was about .20, or 20%. Variance was therefore $.20^2$, or .04. The compound annual return is about $.04/2 = .02$, or 2 percentage points less than the arithmetic average.

If we run the process in reverse and discount the expected cash flow by the expected rate of return, we obtain the value of Big Oil's stock:

$$PV = \frac{110}{1.10} = \$100$$

The expected return of 10% is therefore the correct rate at which to discount the expected cash flow from Big Oil's stock. It is also the opportunity cost of capital for investments that have the same degree of risk as Big Oil.

Now suppose that we observe the returns on Big Oil stock over a large number of years. If the odds are unchanged, the return will be -10% in a third of the years, $+10\%$ in a further third, and $+30\%$ in the remaining years. The arithmetic average of these yearly returns is

$$\frac{-10 + 10 + 30}{3} = +10\%$$

Thus the arithmetic average of the returns correctly measures the opportunity cost of capital for investments of similar risk to Big Oil stock.[6]

The average compound annual return[7] on Big Oil stock would be

$$(.9 \times 1.1 \times 1.3)^{1/3} - 1 = .088, \text{ or } 8.8\%.$$

which is *less* than the opportunity cost of capital. Investors would not be willing to invest in a project that offered an 8.8% expected return if they could get an expected return of 10% in the capital markets. The net present value of such a project would be

$$NPV = -100 + \frac{108.8}{1.1} = -1.1$$

Moral: If the cost of capital is estimated from historical returns or risk premiums, use arithmetic averages, not compound annual rates of return.[8]

Using Historical Evidence to Evaluate Today's Cost of Capital

Suppose there is an investment project that you *know*—don't ask how—has the same risk as Standard and Poor's Composite Index. We will say that it has the same degree of risk as the *market portfolio*, although this is speaking somewhat loosely, because the index does not include all risky securities. What rate should you use to discount this project's forecasted cash flows?

---

[6] You sometimes hear that the arithmetic average correctly measures the opportunity cost of capital for one-year cash flows, but not for more distant ones. Let us check. Suppose that you expect to receive a cash flow of $121 in year 2. We know that one year hence investors will value that cash flow by discounting at 10% (the arithmetic average of possible returns). In other words, at the end of the year they will be willing to pay $PV_1 = 121/1.10 = \$110$ for the expected cash flow. But we already know how to value an asset that pays off $110 in year 1—just discount at the 10% opportunity cost of capital. Thus $PV_0 = PV_1/1.10 = 110/1.10 = \$100$. Our example demonstrates that the arithmetic average (10% in our example) provides a correct measure of the opportunity cost of capital regardless of the timing of the cash flow.

[7] The compound annual return is often referred to as the *geometric average* return.

[8] Our discussion above assumed that we *knew* that the returns of -10, $+10$, and $+30\%$ were equally likely. For an analysis of the effect of uncertainty about the expected return see I. A. Cooper, "Arithmetic Versus Geometric Mean Estimators: Setting Discount Rates for Capital Budgeting," *European Financial Management* 2 (July 1996), pp. 157–167; and E. Jaquier, A. Kane, and A. J. Marcus, "Optimal Estimation of the Risk Premium for the Long Run and Asset Allocation: A Case of Compounded Estimation Risk," *Journal of Financial Econometrics* 3 (2005), pp. 37–55. When future returns are forecasted to distant horizons, the historical arithmetic means are upward-biased. This bias would be small in most corporate-finance applications, however.

Clearly you should use the currently expected rate of return on the market portfolio; that is the return investors would forgo by investing in the proposed project. Let us call this market return r_m. One way to estimate r_m is to assume that the future will be like the past and that today's investors expect to receive the same "normal" rates of return revealed by the averages shown in Table 7.1. In this case, you would set r_m at 11.1%, the average of past market returns.

Unfortunately, this is *not* the way to do it; r_m is not likely to be stable over time. Remember that it is the sum of the risk-free interest rate r_f and a premium for risk. We know that r_f varies. For example, in 1981 the interest rate on Treasury bills was about 15%. It is difficult to believe that investors in that year were content to hold common stocks offering an expected return of only 11.1%.

If you need to estimate the return that investors expect to receive, a more sensible procedure is to take the interest rate on Treasury bills and add 7.1%, the average *risk premium* shown in Table 7.1. For example, in early 2009 the interest rate on Treasury bills was unusually low at .2%. Adding on the average risk premium, therefore, gives

$$r_m(2009) = r_f(2009) + \text{normal risk premium}$$
$$= .002 + .071 = .073, \text{ or } 7.3\%$$

The crucial assumption here is that there is a normal, stable risk premium on the market portfolio, so that the expected *future* risk premium can be measured by the average past risk premium.

Even with over 100 years of data, we can't estimate the market risk premium exactly; nor can we be sure that investors today are demanding the same reward for risk that they were 50 or 100 years ago. All this leaves plenty of room for argument about what the risk premium *really* is.[9]

Many financial managers and economists believe that long-run historical returns are the best measure available. Others have a gut instinct that investors don't need such a large risk premium to persuade them to hold common stocks.[10] For example, surveys of chief financial officers commonly suggest that they expect a market risk premium that is several percentage points below the historical average.[11]

If you believe that the expected market risk premium is less than the historical average, you probably also believe that history has been unexpectedly kind to investors in the United States and that their good luck is unlikely to be repeated. Here are two reasons that history *may* overstate the risk premium that investors demand today.

Reason 1   Since 1900 the United States has been among the world's most prosperous countries. Other economies have languished or been wracked by war or civil unrest. By focusing on equity returns in the United States, we may obtain a biased view of what

---

[9] Some of the disagreements simply reflect the fact that the risk premium is sometimes defined in different ways. Some measure the average difference between stock returns and the returns (or yields) on long-term bonds. Others measure the difference between the compound rate of growth on stocks and the interest rate. As we explained above, this is not an appropriate measure of the cost of capital.

[10] There is some theory behind this instinct. The high risk premium earned in the market seems to imply that investors are extremely risk-averse. If that is true, investors ought to cut back their consumption when stock prices fall and wealth decreases. But the evidence suggests that when stock prices fall, investors spend at nearly the same rate. This is difficult to reconcile with high risk aversion and a high market risk premium. There is active research literature on this "equity premium puzzle." See R. Mehra, "The Equity Premium Puzzle: A Review," *Foundations and Trends in Finance®* 2 (2006), pp. 11–81, and R. Mehra, ed., *Handbook of the Equity Risk Premium* (Amsterdam: Elsevier Handbooks in Finance Series, 2008).

[11] It is difficult to interpret the responses to such surveys precisely. The best known is conducted every quarter by Duke University and *CFO* magazine and reported on at **www.cfosurvey.org**. On average since inception CFOs have predicted a 10-year return on U.S. equities of 3.7% in excess of the return on 10-year Treasury bonds. However, respondents appear to have interpreted the question as asking for their forecast of the *compound* annual return. In this case the comparable *expected* (arithmetic average) premium over *bills* is probably 2 or 3 percentage points higher at about 6%. For a description of the survey data, see J. R. Graham and C. Harvey, "The Long-Run Equity Risk Premium," *Finance Research Letters* 2 (2005), pp. 185–194.

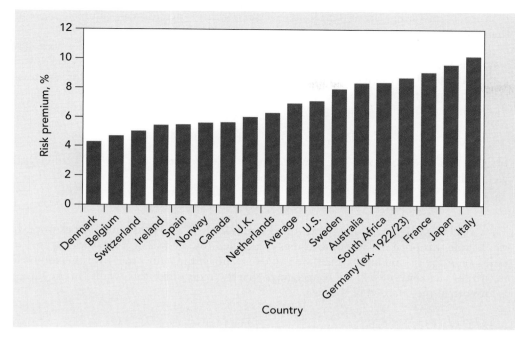

> **FIGURE 7.3**

Average market risk premiums (nominal return on stocks minus nominal return on bills), 1900–2008.

Source: E. Dimson, P. R. Marsh, and M. Staunton, *Triumph of the Optimists: 101 Years of Investment Returns* (Princeton, NJ: Princeton University Press, 2002), with updates provided by the authors.

investors expected. Perhaps the historical averages miss the possibility that the United States could have turned out to be one of these less-fortunate countries.[12]

Figure 7.3 sheds some light on this issue. It is taken from a comprehensive study by Dimson, Marsh, and Staunton of market returns in 17 countries and shows the average risk premium in each country between 1900 and 2008. There is no evidence here that U.S. investors have been particularly fortunate; the U.S. was just about average in terms of returns.

In Figure 7.3 Danish stocks come bottom of the league; the average risk premium in Denmark was only 4.3%. The clear winner was Italy with a premium of 10.2%. Some of these differences between countries may reflect differences in risk. For example, Italian stocks have been particularly variable and investors may have required a higher return to compensate. But remember how difficult it is to make precise estimates of what investors expected. You probably would not be too far out if you concluded that the *expected* risk premium was the same in each country.[13]

Reason 2 Stock prices in the United States have for some years outpaced the growth in company dividends or earnings. For example, between 1950 and 2000 dividend yields in the United States fell from 7.2% to 1.1%. It seems unlikely that investors *expected* such a sharp decline in yields, in which case some part of the actual return during this period was *unexpected*.

Some believe that the low dividend yields at the turn of the century reflected optimism that the new economy would lead to a golden age of prosperity and surging profits, but others attribute the low yields to a reduction in the market risk premium. Perhaps the growth in mutual funds has made it easier for individuals to diversify away part of their risk, or perhaps pension funds and other financial institutions have found that they also could reduce

---

[12] This possibility was suggested in P. Jorion and W. N. Goetzmann, "Global Stock Markets in the Twentieth Century," *Journal of Finance* 54 (June 1999), pp. 953–980.

[13] We are concerned here with the difference between the nominal market return and the nominal interest rate. Sometimes you will see *real* risk premiums quoted—that is, the difference between the *real* market return and the *real* interest rate. If the inflation rate is *i*, then the real risk premium is $(r_m - r_f)/(1 + i)$. For countries such as Italy that have experienced a high degree of inflation, this real risk premium may be significantly lower than the nominal premium.

their risk by investing part of their funds overseas. If these investors can eliminate more of their risk than in the past, they may be content with a lower return.

To see how a rise in stock prices can stem from a fall in the risk premium, suppose that a stock is expected to pay a dividend next year of $12 ($DIV_1 = 12$). The stock yields 3% and the dividend is expected to grow indefinitely by 7% a year ($g = .07$). Therefore the total return that investors expect is $r = 3 + 7 = 10\%$. We can find the stock's value by plugging these numbers into the constant-growth formula that we used in Chapter 4 to value stocks:

$$PV = DIV_1/(r - g) = 12/(.10 - .07) = \$400$$

Imagine that investors now revise downward their required return to $r = 9\%$. The dividend yield falls to 2% and the value of the stock rises to

$$PV = DIV_1/(r - g) = 12/(.09 - .07) = \$600$$

Thus a fall from 10% to 9% in the required return leads to a 50% rise in the stock price. If we include this price rise in our measures of past returns, we will be doubly wrong in our estimate of the risk premium. First, we will overestimate the return that investors required in the past. Second, we will fail to recognize that the return investors require in the future is lower than they needed in the past.

Dividend Yields and the Risk Premium

If there has been a downward shift in the return that investors have required, then past returns will provide an overestimate of the risk premium. We can't wholly get around this difficulty, but we can get another clue to the risk premium by going back to the constant-growth model that we discussed in Chapter 2. If stock prices are expected to keep pace with the growth in dividends, then the expected market return is equal to the dividend yield plus the expected dividend growth—that is, $r = DIV_1/P_0 + g$. Dividend yields in the United States have averaged 4.3% since 1900, and the annual growth in dividends has averaged 5.3%. If this dividend growth is representative of what investors *expected*, then the expected market return over this period was $DIV_1/P_0 + g = 4.3 + 5.3 = 9.6\%$, or 5.6% above the risk-free interest rate. This figure is 1.5% lower than the *realized* risk premium reported in Table 7.1.[14]

Dividend yields have averaged 4.3% since 1900, but, as you can see from Figure 7.4, they have fluctuated quite sharply. At the end of 1917, stocks were offering a yield of 9.0%; by 2000 the yield had plunged to just 1.1%. You sometimes hear financial managers suggest that in years such as 2000, when dividend yields were low, capital was relatively cheap. Is there any truth to this? Should companies be adjusting their cost of capital to reflect these fluctuations in yield?

Notice that there are only two possible reasons for the yield changes in Figure 7.4. One is that in some years investors were unusually optimistic or pessimistic about g, the future growth in dividends. The other is that r, the required return, was unusually high or low. Economists who have studied the behavior of dividend yields have concluded that very little of the variation is related to the subsequent rate of dividend growth. If they are right, the level of yields ought to be telling us something about the return that investors require.

This in fact appears to be the case. A reduction in the dividend yield seems to herald a reduction in the risk premium that investors can expect over the following few years. So, when yields are relatively low, companies may be justified in shaving their estimate

---

[14] See E. F. Fama and K. R. French, "The Equity Premium," *Journal of Finance* 57 (April 2002), pp. 637–659. Fama and French quote even lower estimates of the risk premium, particularly for the second half of the period. The difference partly reflects the fact that they define the risk premium as the difference between market returns and the commercial paper rate. Except for the years 1900–1918, the interest rates used in Table 7.1 are the rates on U.S. Treasury bills.

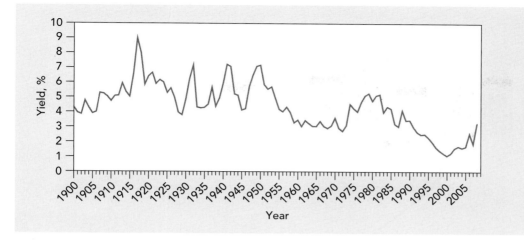

▶ **FIGURE 7.4**

Dividend yields in the U.S.A., 1900–2008.

Source: R.J. Shiller, "Long Term Stock, Bond, Interest Rate and Consumption Data since 1871," www.econ.yale.edu/~shiller/data.htm. Used with permission.

of required returns over the next year or so. However, changes in the dividend yield tell companies next to nothing about the expected risk premium over the next 10 or 20 years. It seems that, when estimating the discount rate for longer term investments, a firm can safely ignore year-to-year fluctuations in the dividend yield.

Out of this debate only one firm conclusion emerges: Do not trust anyone who claims to *know* what returns investors expect. History contains some clues, but ultimately we have to judge whether investors on average have received what they expected. Many financial economists rely on the evidence of history and therefore work with a risk premium of about 7.1%. The remainder generally use a somewhat lower figure. Brealey, Myers, and Allen have no official position on the issue, but we believe that a range of 5% to 8% is reasonable for the risk premium in the United States.

7-2 Measuring Portfolio Risk

You now have a couple of benchmarks. You know the discount rate for safe projects, and you have an estimate of the rate for average-risk projects. But you *don't* know yet how to estimate discount rates for assets that do not fit these simple cases. To do that, you have to learn (1) how to measure risk and (2) the relationship between risks borne and risk premiums demanded.

Figure 7.5 shows the 109 annual rates of return for U.S. common stocks. The fluctuations in year-to-year returns are remarkably wide. The highest annual return was 57.6% in 1933—a partial rebound from the stock market crash of 1929–1932. However, there were losses exceeding 25% in five years, the worst being the −43.9% return in 1931.

Another way of presenting these data is by a histogram or frequency distribution. This is done in Figure 7.6, where the variability of year-to-year returns shows up in the wide "spread" of outcomes.

Variance and Standard Deviation

The standard statistical measures of spread are **variance** and **standard deviation.** The variance of the market return is the expected squared deviation from the expected return. In other words,

$$\text{Variance } (\tilde{r}_m) = \text{the expected value of } (\tilde{r}_m - r_m)^2$$

▶ **FIGURE 7.5**

The stock market has been a profitable but extremely variable investment.

Source: E. Dimson, P. R. Marsh, and M. Staunton, *Triumph of the Optimists: 101 Years of Investment Returns* (Princeton, NJ: Princeton University Press, 2002), with updates provided by the authors.

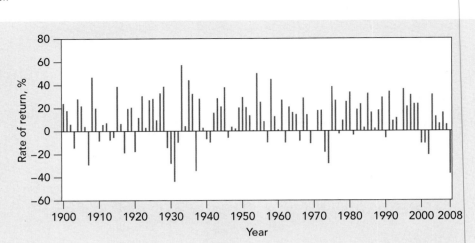

▶ **FIGURE 7.6**

Histogram of the annual rates of return from the stock market in the United States, 1900–2008, showing the wide spread of returns from investment in common stocks.

Source: E. Dimson, P. R. Marsh, and M. Staunton, *Triumph of the Optimists: 101 Years of Investment Returns,* (Princeton, NJ: Princeton University Press, 2002), with updates provided by the authors.

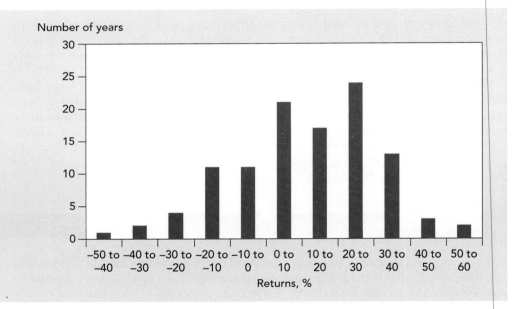

where $\tilde{r}_m$ is the actual return and r_m is the expected return.[15] The standard deviation is simply the square root of the variance:

$$\text{Standard deviation of } \tilde{r}_m = \sqrt{\text{variance}(\tilde{r}_m)}$$

Standard deviation is often denoted by σ and variance by σ^2.

Here is a very simple example showing how variance and standard deviation are calculated. Suppose that you are offered the chance to play the following game. You start by

---

[15] One more technical point: When variance is estimated from a sample of *observed* returns, we add the squared deviations and divide by $N - 1$, where N is the number of observations. We divide by $N - 1$ rather than N to correct for what is called *the loss of a degree of freedom.* The formula is

$$\text{Variance } (\tilde{r}_m) = \frac{1}{N-1}\sum_{t=1}^{N}(\tilde{r}_{mt} - r_m)^2$$

where $\tilde{r}_{mt}$ is the market return in period t and r_m is the mean of the values of $\tilde{r}_{mt}$.

(1) Percent Rate of Return ($\tilde{r}$)	(2) Deviation from Expected Return ($\tilde{r} - r$)	(3) Squared Deviation ($\tilde{r} - r$)²	(4) Probability	(5) Probability × Squared Deviation
+40	+30	900	.25	225
+10	0	0	.5	0
−20	−30	900	.25	225

Variance = expected value of $(\tilde{r} - r)^2$ = 450

Standard deviation = $\sqrt{\text{variance}} = \sqrt{450} = 21$

▶ **TABLE 7.2**

The coin-tossing game: Calculating variance and standard deviation.

investing $100. Then two coins are flipped. For each head that comes up you get back your starting balance *plus* 20%, and for each tail that comes up you get back your starting balance *less* 10%. Clearly there are four equally likely outcomes:

· Head + head: You gain 40%.
· Head + tail: You gain 10%.
· Tail + head: You gain 10%.
· Tail + tail: You lose 20%.

There is a chance of 1 in 4, or .25, that you will make 40%; a chance of 2 in 4, or .5, that you will make 10%; and a chance of 1 in 4, or .25, that you will lose 20%. The game's expected return is, therefore, a weighted average of the possible outcomes:

$$\text{Expected return} = (.25 \times 40) + (.5 \times 10) + (.25 \times -20) = +10\%$$

Table 7.2 shows that the variance of the percentage returns is 450. Standard deviation is the square root of 450, or 21. This figure is in the same units as the rate of return, so we can say that the game's variability is 21%.

One way of defining uncertainty is to say that more things can happen than will happen. The risk of an asset can be completely expressed, as we did for the coin-tossing game, by writing all possible outcomes and the probability of each. In practice this is cumbersome and often impossible. Therefore we use variance or standard deviation to summarize the spread of possible outcomes.[16]

These measures are natural indexes of risk.[17] If the outcome of the coin-tossing game had been certain, the standard deviation would have been zero. The actual standard deviation is positive because we *don't* know what will happen.

Or think of a second game, the same as the first except that each head means a 35% gain and each tail means a 25% loss. Again, there are four equally likely outcomes:

· Head + head: You gain 70%.
· Head + tail: You gain 10%.
· Tail + head: You gain 10%.
· Tail + tail: You lose 50%.

---

[16] Which of the two we use is solely a matter of convenience. Since standard deviation is in the same units as the rate of return, it is generally more convenient to use standard deviation. However, when we are talking about the *proportion* of risk that is due to some factor, it is less confusing to work in terms of the variance.

[17] As we explain in Chapter 8, standard deviation and variance are the correct measures of risk if the returns are normally distributed.

For this game the expected return is 10%, the same as that of the first game. But its standard deviation is double that of the first game, 42 versus 21%. By this measure the second game is twice as risky as the first.

Measuring Variability

In principle, you could estimate the variability of any portfolio of stocks or bonds by the procedure just described. You would identify the possible outcomes, assign a probability to each outcome, and grind through the calculations. But where do the probabilities come from? You can't look them up in the newspaper; newspapers seem to go out of their way to avoid definite statements about prospects for securities. We once saw an article headlined "Bond Prices Possibly Set to Move Sharply Either Way." Stockbrokers are much the same. Yours may respond to your query about possible market outcomes with a statement like this:

> The market currently appears to be undergoing a period of consolidation. For the inter- mediate term, we would take a constructive view, provided economic recovery continues. The market could be up 20% a year from now, perhaps more if inflation continues low. On the other hand, . . .

The Delphic oracle gave advice, but no probabilities.

Most financial analysts start by observing past variability. Of course, there is no risk in hindsight, but it is reasonable to assume that portfolios with histories of high variability also have the least predictable future performance.

The annual standard deviations and variances observed for our three portfolios over the period 1900–2008 were:[18]

Portfolio	Standard Deviation (σ)	Variance (σ^2)
Treasury bills	2.8	7.7
Government bonds	8.3	69.3
Common stocks	20.2	406.4

As expected, Treasury bills were the least variable security, and common stocks were the most variable. Government bonds hold the middle ground.

You may find it interesting to compare the coin-tossing game and the stock market as alternative investments. The stock market generated an average annual return of 11.1% with a standard deviation of 20.2%. The game offers 10% and 21%, respectively—slightly lower return and about the same variability. Your gambling friends may have come up with a crude representation of the stock market.

Figure 7.7 compares the standard deviation of stock market returns in 17 countries over the same 109-year period. Canada occupies low field with a standard deviation of 17.0%, but most of the other countries cluster together with percentage standard deviations in the low 20s.

Of course, there is no reason to suppose that the market's variability should stay the same over more than a century. For example, Germany, Italy, and Japan now have much more stable economies and markets than they did in the years leading up to and including the Second World War.

---

[18] In discussing the riskiness of *bonds*, be careful to specify the time period and whether you are speaking in real or nominal terms. The *nominal* return on a long-term government bond is absolutely certain to an investor who holds on until maturity; in other words, it is risk-free if you forget about inflation. After all, the government can always print money to pay off its debts. However, the real return on Treasury securities is uncertain because no one knows how much each future dollar will buy.

The bond returns were measured annually. The returns reflect year-to-year changes in bond prices as well as interest received. The *one-year* returns on long-term bonds are risky in *both* real and nominal terms.

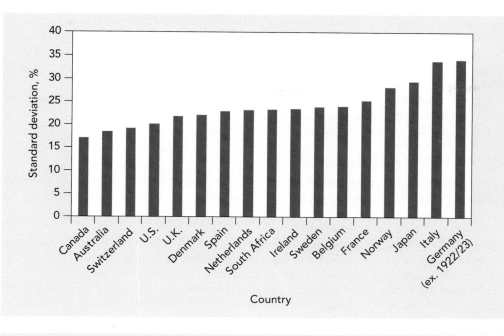

▶ **FIGURE 7.7**

The risk (standard deviation of annual returns) of markets around the world, 1900–2008.

Source: E. Dimson, P. R. Marsh, and M. Staunton, *Triumph of the Optimists: 101 Years of Global Investment Returns* (Princeton, NJ: Princeton University Press, 2002), with updates provided by the authors.

▶ **FIGURE 7.8**

Annualized standard deviation of the preceding 52 weekly changes in the Dow Jones Industrial Average, 1900–2008.

Figure 7.8 does not suggest a long-term upward or downward trend in the volatility of the U.S. stock market.[19] Instead there have been periods of both calm and turbulence. In 2005, an unusually tranquil year, the standard deviation of returns was only 9%, less than half the long-term average. The standard deviation in 2008 was about four times higher at 34%.

Market turbulence over shorter daily, weekly, or monthly periods can be amazingly high. On Black Monday, October 19, 1987, the U.S. market fell by 23% *on a single day*. The market

---

[19] These estimates are derived from *weekly* rates of return. The weekly variance is converted to an annual variance by multiplying by 52. That is, the variance of the weekly return is one-fifty-second of the annual variance. The longer you hold a security or portfolio, the more risk you have to bear.

This conversion assumes that successive weekly returns are statistically independent. This is, in fact, a good assumption, as we will show in Chapter 11.

Because variance is approximately proportional to the length of time interval over which a security or portfolio return is measured, standard deviation is proportional to the square root of the interval.

standard deviation for the week surrounding Black Monday was equivalent to 89% per year. Fortunately volatility dropped back to normal levels within a few weeks after the crash.

At the height of the financial crisis in October and November 2008, the U.S. market standard deviation was running at a rate of about 70% per year. As we write this in August 2009, the standard deviation has fallen back to 25%.[20]

Earlier we quoted 5% to 8% as a reasonable, normal range for the U.S. risk premium. The risk premium has probably increased as a result of the financial crisis. We hope that economic recovery and lower market volatility will allow the risk premium to fall back to normalcy.

How Diversification Reduces Risk

We can calculate our measures of variability equally well for individual securities and portfolios of securities. Of course, the level of variability over 100 years is less interesting for specific companies than for the market portfolio—it is a rare company that faces the same business risks today as it did a century ago.

Table 7.3 presents estimated standard deviations for 10 well-known common stocks for a recent five-year period.[21] Do these standard deviations look high to you? They should. The market portfolio's standard deviation was about 13% during this period. Each of our individual stocks had higher volatility. Amazon was over four times more variable than the market portfolio.

Take a look also at Table 7.4, which shows the standard deviations of some well-known stocks from different countries and of the markets in which they trade. Some of these stocks are more variable than others, but you can see that once again the individual stocks are for the most part more variable than the market indexes.

This raises an important question: The market portfolio is made up of individual stocks, so why doesn't its variability reflect the average variability of its components? The answer is that *diversification reduces variability*.

▶ **TABLE 7.3**
Standard deviations for selected U.S. common stocks, January 2004–December 2008 (figures in percent per year).

Stock	Standard Deviation (σ)	Stock	Standard Deviation (σ)
Amazon	50.9	Boeing	23.7
Ford	47.2	Disney	19.6
Newmont	36.1	Exxon Mobil	19.1
Dell	30.9	Campbell Soup	15.8
Starbucks	30.3	Johnson & Johnson	12.5

▶ **TABLE 7.4**
Standard deviations for selected foreign stocks and market indexes, January 2004–December 2008 (figures in percent per year).

	Standard Deviation (σ)			Standard Deviation (σ)	
	Stock	Market		Stock	Market
BP	20.7	16.0	LVMH	20.6	18.3
Deutsche Bank	28.9	20.6	Nestlé	14.6	13.7
Fiat	35.7	18.9	Nokia	31.6	25.8
Heineken	21.0	20.8	Sony	33.9	16.6
Iberia	35.4	20.4	Telefonica de Argentina	58.6	40.0

---

[20] The standard deviations for 2008 and 2009 are the VIX index of market volatility, published by the Chicago Board Options Exchange (CBOE). We explain the VIX index in Chapter 17. In the meantime, you may wish to check the current level of the VIX on **finance.yahoo** or at the CBOE Web site.

[21] These standard deviations are also calculated from monthly data.

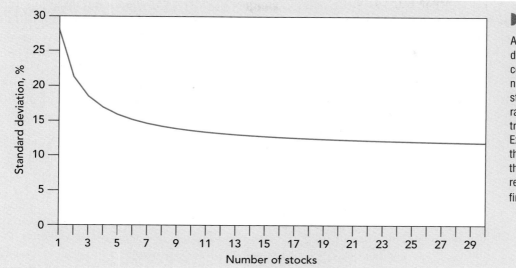

Average risk (standard deviation) of portfolios containing different numbers of stocks. The stocks were selected randomly from stocks traded on the New York Exchange from 2002 through 2007. Notice that diversification reduces risk rapidly at first, then more slowly.

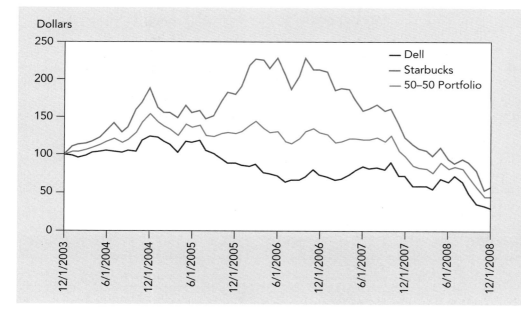

▶ **FIGURE 7.10**

The value of a portfolio evenly divided between Dell and Starbucks was less volatile than either stock on its own. The assumed initial investment is $100.

Even a little diversification can provide a substantial reduction in variability. Suppose you calculate and compare the standard deviations between 2002 and 2007 of one-stock portfolios, two-stock portfolios, five-stock portfolios, etc. You can see from Figure 7.9 that diversification can cut the variability of returns about in half. Notice also that you can get most of this benefit with relatively few stocks: The improvement is much smaller when the number of securities is increased beyond, say, 20 or 30.[22]

Diversification works because prices of different stocks do not move exactly together. Statisticians make the same point when they say that stock price changes are less than perfectly correlated. Look, for example, at Figure 7.10, which plots the prices of Starbucks

---

[22] There is some evidence that in recent years stocks have become individually more risky but have moved less closely together. Consequently, the benefits of diversification have increased. See J. Y. Campbell, M. Lettau, B. C. Malkiel, and Y. Xu, "Have Individual Stocks Become More Volatile? An Empirical Exploration of Idiosyncratic Risk," *Journal of Finance 56* (February 2001), pp. 1–43.

▶ FIGURE 7.11

Diversification eliminates specific risk. But there is some risk that diversification *cannot* eliminate. This is called *market risk*.

(top line) and Dell (bottom line) for the 60-month period ending December 2008. As we showed in Table 7.3, during this period the standard deviation of the monthly returns of both stocks was about 30%. Although the two stocks enjoyed a fairly bumpy ride, they did not move in exact lockstep. Often a decline in the value of Dell was offset by a rise in the price of Starbucks.[23] So, if you had split your portfolio between the two stocks, you could have reduced the monthly fluctuations in the value of your investment. You can see from the blue line in Figure 7.10 that if your portfolio had been evenly divided between Dell and Starbucks, there would have been many more months when the return was just middling and far fewer cases of extreme returns. By diversifying between the two stocks, you would have reduced the standard deviation of the returns to about 20% a year.

The risk that potentially can be eliminated by diversification is called **specific risk.**[24] Specific risk stems from the fact that many of the perils that surround an individual company are peculiar to that company and perhaps its immediate competitors. But there is also some risk that you can't avoid, regardless of how much you diversify. This risk is generally known as **market risk.**[25] Market risk stems from the fact that there are other economywide perils that threaten all businesses. That is why stocks have a tendency to move together. And that is why investors are exposed to market uncertainties, no matter how many stocks they hold.

In Figure 7.11 we have divided risk into its two parts—specific risk and market risk. If you have only a single stock, specific risk is very important; but once you have a portfolio of 20 or more stocks, diversification has done the bulk of its work. For a reasonably well-diversified portfolio, only market risk matters. Therefore, the predominant source of uncertainty for a diversified investor is that the market will rise or plummet, carrying the investor's portfolio with it.

7-3 Calculating Portfolio Risk

We have given you an intuitive idea of how diversification reduces risk, but to understand fully the effect of diversification, you need to know how the risk of a portfolio depends on the risk of the individual shares.

Suppose that 60% of your portfolio is invested in Campbell Soup and the remainder is invested in Boeing. You expect that over the coming year Campbell Soup will give a return of 3.1% and Boeing, 9.5%. The expected return on your portfolio is simply a weighted average of the expected returns on the individual stocks:[26]

$$\text{Expected portfolio return} = (.60 \times 3.1) + (.40 \times 9.5) = 5.7\%$$

---

[23] Over this period the correlation between the returns on the two stocks was .29.

[24] Specific risk may be called *unsystematic risk, residual risk, unique risk,* or *diversifiable risk.*

[25] Market risk may be called *systematic risk* or *undiversifiable risk.*

[26] Let's check this. Suppose you invest $60 in Campbell Soup and $40 in Boeing. The expected dollar return on your Campbell holding is .031 × 60 = $1.86, and on Boeing it is .095 × 40 = $3.80. The expected dollar return on your portfolio is 1.86 + 3.80 = $5.66. The portfolio *rate* of return is 5.66/100 = 0.057, or 5.7%.

The variance of a two-stock portfolio is the sum of these four boxes. x_1, x_2 = proportions invested in stocks 1 and 2; σ_1^2, σ_2^2 = variances of stock returns; σ_{12} = covariance of returns ($\rho_{12}\sigma_1\sigma_2$); ρ_{12} = correlation between returns on stocks 1 and 2.

Calculating the expected portfolio return is easy. The hard part is to work out the risk of your portfolio. In the past the standard deviation of returns was 15.8% for Campbell and 23.7% for Boeing. You believe that these figures are a good representation of the spread of possible *future* outcomes. At first you may be inclined to assume that the standard deviation of the portfolio is a weighted average of the standard deviations of the two stocks, that is, $(.60 \times 15.8) + (.40 \times 23.7) = 19.0\%$. That would be correct *only* if the prices of the two stocks moved in perfect lockstep. In any other case, diversification reduces the risk below this figure.

The exact procedure for calculating the risk of a two-stock portfolio is given in Figure 7.12. You need to fill in four boxes. To complete the top-left box, you weight the variance of the returns on stock 1 (σ_1^2) by the *square* of the proportion invested in it (x_1^2). Similarly, to complete the bottom-right box, you weight the variance of the returns on stock 2 (σ_2^2) by the *square* of the proportion invested in stock 2 (x_2^2).

The entries in these diagonal boxes depend on the variances of stocks 1 and 2; the entries in the other two boxes depend on their **covariance.** As you might guess, the covariance is a measure of the degree to which the two stocks "covary." The covariance can be expressed as the product of the correlation coefficient ρ_{12} and the two standard deviations:[27]

$$\text{Covariance between stocks 1 and 2} = \sigma_{12} = \rho_{12}\sigma_1\sigma_2$$

For the most part stocks tend to move together. In this case the correlation coefficient ρ_{12} is positive, and therefore the covariance σ_{12} is also positive. If the prospects of the stocks were wholly unrelated, both the correlation coefficient and the covariance would be zero; and if the stocks tended to move in opposite directions, the correlation coefficient and the covariance would be negative. Just as you weighted the variances by the square of the proportion invested, so you must weight the covariance by the *product* of the two proportionate holdings x_1 and x_2.

---

[27] Another way to define the covariance is as follows:

$$\text{Covariance between stocks 1 and 2} = \sigma_{12} = \text{expected value of } (\tilde{r}_1 - r_1) \times (\tilde{r}_2 - r_2)$$

Note that any security's covariance with itself is just its variance:

$$\sigma_{11} = \text{expected value of } (\tilde{r}_1 - r_1) \times (\tilde{r}_1 - r_1)$$
$$= \text{expected value of } (\tilde{r}_1 - r_1)^2 = \text{variance of stock 1} = \sigma_1^2$$

Once you have completed these four boxes, you simply add the entries to obtain the portfolio variance:

$$\text{Portfolio variance} = x_1^2\sigma_1^2 + x_2^2\sigma_2^2 + 2(x_1x_2\rho_{12}\sigma_1\sigma_2)$$

The portfolio standard deviation is, of course, the square root of the variance.

Now you can try putting in some figures for Campbell Soup and Boeing. We said earlier that if the two stocks were perfectly correlated, the standard deviation of the portfolio would lie 40% of the way between the standard deviations of the two stocks. Let us check this out by filling in the boxes with $\rho_{12} = +1$.

	Campbell Soup	**Boeing**
Campbell Soup	$x_1^2\sigma_1^2 = (.6)^2 \times (15.8)^2$	$x_1x_2\rho_{12}\sigma_1\sigma_2$ $= (.6) \times (.4) \times 1 \times (15.8) \times (23.7)$
Boeing	$x_1x_2\rho_{12}\sigma_1\sigma_2$ $= (.6) \times (.4) \times 1 \times (15.8) \times (23.7)$	$x_2^2\sigma_2^2 = (.4)^2 \times (23.7)^2$

The variance of your portfolio is the sum of these entries:

$$\text{Portfolio variance} = [(.6)^2 \times (15.8)^2] + [(.4)^2 \times (23.7)^2] + 2(.6 \times .4 \times 1 \times 15.8 \times 23.7)$$
$$= 359.5$$

The standard deviation is $\sqrt{359.5} = 19\%$, or 40% of the way between 15.8 and 23.7.

Campbell Soup and Boeing do not move in perfect lockstep. If past experience is any guide, the correlation between the two stocks is about .18. If we go through the same exercise again with $\rho_{12} = .18$, we find

$$\text{Portfolio variance} = [(.6)^2 \times (15.8)^2] + [(.4)^2 \times (23.7)^2]$$
$$+ 2(.6 \times .4 \times .18 \times 15.8 \times 23.7) = 212.1$$

The standard deviation is $\sqrt{212.1} = 14.6\%$. The risk is now less than 40% of the way between 15.8 and 23.7. In fact, it is less than the risk of investing in Campbell Soup alone.

The greatest payoff to diversification comes when the two stocks are negatively correlated. Unfortunately, this almost never occurs with real stocks, but just for illustration, let us assume it for Campbell Soup and Boeing. And as long as we are being unrealistic, we might as well go whole hog and assume perfect negative correlation ($\rho_{12} = -1$). In this case,

$$\text{Portfolio variance} = [(.6)^2 \times (15.8)^2] + [(.4)^2 \times (23.7)^2]$$
$$+ 2(.6 \times .4 \times (-1) \times 15.8 \times 23.7) = 0$$

When there is perfect negative correlation, there is always a portfolio strategy (represented by a particular set of portfolio weights) that will completely eliminate risk.[28] It's too bad perfect negative correlation doesn't really occur between common stocks.

General Formula for Computing Portfolio Risk

The method for calculating portfolio risk can easily be extended to portfolios of three or more securities. We just have to fill in a larger number of boxes. Each of those down the

---

[28] Since the standard deviation of Boeing is 1.5 times that of Campbell Soup, you need to invest 1.5 times more in Campbell Soup to eliminate risk in this two-stock portfolio.

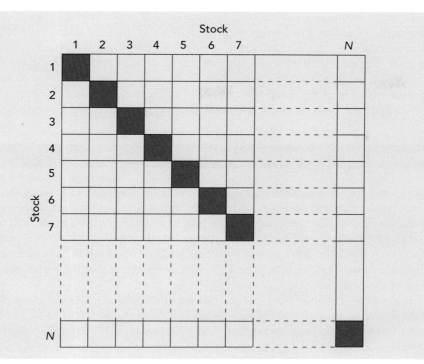

To find the variance of an N-stock portfolio, we must add the entries in a matrix like this. The diagonal cells contain variance terms $(x^2\sigma^2)$ and the off-diagonal cells contain covariance terms $(x_i x_j \sigma_{ij})$.

diagonal—the shaded boxes in Figure 7.13—contains the variance weighted by the square of the proportion invested. Each of the other boxes contains the covariance between that pair of securities, weighted by the product of the proportions invested.[29]

Limits to Diversification

Did you notice in Figure 7.13 how much more important the covariances become as we add more securities to the portfolio? When there are just two securities, there are equal numbers of variance boxes and of covariance boxes. When there are many securities, the number of covariances is much larger than the number of variances. Thus the variability of a well-diversified portfolio reflects mainly the covariances.

Suppose we are dealing with portfolios in which equal investments are made in each of N stocks. The proportion invested in each stock is, therefore, $1/N$. So in each variance box we have $(1/N)^2$ times the variance, and in each covariance box we have $(1/N)^2$ times the covariance. There are N variance boxes and $N^2 - N$ covariance boxes. Therefore,

$$\text{Portfolio variance} = N\left(\frac{1}{N}\right)^2 \times \text{average variance}$$

$$+ \ (N^2 - N)\left(\frac{1}{N}\right)^2 \times \text{average covariance}$$

$$= \frac{1}{N} \times \text{average variance} + \left(1 - \frac{1}{N}\right) \times \text{average covariance}$$

---

[29] The formal equivalent to "add up all the boxes" is

$$\text{Portfolio variance} = \sum_{i=1}^{N}\sum_{j=1}^{N} x_i x_j \sigma_{ij}$$

Notice that when $i = j$, σ_{ij} is just the variance of stock i.

Notice that, as N increases, the portfolio variance steadily approaches the average covariance. If the average covariance were zero, it would be possible to eliminate *all* risk by holding a sufficient number of securities. Unfortunately common stocks move together, not independently. Thus most of the stocks that the investor can actually buy are tied together in a web of positive covariances that set the limit to the benefits of diversification. Now we can understand the precise meaning of the market risk portrayed in Figure 7.11. It is the average covariance that constitutes the bedrock of risk remaining after diversification has done its work.

7-4   How Individual Securities Affect Portfolio Risk

We presented earlier some data on the variability of 10 individual U.S. securities. Amazon had the highest standard deviation and Johnson & Johnson had the lowest. If you had held Amazon on its own, the spread of possible returns would have been more than four times greater than if you had held Johnson & Johnson on its own. But that is not a very interesting fact. Wise investors don't put all their eggs into just one basket: They reduce their risk by diversification. They are therefore interested in the effect that each stock will have on the risk of their portfolio.

This brings us to one of the principal themes of this chapter. *The risk of a well-diversified portfolio depends on the market risk of the securities included in the portfolio.* Tattoo that statement on your forehead if you can't remember it any other way. It is one of the most important ideas in this book.

Market Risk Is Measured by Beta

If you want to know the contribution of an individual security to the risk of a well-diversified portfolio, it is no good thinking about how risky that security is if held in isolation—you need to measure its *market risk*, and that boils down to measuring how sensitive it is to market movements. This sensitivity is called **beta** (β).

Stocks with betas greater than 1.0 tend to amplify the overall movements of the market. Stocks with betas between 0 and 1.0 tend to move in the same direction as the market, but not as far. Of course, the market is the portfolio of all stocks, so the "average" stock has a beta of 1.0. Table 7.5 reports betas for the 10 well-known common stocks we referred to earlier.

Over the five years from January 2004 to December 2008, Dell had a beta of 1.41. If the future resembles the past, this means that *on average* when the market rises an extra 1%, Dell's stock price will rise by an extra 1.41%. When the market falls an extra 2%, Dell's stock prices will fall an extra $2 \times 1.41 = 2.82\%$. Thus a line fitted to a plot of Dell's returns versus market returns has a slope of 1.41. See Figure 7.14.

Of course Dell's stock returns are not perfectly correlated with market returns. The company is also subject to specific risk, so the actual returns will be scattered about the line in Figure 7.14. Sometimes Dell will head south while the market goes north, and vice versa.

▶ **TABLE 7.5**

Betas for selected U.S. common stocks, January 2004–December 2008.

Stock	Beta (β)	Stock	Beta (β)
Amazon	2.16	Disney	.96
Ford	1.75	Newmont	.63
Dell	1.41	Exxon Mobil	.55
Starbucks	1.16	Johnson & Johnson	.50
Boeing	1.14	Campbell Soup	.30

Of the 10 stocks in Table 7.5 Dell has one of the highest betas. Campbell Soup is at the other extreme. A line fitted to a plot of Campbell Soup's returns versus market returns would be less steep: Its slope would be only .30. Notice that many of the stocks that have high standard deviations also have high betas. But that is not always so. For example, Newmont, which has a relatively high standard deviation, has joined the low-beta stocks in the right-hand column of Table 7.5. It seems that while Newmont is a risky investment if held on its own, it makes a relatively low contribution to the risk of a diversified portfolio.

▶ FIGURE 7.14

The return on Dell stock changes on average by 1.41% for each additional 1% change in the market return. Beta is therefore 1.41.

Just as we can measure how the returns of a U.S. stock are affected by fluctuations in the U.S. market, so we can measure how stocks in other countries are affected by movements in *their* markets. Table 7.6 shows the betas for the sample of stocks from other countries.

Why Security Betas Determine Portfolio Risk

Let us review the two crucial points about security risk and portfolio risk:

• Market risk accounts for most of the risk of a well-diversified portfolio.
• The beta of an individual security measures its sensitivity to market movements.

It is easy to see where we are headed: In a portfolio context, a security's risk is measured by beta. Perhaps we could just jump to that conclusion, but we would rather explain it. Here is an intuitive explanation. We provide a more technical one in footnote 31.

Where's Bedrock?   Look back to Figure 7.11, which shows how the standard deviation of portfolio return depends on the number of securities in the portfolio. With more securities, and therefore better diversification, portfolio risk declines until all specific risk is eliminated and only the bedrock of market risk remains.

Where's bedrock? It depends on the average beta of the securities selected.

Suppose we constructed a portfolio containing a large number of stocks—500, say— drawn randomly from the whole market. What would we get? The market itself, or a port- folio *very* close to it. The portfolio beta would be 1.0, and the correlation with the market would be 1.0. If the standard deviation of the market were 20% (roughly its average for 1900–2008), then the portfolio standard deviation would also be 20%. This is shown by the green line in Figure 7.15.

Stock	Beta (β)	Stock	Beta (β)
BP	.49	LVMH	.86
Deutsche Bank	1.07	Nestlé	.35
Fiat	1.11	Nokia	1.07
Heineken	.53	Sony	1.32
Iberia	.59	Telefonica de Argentina	.42

▶ TABLE 7.6

Betas for selected foreign stocks, January 2004–December 2008 (beta is measured rela- tive to the stock's home market).

The green line shows that a well-diversified portfolio of randomly selected stocks ends up with $\beta = 1$ and a standard deviation equal to the market's—in this case 20%. The upper, red line shows that a well-diversified portfolio with $\beta = 1.5$ has a standard deviation of about 30%—1.5 times that of the market. The lower, brown line shows that a well-diversified portfolio with $\beta = .5$ has a standard deviation of about 10%—half that of the market.

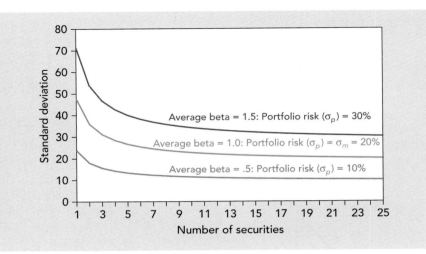

But suppose we constructed the portfolio from a large group of stocks with an average beta of 1.5. Again we would end up with a 500-stock portfolio with virtually no specific risk—a portfolio that moves almost in lockstep with the market. However, *this* portfolio's standard deviation would be 30%, 1.5 times that of the market.[30] A well-diversified portfolio with a beta of 1.5 will amplify every market move by 50% and end up with 150% of the market's risk. The upper red line in Figure 7.15 shows this case.

Of course, we could repeat the same experiment with stocks with a beta of .5 and end up with a well-diversified portfolio half as risky as the market. You can see this also in Figure 7.15.

The general point is this: The risk of a well-diversified portfolio is proportional to the portfolio beta, which equals the average beta of the securities included in the portfolio. This shows you how portfolio risk is driven by security betas.

Calculating Beta   A statistician would define the beta of stock i as

$$\beta_i = \sigma_{im}/\sigma_m^2$$

where σ_{im} is the *covariance* between the stock returns and the market returns and σ_m^2 is the variance of the returns on the market. It turns out that this ratio of covariance to variance measures a stock's contribution to portfolio risk.[31]

---

[30] A 500-stock portfolio with $\beta = 1.5$ would still have some specific risk because it would be unduly concentrated in high-beta industries. Its actual standard deviation would be a bit higher than 30%. If that worries you, relax; we will show you in Chapter 8 how you can construct a fully diversified portfolio with a beta of 1.5 by borrowing and investing in the market portfolio.

[31] To understand why, skip back to Figure 7.13. Each row of boxes in Figure 7.13 represents the contribution of that particular security to the portfolio's risk. For example, the contribution of stock 1 is

$$x_1 x_1 \sigma_{11} + x_1 x_2 \sigma_{12} + \cdots = x_1 (x_1 \sigma_{11} + x_2 \sigma_{12} + \cdots)$$

where x_i is the proportion invested in stock i, and σ_{ij} is the covariance between stocks i and j (note: σ_{ii} is equal to the variance of stock i). In other words, the contribution of stock 1 to portfolio risk is equal to the relative size of the holding (x_1) times the average covariance between stock 1 and all the stocks in the portfolio. We can write this more concisely by saying that the contribution of stock 1 to portfolio risk is equal to the holding size (x_1) times the covariance between stock 1 and the entire portfolio (σ_{1p}).

To find stock 1's *relative* contribution to risk we simply divide by the portfolio variance to give $x_1(\sigma_{1p}/\sigma_p^2)$. In other words, it is equal to the holding size (x_1) times the beta of stock 1 relative to the portfolio (σ_{1p}/σ_p^2).

We can calculate the beta of a stock relative to *any* portfolio by simply taking its covariance with the portfolio and dividing by the portfolio's variance. If we wish to find a stock's beta *relative to the market portfolio* we just calculate its covariance with the market portfolio and divide by the variance of the market:

$$\text{Beta relative to market portfolio} = \frac{\text{covariance with the market}}{\text{variance of market}} = \frac{\sigma_{im}}{\sigma_m^2}$$
$$\text{(or, more simply, beta)}$$

(1)	(2)	(3)	(4)	(5)	(6)	(7)
						Product of
			Deviation	Deviation	Squared	deviations
			from	from average	deviation	from average
	Market	Anchovy Q	average	Anchovy Q	from average	returns
Month	return	return	market return	return	market return	(cols 4 × 5)
1	–8%	–11%	–10	–13	100	130
2	4	8	2	6	4	12
3	12	19	10	17	100	170
4	–6	–13	–8	–15	64	120
5	2	3	0	1	0	0
6	8	6	6	4	36	24
Average	2	2		Total	304	456

$$\text{Variance} = \sigma_m^2 = 304/6 = 50.67$$
$$\text{Covariance} = \sigma_{im} = 456/6 = 76$$
$$\text{Beta } (\beta) = \sigma_{im}/\sigma_m^2 = 76/50.67 = 1.5$$

▶ **TABLE 7.7**   Calculating the variance of the market returns and the covariance between the returns on the market and those of Anchovy Queen. Beta is the ratio of the variance to the covariance (i.e., $\beta = \sigma_{im}/\sigma_m^2$).

Here is a simple example of how to do the calculations. Columns 2 and 3 in Table 7.7 show the returns over a particular six-month period on the market and the stock of the Anchovy Queen restaurant chain. You can see that, although both investments provided an average return of 2%, Anchovy Queen's stock was particularly sensitive to market movements, rising more when the market rises and falling more when the market falls.

Columns 4 and 5 show the deviations of each month's return from the average. To calculate the market variance, we need to average the squared deviations of the market returns (column 6). And to calculate the covariance between the stock returns and the market, we need to average the product of the two deviations (column 7). Beta is the ratio of the covariance to the market variance, or 76/50.67 = 1.50. A diversified portfolio of stocks with the same beta as Anchovy Queen would be one-and-a-half times as volatile as the market.

7-5   Diversification and Value Additivity

We have seen that diversification reduces risk and, therefore, makes sense for investors. But does it also make sense for the firm? Is a diversified firm more attractive to investors than an undiversified one? If it is, we have an *extremely* disturbing result. If diversification is an appropriate corporate objective, each project has to be analyzed as a potential addition to the firm's portfolio of assets. The value of the diversified package would be greater than the sum of the parts. So present values would no longer add.

Diversification is undoubtedly a good thing, but that does not mean that firms should practice it. If investors were *not* able to hold a large number of securities, then they might want firms to diversify for them. But investors *can* diversify.[32] In many ways they can do so more easily than firms. Individuals can invest in the steel industry this week and pull out next week. A firm cannot do that. To be sure, the individual would have to pay brokerage fees on the purchase and sale of steel company shares, but think of the time and expense for a firm to acquire a steel company or to start up a new steel-making operation.

You can probably see where we are heading. If investors can diversify on their own account, they will not pay any *extra* for firms that diversify. And if they have a sufficiently wide choice of securities, they will not pay any *less* because they are unable to invest separately in each factory. Therefore, in countries like the United States, which have large and competitive capital markets, diversification does not add to a firm's value or subtract from it. The total value is the sum of its parts.

This conclusion is important for corporate finance, because it justifies adding present values. The concept of *value additivity* is so important that we will give a formal definition of it. If the capital market establishes a value PV(A) for asset A and PV(B) for B, the market value of a firm that holds only these two assets is

$$PV(AB) = PV(A) + PV(B)$$

A three-asset firm combining assets A, B, and C would be worth PV(ABC) = PV(A) + PV(B) + PV(C), and so on for any number of assets.

We have relied on intuitive arguments for value additivity. But the concept is a general one that can be proved formally by several different routes. The concept seems to be widely accepted, for thousands of managers add thousands of present values daily, usually without thinking about it.

---

[32] One of the simplest ways for an individual to diversify is to buy shares in a mutual fund that holds a diversified portfolio.

● ● ● ● ●

SUMMARY

Our review of capital market history showed that the returns to investors have varied according to the risks they have borne. At one extreme, very safe securities like U.S. Treasury bills have provided an average return over 109 years of only 4.0% a year. The riskiest securities that we looked at were common stocks. The stock market provided an average return of 11.1%, a premium of 7.1% over the safe rate of interest.

This gives us two benchmarks for the opportunity cost of capital. If we are evaluating a safe project, we discount at the current risk-free rate of interest. If we are evaluating a project of average risk, we discount at the expected return on the average common stock. Historical evidence suggests that this return is 7.1% above the risk-free rate, but many financial managers and economists opt for a lower figure. That still leaves us with a lot of assets that don't fit these simple cases. Before we can deal with them, we need to learn how to measure risk.

Risk is best judged in a portfolio context. Most investors do not put all their eggs into one basket: They diversify. Thus the effective risk of any security cannot be judged by an examination of that security alone. Part of the uncertainty about the security's return is diversified away when the security is grouped with others in a portfolio.

Risk in investment means that future returns are unpredictable. This spread of possible outcomes is usually measured by standard deviation. The standard deviation of the *market portfolio*, generally represented by the Standard and Poor's Composite Index, is around 15% to 20% a year.

Most individual stocks have higher standard deviations than this, but much of their variability represents *specific* risk that can be eliminated by diversification. Diversification cannot eliminate *market* risk. Diversified portfolios are exposed to variation in the general level of the market.

A security's contribution to the risk of a well-diversified portfolio depends on how the security is liable to be affected by a general market decline. This sensitivity to market movements is known as *beta* (β). Beta measures the amount that investors expect the stock price to change for each additional 1% change in the market. The average beta of all stocks is 1.0. A stock with a beta greater than 1 is unusually sensitive to market movements; a stock with a beta below 1 is unusually insensitive to market movements. The standard deviation of a well-diversified portfolio is proportional to its beta. Thus a diversified portfolio invested in stocks with a beta of 2.0 will have twice the risk of a diversified portfolio with a beta of 1.0.

One theme of this chapter is that diversification is a good thing *for the investor*. This does not imply that *firms* should diversify. Corporate diversification is redundant if investors can diversify on their own account. Since diversification does not affect the value of the firm, present values add even when risk is explicitly considered. Thanks to *value additivity*, the net present value rule for capital budgeting works even under uncertainty.

In this chapter we have introduced you to a number of formulas. They are reproduced in the endpapers to the book. You should take a look and check that you understand them.

Near the end of Chapter 9 we list some Excel functions that are useful for measuring the risk of stocks and portfolios.

FURTHER READING

For international evidence on market returns since 1900, see:

E. Dimson, P. R. Marsh, and M. Staunton, *Triumph of the Optimists: 101 Years of Investment Returns* (Princeton, NJ: Princeton University Press, 2002). More recent data is available in The Credit Suisse Global Investment Returns Yearbook at **www.tinyurl.com/DMSyearbook**.

The Ibbotson Yearbook is a valuable record of the performance of U.S. securities since 1926:

Ibbotson Stocks, Bonds, Bills, and Inflation 2009 Yearbook (Chicago, IL: Morningstar, Inc., 2009).

Useful books and reviews on the equity risk premium include:

B. Cornell, *The Equity Risk Premium: The Long-Run Future of the Stock Market* (New York: Wiley, 1999).

W. Goetzmann and R. Ibbotson, *The Equity Risk Premium: Essays and Explorations* (Oxford University Press, 2006).

R. Mehra (ed.), *Handbook of Investments: Equity Risk Premium 1* (Amsterdam, North-Holland, 2007).

R. Mehra and E. C. Prescott, "The Equity Risk Premium in Prospect," in *Handbook of the Economics of Finance,* eds. G. M. Constantinides, M. Harris, and R. M. Stulz (Amsterdam, North-Holland, 2003).

PROBLEM SETS

BASIC

1. A game of chance offers the following odds and payoffs. Each play of the game costs $100, so the net profit per play is the payoff less $100.

Probability	Payoff	Net Profit
.10	$500	$400
.50	100	0
.40	0	−100

What are the expected cash payoff and expected rate of return? Calculate the variance and standard deviation of this rate of return.

Visit us at
www.mhhe.com/bma

2. The following table shows the nominal returns on U.S. stocks and the rate of inflation.

   a. What was the standard deviation of the market returns?

   b. Calculate the average real return.

Year	Nominal Return (%)	Inflation (%)
2004	+12.5	+3.3
2005	+6.4	+3.4
2006	+15.8	+2.5
2007	+5.6	+4.1
2008	−37.2	+0.1

3. During the boom years of 2003–2007, ace mutual fund manager Diana Sauros produced the following percentage rates of return. Rates of return on the market are given for comparison.

	2003	2004	2005	2006	2007
Ms. Sauros	+39.1	+11.0	+2.6	+18.0	+2.3
S&P 500	+31.6	+12.5	+6.4	+15.8	+5.6

Calculate the average return and standard deviation of Ms. Sauros's mutual fund. Did she do better or worse than the market by these measures?

4. True or false?

   a. Investors prefer diversified companies because they are less risky.

   b. If stocks were perfectly positively correlated, diversification would not reduce risk.

   c. Diversification over a large number of assets completely eliminates risk.

   d. Diversification works only when assets are uncorrelated.

   e. A stock with a low standard deviation always contributes less to portfolio risk than a stock with a higher standard deviation.

   f. The contribution of a stock to the risk of a well-diversified portfolio depends on its market risk.

   g. A well-diversified portfolio with a beta of 2.0 is twice as risky as the market portfolio.

   h. An undiversified portfolio with a beta of 2.0 is less than twice as risky as the market portfolio.

5. In which of the following situations would you get the largest reduction in risk by spreading your investment across two stocks?

   a. The two shares are perfectly correlated.

   b. There is no correlation.

   c. There is modest negative correlation.

   d. There is perfect negative correlation.

6. To calculate the variance of a three-stock portfolio, you need to add nine boxes:

Use the same symbols that we used in this chapter; for example, x_1 = proportion invested in stock 1 and σ_{12} = covariance between stocks 1 and 2. Now complete the nine boxes.

7. Suppose the standard deviation of the market return is 20%.
   a. What is the standard deviation of returns on a well-diversified portfolio with a beta of 1.3?
   b. What is the standard deviation of returns on a well-diversified portfolio with a beta of 0?
   c. A well-diversified portfolio has a standard deviation of 15%. What is its beta?
   d. A poorly diversified portfolio has a standard deviation of 20%. What can you say about its beta?

8. A portfolio contains equal investments in 10 stocks. Five have a beta of 1.2; the remainder have a beta of 1.4. What is the portfolio beta?
   a. 1.3.
   b. Greater than 1.3 because the portfolio is not completely diversified.
   c. Less than 1.3 because diversification reduces beta.

9. What is the beta of each of the stocks shown in Table 7.8?

Stock	Stock Return if Market Return Is:	
	−10%	**+10%**
A	0	+20
B	−20	+20
C	−30	0
D	+15	+15
E	+10	−10

▶ **TABLE 7.8**
See Problem 9.

INTERMEDIATE

10. Here are inflation rates and U.S. stock market and Treasury bill returns between 1929 and 1933:

Year	Inflation	Stock Market Return	T-Bill Return
1929	−.2	−14.5	4.8
1930	−6.0	−28.3	2.4
1931	−9.5	−43.9	1.1
1932	−10.3	−9.9	1.0
1933	.5	57.3	.3

Visit us at
www.mhhe.com/bma

a. What was the real return on the stock market in each year?
b. What was the average real return?
c. What was the risk premium in each year?
d. What was the average risk premium?
e. What was the standard deviation of the risk premium?

11. Each of the following statements is dangerous or misleading. Explain why.

    a. A long-term United States government bond is always absolutely safe.

    b. All investors should prefer stocks to bonds because stocks offer higher long-run rates of return.

    c. The best practical forecast of future rates of return on the stock market is a 5- or 10-year average of historical returns.

12. Hippique s.a., which owns a stable of racehorses, has just invested in a mysterious black stallion with great form but disputed bloodlines. Some experts in horseflesh predict the horse will win the coveted Prix de Bidet; others argue that it should be put out to grass. Is this a risky investment for Hippique shareholders? Explain.

13. Lonesome Gulch Mines has a standard deviation of 42% per year and a beta of $+.10$. Amalgamated Copper has a standard deviation of 31% a year and a beta of $+.66$. Explain why Lonesome Gulch is the safer investment for a diversified investor.

Visit us at
www.mhhe.com/bma

14. Hyacinth Macaw invests 60% of her funds in stock I and the balance in stock J. The standard deviation of returns on I is 10%, and on J it is 20%. Calculate the variance of portfolio returns, assuming

    a. The correlation between the returns is 1.0.

    b. The correlation is .5.

    c. The correlation is 0.

15. a. How many variance terms and how many covariance terms do you need to calculate the risk of a 100-share portfolio?

    b. Suppose all stocks had a standard deviation of 30% and a correlation with each other of .4. What is the standard deviation of the returns on a portfolio that has equal holdings in 50 stocks?

    c. What is the standard deviation of a fully diversified portfolio of such stocks?

16. Suppose that the standard deviation of returns from a typical share is about .40 (or 40%) a year. The correlation between the returns of each pair of shares is about .3.

    a. Calculate the variance and standard deviation of the returns on a portfolio that has equal investments in 2 shares, 3 shares, and so on, up to 10 shares.

    b. Use your estimates to draw a graph like Figure 7.11. How large is the underlying market risk that cannot be diversified away?

    c. Now repeat the problem, assuming that the correlation between each pair of stocks is zero.

Visit us at
www.mhhe.com/bma

17. Table 7.9 shows standard deviations and correlation coefficients for eight stocks from different countries. Calculate the variance of a portfolio with equal investments in each stock.

Visit us at
www.mhhe.com/bma

18. Your eccentric Aunt Claudia has left you $50,000 in Canadian Pacific shares plus $50,000 cash. Unfortunately her will requires that the Canadian Pacific stock not be sold for one year and the $50,000 cash must be entirely invested in one of the stocks shown in Table 7.9. What is the safest attainable portfolio under these restrictions?

19. There are few, if any, real companies with negative betas. But suppose you found one with $\beta = -.25$.

    a. How would you expect this stock's rate of return to change if the overall market rose by an extra 5%? What if the market fell by an extra 5%?

    b. You have $1 million invested in a well-diversified portfolio of stocks. Now you receive an additional $20,000 bequest. Which of the following actions will yield the safest overall portfolio return?

        i.   Invest $20,000 in Treasury bills (which have $\beta = 0$).

        ii. Invest $20,000 in stocks with $\beta = 1$.

        iii. Invest $20,000 in the stock with $\beta = -.25$.

        Explain your answer.

	BP	Canadian Pacific	Deutsche Bank	Fiat	Heineken	LVMH	Nestlé	Tata Motors	Standard Deviation
					Correlation Coefficients				
BP	1	0.19	0.23	0.20	0.34	0.30	0.16	0.09	22.2%
Canadian Pacific		1	0.43	0.31	0.39	0.34	0.17	0.40	23.9
Deutsche Bank			1	0.74	0.73	0.73	0.49	0.68	29.2
Fiat				1	0.66	0.64	0.47	0.53	35.7
Heineken					1	0.64	0.51	0.50	18.9
LVMH						1	0.52	0.60	20.8
Nestlé							1	0.43	15.4
Tata Motors								1	43.0

▶ **TABLE 7.9** Standard deviations of returns and correlation coefficients for a sample of eight stocks.

Note: Correlations and standard deviations are calculated using returns in each country's own currency; in other words, they assume that the investor is protected against exchange risk.

20. You can form a portfolio of two assets, A and B, whose returns have the following characteristics:

Stock	Expected Return	Standard Deviation	Correlation
A	10%	20%	
			.5
B	15	40	

If you demand an expected return of 12%, what are the portfolio weights? What is the portfolio's standard deviation?

CHALLENGE

21. Here are some historical data on the risk characteristics of Dell and McDonald's:

	Dell	McDonald's
β (beta)	1.41	.77
Yearly standard deviation of return (%)	30.9	17.2

Assume the standard deviation of the return on the market was 15%.

a. The correlation coefficient of Dell's return versus McDonald's is .31. What is the standard deviation of a portfolio invested half in Dell and half in McDonald's?

b. What is the standard deviation of a portfolio invested one-third in Dell, one-third in McDonald's, and one-third in risk-free Treasury bills?

c. What is the standard deviation if the portfolio is split evenly between Dell and McDonald's and is financed at 50% margin, i.e., the investor puts up only 50% of the total amount and borrows the balance from the broker?

d. What is the *approximate* standard deviation of a portfolio composed of 100 stocks with betas of 1.41 like Dell? How about 100 stocks like McDonald's? (*Hint:* Part (d) should not require anything but the simplest arithmetic to answer.)

22. Suppose that Treasury bills offer a return of about 6% and the expected market risk premium is 8.5%. The standard deviation of Treasury-bill returns is zero and the standard deviation of market returns is 20%. Use the formula for portfolio risk to calculate the standard deviation of portfolios with different proportions in Treasury bills and the market. (*Note:* The covariance of two rates of return must be zero when the standard deviation of one return is zero.) Graph the expected returns and standard deviations.

23. Calculate the beta of each of the stocks in Table 7.9 relative to a portfolio with equal investments in each stock.

eXcel

Visit us at
www.mhhe.com/bma

● ● ● ● ●

**REAL-TIME
DATA ANALYSIS**

STANDARD
&POOR'S

STANDARD
&POOR'S

You can download data for the following questions from the Standard & Poor's Market Insight Web site (www.mhhe.com/edumarketinsight)—see the "Monthly Adjusted Prices" spreadsheet—or from finance.yahoo.com. Refer to the Useful Spreadsheet Functions box near the end of Chapter 9 for information on Excel functions.

1. Download to a spreadsheet the last three years of monthly adjusted stock prices for Coca-Cola (KO), Citigroup (C), and Pfizer (PFE).

   a. Calculate the monthly returns.

   b. Calculate the monthly standard deviation of those returns (see Section 7–2). Use the Excel function STDEVP to check your answer. Find the annualized standard deviation by multiplying by the square root of 12.

   c. Use the Excel function CORREL to calculate the correlation coefficient between the monthly returns for each pair of stocks. Which pair provides the greatest gain from diversification?

   d. Calculate the standard deviation of returns for a portfolio with equal investments in the three stocks.

2. Download to a spreadsheet the last five years of monthly adjusted stock prices for each of the companies in Table 7.5 and for the Standard & Poor's Composite Index (S&P 500).

   a. Calculate the monthly returns.

   b. Calculate beta for each stock using the Excel function SLOPE, where the "y" range refers to the stock return (the dependent variable) and the "x" range is the market return (the independent variable).

   c. How have the betas changed from those reported in Table 7.5?

3. A large mutual fund group such as Fidelity offers a variety of funds. They include *sector funds* that specialize in particular industries and *index funds* that simply invest in the market index. Log on to www.fidelity.com and find first the standard deviation of returns on the Fidelity Spartan 500 Index Fund, which replicates the S&P 500. Now find the standard deviations for different sector funds. Are they larger or smaller than the figure for the index fund? How do you interpret your findings?

RISK

Portfolio Theory and the Capital Asset Pricing Model

▶ **In Chapter 7** we began to come to grips with the problem of measuring risk. Here is the story so far.

The stock market is risky because there is a spread of possible outcomes. The usual measure of this spread is the standard deviation or variance. The risk of any stock can be broken down into two parts. There is the *specific* or *diversifiable risk* that is peculiar to that stock, and there is the *market risk* that is associated with marketwide variations. Investors can eliminate specific risk by holding a well-diversified portfolio, but they cannot eliminate market risk. *All* the risk of a fully diversified portfolio is market risk.

A stock's contribution to the risk of a fully diversified portfolio depends on its sensitivity to market changes. This sensitivity is generally known as *beta*. A security with a beta of 1.0 has average market risk—a well-diversified portfolio of such securities has the same standard deviation as the market index. A security with a beta of .5 has below-average market risk—a well-diversified portfolio of these securities tends to move half as far as the market moves and has half the market's standard deviation.

In this chapter we build on this newfound knowledge. We present leading theories linking risk and return in a competitive economy, and we show how these theories can be used to estimate the returns required by investors in different stock-market investments. We start with the most widely used theory, the capital asset pricing model, which builds directly on the ideas developed in the last chapter. We will also look at another class of models, known as arbitrage pricing or factor models. Then in Chapter 9 we show how these ideas can help the financial manager cope with risk in practical capital budgeting situations.

● ● ● ● ●

8-1 Harry Markowitz and the Birth of Portfolio Theory

Most of the ideas in Chapter 7 date back to an article written in 1952 by Harry Markowitz.[1] Markowitz drew attention to the common practice of portfolio diversification and showed exactly how an investor can reduce the standard deviation of portfolio returns by choosing stocks that do not move exactly together. But Markowitz did not stop there; he went on to work out the basic principles of portfolio construction. These principles are the foundation for much of what has been written about the relationship between risk and return.

We begin with Figure 8.1, which shows a histogram of the daily returns on IBM stock from 1988 to 2008. On this histogram we have superimposed a bell-shaped normal

---

[1] H. M. Markowitz, "Portfolio Selection," *Journal of Finance* 7 (March 1952), pp. 77–91.

▶ **FIGURE 8.1**

Daily price changes for
IBM are approximately
normally distributed.
This plot spans 1988
to 2008.

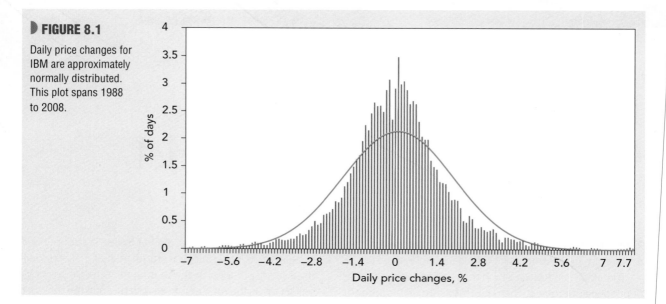

distribution. The result is typical: When measured over a short interval, the past rates of return on any stock conform fairly closely to a normal distribution.[2]

Normal distributions can be completely defined by two numbers. One is the average or expected return; the other is the variance or standard deviation. Now you can see why in Chapter 7 we discussed the calculation of expected return and standard deviation. They are not just arbitrary measures: If returns are normally distributed, expected return and standard deviation are the *only* two measures that an investor need consider.

Figure 8.2 pictures the distribution of possible returns from three investments. A and B offer an expected return of 10%, but A has the much wider spread of possible outcomes. Its standard deviation is 15%; the standard deviation of B is 7.5%. Most investors dislike uncertainty and would therefore prefer B to A.

Now compare investments B and C. This time both have the *same* standard deviation, but the expected return is 20% from stock C and only 10% from stock B. Most investors like high expected return and would therefore prefer C to B.

Combining Stocks into Portfolios

Suppose that you are wondering whether to invest in the shares of Campbell Soup or Boeing. You decide that Campbell offers an expected return of 3.1% and Boeing offers an expected return of 9.5%. After looking back at the past variability of the two stocks, you also decide that the standard deviation of returns is 15.8% for Campbell Soup and 23.7% for Boeing. Boeing offers the higher expected return, but it is more risky.

Now there is no reason to restrict yourself to holding only one stock. For example, in Section 7–3 we analyzed what would happen if you invested 60% of your money in Campbell Soup and 40% in Boeing. The expected return on this portfolio is about 5.7%, simply a weighted average of the expected returns on the two holdings. What about the risk of such a portfolio? We know that thanks to diversification the portfolio risk is less than the average

---

[2] If you were to measure returns over *long* intervals, the distribution would be skewed. For example, you would encounter returns greater than 100% but none less than −100%. The distribution of returns over periods of, say, one year would be better approximated by a *lognormal* distribution. The lognormal distribution, like the normal, is completely specified by its mean and standard deviation.

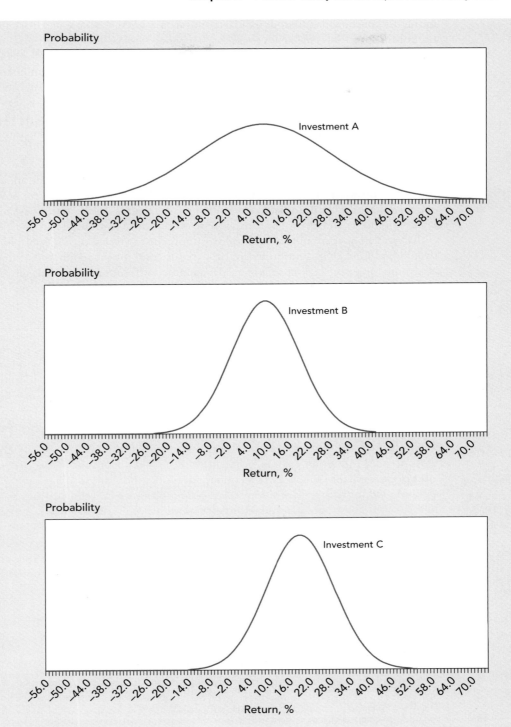

▶ FIGURE 8.2

Investments A and B both have an *expected* return of 10%, but because investment A has the greater spread of *possible* returns, it is more risky than B. We can measure this spread by the standard deviation. Investment A has a standard deviation of 15%; B, 7.5%. Most investors would prefer B to A. Investments B and C both have the same standard deviation, but C offers a higher expected return. Most investors would prefer C to B.

of the risks of the separate stocks. In fact, on the basis of past experience the standard deviation of this portfolio is 14.6%.[3]

The curved blue line in Figure 8.3 shows the expected return and risk that you could achieve by different combinations of the two stocks. Which of these combinations is best depends on your stomach. If you want to stake all on getting rich quickly, you should put all your money in Boeing. If you want a more peaceful life, you should invest most of your money in Campbell Soup, but you should keep at least a small investment in Boeing.[4]

We saw in Chapter 7 that the gain from diversification depends on how highly the stocks are correlated. Fortunately, on past experience there is only a small positive correlation between the returns of Campbell Soup and Boeing ($\rho = +.18$). If their stocks moved in exact lockstep ($\rho = +1$), there would be no gains at all from diversification. You can see this by the brown dotted line in Figure 8.3. The red dotted line in the figure shows a second extreme (and equally unrealistic) case in which the returns on the two stocks are perfectly *negatively* correlated ($\rho = -1$). If this were so, your portfolio would have no risk.

In practice, you are not limited to investing in just two stocks. For example, you could decide to choose a portfolio from the 10 stocks listed in the first column of Table 8.1. After analyzing the prospects for each firm, you come up with forecasts of their returns. You are most optimistic about the outlook for Amazon, and forecast that it will provide a return of 22.8%. At the other extreme, you are cautious about the prospects for Johnson & Johnson and predict a return of 3.8%. You use data for the past five years to estimate the risk of each stock and the correlation between the returns on each pair of stocks.[5]

Now look at Figure 8.4. Each diamond marks the combination of risk and return offered by a different individual security. For example, Amazon has both the highest standard deviation and the highest expected return. It is represented by the upper-right diamond in the figure.

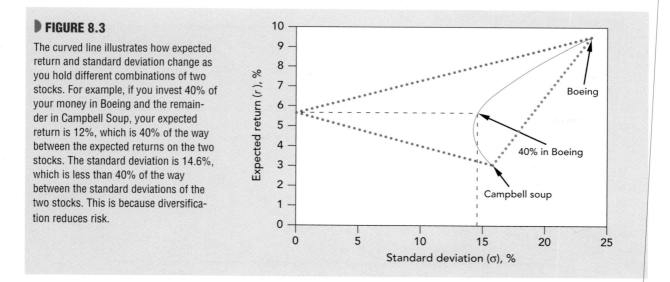

▶ **FIGURE 8.3**

The curved line illustrates how expected return and standard deviation change as you hold different combinations of two stocks. For example, if you invest 40% of your money in Boeing and the remainder in Campbell Soup, your expected return is 12%, which is 40% of the way between the expected returns on the two stocks. The standard deviation is 14.6%, which is less than 40% of the way between the standard deviations of the two stocks. This is because diversification reduces risk.

---

[3] We pointed out in Section 7–3 that the correlation between the returns of Campbell Soup and Boeing has been about .18. The variance of a portfolio which is invested 60% in Campbell and 40% in Boeing is

$$\text{Variance} = x_1^2\sigma_1^2 + x_2^2\sigma_2^2 + 2x_1x_2\rho_{12}\sigma_1\sigma_2$$
$$= [(.6)^2 \times (15.8)^2] + [(.4)^2 \times (23.7)^2] + 2(.6 \times .4 \times .18 \times 15.8 \times 23.7)$$
$$= 212.1$$

The portfolio standard deviation is $\sqrt{212.1} = 14.6\%$.

[4] The portfolio with the minimum risk has 73.1% in Campbell Soup. We assume in Figure 8.3 that you may not take negative positions in either stock, i.e., we rule out short sales.

[5] There are 45 different correlation coefficients, so we have not listed them in Table 8.1.

Stock	Expected Return	Standard Deviation	Efficient Portfolios—Percentages Allocated to Each Stock		
			A	B	C
Amazon	22.8%	50.9%	100	10.9	
Ford	19.0	47.2		11.0	
Dell	13.4	30.9		10.3	
Starbucks	9.0	30.3		10.7	3.6
Boeing	9.5	23.7		10.5	
Disney	7.7	19.6		11.2	
Newmont	7.0	36.1		9.9	10.2
Exxon Mobil	4.7	19.1		9.7	18.4
Johnson & Johnson	3.8	12.5		7.4	33.9
Campbell Soup	3.1	15.8		8.4	33.9
Expected portfolio return			22.8	10.5	4.2
Portfolio standard deviation			50.9	16.0	8.8

▶ **TABLE 8.1**   Examples of efficient portfolios chosen from 10 stocks.

Note: Standard deviations and the correlations between stock returns were estimated from monthly returns, January 2004–December 2008. Efficient portfolios are calculated assuming that short sales are prohibited.

By holding different proportions of the 10 securities, you can obtain an even wider selection of risk and return: In fact, *anywhere* in the shaded area in Figure 8.4. But where in the shaded area is best? Well, what is your goal? Which direction do you want to go? The answer should be obvious: you want to go up (to increase expected return) and to the left (to reduce risk). Go as far as you can, and you will end up with one of the portfolios that lies along the heavy solid line. Markowitz called them **efficient portfolios.** They offer the highest expected return for any level of risk.

We will not calculate this set of efficient portfolios here, but you may be interested in how to do it. Think back to the capital rationing problem in Section 5–4. There we wanted to deploy a limited amount of capital investment in a mixture of projects to give the highest NPV. Here we want to deploy an investor's funds to give the highest expected return for a given standard deviation. In principle, both problems can be solved by hunting and pecking—but only in principle. To solve the capital rationing problem, we can employ linear programming; to solve the portfolio problem, we would turn to a variant of linear programming known as *quadratic programming.* Given the expected return and standard deviation for each stock, as well as the correlation between each pair of stocks, we could use a standard quadratic computer program to calculate the set of efficient portfolios.

Three of these efficient portfolios are marked in Figure 8.4. Their compositions are summarized in Table 8.1. Portfolio A offers the highest expected return: It is invested entirely in one stock, Amazon. Portfolio C offers the minimum risk; you can see from Table 8.1 that it has large holdings in Johnson & Johnson and Campbell Soup, which have the lowest standard deviations. However, the portfolio also has a sizable holding in Newmont even though it is individually very risky. The reason? On past evidence the fortunes of gold-mining shares, such as Newmont, are almost uncorrelated with those of other stocks and so provide additional diversification.

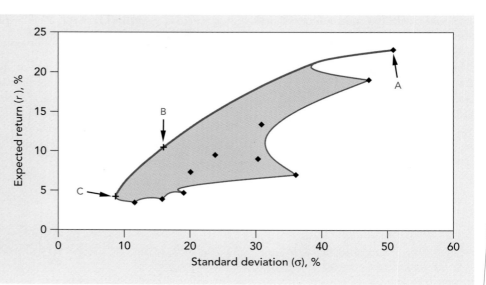

▶ **FIGURE 8.4**

Each diamond shows the expected return and standard deviation of 1 of the 10 stocks in Table 8.1. The shaded area shows the possible combinations of expected return and standard deviation from investing in a *mixture* of these stocks. If you like high expected returns and dislike high standard deviations, you will prefer portfolios along the heavy line. These are *efficient* portfolios. We have marked the three efficient portfolios described in Table 8.1 (A, B, and C).

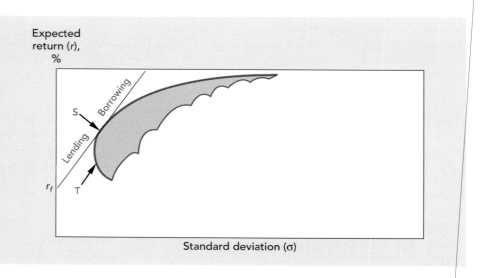

▶ **FIGURE 8.5**

Lending and borrowing extend the range of investment possibilities. If you invest in portfolio S and lend or borrow at the risk-free interest rate, r_f, you can achieve any point along the straight line from r_f through S. This gives you a higher expected return for any level of risk than if you just invest in common stocks.

Table 8.1 also shows the compositions of a third efficient portfolio with intermediate levels of risk and expected return.

Of course, large investment funds can choose from thousands of stocks and thereby achieve a wider choice of risk and return. This choice is represented in Figure 8.5 by the shaded, broken-egg-shaped area. The set of efficient portfolios is again marked by the heavy curved line.

We Introduce Borrowing and Lending

Now we introduce yet another possibility. Suppose that you can also lend or borrow money at some risk-free rate of interest r_f. If you invest some of your money in Treasury bills (i.e., lend money) and place the remainder in common stock portfolio S, you can obtain any combination of expected return and risk along the straight line joining r_f and

S in Figure 8.5. Since borrowing is merely negative lending, you can extend the range of possibilities to the right of S by borrowing funds at an interest rate of r_f and investing them as well as your own money in portfolio S.

Let us put some numbers on this. Suppose that portfolio S has an expected return of 15% and a standard deviation of 16%. Treasury bills offer an interest rate (r_f) of 5% and are risk-free (i.e., their standard deviation is zero). If you invest half your money in portfolio S and lend the remainder at 5%, the expected return on your investment is likewise halfway between the expected return on S and the interest rate on Treasury bills:

$$r = (\tfrac{1}{2} \times \text{expected return on S}) + (\tfrac{1}{2} \times \text{interest rate})$$
$$= 10\%$$

And the standard deviation is halfway between the standard deviation of S and the standard deviation of Treasury bills:[6]

$$\sigma = (\tfrac{1}{2} \times \text{standard deviation of S}) + (\tfrac{1}{2} \times \text{standard deviation of bills})$$
$$= 8\%$$

Or suppose that you decide to go for the big time: You borrow at the Treasury bill rate an amount equal to your initial wealth, and you invest everything in portfolio S. You have twice your own money invested in S, but you have to *pay* interest on the loan. Therefore your expected return is

$$r = (2 \times \text{expected return on S}) - (1 \times \text{interest rate})$$
$$= 25\%$$

And the standard deviation of your investment is

$$\sigma = (2 \times \text{standard deviation of S}) - (1 \times \text{standard deviation of bills})$$
$$= 32\%$$

You can see from Figure 8.5 that when you lend a portion of your money, you end up partway between r_f and S; if you can borrow money at the risk-free rate, you can extend your possibilities beyond S. You can also see that regardless of the level of risk you choose, you can get the highest expected return by a mixture of portfolio S and borrowing or lending. S is the *best* efficient portfolio. There is no reason ever to hold, say, portfolio T.

If you have a graph of efficient portfolios, as in Figure 8.5, finding this best efficient portfolio is easy. Start on the vertical axis at r_f and draw the steepest line you can to the curved heavy line of efficient portfolios. That line will be tangent to the heavy line. The efficient portfolio at the tangency point is better than all the others. Notice that it offers the highest *ratio* of risk premium to standard deviation. This ratio of the risk premium to the standard deviation is called the *Sharpe ratio:*

$$\text{Sharpe ratio} = \frac{\text{Risk premium}}{\text{Standard deviation}} = \frac{r - r_f}{\sigma}$$

Investors track Sharpe ratios to measure the risk-adjusted performance of investment managers. (Take a look at the mini-case at the end of this chapter.)

We can now separate the investor's job into two stages. First, the best portfolio of common stocks must be selected—S in our example. Second, this portfolio must be blended with borrowing or lending to obtain an exposure to risk that suits the particular investor's taste. Each investor, therefore, should put money into just two benchmark investments—a risky portfolio S and a risk-free loan (borrowing or lending).

---

[6] If you want to check this, write down the formula for the standard deviation of a two-stock portfolio:

$$\text{Standard deviation} = \sqrt{x_1^2\sigma_1^2 + x_2^2\sigma_2^2 + 2x_1x_2\rho_{12}\sigma_1\sigma_2}$$

Now see what happens when security 2 is riskless, i.e., when $\sigma_2 = 0$.

What does portfolio S look like? If you have better information than your rivals, you will want the portfolio to include relatively large investments in the stocks you think are undervalued. But in a competitive market you are unlikely to have a monopoly of good ideas. In that case there is no reason to hold a different portfolio of common stocks from anybody else. In other words, you might just as well hold the market portfolio. That is why many professional investors invest in a market-index portfolio and why most others hold well-diversified portfolios.

8-2   The Relationship Between Risk and Return

In Chapter 7 we looked at the returns on selected investments. The least risky investment was U.S. Treasury bills. Since the return on Treasury bills is fixed, it is unaffected by what happens to the market. In other words, Treasury bills have a beta of 0. We also considered a much riskier investment, the market portfolio of common stocks. This has average market risk: its beta is 1.0.

Wise investors don't take risks just for fun. They are playing with real money. Therefore, they require a higher return from the market portfolio than from Treasury bills. The difference between the return on the market and the interest rate is termed the *market risk premium*. Since 1900 the market risk premium ($r_m - r_f$) has averaged 7.1% a year.

In Figure 8.6 we have plotted the risk and expected return from Treasury bills and the market portfolio. You can see that Treasury bills have a beta of 0 and a risk premium of 0.[7] The market portfolio has a beta of 1 and a risk premium of $r_m - r_f$. This gives us two benchmarks for the expected risk premium. But what is the expected risk premium when beta is not 0 or 1?

In the mid-1960s three economists—William Sharpe, John Lintner, and Jack Treynor—produced an answer to this question.[8] Their answer is known as the **capital asset pricing**

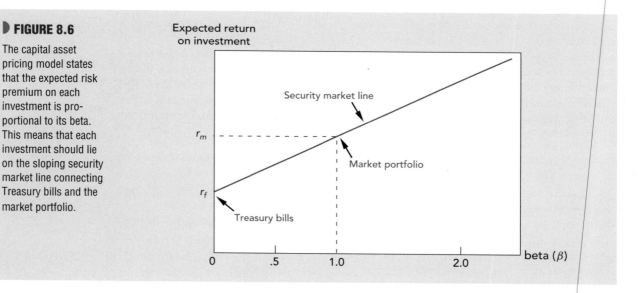

▶ **FIGURE 8.6**

The capital asset pricing model states that the expected risk premium on each investment is proportional to its beta. This means that each investment should lie on the sloping security market line connecting Treasury bills and the market portfolio.

---

[7] Remember that the risk premium is the difference between the investment's expected return and the risk-free rate. For Treasury bills, the difference is zero.

[8] W. F. Sharpe, "Capital Asset Prices: A Theory of Market Equilibrium under Conditions of Risk," *Journal of Finance* 19 (September 1964), pp. 425–442; and J. Lintner, "The Valuation of Risk Assets and the Selection of Risky Investments in Stock Portfolios and Capital Budgets," *Review of Economics and Statistics* 47 (February 1965), pp. 13–37. Treynor's article has not been published.

model, or **CAPM.** The model's message is both startling and simple. In a competitive market, the expected risk premium varies in direct proportion to beta. This means that in Figure 8.6 all investments must plot along the sloping line, known as the **security market line.** The expected risk premium on an investment with a beta of .5 is, therefore, *half* the expected risk premium on the market; the expected risk premium on an investment with a beta of 2 is *twice* the expected risk premium on the market. We can write this relationship as

$$\text{Expected risk premium on stock} = \text{beta} \times \text{expected risk premium on market}$$
$$r - r_f = \beta(r_m - r_f)$$

Some Estimates of Expected Returns

Before we tell you where the formula comes from, let us use it to figure out what returns investors are looking for from particular stocks. To do this, we need three numbers: β, r_f, and $r_m - r_f$. We gave you estimates of the betas of 10 stocks in Table 7.5. In February 2009 the interest rate on Treasury bills was about .2%.

How about the market risk premium? As we pointed out in the last chapter, we can't measure $r_m - r_f$ with precision. From past evidence it appears to be 7.1%, although many economists and financial managers would forecast a slightly lower figure. Let us use 7% in this example.

Table 8.2 puts these numbers together to give an estimate of the expected return on each stock. The stock with the highest beta in our sample is Amazon. Our estimate of the expected return from Amazon is 15.4%. The stock with the lowest beta is Campbell Soup. Our estimate of its expected return is 2.4%, 2.2% more than the interest rate on Treasury bills. Notice that these expected returns are not the same as the hypothetical forecasts of return that we assumed in Table 8.1 to generate the efficient frontier.

You can also use the capital asset pricing model to find the discount rate for a new capital investment. For example, suppose that you are analyzing a proposal by Dell to expand its capacity. At what rate should you discount the forecasted cash flows? According to Table 8.2, investors are looking for a return of 10.2% from businesses with the risk of Dell. So the cost of capital for a further investment in the same business is 10.2%.[9]

Stock	Beta (β)	Expected Return $[r_f + \beta(r_m - r_f)]$
Amazon	2.16	15.4
Ford	1.75	12.6
Dell	1.41	10.2
Starbucks	1.16	8.4
Boeing	1.14	8.3
Disney	.96	7.0
Newmont	.63	4.7
Exxon Mobil	.55	4.2
Johnson & Johnson	.50	3.8
Campbell Soup	.30	2.4

▶ **TABLE 8.2**
These estimates of the returns expected by investors in February 2009 were based on the capital asset pricing model. We assumed .2% for the interest rate r_f and 7% for the expected risk premium $r_m - r_f$.

[9] Remember that instead of investing in plant and machinery, the firm could return the money to the shareholders. The opportunity cost of investing is the return that shareholders could expect to earn by buying financial assets. This expected return depends on the market risk of the assets.

In practice, choosing a discount rate is seldom so easy. (After all, you can't expect to be paid a fat salary just for plugging numbers into a formula.) For example, you must learn how to adjust the expected return for the extra risk caused by company borrowing. Also you need to consider the difference between short- and long-term interest rates. In early 2009 short-term interest rates were at record lows and well below long-term rates. It is possible that investors were content with the prospect of quite modest equity returns in the short run, but they almost certainly required higher long-run returns than the figures shown in Table 8.2.[10] If that is so, a cost of capital based on short-term rates may be inappropriate for long-term capital investments. But these refinements can wait until later.

Review of the Capital Asset Pricing Model

Let us review the basic principles of portfolio selection:

1. Investors like high expected return and low standard deviation. Common stock portfolios that offer the highest expected return for a given standard deviation are known as *efficient portfolios*.

2. If the investor can lend or borrow at the risk-free rate of interest, one efficient portfolio is better than all the others: the portfolio that offers the highest ratio of risk premium to standard deviation (that is, portfolio S in Figure 8.5). A risk-averse investor will put part of his money in this efficient portfolio and part in the risk-free asset. A risk-tolerant investor may put all her money in this portfolio or she may borrow and put in even more.

3. The composition of this best efficient portfolio depends on the investor's assessments of expected returns, standard deviations, and correlations. But suppose everybody has the same information and the same assessments. If there is no superior information, each investor should hold the same portfolio as everybody else; in other words, everyone should hold the market portfolio.

Now let us go back to the risk of individual stocks:

4. Do not look at the risk of a stock in isolation but at its contribution to portfolio risk. This contribution depends on the stock's sensitivity to changes in the value of the portfolio.

5. A stock's sensitivity to changes in the value of the *market* portfolio is known as *beta*. Beta, therefore, measures the marginal contribution of a stock to the risk of the market portfolio.

Now if everyone holds the market portfolio, and if beta measures each security's contribution to the market portfolio risk, then it is no surprise that the risk premium demanded by investors is proportional to beta. That is what the CAPM says.

What If a Stock Did Not Lie on the Security Market Line?

Imagine that you encounter stock A in Figure 8.7. Would you buy it? We hope not[11]—if you want an investment with a beta of .5, you could get a higher expected return by investing half your money in Treasury bills and half in the market portfolio. If everybody shares your view of the stock's prospects, the price of A will have to fall until the expected return matches what you could get elsewhere.

---

[10] The estimates in Table 8.2 may also be too low for the *short term* if investors required a higher risk premium in the short term to compensate for the unusual market volatility in 2009.

[11] Unless, of course, we were trying to sell it.

▶ **FIGURE 8.7**

In equilibrium no stock can lie below the security market line. For example, instead of buying stock A, investors would prefer to lend part of their money and put the balance in the market portfolio. And instead of buying stock B, they would prefer to borrow and invest in the market portfolio.

What about stock B in Figure 8.7? Would you be tempted by its high return? You wouldn't if you were smart. You could get a higher expected return for the same beta by borrowing 50 cents for every dollar of your own money and investing in the market portfolio. Again, if everybody agrees with your assessment, the price of stock B cannot hold. It will have to fall until the expected return on B is equal to the expected return on the combination of borrowing and investment in the market portfolio.[12]

We have made our point. An investor can always obtain an expected risk premium of $\beta(r_m - r_f)$ by holding a mixture of the market portfolio and a risk-free loan. So in well-functioning markets nobody will hold a stock that offers an expected risk premium of *less* than $\beta(r_m - r_f)$. But what about the other possibility? Are there stocks that offer a higher expected risk premium? In other words, are there any that lie above the security market line in Figure 8.7? If we take all stocks together, we have the market portfolio. Therefore, we know that stocks *on average* lie on the line. Since none lies *below* the line, then there also can't be any that lie *above* the line. Thus each and every stock must lie on the security market line and offer an expected risk premium of

$$r - r_f = \beta(r_m - r_f)$$

8-3 Validity and Role of the Capital Asset Pricing Model

Any economic model is a simplified statement of reality. We need to simplify in order to interpret what is going on around us. But we also need to know how much faith we can place in our model.

Let us begin with some matters about which there is broad agreement. First, few people quarrel with the idea that investors require some extra return for taking on risk. That is why common stocks have given on average a higher return than U.S. Treasury bills. Who would want to invest in risky common stocks if they offered only the *same* expected return as bills? We would not, and we suspect you would not either.

Second, investors do appear to be concerned principally with those risks that they cannot eliminate by diversification. If this were not so, we should find that stock prices increase whenever two companies merge to spread their risks. And we should find that investment

---

[12] Investing in A or B only would be stupid; you would hold an undiversified portfolio.

companies which invest in the shares of other firms are more highly valued than the shares they hold. But we do not observe either phenomenon. Mergers undertaken just to spread risk do not increase stock prices, and investment companies are no more highly valued than the stocks they hold.

The capital asset pricing model captures these ideas in a simple way. That is why financial managers find it a convenient tool for coming to grips with the slippery notion of risk and why nearly three-quarters of them use it to estimate the cost of capital.[13] It is also why economists often use the capital asset pricing model to demonstrate important ideas in finance even when there are other ways to prove these ideas. But that does not mean that the capital asset pricing model is ultimate truth. We will see later that it has several unsatisfactory features, and we will look at some alternative theories. Nobody knows whether one of these alternative theories is eventually going to come out on top or whether there are other, better models of risk and return that have not yet seen the light of day.

Tests of the Capital Asset Pricing Model

Imagine that in 1931 ten investors gathered together in a Wall Street bar and agreed to establish investment trust funds for their children. Each investor decided to follow a different strategy. Investor 1 opted to buy the 10% of the New York Stock Exchange stocks with the lowest estimated betas; investor 2 chose the 10% with the next-lowest betas; and so on, up to investor 10, who proposed to buy the stocks with the highest betas. They also planned that at the end of each year they would reestimate the betas of all NYSE stocks and reconstitute their portfolios.[14] And so they parted with much cordiality and good wishes.

In time the 10 investors all passed away, but their children agreed to meet in early 2009 in the same bar to compare the performance of their portfolios. Figure 8.8 shows how they had fared. Investor 1's portfolio turned out to be much less risky than the market; its beta was only .49. However, investor 1 also realized the lowest return, 8.0% above the risk-free rate of interest. At the other extreme, the beta of investor 10's portfolio was 1.53, about three times that of investor 1's portfolio. But investor 10 was rewarded with the highest return, averaging 14.3% a year above the interest rate. So over this 77-year period returns did indeed increase with beta.

As you can see from Figure 8.8, the market portfolio over the same 77-year period provided an average return of 11.8% above the interest rate[15] and (of course) had a beta of 1.0. The CAPM predicts that the risk premium should increase in proportion to beta, so that the returns of each portfolio should lie on the upward-sloping security market line in Figure 8.8. Since the market provided a risk premium of 11.8%, investor 1's portfolio, with a beta of .49, should have provided a risk premium of 5.8% and investor 10's portfolio, with a beta of 1.53, should have given a premium of 18.1%. You can see that, while high-beta stocks performed better than low-beta stocks, the difference was not as great as the CAPM predicts.

Although Figure 8.8 provides broad support for the CAPM, critics have pointed out that the slope of the line has been particularly flat in recent years. For example, Figure 8.9 shows how our 10 investors fared between 1966 and 2008. Now it is less clear who is buying the drinks: Returns are pretty much in line with the CAPM with the important exception of the

---

[13] See J. R. Graham and C. R. Harvey, "The Theory and Practice of Corporate Finance: Evidence from the Field," *Journal of Financial Economics* 61 (2001), pp. 187–243. A number of the managers surveyed reported using more than one method to estimate the cost of capital. Seventy-three percent used the capital asset pricing model, while 39% stated they used the average historical stock return and 34% used the capital asset pricing model with some extra risk factors.

[14] Betas were estimated using returns over the previous 60 months.

[15] In Figure 8.8 the stocks in the "market portfolio" are weighted equally. Since the stocks of small firms have provided higher average returns than those of large firms, the risk premium on an equally weighted index is higher than on a value-weighted index. This is one reason for the difference between the 11.8% market risk premium in Figure 8.8 and the 7.1% premium reported in Table 7.1.

FIGURE 8.8

The capital asset pricing model states that the expected risk premium from any investment should lie on the security market line. The dots show the actual average risk premiums from portfolios with different betas. The high-beta portfolios generated higher average returns, just as predicted by the CAPM. But the high-beta portfolios plotted below the market line, and the low-beta portfolios plotted above. A line fitted to the 10 portfolio returns would be "flatter" than the market line.

Source: F. Black, "Beta and Return," *Journal of Portfolio Management* 20 (Fall 1993), pp. 8–18. © 1993 Institutional Investor. Used with permission. We are grateful to Adam Kolasinski for updating the calculations.

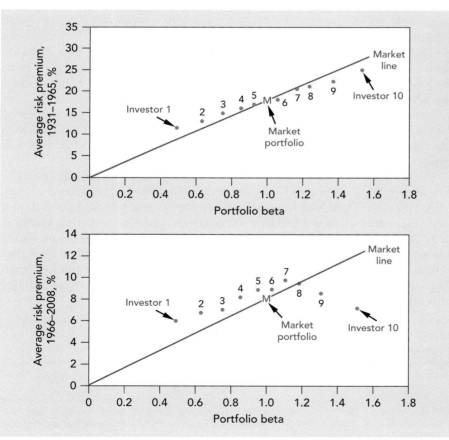

FIGURE 8.9

The relationship between beta and actual average return has been weaker since the mid-1960s. Stocks with the highest betas have provided poor returns.

Source: F. Black, "Beta and Return," *Journal of Portfolio Management* 20 (Fall 1993), pp. 8–18. © 1993 Institutional Investor. Used with permission. We are grateful to Adam Kolasinski for updating the calculations.

two highest-risk portfolios. Investor 10, who rode the roller coaster of a high-beta portfolio, earned a return that was below that of the market. Of course, before 1966 the line was correspondingly steeper. This is also shown in Figure 8.9.

What is going on here? It is hard to say. Defenders of the capital asset pricing model emphasize that it is concerned with *expected* returns, whereas we can observe only *actual* returns. Actual stock returns reflect expectations, but they also embody lots of "noise"—the steady flow of surprises that conceal whether on average investors have received the returns they expected. This noise may make it impossible to judge whether the model holds better in one period than another.[16] Perhaps the best that we can do is to focus on the longest period for which there is reasonable data. This would take us back to Figure 8.8, which suggests that expected returns do indeed increase with beta, though less rapidly than the simple version of the CAPM predicts.[17]

The CAPM has also come under fire on a second front: Although return has not risen with beta in recent years, it has been related to other measures. For example, the red line in Figure 8.10 shows the cumulative difference between the returns on small-firm stocks and large-firm stocks. If you had bought the shares with the smallest market capitalizations and sold those with the largest capitalizations, this is how your wealth would have changed. You can see that small-cap stocks did not always do well, but over the long haul their owners have made substantially higher returns. Since the end of 1926 the average annual difference between the returns on the two groups of stocks has been 3.6%.

Now look at the green line in Figure 8.10, which shows the cumulative difference between the returns on value stocks and growth stocks. Value stocks here are defined as those with high ratios of book value to market value. Growth stocks are those with low ratios of book to market. Notice that value stocks have provided a higher long-run return than growth stocks.[18] Since 1926 the average annual difference between the returns on value and growth stocks has been 5.2%.

Figure 8.10 does not fit well with the CAPM, which predicts that beta is the *only* reason that expected returns differ. It seems that investors saw risks in "small-cap" stocks and value stocks that were not captured by beta.[19] Take value stocks, for example. Many of these stocks may have sold below book value because the firms were in serious trouble; if the economy slowed unexpectedly, the firms might have collapsed altogether. Therefore, investors, whose jobs could also be on the line in a recession, may have regarded these stocks as particularly risky and demanded compensation in the form of higher expected returns. If that were the case, the simple version of the CAPM cannot be the whole truth.

Again, it is hard to judge how seriously the CAPM is damaged by this finding. The relationship among stock returns and firm size and book-to-market ratio has been well documented. However, if you look long and hard at past returns, you are bound to find some strategy that just by chance would have worked in the past. This practice is known as "data-mining" or "data snooping." Maybe the size and book-to-market effects are simply chance results that stem from data snooping. If so, they should have vanished once they were discovered. There is some evidence that this is the case. For example, if you look again at Figure 8.10, you will see that in the past 25 years small-firm stocks have underperformed just about as often as they have overperformed.

---

[16] A second problem with testing the model is that the market portfolio should contain all risky investments, including stocks, bonds, commodities, real estate—even human capital. Most market indexes contain only a sample of common stocks.

[17] We say "simple version" because Fischer Black has shown that if there are borrowing restrictions, there should still exist a positive relationship between expected return and beta, but the security market line would be less steep as a result. See F. Black, "Capital Market Equilibrium with Restricted Borrowing," *Journal of Business* 45 (July 1972), pp. 444–455.

[18] Fama and French calculated the returns on portfolios designed to take advantage of the size effect and the book-to-market effect. See E. F. Fama and K. R. French, "The Cross-Section of Expected Stock Returns," *Journal of Financial Economics* 47 (June 1992), pp. 427–465. When calculating the returns on these portfolios, Fama and French control for differences in firm size when comparing stocks with low and high book-to-market ratios. Similarly, they control for differences in the book-to-market ratio when comparing small- and large-firm stocks. For details of the methodology and updated returns on the size and book-to-market factors see Kenneth French's Web site (mba.tuck.dartmouth.edu/pages/faculty/ken.french/data_library.html).

[19] An investor who bought small-company stocks and sold large-company stocks would have incurred some risk. Her portfolio would have had a beta of .28. This is not nearly large enough to explain the difference in returns. There is no simple relationship between the return on the value- and growth-stock portfolios and beta.

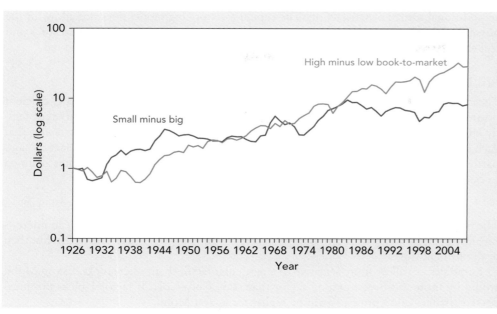

▶ **FIGURE 8.10**

The red line shows the cumulative difference between the returns on small-firm and large-firm stocks. The green line shows the cumulative difference between the returns on high book-to-market-value stocks (i.e., value stocks) and low book-to-market-value stocks (i.e., growth stocks).

Source: Kenneth French's Web site, mba.tuck .dartmouth.edu/pages/ faculty/ken.french/data_ library.html. Used with permission.

There is no doubt that the evidence on the CAPM is less convincing than scholars once thought. But it will be hard to reject the CAPM beyond all reasonable doubt. Since data and statistics are unlikely to give final answers, the plausibility of the CAPM *theory* will have to be weighed along with the empirical "facts."

Assumptions behind the Capital Asset Pricing Model

The capital asset pricing model rests on several assumptions that we did not fully spell out. For example, we assumed that investment in U.S. Treasury bills is risk-free. It is true that there is little chance of default, but bills do not guarantee a *real* return. There is still some uncertainty about inflation. Another assumption was that investors can *borrow* money at the same rate of interest at which they can lend. Generally borrowing rates are higher than lending rates.

It turns out that many of these assumptions are not crucial, and with a little pushing and pulling it is possible to modify the capital asset pricing model to handle them. The really important idea is that investors are content to invest their money in a limited number of benchmark portfolios. (In the basic CAPM these benchmarks are Treasury bills and the market portfolio.)

In these modified CAPMs expected return still depends on market risk, but the definition of market risk depends on the nature of the benchmark portfolios. In practice, none of these alternative capital asset pricing models is as widely used as the standard version.

8-4 Some Alternative Theories

The capital asset pricing model pictures investors as solely concerned with the level and uncertainty of their future wealth. But this could be too simplistic. For example, investors may become accustomed to a particular standard of living, so that poverty tomorrow may be particularly difficult to bear if you were wealthy yesterday. Behavioral psychologists have also observed that investors do not focus solely on the *current* value of their holdings, but look back at whether their investments are showing a profit. A gain, however small, may be an additional source of satisfaction. The capital asset pricing model does not allow for the possibility that investors may take account of the price at which they purchased stock and feel elated when their investment is in the black and depressed when it is in the red.[20]

Arbitrage Pricing Theory

The capital asset pricing theory begins with an analysis of how investors construct efficient portfolios. Stephen Ross's **arbitrage pricing theory,** or **APT,** comes from a different family entirely. It does not ask which portfolios are efficient. Instead, it starts by *assuming* that each stock's return depends partly on pervasive macroeconomic influences or "factors" and partly on "noise"—events that are unique to that company. Moreover, the return is assumed to obey the following simple relationship:

$$\text{Return} = a + b_1(r_{\text{factor 1}}) + b_2(r_{\text{factor 2}}) + b_3(r_{\text{factor 3}}) + \cdots + \text{noise}$$

The theory does not say what the factors are: There could be an oil price factor, an interest-rate factor, and so on. The return on the market portfolio *might* serve as one factor, but then again it might not.

Some stocks will be more sensitive to a particular factor than other stocks. Exxon Mobil would be more sensitive to an oil factor than, say, Coca-Cola. If factor 1 picks up unexpected changes in oil prices, b_1 will be higher for Exxon Mobil.

For any individual stock there are two sources of risk. First is the risk that stems from the pervasive macroeconomic factors. This cannot be eliminated by diversification. Second is the risk arising from possible events that are specific to the company. Diversification eliminates specific risk, and diversified investors can therefore ignore it when deciding whether to buy or sell a stock. The expected risk premium on a stock is affected by factor or macroeconomic risk; it is *not* affected by specific risk.

Arbitrage pricing theory states that the expected risk premium on a stock should depend on the expected risk premium associated with each factor and the stock's sensitivity to each of the factors (b_1, b_2, b_3, etc.). Thus the formula is[21]

$$\text{Expected risk premium} = r - r_f$$
$$= b_1(r_{\text{factor 1}} - r_f) + b_2(r_{\text{factor 2}} - r_f) + \cdots$$

Notice that this formula makes two statements:

1. If you plug in a value of zero for each of the *b*'s in the formula, the expected risk premium is zero. A diversified portfolio that is constructed to have zero sensitivity to each macroeconomic factor is essentially risk-free and therefore must be priced to offer the risk-free rate of interest. If the portfolio offered a higher return, investors could make a risk-free (or "arbitrage") profit by borrowing to buy the portfolio. If it offered a lower return, you could make an arbitrage profit by running the strategy in reverse; in other words, you would *sell* the diversified zero-sensitivity portfolio and *invest* the proceeds in U.S. Treasury bills.

2. A diversified portfolio that is constructed to have exposure to, say, factor 1, will offer a risk premium, which will vary in direct proportion to the portfolio's sensitivity to that factor. For example, imagine that you construct two portfolios, A and B, that are affected only by factor 1. If portfolio A is twice as sensitive as portfolio B to factor 1,

---

[20] We discuss aversion to loss again in Chapter 11. The implications for asset pricing are explored in S. Benartzi and R. Thaler, "Myopic Loss Aversion and the Equity Premium Puzzle," *Quarterly Journal of Economics* 110 (1995), pp. 75–92; and in N. Barberis, M. Huang, and T. Santos, "Prospect Theory and Asset Prices," *Quarterly Journal of Economics* 116 (2001), pp. 1–53.

[21] There may be some macroeconomic factors that investors are simply not worried about. For example, some macroeconomists believe that money supply doesn't matter and therefore investors are not worried about inflation. Such factors would not command a risk premium. They would drop out of the APT formula for expected return.

portfolio A must offer twice the risk premium. Therefore, if you divided your money equally between U.S. Treasury bills and portfolio A, your combined portfolio would have exactly the same sensitivity to factor 1 as portfolio B and would offer the same risk premium.

Suppose that the arbitrage pricing formula did *not* hold. For example, suppose that the combination of Treasury bills and portfolio A offered a higher return. In that case investors could make an arbitrage profit by selling portfolio B and investing the proceeds in the mixture of bills and portfolio A.

The arbitrage that we have described applies to well-diversified portfolios, where the specific risk has been diversified away. But if the arbitrage pricing relationship holds for all diversified portfolios, it must generally hold for the individual stocks. Each stock must offer an expected return commensurate with its contribution to portfolio risk. In the APT, this contribution depends on the sensitivity of the stock's return to unexpected changes in the macroeconomic factors.

A Comparison of the Capital Asset Pricing Model and Arbitrage Pricing Theory

Like the capital asset pricing model, arbitrage pricing theory stresses that expected return depends on the risk stemming from economywide influences and is not affected by specific risk. You can think of the factors in arbitrage pricing as representing special portfolios of stocks that tend to be subject to a common influence. If the expected risk premium on each of these portfolios is proportional to the portfolio's market beta, then the arbitrage pricing theory and the capital asset pricing model will give the same answer. In any other case they will not.

How do the two theories stack up? Arbitrage pricing has some attractive features. For example, the market portfolio that plays such a central role in the capital asset pricing model does not feature in arbitrage pricing theory.[22] So we do not have to worry about the problem of measuring the market portfolio, and in principle we can test the arbitrage pricing theory even if we have data on only a sample of risky assets.

Unfortunately you win some and lose some. Arbitrage pricing theory does not tell us what the underlying factors are—unlike the capital asset pricing model, which collapses *all* macroeconomic risks into a well-defined *single* factor, the return on the market portfolio.

The Three-Factor Model

Look back at the equation for APT. To estimate expected returns, you first need to follow three steps:

> *Step 1:* Identify a reasonably short list of macroeconomic factors that could affect stock returns.
>
> *Step 2:* Estimate the expected risk premium on each of these factors ($r_{factor\ 1} - r_f$, etc.).
>
> *Step 3:* Measure the sensitivity of each stock to the factors (b_1, b_2, etc.).

One way to shortcut this process is to take advantage of the research by Fama and French, which showed that stocks of small firms and those with a high book-to-market ratio have provided above-average returns. This could simply be a coincidence. But there is also some evidence that these factors are related to company profitability and therefore may be picking up risk factors that are left out of the simple CAPM.[23]

---

[22] Of course, the market portfolio *may* turn out to be one of the factors, but that is not a necessary implication of arbitrage pricing theory.

[23] E. F. Fama and K. R. French, "Size and Book-to-Market Factors in Earnings and Returns," *Journal of Finance* 50 (1995), pp. 131–155.

If investors do demand an extra return for taking on exposure to these factors, then we have a measure of the expected return that looks very much like arbitrage pricing theory:

$$r - r_f = b_{\text{market}}(r_{\text{market factor}}) + b_{\text{size}}(r_{\text{size factor}}) + b_{\text{book-to-market}}(r_{\text{book-to-market factor}})$$

This is commonly known as the Fama–French three-factor model. Using it to estimate expected returns is the same as applying the arbitrage pricing theory. Here is an example.[24]

Step 1: Identify the Factors   Fama and French have already identified the three factors that appear to determine expected returns. The returns on each of these factors are

Factor	Measured by
Market factor	Return on market index *minus* risk-free interest rate
Size factor	Return on small-firm stocks *less* return on large-firm stocks
Book-to-market factor	Return on high book-to-market-ratio stocks *less* return on low book-to-market-ratio stocks

Step 2: Estimate the Risk Premium for Each Factor   We will keep to our figure of 7% for the market risk premium. History may provide a guide to the risk premium for the other two factors. As we saw earlier, between 1926 and 2008 the difference between the annual returns on small and large capitalization stocks averaged 3.6% a year, while the difference between the returns on stocks with high and low book-to-market ratios averaged 5.2%.

Step 3: Estimate the Factor Sensitivities   Some stocks are more sensitive than others to fluctuations in the returns on the three factors. You can see this from the first three columns of numbers in Table 8.3, which show some estimates of the factor sensitivities of 10 industry groups for the 60 months ending in December 2008. For example, an increase of 1% in the return on the book-to-market factor *reduces* the return on computer stocks by .87% but *increases* the return on utility stocks by .77%. In other words, when value stocks (high book-to-market) outperform growth stocks (low book-to-market), computer stocks tend to perform relatively badly and utility stocks do relatively well.

Once you have estimated the factor sensitivities, it is a simple matter to multiply each of them by the expected factor return and add up the results. For example, the expected risk premium on computer stocks is $r - r_f = (1.43 \times 7) + (.22 \times 3.6) - (.87 \times 5.2) = 6.3\%$. To calculate the return that investors expected in 2008 we need to add on the risk-free interest rate of about .2%. Thus the three-factor model suggests that expected return on computer stocks in 2008 was $.2 + 6.3 = 6.5\%$.

Compare this figure with the expected return estimate using the capital asset pricing model (the final column of Table 8.3). The three-factor model provides a substantially lower estimate of the expected return for computer stocks. Why? Largely because computer stocks are growth stocks with a low exposure ($-.87$) to the book-to-market factor. The three-factor model produces a lower expected return for growth stocks, but it produces a higher figure for value stocks such as those of auto and construction companies which have a high book-to-market ratio.

---

[24] The three-factor model was first used to estimate the cost of capital for different industry groups by Fama and French. See E. F. Fama and K. R. French, "Industry Costs of Equity," *Journal of Financial Economics* 43 (1997), pp. 153–193. Fama and French emphasize the imprecision in using either the CAPM or an APT-style model to estimate the returns that investors expect.

| | Three-Factor Model | | | | CAPM |
| | Factor Sensitivities | | | | |
	b_{market}	b_{size}	$b_{book\text{-}to\text{-}market}$	Expected Return*	Expected Return**
Autos	1.51	.07	.91	15.7	7.9
Banks	1.16	−.25	.72	11.1	6.2
Chemicals	1.02	−.07	.61	10.2	5.5
Computers	1.43	.22	−.87	6.5	12.8
Construction	1.40	.46	.98	16.6	7.6
Food	.53	−.15	.47	5.8	2.7
Oil and gas	.85	−.13	.54	8.5	4.3
Pharmaceuticals	.50	−.32	−.13	1.9	4.3
Telecoms	1.05	−.29	−.16	5.7	7.3
Utilities	.61	−.01	.77	8.4	2.4

▶ **TABLE 8.3** Estimates of expected equity returns for selected industries using the Fama–French three-factor model and the CAPM.

*The expected return equals the risk-free interest rate plus the factor sensitivities multiplied by the factor risk premiums, that is, $r_f + (b_{market} \times 7) + (b_{size} \times 3.6) + (b_{book\text{-}to\text{-}market} \times 5.2)$.

**Estimated as $r_f + \beta(r_m - r_f)$, that is, $r_f + \beta \times 7$. Note that we used *simple* regression to estimate β in the CAPM formula. This beta may, therefore, be different from b_{market} that we estimated from a *multiple* regression of stock returns on the three factors.

The basic principles of portfolio selection boil down to a commonsense statement that investors try to increase the expected return on their portfolios and to reduce the standard deviation of that return. A portfolio that gives the highest expected return for a given standard deviation, or the lowest standard deviation for a given expected return, is known as an *efficient portfolio*. To work out which portfolios are efficient, an investor must be able to state the expected return and standard deviation of each stock and the degree of correlation between each pair of stocks.

SUMMARY

Investors who are restricted to holding common stocks should choose efficient portfolios that suit their attitudes to risk. But investors who can also borrow and lend at the risk-free rate of interest should choose the *best* common stock portfolio *regardless* of their attitudes to risk. Having done that, they can then set the risk of their overall portfolio by deciding what proportion of their money they are willing to invest in stocks. The best efficient portfolio offers the highest ratio of forecasted risk premium to portfolio standard deviation.

For an investor who has only the same opportunities and information as everybody else, the best stock portfolio is the same as the best stock portfolio for other investors. In other words, he or she should invest in a mixture of the market portfolio and a risk-free loan (i.e., borrowing or lending).

A stock's marginal contribution to portfolio risk is measured by its sensitivity to changes in the value of the portfolio. The marginal contribution of a stock to the risk of the *market portfolio* is measured by *beta*. That is the fundamental idea behind the capital asset pricing model (CAPM), which concludes that each security's expected risk premium should increase in proportion to its beta:

$$\text{Expected risk premium} = \text{beta} \times \text{market risk premium}$$
$$r - r_f = \beta(r_m - r_f)$$

The capital asset pricing theory is the best-known model of risk and return. It is plausible and widely used but far from perfect. Actual returns are related to beta over the long run, but the relationship is not as strong as the CAPM predicts, and other factors seem to explain returns better since the mid-1960s. Stocks of small companies, and stocks with high book values relative to market prices, appear to have risks not captured by the CAPM.

Visit us at www.mhhe.com/bma

The arbitrage pricing theory offers an alternative theory of risk and return. It states that the expected risk premium on a stock should depend on the stock's exposure to several pervasive macroeconomic factors that affect stock returns:

$$\text{Expected risk premium} = b_1(r_{\text{factor 1}} - r_f) + b_2(r_{\text{factor 2}} - r_f) + \cdots$$

Here b's represent the individual security's sensitivities to the factors, and $r_{\text{factor}} - r_f$ is the risk premium demanded by investors who are exposed to this factor.

Arbitrage pricing theory does not say what these factors are. It asks for economists to hunt for unknown game with their statistical toolkits. Fama and French have suggested three factors:

- The return on the market portfolio less the risk-free rate of interest.
- The difference between the return on small- and large-firm stocks.
- The difference between the return on stocks with high book-to-market ratios and stocks with low book-to-market ratios.

In the Fama–French three-factor model, the expected return on each stock depends on its exposure to these three factors.

Each of these different models of risk and return has its fan club. However, all financial economists agree on two basic ideas: (1) Investors require extra expected return for taking on risk, and (2) they appear to be concerned predominantly with the risk that they cannot eliminate by diversification.

Near the end of Chapter 9 we list some Excel functions that are useful for measuring the risk of stocks and portfolios.

● ● ● ● ●

FURTHER READING

A number of textbooks on portfolio selection explain both Markowitz's original theory and some ingenious simplified versions. See, for example:

E. J. Elton, M. J. Gruber, S. J. Brown, and W. N. Goetzmann, *Modern Portfolio Theory and Investment Analysis,* 7th ed. (New York: John Wiley & Sons, 2007).

The literature on the capital asset pricing model is enormous. There are dozens of published tests of the capital asset pricing model. Fischer Black's paper is a very readable example. Discussions of the theory tend to be more uncompromising. Two excellent but advanced examples are Campbell's survey paper and Cochrane's book.

F. Black, "Beta and Return," *Journal of Portfolio Management* 20 (Fall 1993), pp. 8–18.

J. Y. Campbell, "Asset Pricing at the Millennium," *Journal of Finance* 55 (August 2000), pp. 1515–1567.

J. H. Cochrane, *Asset Pricing,* revised ed. (Princeton, NJ: Princeton University Press, 2004).

● ● ● ● ●

PROBLEM SETS

BASIC

1. Here are returns and standard deviations for four investments.

	Return	Standard Deviation
Treasury bills	6 %	0%
Stock P	10	14
Stock Q	14.5	28
Stock R	21	26

Calculate the standard deviations of the following portfolios.
a. 50% in Treasury bills, 50% in stock P.
b. 50% each in Q and R, assuming the shares have

- Perfect positive correlation.
- Perfect negative correlation.
- No correlation.

c. Plot a figure like Figure 8.3 for Q and R, assuming a correlation coefficient of .5.
d. Stock Q has a lower return than R but a higher standard deviation. Does that mean that Q's price is too high or that R's price is too low?

2. For each of the following pairs of investments, state which would always be preferred by a rational investor (assuming that these are the *only* investments available to the investor):

a. Portfolio A $r = 18\%$ $\sigma = 20\%$
   Portfolio B $r = 14\%$ $\sigma = 20\%$

b. Portfolio C $r = 15\%$ $\sigma = 18\%$
   Portfolio D $r = 13\%$ $\sigma = 8\%$

c. Portfolio E $r = 14\%$ $\sigma = 16\%$
   Portfolio F $r = 14\%$ $\sigma = 10\%$

3. Use the long-term data on security returns in Sections 7–1 and 7–2 to calculate the historical level of the Sharpe ratio of the market portfolio.

4. Figure 8.11 below purports to show the range of attainable combinations of expected return and standard deviation.
a. Which diagram is incorrectly drawn and why?
b. Which is the efficient set of portfolios?
c. If r_f is the rate of interest, mark with an X the optimal stock portfolio.

5. a. Plot the following risky portfolios on a graph:

	Portfolio							
	A	**B**	**C**	**D**	**E**	**F**	**G**	**H**
Expected return (r), %	10	12.5	15	16	17	18	18	20
Standard deviation (σ), %	23	21	25	29	29	32	35	45

b. Five of these portfolios are efficient, and three are not. Which are *in*efficient ones?
c. Suppose you can also borrow and lend at an interest rate of 12%. Which of the above portfolios has the highest Sharpe ratio?

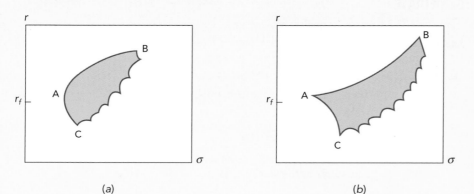

(a)   (b)

▶ **FIGURE 8.11**

See Problem 4.

d. Suppose you are prepared to tolerate a standard deviation of 25%. What is the maximum expected return that you can achieve if you cannot borrow or lend?

e. What is your optimal strategy if you can borrow or lend at 12% and are prepared to tolerate a standard deviation of 25%? What is the maximum expected return that you can achieve with this risk?

6. Suppose that the Treasury bill rate were 6% rather than 4%. Assume that the expected return on the market stays at 10%. Use the betas in Table 8.2.

a. Calculate the expected return from Dell.

b. Find the highest expected return that is offered by one of these stocks.

c. Find the lowest expected return that is offered by one of these stocks.

d. Would Ford offer a higher or lower expected return if the interest rate were 6% rather than 4%? Assume that the expected market return stays at 10%.

e. Would Exxon Mobil offer a higher or lower expected return if the interest rate were 8%?

7. True or false?

a. The CAPM implies that if you could find an investment with a negative beta, its expected return would be less than the interest rate.

b. The expected return on an investment with a beta of 2.0 is twice as high as the expected return on the market.

c. If a stock lies below the security market line, it is undervalued.

8. Consider a three-factor APT model. The factors and associated risk premiums are

Factor	Risk Premium
Change in GNP	5%
Change in energy prices	−1
Change in long-term interest rates	+2

Calculate expected rates of return on the following stocks. The risk-free interest rate is 7%.

a. A stock whose return is uncorrelated with all three factors.

b. A stock with average exposure to each factor (i.e., with $b = 1$ for each).

c. A pure-play energy stock with high exposure to the energy factor ($b = 2$) but zero exposure to the other two factors.

d. An aluminum company stock with average sensitivity to changes in interest rates and GNP, but negative exposure of $b = -1.5$ to the energy factor. (The aluminum company is energy-intensive and suffers when energy prices rise.)

INTERMEDIATE

9. True or false? Explain or qualify as necessary.

a. Investors demand higher expected rates of return on stocks with more variable rates of return.

b. The CAPM predicts that a security with a beta of 0 will offer a zero expected return.

c. An investor who puts $10,000 in Treasury bills and $20,000 in the market portfolio will have a beta of 2.0.

d. Investors demand higher expected rates of return from stocks with returns that are highly exposed to macroeconomic risks.

e. Investors demand higher expected rates of return from stocks with returns that are very sensitive to fluctuations in the stock market.

10. Look back at the calculation for Campbell Soup and Boeing in Section 8–1. Recalculate the expected portfolio return and standard deviation for different values of x_1 and x_2, assuming the correlation coefficient $\rho_{12} = 0$. Plot the range of possible combinations of expected return and standard deviation as in Figure 8.3. Repeat the problem for $\rho_{12} = +.5$.

11. Mark Harrywitz proposes to invest in two shares, X and Y. He expects a return of 12% from X and 8% from Y. The standard deviation of returns is 8% for X and 5% for Y. The correlation coefficient between the returns is .2.

    a. Compute the expected return and standard deviation of the following portfolios:

Portfolio	Percentage in X	Percentage in Y
1	50	50
2	25	75
3	75	25

    b. Sketch the set of portfolios composed of X and Y.

    c. Suppose that Mr. Harrywitz can also borrow or lend at an interest rate of 5%. Show on your sketch how this alters his opportunities. Given that he can borrow or lend, what proportions of the common stock portfolio should be invested in X and Y?

12. Ebenezer Scrooge has invested 60% of his money in share A and the remainder in share B. He assesses their prospects as follows:

	A	B
Expected return (%)	15	20
Standard deviation (%)	20	22
Correlation between returns		.5

    a. What are the expected return and standard deviation of returns on his portfolio?

    b. How would your answer change if the correlation coefficient were 0 or $-.5$?

    c. Is Mr. Scrooge's portfolio better or worse than one invested entirely in share A, or is it not possible to say?

13. Look back at Problem 3 in Chapter 7. The risk-free interest rate in each of these years was as follows:

	2003	2004	2005	2006	2007
Interest rate%	1.01	1.37	3.15	4.73	4.36

    a. Calculate the average return and standard deviation of returns for Ms. Sauros's portfolio and for the market. Use these figures to calculate the Sharpe ratio for the portfolio and the market. On this measure did Ms. Sauros perform better or worse than the market?

    b. Now calculate the average return that you could have earned over this period if you had held a combination of the market and a risk-free loan. Make sure that the combination has the same beta as Ms. Sauros's portfolio. Would your average return on this portfolio have been higher or lower?

    Explain your results.

14. Look back at Table 7.5 on page 174.

    a. What is the beta of a portfolio that has 40% invested in Disney and 60% in Exxon Mobil?

b. Would you invest in this portfolio if you had no superior information about the prospects for these stocks? Devise an alternative portfolio with the same expected return and less risk.

c. Now repeat parts (a) and (b) with a portfolio that has 40% invested in Amazon and 60% in Dell.

15. The Treasury bill rate is 4%, and the expected return on the market portfolio is 12%. Using the capital asset pricing model:

a. Draw a graph similar to Figure 8.6 showing how the expected return varies with beta.

b. What is the risk premium on the market?

c. What is the required return on an investment with a beta of 1.5?

d. If an investment with a beta of .8 offers an expected return of 9.8%, does it have a positive NPV?

e. If the market expects a return of 11.2% from stock X, what is its beta?

16. Percival Hygiene has $10 million invested in long-term corporate bonds. This bond portfolio's expected annual rate of return is 9%, and the annual standard deviation is 10%.

Amanda Reckonwith, Percival's financial adviser, recommends that Percival consider investing in an index fund that closely tracks the Standard & Poor's 500 index. The index has an expected return of 14%, and its standard deviation is 16%.

a. Suppose Percival puts all his money in a combination of the index fund and Treasury bills. Can he thereby improve his expected rate of return without changing the risk of his portfolio? The Treasury bill yield is 6%.

b. Could Percival do even better by investing equal amounts in the corporate bond portfolio and the index fund? The correlation between the bond portfolio and the index fund is +.1.

17. Epsilon Corp. is evaluating an expansion of its business. The cash-flow forecasts for the project are as follows:

Years	Cash Flow ($ millions)
0	−100
1–10	+15

The firm's existing assets have a beta of 1.4. The risk-free interest rate is 4% and the expected return on the market portfolio is 12%. What is the project's NPV?

18. Some true or false questions about the APT:

a. The APT factors cannot reflect diversifiable risks.

b. The market rate of return cannot be an APT factor.

c. There is no theory that specifically identifies the APT factors.

d. The APT model could be true but not very useful, for example, if the relevant factors change unpredictably.

19. Consider the following simplified APT model:

Factor	Expected Risk Premium
Market	6.4%
Interest rate	−.6
Yield spread	5.1

Calculate the expected return for the following stocks. Assume $r_f = 5\%$.

	Factor Risk Exposures		
	Market	Interest Rate	Yield Spread
Stock	(b_1)	(b_2)	(b_3)
P	1.0	−2.0	−.2
P^2	1.2	0	.3
P^3	.3	.5	1.0

20. Look again at Problem 19. Consider a portfolio with equal investments in stocks P, P^2, and P^3.

   a. What are the factor risk exposures for the portfolio?

   b. What is the portfolio's expected return?

21. The following table shows the sensitivity of four stocks to the three Fama–French factors. Estimate the expected return on each stock assuming that the interest rate is .2%, the expected risk premium on the market is 7%, the expected risk premium on the size factor is 3.6%, and the expected risk premium on the book-to-market factor is 5.2%.

	Boeing	Johnson & Johnson	Dow Chemical	Microsoft
Market	0.66	0.54	1.05	0.91
Size	1.19	−0.58	−0.15	−0.04
Book-to-market	−0.76	0.19	0.77	−0.40

CHALLENGE

22. In footnote 4 we noted that the minimum-risk portfolio contained an investment of 73.1% in Campbell Soup and 26.9% in Boeing. Prove it. (*Hint:* You need a little calculus to do so.)

23. Look again at the set of the three efficient portfolios that we calculated in Section 8–1.

   a. If the interest rate is 10%, which of the four efficient portfolios should you hold?

   b. What is the beta of each holding relative to that portfolio? (*Hint:* Note that if a portfolio is efficient, the expected risk premium on each holding must be proportional to the beta of the stock *relative to that portfolio.*)

   c. How would your answers to (a) and (b) change if the interest rate were 5%?

24. The following question illustrates the APT. Imagine that there are only two pervasive macroeconomic factors. Investments X, Y, and Z have the following sensitivities to these two factors:

Investment	b_1	b_2
X	1.75	.25
Y	−1.00	2.00
Z	2.00	1.00

We assume that the expected risk premium is 4% on factor 1 and 8% on factor 2. Treasury bills obviously offer zero risk premium.

   a. According to the APT, what is the risk premium on each of the three stocks?

   b. Suppose you buy $200 of X and $50 of Y and sell $150 of Z. What is the sensitivity of your portfolio to each of the two factors? What is the expected risk premium?

c. Suppose you buy $80 of X and $60 of Y and sell $40 of Z. What is the sensitivity of your portfolio to each of the two factors? What is the expected risk premium?

d. Finally, suppose you buy $160 of X and $20 of Y and sell $80 of Z. What is your portfolio's sensitivity now to each of the two factors? And what is the expected risk premium?

e. Suggest two possible ways that you could construct a fund that has a sensitivity of .5 to factor 1 only. (*Hint:* One portfolio contains an investment in Treasury bills.) Now compare the risk premiums on each of these two investments.

f. Suppose that the APT did *not* hold and that X offered a risk premium of 8%, Y offered a premium of 14%, and Z offered a premium of 16%. Devise an investment that has zero sensitivity to each factor and that has a positive risk premium.

You can download data for the following questions from the Standard & Poor's Market Insight Web site (www.mhhe.com/edumarketinsight)—see the "Monthly Adjusted Prices" spreadsheet—or from finance.yahoo.com.

Note: When we calculated the efficient portfolios in Table 8.1, we assumed that the investor could not hold short positions (i.e., have negative holdings). The book's Web site (www.mhhe.com/bma) contains an Excel program for calculating the efficient frontier with short sales. (We are grateful to Simon Gervais for providing us with a copy of this program.) Excel functions SLOPE, STDEV, and CORREL are especially useful for answering the following questions.

1. a. Look at the efficient portfolios constructed from the 10 stocks in Table 8.1. How does the possibility of short sales improve the choices open to the investor?

   b. Now download up to 10 years of monthly returns for 10 different stocks and enter them into the Excel program. Enter some plausible figures for the expected return on each stock and find the set of efficient portfolios.

2. Find a low-risk stock—Exxon Mobil or Kellogg would be a good candidate. Use monthly returns for the most recent three years to confirm that the beta is less than 1.0. Now estimate the annual standard deviation for the stock and the S&P index, and the correlation between the returns on the stock and the index. Forecast the expected return for the stock, assuming the CAPM holds, with a market return of 12% and a risk-free rate of 5%.

   a. Plot a graph like Figure 8.5 showing the combinations of risk and return from a portfolio invested in your low-risk stock and the market. Vary the fraction invested in the stock from 0 to 100%.

   b. Suppose that you can borrow or lend at 5%. Would you invest in some combination of your low-risk stock and the market, or would you simply invest in the market? Explain.

   c. Suppose that you forecasted a return on the stock that is 5 percentage points higher than the CAPM return used in part (b). Redo parts (a) and (b) with the higher forecasted return.

   d. Find a high-risk stock and redo parts (a) and (b).

3. Recalculate the betas for the stocks in Table 8.2 using the latest 60 monthly returns. Recalculate expected rates of return from the CAPM formula, using a current risk-free rate and a market risk premium of 7%. How have the expected returns changed from Table 8.2?

MINI-CASE ● ● ● ● ●

John and Marsha on Portfolio Selection

The scene: John and Marsha hold hands in a cozy French restaurant in downtown Manhattan, several years before the mini-case in Chapter 9. Marsha is a futures-market trader. John manages a $125 million common-stock portfolio for a large pension fund. They have just ordered tournedos financiere for the main course and flan financiere for dessert. John reads the financial pages of *The Wall Street Journal* by candlelight.

John: Wow! Potato futures hit their daily limit. Let's add an order of gratin dauphinoise. Did you manage to hedge the forward interest rate on that euro loan?

Marsha: John, please fold up that paper. (*He does so reluctantly.*) John, I love you. Will you marry me?

John: Oh, Marsha, I love you too, but . . . there's something you must know about me— something I've never told anyone.

Marsha (concerned): John, what is it?

John: I think I'm a closet indexer.

Marsha: What? Why?

John: My portfolio returns always seem to track the S&P 500 market index. Sometimes I do a little better, occasionally a little worse. But the correlation between my returns and the market returns is over 90%.

Marsha: What's wrong with that? Your client wants a diversified portfolio of large-cap stocks. Of course your portfolio will follow the market.

John: Why doesn't my client just buy an index fund? Why is he paying *me?* Am I really adding value by active management? I try, but I guess I'm just an . . . indexer.

Marsha: Oh, John, I know you're adding value. You were a star security analyst.

John: It's not easy to find stocks that are truly over- or undervalued. I have firm opinions about a few, of course.

Marsha: You were explaining why Pioneer Gypsum is a good buy. And you're bullish on Global Mining.

John: Right, Pioneer. (*Pulls handwritten notes from his coat pocket.*) Stock price $87.50. I estimate the expected return as 11% with an annual standard deviation of 32%.

Marsha: Only 11%? You're forecasting a market return of 12.5%.

John: Yes, I'm using a market risk premium of 7.5% and the risk-free interest rate is about 5%. That gives 12.5%. But Pioneer's beta is only .65. I was going to buy 30,000 shares this morning, but I lost my nerve. I've got to stay diversified.

Marsha: Have you tried modern portfolio theory?

John: MPT? Not practical. Looks great in textbooks, where they show efficient frontiers with 5 or 10 stocks. But I choose from hundreds, maybe thousands, of stocks. Where do I get the inputs for 1,000 stocks? That's a million variances and covariances!

Marsha: Actually only about 500,000, dear. The covariances above the diagonal are the same as the covariances below. But you're right, most of the estimates would be out-of-date or just garbage.

John: To say nothing about the expected returns. Garbage in, garbage out.

Marsha: But John, you don't need to solve for 1,000 portfolio weights. You only need a handful. Here's the trick: Take your benchmark, the S&P 500, as security 1. That's what you would end up with as an indexer. Then consider a few securities you really know something about. Pioneer could be security 2, for example. Global, security 3. And so on. Then you could put your wonderful financial mind to work.

John: I get it: Active management means selling off some of the benchmark portfolio and investing the proceeds in specific stocks like Pioneer. But how do I decide whether Pioneer really improves the portfolio? Even if it does, how much should I buy?

Marsha: Just maximize the Sharpe ratio, dear.

John: I've got it! The answer is yes!

Marsha: What's the question?

John: You asked me to marry you. The answer is yes. Where should we go on our honeymoon?

Marsha: How about Australia? I'd love to visit the Sydney Futures Exchange.

QUESTIONS

1. Table 8.4 reproduces John's notes on Pioneer Gypsum and Global Mining. Calculate the expected return, risk premium, and standard deviation of a portfolio invested partly in the market and partly in Pioneer. (You can calculate the necessary inputs from the betas and standard deviations given in the table.) Does adding Pioneer to the market benchmark improve the Sharpe ratio? How much should John invest in Pioneer and how much in the market?

2. Repeat the analysis for Global Mining. What should John do in this case? Assume that Global accounts for .75% of the S&P index.

▶ TABLE 8.4   John's notes on Pioneer Gypsum and Global Mining.

	Pioneer Gypsum	Global Mining
Expected return	11.0%	12.9%
Standard deviation	32%	20%
Beta	.65	1.22
Stock price	$87.50	$105.00

Risk and the Cost of Capital

▶ **Long before the** development of modern theories linking risk and return, smart financial managers adjusted for risk in capital budgeting. They knew that risky projects are, other things equal, less valuable than safe ones—that is just common sense. Therefore they demanded higher rates of return from risky projects, or they based their decisions about risky projects on conservative forecasts of project cash flows.

Today most companies start with the *company cost of capital* as a benchmark risk-adjusted discount rate for new investments. The company cost of capital is the right discount rate only for investments that have the same risk as the company's overall business. For riskier projects the opportunity cost of capital is greater than the company cost of capital. For safer projects it is less.

The company cost of capital is usually estimated as a weighted-average cost of capital, that is, as the average rate of return demanded by investors in the company's debt and equity. The hardest part of estimating the weighted-average cost of capital is figuring out the cost of equity, that is, the expected rate of return to investors in the firm's common stock. Many firms turn to the capital asset pricing model (CAPM) for an answer. The CAPM states that the expected rate of return equals the risk-free interest rate plus a risk premium that depends on beta and the market risk premium.

We explained the CAPM in the last chapter, but didn't show you how to estimate betas. You can't look up betas in a newspaper or see them clearly by tracking a few day-to-day changes in stock price. But you can get useful statistical estimates from the history of stock and market returns.

Now suppose you're responsible for a specific investment project. How do you know if the project is average risk or above- or below-average risk? We suggest you check whether the project's cash flows are more or less sensitive to the business cycle than the average project. Also check whether the project has higher or lower fixed operating costs (higher or lower operating leverage) and whether it requires large future investments.

Remember that a project's cost of capital depends only on market risk. Diversifiable risk can affect project cash flows but does not increase the cost of capital. Also don't be tempted to add arbitrary fudge factors to discount rates. Fudge factors are too often added to discount rates for projects in unstable parts of the world, for example.

Risk varies from project to project. Risk can also vary over time for a given project. For example, some projects are riskier in youth than in old age. But financial managers usually assume that project risk will be the same in every future period, and they use a single risk-adjusted discount rate for all future cash flows. We close the chapter by introducing certainty equivalents, which illustrate how risk can change over time.

●●●●●

9-1   Company and Project Costs of Capital

The **company cost of capital** is defined as the expected return on a portfolio of all the company's existing securities. It is the opportunity cost of capital for investment in the firm's assets, and therefore the appropriate discount rate for the firm's average-risk projects.

If the firm has no debt outstanding, then the company cost of capital is just the expected rate of return on the firm's stock. Many large, successful companies pretty well fit this special case, including Johnson & Johnson (J&J). In Table 8.2 we estimated that investors require a return of 3.8% from J&J common stock. If J&J is contemplating an expansion of its existing business, it would make sense to discount the forecasted cash flows at 3.8%.[1]

The company cost of capital is *not* the correct discount rate if the new projects are more or less risky than the firm's existing business. Each project should in principle be evaluated at its *own* opportunity cost of capital. This is a clear implication of the value-additivity principle introduced in Chapter 7. For a firm composed of assets A and B, the firm value is

$$\text{Firm value} = PV(AB) = PV(A) + PV(B)$$
$$= \text{sum of separate asset values}$$

Here PV(A) and PV(B) are valued just as if they were mini-firms in which stockholders could invest directly. Investors would value A by discounting its forecasted cash flows at a rate reflecting the risk of A. They would value B by discounting at a rate reflecting the risk of B. The two discount rates will, in general, be different. If the present value of an asset depended on the identity of the company that bought it, present values would *not* add up, and we know they do add up. (Consider a portfolio of $1 million invested in J&J and $1 million invested in Toyota. Would any reasonable investor say that the portfolio is worth anything more or less than $2 million?)

If the firm considers investing in a third project C, it should also value C as if C were a mini-firm. That is, the firm should discount the cash flows of C at the expected rate of return that investors would demand if they could make a separate investment in C. *The opportunity cost of capital depends on the use to which that capital is put.*

Perhaps we're saying the obvious. Think of J&J: It is a massive health care and consumer products company, with $64 billion in sales in 2008. J&J has well-established consumer products, including Band-Aid® bandages, Tylenol®, and products for skin care and babies. It also invests heavily in much chancier ventures, such as biotech research and development (R&D). Do you think that a new production line for baby lotion has the same cost of capital as an investment in biotech R&D? We don't, though we admit that estimating the cost of capital for biotech R&D could be challenging.

Suppose we measure the risk of each project by its beta. Then J&J should accept any project lying above the upward-sloping security market line that links expected return to risk in Figure 9.1. If the project is high-risk, J&J needs a higher prospective return than if the project is low-risk. That is different from the company cost of capital rule, which accepts any project *regardless of its risk* as long as it offers a higher return than the *company's* cost of capital. The rule tells J&J to accept any project above the horizontal cost of capital line in Figure 9.1, that is, any project offering a return of more than 3.8%.

It is clearly silly to suggest that J&J should demand the same rate of return from a very safe project as from a very risky one. If J&J used the company cost of capital rule, it would reject many good low-risk projects and accept many poor high-risk projects. It is also silly to

---

[1] If 3.8% seems like a very low number, recall that short-term interest rates were at historic lows in 2009. Long-term interest rates were higher, and J&J probably would use a higher discount rate for cash flows spread out over many future years. We return to this distinction later in the chapter. We have also simplified by treating J&J as all-equity-financed. J&J's market-value debt ratio is very low, but not zero. We discuss debt financing and the weighted-average cost of capital below.

▶ **FIGURE 9.1**

A comparison between the company cost of capital rule and the required return from the capital asset pricing model. J&J's company cost of capital is about 3.8%. This is the correct discount rate only if the project beta is .50. In general, the correct discount rate increases as project beta increases. J&J should accept projects with rates of return above the security market line relating required return to beta.

suggest that, just because another company has a low company cost of capital, it is justified in accepting projects that J&J would reject.

Perfect Pitch and the Cost of Capital

The true cost of capital depends on project risk, not on the company undertaking the project. So why is so much time spent estimating the company cost of capital?

There are two reasons. First, many (maybe most) projects can be treated as average risk, that is, neither more nor less risky than the average of the company's other assets. For these projects the company cost of capital is the right discount rate. Second, the company cost of capital is a useful starting point for setting discount rates for unusually risky or safe projects. It is easier to add to, or subtract from, the company cost of capital than to estimate each project's cost of capital from scratch.

There is a good musical analogy here. Most of us, lacking perfect pitch, need a well-defined reference point, like middle C, before we can sing on key. But anyone who can carry a tune gets *relative* pitches right. Businesspeople have good intuition about *relative* risks, at least in industries they are used to, but not about absolute risk or required rates of return. Therefore, they set a companywide cost of capital as a benchmark. This is not the right discount rate for everything the company does, but adjustments can be made for more or less risky ventures.

That said, we have to admit that many large companies use the company cost of capital not just as a benchmark, but also as an all-purpose discount rate for every project proposal. Measuring differences in risk is difficult to do objectively, and financial managers shy away from intracorporate squabbles. (You can imagine the bickering: "My projects are safer than yours! I want a lower discount rate!" "No they're not! Your projects are riskier than a naked call option!")[2]

When firms force the use of a single company cost of capital, risk adjustment shifts from the discount rate to project cash flows. Top management may demand extra-conservative cash-flow forecasts from extra-risky projects. They may refuse to sign off on an extra-risky project unless NPV, computed at the company cost of capital, is well above zero. Rough-and-ready risk adjustments are better than none at all.

---

[2] A "naked" call option is an option purchased with no offsetting (hedging) position in the underlying stock or in other options. We discuss options in Chapter 16.

Debt and the Company Cost of Capital

We defined the company cost of capital as "the expected return on a portfolio of all the company's existing securities." That portfolio usually includes debt as well as equity. Thus the cost of capital is estimated as a blend of the *cost of debt* (the interest rate) and the *cost of equity* (the expected rate of return demanded by investors in the firm's common stock).

Suppose the company's market-value balance sheet looks like this:

Asset value	100	Debt	$D = 30$ at 7.5%
		Equity	$E = 70$ at 15%
Asset value	100	Firm value	$V = 100$

The values of debt and equity add up to overall firm value ($D + E = V$) and firm value V equals asset value. These figures are all market values, not book (accounting) values. The market value of equity is often much larger than the book value, so the market debt ratio D/V is often much lower than a debt ratio computed from the book balance sheet.

The 7.5% cost of debt is the opportunity cost of capital for the investors who hold the firm's debt. The 15% cost of equity is the opportunity cost of capital for the investors who hold the firm's shares. Neither measures the *company* cost of capital, that is, the opportunity cost of investing in the firm's *assets*. The cost of debt is less than the company cost of capital, because debt is safer than the assets. The cost of equity is greater than the company cost of capital, because the equity of a firm that borrows is riskier than the assets. Equity is not a direct claim on the firm's free cash flow. It is a residual claim that stands behind debt.

The company cost of capital is not equal to the cost of debt or to the cost of equity but is a blend of the two. Suppose you purchased a portfolio consisting of 100% of the firm's debt and 100% of its equity. Then you would own 100% of its assets lock, stock, and barrel. You would not share the firm's free cash flow with anyone; every dollar that the firm pays out would be paid to you.

The expected rate of return on your hypothetical portfolio is the company cost of capital. The expected rate of return is just a weighted average of the cost of debt ($r_D = 7.5\%$) and the cost of equity ($r_E = 15\%$). The weights are the relative market values of the firm's debt and equity, that is, $D/V = 30\%$ and $E/V = 70\%$.[3]

$$\text{Company cost of capital} = r_D D/V + r_E E/V$$
$$= 7.5 \times .30 + 15 \times .70 = 12.75\%$$

This blended measure of the company cost of capital is called the **weighted-average cost of capital** or **WACC** (pronounced "whack"). Calculating WACC is a bit more complicated than our example suggests, however. For example, interest is a tax-deductible expense for corporations, so the after-tax cost of debt is $(1 - T_c)r_D$, where T_c is the marginal corporate tax rate. Suppose $T_c = 35\%$. Then *after-tax WACC* is

$$\text{After-tax WACC} = (1 - T_c)r_D D/V + r_E E/V$$
$$= (1 - .35) \times 7.5 \times .30 + 15 \times .70 = 12.0\%$$

We give another example of the after-tax WACC later in this chapter, and we cover the topic in much more detail in Chapter 15. But now we turn to the hardest part of calculating WACC, estimating the cost of equity.

---

[3] Recall that the 30% and 70% weights in your hypothetical portfolio are based on market, not book, values. Now you can see why. If the portfolio were constructed with different book weights, say 50-50, then the portfolio returns could not equal the asset returns.

To calculate the weighted-average cost of capital, you need an estimate of the cost of equity. You decide to use the capital asset pricing model (CAPM). Here you are in good company: as we saw in the last chapter, most large U.S. companies do use the CAPM to estimate the cost of equity, which is the expected rate of return on the firm's common stock.[4] The CAPM says that

$$\text{Expected stock return} = r_f + \beta(r_m - r_f)$$

Now you have to estimate beta. Let us see how that is done in practice.

Estimating Beta

In principle we are interested in the future beta of the company's stock, but lacking a crystal ball, we turn first to historical evidence. For example, look at the scatter diagram at the top left of Figure 9.2. Each dot represents the return on Amazon stock and the return on the market in a particular month. The plot starts in January 1999 and runs to December 2003, so there are 60 dots in all.

The second diagram on the left shows a similar plot for the returns on Disney stock, and the third shows a plot for Campbell Soup. In each case we have fitted a line through the points. The slope of this line is an estimate of beta.[5] It tells us how much on average the stock price changed when the market return was 1% higher or lower.

The right-hand diagrams show similar plots for the same three stocks during the subsequent period ending in December 2008. Although the slopes varied from the first period to the second, there is little doubt that Campbell Soup's beta is much less than Amazon's or that Disney's beta falls somewhere between the two. If you had used the past beta of each stock to predict its future beta, you would not have been too far off.

Only a small portion of each stock's total risk comes from movements in the market. The rest is firm-specific, diversifiable risk, which shows up in the scatter of points around the fitted lines in Figure 9.2. *R-squared* (R^2) measures the proportion of the total variance in the stock's returns that can be explained by market movements. For example, from 2004 to 2008, the R^2 for Disney was .395. In other words, about 40% of Disney's risk was market risk and 60% was diversifiable risk. The variance of the returns on Disney stock was 383.[6] So we could say that the variance in stock returns that was due to the market was $.4 \times 383 = 153$, and the variance of diversifiable returns was $.6 \times 383 = 230$.

The estimates of beta shown in Figure 9.2 are just that. They are based on the stocks' returns in 60 particular months. The noise in the returns can obscure the true beta.[7] Therefore, statisticians calculate the *standard error* of the estimated beta to show the extent of possible mismeasurement. Then they set up a *confidence interval* of the estimated value plus or minus two standard errors. For example, the standard error of Disney's

---

[4] The CAPM is not the last word on risk and return, of course, but the principles and procedures covered in this chapter work just as well with other models such as the Fama–French three-factor model. See Section 8–4.

[5] Notice that to estimate beta you must regress the *returns* on the stock on the market *returns*. You would get a very similar estimate if you simply used the percentage *changes* in the stock price and the market index. But sometimes people make the mistake of regressing the stock price *level* on the *level* of the index and obtain nonsense results.

[6] This is an annual figure; we annualized the monthly variance by multiplying by 12 (see footnote 18 in Chapter 7). The standard deviation was $\sqrt{383} = 19.6\%$.

[7] Estimates of beta may be distorted if there are extreme returns in one or two months. This is a potential problem in our estimates for 2004–2008, since you can see in Figure 9.2 that there was one month (October 2008) when the market fell by over 16%. The performance of each stock that month has an excessive effect on the estimated beta. In such cases statisticians may prefer to give less weight to the extreme observations or even to omit them entirely.

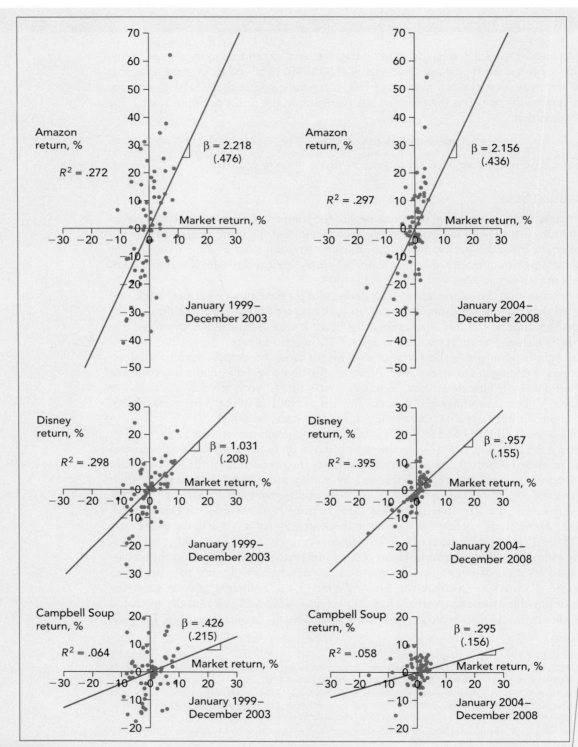

▶ **FIGURE 9.2**

We have used past returns to estimate the betas of three stocks for the periods January 1999 to December 2003 (left-hand diagrams) and January 2004 to December 2008 (right-hand diagrams). Beta is the slope of the fitted line. Notice that in both periods Amazon had the highest beta and Campbell Soup the lowest. Standard errors are in parentheses below the betas. The standard error shows the range of possible error in the beta estimate. We also report the proportion of total risk that is due to market movements (R^2).

estimated beta in the most recent period is about .16. Thus the confidence interval for Disney's beta is .96 plus or minus 2 × .16. If you state that the *true* beta for Disney is between .64 and 1.28, you have a 95% chance of being right. Notice that we can be equally confident of our estimate of Campbell Soup's beta, but much less confident of Amazon's.

Usually you will have more information (and thus more confidence) than this simple, and somewhat depressing, calculation suggests. For example, you know that Campbell Soup's estimated beta was well below 1 in two successive five-year periods. Amazon's estimated beta was well above 1 in both periods. Nevertheless, there is always a large margin for error when estimating the beta for individual stocks.

Fortunately, the estimation errors tend to cancel out when you estimate betas of *portfolios*.[8] That is why financial managers often turn to *industry betas*. For example, Table 9.1 shows estimates of beta and the standard errors of these estimates for the common stocks of six large railroad companies. Five of the standard errors are above .2. Kansas City Southern's is .29, large enough to preclude a price estimate of that railroad's beta. However, the table also shows the estimated beta for a portfolio of all six railroad stocks. Notice that the estimated industry beta is somewhat more reliable. This shows up in the lower standard error.

The Expected Return on Union Pacific Corporation's Common Stock

Suppose that in early 2009 you had been asked to estimate the company cost of capital of Union Pacific. Table 9.1 provides two clues about the true beta of Union Pacific's stock: the direct estimate of 1.16 and the average estimate for the industry of 1.24. We will use the direct estimate of 1.16.[9]

The next issue is what value to use for the risk-free interest rate. By the first months of 2009, the U.S. Federal Reserve Board had pushed down Treasury bill rates to about .2% in an attempt to reverse the financial crisis and recession. The one-year interest rate was only a little higher, at about .7%. Yields on longer-maturity U.S. Treasury bonds were higher still, at about 3.3% on 20-year bonds.

The CAPM is a short-term model. It works period by period and calls for a short-term interest rate. But could a .2% three-month risk-free rate give the right discount rate for cash flows 10 or 20 years in the future? Well, now that you mention it, probably not.

Financial managers muddle through this problem in one of two ways. The first way simply uses a long-term risk-free rate in the CAPM formula. If this short-cut is used, then

	Beta	Standard Error
Burlington Northern Santa Fe	1.01	.19
Canadian Pacific	1.34	.23
CSX	1.14	.22
Kansas City Southern	1.75	.29
Norfolk Southern	1.05	.24
Union Pacific	1.16	.21
Industry portfolio	1.24	.18

▶ **TABLE 9.1** Estimates of betas and standard errors for a sample of large railroad companies and for an equally weighted portfolio of these companies, based on monthly returns from January 2004 to December 2008. The portfolio beta is more reliable than the betas of the individual companies. Note the lower standard error for the portfolio.

---

[8] If the observations are independent, the standard error of the estimated mean beta declines in proportion to the square root of the number of stocks in the portfolio.

[9] One reason that Union Pacific's beta is less than that of the average railroad is that the company has below-average debt ratio. Chapter 15 explains how to adjust betas for differences in debt ratios.

the market risk premium must be restated as the average difference between market returns and returns on *long-term* Treasuries.[10]

The second way retains the usual definition of the market risk premium as the difference between market returns and returns on *short-term* Treasury bill rates. But now you have to forecast the expected return from holding Treasury bills over the life of the project. In Chapter 3 we observed that investors require a risk premium for holding long-term bonds rather than bills. Table 7.1 showed that over the past century this risk premium has averaged about 1.5%. So to get a rough but reasonable estimate of the expected long-term return from investing in Treasury bills, we need to subtract 1.5% from the current yield on long-term bonds. In our example

$$\text{Expected long-term return from bills} = \text{yield on long-term bonds} - 1.5\%$$
$$= 3.3 - 1.5 = 1.8\%$$

This is a plausible estimate of the expected average future return on Treasury bills. We therefore use this rate in our example.

Returning to our Union Pacific example, suppose you decide to use a market risk premium of 7%. Then the resulting estimate for Union Pacific's cost of equity is about 9.9%:

$$\text{Cost of equity} = \text{expected return} = r_f + \beta(r_m - r_f)$$
$$= 1.8 + 1.16 \times 7.0 = 9.9\%$$

Union Pacific's After-Tax Weighted-Average Cost of Capital

Now you can calculate Union Pacific's after-tax WACC in early 2009. The company's cost of debt was about 7.8%. With a 35% corporate tax rate, the after-tax cost of debt was $r_D(1 - T_c) = 7.8 \times (1 - .35) = 5.1\%$. The ratio of debt to overall company value was $D/V = 31.5\%$. Therefore:

$$\text{After-tax WACC} = (1 - T_c)r_D D/V + r_E E/V$$
$$= (1 - .35) \times 7.8 \times .315 + 9.9 \times .685 = 8.4\%$$

Union Pacific should set its overall cost of capital to 8.4%, assuming that its CFO agrees with our estimates.

Warning The cost of debt is always less than the cost of equity. The WACC formula blends the two costs. The formula is dangerous, however, because it suggests that the average cost of capital could be reduced by substituting cheap debt for expensive equity. It doesn't work that way! As the debt ratio D/V increases, the cost of the remaining equity also increases, offsetting the apparent advantage of more cheap debt. We show how and why this offset happens in Chapter 13.

Debt does have a tax advantage, however, because interest is a tax-deductible expense. That is why we use the after-tax cost of debt in the after-tax WACC. We cover debt and taxes in much more detail in Chapters 14 and 15.

Union Pacific's Asset Beta

The after-tax WACC depends on the average risk of the company's assets, but it also depends on taxes and financing. It's easier to think about project risk if you measure it directly. The direct measure is called the **asset beta.**

---

[10] This approach gives a security market line with a higher intercept and a lower market risk premium. Using a "flatter" security market line is perhaps a better match to the historical evidence, which shows that the slope of average returns against beta is not as steeply upward-sloping as the CAPM predicts. See Figures 8.8 and 8.9.

We calculate the asset beta as a blend of the separate betas of debt (β_D) and equity (β_E). For Union Pacific we have $\beta_E = 1.16$, and we'll assume $\beta_D = .3$.[11] The weights are the fractions of debt and equity financing, $D/V = .315$ and $E/V = .685$:

$$\text{Asset beta} = \beta_A = \beta_D(D/V) + \beta_E(E/V)$$
$$\beta_A = .3 \times .315 + 1.16 \times .685 = .89$$

Calculating an asset beta is similar to calculating a weighted-average cost of capital. The debt and equity weights D/V and E/V are the same. The logic is also the same: Suppose you purchased a portfolio consisting of 100% of the firm's debt and 100% of its equity. Then you would own 100% of its assets lock, stock, and barrel, and the beta of your portfolio would equal the beta of the assets. The portfolio beta is of course just a weighted average of the betas of debt and equity.

This asset beta is an estimate of the average risk of Union Pacific's railroad business. It is a useful benchmark, but it can take you only so far. Not all railroad investments are average risk. And if you are the first to use railroad-track networks as interplanetary transmission antennas, you will have no asset beta to start with.

How can you make informed judgments about costs of capital for projects or lines of business when you suspect that risk is *not* average? That is our next topic.

9-3 Analyzing Project Risk

Suppose that a coal-mining corporation wants to assess the risk of investing in commercial real estate, for example, in a new company headquarters. The asset beta for coal mining is not helpful. You need to know the beta of real estate. Fortunately, portfolios of commercial real estate are traded. For example, you could estimate asset betas from returns on Real Estate Investment Trusts (REITs) specializing in commercial real estate.[12] The REITs would serve as traded *comparables* for the proposed office building. You could also turn to indexes of real estate prices and returns derived from sales and appraisals of commercial properties.[13]

A company that wants to set a cost of capital for one particular line of business typically looks for *pure plays* in that line of business. Pure-play companies are public firms that specialize in one activity. For example, suppose that J&J wants to set a cost of capital for its pharmaceutical business. It could estimate the average asset beta or cost of capital for pharmaceutical companies that have *not* diversified into consumer products like Band-Aid® bandages or baby powder.

Overall company costs of capital are almost useless for *conglomerates*. Conglomerates diversify into several unrelated industries, so they have to consider industry-specific costs of capital. They therefore look for pure plays in the relevant industries. Take Richard Branson's Virgin Group as an example. The group combines many different companies, including airlines (Virgin Atlantic) and retail outlets for music, books, and movies (Virgin Megastores). Fortunately there are many examples of pure-play airlines and pure-play retail

---

[11]Why is the debt beta positive? Two reasons: First, debt investors worry about the risk of default. Corporate bond prices fall, relative to Treasury-bond prices, when the economy goes from expansion to recession. The risk of default is therefore partly a macroeconomic and market risk. Second, all bonds are exposed to uncertainty about interest rates and inflation. Even Treasury bonds have positive betas when long-term interest rates and inflation are volatile and uncertain.

[12] REITs are investment funds that invest in real estate. You would have to be careful to identify REITs investing in commercial properties similar to the proposed office building. There are also REITs that invest in other types of real estate, including apartment buildings, shopping centers, and timberland.

[13] See Chapter 23 in D. Geltner, N. G. Miller, J. Clayton, and P. Eichholtz, *Commercial Real Estate Analysis and Investments*, 2nd ed. (South-Western College Publishing, 2006).

chains. The trick is picking the comparables with business risks that are most similar to Virgin's companies.

Sometimes good comparables are not available or not a good match to a particular project. Then the financial manager has to exercise his or her judgment. Here we offer the following advice:

1. *Think about the determinants of asset betas.* Often the characteristics of high- and low-beta assets can be observed when the beta itself cannot be.
2. *Don't be fooled by diversifiable risk.*
3. *Avoid fudge factors.* Don't give in to the temptation to add fudge factors to the discount rate to offset things that could go wrong with the proposed investment. Adjust cash-flow forecasts first.

What Determines Asset Betas?

Cyclicality   Many people's intuition associates risk with the variability of earnings or cash flow. But much of this variability reflects diversifiable risk. Lone prospectors searching for gold look forward to extremely uncertain future income, but whether they strike it rich is unlikely to depend on the performance of the market portfolio. Even if they do find gold, they do not bear much market risk. Therefore, an investment in gold prospecting has a high standard deviation but a relatively low beta.

What really counts is the strength of the relationship between the firm's earnings and the aggregate earnings on all real assets. We can measure this either by the *earnings beta* or by the *cash-flow beta*. These are just like a real beta except that changes in earnings or cash flow are used in place of rates of return on securities. We would predict that firms with high earnings or cash-flow betas should also have high asset betas.

This means that cyclical firms—firms whose revenues and earnings are strongly dependent on the state of the business cycle—tend to be high-beta firms. Thus you should demand a higher rate of return from investments whose performance is strongly tied to the performance of the economy. Examples of cyclical businesses include airlines, luxury resorts and restaurants, construction, and steel. (Much of the demand for steel depends on construction and capital investment.) Examples of less-cyclical businesses include food and tobacco products and established consumer brands such as J&J's baby products. MBA programs are another example, because spending a year or two at a business school is an easier choice when jobs are scarce. Applications to top MBA programs increase in recessions.

Operating Leverage   A production facility with high fixed costs, relative to variable costs, is said to have high *operating leverage*. High operating leverage means a high asset beta. Let us see how this works.

The cash flows generated by an asset can be broken down into revenue, fixed costs, and variable costs:

$$\text{Cash flow} = \text{revenue} - \text{fixed cost} - \text{variable cost}$$

Costs are variable if they depend on the rate of output. Examples are raw materials, sales commissions, and some labor and maintenance costs. Fixed costs are cash outflows that occur regardless of whether the asset is active or idle, for example, property taxes or the wages of workers under contract.

We can break down the asset's present value in the same way:

$$\text{PV(asset)} = \text{PV(revenue)} - \text{PV(fixed cost)} - \text{PV(variable cost)}$$

Or equivalently

$$PV(revenue) = PV(fixed\ cost) + PV(variable\ cost) + PV(asset)$$

Those who *receive* the fixed costs are like debtholders in the project; they simply get a fixed payment. Those who receive the net cash flows from the asset are like holders of common stock; they get whatever is left after payment of the fixed costs.

We can now figure out how the asset's beta is related to the betas of the values of revenue and costs. The beta of PV(revenue) is a weighted average of the betas of its component parts:

$$\beta_{revenue} = \beta_{fixed\ cost} \frac{PV(fixed\ cost)}{PV(revenue)}$$

$$+ \beta_{variable\ cost} \frac{PV(variable\ cost)}{PV(revenue)} + \beta_{assets} \frac{PV(asset)}{PV(revenue)}$$

The fixed-cost beta should be about zero; whoever receives the fixed costs receives a fixed stream of cash flows. The betas of the revenues and variable costs should be approximately the same, because they respond to the same underlying variable, the rate of output. Therefore we can substitute $\beta_{revenue}$ for $\beta_{variable\ cost}$ and solve for the asset beta. Remember, we are assuming $\beta_{fixed\ cost} = 0$. Also, PV(revenue) − PV(variable cost) = PV(asset) + PV(fixed cost).[14]

$$\beta_{assets} = \beta_{revenue} \frac{PV(revenue) - PV(variable\ cost)}{PV(asset)}$$

$$= \beta_{revenue} \left[1 + \frac{PV(fixed\ cost)}{PV(asset)} \right]$$

Thus, given the cyclicality of revenues (reflected in $\beta_{revenue}$), the asset beta is proportional to the ratio of the present value of fixed costs to the present value of the project.

Now you have a rule of thumb for judging the relative risks of alternative designs or technologies for producing the same project. Other things being equal, the alternative with the higher ratio of fixed costs to project value will have the higher project beta. Empirical tests confirm that companies with high operating leverage actually do have high betas.[15]

We have interpreted fixed costs as costs of production, but fixed costs can show up in other forms, for example, as future investment outlays. Suppose that an electric utility commits to build a large electricity-generating plant. The plant will take several years to build, and the cost is fixed. Our operating leverage formula still applies, but with PV(future investment) included in PV(fixed costs). The commitment to invest therefore increases the plant's asset beta. Of course PV(future investment) decreases as the plant is constructed and disappears when the plant is up and running. Therefore the plant's asset beta is only temporarily high during construction.

Other Sources of Risk So far we have focused on cash flows. Cash-flow risk is not the only risk. A project's value is equal to the expected cash flows discounted at the risk-adjusted discount rate *r*. If either the risk-free rate or the market risk premium changes, then *r* will change and so will the project value. A project with very long-term cash flows is more exposed to such

---

[14] In Chapter 10 we describe an accounting measure of the degree of operating leverage (DOL), defined as DOL = 1 + fixed costs/profits. DOL measures the percentage change in profits for a 1% change in revenue. We have derived here a version of DOL expressed in PVs and betas.

[15] See B. Lev, "On the Association between Operating Leverage and Risk," *Journal of Financial and Quantitative Analysis* 9 (September 1974), pp. 627–642; and G. N. Mandelker and S. G. Rhee, "The Impact of the Degrees of Operating and Financial Leverage on Systematic Risk of Common Stock," *Journal of Financial and Quantitative Analysis* 19 (March 1984), pp. 45–57.

shifts in the discount rate than one with short-term cash flows. This project will, therefore, have a high beta even though it may not have high operating leverage and cyclicality.[16]

You cannot hope to estimate the relative risk of assets with any precision, but good managers examine any project from a variety of angles and look for clues as to its riskiness. They know that high market risk is a characteristic of cyclical ventures, of projects with high fixed costs, and of projects that are sensitive to marketwide changes in the discount rate. They think about the major uncertainties affecting the economy and consider how projects are affected by these uncertainties.

Don't Be Fooled by Diversifiable Risk

In this chapter we have defined risk as the asset beta for a firm, industry, or project. But in everyday usage, "risk" simply means "bad outcome." People think of the risks of a project as a list of things that can go wrong. For example,

- A geologist looking for oil worries about the risk of a dry hole.
- A pharmaceutical-company scientist worries about the risk that a new drug will have unacceptable side effects.
- A plant manager worries that new technology for a production line will fail to work, requiring expensive changes and repairs.
- A telecom CFO worries about the risk that a communications satellite will be damaged by space debris. (This was the fate of an Iridium satellite in 2009, when it collided with Russia's defunct Cosmos 2251. Both were blown to smithereens.)

Notice that these risks are all diversifiable. For example, the Iridium-Cosmos collision was definitely a zero-beta event. These hazards do not affect asset betas and should not affect the discount rate for the projects.

Sometimes financial managers increase discount rates in an attempt to offset these risks. This makes no sense. Diversifiable risks should not increase the cost of capital.

EXAMPLE 9.1 ● Allowing for Possible Bad Outcomes

Project Z will produce just one cash flow, forecasted at $1 million at year 1. It is regarded as average risk, suitable for discounting at a 10% company cost of capital:

$$PV = \frac{C_1}{1 + r} = \frac{1,000,000}{1.1} = \$909,100$$

But now you discover that the company's engineers are behind schedule in developing the technology required for the project. They are confident it will work, but they admit to a small chance that it will not. You still see the *most likely* outcome as $1 million, but you also see some chance that project Z will generate *zero* cash flow next year.

Now the project's prospects are clouded by your new worry about technology. It must be worth less than the $909,100 you calculated before that worry arose. But how much less? There is *some* discount rate (10% plus a fudge factor) that will give the right value, but we do not know what that adjusted discount rate is.

We suggest you reconsider your original $1 million forecast for project Z's cash flow. Project cash flows are supposed to be *unbiased* forecasts that give due weight to all possible outcomes, favorable and unfavorable. Managers making unbiased forecasts are correct on

---

[16] See J. Y. Campbell and J. Mei, "Where Do Betas Come From? Asset Price Dynamics and the Sources of Systematic Risk," *Review of Financial Studies* 6 (Fall 1993), pp. 567–592. Cornell discusses the effect of duration on project risk in B. Cornell, "Risk, Duration and Capital Budgeting: New Evidence on Some Old Questions," *Journal of Business* 72 (April 1999), pp. 183–200.

average. Sometimes their forecasts will turn out high, other times low, but their errors will average out over many projects.

If you forecast a cash flow of $1 million for projects like Z, you will overestimate the average cash flow, because every now and then you will hit a zero. Those zeros should be "averaged in" to your forecasts.

For many projects, the most likely cash flow is also the unbiased forecast. If there are three possible outcomes with the probabilities shown below, the unbiased forecast is $1 million. (The unbiased forecast is the sum of the probability-weighted cash flows.)

Possible Cash Flow	Probability	Probability-Weighted Cash Flow	Unbiased Forecast
1.2	.25	.3	
1.0	.50	.5	1.0, or $1 million
.8	.25	.2	

This might describe the initial prospects of project Z. But if technological uncertainty introduces a 10% chance of a zero cash flow, the unbiased forecast could drop to $900,000:

Possible Cash Flow	Probability	Probability-Weighted Cash Flow	Unbiased Forecast
1.2	.225	.27	
1.0	.45	.45	.90, or $900,000
.8	.225	.18	
0	.10	.0	

The present value is

$$PV = \frac{.90}{1.1} = .818, \text{ or } \$818,000$$

• • • • •

Managers often work out a range of possible outcomes for major projects, sometimes with explicit probabilities attached. We give more elaborate examples and further discussion in Chapter 10. But even when outcomes and probabilities are not explicitly written down, the manager can still consider the good and bad outcomes as well as the most likely one. When the bad outcomes outweigh the good, the cash-flow forecast should be reduced until balance is regained.

Step 1, then, is to do your best to make unbiased forecasts of a project's cash flows. Unbiased forecasts incorporate all risks, including diversifiable risks as well as market risks. Step 2 is to consider whether *diversified* investors would regard the project as more or less risky than the average project. In this step only market risks are relevant.

Avoid Fudge Factors in Discount Rates

Think back to our example of project Z, where we reduced forecasted cash flows from $1 million to $900,000 to account for a possible failure of technology. The project's PV was reduced from $909,100 to $818,000. You could have gotten the right answer by adding a fudge factor to the discount rate and discounting the original forecast of $1 million. But you have to think through the possible cash flows to get the fudge factor, and once you forecast the cash flows correctly, you don't need the fudge factor.

Fudge factors in discount rates are dangerous because they displace clear thinking about future cash flows. Here is an example.

EXAMPLE 9.2 ● Correcting for Optimistic Forecasts

The CFO of EZ^2 Corp. is disturbed to find that cash-flow forecasts for its investment projects are almost always optimistic. On average they are 10% too high. He therefore decides to compensate by adding 10% to EZ^2's WACC, increasing it from 12% to 22%.[17]

Suppose the CEO is right about the 10% upward bias in cash-flow forecasts. Can he just add 10% to the discount rate?

Project ZZ has level forecasted cash flows of $1,000 per year lasting for 15 years. The first two lines of Table 9.2 show these forecasts and their PVs discounted at 12%. Lines 3 and 4 show the corrected forecasts, each reduced by 10%, and the corrected PVs, which are (no surprise) also reduced by 10% (line 5). Line 6 shows the PVs when the uncorrected forecasts are discounted at 22%. The final line 7 shows the percentage reduction in PVs at the 22% discount rate, compared to the unadjusted PVs in line 2.

Line 5 shows the correct adjustment for optimism (10%). Line 7 shows what happens when a 10% fudge factor is added to the discount rate. The effect on the first year's cash flow is a PV "haircut" of about 8%, 2% less than the CFO expected. But later present values are knocked down by much more than 10%, because the fudge factor is compounded in the 22% discount rate. By years 10 and 15, the PV haircuts are 57% and 72%, far more than the 10% bias that the CFO started with.

Did the CFO really think that bias accumulated as shown in line 7 of Table 9.2? We doubt that he ever asked that question. If he was right in the first place, and the true bias is 10%, then adding a 10% fudge factor to the discount rate understates PV. The fudge factor also makes long-lived projects look much worse than quick-payback projects.[18]

Year:	1	2	3	4	5	. . .	10	. . .	15
1. Original cash-flow forecast	$1,000.00	$1,000.00	$1,000.00	$1,000.00	$1,000.00	. . .	$1,000.00	. . .	$1,000.00
2. PV at 12%	$ 892.90	$ 797.20	$ 711.80	$ 635.50	$ 567.40	. . .	$ 322.00	. . .	$ 182.70
3. Corrected cash-flow forecast	$ 900.00	$ 900.00	$ 900.00	$ 900.00	$ 900.00	. . .	$ 900.00	. . .	$ 900.00
4. PV at 12%	$ 803.60	$ 717.50	$ 640.60	$ 572.00	$ 510.70	. . .	$ 289.80	. . .	$ 164.40
5. PV correction	−10.0%	−10.0%	−10.0%	−10.0%	−10.0%	. . .	−10.0%	. . .	−10.0%
6. Original forecast discounted at 22%	$ 819.70	$ 671.90	$ 550.70	$ 451.40	$ 370.00	. . .	$ 136.90	. . .	$ 50.70
7. PV "correction" at 22% discount rate	−8.2%	−15.7%	−22.6%	−29.0%	−34.8%	. . .	−57.5%	. . .	−72.3%

▶ **TABLE 9.2**   The original cash-flow forecasts for the ZZ project (line 1) are too optimistic. The forecasts and PVs should be reduced by 10% (lines 3 and 4). But adding a 10% fudge factor to the discount rate reduces PVs by far more than 10% (line 6). The fudge factor overcorrects for bias and would penalize long-lived projects.

---

[17] The CFO is ignoring Brealey, Myers, and Allen's Second Law, which we cover in the next chapter.

[18] The optimistic bias could be worse for distant than near cash flows. If so, the CFO should make the time-pattern of bias explicit and adjust the cash-flow forecasts accordingly.

● ● ● ● ●

Discount Rates for International Projects

In this chapter we have concentrated on investments in the U.S., but we should also warn against adding fudge factors to discount rates for projects in developing economies. Such fudge factors are too often seen in practice.

It's true that markets are more volatile in developing economies, but much of that risk is diversifiable for investors in the U.S., Europe, and other developed countries. It's also true that more things can go wrong for projects in developing economies, particularly in countries that are unstable politically. Expropriations happen. Sometimes governments default on their obligations to international investors. Thus it's especially important to think through the downside risks and to give them weight in cash-flow forecasts.

Some international projects are at least partially protected from these downsides. For example, an opportunistic government would gain little or nothing by expropriating the local IBM affiliate, because the affiliate would have little value without the IBM brand name, products, and customer relationships. A privately owned toll road would be a more tempting target, because the toll road would be relatively easy for the local government to maintain and operate.

9-4 Certainty Equivalents—Another Way to Adjust for Risk

In practical capital budgeting, a single risk-adjusted rate is used to discount all future cash flows. This assumes that project risk does not change over time, but remains constant year-in and year-out. We know that this cannot be strictly true, for the risks that companies are exposed to are constantly shifting. We are venturing here onto somewhat difficult ground, but there is a way to think about risk that can suggest a route through. It involves converting the expected cash flows to **certainty equivalents.** First we work through an example showing what certainty equivalents are. Then, as a reward for your investment, we use certainty equivalents to uncover what you are really assuming when you discount a series of future cash flows at a single risk-adjusted discount rate. We also value a project where risk changes over time and ordinary discounting fails. Your investment will be rewarded still more when we cover options in Chapters 16 and 17. Option-pricing formulas discount certainty equivalents.

Valuation by Certainty Equivalents

Think back to the simple real estate investment that we used in Chapter 2 to introduce the concept of present value. You are considering construction of an office building that you plan to sell after one year for $420,000. That cash flow is uncertain with the same risk as the market, so $\beta = 1$. Given $r_f = 5\%$ and $r_m - r_f = 7\%$, you discount at a risk-adjusted discount rate of $5 + 1 \times 7 = 12\%$ rather than the 5% risk-free rate of interest. This gives a present value of $420,000/1.12 = \$375,000$.

Suppose a real estate company now approaches and offers to fix the price at which it will buy the building from you at the end of the year. This guarantee would remove any uncertainty about the payoff on your investment. So you would accept a lower figure than the uncertain payoff of $420,000. But how much less? If the building has a present value of $375,000 and the interest rate is 5%, then

$$PV = \frac{\text{Certain cash flow}}{1.05} = 375,000$$

Certain cash flow $= \$393,750$

In other words, a certain cash flow of $393,750 has exactly the same present value as an expected but uncertain cash flow of $420,000. The cash flow of $393,750 is therefore known as the *certainty-equivalent cash flow*. To compensate for both the delayed payoff and the uncertainty in real estate prices, you need a return of $420,000 - 375,000 = $45,000. One part of this difference compensates for the time value of money. The other part ($420,000 - 393,750 = $26,250) is a markdown or haircut to compensate for the risk attached to the forecasted cash flow of $420,000.

Our example illustrates two ways to value a risky cash flow:

Method 1: Discount the risky cash flow at a *risk-adjusted discount rate r* that is greater than r_f.[19] The risk-adjusted discount rate adjusts for both time and risk. This is illustrated by the clockwise route in Figure 9.3.

Method 2: Find the certainty-equivalent cash flow and discount at the risk-free interest rate r_f. When you use this method, you need to ask, What is the smallest *certain* payoff for which I would exchange the risky cash flow? This is called the *certainty equivalent*, denoted by CEQ. Since CEQ is the value equivalent of a safe cash flow, it is discounted at the risk-free rate. The certainty-equivalent method makes *separate* adjustments for risk and time. This is illustrated by the counterclockwise route in Figure 9.3.

We now have two identical expressions for the PV of a cash flow at period 1:[20]

$$PV = \frac{C_1}{1 + r} = \frac{CEQ_1}{1 + r_f}$$

For cash flows two, three, or *t* years away,

$$PV = \frac{C_t}{(1 + r)^t} = \frac{CEQ_t}{(1 + r_f)^t}$$

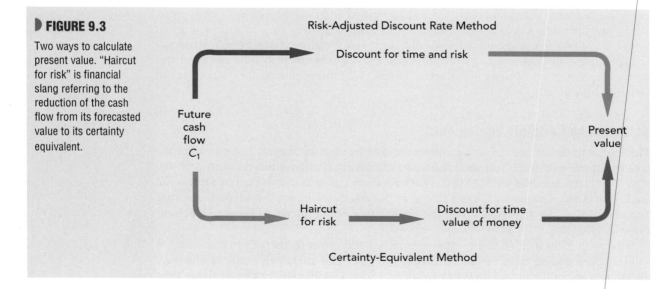

▶ **FIGURE 9.3**

Two ways to calculate present value. "Haircut for risk" is financial slang referring to the reduction of the cash flow from its forecasted value to its certainty equivalent.

Risk-Adjusted Discount Rate Method

Discount for time and risk

Future cash flow C_1

Present value

Haircut for risk   Discount for time value of money

Certainty-Equivalent Method

---

[19] The discount rate *r* can be less than r_f for assets with negative betas. But actual betas are almost always positive.

[20] CEQ_1 can be calculated directly from the capital asset pricing model. The certainty-equivalent form of the CAPM states that the certainty-equivalent value of the cash flow C_1 is $C_1 - \lambda \text{ cov } (\tilde{C}_1, \tilde{r}_m)$. $\text{Cov}(\tilde{C}_1, \tilde{r}_m)$ is the covariance between the uncertain cash flow, and the return on the market, $\tilde{r}_m$. Lambda, λ, is a measure of the market price of risk. It is defined as $(r_m - r_f)/\sigma_m^2$. For example, if $r_m - r_f = .08$ and the standard deviation of market returns is $\sigma_m = .20$, then lambda $= .08/.20^2 = 2$. We show on our Web site (**www.mhhe.com/bma**) how the CAPM formula can be restated in this certainty-equivalent form.

When to Use a Single Risk-Adjusted Discount Rate for Long-Lived Assets

We are now in a position to examine what is implied when a constant risk-adjusted discount rate is used to calculate a present value.

Consider two simple projects. Project A is expected to produce a cash flow of $100 million for each of three years. The risk-free interest rate is 6%, the market risk premium is 8%, and project A's beta is .75. You therefore calculate A's opportunity cost of capital as follows:

$$r = r_f + \beta (r_m - r_f)$$
$$= 6 + .75(8) = 12\%$$

Discounting at 12% gives the following present value for each cash flow:

Project A		
Year	**Cash Flow**	**PV at 12%**
1	100	89.3
2	100	79.7
3	100	71.2
	Total PV	240.2

Now compare these figures with the cash flows of project B. Notice that B's cash flows are lower than A's; but B's flows are safe, and therefore they are discounted at the risk-free interest rate. The *present value* of each year's cash flow is identical for the two projects.

Project B		
Year	**Cash Flow**	**PV at 6%**
1	94.6	89.3
2	89.6	79.7
3	84.8	71.2
	Total PV	240.2

In year 1 project A has a risky cash flow of 100. This has the same PV as the safe cash flow of 94.6 from project B. Therefore 94.6 is the certainty equivalent of 100. Since the two cash flows have the same PV, investors must be willing to give up $100 - 94.6 = 5.4$ in expected year-1 income in order to get rid of the uncertainty.

In year 2 project A has a risky cash flow of 100, and B has a safe cash flow of 89.6. Again both flows have the same PV. Thus, to eliminate the uncertainty in year 2, investors are prepared to give up $100 - 89.6 = 10.4$ of future income. To eliminate uncertainty in year 3, they are willing to give up $100 - 84.8 = 15.2$ of future income.

To value project A, you discounted each cash flow at the same risk-adjusted discount rate of 12%. Now you can see what is implied when you did that. By using a constant rate, you effectively made a larger deduction for risk from the later cash flows:

Year	Forecasted Cash Flow for Project A	Certainty-Equivalent Cash Flow	Deduction for Risk
1	100	94.6	5.4
2	100	89.6	10.4
3	100	84.8	15.2

The second cash flow is riskier than the first because it is exposed to two years of market risk. The third cash flow is riskier still because it is exposed to three years of market risk. This increased risk is reflected in the certainty equivalents that decline by a constant proportion each period.

Therefore, use of a constant risk-adjusted discount rate for a stream of cash flows assumes that risk accumulates at a constant rate as you look farther out into the future.

A Common Mistake

You sometimes hear people say that because distant cash flows are riskier, they should be discounted at a higher rate than earlier cash flows. That is quite wrong: We have just seen that using the same risk-adjusted discount rate for each year's cash flow implies a larger deduction for risk from the later cash flows. The reason is that the discount rate compensates for the risk borne *per period*. The more distant the cash flows, the greater the number of periods and the larger the *total* risk adjustment.

When You Cannot Use a Single Risk-Adjusted Discount Rate for Long-Lived Assets

Sometimes you will encounter problems where the use of a single risk-adjusted discount rate will get you into trouble. For example, later in the book we look at how options are valued. Because an option's risk is continually changing, the certainty-equivalent method needs to be used.

Here is a disguised, simplified, and somewhat exaggerated version of an actual project proposal that one of the authors was asked to analyze. The scientists at Vegetron have come up with an electric mop, and the firm is ready to go ahead with pilot production and test marketing. The preliminary phase will take one year and cost $125,000. Management feels that there is only a 50% chance that pilot production and market tests will be successful. If they are, then Vegetron will build a $1 million plant that would generate an expected annual cash flow in perpetuity of $250,000 a year after taxes. If they are not successful, the project will have to be dropped.

The expected cash flows (in thousands of dollars) are

$$C_0 = -125$$
$$C_1 = 50\% \text{ chance of } -1{,}000 \text{ and } 50\% \text{ chance of } 0$$
$$= .5(-1{,}000) + .5(0) = -500$$
$$C_t \text{ for } t = 2{,}3{,}\ldots = 50\% \text{ chance of } 250 \text{ and } 50\% \text{ chance of } 0$$
$$= .5(250) + .5(0) = 125$$

Management has little experience with consumer products and considers this a project of extremely high risk.[21] Therefore management discounts the cash flows at 25%, rather than at Vegetron's normal 10% standard:

$$\text{NPV} = -125 - \frac{500}{1.25} + \sum_{t=2}^{\infty} \frac{125}{(1.25)^t} = -125, \text{ or } -\$125{,}000$$

This seems to show that the project is not worthwhile.

Management's analysis is open to criticism if the first year's experiment resolves a high proportion of the risk. If the test phase is a failure, then there is no risk at all—the project is *certain* to be worthless. If it is a success, there could well be only normal risk from then on. That means there is a 50% chance that in one year Vegetron will have the opportunity to invest in a project of *normal* risk, for which the *normal* discount rate of 10% would be

---

[21] We will assume that they mean high *market risk* and that the difference between 25% and 10% is *not* a fudge factor introduced to offset optimistic cash-flow forecasts.

Estimating Stock and Market Risk

▶ Spreadsheets such as Excel have some built-in statistical functions that are useful for calculating risk measures. You can find these functions by pressing *fx* on the Excel toolbar. If you then click on the function that you wish to use, Excel will ask you for the inputs that it needs. At the bottom left of the function box there is a Help facility with an example of how the function is used.

Here is a list of useful functions for estimating stock and market risk. You can enter the inputs for all these functions as numbers or as the addresses of cells that contain the numbers.

1. **VARP** and **STDEVP:** Calculate variance and standard deviation of a series of numbers, as shown in Section 7–2.

2. **VAR** and **STDEV:** Footnote 15 on page 223 noted that when variance is estimated from a sample of observations (the usual case), a correction should be made for the loss of a degree of freedom. VAR and STDEV provide the corrected measures. For any large sample VAR and VARP will be similar.

3. **SLOPE:** Useful for calculating the beta of a stock or portfolio.

4. **CORREL:** Useful for calculating the correlation between the returns on any two investments.

5. **RSQ:** R-squared is the square of the correlation coefficient and is useful for measuring the proportion of the variance of a stock's returns that can be explained by the market.

6. **AVERAGE:** Calculates the average of any series of numbers.

If, say, you need to know the standard error of your estimate of beta, you can obtain more detailed statistics by going to the *Tools* menu and clicking on *Data Analysis* and then on *Regression*.

SPREADSHEET QUESTIONS

The following questions provide opportunities to practice each of the Excel functions.

9.1 (VAR and STDEV) Choose two well-known stocks and download the latest 61 months of adjusted prices from **finance.yahoo.com**. Calculate the monthly returns for each stock. Now find the variance and standard deviation of the returns for each stock by using VAR and STDEV. Annualize the variance by multiplying by 12 and the standard deviation by multiplying by the square root of 12.

9.2 (AVERAGE, VAR, and STDEV) Now calculate the annualized variance and standard deviation for a portfolio that each month has equal holdings in the two stocks. Is the result more or less than the average of the standard deviations of the two stocks? Why?

9.3 (SLOPE) Download the Standard & Poor's index for the same period (its symbol is ^GSPC). Find the beta of each stock and of the portfolio. (*Note:* You need to enter the stock returns as the Y-values and market returns as the X-values.) Is the beta of the portfolio more or less than the average of the betas of the two stocks?

9.4 (CORREL) Calculate the correlation between the returns on the two stocks. Use this measure and your earlier estimates of each stock's variance to calculate the variance of a portfolio that is evenly divided between the two stocks. (You may need to reread Section 7–3 to refresh your memory of how to do this.) Check that you get the same answer as when you calculated the portfolio variance directly.

9.5 (RSQ) For each of the two stocks calculate the proportion of the variance explained by the market index. Do the results square with your intuition?

9.6 Use the *Regression* facility under the *Data Analysis* menu to calculate the beta of each stock and of the portfolio (beta here is called the coefficient of the X-variable). Look at the standard error of the estimate in the cell to the right. How confident can you be of your estimates of the betas of each stock? How about your estimate of the portfolio beta?

	SLOPE	▾ X ✓ ƒx	=SLOPE(B1:B9,A1:A9)					
	A	B	C	D	E	F	G	H
1	0.8	20.1						
2	-7.5	-25.4						
3	-16.8	-21.3						
4	-9.2	-10.0						
5	1.2	5.9						
6	-1.0	4.1						
7	-8.6	-10.2						
8	1.1	3.8						
9	4.8	10.3						
10								
11	A1:A9							
12								

Function Arguments ☒

SLOPE

Known_y's B1:B9   = {20.0936768149883

Known_x's A1:A9   = {0.78215656520575

= 1.83972892

Returns the slope of the linear regression line through the given data points.

Known_x's is the set of independent data points and can be numbers or names, arrays, or references that contain numbers.

Formula result = 1.83972892

Help on this function   OK   Cancel

appropriate. Thus the firm has a 50% chance to invest $1 million in a project with a net present value of $1.5 million:

$$\text{Success} \rightarrow \text{NPV} = -1{,}000 + \frac{250}{.10} = +1{,}500 \ (50\% \text{ chance})$$

Pilot production
and market tests

$$\text{Failure} \rightarrow \text{NPV} = 0 \ (50\% \text{ chance})$$

Thus we could view the project as offering an expected payoff of $.5(1{,}500) + .5(0) = 750$, or $750,000, at $t = 1$ on a $125,000 investment at $t = 0$. Of course, the certainty equivalent of the payoff is less than $750,000, but the difference would have to be very large to justify rejecting the project. For example, if the certainty equivalent is half the forecasted cash flow (an extremely large cash-flow haircut) and the risk-free rate is 7%, the project is worth $225,500:

$$\text{NPV} = C_0 + \frac{\text{CEQ}_1}{1 + r}$$

$$= -125 + \frac{.5(750)}{1.07} = 225.5, \text{ or } \$225{,}500$$

This is not bad for a $125,000 investment—and quite a change from the negative-NPV that management got by discounting all future cash flows at 25%.

• • • • •

SUMMARY

In Chapter 8 we set out the basic principles for valuing risky assets. This chapter shows you how to apply those principles when valuing capital investment projects.

Suppose the project has the same market risk as the company's existing assets. In this case, the project cash flows can be discounted at the *company cost of capital*. The company cost of capital is the rate of return that investors require on a portfolio of all of the company's outstanding debt and equity. It is usually calculated as an after-tax *weighted-average cost of capital* (after-tax WACC), that is, as the weighted average of the after-tax cost of debt and the cost of equity. The weights are the relative market values of debt and equity. The cost of debt is calculated after tax because interest is a tax-deductible expense.

The hardest part of calculating the after-tax WACC is estimation of the cost of equity. Most large, public corporations use the capital asset pricing model (CAPM) to do this. They generally estimate the firm's equity beta from past rates of return for the firm's common stock and for the market, and they check their estimate against the average beta of similar firms.

The after-tax WACC is the correct discount rate for projects that have the same market risk as the company's existing business. Many firms, however, use the after-tax WACC as the discount rate for all projects. This is a dangerous procedure. If the procedure is followed strictly, the firm will accept too many high-risk projects and reject too many low-risk projects. It is *project* risk that counts: The true cost of capital depends on the use to which the capital is put.

Managers, therefore, need to understand why a particular project may have above- or below-average risk. You can often identify the characteristics of a high- or low-beta project even when the beta cannot be estimated directly. For example, you can figure out how much the project's cash flows are affected by the performance of the entire economy. Cyclical projects are generally high-beta projects. You can also look at operating leverage. Fixed production costs increase beta.

Don't be fooled by diversifiable risk. Diversifiable risks do not affect asset betas or the cost of capital, but the possibility of bad outcomes should be incorporated in the cash-flow forecasts. Also be careful not to offset worries about a project's future performance by adding a fudge factor to the discount rate. Fudge factors don't work, and they may seriously undervalue long-lived projects.

There is one more fence to jump. Most projects produce cash flows for several years. Firms generally use the same risk-adjusted rate to discount each of these cash flows. When they do this, they are implicitly assuming that cumulative risk increases at a constant rate as you look further into the future. That assumption is usually reasonable. It is precisely true when the project's future beta will be constant, that is, when risk *per period* is constant.

But exceptions sometimes prove the rule. Be on the alert for projects where risk clearly does not increase steadily. In these cases, you should break the project into segments within which the same discount rate can be reasonably used. Or you should use the certainty-equivalent version of the DCF model, which allows separate risk adjustments to each period's cash flow.

The nearby box (on page 231) provides useful spreadsheet functions for estimating stock and market risk.

● ● ● ● ●

FURTHER READING

Michael Brennan provides a useful, but quite difficult, survey of the issues covered in this chapter:

M. J. Brennan, "Corporate Investment Policy," *Handbook of the Economics of Finance, Volume 1A, Corporate Finance,* eds. G. M. Constantinides, M. Harris, and R. M. Stulz (Amsterdam: Elsevier BV, 2003).

● ● ● ● ●

PROBLEM SETS

BASIC

1. Suppose a firm uses its company cost of capital to evaluate all projects. Will it underestimate or overestimate the value of high-risk projects?

2. A company is 40% financed by risk-free debt. The interest rate is 10%, the expected market risk premium is 8%, and the beta of the company's common stock is .5. What is the company cost of capital? What is the after-tax WACC, assuming that the company pays tax at a 35% rate?

3. Look back to the top-right panel of Figure 9.2. What proportion of Amazon's returns was explained by market movements? What proportion of risk was diversifiable? How does the diversifiable risk show up in the plot? What is the range of possible errors in the estimated beta?

4. Define the following terms:
   a. Cost of debt.
   b. Cost of equity.
   c. After-tax WACC.
   d. Equity beta.
   e. Asset beta.
   f. Pure-play comparable.
   g. Certainty equivalent.

5. EZCUBE Corp. is 50% financed with long-term bonds and 50% with common equity. The debt securities have a beta of .15. The company's equity beta is 1.25. What is EZCUBE's asset beta?

6. Many investment projects are exposed to diversifiable risks. What does "diversifiable" mean in this context? How should diversifiable risks be accounted for in project valuation? Should they be ignored completely?

7. John Barleycorn estimates his firm's after-tax WACC at only 8%. Nevertheless he sets a 15% companywide discount rate to offset the optimistic biases of project sponsors and to

impose "discipline" on the capital-budgeting process. Suppose Mr. Barleycorn is correct about the project sponsors, who are in fact optimistic by 7% on average. Will the increase in the discount rate from 8% to 15% offset the bias?

8. Which of these projects is likely to have the higher asset beta, other things equal? Why?

   a. The sales force for project A is paid a fixed annual salary. Project B's sales force is paid by commissions only.

   b. Project C is a first-class-only airline. Project D is a well-established line of breakfast cereals.

9. True or false?

   a. The company cost of capital is the correct discount rate for all projects, because the high risks of some projects are offset by the low risk of other projects.

   b. Distant cash flows are riskier than near-term cash flows. Therefore long-term projects require higher risk-adjusted discount rates.

   c. Adding fudge factors to discount rates undervalues long-lived projects compared with quick-payoff projects.

10. A project has a forecasted cash flow of $110 in year 1 and $121 in year 2. The interest rate is 5%, the estimated risk premium on the market is 10%, and the project has a beta of .5. If you use a constant risk-adjusted discount rate, what is

    a. The PV of the project?

    b. The certainty-equivalent cash flow in year 1 and year 2?

    c. The ratio of the certainty-equivalent cash flows to the expected cash flows in years 1 and 2?

INTERMEDIATE

11. The total market value of the common stock of the Okefenokee Real Estate Company is $6 million, and the total value of its debt is $4 million. The treasurer estimates that the beta of the stock is currently 1.5 and that the expected risk premium on the market is 6%. The Treasury bill rate is 4%. Assume for simplicity that Okefenokee debt is risk-free and the company does not pay tax.

    a. What is the required return on Okefenokee stock?

    b. Estimate the company cost of capital.

    c. What is the discount rate for an expansion of the company's present business?

    d. Suppose the company wants to diversify into the manufacture of rose-colored spectacles. The beta of unleveraged optical manufacturers is 1.2. Estimate the required return on Okefenokee's new venture.

12. Nero Violins has the following capital structure:

Security	Beta	Total Market Value ($ millions)
Debt	0	$100
Preferred stock	.20	40
Common stock	1.20	299

    a. What is the firm's asset beta? (*Hint:* What is the beta of a portfolio of all the firm's securities?)

    b. Assume that the CAPM is correct. What discount rate should Nero set for investments that expand the scale of its operations without changing its asset beta? Assume a risk-free interest rate of 5% and a market risk premium of 6%.

13. The following table shows estimates of the risk of two well-known Canadian stocks:

	Standard Deviation, (%)	R^2	Beta	Standard Error of Beta
Toronto Dominion Bank	25	.25	.82	.18
Canadian Pacific	28	.30	1.04	.20

a. What proportion of each stock's risk was market risk, and what proportion was specific risk?

b. What is the variance of Toronto Dominion? What is the specific variance?

c. What is the confidence interval on Canadian Pacific's beta?

d. If the CAPM is correct, what is the expected return on Toronto Dominion? Assume a risk-free interest rate of 5% and an expected market return of 12%.

e. Suppose that next year the market provides a zero return. Knowing this, what return would you expect from Toronto Dominion?

14. You are given the following information for Golden Fleece Financial:

Long-term debt outstanding:	$300,000
Current yield to maturity (r_{debt}):	8%
Number of shares of common stock:	10,000
Price per share:	$50
Book value per share:	$25
Expected rate of return on stock (r_{equity}):	15%

Calculate Golden Fleece's company cost of capital. Ignore taxes.

15. Look again at Table 9.1. This time we will concentrate on Burlington Northern Santa Fe.

a. Calculate Burlington's cost of equity from the CAPM using its own beta estimate and the industry beta estimate. How different are your answers? Assume a risk-free rate of 5% and a market risk premium of 7%.

b. Can you be confident that Burlington's true beta is *not* the industry average?

c. Under what circumstances might you advise Burlington to calculate its cost of equity based on its own beta estimate?

16. What types of firms need to estimate industry asset betas? How would such a firm make the estimate? Describe the process step by step.

17. Binomial Tree Farm's financing includes $5 million of bank loans. Its common equity is shown in Binomial's *Annual Report* at $6.67 million. It has 500,000 shares of common stock outstanding, which trade on the Wichita Stock Exchange at $18 per share. What debt ratio should Binomial use to calculate its WACC or asset beta? Explain.

18. You run a perpetual encabulator machine, which generates revenues averaging $20 million per year. Raw material costs are 50% of revenues. These costs are variable—they are always proportional to revenues. There are no other operating costs. The cost of capital is 9%. Your firm's long-term borrowing rate is 6%.

Now you are approached by Studebaker Capital Corp., which proposes a fixed-price contract to supply raw materials at $10 million per year for 10 years.

a. What happens to the operating leverage and business risk of the encabulator machine if you agree to this fixed-price contract?

b. Calculate the present value of the encabulator machine with and without the fixed-price contract.

19. Mom and Pop Groceries has just dispatched a year's supply of groceries to the government of the Central Antarctic Republic. Payment of $250,000 will be made one year hence after the shipment arrives by snow train. Unfortunately there is a good chance of a coup d'état, in which case the new government will not pay. Mom and Pop's controller therefore decides to discount the payment at 40%, rather than at the company's 12% cost of capital.

    a. What's wrong with using a 40% rate to offset political risk?

    b. How much is the $250,000 payment really worth if the odds of a coup d'état are 25%?

20. An oil company is drilling a series of new wells on the perimeter of a producing oil field. About 20% of the new wells will be dry holes. Even if a new well strikes oil, there is still uncertainty about the amount of oil produced: 40% of new wells that strike oil produce only 1,000 barrels a day; 60% produce 5,000 barrels per day.

    a. Forecast the annual cash revenues from a new perimeter well. Use a future oil price of $50 per barrel.

    b. A geologist proposes to discount the cash flows of the new wells at 30% to offset the risk of dry holes. The oil company's normal cost of capital is 10%. Does this proposal make sense? Briefly explain why or why not.

21. A project has the following forecasted cash flows:

Cash Flows, ($ thousands)			
C_0	C_1	C_2	C_3
−100	+40	+60	+50

    The estimated project beta is 1.5. The market return r_m is 16%, and the risk-free rate r_f is 7%.

    a. Estimate the opportunity cost of capital and the project's PV (using the same rate to discount each cash flow).

    b. What are the certainty-equivalent cash flows in each year?

    c. What is the ratio of the certainty-equivalent cash flow to the expected cash flow in each year?

    d. Explain why this ratio declines.

22. The McGregor Whisky Company is proposing to market diet Scotch. The product will first be test-marketed for two years in southern California at an initial cost of $500,000. This test launch is not expected to produce any profits but should reveal consumer preferences. There is a 60% chance that demand will be satisfactory. In this case McGregor will spend $5 million to launch the Scotch nationwide and will receive an expected annual profit of $700,000 in perpetuity. If demand is not satisfactory, diet Scotch will be withdrawn.

    Once consumer preferences are known, the product will be subject to an average degree of risk, and, therefore, McGregor requires a return of 12% on its investment. However, the initial test-market phase is viewed as much riskier, and McGregor demands a return of 20% on this initial expenditure.

    What is the NPV of the diet Scotch project?

CHALLENGE

23. Suppose you are valuing a future stream of high-risk (high-beta) cash *outflows*. High risk means a high discount rate. But the higher the discount rate, the less the present value. This seems to say that the higher the risk of cash outflows, the less you should worry about them! Can that be right? Should the sign of the cash flow affect the appropriate discount rate? Explain.

24. An oil company executive is considering investing $10 million in one or both of two wells: Well 1 is expected to produce oil worth $3 million a year for 10 years; well 2 is expected to produce $2 million for 15 years. These are *real* (inflation-adjusted) cash flows.

The beta for *producing wells* is .9. The market risk premium is 8%, the nominal risk-free interest rate is 6%, and expected inflation is 4%.

The two wells are intended to develop a previously discovered oil field. Unfortunately there is still a 20% chance of a dry hole in each case. A dry hole means zero cash flows and a complete loss of the $10 million investment.

Ignore taxes and make further assumptions as necessary.

a. What is the correct real discount rate for cash flows from developed wells?

b. The oil company executive proposes to add 20 percentage points to the real discount rate to offset the risk of a dry hole. Calculate the NPV of each well with this adjusted discount rate.

c. What do *you* say the NPVs of the two wells are?

d. Is there any *single* fudge factor that could be added to the discount rate for developed wells that would yield the correct NPV for both wells? Explain.

● ● ● ● ●

REAL-TIME DATA ANALYSIS

You can download data for the following questions from Standard & Poor's Market Insight Web site (**www.mhhe.com/edumarketinsight**)—see the "Monthly Adjusted Prices" spreadsheet—or from **finance.yahoo.com**.

1. Look at the companies listed in Table 8.2. Calculate monthly rates of return for two successive five-year periods. Calculate betas for each subperiod using the Excel SLOPE function. How stable was each company's beta? Suppose that you had used these betas to estimate expected rates of return from the CAPM. Would your estimates have changed significantly from period to period?

2. Identify a sample of food companies. For example, you could try Campbell Soup (CPB), General Mills (GIS), Kellogg (K), Kraft Foods (KFT), and Sara Lee (SLE).

   STANDARD &POOR'S

   a. Estimate beta and R^2 for each company, using five years of monthly returns and Excel functions SLOPE and RSQ.

   b. Average the returns for each month to give the return on an equally weighted portfolio of the stocks. Then calculate the industry beta using these portfolio returns. How does the R^2 of this portfolio compare with the average R^2 of the individual stocks?

   c. Use the CAPM to calculate an average cost of equity (r_{equity}) for the food industry. Use current interest rates—take a look at the end of Section 9–2—and a reasonable estimate of the market risk premium.

MINI-CASE ● ● ● ● ●

The Jones Family, Incorporated

The Scene: Early evening in an ordinary family room in Manhattan. Modern furniture, with old copies of *The Wall Street Journal* and the *Financial Times* scattered around. Autographed photos of Alan Greenspan and George Soros are prominently displayed. A picture window reveals a distant view of lights on the Hudson River. John Jones sits at a computer terminal, glumly sipping a glass of chardonnay and putting on a carry trade in Japanese yen over the Internet. His wife Marsha enters.

Marsha: Hi, honey. Glad to be home. Lousy day on the trading floor, though. Dullsville. No volume. But I did manage to hedge next year's production from our copper mine. I couldn't get a good quote on the right package of futures contracts, so I arranged a commodity swap.

John doesn't reply.

Marsha: John, what's wrong? Have you been selling yen again? That's been a losing trade for weeks.

John: Well, yes. I shouldn't have gone to Goldman Sachs's foreign exchange brunch. But I've got to get out of the house somehow. I'm cooped up here all day calculating covariances and efficient risk-return trade-offs while you're out trading commodity futures. You get all the glamour and excitement.

Marsha: Don't worry, dear, it will be over soon. We only recalculate our most efficient common stock portfolio once a quarter. Then you can go back to leveraged leases.

John: You trade, and I do all the worrying. Now there's a rumor that our leasing company is going to get a hostile takeover bid. I knew the debt ratio was too low, and you forgot to put on the poison pill. And now you've made a negative-NPV investment!

Marsha: What investment?

John: That wildcat oil well. Another well in that old Sourdough field. It's going to cost $5 million! Is there any oil down there?

Marsha: That Sourdough field has been good to us, John. Where do you think we got the capital for your yen trades? I bet we'll find oil. Our geologists say there's only a 30% chance of a dry hole.

John: Even if we hit oil, I bet we'll only get 150 barrels of crude oil per day.

Marsha: That's 150 barrels day in, day out. There are 365 days in a year, dear.

John and Marsha's teenage son Johnny bursts into the room.

Johnny: Hi, Dad! Hi, Mom! Guess what? I've made the junior varsity derivatives team! That means I can go on the field trip to the Chicago Board Options Exchange. (*Pauses.*) What's wrong?

John: Your mother has made another negative-NPV investment. A wildcat oil well, way up on the North Slope of Alaska.

Johnny: That's OK, Dad. Mom told me about it. I was going to do an NPV calculation yesterday, but I had to finish calculating the junk-bond default probabilities for my corporate finance homework. (*Grabs a financial calculator from his backpack.*) Let's see: 150 barrels a day times 365 days per year times $50 per barrel when delivered in Los Angeles . . . that's $2.7 million per year.

John: That's $2.7 million *next* year, assuming that we find any oil at all. The production will start declining by 5% every year. And we still have to pay $10 per barrel in pipeline and tanker charges to ship the oil from the North Slope to Los Angeles. We've got some serious operating leverage here.

Marsha: On the other hand, our energy consultants project increasing oil prices. If they increase with inflation, price per barrel should increase by roughly 2.5% per year. The wells ought to be able to keep pumping for at least 15 years.

Johnny: I'll calculate NPV after I finish with the default probabilities. The interest rate is 6%. Is it OK if I work with the beta of .8 and our usual figure of 7% for the market risk premium?

Marsha: I guess so, Johnny. But I am concerned about the fixed shipping costs.

John: (*Takes a deep breath and stands up.*) Anyway, how about a nice family dinner? I've reserved our usual table at the Four Seasons.

Everyone exits.

Announcer: Is the wildcat well really negative-NPV? Will John and Marsha have to fight a hostile takeover? Will Johnny's derivatives team use Black–Scholes or the binomial method? Find out in the next episode of The Jones Family, Incorporated.

You may not aspire to the Jones family's way of life, but you will learn about all their activities, from futures contracts to binomial option pricing, later in this book. Meanwhile, you may wish to replicate Johnny's NPV analysis.

QUESTIONS

1. Calculate the NPV of the wildcat oil well, taking account of the probability of a dry hole, the shipping costs, the decline in production, and the forecasted increase in oil prices. How long does production have to continue for the well to be a positive-NPV investment? Ignore taxes and other possible complications.

2. Now consider operating leverage. How should the shipping costs be valued, assuming that output is known and the costs are fixed? How would your answer change if the shipping costs were proportional to output? Assume that unexpected fluctuations in output are zero-beta and diversifiable. (*Hint:* The Jones's oil company has an excellent credit rating. Its long-term borrowing rate is only 7%.)

10

Project Analysis

▶ **Having read our** earlier chapters on capital budgeting, you may have concluded that the choice of which projects to accept or reject is a simple one. You just need to draw up a set of cash-flow forecasts, choose the right discount rate, and crank out net present value. But finding projects that create value for the shareholders can never be reduced to a mechanical exercise. We therefore devote this chapter to ways in which companies can stack the odds in their favor when making investment decisions.

Investment proposals may emerge from many different parts of the organization. So companies need procedures to ensure that every project is assessed consistently. Our first task in this chapter is to review how firms develop plans and budgets for capital investments, how they authorize specific projects, and how they check whether projects perform as promised.

When managers are presented with investment proposals, they do not accept the cash flow forecasts at face value. Instead, they try to understand what makes a project tick and what could go wrong with it. Remember Murphy's law, "if anything can go wrong, it will," and O'Reilly's corollary, "at the worst possible time."

Once you know what makes a project tick, you may be able to reconfigure it to improve its chance of success. And if you understand why the venture could fail, you can decide whether it is worth trying to rule out the possible causes of failure. Maybe further expenditure on market research would clear up those doubts about

acceptance by consumers, maybe another drill hole would give you a better idea of the size of the ore body, and maybe some further work on the test bed would confirm the durability of those welds.

If the project really has a negative NPV, the sooner you can identify it, the better. And even if you decide that it is worth going ahead without further analysis, you do not want to be caught by surprise if things go wrong later. You want to know the danger signals and the actions that you might take.

Our second task in this chapter is to show how managers use *sensitivity analysis, break-even analysis,* and *Monte Carlo simulation* to identify the crucial assumptions in investment proposals and to explore what can go wrong. There is no magic in these techniques, just computer-assisted common sense. You do not need a license to use them.

Discounted-cash-flow analysis commonly assumes that companies hold assets passively, and it ignores the opportunities to expand the project if it is successful or to bail out if it is not. However, wise managers recognize these opportunities when considering whether to invest. They look for ways to capitalize on success and to reduce the costs of failure, and they are prepared to pay up for projects that give them this flexibility. Opportunities to modify projects as the future unfolds are known as *real options*. In the final section of the chapter we describe several important real options, and we show how to use *decision trees* to set out the possible future choices.

● ● ● ● ●

10-1   The Capital Investment Process

Senior management needs some forewarning of future investment outlays. So for most large firms, the investment process starts with the preparation of an annual **capital budget,** which is a list of investment projects planned for the coming year.

Most firms let project proposals bubble up from plants for review by divisional management and then from divisions for review by senior management and their planning staff. Of course middle managers cannot identify all worthwhile projects. For example, the managers of plants A and B cannot be expected to see the potential economies of closing their plants and consolidating production at a new plant C. Divisional managers would propose plant C. But the managers of divisions 1 and 2 may not be eager to give up their own computers to a corporation-wide information system. That proposal would come from senior management, for example, the company's chief information officer.

Inconsistent assumptions often creep into expenditure plans. For example, suppose the manager of your furniture division is bullish on housing starts, but the manager of your appliance division is bearish. The furniture division may push for a major investment in new facilities, while the appliance division may propose a plan for retrenchment. It would be better if both managers could agree on a common estimate of housing starts and base their investment proposals on it. That is why many firms begin the capital budgeting process by establishing consensus forecasts of economic indicators, such as inflation and growth in national income, as well as forecasts of particular items that are important to the firm's business, such as housing starts or the prices of raw materials. These forecasts are then used as the basis for the capital budget.

Preparation of the capital budget is not a rigid, bureaucratic exercise. There is plenty of give-and-take and back-and-forth. Divisional managers negotiate with plant managers and fine-tune the division's list of projects. The final capital budget must also reflect the corporation's strategic planning. Strategic planning takes a top-down view of the company. It attempts to identify businesses where the company has a competitive advantage. It also attempts to identify businesses that should be sold or allowed to run down.

A firm's capital investment choices should reflect both bottom-up and top-down views of the business—capital budgeting and strategic planning, respectively. Plant and division managers, who do most of the work in bottom-up capital budgeting, may not see the forest for the trees. Strategic planners may have a mistaken view of the forest because they do not look at the trees one by one.

Project Authorizations—and the Problem of Biased Forecasts

Once the capital budget has been approved by top management and the board of directors, it is the official plan for the ensuing year. However, it is not the final sign-off for specific projects. Most companies require **appropriation requests** for each proposal. These requests include detailed forecasts, discounted-cash-flow analyses, and back-up information.

Many investment projects carry a high price tag; they also determine the shape of the firm's business 10 or 20 years in the future. Hence final approval of appropriation requests tends to be reserved for top management. Companies set ceilings on the size of projects that divisional managers can authorize. Often these ceilings are surprisingly low. For example, a large company, investing $400 million per year, might require top management to approve all projects over $500,000.

This centralized decision making brings its problems: Senior management can't process detailed information about hundreds of projects and must rely on forecasts put together by project sponsors. A smart manager quickly learns to worry whether these forecasts are realistic.

Even when the forecasts are not consciously inflated, errors creep in. For example, most people tend to be overconfident when they forecast. Events they think are almost certain to occur may actually happen only 80% of the time, and events they believe are impossible may happen 20% of the time. Therefore project risks are understated. Anyone who is keen to get a project accepted is also likely to look on the bright side when forecasting the project's cash flows. Such overoptimism seems to be a common feature in financial forecasts. Overoptimism afflicts governments too, probably more than private businesses. How often have you heard of a new dam, highway, or military aircraft that actually cost *less* than was originally forecasted?

You can expect plant or divisional managers to look on the bright side when putting forward investment proposals. That is not altogether bad. Psychologists stress that optimism and confidence are likely to increase effort, commitment, and persistence. The problem is that hundreds of appropriation requests may reach senior management each year, all essentially sales documents presented by united fronts and designed to persuade. Alternative schemes have been filtered out at earlier stages.

It is probably impossible to eliminate bias completely, but senior managers should take care not to encourage it. For example, if managers believe that success depends on having the largest division rather than the most profitable one, they will propose large expansion projects that they do not truly believe have positive NPVs. Or if new plant managers are pushed to generate increased earnings right away, they will be tempted to propose quick-payback projects even when NPV is sacrificed.

Sometimes senior managers try to offset bias by increasing the hurdle rate for capital expenditure. Suppose the true cost of capital is 10%, but the CFO is frustrated by the large fraction of projects that don't earn 10%. She therefore directs project sponsors to use a 15% discount rate. In other words, she adds a 5% fudge factor in an attempt to offset forecast bias. But it doesn't work; it *never* works. Brealey, Myers, and Allen's Second Law[1] explains why. The law states: *The proportion of proposed projects having positive NPVs at the corporate hurdle rate is independent of the hurdle rate.*

The law is not a facetious conjecture. It was tested in a large oil company where staff kept careful statistics on capital investment projects. About 85% of projects had positive NPVs. (The remaining 15% were proposed for other reasons, for example, to meet environmental standards.) One year, after several quarters of disappointing earnings, top management decided that more financial discipline was called for and increased the corporate hurdle rate by several percentage points. But in the following year the fraction of projects with positive NPVs stayed rock-steady at 85%.

If you're worried about bias in forecasted cash flows, the only remedy is careful analysis of the forecasts. *Do not add fudge factors to the cost of capital.*[2]

Postaudits

Most firms keep a check on the progress of large projects by conducting **postaudits** shortly after the projects have begun to operate. Postaudits identify problems that need fixing, check the accuracy of forecasts, and suggest questions that should have been asked before the project was undertaken. Postaudits pay off mainly by helping managers to do a better job when it comes to the next round of investments. After a postaudit the controller may say, "We should have anticipated the extra training required for production workers." When the next proposal arrives, training will get the attention it deserves.

---

[1] There is no First Law. We think "Second Law" sounds better. There is a Third Law, but that is for another chapter.

[2] Adding a fudge factor to the cost of capital also favors quick-payback projects and penalizes longer-lived projects, which tend to have lower rates of return but higher NPVs. Adding a 5% fudge factor to the discount rate is roughly equivalent to reducing the forecast and present value of the first year's cash flow by 5%. The impact on the present value of a cash flow 10 years in the future is much greater, because the fudge factor is compounded in the discount rate. The fudge factor is not too much of a burden for a 2- or 3-year project, but an enormous burden for a 10- or 20-year project.

Postaudits may not be able to measure all of a project's costs and benefits. It may be impossible to split the project away from the rest of the business. Suppose that you have just taken over a trucking firm that operates a delivery service for local stores. You decide to improve service by installing custom software to keep track of packages and to schedule trucks. You also construct a dispatching center and buy five new diesel trucks. A year later you try a postaudit of the investment in software. You verify that it is working properly and check actual costs of purchase, installation, and operation against projections. But how do you identify the incremental cash inflows? No one has kept records of the extra diesel fuel that *would have been* used or the extra shipments that *would have been* lost absent the software. You may be able to verify that service is better, but how much of the improvement comes from the new trucks, how much from the dispatching center, and how much from the software? The only meaningful measures of success are for the delivery business as a whole.

10-2 Sensitivity Analysis

Uncertainty means that more things can happen than will happen. Whenever you are confronted with a cash-flow forecast, you should try to discover what else can happen.

Put yourself in the well-heeled shoes of the treasurer of the Otobai Company in Osaka, Japan. You are considering the introduction of an electrically powered motor scooter for city use. Your staff members have prepared the cash-flow forecasts shown in Table 10.1. Since NPV is positive at the 10% opportunity cost of capital, it appears to be worth going ahead.

$$\text{NPV} = -15 + \sum_{t=1}^{10} \frac{3}{(1.10)^t} = +\text{¥}3.43 \text{ billion}$$

Before you decide, you want to delve into these forecasts and identify the key variables that determine whether the project succeeds or fails. It turns out that the marketing department has estimated revenue as follows:

$$\text{Unit sales} = \text{new product's share of market} \times \text{size of scooter market}$$
$$= .1 \times 1 \text{ million} = 100,000 \text{ scooters}$$
$$\text{Revenue} = \text{unit sales} \times \text{price per unit}$$
$$= 100,000 \times 375,000 = \text{¥}37.5 \text{ billion}$$

The production department has estimated variable costs per unit as ¥300,000. Since projected volume is 100,000 scooters per year, total variable cost is ¥30 billion. Fixed costs are ¥3 billion per year. The initial investment can be depreciated on a straight-line basis over the 10-year period, and profits are taxed at a rate of 50%.

	Year 0	Years 1–10
1 Investment	15	
2 Revenue		37.5
3 Variable cost		30
4 Fixed cost		3
5 Depreciation		1.5
6 Pretax profit		3
7 Tax		1.5
8 Net profit		1.5
Operating cash flow		3
Net cash flow	−15	3

▶ **TABLE 10.1** Preliminary cash-flow forecasts for Otobai's electric scooter project (figures in ¥ billions).

Assumptions:
1. Investment is depreciated over 10 years straight-line.
2. Income is taxed at a rate of 50%.

"Live" Excel versions of Tables 10.1 to 10.5 are available on the book's Web site, **www.mhhe.com/bma**.

eXcel

Visit us at
www.mhhe.com/bma

These seem to be the important things you need to know, but look out for unidentified variables. Perhaps there are patent problems, or perhaps you will need to invest in service stations that will recharge the scooter batteries. The greatest dangers often lie in these *unknown* unknowns, or "unk-unks," as scientists call them.

Having found no unk-unks (no doubt you will find them later), you conduct a **sensitivity analysis** with respect to market size, market share, and so on. To do this, the marketing and production staffs are asked to give optimistic and pessimistic estimates for the underlying variables. These are set out in the left-hand columns of Table 10.2. The right-hand side shows what happens to the project's net present value if the variables are set *one at a time* to their optimistic and pessimistic values. Your project appears to be by no means a sure thing. The most dangerous variables are market share and unit variable cost. If market share is only .04 (and all other variables are as expected), then the project has an NPV of −¥10.4 billion. If unit variable cost is ¥360,000 (and all other variables are as expected), then the project has an NPV of −¥15 billion.

Value of Information

Now you can check whether you could resolve some of the uncertainty *before* your company parts with the ¥15 billion investment. Suppose that the pessimistic value for unit variable cost partly reflects the production department's worry that a particular machine will not work as designed and that the operation will have to be performed by other methods at an extra cost of ¥20,000 per unit. The chance that this will occur is only 1 in 10. But, if it does occur, the extra ¥20,000 unit cost will reduce after-tax cash flow by

$$\text{Unit sales} \times \text{additional unit cost} \times (1 - \text{tax rate})$$
$$= 100,000 \times 20,000 \times .50 = \text{¥1 billion}$$

It would reduce the NPV of your project by

$$\sum_{t=1}^{10} \frac{1}{(1.10)^t} = \text{¥6.14 billion,}$$

putting the NPV of the scooter project underwater at +3.43 − 6.14 = −¥2.71 billion. It is possible that a relatively small change in the scooter's design would remove the need for the new machine. Or perhaps a ¥10 million pretest of the machine will reveal whether it will work and allow you to clear up the problem. It clearly pays to invest ¥10 million to avoid a 10% probability of a ¥6.14 billion fall in NPV. You are ahead by −10 + .10 × 6,140 = +¥604 million.

On the other hand, the value of additional information about market size is small. Because the project is acceptable even under pessimistic assumptions about market size, you are unlikely to be in trouble if you have misestimated that variable.

Variable	Range			NPV, ¥ billions		
	Pessimistic	Expected	Optimistic	Pessimistic	Expected	Optimistic
Market size, million	0.9	1	1.1	1.1	3.4	5.7
Market share	0.04	0.10	0.16	−10.4	3.4	17.3
Unit price, yen	350,000	375,000	380,000	−4.2	3.4	5.0
Unit variable cost, yen	360,000	300,000	275,000	−15.0	3.4	11.1
Fixed cost, ¥ billions	4	3	2	0.4	3.4	6.5

▶ **TABLE 10.2**   To undertake a sensitivity analysis of the electric scooter project, we set each variable in turn at its most pessimistic or optimistic value and recalculate the NPV of the project.

Visit us at
www.mhhe.com/bma.

Limits to Sensitivity Analysis

Sensitivity analysis boils down to expressing cash flows in terms of key project variables and then calculating the consequences of misestimating the variables. It forces the manager to identify the underlying variables, indicates where additional information would be most useful, and helps to expose inappropriate forecasts.

One drawback to sensitivity analysis is that it always gives somewhat ambiguous results. For example, what exactly does *optimistic* or *pessimistic* mean? The marketing department may be interpreting the terms in a different way from the production department. Ten years from now, after hundreds of projects, hindsight may show that the marketing department's pessimistic limit was exceeded twice as often as the production department's; but what you may discover 10 years hence is no help now. Of course, you could specify that, when you use the terms "pessimistic" and "optimistic," you mean that there is only a 10% chance that the actual value will prove to be worse than the pessimistic figure or better than the optimistic one. However, it is far from easy to extract a forecaster's notion of the true probabilities of possible outcomes.[3]

Another problem with sensitivity analysis is that the underlying variables are likely to be interrelated. What sense does it make to look at the effect in isolation of an increase in market size? If market size exceeds expectations, it is likely that demand will be stronger than you anticipated and unit prices will be higher. And why look in isolation at the effect of an increase in price? If inflation pushes prices to the upper end of your range, it is quite probable that costs will also be inflated.

Sometimes the analyst can get around these problems by defining underlying variables so that they are roughly independent. But you cannot push *one-at-a-time* sensitivity analysis too far. It is impossible to obtain expected, optimistic, and pessimistic values for total *project* cash flows from the information in Table 10.2.

Scenario Analysis

If the variables are interrelated, it may help to consider some alternative plausible scenarios. For example, perhaps the company economist is worried about the possibility of another sharp rise in world oil prices. The direct effect of this would be to encourage the use of electrically powered transportation. The popularity of compact cars after the oil price increases in 2007 leads you to estimate that an immediate 20% rise in the price of oil would enable you to capture an extra 3% of the scooter market. On the other hand, the economist also believes that higher oil prices would prompt a world recession and at the same time stimulate inflation. In that case, market size might be in the region of .8 million scooters and both prices and cost might be 15% higher than your initial estimates. Table 10.3 shows that this scenario of higher oil prices and recession would on balance help your new venture. Its NPV would increase to ¥6.4 billion.

Managers often find **scenario analysis** helpful. It allows them to look at different but *consistent* combinations of variables. Forecasters generally prefer to give an estimate of revenues or costs under a particular scenario than to give some absolute optimistic or pessimistic value.

Break-Even Analysis

When we undertake a sensitivity analysis of a project or when we look at alternative scenarios, we are asking how serious it would be if sales or costs turned out to be worse than we forecasted. Managers sometimes prefer to rephrase this question and ask how bad sales

---

[3] If you doubt this, try some simple experiments. Ask the person who repairs your dishwasher to state a numerical probability that it will work for at least one more year. Or construct your own subjective probability distribution of the number of telephone calls you will receive next week. That ought to be easy. Try it.

can get before the project begins to lose money. This exercise is known as **break-even analysis.**

In the left-hand portion of Table 10.4 we set out the revenues and costs of the electric scooter project under different assumptions about annual sales.[4] In the right-hand portion of the table we discount these revenues and costs to give the *present value* of the inflows and the *present value* of the outflows. Net present value is of course the difference between these numbers.

You can see that NPV is strongly negative if the company does not produce a single scooter. It is just positive if (as expected) the company sells 100,000 scooters and is strongly positive if it sells 200,000. Clearly the *zero*-NPV point occurs at a little under 100,000 scooters.

	Cash Flows, Years 1–10, ¥ billions		
	Base Case	High Oil Prices and Recession Case	
1 Revenue	37.5	44.9	
2 Variable cost	30	35.9	
3 Fixed cost	3	3.5	
4 Depreciation	1.5	1.5	
5 Pretax profit	3	4.0	
6 Tax	1.5	2.0	
7 Net profit	1.5	2.0	
8 Net cash flow	3	3.5	
PV of cash flows	18.4	21.4	
NPV	3.4	6.4	
	Assumptions		
	Base Case	High Oil Prices and Recession Case	
Market size, million	1	0.8	
Market share	0.10	0.13	
Unit price, yen	375,000	431,300	
Unit variable cost, yen	300,000	345,000	
Fixed cost, ¥ billions	3	3.5	

▶ **TABLE 10.3**   How the NPV of the electric scooter project would be affected by higher oil prices and a world recession.

Visit us at
www.mhhe.com/bma.

Inflows			Outflows					
		Year 0	Years 1–10					
Unit Sales, Thousands	Revenues, Years 1–10	Investment	Variable Costs	Fixed Costs	Taxes	PV Inflows	PV Outflows	NPV
0	0	15	0	3	−2.25	0	19.6	−19.6
100	37.5	15	30	3	1.5	230.4	227.0	3.4
200	75.0	15	60	3	5.25	460.8	434.4	26.5

▶ **TABLE 10.4**   NPV of electric scooter project under different assumptions about unit sales (figures in ¥ billions except as noted).

Visit us at
www.mhhe.com/bma.

---

[4] Notice that if the project makes a loss, this loss can be used to reduce the tax bill on the rest of the company's business. In this case the project produces a tax saving—the tax outflow is negative.

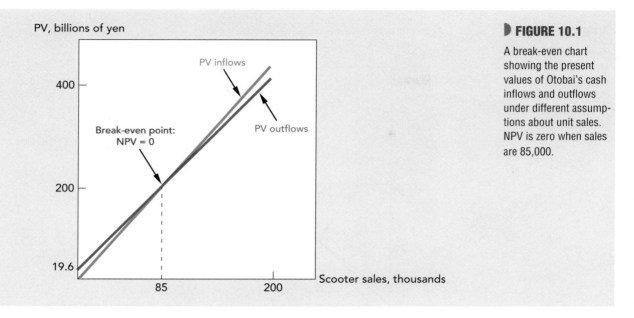

▶ **FIGURE 10.1**

A break-even chart showing the present values of Otobai's cash inflows and outflows under different assumptions about unit sales. NPV is zero when sales are 85,000.

Unit Sales, Thousands	Revenues Years 1–10	Variable Costs	Fixed Costs	Depreciation	Taxes	Total Costs	Profit after Tax
0	0	0	3	1.5	−2.25	2.25	−2.25
100	37.5	30	3	1.5	1.5	36.0	1.5
200	75.0	60	3	1.5	5.25	69.75	5.25

▶ **TABLE 10.5** The electric scooter project's accounting profit under different assumptions about unit sales (figures in ¥ billions except as noted).

In Figure 10.1 we have plotted the present value of the inflows and outflows under different assumptions about annual sales. The two lines cross when sales are 85,000 scooters. This is the point at which the project has zero NPV. As long as sales are greater than 85,000, the project has a positive NPV.[5]

Managers frequently calculate break-even points in terms of accounting profits rather than present values. Table 10.5 shows Otobai's after-tax profits at three levels of scooter sales. Figure 10.2 once again plots revenues and costs against sales. But the story this time is different. Figure 10.2, which is based on accounting profits, suggests a breakeven of 60,000 scooters. Figure 10.1, which is based on present values, shows a breakeven at 85,000 scooters. Why the difference?

When we work in terms of accounting profit, we deduct depreciation of ¥1.5 billion each year to cover the cost of the initial investment. If Otobai sells 60,000 scooters a year, revenues will be sufficient both to pay operating costs and to recover the initial

---

[5] We could also calculate break-even sales by plotting equivalent annual costs and revenues. Of course, the break-even point would be identical at 85,000 scooters.

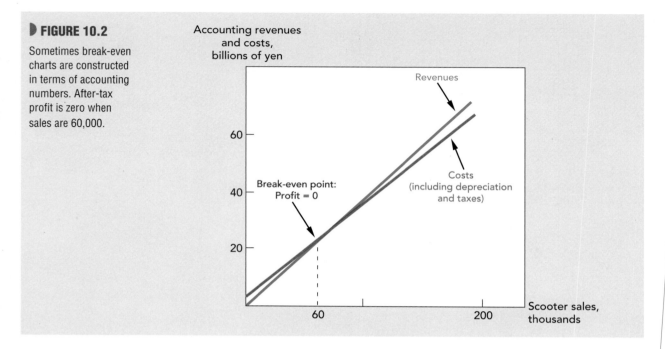

FIGURE 10.2

Sometimes break-even charts are constructed in terms of accounting numbers. After-tax profit is zero when sales are 60,000.

outlay of ¥15 billion. But they will *not* be sufficient to repay the *opportunity cost of capital* on that ¥15 billion. A project that breaks even in accounting terms will surely have a negative NPV.

Operating Leverage and the Break-Even Point

A project's break-even point depends on the extent to which its costs vary with the level of sales. Suppose that electric scooters fall out of favor. The bad news is that Otobai's sales revenue is less than you'd hoped, but you have the consolation that the variable costs also decline. On the other hand, even if Otobai is unable to sell a single scooter, it must make the up-front investment of ¥15 billion and pay the fixed costs of ¥3 billion a year.

Suppose that Otobai's *entire* costs were fixed at ¥33 billion. Then it would need only a 3% shortfall in revenues (from ¥37.5 billion to ¥36.4 billion) to turn the project into a negative-NPV investment. Thus, when costs are largely fixed, a shortfall in sales has a greater impact on profitability and the break-even point is higher. Of course, a high propor-tion of fixed costs is not all bad. The firm whose costs are fixed fares poorly when demand is low, but makes a killing during a boom.

A business with high fixed costs is said to have high **operating leverage.** Operating lever-age is usually defined in terms of accounting profits rather than cash flows[6] and is measured by the percentage change in profits for each 1% change in sales. Thus **degree of operating leverage (DOL)** is

$$DOL = \frac{\text{percentage change in profits}}{\text{percentage change in sales}}$$

---

[6] In Chapter 9 we developed a measure of operating leverage that was expressed in terms of cash flows and their present values. We used this measure to show how beta depends on operating leverage.

Industries with High Operating Leverage		Industries with Low Operating Leverage	
Industry	**DOL**	**Industry**	**DOL**
Steel	2.20	Electric utilities	.56
Railroads	1.99	Food	.79
Autos	1.57	Clothing	.88

▶ **TABLE 10.6**   Estimated degree of operating leverage (DOL) for large U.S. companies by industry.

Note: DOL is estimated as the median ratio of the change in profits to the change in sales for firms in Standard & Poor's index, 1998–2008.

The following simple formula[7] shows how DOL is related to the business's fixed costs (including depreciation) as a proportion of pretax profits:

$$DOL = 1 + \frac{\text{fixed costs}}{\text{profits}}$$

In the case of Otobai's scooter project

$$DOL = 1 + \frac{(3 + 1.5)}{3} = 2.5$$

A 1% shortfall in the scooter project's revenues would result in a 2.5% shortfall in profits.

Look now at Table 10.6, which shows how much the profits of some large U.S. companies have typically changed as a proportion of the change in sales. For example, notice that each 1% drop in sales has reduced steel company profits by 2.20%. This suggests that steel companies have an estimated operating leverage of 2.20. You would expect steel stocks therefore to have correspondingly high betas and this is indeed the case.

10-3 Monte Carlo Simulation

Sensitivity analysis allows you to consider the effect of changing one variable at a time. By looking at the project under alternative scenarios, you can consider the effect of a *limited number* of plausible combinations of variables. **Monte Carlo simulation** is a tool for considering *all* possible combinations. It therefore enables you to inspect the entire distribution of project outcomes.

Imagine that you are a gambler at Monte Carlo. You know nothing about the laws of probability (few casual gamblers do), but a friend has suggested to you a complicated strategy for playing roulette. Your friend has not actually tested the strategy but is confident that it will *on the average* give you a 2½% return for every 50 spins of the wheel. Your friend's optimistic estimate for any series of 50 spins is a profit of 55%; your friend's pessimistic estimate is a loss of 50%. How can you find out whether these really are the odds? An easy but possibly expensive way is to start playing and record the outcome at the end of

---

[7] This formula for DOL can be derived as follows. If sales increase by 1%, then variable costs will also increase by 1%, and profits will increase by .01 × (sales − variable costs) = .01 × (pretax profits + fixed costs). Now recall the definition of DOL:

$$DOL = \frac{\text{percentage change in profits}}{\text{percentage change in sales}} = \frac{(\text{change in profits})/(\text{level of profits})}{.01}$$

$$= 100 \times \frac{\text{change in profits}}{\text{level of profits}} = 100 \times \frac{.01 \times (\text{profits} + \text{fixed costs})}{\text{level of profits}}$$

$$= 1 + \frac{\text{fixed costs}}{\text{profits}}$$

each series of 50 spins. After, say, 100 series of 50 spins each, plot a frequency distribution of the outcomes and calculate the average and upper and lower limits. If things look good, you can then get down to some serious gambling.

An alternative is to tell a computer to simulate the roulette wheel and the strategy. In other words, you could instruct the computer to draw numbers out of its hat to determine the outcome of each spin of the wheel and then to calculate how much you would make or lose from the particular gambling strategy.

That would be an example of Monte Carlo simulation. In capital budgeting we replace the gambling strategy with a model of the project, and the roulette wheel with a model of the world in which the project operates. Let us see how this might work with our project for an electrically powered scooter.

Simulating the Electric Scooter Project

Step 1: Modeling the Project   The first step in any simulation is to give the computer a precise model of the project. For example, the sensitivity analysis of the scooter project was based on the following implicit model of cash flow:

$$\text{Cash flow} = (\text{revenues} - \text{costs} - \text{depreciation}) \times (1 - \text{tax rate}) + \text{depreciation}$$
$$\text{Revenues} = \text{market size} \times \text{market share} \times \text{unit price}$$
$$\text{Costs} = (\text{market size} \times \text{market share} \times \text{variable unit cost}) + \text{fixed cost}$$

This model of the project was all that you needed for the simpleminded sensitivity analysis that we described above. But if you wish to simulate the whole project, you need to think about how the variables are interrelated.

For example, consider the first variable—market size. The marketing department has estimated a market size of 1 million scooters in the first year of the project's life, but of course you do not know how things will work out. Actual market size will exceed or fall short of expectations by the amount of the department's forecast error:

$$\text{Market size, year 1} = \text{expected market size, year 1} \times (1 + \text{forecast error, year 1})$$

You *expect* the forecast error to be zero, but it could turn out to be positive or negative. Suppose, for example, that the actual market size turns out to be 1.1 million. That means a forecast error of 10%, or +.1:

$$\text{Market size, year 1} = 1 \times (1 + .1) = 1.1 \text{ million}$$

You can write the market size in the second year in exactly the same way:

$$\text{Market size, year 2} = \text{expected market size, year 2} \times (1 + \text{forecast error, year 2})$$

But at this point you must consider how the expected market size in year 2 is affected by what happens in year 1. If scooter sales are below expectations in year 1, it is likely that they will continue to be below in subsequent years. Suppose that a shortfall in sales in year 1 would lead you to revise down your forecast of sales in year 2 by a like amount. Then

$$\text{Expected market size, year 2} = \text{actual market size, year 1}$$

Now you can rewrite the market size in year 2 in terms of the actual market size in the previous year plus a forecast error:

$$\text{Market size, year 2} = \text{market size, year 1} \times (1 + \text{forecast error, year 2})$$

In the same way you can describe the expected market size in year 3 in terms of market size in year 2 and so on.

This set of equations illustrates how you can describe interdependence between different *periods*. But you also need to allow for interdependence between different *variables*. For example, the price of electrically powered scooters is likely to increase with market size. Suppose that this is the only uncertainty and that a 10% addition to market size would lead you to predict a 3% increase in price. Then you could model the first year's price as follows:

Price, year 1 = expected price, year 1 × (1 + .3 × error in market size forecast, year 1)

Then, if variations in market size exert a permanent effect on price, you can define the second year's price as

Price, year 2 = expected price, year 2 × (1 + .3 × error in market size forecast, year 2)
= actual price, year 1 × (1 + .3 × error in market size forecast, year 2)

Notice how we have linked each period's selling price to the *actual* selling prices (including forecast error) in all previous periods. We used the same type of linkage for market size. These linkages mean that forecast errors accumulate; they do not cancel out over time. Thus, uncertainty *increases* with time: The farther out you look into the future, the more the actual price or market size may depart from your original forecast.

The complete model of your project would include a set of equations for each of the variables: market size, price, market share, unit variable cost, and fixed cost. Even if you allowed for only a few interdependencies between variables and across time, the result would be quite a complex list of equations.[8] Perhaps that is not a bad thing if it forces you to understand what the project is all about. Model building is like spinach: You may not like the taste, but it is good for you.

Step 2: Specifying Probabilities   Remember the procedure for simulating the gambling strategy? The first step was to specify the strategy, the second was to specify the numbers on the roulette wheel, and the third was to tell the computer to select these numbers at random and calculate the results of the strategy:

The steps are just the same for your scooter project:

Think about how you might go about specifying your possible errors in forecasting market size. You *expect* market size to be 1 million scooters. You obviously don't think that you are underestimating or overestimating, so the expected forecast error is zero. On the other hand, the marketing department has given you a range of possible estimates. Market size could be as low as .85 million scooters or as high as 1.15 million scooters. Thus the forecast error has an expected value of 0 and a range of plus or minus 15%. If the marketing

---

[8] Specifying the interdependencies is the hardest and most important part of a simulation. If all components of project cash flows were unrelated, simulation would rarely be necessary.

department has in fact given you the lowest and highest possible outcomes, actual market size should fall somewhere within this range with near certainty.[9]

That takes care of market size; now you need to draw up similar estimates of the possible forecast errors for each of the other variables that are in your model.

Step 3: Simulate the Cash Flows   The computer now *samples* from the distribution of the forecast errors, calculates the resulting cash flows for each period, and records them. After many iterations you begin to get accurate estimates of the probability distributions of the project cash flows—accurate, that is, only to the extent that your model and the probability distributions of the forecast errors are accurate. Remember the GIGO principle: "Garbage in, garbage out."

Figure 10.3 shows part of the output from an actual simulation of the electric scooter project.[10] Note the positive skewness of the outcomes—very large outcomes are more likely than very small ones. This is common when forecast errors accumulate over time. Because of the skewness the average cash flow is somewhat higher than the most likely outcome; in other words, a bit to the right of the peak of the distribution.[11]

▶ FIGURE 10.3

Simulation of cash flows for year 10 of the electric scooter project.

---

[9] Suppose "near certainty" means "99% of the time." If forecast errors are normally distributed, this degree of certainty requires a range of plus or minus three standard deviations.

Other distributions could, of course, be used. For example, the marketing department may view any market size between .85 and 1.15 million scooters as *equally likely*. In that case the simulation would require a uniform (rectangular) distribution of forecast errors.

[10] These are actual outputs from Crystal Ball™ software. The simulation assumed annual forecast errors were normally distributed and ran through 10,000 trials. We thank Christopher Howe for running the simulation. An Excel program to simulate the Otobai project was kindly provided by Marek Jochec and is available on the Web site, **www.mhhe.com/bma**.

[11] When you are working with cash-flow forecasts, bear in mind the distinction between the expected value and the most likely (or modal) value. Present values are based on *expected* cash flows—that is, the probability-weighted average of the possible future cash flows. If the distribution of possible outcomes is skewed to the right as in Figure 10.3, the expected cash flow will be greater than the most likely cash flow.

Step 4: Calculate Present Value   The distributions of project cash flows should allow you to calculate the expected cash flows more accurately. In the final step you need to discount these expected cash flows to find present value.

Simulation, though complicated, has the obvious merit of compelling the forecaster to face up to uncertainty and to interdependencies. Once you have set up your simulation model, it is a simple matter to analyze the principal sources of uncertainty in the cash flows and to see how much you could reduce this uncertainty by improving the forecasts of sales or costs. You may also be able to explore the effect of possible modifications to the project.

Simulation may sound like a panacea for the world's ills, but, as usual, you pay for what you get. Sometimes you pay for more than you get. It is not just a matter of the time spent in building the model. It is extremely difficult to estimate interrelationships between variables and the underlying probability distributions, even when you are trying to be honest. But in capital budgeting, forecasters are seldom completely impartial and the probability distributions on which simulations are based can be highly biased.

In practice, a simulation that attempts to be realistic will also be complex. Therefore the decision maker may delegate the task of constructing the model to management scientists or consultants. The danger here is that, even if the builders understand their creation, the decision maker cannot and therefore does not rely on it. This is a common but ironic experience.

10-4   Real Options and Decision Trees

When you use discounted cash flow (DCF) to value a project, you implicitly assume that the firm will hold the assets passively. But managers are not paid to be dummies. After they have invested in a new project, they do not simply sit back and watch the future unfold. If things go well, the project may be expanded; if they go badly, the project may be cut back or abandoned altogether. Projects that can be modified in these ways are more valuable than those that do not provide such flexibility. The more uncertain the outlook, the more valuable this flexibility becomes.

That sounds obvious, but notice that sensitivity analysis and Monte Carlo simulation do not recognize the opportunity to modify projects.[12] For example, think back to the Otobai electric scooter project. In real life, if things go wrong with the project, Otobai would abandon to cut its losses. If so, the worst outcomes would not be as devastating as our sensitivity analysis and simulation suggested.

Options to modify projects are known as **real options.** Managers may not always use the term "real option" to describe these opportunities; for example, they may refer to "intangible advantages" of easy-to-modify projects. But when they review major investment proposals, these option intangibles are often the key to their decisions.

The Option to Expand

Long-haul airfreight businesses such as FedEx need to move a massive amount of goods each day. Therefore, when Airbus announced delays to its A380 superjumbo freighter, FedEx turned to Boeing and ordered 15 of its 777 freighters to be delivered between 2009 and 2011. If business continues to expand, FedEx will need more aircraft. But rather than placing additional firm orders, the company secured a place in Boeing's production line by acquiring *options* to buy a further 15 aircraft at a predetermined price. These options did not commit FedEx to expand but gave it the flexibility to do so.

---

[12] Some simulation models *do* recognize the possibility of changing policy. For example, when a pharmaceutical company uses simulation to analyze its R&D decisions, it allows for the possibility that the company can abandon the development at each phase.

Figure 10.4 displays FedEx's expansion option as a simple **decision tree.** You can think of it as a game between FedEx and fate. Each square represents an action or decision by the company. Each circle represents an outcome revealed by fate. In this case there is only one outcome—when fate reveals the airfreight demand and FedEx's capacity needs. FedEx then decides whether to exercise its options and buy additional 777s. Here the future decision is easy: Buy the airplanes only if demand is high and the company can operate them profitably. If demand is low, FedEx walks away and leaves Boeing with the problem of finding another customer for the planes that were reserved for FedEx.

You can probably think of many other investments that take on added value because of the further options they provide. For example,

- When launching a new product, companies often start with a pilot program to iron out possible design problems and to test the market. The company can evaluate the pilot project and then decide whether to expand to full-scale production.
- When designing a factory, it can make sense to provide extra land or floor space to reduce the future cost of a second production line.
- When building a four-lane highway, it may pay to build six-lane bridges so that the road can be converted later to six lanes if traffic volumes turn out to be higher than expected.
- When building production platforms for offshore oil and gas fields, companies usually allow ample vacant deck space. The vacant space costs more up front but reduces the cost of installing extra equipment later. For example, vacant deck space could provide an option to install water-flooding equipment if oil or gas prices turn out high enough to justify this investment.

Expansion options do not show up on accounting balance sheets, but managers and investors are well aware of their importance. For example, in Chapter 4 we showed how the present value of growth opportunities (PVGO) contributes to the value of a company's common stock. PVGO equals the forecasted total NPV of future investments. But it is better to think of PVGO as the value of the firm's *options* to invest and expand. The firm is not obliged to grow. It can invest more if the number of positive-NPV projects turns out high or slow down if that number turns out low. The flexibility to adapt investment to future opportunities is one of the factors that makes PVGO so valuable.

The Option to Abandon

If the option to expand has value, what about the decision to bail out? Projects do not just go on until assets expire of old age. The decision to terminate a project is usually taken by

▶ FIGURE 10.4

FedEx's expansion option expressed as a simple decision tree.

management, not by nature. Once the project is no longer profitable, the company will cut its losses and exercise its option to abandon the project.

Some assets are easier to bail out of than others. Tangible assets are usually easier to sell than intangible ones. It helps to have active secondhand markets, which really exist only for standardized items. Real estate, airplanes, trucks, and certain machine tools are likely to be relatively easy to sell. On the other hand, the knowledge accumulated by a software company's research and development program is a specialized intangible asset and probably would not have significant abandonment value. (Some assets, such as old mattresses, even have *negative* abandonment value; you have to pay to get rid of them. It is costly to decommission nuclear power plants or to reclaim land that has been strip-mined.)

EXAMPLE 10.1 ● Bailing Out of the Outboard-Engine Project

Managers should recognize the option to abandon when they make the initial investment in a new project or venture. For example, suppose you must choose between two technologies for production of a Wankel-engine outboard motor.

1. Technology A uses computer-controlled machinery custom-designed to produce the complex shapes required for Wankel engines in high volumes and at low cost. But if the Wankel outboard does not sell, this equipment will be worthless.

2. Technology B uses standard machine tools. Labor costs are much higher, but the machinery can be sold for $17 million if demand turns out to be low.

Just for simplicity, assume that the initial capital outlays are the same for both technologies. If demand in the first year is buoyant, technology A will provide a payoff of $24 million. If demand is sluggish, the payoff from A is $16 million. Think of these payoffs as the project's cash flow in the first year of production plus the value in year 1 of all future cash flows. The corresponding payoffs to technology B are $22.5 million and $15 million:

Payoffs from Producing Outboard ($ millions)		
	Technology A	**Technology B**
Buoyant demand	$24.0	$22.5
Sluggish demand	16.0	15.0*

* Composed of a cash flow of $1.5 million and a PV in year 1 of 13.5 million.

Technology A looks better in a DCF analysis of the new product because it was designed to have the lowest possible cost at the planned production volume. Yet you can sense the advantage of the flexibility provided by technology B if you are unsure whether the new outboard will sink or swim in the marketplace. If you adopt technology B and the outboard is not a success, you are better off collecting the first year's cash flow of $1.5 million and then selling the plant and equipment for $17 million.

● ● ● ● ●

Figure 10.5 summarizes Example 10.1 as a decision tree. The abandonment option occurs at the right-hand boxes for technology B. The decisions are obvious: Continue if demand is buoyant, abandon otherwise. Thus the payoffs to technology B are

Buoyant demand →   continue production   →   payoff of $22.5 million

Sluggish demand → exercise option to sell assets → payoff of 1.5 + 17 = $18.5 million

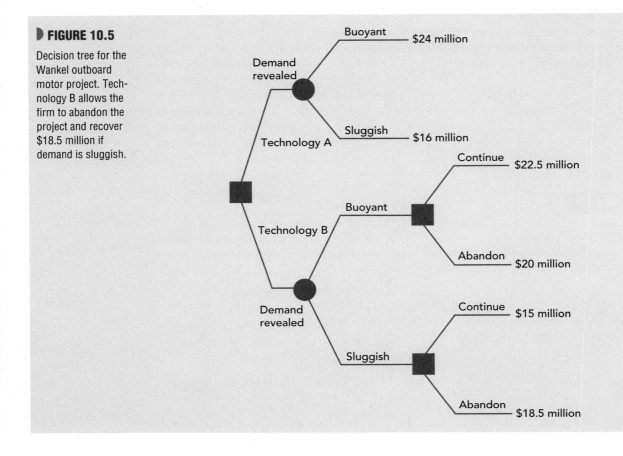

FIGURE 10.5

Decision tree for the Wankel outboard motor project. Technology B allows the firm to abandon the project and recover $18.5 million if demand is sluggish.

Technology B provides an insurance policy: If the outboard's sales are disappointing, you can abandon the project and receive $18.5 million. The total value of the project with technology B is its DCF value, assuming that the company does not abandon, *plus* the value of the option to sell the assets for $17 million. When you value this abandonment option, you are placing a value on flexibility.

Production Options

When companies undertake new investments, they generally think about the possibility that at a later stage they may wish to modify the project. After all, today everybody may be demanding round pegs, but, who knows, tomorrow square ones may be all the rage. In that case you need a plant that provides the flexibility to produce a variety of peg shapes. In just the same way, it may be worth paying up front for the flexibility to vary the inputs. For example, electric utilities often build in the option to switch between burning oil and burning natural gas. We refer to these opportunities as *production options*.

Timing Options

The fact that a project has a positive NPV does not mean that it is best undertaken now. It might be even more valuable to delay.

Timing decisions are fairly straightforward under conditions of certainty. You need to examine alternative dates for making the investment and calculate its net future value at each of these dates. Then, to find which of the alternatives would add most to the firm's *current* value, you must discount these net future values back to the present:

$$\text{Net present value of investment if undertaken at time } t = \frac{\text{Net future value at date } t}{(1 + r)^t}$$

The optimal date to undertake the investment is the one that maximizes its contribution to the value of your firm today. This procedure should already be familiar to you from Chapter 6, where we worked out when it was best to cut a tract of timber.

In the timber-cutting example we assumed that there was no uncertainty about the cash flows, so that you knew the optimal time to exercise your option. When there is uncertainty, the timing option is much more complicated. An opportunity not taken at $t = 0$ might be more or less attractive at $t = 1$; there is rarely any way of knowing for sure. Perhaps it is better to strike while the iron is hot even if there is a chance that it will become hotter. On the other hand, if you wait a bit you might obtain more information and avoid a bad mistake. That is why you often find that managers choose not to invest today in projects where the NPV is only marginally positive and there is much to be learned by delay.

More on Decision Trees

In Chapters 16 and 17, we provide an introduction to the topic of option valuation. But we will end this chapter with a closer look at decision trees.

Decision trees are commonly used to describe the real options imbedded in capital investment projects. But decision trees were used in the analysis of projects years before real options were first explicitly identified. Decision trees can help to understand project risk and how future decisions will affect project cash flows. Even if you never learn or use option-valuation theory, decision trees belong in your financial toolkit.

The best way to appreciate how decision trees can be used in project analysis is to work through a detailed example.

EXAMPLE 10.2 ● A Decision Tree for Pharmaceutical R&D

Drug development programs may last decades. Usually hundreds of thousands of compounds may be tested to find a few with promise. Then these compounds must survive several stages of investment and testing to gain approval from the Food and Drug Administration (FDA). Only then can the drug be sold commercially. The stages are as follows:

1. *Phase I clinical trials.* After laboratory and clinical tests are concluded, the new drug is tested for safety and dosage in a small sample of humans.

2. *Phase II clinical trials.* The new drug is tested for efficacy (Does it work as predicted?) and for potentially harmful side effects.

3. *Phase III clinical trials.* The new drug is tested on a larger sample of humans to confirm efficacy and to rule out harmful side effects.

4. *Prelaunch.* If FDA approval is gained, there is investment in production facilities and initial marketing. Some clinical trials continue.

5. *Commercial launch.* After making a heavy initial investment in marketing and sales, the company begins to sell the new drug to the public.

Once a drug is launched successfully, sales usually continue for about 10 years, until the drug's patent protection expires and competitors enter with generic versions of the same chemical compound. The drug may continue to be sold off-patent, but sales volume and profits are much lower.

The commercial success of FDA-approved drugs varies enormously. The PV of a "blockbuster" drug at launch can be 5 or 10 times the PV of an average drug. A few blockbusters can generate most of a large pharmaceutical company's profits.[13]

No company hesitates to invest in R&D for a drug that it *knows* will be a blockbuster. But the company will not find out for sure until after launch. Sometimes a company thinks it has a blockbuster, only to discover that a competitor has launched a better drug first.

Sometimes the FDA approves a drug but limits its scope of use. Some drugs, though effective, can only be prescribed for limited classes of patients; other drugs can be prescribed much more widely. Thus the manager of a pharmaceutical R&D program has to assess the odds of clinical success and the odds of commercial success. A new drug may be abandoned if it fails clinical trials—for example, because of dangerous side effects—or if the outlook for profits is discouraging.

Figure 10.6 is a decision tree that illustrates these decisions. We have assumed that a new drug has passed phase I clinical trials with flying colors. Now it requires an investment of $18 million for phase II trials. These trials take two years. The probability of success is 44%.

If the trials are successful, the manager learns the commercial potential of the drug, which depends on how widely it can be used. Suppose that the forecasted PV at launch depends on the scope of use allowed by the FDA. These PVs are shown at the far right of the decision tree: an upside outcome of NPV = $700 million if the drug can be widely used, a most likely case with NPV = $300 million, and a downside case of NPV = $100 million if the drug's scope is greatly restricted.[14] The NPVs are the payoffs at launch after investment in marketing. Launch comes three years after the start of phase III if the drug is approved by the FDA. The probabilities of the upside, most likely, and downside outcomes are 25%, 50%, and 25%, respectively.

A further R&D investment of $130 million is required for phase III trials and for the prelaunch period. (We have combined phase III and prelaunch for simplicity.) The probability of FDA approval and launch is 80%.

Now let's value the investments in Figure 10.6. We assume a risk-free rate of 4% and market risk premium of 7%. If FDA-approved pharmaceutical products have asset betas of .8, the opportunity cost of capital is $4 + .8 \times 7 = 9.6\%$.

We work back through the tree from right to left. The NPVs at the start of phase III trials are:

$$\text{NPV(upside)} \quad = -130 + .8 \times \frac{700}{(1.096)^3} = +\$295 \text{ million}$$

$$\text{NPV(most likely)} = -130 + .8 \times \frac{300}{(1.096)^3} = +\$52 \text{ million}$$

$$\text{NPV(downside)} \quad = -130 + .8 \times \frac{100}{(1.096)^3} = -\$69 \text{ million}$$

Since the downside NPV is negative at −$69 million, the $130 million investment at the start of phase III should *not* be made in the downside case. There is no point investing

---

[13] The Web site of the Tufts Center for the Study of Drug Development (**http://csdd.tufts.edu**) provides a wealth of information about the costs and risks of pharmaceutical R&D.

[14] The most likely case is not the average outcome, because PVs in the pharmaceutical business are skewed to the upside. The average PV is $.25 \times 700 + .5 \times 300 + .25 \times 100 = \$350$ million.

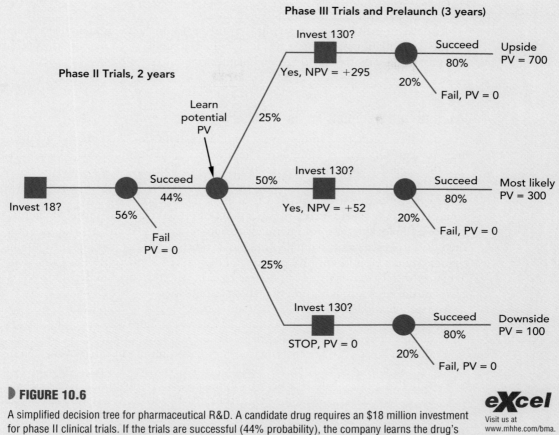

▶ **FIGURE 10.6**

A simplified decision tree for pharmaceutical R&D. A candidate drug requires an $18 million investment for phase II clinical trials. If the trials are successful (44% probability), the company learns the drug's scope of use and updates its forecast of the drug's PV at commercial launch. The investment required for the phase III trials and prelaunch outlays is $130 million. The probability of success in phase III and prelaunch is 80%.

$130 million for an 80% chance of a $100 million payoff three years later. Therefore the value of the R&D program at this point in the decision tree is not −$69 million, but zero.

Now calculate the NPV at the initial investment decision for phase II trials. The payoff two years later depends on whether the drug delivers on the upside, most likely, or downside: a 25% chance of NPV = +$295 million, a 50% chance of NPV = +$52 million, and a 25% chance of cancellation and NPV = 0. These NPVs are achieved only if the phase II trials are successful: There is a 44% chance of success and a 56% chance of failure. The initial investment is $18 million. Therefore NPV is

$$NPV = -18 + .44 \times \frac{.25 \times 295 + .5 \times 52 + .25 \times 0}{(1.096)^2} = -18 + 37 = +\$19 \text{ million}$$

Thus the phase II R&D is a worthwhile investment, even though the drug has only a 33% chance of making it to launch (.44 × .75 = .33, or 33%).

Notice that we did not increase the 9.6% discount rate to offset the risks of failure in clinical trials or the risk that the drug will fail to generate profits. Concerns about the drug's efficacy, possible side effects, and scope of use are diversifiable risks, which do not increase the risk of the R&D project to the company's diversified stockholders. We were careful to take these concerns into account in the cash-flow forecasts, however. The decision tree in Figure 10.6 keeps track of the probabilities of success or failure and the probabilities of upside and downside outcomes.[15]

While Figures 10.5 and 10.6 set out the possible future abandonment decisions, a more complete calculation of net present value would need to take advantage of the option valuation techniques that we introduce in Chapters 16 and 17.

● ● ● ● ●

Pro and Con Decision Trees

Any cash-flow forecast rests on some assumption about the firm's future investment and operating strategy. Often that assumption is implicit. Decision trees force the underlying strategy into the open. By displaying the links between today's decisions and tomorrow's decisions, they help the financial manager to find the strategy with the highest net present value.

The decision tree in Figure 10.6 is a simplified version of reality. For example, you could expand the tree to include a wider range of NPVs at launch, possibly including some chance of a blockbuster or of intermediate outcomes. You could allow information about the NPVs to arrive gradually, rather than just at the start of phase III. You could introduce the investment decision at phase I trials and separate the phase III and prelaunch stages. You may wish to draw a new decision tree covering these events and decisions. You will see how fast the circles, squares, and branches accumulate.

The trouble with decision trees is that they get so _____ complex so _____ quickly (insert your own expletives). Life is complex, however, and there is very little we can do about it. It is therefore unfair to criticize decision trees because they can become complex. Our criticism is reserved for analysts who let the complexity become overwhelming. The point of decision trees is to allow explicit analysis of possible future events and decisions. They should be judged not on their comprehensiveness but on whether they show the most important links between today's and tomorrow's decisions. Decision trees used in real life will be more complex than Figure 10.6, but they will nevertheless display only a small fraction of possible future events and decisions. Decision trees are like grapevines: They are productive only if they are vigorously pruned.

---

[15] The market risk attaching to the PVs at launch is recognized in the 9.6% discount rate.

● ● ● ● ●

SUMMARY

Earlier chapters explained how companies calculate a project's NPV by forecasting the cash flows and discounting them at a rate that reflects project risk. The end result is the project's contribution to shareholder wealth. Understanding discounted-cash-flow analysis is important, but there is more to good capital budgeting practice than an ability to discount.

First, companies need to establish a set of capital budgeting procedures to ensure that decisions are made in an orderly manner. Most companies prepare an annual capital budget, which is a list of investment projects planned for the coming year. Inclusion of a project in the capital budget does not constitute final approval for the expenditure. Before the plant or division can go ahead with a proposal, it will usually need to submit an appropriation request that includes detailed forecasts, a discounted-cash-flow analysis, and back-up information.

Sponsors of capital investment projects are tempted to overstate future cash flows and understate risks. Therefore firms need to encourage honest and open discussion. They also need procedures to ensure that projects fit in with the company's strategic plans and are developed on a consistent basis. (These procedures should _not_ include fudge factors added to project hurdle rates in an attempt to offset optimistic forecasts.) Later, after a project has begun to operate, the firm can follow up with a postaudit. Postaudits identify problems that need fixing and help the firm learn from its mistakes.

Visit us at www.mhhe.com/bma

Good capital budgeting practice also tries to identify the major uncertainties in project proposals. An awareness of these uncertainties may suggest ways that the project can be reconfigured to reduce the dangers, or it may point out some additional research that will confirm whether the project is worthwhile.

There are several ways in which companies try to identify and evaluate the threats to a project's success. The first is *sensitivity analysis*. Here the manager considers in turn each forecast or assumption that drives cash flows and recalculates NPV at optimistic and pessimistic values of that variable. The project is "sensitive to" that variable if the resulting range of NPVs is wide, particularly on the pessimistic side.

Sensitivity analysis often moves on to *break-even analysis*, which identifies break-even values of key variables. Suppose the manager is concerned about a possible shortfall in sales. Then he or she can calculate the sales level at which the project just breaks even (NPV = 0) and consider the odds that sales will fall that far. Break-even analysis is also done in terms of accounting income, although we do not recommend this application.

Sensitivity analysis and break-even analysis are easy, and they identify the forecasts and assumptions that really count for the project's success or failure. The important variables do not change one at a time, however. For example, when raw material prices are higher than forecasted, it's a good bet that selling prices will be higher too. The logical response is *scenario analysis*, which examines the effects on NPV of changing several variables at a time.

Scenario analysis looks at a limited number of combinations of variables. If you want to go whole hog and look at all possible combinations, you will have to turn to *Monte Carlo simulation*. In that case, you must build a financial model of the project and specify the probability distribution of each variable that determines cash flow. Then you ask the computer to draw random values for each variable and work out the resulting cash flows. In fact you ask the computer to do this thousands of times, in order to generate complete distributions of future cash flows. With these distributions in hand, you can get a better handle on expected cash flows and project risks. You can also experiment to see how the distributions would be affected by altering project scope or the ranges for any of the variables.

Elementary treatises on capital budgeting sometimes create the impression that, once the manager has made an investment decision, there is nothing to do but sit back and watch the cash flows unfold. In practice, companies are constantly modifying their operations. If cash flows are better than anticipated, the project may be expanded; if they are worse, it may be contracted or abandoned altogether. Options to modify projects are known as *real options*. In this chapter we introduced the main categories of real options: *expansion* options, *abandonment* options, *timing* options, and options providing *flexibility in production*.

Good managers take account of real options when they value a project. One convenient way to summarize real options and their cash-flow consequences is to create a *decision tree*. You identify the things that could happen to the project and the main counteractions that you might take. Then, working back from the future to the present, you can consider which action you *should* take in each case.

Decision trees can help to identify the possible impact of real options on project cash flows, but we largely skirted the issue of how to value real options.

● ● ● ● ●

FURTHER READING

Three not-too-technical references on real options are listed below.

A. Dixit and R. Pindyck, "The Options Approach to Capital Investment," *Harvard Business Review* 73 (May–June 1995), pp. 105–115.

W. C. Kester, "Today's Options for Tomorrow's Growth," *Harvard Business Review* 62 (March–April 1984), pp. 153–160.

A. Triantis and A. Borison, "Real Options: State of the Practice," *Journal of Applied Corporate Finance* 14 (Summer 2001), pp. 8–24.

Visit us at www.mhhe.com/bma

● ● ● ● ●

PROBLEM SETS   **BASIC**

1. True or false?
   a. The approval of a capital budget allows managers to go ahead with any project included in the budget.
   b. Capital budgets and project authorizations are mostly developed "bottom up." Strategic planning is a "top-down" process.
   c. Project sponsors are likely to be overoptimistic.

2. Explain how each of the following actions or problems can distort or disrupt the capital budgeting process.
   a. Overoptimism by project sponsors.
   b. Inconsistent forecasts of industry and macroeconomic variables.
   c. Capital budgeting organized solely as a bottom-up process.

3. Define and briefly explain each of the following terms or procedures:
   a. Sensitivity analysis
   b. Scenario analysis
   c. Break-even analysis
   d. Monte Carlo simulation
   e. Decision tree
   f. Real option
   g. Abandonment value
   h. Expansion value

4. True or false?
   a. Sensitivity analysis is unnecessary for projects with asset betas that are equal to 0.
   b. Sensitivity analysis can be used to identify the variables most crucial to a project's success.
   c. If only one variable is uncertain, sensitivity analysis gives "optimistic" and "pessimistic" values for project cash flow and NPV.
   d. The break-even sales level of a project is higher when *breakeven* is defined in terms of NPV rather than accounting income.
   e. Risk is reduced when a high proportion of costs are fixed.
   f. Monte Carlo simulation can be used to help forecast cash flows.

5. Suppose a manager has already estimated a project's cash flows, calculated its NPV, and done a sensitivity analysis like the one shown in Table 10.2. List the additional steps required to carry out a Monte Carlo simulation of project cash flows.

6. True or false?
   a. Decision trees can help identify and describe real options.
   b. The option to expand increases PV.
   c. High abandonment value decreases PV.
   d. If a project has positive NPV, the firm should always invest immediately.

7. Explain why setting a higher discount rate is not a cure for upward-biased cash-flow forecasts.

INTERMEDIATE

8. Draw up an outline or flowchart tracing the capital budgeting process from the initial idea for a new investment project to the completion of the project and the start of operations.

Assume the idea for a new obfuscator machine comes from a plant manager in the Deconstruction Division of the Modern Language Corporation.

Here are some questions your outline or flowchart should consider: Who will prepare the original proposal? What information will the proposal contain? Who will evaluate it? What approvals will be needed, and who will give them? What happens if the machine costs 40% more to purchase and install than originally forecasted? What will happen when the machine is finally up and running?

9. Look back to the cash flows for projects F and G in Section 5–3. The cost of capital was assumed to be 10%. Assume that the forecasted cash flows for projects of this type are overstated by 8% on average. That is, the forecast for each cash flow from each project should be reduced by 8%. But a lazy financial manager, unwilling to take the time to argue with the projects' sponsors, instructs them to use a discount rate of 18%.

   a. What are the projects' true NPVs?

   b. What are the NPVs at the 18% discount rate?

   c. Are there any circumstances in which the 18% discount rate would give the correct NPVs? (*Hint:* Could upward bias be more severe for more-distant cash flows?)

10. What is the NPV of the electric scooter project under the following scenario?

Market size	1.1 million
Market share	.1
Unit price	¥400,000
Unit variable cost	¥360,000
Fixed cost	¥2 billion

11. Otobai's staff (see Section 10–2) has come up with the following revised estimates for the electric scooter project:

Visit us at
www.mhhe.com/bma

	Pessimistic	Expected	Optimistic
Market size	.8 million	1.0 million	1.2 million
Market share	.04	.1	.16
Unit price	¥300,000	¥375,000	¥400,000
Unit variable cost	¥350,000	¥300,000	¥275,000
Fixed cost	¥5 billion	¥3 billion	¥1 billion

Conduct a sensitivity analysis using the "live" spreadsheets (available at **www.mhhe.com/bma**). What are the principal uncertainties in the project?

12. Otobai is considering still another production method for its electric scooter (see Section 10–2). It would require an additional investment of ¥15 billion but would reduce variable costs by ¥40,000 per unit. Other assumptions follow Table 10.1.

   a. What is the NPV of this alternative scheme?

   b. Draw break-even charts for this alternative scheme along the lines of Figure 10.1.

   c. Explain how you would interpret the break-even figure.

   d. Now suppose Otobai's management would like to know the figure for variable cost per unit at which the electric scooter project in Section 10–2 would break even. Calculate the level of costs at which the project would earn zero profit and at which it would have zero NPV. Assume that the initial investment is ¥15 billion.

   e. Recalculate DOL.

13. The Rustic Welt Company is proposing to replace its old welt-making machinery with more modern equipment. The new equipment costs $9 million (the existing equipment has zero salvage value). The attraction of the new machinery is that it is expected to cut manufacturing costs from their current level of $8 a welt to $4. However, as the following table shows, there is some uncertainty both about future sales and about the performance of the new machinery:

	Pessimistic	Expected	Optimistic
Sales, millions of welts	.4	.5	.7
Manufacturing cost with new machinery, dollars per welt	6	4	3
Economic life of new machinery, years	7	10	13

Conduct a sensitivity analysis of the replacement decision, assuming a discount rate of 12%. Rustic Welt does not pay taxes.

14. Suppose that the expected variable costs of Otobai's project are ¥33 billion a year and that fixed costs are zero. How does this change the degree of operating leverage? Now recompute the operating leverage assuming that the entire ¥33 billion of costs are fixed.

15. Operating leverage is often measured as the percentage increase in pretax profits after depreciation for a 1% increase in sales.

   a. Calculate the operating leverage for the electric scooter project assuming unit sales are 100,000 (see Section 10–2).

   b. Now show that this figure is equal to 1 + (fixed costs including depreciation divided by pretax profits).

   c. Would operating leverage be higher or lower if sales were 200,000 scooters?

16. Look back at the Vegetron electric mop project in Section 9–4. Assume that if tests fail and Vegetron continues to go ahead with the project, the $1 million investment would generate only $75,000 a year. Display Vegetron's problem as a decision tree.

17. Our Web site (**www.mhhe.com/bma**) contains an Excel program for simulating the cash flows from the Otobai project. Use this program to examine which are the principal uncertainties surrounding the project. Suppose that some more analysis could effectively remove uncertainty about *one* of the variables. Suggest where it could be most usefully applied.

18. Describe the real option in each of the following cases:

   a. Deutsche Metall postpones a major plant expansion. The expansion has positive NPV on a discounted-cash-flow basis but top management wants to get a better fix on product demand before proceeding.

   b. Western Telecom commits to production of digital switching equipment specially designed for the European market. The project has a negative NPV, but it is justified on strategic grounds by the need for a strong market position in the rapidly growing, and potentially very profitable, market.

   c. Western Telecom vetoes a fully integrated, automated production line for the new digital switches. It relies on standard, less-expensive equipment. The automated production line is more efficient overall, according to a discounted-cash-flow calculation.

   d. Mount Fuji Airways buys a jumbo jet with special equipment that allows the plane to be switched quickly from freight to passenger use or vice versa.

19. Look again at the decision tree in Figure 10.6. Expand the possible outcomes as follows:

   • Blockbuster: PV = $1.5 billion with 5% probability.

   • Above average: PV = $700 million with 20% probability.

   • Average: PV = $300 million with 40% probability.

   • Below average: PV = $100 million with 25% probability.

   • "Dog": PV = $40 million with 10% probability.

Redraw the decision tree. Is the $18 million investment in phase II trials still positive NPV?

20. Look again at the example in Figure 10.6. The R&D team has put forward a proposal to invest an extra $20 million in expanded phase II trials. The object is to prove that the drug can be administered by a simple inhaler rather than as a liquid. If successful, the scope of use is broadened and the upside PV increases to $1 billion. The probabilities of success are unchanged. Go to the "live" Excel spreadsheet version of Figure 10.6 at **www.mhhe.com/ bma**. Is the extra $20 million investment worthwhile? Would your answer change if the probability of success in the phase III trials falls to 75%?

CHALLENGE

21. Magna Charter is a new corporation formed by Agnes Magna to provide an executive flying service for the southeastern United States. The founder thinks there will be a ready demand from businesses that cannot justify a full-time company plane but nevertheless need one from time to time. However, the venture is not a sure thing. There is a 40% chance that demand in the first year will be low. If it is low, there is a 60% chance that it will remain low in subsequent years. On the other hand, if the initial demand is high, there is an 80% chance that it will stay high. The immediate problem is to decide what kind of plane to buy. A turboprop costs $550,000. A piston-engine plane costs only $250,000 but has less capacity. Moreover, the piston-engine plane is an old design and likely to depreciate rapidly. Ms. Magna thinks that next year secondhand piston aircraft will be available for only $150,000.

    Table 10.7 shows how the payoffs in years 1 and 2 from both planes depend on the pattern of demand. You can see, for example, that if demand is high in both years 1 and 2, the turbo will provide a payoff of $960,000 in year 2. If demand is high in year 1 but low in year 2, the turbo's payoff in the second year is only $220,000. Think of the payoffs in the second year as the cash flow that year plus the year-2 value of any subsequent cash flows. Also think of these cash flows as certainty equivalents, which can therefore be discounted at the risk-free interest rate of 10%.

    Ms. Magna now has an idea: Why not start out with one piston plane. If demand is low in the first year, Magna Charter can sit tight with this one relatively inexpensive aircraft. On the other hand, if demand is high in the first year she can buy a second piston-engine plane for only $150,000. In this case, if demand continues to be high, the payoff in year 2 from the two piston planes will be $800,000. However, if demand in year 2 were to decline, the payoff would be only $100,000.

    a. Draw a decision tree setting out Magna Charter's choices.

    b. If Magna Charter buys a piston plane, should it expand if demand turns out to be high in the first year?

Payoffs from the Turboprop				
Year 1 demand	**High (.6)**		**Low (.4)**	
Year 1 payoff	$150		$30	
Year 2 demand	**High (.8)**	**Low (.2)**	**High (.4)**	**Low (.6)**
Year 2 payoff	$960	$220	$930	$140
Payoffs from the Piston Engine				
Year 1 demand	**High (.6)**		**Low (.4)**	
Year 1 payoff	$100		$50	
Year 2 demand	**High (.8)**	**Low (.2)**	**High (.4)**	**Low (.6)**
Year 2 payoff	$410	$180	$220	$100

▶ **TABLE 10.7**   The possible payoffs from Ms. Magna's flying service. (All figures are in thousands. Probabilities are in parentheses.)

c. Given your answer to (b), would you recommend that Ms. Magna buys the turboprop or the piston-engine plane today?

d. What would be the NPV of an investment in a piston plane if there were no option to expand? How much extra value is contributed by the option to expand?

22. Look back at the guano project in Section 6–2. Use the Crystal Ball™ software to simulate how uncertainty about inflation could affect the project's cash flows.

MINI-CASE ● ● ● ● ●

Waldo County

Waldo County, the well-known real estate developer, worked long hours, and he expected his staff to do the same. So George Chavez was not surprised to receive a call from the boss just as George was about to leave for a long summer's weekend.

Mr. County's success had been built on a remarkable instinct for a good site. He would exclaim "Location! Location! Location!" at some point in every planning meeting. Yet finance was not his strong suit. On this occasion he wanted George to go over the figures for a new $90 million outlet mall designed to intercept tourists heading downeast toward Maine. "First thing Monday will do just fine," he said as he handed George the file. "I'll be in my house in Bar Harbor if you need me."

George's first task was to draw up a summary of the projected revenues and costs. The results are shown in Table 10.8. Note that the mall's revenues would come from two sources: The company would charge retailers an annual rent for the space they occupied, and in addition it would receive 5% of each store's gross sales.

Construction of the mall was likely to take three years. The construction costs could be depreciated straight-line over 15 years starting in year 3. As in the case of the company's other developments, the mall would be built to the highest specifications and would not need to be rebuilt until year 17. The land was expected to retain its value, but could not be depreciated for tax purposes.

Construction costs, revenues, operating and maintenance costs, and real estate taxes were all likely to rise in line with inflation, which was forecasted at 2% a year. The company's tax rate was 35% and the cost of capital was 9% in nominal terms.

George decided first to check that the project made financial sense. He then proposed to look at some of the things that might go wrong. His boss certainly had a nose for a good retail project, but he was not infallible. The Salome project had been a disaster because store sales

▶ TABLE 10.8
Projected revenues and costs in real terms for the Downeast Tourist Mall (figures in $ millions).

	Year					
	0	1	2	3	4	5–17
Investment:						
Land	30					
Construction	20	30	10			
Operations:						
Rentals				12	12	12
Share of retail sales				24	24	24
Operating and maintenance costs	2	4	4	10	10	10
Real estate taxes	2	2	3	4	4	4

had turned out to be 40% below forecast. What if that happened here? George wondered just how far sales could fall short of forecast before the project would be underwater.

Inflation was another source of uncertainty. Some people were talking about a zero long-term inflation rate, but George also wondered what would happen if inflation jumped to, say, 10%.

A third concern was possible construction cost overruns and delays due to required zoning changes and environmental approvals. George had seen cases of 25% construction cost overruns and delays up to 12 months between purchase of the land and the start of construction. He decided that he should examine the effect that this scenario would have on the project's profitability.

"Hey, this might be fun," George exclaimed to Mr. Waldo's secretary, Fifi, who was heading for Old Orchard Beach for the weekend. "I might even try Monte Carlo."

"Waldo went to Monte Carlo once," Fifi replied. "Lost a bundle at the roulette table. I wouldn't remind him. Just show him the bottom line. Will it make money or lose money? That's the bottom line."

"OK, no Monte Carlo," George agreed. But he realized that building a spreadsheet and running scenarios was not enough. He had to figure out how to summarize and present his results to Mr. County.

QUESTIONS

1. What is the project's NPV, given the projections in Table 10.8?
2. Conduct a sensitivity and a scenario analysis of the project. What do these analyses reveal about the project's risks and potential value?

11

Efficient Markets and Behavioral Finance

▶ **Up to this** point we have concentrated almost exclusively on the left-hand side of the balance sheet—the firm's capital investment decision. Now we move to the right-hand side and to the problems involved in financing the capital investments. To put it crudely, you've learned how to spend money, now learn how to raise it.

Of course we haven't totally ignored financing in earlier chapters. We introduced the weighted-average cost of capital, for example. But in most places we have looked past financing issues and used estimates of the opportunity cost of capital to discount future cash flows. We didn't ask how the cost of capital might be affected by financing.

Now we are turning the problem around. We take the firm's present portfolio of real assets and its future investment strategy as given, and then we determine the best financing strategy. For example,

- Should the firm reinvest most of its earnings in the business, or distribute the cash to shareholders?

- If the firm needs more money, should it issue more stock or should it borrow?

- Should it borrow short term or long term?

- Should it borrow by issuing a normal long-term bond or a convertible bond (a bond which can be exchanged for stock by the bondholders)?

There are countless other financing trade-offs, as you will see.

The purpose of holding the firm's capital investment decision constant is to separate that decision from the financing decision. Strictly speaking, this assumes that investment and financing decisions are *independent*. In many circumstances this is a reasonable assumption. The firm is generally free to change its capital structure by repurchasing one security and issuing another. In that case there is no need to associate a particular investment project with a particular source of cash. The firm can think, first, about which projects to accept and, second, about how they should be financed.

Sometimes decisions about capital structure depend on project choice or vice versa, and in those cases the investment and financing decisions have to be considered jointly. However, we defer discussion of such interactions of financing and investment decisions until Chapter 15.

We start this chapter by contrasting investment and financing decisions. The objective in each case is the same—to maximize NPV. However, it may be harder to find positive-NPV financing opportunities. The reason it is difficult to add value by clever financing decisions is that capital markets are usually efficient. By this we mean that fierce competition between investors eliminates profit opportunities and causes debt and equity issues to be fairly priced. If you think that sounds like a sweeping statement, you are right. That is why we have devoted this chapter to explaining and evaluating the efficient-market hypothesis.

You may ask why we start our discussion of financing issues with this conceptual point, before you have even the most basic knowledge about securities and issue procedures. We do it this way because financing decisions seem overwhelmingly complex if you don't learn to ask the right questions. We are afraid you might flee from confusion to the myths that often dominate popular discussion of corporate financing. You need to understand the efficient-market hypothesis not because it is *universally* true but because it leads you to ask the right questions.

We define the efficient-market hypothesis more carefully in Section 11–2. The hypothesis comes in different strengths, depending on the information available to investors. Sections 11–2 through 11–4 review the evidence for and against efficient markets. The evidence "for" is considerable, but over the years a number of puzzling anomalies have accumulated.

Advocates for rational and efficient markets also have a hard time explaining *bubbles*. Every decade seems to find its own bubble: the 1980s real estate and stock market bubble in Japan, the 1990s technology stock bubble, and the recent real estate bubble that triggered the subprime crisis. Part of the blame for bubbles goes to the incentive and agency problems that can plague even the most rational people, particularly when they are investing other people's money. But bubbles may also reflect patterns of irrational behavior that have been well documented by behavioral psychologists. We describe the main features of *behavioral finance* and the challenge that it poses to the efficient-market hypothesis.

The chapter closes with the six lessons of market efficiency.

● ● ● ● ●

11-1 We Always Come Back to NPV

Although it is helpful to separate investment and financing decisions, there are basic similarities in the criteria for making them. The decisions to purchase a machine tool and to sell a bond each involve valuation of a risky asset. The fact that one asset is real and the other is financial doesn't matter. In both cases we end up computing net present value.

The phrase *net present value of borrowing* may seem odd to you. But the following example should help to explain what we mean: As part of its policy of encouraging small business, the government offers to lend your firm $100,000 for 10 years at 3%. This means that the firm is liable for interest payments of $3,000 in each of the years 1 through 10 and that it is responsible for repaying the $100,000 in the final year. Should you accept this offer?

We can compute the NPV of the loan agreement in the usual way. The one difference is that the first cash flow is *positive* and the subsequent flows are *negative:*

$$NPV = \text{amount borrowed} - \text{present value of interest payments}$$
$$- \text{present value of loan repayment}$$
$$= +100,000 - \sum_{t=1}^{10} \frac{3,000}{(1 + r)^t} - \frac{100,000}{(1 + r)^{10}}$$

The only missing variable is r, the opportunity cost of capital. You need that to value the liability created by the loan. We reason this way: The government's loan to you is a financial asset, a piece of paper representing your promise to pay $3,000 per year plus the final repayment of $100,000. How much would that paper sell for if freely traded in the capital market? It would sell for the present value of those cash flows, discounted at r, the rate of return offered by other securities issued by your firm. All you have to do to determine r is to answer the question, What interest rate would my firm need to pay to borrow money directly from the capital markets rather than from the government?

Suppose that this rate is 10%. Then

$$NPV = +100,000 - \sum_{t=1}^{10} \frac{3,000}{(1.10)^t} - \frac{100,000}{(1.10)^{10}}$$
$$= +100,000 - 56,988 = +\$43,012$$

Of course, you don't need any arithmetic to tell you that borrowing at 3% is a good deal when the fair rate is 10%. But the NPV calculations tell you just how much that opportunity is worth ($43,012).[1] It also brings out the essential similarity between investment and financing decisions.

---

[1] We ignore here any tax consequences of borrowing. These are discussed in Chapter 14.

Differences between Investment and Financing Decisions

In some ways, financing decisions are more complicated than investment decisions. For example, the number of different securities and financing strategies is well into the hundreds (we have stopped counting). But there are also ways in which financing decisions are much easier than investment decisions. First, financing decisions do not have the same degree of finality as investment decisions. They are easier to reverse. That is, their abandonment value is higher. Second, it's harder to make money by smart financing strategies. The reason is that financial markets are more competitive than product markets. This means it is more difficult to find positive-NPV financing strategies than positive-NPV investment strategies.

When the firm looks at capital investment decisions, it does *not* assume that it is facing perfect, competitive markets. It may have only a few competitors that specialize in the same line of business in the same geographical area. And it may own some unique assets that give it an edge over its competitors. Often these assets are intangible, such as patents, expertise, or reputation. All this opens up the opportunity to make superior profits and find projects with positive NPVs.

In financial markets your competition is all other corporations seeking funds, to say nothing of the state, local, and federal governments that go to New York, London, and other financial centers to raise money. The investors who supply financing are comparably numerous, and they are smart: Money attracts brains. The financial amateur often views capital markets as *segmented*, that is, broken down into distinct sectors. But money moves between those sectors, and it usually moves fast. In general, as we shall see, firms should assume that the securities they issue are fairly priced. That takes us into the main topic of this chapter: efficient capital markets.

11-2 What Is an Efficient Market?

A Startling Discovery: Price Changes Are Random

As is so often the case with important ideas, the concept of efficient capital markets stemmed from a chance discovery. In 1953 Maurice Kendall, a British statistician, presented a controversial paper to the Royal Statistical Society on the behavior of stock and commodity prices.[2] Kendall had expected to find regular price cycles, but to his surprise they did not seem to exist. Each series appeared to be "a 'wandering' one, almost as if once a week the Demon of Chance drew a random number . . . and added it to the current price to determine the next week's price." In other words, the prices of stocks and commodities seemed to follow a *random walk.*

If you are not sure what we mean by "random walk," you might like to think of the following example: You are given $100 to play a game. At the end of each week a coin is tossed. If it comes up heads, you win 3% of your investment; if it is tails, you lose 2.5%. Therefore, your capital at the end of the first week is either $103.00 or $97.50.

---

[2] See M. G. Kendall, "The Analysis of Economic Time Series, Part I. Prices," *Journal of the Royal Statistical Society* 96 (1953), pp. 11–25. Kendall's idea was not wholly new. It had been proposed in an almost forgotten thesis written 53 years earlier by a French doctoral student, Louis Bachelier. Bachelier's accompanying development of the mathematical theory of random processes anticipated by five years Einstein's famous work on the random Brownian motion of colliding gas molecules. See L. Bachelier, *Théorie de la Speculation* (Paris: Gauthiers-Villars, 1900). Reprinted in English (A. J. Boness, trans.) in P. H. Cootner (ed.), *The Random Character of Stock Market Prices* (Cambridge, MA: MIT Press, 1964), pp. 17–78.

At the end of the second week the coin is tossed again. Now the possible outcomes are:

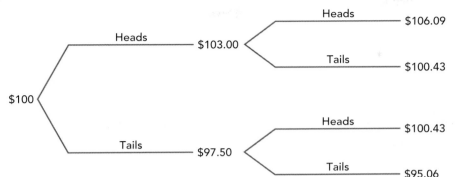

This process is a random walk with a positive drift of .25% per week.[3] It is a random walk because successive changes in value are independent. That is, the odds each week are the same, regardless of the value at the start of the week or of the pattern of heads and tails in the previous weeks.

If you find it difficult to believe that there are no patterns in share price changes, look at the two charts in Figure 11.1. One of these charts shows the outcome from playing our game for five years; the other shows the actual performance of the Standard and Poor's Index for a five-year period. Can you tell which one is which?[4]

When Maurice Kendall suggested that stock prices follow a random walk, he was implying that the price changes are independent of one another just as the gains and losses in our coin-tossing game were independent. Figure 11.2 illustrates this for four stocks, Microsoft, BP, Philips, and Sony. Each panel shows the change in price of the stock on successive days. The circled dot in the southeast quadrant of the Microsoft panel refers to a pair of days in which a 3% increase was followed by a 3% decrease. If there were a systematic tendency for increases to be followed by decreases, there would be many dots in the southeast quadrant and few in the northeast quadrant. It is obvious from a glance that there is very little pattern in these price movements, but we can test this more precisely by calculating the coefficient of correlation between each day's price change and the next. If price movements persisted, the correlation would be positive; if there were no relationship, it would be 0. In our

▶ **FIGURE 11.1**

This chart show the Standard and Poor's Index for a five-year period and the results of playing our coin-tossing game for five years. Can you tell which line is which?

---

[3] The drift is equal to the expected outcome: $(1/2)(3) + (1/2)(-2.5) = .25\%$.

[4] The blue in Figure 11.1 shows the actual Standard and Poor's Index for February 2002 to February 2007; the red is a series of cumulated random numbers. Of course, 50% of you are likely to have guessed right, but we bet it was just a guess.

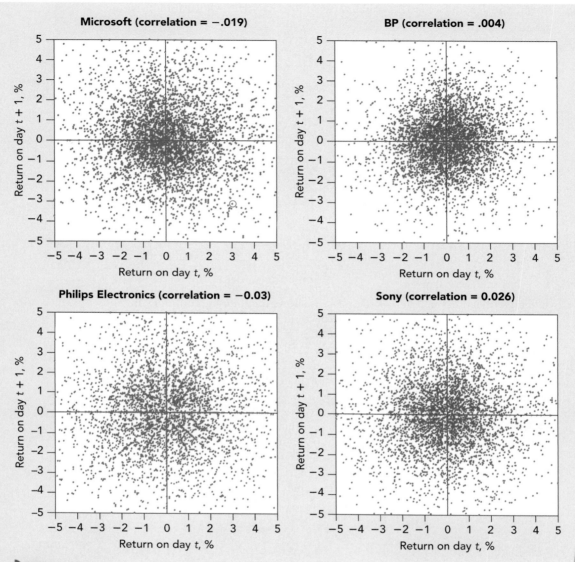

▶ FIGURE 11.2

Each dot shows a pair of returns for a stock on two successive days between January 1990 and May 2009. The circled dot for Microsoft records a daily return of +3% and then −3% on the next day. The scatter diagram shows no significant relationship between returns on successive days.

example, the correlation between successive price changes in Microsoft stock was −.019; there was a negligible tendency for price rises to be followed by price falls.[5] For Philips this correlation was also negative at −.030. However, for BP and Sony the correlations were positive at +.004 and +.026, respectively. In these cases there was a negligible tendency for price rises to be followed by further price rises.

Figure 11.2 suggests that successive price changes of all four stocks were effectively uncorrelated. Today's price change gave investors almost no clue as to the likely change

---

[5] The correlation coefficient between successive observations is known as the *autocorrelation coefficient*. An autocorrelation of −.019 implies that, if Microsoft's stock price rose by 1% more than the average yesterday, your best forecast of today's change would be .019% *less* than the average.

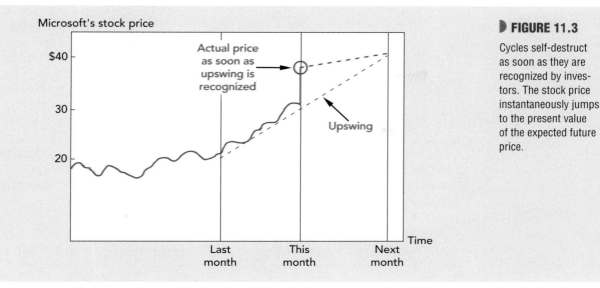

Microsoft's stock price

Actual price as soon as upswing is recognized

Upswing

$40

30

20

Last month

This month

Next month

Time

FIGURE 11.3

Cycles self-destruct as soon as they are recognized by investors. The stock price instantaneously jumps to the present value of the expected future price.

tomorrow. Does that surprise you? If so, imagine that it were not the case and that changes in Microsoft's stock price were expected to persist for several months. Figure 11.3 provides an example of such a predictable cycle. You can see that an upswing in Microsoft's stock price started last month, when the price was $20, and it is expected to carry the price to $40 next month. What will happen when investors perceive this bonanza? It will self-destruct. Since Microsoft stock is a bargain at $30, investors will rush to buy. They will stop buying only when the stock offers a normal rate of return. Therefore, as soon as a cycle becomes apparent to investors, they immediately eliminate it by their trading.

Three Forms of Market Efficiency

You should see now why prices in competitive markets must follow a random walk. If past price changes could be used to predict future price changes, investors could make easy profits. But in competitive markets easy profits don't last. As investors try to take advantage of the information in past prices, prices adjust immediately until the superior profits from studying past price movements disappear. As a result, all the information in past prices will be reflected in *today's* stock price, not tomorrow's. Patterns in prices will no longer exist and price changes in one period will be independent of changes in the next. In other words, the share price will follow a random walk.

In competitive markets today's stock price must already reflect the information in past prices. But why stop there? If markets are competitive, shouldn't today's stock price reflect *all* the information that is available to investors? If so, securities will be fairly priced and security returns will be unpredictable. No one earns consistently superior returns in such a market. Collecting more information won't help, because all available information is already impounded in today's stock prices.

Economists define three levels of market efficiency, which are distinguished by the degree of information reflected in security prices. In the first level, prices reflect the information contained in the record of past prices. This is called *weak market efficiency*. If markets are efficient in the weak sense, then it is impossible to make consistently superior profits by studying past returns. Prices will follow a random walk.

The second level of efficiency requires that prices reflect not just past prices but all other public information, for example, from the Internet or the financial press. This is known as *semistrong market efficiency*. If markets are semistrong efficient, then prices will adjust immediately to public information such as the announcement of the last quarter's earnings, a new issue of stock, or a proposal to merge two companies.

With *strong-market efficiency,* prices reflect *all* the information that can be acquired by painstaking analysis of the company and the economy. In such a market we would observe lucky and unlucky investors, but we wouldn't find any superior investment managers who can consistently beat the market.

Efficient Markets: The Evidence

In the years that followed Maurice Kendall's discovery, financial journals were packed with tests of the efficient-market hypothesis. To test the weak form of the hypothesis, researchers measured the profitability of some of the trading rules used by those investors who claim to find patterns in security prices. They also employed statistical tests, including the test we used to look for patterns in the returns on Microsoft, BP, Philips, and Sony stock. It appears that throughout the world there are few patterns in day-to-day returns.

To analyze the semistrong form of the efficient-market hypothesis, researchers have measured how rapidly security prices respond to different items of news, such as earnings or dividend announcements, news of a takeover, or macroeconomic information.

Before we describe what they found, we should explain how to isolate the effect of an announcement on the price of a stock. Suppose, for example, that you need to understand how stock prices of takeover targets respond when the takeovers are first announced. As a first stab, you could simply calculate the average return on target-company stocks in the days leading up to the announcement and immediately after it. With daily returns on a large sample of targets, the average announcement effect should be clear. There won't be too much contamination from movements in the overall market around the announcement dates, because daily market returns average out to a very small number.[6] The potential contamination increases for weekly or monthly returns, however. Thus you will usually want to adjust for market movements. For example, you can simply subtract out the return on the market:

$$\text{Adjusted stock return} = \text{return on stock} - \text{return on market index}$$

Chapter 8 suggests a refined adjustment based on betas. (Just subtracting the market return assumes that target-firm betas equal 1.0.) This adjustment is called the *market model:*

$$\text{Expected stock return} = \alpha + \beta \times \text{return on market index}$$

Alpha (α) states how much on average the stock price changed when the market index was unchanged. Beta (β) tells us how much *extra* the stock price moved for each 1% change in the market index.[7] Suppose that subsequently the stock price return is $\tilde{r}$ in a month when the market return is $\tilde{r}_m$. In that case we would conclude that the *abnormal return* for that month is

$$\text{Abnormal stock return} = \text{actual stock return} - \text{expected stock return}$$
$$= \tilde{r} - (\alpha + \beta\tilde{r}_m)$$

This abnormal return should reflect firm-specific news only.[8]

---

[6] Suppose, for example, that the market return is 12% per year. With 250 trading days in the year, the average daily return is $(1.12)^{1/250} - 1 = .00045$, or .045%.

[7] It is important when estimating α and β that you choose a period in which you believe that the stock behaved normally. If its performance was abnormal, then estimates of α and β cannot be used to measure the returns that investors expected. As a precaution, ask yourself whether your estimates of expected returns look sensible. Methods for estimating abnormal returns are analyzed in A. C. MacKinlay, "Event Studies in Economics and Finance," *Journal of Economic Literature* 35 (1997), pp. 13–39; and also S. P. Kothari and J. B. Warner, "Econometrics of Event Studies," in B. E. Eckbo (ed.), *The Handbook of Empirical Corporate Finance* (Amsterdam: Elsevier/North-Holland, 2007), Chapter 1.

[8] Abnormal returns are also often calculated using the Fama–French three-factor model, which we discussed in Chapter 8. The stock return is adjusted for the market return, the difference between small- and large-stock returns, and the difference between returns on high and low book-to-market firms.

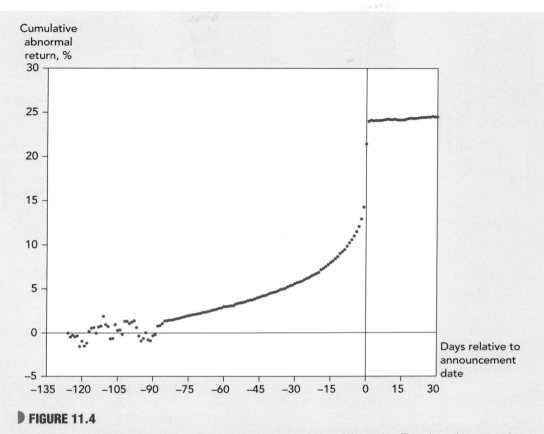

▶ FIGURE 11.4

The performance of the stocks of target companies compared with that of the market. The prices of target stocks jump up on the announcement day, but from then on there are no unusual price movements. The announcement of the takeover attempt seems to be fully reflected in the stock price on the announcement day.

Source: A. Keown and J. Pinkerton, "Merger Announcements and Insider Trading Activity," *Journal of Finance* 36 (September 1981), pp. 855–869. © 1981. Reprinted with permission of Blackwell Publishers Journal Rights. We are grateful to Jinghua Yan for updating the calculations to the period 1979–2004.

Figure 11.4 illustrates how the release of news affects abnormal returns. The graph shows the abnormal return on a sample of nearly 17,000 firms that were targets of takeover attempts. Acquiring firms usually have to pay a substantial *takeover premium* to get the deal done, so the target firm's stock price increases as soon as the takeover bid is announced. Figure 11.4 shows the average pattern of the target's stock returns before and after the announcement of a takeover (day 0 in the figure). Stock prices drift up before date zero, as investors gradually realize that a takeover may be coming. On the announcement day, prices jump up dramatically.[9] The stock-price adjustment is immediate and complete. After the big price move on the public announcement day, the run-up is over, and there is no significant further drift in the stock price, either upward or downward. Thus within the day, the new stock prices reflect (at least on average) the magnitude of the takeover premium.

Tests of the strong form of the hypothesis have examined the recommendations of professional security analysts and have looked for mutual funds or pension funds that could predictably outperform the market. Some researchers have found a slight persistent

---

[9] Big profits await if you can identify target firms before the takeover announcement. Purchases based on confidential inside information are illegal, however, and could land you in jail.

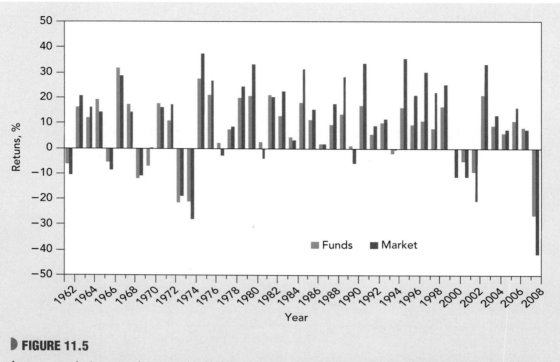

FIGURE 11.5

Average annual returns on a large sample of U.S. mutual funds and the market index, 1962–2008. Notice that mutual funds underperform the market in approximately two-thirds of the years.

Source: M. M. Carhart, "On Persistence in Mutual Fund Performance," *Journal of Finance* 52 (March 1997), pp. 57–82. © 1997 Blackwell Publishers. We are grateful to Jinghua Yan for updating the calculations.

outperformance, but just as many have concluded that professionally managed funds fail to recoup the costs of management. Look, for example, at Figure 11.5, which is an updated version of a study by Mark Carhart of the average return on a large sample of U.S. mutual funds. You can see that in some years the mutual funds beat the market, but roughly two-thirds of the time it was the other way around. Figure 11.5 provides a fairly crude comparison, for mutual funds have tended to specialize in particular sectors of the market, such as low-beta stocks or large-firm stocks, that may have given below-average returns. To control for such differences, each fund needs to be compared with a benchmark portfolio of similar securities. The study by Mark Carhart did this, but the message was unchanged: The funds earned a lower return than the benchmark portfolios *after* expenses and roughly matched the benchmarks *before* expenses.

It would be surprising if some managers were not smarter than others and could earn superior returns. But it seems difficult to spot the smart ones, and the top-performing managers one year have about an average chance of falling on their faces the next year.[10]

The evidence on efficient markets has convinced many professional and individual investors to give up pursuit of superior performance. They simply "buy the index," which maximizes diversification and cuts costs to the bone. Individual investors can buy *index*

---

[10] See, for example, B. G. Malkiel, "Returns from Investing in Equity Mutual Funds 1971 to 1991," *Journal of Finance* 50 (June 1995), pp. 549–572. Some contrary evidence that good performance does persist is provided in R. Kosowski, A. Timmerman, R. Wermers, and H. White, "Can Mutual Fund 'Stars' Really Pick Stocks? New Evidence from a Bootstrap Analysis," *Journal of Finance* 61 (December 2006), pp. 2551–2595. See also M. J. Gruber, "Another Puzzle: The Growth in Actively Managed Mutual Funds," *Journal of Finance* 51 (July 1996), pp. 783–810.

funds, which are mutual funds that track stock market indexes. There is no active management, so costs are very low. For example, management fees for the Vanguard 500 Index Fund, which tracks the S&P 500 Index, were .18% per year in 2009 (.09% per year for investments over $100,000). The size of this fund was $73 billion.

How far could indexing go? Not to 100%: If all investors hold index funds, then nobody will be collecting information and prices will not respond to new information when it arrives. An efficient market needs some smart investors who gather information and attempt to profit from it. To provide incentives to gather costly information, prices cannot reflect *all* information.[11] There must be some profits available to allow the costs of information to be recouped. But if the costs are small, relative to the total market value of traded securities, then the financial market can still be close to perfectly efficient.

11-3 The Evidence Against Market Efficiency

Almost without exception, early researchers concluded that the efficient-market hypothesis was a remarkably good description of reality. So powerful was the evidence that any dissenting research was regarded with suspicion. But eventually the readers of finance journals grew weary of hearing the same message. The interesting articles became those that turned up some puzzle. Soon the journals were packed with evidence of anomalies that investors have apparently failed to exploit.

What exactly is an anomaly? So far we have connected market efficiency to the absence of opportunities to make money. Let's be more precise: In an efficient market it is not possible to find expected returns greater (or less) than the risk-adjusted opportunity cost of capital. This implies that every security trades at its fundamental value, based on future cash flows (C_t) and the opportunity cost of capital (r):

$$P = \sum_{t=1}^{\infty} \frac{C_t}{(1 + r)^t}$$

If price equals fundamental value, the expected rate of return is the opportunity cost of capital, no more and no less. If price differs from fundamental value, then investors can earn more than the cost of capital, by selling if the price is too high and buying when it is too low.

You will recall these principles from our discussion of common stock values in Chapter 4. Here the principles tell us that you can't identify a superior return unless you know what the normal expected return is. Therefore, if you try to determine whether a market is efficient, you usually have to adopt an asset pricing model that specifies the relationship between risk and expected return. Any test of market efficiency is then a combined test of efficiency and the asset pricing model. Any test of an asset pricing model is also a combined test of the model and market efficiency.

The most commonly used asset pricing model is the CAPM. Chapter 8 pointed to some apparent violations of the CAPM, including the abnormally high returns on the stocks of small firms. For example, look back at Figure 8.10, which shows the cumulative difference between the returns on small-firm stocks and large-firm stocks. You can see that since 1926 the stocks of the firms with the lowest market capitalizations have performed substantially better than those with the highest capitalizations.

Now this may mean one (or more) of several things. First, it could be that investors have demanded a higher expected return from small firms to compensate for some extra risk factor that is not captured in the simple capital asset pricing model.

---

[11] See S. J. Grossman and J. E. Stiglitz, "On the Impossibility of Informationally Efficient Markets," *American Economic Review* 70 (June 1980), pp. 393–408.

Second, the superior performance of small firms could simply be a coincidence, a finding that stems from the efforts of many researchers to find interesting patterns in the data. There is evidence for and against the coincidence theory. Those who believe that the small-firm effect is a pervasive phenomenon can point to the fact that small-firm stocks have provided a higher return in many other countries. On the other hand, you can see from Figure 8.10 that the small-firm effect seems to have disappeared as soon as it was first documented in 1981. Perhaps investors did underestimate the returns on small firms before 1981, but then bid up the firms' stock prices as soon as the mispricing was identified.

Third, the small-firm effect could be an important exception to the efficient-market theory, an exception that gave investors the opportunity for consistently superior returns over a period of several decades. If these anomalies offer easy pickings, you would expect to find a number of investors eager to take advantage of them. It turns out that, while many investors do try to exploit such anomalies, it is surprisingly difficult to get rich by doing so. For example, Professor Richard Roll, who probably knows as much as anyone about market anomalies, confesses

> Over the past decade, I have attempted to exploit many of the seemingly most promising "inefficiencies" by actually trading significant amounts of money according to a trading rule suggested by the "inefficiencies" . . . I have never yet found one that worked in practice, in the sense that it returned more after cost than a buy-and-hold strategy.[12]

Do Investors Respond Slowly to New Information?

We have dwelt on the small-firm effect, but there is no shortage of other puzzles and anomalies. Some of them relate to the short-term behavior of stock prices. For example, returns appear to be higher in January than in other months, they seem to be lower on a Monday than on other days of the week, and most of the daily return comes at the beginning and end of the day.

To have any chance of making money from such short-term patterns, you need to be a professional trader, with one eye on the computer screen and the other on your annual bonus. If you are a corporate financial manager, these short-term patterns in stock prices may be intriguing conundrums, but they are unlikely to change the major financial decisions about which projects to invest in and how they should be financed.

Corporate financial managers should be more concerned about mispricing that lasts months or years. Here are two examples of possible longer-lasting inefficiency.

The Earnings Announcement Puzzle   The earnings announcement puzzle is summarized in Figure 11.6, which shows stock performance following the announcement of unexpectedly good or bad earnings during the years 1972 to 2001. The 10% of the stocks of firms with the best earnings news outperform those with the worst news by about 1% per month over the six-month period following the announcement. It seems that investors underreact to the earnings announcement and become aware of the full significance only as further information arrives.

The New-Issue Puzzle   When firms issue stock to the public, investors typically rush to buy. On average those lucky enough to receive stock receive an immediate capital gain. However, researchers have found that these early gains often turn into losses. For example, suppose that you bought stock immediately following each initial public offering (IPO) and then held that stock for five years. Over the period 1970–2007 your average annual return would have been 3.8% less than the return on a portfolio of similar-sized stocks.

---

[12] R. Roll, "What Every CFO Should Know about Scientific Progress in Financial Economics: What Is Known and What Remains to Be Resolved," *Financial Management* 23 (Summer 1994), pp. 69–75.

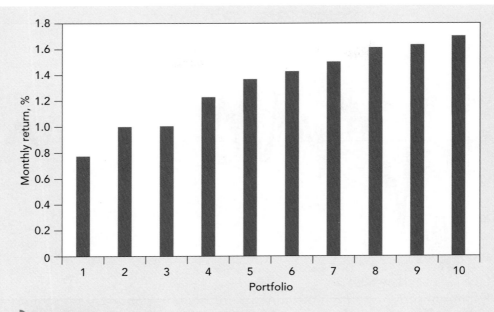

▶ **FIGURE 11.6**

The average return 1972–2001 on stocks of firms over the six months following an announcement of quarterly earnings. The 10% of stocks with the best earnings news (portfolio 10) outperformed those with the worst news (portfolio 1) by about 1% per month.

Source: T. Chordia and L. Shivakumar, "Inflation Illusion and the Post-earnings Announcement Drift," *Journal of Accounting Research* 43 (2005), pp. 521–556.

The jury is still out on these studies of long-term anomalies. Take, for example, the new-issue puzzle. Most new issues during the past 30 years have involved growth stocks with high market values and limited book assets. When the long-run performance of new issues is compared with a portfolio that is matched in terms of both size and book-to-market ratios, the difference in performance almost halves.[13] So the new-issue puzzle could turn out to be just the book-to-market ratio puzzle in disguise.[14]

Anomalies such as the new-issue puzzle may be a sign of inadequate asset pricing models, and so for many people they are not convincing evidence against market efficiency. However, there are other anomalies that cannot be dismissed so easily. One example is that of "Siamese twins," two securities with claims on the same cash flows, which nevertheless trade separately. Before the two companies merged in July 2005, the Dutch company Royal Dutch Petroleum and the British company Shell Transport & Trading (T&T) were Siamese twins, each with a fixed share in the profits and dividends of the oil giant. Since both companies participated in the same underlying cash flows, you would expect the stock prices to have moved in exact lockstep. But, as you can see from Figure 11.7, the prices of the two shares sometimes diverged substantially.[15]

---

[13] The long-run underperformance of new issues was documented in R. Loughran and J. R. Ritter, "The New Issues Puzzle," *Journal of Finance* 50 (1995), pp. 23–51. The figures are updated on Jay Ritter's Web site, where IPO returns are compared with those of a portfolio that is matched in terms of size and book-to-market ratio. (See **bear.cba.ufl.edu/ritter**.)

[14] There may be still other reasons for the poor long-term performance of IPOs, including tax effects. Portfolios of IPOs generate many extreme winners and losers. Investors can sell the losers, deducting the losses against other capital gains, and hold the winners, thus deferring taxes. IPO stocks are a good venue for this tax strategy, so tax-savvy investors may have bid up IPO stock prices.

[15] For evidence on the pricing of Siamese twins see K. A. Froot and E. Dabora, "How Are Stock Prices Affected by the Location of Trade?" *Journal of Financial Economics* 53 (August 1999), pp. 189–216, and, for more recent data, A. De Jong, L. Rosenthal, and M. A. Van Dijk, "The Risk and Return of Arbitrage in Dual-Listed Companies," *Review of Finance* 13 (2009), pp. 495–520.

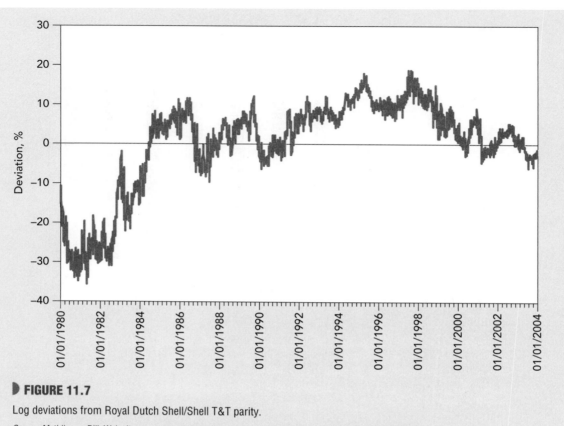

▶ **FIGURE 11.7**

Log deviations from Royal Dutch Shell/Shell T&T parity.

Source: Mathijs van Dijk Web site, **www.mathijsavandijk.com/dual-listed-companies**. Used with permission.

Bubbles and Market Efficiency

Cases such as the Siamese twins suggest that there are occasions when prices of individual stocks can get out of line. But are there also cases in which prices as a whole can no longer be justified by fundamentals? We will look at the evidence in a moment, but first we should note how difficult it is to value common stocks and to determine whether their prices are irrational.

For example, imagine that in May 2009 you wanted to check whether the stocks forming Standard & Poor's Composite Index were fairly valued. As a first stab you might use the constant-growth formula that we introduced in Chapter 4. In 2009 the annual dividends paid by the companies in the index came to about $217 billion. Suppose that these dividends were expected to grow at a steady rate of 4.1% and that investors required a return of 7.2%. Then the constant-growth formula gives a value for the common stocks of

$$\text{PV common stocks} = \frac{\text{DIV}}{r - g} = \frac{217}{.072 - .041} = \$7,000 \text{ billion}$$

which was roughly their value in May 2009. But how confident could you be about these figures? Perhaps the likely dividend growth was only 3.6% per year. In that case your estimate of the value of the common stocks would decline to

$$\text{PV common stocks} = \frac{\text{DIV}}{r - g} = \frac{217}{.072 - .036} = \$6,028 \text{ billion}$$

In other words, a reduction of just half a percentage point in the expected rate of dividend growth would reduce the value of common stocks by about 14%.

The extreme difficulty of valuing common stocks from scratch has two important consequences. First, investors find it easier to price a common stock relative to yesterday's price or relative to today's price of comparable securities. In other words, they generally take yesterday's price as correct, adjusting upward or downward on the basis of today's information. If information arrives smoothly, then, as time passes, investors become increasingly confident that today's price level is correct. But when investors lose confidence in the benchmark of yesterday's price, there may be a period of confused trading and volatile prices before a new benchmark is established.

Second, most of the tests of market efficiency are concerned with *relative* prices and focus on whether there are easy profits to be made. It is almost impossible to test whether stocks are *correctly valued*, because no one can measure true value with any precision. Take, for example, Hershey stock, which sold for $36 in April 2009. Could we prove that this was its true value? Of course not, but we could be more confident that the price of Hershey should not be very different from that of Smucker's ($39), because both companies had similar earnings and dividends per share and both had similar growth prospects.

It may be impossible to *prove* that market levels are, or are not, consistent with fundamentals. However, every now and again investors seem to be caught up in a speculative frenzy, and asset prices then reach levels that (at least with hindsight) cannot easily be justified by the outlook for profits and dividends. Investors refer to such occasions as *bubbles*. Bubbles can result when prices rise rapidly, and more and more investors join the game on the assumption that prices will *continue* to rise. These bubbles can be self-sustaining for a while. It can be rational to jump on the bandwagon as long as you are sure that there will be greater fools that you can sell out to. But remember that lots of money will be lost, perhaps by you, when the bubble bursts.[16]

The Japanese bubble is a good example. The Nikkei 225 Index rose about 300% between the start of 1985 and December 1989. After a sharp increase in interest rates at the beginning of 1990, stock prices began to fall. By October the Nikkei had sunk to about half its peak. In March 2009, the Nikkei was still down 80% from its peak 19 years before.

The boom in Japanese stock prices was matched by an even greater explosion in land prices. For example, Ziemba and Schwartz document that the few hundred acres of land under the Emperor's Palace in Tokyo, evaluated at neighborhood land prices, was worth as much as all the land in Canada or California.[17] But then the real estate bubble also burst. By 2005 land prices in the six major Japanese cities had slumped to just 13% of their peak.

Such bubbles are not confined to Japan. Toward the end of the twentieth century investors in technology stocks saw a remarkable run-up in the value of their holdings. The Nasdaq Composite Index, which has a heavy weighting in high-tech stocks, rose 580% from the start of 1995 to its high in March 2000. Then, as rapidly as it began, the boom ended, and by October 2002 the Nasdaq index had fallen 78% from its peak.

Some of the largest gains and losses were experienced by dot.com stocks. For example, Yahoo! shares, which began trading in April 1996, appreciated by 1,400% in four years. In these heady days some companies found that they could boost their stock price simply by adding "dot.com" to the company name.[18]

Looking back at the Japanese and dot.com bubbles, it seems difficult to believe that future cash flows could ever have been sufficient to provide investors with a reasonable return.[19] If that is the case, we have two important exceptions to the theory of efficient markets.

---

[16] Bubbles are not necessarily irrational. See M. Brunnermeier, *Asset Pricing under Asymmetric Information: Bubbles, Crashes, Technical Analysis and Herding* (Oxford: Oxford University Press, 2001).

[17] See W. T. Ziemba and S. L. Schwartz, *Invest Japan* (Chicago, IL: Probus Publishing Co., 1992), p. 109.

[18] P. R. Rau, O. Dimitrov, and M. Cooper, "A Rose.com by Any Other Name," *Journal of Finance* 56 (2001), pp. 2371–2388.

[19] For an analysis of Japanese stock prices, see K. French and J. M. Poterba, "Were Japanese Stock Prices Too High?" *Journal of Financial Economics* 29 (October 1991), pp. 337–364. For more on dot.com stock prices, see E. Ofek and M. Richardson, "The Valuation and Market Rationality of Internet Stock Prices," *Oxford Review of Economic Policy* 18 (Autumn 2002), pp. 265–287.

11-4 Behavioral Finance

Why might prices depart from fundamental values? Some believe that the answer lies in behavioral psychology. People are not 100% rational 100% of the time. This shows up in investors' attitudes to risk and the way they assess probabilities.

1. *Attitudes toward risk.* Psychologists have observed that, when making risky decisions, people are particularly loath to incur losses. It seems that investors do not focus solely on the current value of their holdings, but look back at whether their investments are showing a profit or a loss. For example, if I sell my holding of IBM stock for $10,000, I may feel on top of the world if the stock only cost me $5,000, but I will be much less happy if it had cost $11,000. This observation is the basis for *prospect theory.*[20] Prospect theory states that (a) the value investors place on a particular outcome is determined by the gains or losses that they have made since the asset was acquired or the holding last reviewed, and (b) investors are particularly averse to the possibility of even a very small loss and need a high return to compensate for it.

   The pain of loss seems also to depend on whether it comes on the heels of earlier losses. Once investors have suffered a loss, they may be even more concerned not to risk a further loss. Conversely, just as gamblers are known to be more willing to make large bets when they are ahead, so investors may be more prepared to run the risk of a stock market dip after they have enjoyed a run of unexpectedly high returns.[21] If they do then suffer a small loss, they at least have the consolation of still being ahead for the year.

   When we discussed portfolio theory in Chapters 7 and 8, we pictured investors as forward-looking only. Past gains or losses were not mentioned. All that mattered was the investor's current wealth and the expectation and risk of future wealth. We did not allow for the possibility that Nicholas would be elated because his investment is in the black, while Nicola with an equal amount of wealth would be despondent because hers is in the red.

2. *Beliefs about probabilities.* Most investors do not have a PhD in probability theory and may make systematic errors in assessing the probability of uncertain events. Psychologists have found that, when judging possible future outcomes, individuals tend to look back at what happened in a few similar situations. As a result, they are led to place too much weight on a small number of recent events. For example, an investor might judge that an investment manager is particularly skilled because he has "beaten the market" for three years in a row, or that three years of rapidly rising prices are a good indication of future profits from investing in the stock market. The investor may not stop to reflect on how little one can learn about expected returns from three years' experience.

   Most individuals are also too *conservative,* that is, too slow to update their beliefs in the face of new evidence. People tend to update their beliefs in the correct direction but the magnitude of the change is less than rationality would require.

   Another systematic bias is *overconfidence.* Most of us believe that we are better-than-average drivers and most investors think they are better-than-average stock pickers. Two speculators who trade with each other cannot both make money, but may be prepared to continue trading because each is confident that the other is the patsy. Overconfidence also shows up in the certainty that people express about their judgments. They consistently overestimate the odds that the future will turn out as they say and underestimate the chances of unlikely events.

---

[20] Prospect theory was first set out in D. Kahneman and A. Tversky, "Prospect Theory: An Analysis of Decision under Risk," *Econometrica* 47 (1979), pp. 263–291.

[21] The effect is described in R. H. Thaler and E. J. Johnson, "Gambling with the House Money and Trying to Break Even: The Effects of Prior Outcomes on Risky Choice," *Management Science* 36 (1990), pp. 643–660. The implications of prospect theory for stock returns are explored in N. Barberis, M. Huang, and T. Santos, "Prospect Theory and Asset Prices," *Quarterly Journal of Economics* 116 (February 2001), pp. 1–53.

You can see how these behavioral characteristics may help to explain the Japanese and dot.com bubbles. As prices rose, they generated increased optimism about the future and stimulated additional demand. The more that investors racked up profits, the more confident they became in their views and the more willing they became to bear the risk that next month might not be so good.

Limits to Arbitrage

It is not difficult to believe that amateur investors may sometimes be caught up in a scatty whirl of irrational exuberance.[22] But there are plenty of hard-headed professional investors managing huge sums of money. Why don't these investors bail out of overpriced stocks and force their prices down to fair value? One reason is that there are *limits to arbitrage*, that is, limits on the ability of the rational investors to exploit market inefficiencies.

Strictly speaking, *arbitrage* means an investment strategy that guarantees superior returns without any risk. In practice, arbitrage is defined more casually as a strategy that exploits market inefficiency and generates superior returns if and when prices return to fundamental values. Such strategies can be very rewarding, but they are rarely risk-free.

In an efficient market, if prices get out of line, then arbitrage forces them back. The arbitrageur buys the underpriced securities (pushing up their prices) and sells the overpriced securities (pushing down their prices). The arbitrageur earns a profit by buying low and selling high and waiting for prices to converge to fundamentals. Thus arbitrage trading is often called *convergence trading*.

In practice arbitrage is harder than it looks. Trading costs can be significant and some trades are difficult to execute. For example, suppose that you identify an overpriced security that is *not* in your existing portfolio. You want to "sell high," but how do you sell a stock that you don't own? It can be done, but you have to *sell short*.

To sell a stock short, you borrow shares from another investor's portfolio, sell them, and then wait hopefully until the price falls and you can buy the stock back for less than you sold it for. If you're wrong and the stock price increases, then sooner or later you will be forced to repurchase the stock at a higher price (therefore at a loss) to return the borrowed shares to the lender. But if you're right and the price does fall, you repurchase, pocket the difference between the sale and repurchase prices, and return the borrowed shares. Sounds easy, once you see how short selling works, but there are costs and fees to be paid, and in some cases you will not be able to find shares to borrow.[23]

The perils of selling short were dramatically illustrated in 2008. Given the gloomy outlook for the automobile industry, a number of hedge funds decided to sell Volkswagen (VW) shares short in the expectation of buying them back at a lower price. Then in a surprise announcement Porsche revealed that it had effectively gained control of 74% of VW's shares. Since a further 20% was held by the state of Lower Saxony, there was not enough stock available for the short sellers to buy back. As they scrambled to cover their positions, the price of VW stock rose in just two days from €209 to a high of €1005, making VW the most highly valued company in the world. Although the stock price drifted rapidly down, those short-sellers who were caught in the *short squeeze* suffered large losses.

The VW example illustrates that the most important limit to arbitrage is the risk that prices will diverge even further before they converge. Thus an arbitrageur has to have the guts and resources to hold on to a position that may get much worse before it gets better.

---

[22] The term "irrational exuberance" was coined by Alan Greenspan, former chairman of the Federal Reserve Board, to describe the dot.com boom. It was also the title of a book by Robert Shiller that examined the boom. See R. Shiller, *Irrational Exuberance* (New York: Broadway Books, 2001).

[23] Investment and brokerage firms identify shares eligible for lending and arrange to make them available to short-sellers. The supply of shares that can be borrowed is limited. You are charged a fee for borrowing the stock, and you are required to put up collateral to protect the lender in case the share price rises and the short-seller is unable to repurchase and return the shares. Putting up collateral is costless if the short-seller gets a market interest rate, but sometimes only lower interest rates are offered.

Take another look at the relative prices of Royal Dutch and Shell T&T in Figure 11.7. Suppose that you were a professional money manager in 1980, when Royal Dutch was about 12% below parity. You decided to buy Royal Dutch, sell Shell T&T short, and wait confidently for prices to converge to parity. It was a long wait. The first time you would have seen any profit on your position was in 1983. In the meantime the mispricing got worse, not better. Royal Dutch fell to more than 30% below parity in mid-1981. Therefore, you had to report a substantial loss on your "arbitrage" strategy in that year. You were fired and took up a new career as a used-car salesman.

The demise in 1998 of Long Term Capital Management (LTCM) provides another example of the problems with convergence trades. LTCM, one of the largest and most profitable hedge funds of the 1990s, believed that interest rates in the different euro zone countries would converge when the euro replaced the countries' previous currencies. LTCM had taken massive positions to profit from this convergence, as well as massive positions designed to exploit other pricing discrepancies. After the Russian government announced a moratorium on some of its debt payments in August 1998, there was great turbulence in the financial markets, and many of the discrepancies that LTCM was betting on suddenly got much larger.[24] LTCM was losing hundreds of millions of dollars daily. The fund's capital was nearly gone when the Federal Reserve Bank of New York arranged for a group of LTCM's creditor banks to take over LTCM's remaining assets and shut down what was left in an orderly fashion.

LTCM's sudden meltdown has not prevented rapid growth in the hedge fund industry in the 2000s. If hedge funds can push back the limits to arbitrage and avoid the kinds of problems that LTCM ran into, markets will be more efficient going forward. But asking for complete efficiency is probably asking too much. Prices can get out of line and stay out if the risks of an arbitrage strategy outweigh the expected returns.

Incentive Problems and the Subprime Crisis

The limits to arbitrage open the door to individual investors with built-in biases and misconceptions that can push prices away from fundamental values. But there can also be incentive problems that get in the way of a rational focus on fundamentals. We illustrate with a brief look at the subprime crisis in the United States.

Few U.S. homeowners foresaw a collapse in the price of their home. After all, the average house price in the U.S. had not fallen since the Great Depression of the 1930s. But in 2005 *The Economist* surveyed the widespread increase in property prices and warned:

> [T]he total value of the residential property in developed economies rose by more than $30 trillion over the past five years to over $70 trillion, an increase equivalent to 100% of those countries' combined GDPs. Not only does this dwarf any previous house-price boom, it is larger than the global stock market bubble in the late 1920s (55% of GDP). In other words it looks like the biggest bubble in history.[25]

Shortly afterward the bubble burst. By March 2009, U.S. house prices had fallen by nearly a third from their peak in 2006.[26]

How could such a boom and crash arise? In part because banks, credit rating agencies, and other financial institutions all had distorted incentives. Purchases of real estate are generally financed with mortgage loans from banks. In most parts of the U.S., borrowers can default on their mortgages with relatively small penalties. If property prices fall, they can simply walk away. But, if prices rise, they make money. Thus borrowers may be willing to take large risks, especially if the fraction of the purchase price financed with their own money is small.

---

[24] The Russian debt moratorium was unexpected and unusual, because the debt had only recently been issued and was denominated in *roubles*. The government preferred to default rather than to print roubles to service the debt.

[25] "In Come the Waves," *The Economist*, June 16, 2005.

[26] Investors who did foresee that the fall in house prices would lead to the subprime debacle were able to earn high profits. For example, John Paulson, the hedge fund manager, earned $3.7 billion in 2007 as a result (*Financial Times*, January 15, 2008, and June 18, 2008).

Why, then, are banks willing to lend money to people who are bound to default if property prices fall significantly? Since the borrowers benefited most of the time, they were willing to pay attractive up-front fees to banks to get mortgage loans. But the banks could pass on the default risk to somebody else by packaging and reselling the mortgages as mortgage-backed securities (MBSs). Many MBS buyers assumed that they were safe investments, because the credit rating agencies said so. As it turned out, the credit ratings were a big mistake. (The rating agencies introduced another agency problem, because issuers paid the agencies to rate the MBS issues, and the agencies consulted with issuers over how MBS issues should be structured.)

The "somebody else" was also the government. Many subprime mortgages were sold to FNMA and FMAC ("Fannie Mae" and "Freddie Mac"). These were private corporations with a special advantage: government credit backup. (The backup was implicit, but quickly became explicit when Fannie and Freddie got into trouble in 2008. The U.S. Treasury had to take them over.) Thus these companies were able to borrow at artificially low rates, channeling money into the mortgage market.

The government was also on the hook because large banks that held subprime MBSs were "too big to fail" in a financial crisis. So the original incentive problem—the temptation of home buyers to take out a large mortgage and hope for higher real estate prices—was never corrected. The government could have cut its exposure by reining in Fannie and Freddie before the crisis but did not do so.

Agency and incentive problems do not arise just in real estate. They are widespread in the financial services industry. In the U.S. and many other countries, people engage financial institutions such as pension funds and mutual funds to invest their money. These institutions are the investors' agents, but the agents' incentives do not always match the investors' interests. Just as with real estate, these agency relationships can lead to mispricing, and potentially bubbles.[27]

11-5   The Six Lessons of Market Efficiency

The efficient-market hypothesis emphasizes that arbitrage will rapidly eliminate any profit opportunities and drive market prices back to fair value. Behavioral-finance specialists may concede that there are no easy profits, but argue that arbitrage is costly and sometimes slow-working, so that deviations from fair value may persist.

Sorting out the puzzles will take time, but we suggest that financial managers should assume, at least as a starting point, that there are no free lunches to be had on Wall Street.

The "no free lunch" principle gives us the following six lessons of market efficiency. After reviewing these lessons, we consider what market *in*efficiency can mean for the financial manager.

Lesson 1: Markets Have No Memory

The weak form of the efficient-market hypothesis states that the sequence of past price changes contains no information about future changes. Economists express the same idea more concisely when they say that the market has no memory. Sometimes financial managers *seem* to act as if this were not the case. For example, after an abnormal market rise, managers prefer to issue equity rather than debt.[28] The idea is to catch the market while it is high. Similarly, they are often reluctant to issue stock after a fall in price. They are inclined

---

[27] See F. Allen, "Do Financial Institutions Matter?" *Journal of Finance* 56 (2001), pp. 1165–1175.

[28] See, for example, P. Asquith and D. W. Mullins, Jr., "Equity Issues and Offering Dilution," *Journal of Financial Economics* 15 (January–February 1986), pp. 16–89; and (for the U.K.) P. R. Marsh, "The Choice between Debt and Equity: An Empirical Study," *Journal of Finance* 37 (March 1982), pp. 121–144.

to wait for a rebound. But we know that the market has no memory and the cycles that financial managers seem to rely on do not exist.[29]

Sometimes a financial manager will have inside information indicating that the firm's stock is overpriced or underpriced. Suppose, for example, that there is some good news that the market does not know but you do. The stock price will rise sharply when the news is revealed. Therefore, if your company sells shares at the current price, it would offer a bargain to new investors at the expense of present stockholders.

Naturally, managers are reluctant to sell new shares when they have favorable inside information. But such information has nothing to do with the history of the stock price. Your firm's stock could be selling at half its price of a year ago, and yet you could have special information suggesting that it is *still* grossly overvalued. Or it may be undervalued at twice last year's price.

Lesson 2: Trust Market Prices

In an efficient market you can trust prices, for they impound all available information about the value of each security. This means that in an efficient market, there is no way for most investors to achieve consistently superior rates of return. To do so, you not only need to know more than *anyone* else; you also need to know more than *everyone* else. This message is important for the financial manager who is responsible for the firm's exchange-rate policy or for its purchases and sales of debt. If you operate on the basis that you are smarter than others at predicting currency changes or interest-rate moves, you will trade a consistent financial policy for an elusive will-o'-the-wisp.

The company's assets may also be directly affected by management's faith in its investment skills. For example, one company may purchase another simply because its management thinks that the stock is undervalued. On approximately half the occasions the stock of the acquired firm will with hindsight turn out to be undervalued. But on the other half it will be overvalued. On average the value will be correct, so the acquiring company is playing a fair game except for the costs of the acquisition.

Lesson 3: Read the Entrails

If the market is efficient, prices impound all available information. Therefore, if we can only learn to read the entrails, security prices can tell us a lot about the future. For example, the market's assessment of the company's securities can provide important information about the firm's prospects. Thus, if the company's bonds are trading at low prices, you can deduce that the firm is probably in trouble.

Here is another example: Suppose that investors are confident that interest rates are set to rise over the next year. In that case, they will prefer to wait before they make long-term loans, and any firm that wants to borrow long-term money today will have to offer the inducement of a higher rate of interest. In other words, the long-term rate of interest will have to be higher than the one-year rate. Differences between the long-term interest rate and the short-term rate tell you something about what investors expect to happen to short-term rates in the future.

The nearby box shows how market prices reveal opinions about issues as diverse as a presidential election, the weather, or the demand for a new product.

---

[29] If high stock prices signal expanded investment opportunities and the need to finance these new investments, we would expect to see firms raise more money *in total* when stock prices are historically high. But this does not explain why firms prefer to raise the extra cash at these times by an issue of equity rather than debt.

Prediction Markets

▶ Stock markets allow investors to bet on their favorite stocks. Prediction markets allow them to bet on almost anything else. These markets reveal the collective guess of traders on issues as diverse as New York City snowfall, an avian flu outbreak, and the occurrence of a major earthquake.

Prediction markets are conducted on the major futures exchanges and on a number of smaller online exchanges such as Intrade (**www.intrade.com**) and the Iowa Electronic Markets (**www.biz.uiowa.edu/iem**). Take the 2008 presidential race as an example. On the Iowa Electronic Markets you could bet that Barack Obama would win by buying one of his contracts. Each Obama contract paid $1 if he won the presidency and nothing if he lost. If you thought that the probability of an Obama victory was 55% (say), you would have been prepared to pay up to $.55 for his contract. Someone who was relatively pessimistic about Obama's chances would have been happy to *sell* you such a contract, for that sale would turn a profit if Obama were to lose. With many participants buying and selling, the market price of a contract revealed the collective wisdom of the crowd.

Take a look at the accompanying figure from the Iowa Electronic Markets. It shows the contract prices for the two contenders for the White House between June and November 2008. Following the Republican convention at the start of September, the price of a McCain contract reached a maximum of $.47. From then on the market suggested a steady fall in the probability of a McCain victory.

Participants in prediction markets are putting their money where their mouth is. So the forecasting accuracy of these markets compares favorably with those of major polls. Some businesses have also formed internal prediction markets to survey the views of their staff. For example, Google operates an internal market to forecast product launch dates, the number of Gmail users, and other strategic questions.*

---

*Google's experience is analyzed in B. Cowgill, J. Wolfers, and E. Zitzewitz, "Using Prediction Markets to Track Information Flows: Evidence from Google," working paper, Dartmouth College, January 2009.

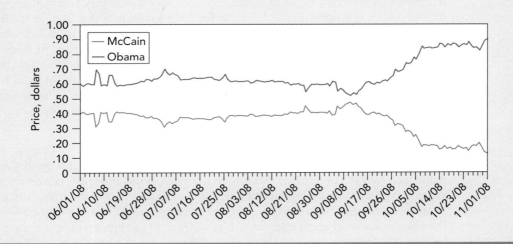

Lesson 4: There Are No Financial Illusions

In an efficient market there are no financial illusions. Investors are unromantically concerned with the firm's cash flows and the portion of those cash flows to which they are entitled. However, there are occasions on which managers seem to assume that investors suffer from financial illusion.

For example, some firms devote considerable ingenuity to the task of manipulating earnings reported to stockholders. This is done by "creative accounting," that is, by choosing accounting methods that stabilize and increase reported earnings. Presumably firms go to this trouble because management believes that stockholders take the figures at face value.[30]

One way that companies can affect their reported earnings is through the way that they cost the goods taken out of inventory. Companies can choose between two methods. Under the FIFO (first-in, first-out) method, the firm deducts the cost of the first goods to have been placed in inventory. Under the LIFO (last-in, first-out) method companies deduct the cost of the latest goods to arrive in the warehouse. When inflation is high, the cost of the goods that were bought first is likely to be lower than the cost of those that were bought last. So earnings calculated under FIFO appear higher than those calculated under LIFO.

Now, if it were just a matter of presentation, there would be no harm in switching from LIFO to FIFO. But the IRS insists that the same method that is used to report to shareholders also be used to calculate the firm's taxes. So the lower apparent earnings from using the LIFO method also bring lower immediate tax payments.

If markets are efficient, investors should welcome a change to LIFO accounting, even though it reduces earnings. Biddle and Lindahl, who studied the matter, concluded that this is exactly what happens, so that the move to LIFO is associated with an abnormal rise in the stock price.[31] It seems that shareholders look behind the figures and focus on the amount of the tax savings.

Lesson 5: The Do-It-Yourself Alternative

In an efficient market investors will not pay others for what they can do equally well themselves. As we shall see, many of the controversies in corporate financing center on how well individuals can replicate corporate financial decisions. For example, companies often justify mergers on the grounds that they produce a more diversified and hence more stable firm. But if investors can hold the stocks of both companies, why should they thank the companies for diversifying? It is much easier and cheaper for them to diversify than it is for the firm.

The financial manager needs to ask the same question when considering whether it is better to issue debt or common stock. If the firm issues debt, it will create financial leverage. As a result, the stock will be more risky and it will offer a higher expected return. But stockholders can obtain financial leverage without the firm's issuing debt; they can borrow on their own accounts. The problem for the financial manager is, therefore, to decide whether the company can issue debt more cheaply than the individual shareholder.

Lesson 6: Seen One Stock, Seen Them All

The elasticity of demand for any article measures the percentage change in the quantity demanded for each percentage addition to the price. If the article has close substitutes, the elasticity will be strongly negative; if not, it will be near zero. For example, coffee, which is a staple commodity, has a demand elasticity of about $-.2$. This means that a 5% increase in the price of coffee changes sales by $-.2 \times .05 = -.01$; in other words, it reduces demand by only 1%. Consumers are likely to regard different *brands* of coffee as much closer substitutes for each other. Therefore, the demand elasticity for a particular brand could be in the region of, say, -2.0. A 5% increase in the price of Maxwell House relative to that of Folgers would in this case reduce demand by 10%.

---

[30] For a discussion of the evidence that investors are not fooled by earnings manipulation, see R. Watts, "Does It Pay to Manipulate EPS?" in J. M. Stern and D. H. Chew, Jr. (eds.), *The Revolution in Corporate Finance* (Oxford: Basil Blackwell, 1992).

[31] G. C. Biddle and F. W. Lindahl, "Stock Price Reactions to LIFO Adoptions: The Association between Excess Returns and LIFO Tax Savings," *Journal of Accounting Research* 20 (Autumn 1982, Part 2), pp. 551–588.

Investors don't buy a stock for its unique qualities; they buy it because it offers the prospect of a fair return for its risk. This means that stocks should be like *very* similar brands of coffee, almost perfect substitutes. Therefore, the demand for a company's stock should be highly elastic. If its prospective return is too low relative to its risk, *nobody* will want to hold that stock. If the reverse is true, *everybody* will scramble to buy.

Suppose that you want to sell a large block of stock. Since demand is elastic, you naturally conclude that you need to cut the offering price only very slightly to sell your stock. Unfortunately, that doesn't necessarily follow. When you come to sell your stock, other investors may suspect that you want to get rid of it because you know something they don't. Therefore, they will revise their assessment of the stock's value downward. Demand is still elastic, but the whole demand curve moves down. Elastic demand does not imply that stock prices never change when a large sale or purchase occurs; it *does* imply that you can sell large blocks of stock at close to the market price *as long as you can convince other investors that you have no private information.*

Here again we encounter an apparent contradiction with practice. State and federal regulatory commissions, which set the prices charged by local telephone companies, electric companies, and other utilities, have sometimes allowed significantly higher earnings to compensate the firm for price "pressure." This pressure is the decline in the firm's stock price that is supposed to occur when new shares are offered to investors. Yet Paul Asquith and David Mullins, who searched for evidence of pressure, found that new stock issues by utilities drove down their stock prices on average by only .9%.[32]

What If Markets Are Not Efficient? Implications for the Financial Manager

Our six lessons depend on efficient markets. What should financial managers do when markets are *not* efficient? The answer depends on the nature of the inefficiency.

Trading Opportunities—Are They Really There for Nonfinancial Corporations? Suppose that the treasurer's staff in your firm notices mispricing in fixed-income or commodities markets, the kind of mispricing that a hedge fund would attempt to exploit in a convergence trade. Should the treasurer authorize the staff to undertake a similar convergence trade? In most cases, the answer should be *no*. First, the corporation faces the same limits to arbitrage that afflict hedge funds and other investors. Second, the corporation probably has no competitive edge in the convergence-trade business.

Procter & Gamble (P&G) supplied a costly example of this point in early 1994, when it lost $102 million in short order. It seems that in 1993 P&G's treasury staff believed that interest rates would be stable and decided to act on this belief to reduce P&G's borrowing costs. They committed P&G to deals with Bankers Trust designed to do just that. Of course there was no free lunch. In exchange for a reduced interest rate, P&G agreed to compensate Bankers Trust if interest rates rose sharply. Rates did increase dramatically in early 1994, and P&G was on the hook.

Then P&G accused Bankers Trust of misrepresenting the transactions—an embarrassing allegation, since P&G was hardly investing as a widow or orphan—and sued Bankers Trust.

We take no stand on the merits of this litigation, which was eventually settled. But think of P&G's competition when it traded in the fixed-income markets. Its competition included the trading desks of all the major investment banks, hedge funds like LTCM, and fixed-income portfolio managers. P&G had no special insights or competitive advantages on the fixed-income playing field. There was no evident reason to expect positive NPV on

---

[32] See P. Asquith and D. W. Mullins, "Equity Issues and Offering Dilution," *Journal of Financial Economics* 15 (January–February 1986), pp. 61–89.

the trades it committed to. Why was it trading at all? P&G would never invest to enter a new consumer market if it had no competitive advantage in that market.

A corporation should not invest unless it can identify a competitive advantage that provides a source of superior profits. Market inefficiencies may offer superior profits from convergence trades, but few corporations have a competitive edge in pursuing these opportunities. As a general rule, nonfinancial corporations gain nothing, on average, by speculation in financial markets. They should not try to imitate hedge funds.[33]

What If Your Company's Shares Are Mispriced?   The financial manager may not have special information about future interest rates, but definitely has special information about the value of his or her own company's shares. The strong form of market efficiency does not always hold, so the financial manager will often have information that outside investors do not have. Or investors may have the same information as management, but be slow in reacting to that information or may be infected with behavioral biases.

Sometimes you hear managers thinking out loud like this:

> Great! Our stock is clearly overpriced. This means we can raise capital cheaply and invest in Project X. Our high stock price gives us a big advantage over our competitors who could not possibly justify investing in Project X.

But that doesn't make sense. If your stock is truly overpriced, you can help your current shareholders by selling additional stock and using the cash to invest in other capital market securities. But you should *never* issue stock to invest in a project that offers a lower rate of return than you could earn elsewhere in the capital market. Such a project would have a negative NPV. You can always do better than investing in a negative-NPV project: Your company can go out and buy common stocks. In an efficient market, such purchases are always *zero* NPV.

What about the reverse? Suppose you know that your stock is *underpriced*. In that case, it certainly would not help your current shareholders to sell additional "cheap" stock to invest in other fairly priced stocks. If your stock is sufficiently underpriced, it may even pay to forgo an opportunity to invest in a positive-NPV project rather than to allow new investors to buy into your firm at a low price. Financial managers who believe that their firm's stock is underpriced may be justifiably reluctant to issue more stock, but they may instead be able to finance their investment program by an issue of debt. In this case the market inefficiency would affect the firm's choice of financing but not its real investment decisions.

What If Your Firm Is Caught in a Bubble?   Once in a lifetime, your company's stock price may be swept up in a bubble like the dot.com boom of the late 1990s. Bubbles can be exhilarating. It's hard not to join in the enthusiasm of the crowds of investors bidding up your firm's stock price.[34] On the other hand, financial management *inside* a bubble poses difficult personal and ethical challenges. Managers don't want to "talk down" a high-flying stock price, especially when bonuses and stock-option payoffs depend on it. The temptation to cover up bad news or manufacture good news can be very strong. But the longer a bubble lasts, the greater the damage when it finally bursts. When it does burst, there will be lawsuits and possibly jail time for managers who have resorted to tricky accounting or misleading public statements in an attempt to sustain the inflated stock price.

---

[33] There are of course some likely exceptions. Hershey and Nestlé are credible traders in cocoa futures markets. The major oil companies probably have special skills and knowledge relevant to energy markets.

[34] See J. C. Stein, "Rational Capital Budgeting in an Irrational World," *Journal of Business* 69 (October 1996), pp. 429–455.

When a firm's stock price is swept upward in a bubble, CEOs and financial managers are tempted to acquire another firm using the stock as currency. One extreme example where this arguably happened is AOL's acquisition of Time Warner at the height of the dot.com bubble in 2000. AOL was a classic dot.com company. Its stock rose from $2.34 at the end of 1995 to $75.88 at the end of 1999. Time Warner's stock price also increased during this period, but only from $18.94 to $72.31. AOL's total market capitalization was a small fraction of Time Warner's in 1995, but overtook Time Warner's in 1998. By the end of 1999 AOL's outstanding shares were worth $173 billion, compared with Time Warner's $95 billion. AOL managed to complete the acquisition before the Internet bubble burst. AOL–Time Warner's stock then plummeted, but not by nearly as much as the stocks of dot.com companies that had not managed to find and acquire safer partners.[35]

---

[35] Pavel Savor and Qi Lu provide evidence that many other firms were able to benefit from stock acquisitions. See "Do Stock Mergers Create Value for Acquirers?" *Journal of Finance* 64 (June 2009), pp. 1061–1097.

SUMMARY

The patron saint of the Bolsa (stock exchange) in Barcelona, Spain, is Nuestra Señora de la Esperanza—Our Lady of Hope. She is the perfect patroness, for we all hope for superior returns when we invest. But competition between investors will tend to produce an efficient market. In such a market, prices will rapidly impound any new information, and it will be difficult to make consistently superior returns. We may indeed hope, but all we can rationally *expect* in an efficient market is a return just sufficient to compensate us for the time value of money and for the risks we bear.

The efficient-market hypothesis comes in three different flavors. The weak form of the hypothesis states that prices efficiently reflect all the information in the past series of stock prices. In this case it is impossible to earn superior returns simply by looking for patterns in stock prices; in other words, price changes are random. The semistrong form of the hypothesis states that prices reflect all published information. That means it is impossible to make consistently superior returns just by reading the newspaper, looking at the company's annual accounts, and so on. The strong form of the hypothesis states that stock prices effectively impound all available information. It tells us that superior information is hard to find because in pursuing it you are in competition with thousands, perhaps millions, of active, intelligent, and greedy investors. The best you can do in this case is to assume that securities are fairly priced and to hope that one day Nuestra Señora will reward your humility.

During the 1960s and 1970s every article on the topic seemed to provide additional evidence that markets are efficient. But then readers became tired of hearing the same message and wanted to read about possible exceptions. During the 1980s and 1990s more and more anomalies and puzzles were uncovered. Bubbles, including the dot.com bubble of the 1990s and the real estate bubble of the 2000s, cast doubt on whether markets were always and everywhere efficient.

Limits to arbitrage can explain why asset prices may get out of line with fundamental values. Behavioral finance, which relies on psychological evidence to interpret investor behavior, is consistent with many of the deviations from market efficiency. Behavioral finance says that investors are averse to even small losses, especially when recent investment returns have been disappointing. Investors may rely too much on a few recent events in predicting the future. They may be overconfident in their predictions and may be sluggish in reacting to new information.

There are plenty of quirks and biases in human behavior, so behavioral finance has plenty of raw material. But if every puzzle or anomaly can be explained by some recipe of quirks, biases, and hindsight, what have we learned? Research in behavioral finance literature is informative and intriguing, but not yet at the stage where a few parsimonious models can account for most of the deviations from market efficiency.

For the corporate treasurer who is concerned with issuing or purchasing securities, the efficient-market theory has obvious implications. In one sense, however, it raises more questions than it answers. The existence of efficient markets does not mean that the financial manager can let financing take care of itself. It provides only a starting point for analysis. It is time to look at the principal financing decisions.

● ● ● ● ●

FURTHER READING

Malkiel's book is an-easy-to-read book on market efficiency. Fama has written two classic review articles on the topic:

B. G. Malkiel, *A Random Walk Down Wall Street,* 8th ed. (New York: W.W. Norton, 2004).

E. F. Fama, "Efficient Capital Markets: A Review of Theory and Empirical Work," *Journal of Finance* 25 (May 1970), pp. 383–417.

E. F. Fama, "Efficient Capital Markets: II," *Journal of Finance* 46 (December 1991), pp. 1575–1617.

There are several useful surveys of behavioral finance:

N. Barberis and R. H. Thaler, "A Survey of Behavioral Finance," in G. M. Constantinides, M. Harris, and R. M. Stulz (eds.), *Handbook of the Economics of Finance* (Amsterdam: Elsevier Science, 2003).

M. Baker, R. S. Ruback, and J. Wurgler, "Behavioral Corporate Finance," in B. E. Eckbo (ed.), *The Handbook of Empirical Corporate Finance* (Amsterdam: Elsevier/North-Holland, 2007), Chapter 4.

R. J. Shiller, "Human Behavior and the Efficiency of the Financial System," in J. B. Taylor and M. Woodford (eds.), *Handbook of Macroeconomics* (Amsterdam: North-Holland, 1999).

A. Shleifer, *Inefficient Markets: An Introduction to Behavioral Finance* (Oxford: Oxford University Press, 2000).

R. H. Thaler (ed.), *Advances in Behavioral Finance* (New York: Russell Sage Foundation, 1993).

Some conflicting views on market efficiency are provided by:

G. W. Schwert, "Anomalies and Market Efficiency," in G. M. Constantinides, M. Harris, and R. M. Stulz (eds.), *Handbook of the Economics of Finance* (Amsterdam: Elsevier Science, 2003).

M. Rubinstein, "Rational Markets: Yes or No? The Affirmative Case?" *Financial Analysts Journal* 57 (May–June 2001), pp. 15–29.

B. G. Malkiel, "The Efficient Market Hypothesis and Its Critics," *Journal of Economic Perspectives* 17 (Winter 2003), pp. 59–82.

R. J. Shiller, "From Efficient Markets Theory to Behavioral Finance," *Journal of Economic Perspectives* 17 (Winter 2003), pp. 83–104.

E. F. Fama and K. R. French, "Dissecting Anomalies," *Journal of Finance* 63 (August 2008), pp. 1653–1678.

Bubbles are discussed in:

M. Brunnermeier, *Asset Pricing under Asymmetric Information: Bubbles, Crashes, Technical Analysis, and Herding* (Oxford: Oxford University Press, 2001).

R. J. Shiller, *Irrational Exuberance*, 2nd ed. (Princeton, NJ: Princeton University Press, 2005).

BASIC

1. Which (if any) of these statements are true? Stock prices appear to behave as though successive values (a) are random numbers, (b) follow regular cycles, (c) differ by a random number.

2. Supply the missing words:

   "There are three forms of the efficient-market hypothesis. Tests of randomness in stock returns provide evidence for the _____ form of the hypothesis. Tests of stock price reaction to well-publicized news provide evidence for the _____ form, and tests of the performance of professionally managed funds provide evidence for the _____ form. Market efficiency results from competition between investors. Many investors search for new information about the company's business that would help them to value the stock more accurately. Such research helps to ensure that prices reflect all available information; in other words, it helps to keep the market efficient in the _____ form. Other investors study past stock prices for recurrent patterns that would allow them to make superior profits. Such research helps to ensure that prices reflect all the information contained in past stock prices; in other words, it helps to keep the market efficient in the _____ form."

3. True or false? The efficient-market hypothesis assumes that
   a. There are no taxes.
   b. There is perfect foresight.
   c. Successive price changes are independent.
   d. Investors are irrational.
   e. There are no transaction costs.
   f. Forecasts are unbiased.

4. True or false?
   a. Financing decisions are less easily reversed than investment decisions.
   b. Tests have shown that there is almost perfect negative correlation between successive price changes.
   c. The semistrong form of the efficient-market hypothesis states that prices reflect all publicly available information.
   d. In efficient markets the expected return on each stock is the same.

5. Analysis of 60 monthly rates of return on United Futon common stock indicates a beta of 1.45 and an alpha of −.2% per month. A month later, the market is up by 5%, and United Futon is up by 6%. What is Futon's abnormal rate of return?

6. True or false?
   a. Analysis by security analysts and investors helps keep markets efficient.
   b. Psychologists have found that, once people have suffered a loss, they are more relaxed about the possibility of incurring further losses.
   c. Psychologists have observed that people tend to put too much weight on recent events when forecasting.
   d. If the efficient-market hypothesis is correct, managers will not be able to increase stock prices by creative accounting that boosts reported earnings.

7. Geothermal Corporation has just received good news: Its earnings increased by 20% from last year's value. Most investors are anticipating an increase of 25%. Will Geothermal's stock price increase or decrease when the announcement is made?

8. Here again are the six lessons of market efficiency. For each lesson give an example showing the lesson's relevance to financial managers.

   a. Markets have no memory.

   b. Trust market prices.

   c. Read the entrails.

   d. There are no financial illusions.

   e. The do-it-yourself alternative.

   f. Seen one stock, seen them all.

9. Give two or three examples of research results or events that raise doubts about market efficiency. Briefly explain why.

INTERMEDIATE

10. How would you respond to the following comments?

    a. "Efficient market, my eye! I know lots of investors who do crazy things."

    b. "Efficient market? Balderdash! I know at least a dozen people who have made a bundle in the stock market."

    c. "The trouble with the efficient-market theory is that it ignores investors' psychology."

    d. "Despite all the limitations, the best guide to a company's value is its written-down book value. It is much more stable than market value, which depends on temporary fashions."

11. Respond to the following comments:

    a. "The random-walk theory, with its implication that investing in stocks is like playing roulette, is a powerful indictment of our capital markets."

    b. "If everyone believes you can make money by charting stock prices, then price changes won't be random."

    c. "The random-walk theory implies that events are random, but many events are not random. If it rains today, there's a fair bet that it will rain again tomorrow."

12. Which of the following observations *appear* to indicate market inefficiency? Explain whether the observation appears to contradict the weak, semistrong, or strong form of the efficient-market hypothesis.

    a. Tax-exempt municipal bonds offer lower pretax returns than taxable government bonds.

    b. Managers make superior returns on their purchases of their company's stock.

    c. There is a positive relationship between the return on the market in one quarter and the change in aggregate profits in the next quarter.

    d. There is disputed evidence that stocks that have appreciated unusually in the recent past continue to do so in the future.

    e. The stock of an acquired firm tends to appreciate in the period before the merger announcement.

    f. Stocks of companies with unexpectedly high earnings appear to offer high returns for several months after the earnings announcement.

    g. Very risky stocks on average give higher returns than safe stocks.

13. Here are alphas and betas for Intel and Conagra for the 60 months ending April 2009. Alpha is expressed as a percent per month.

	Alpha	Beta
Intel	−.57	1.08
Conagra	−.46	.65

Explain how these estimates would be used to calculate an abnormal return.

14. "If the efficient-market hypothesis is true, the pension fund manager might as well select a portfolio with a pin." Explain why this is not so.

15. Two financial managers, Alpha and Beta, are contemplating a chart showing the actual performance of the Standard and Poor's Composite Index over a five-year period. Each manager's company needs to issue new shares of common stock sometime in the next year.

    Alpha: My company's going to issue right away. The stock market cycle has obviously topped out, and the next move is almost surely down. Better to issue now and get a decent price for the shares.

    Beta: You're too nervous; we're waiting. It's true that the market's been going nowhere for the past year or so, but the figure clearly shows a basic upward trend. The market's on the way up to a new plateau.

    What would you say to Alpha and Beta?

16. What does the efficient-market hypothesis have to say about these two statements?

    a. "I notice that short-term interest rates are about 1% below long-term rates. We should borrow short-term."

    b. "I notice that interest rates in Japan are lower than rates in the United States. We would do better to borrow Japanese yen rather than U.S. dollars."

17. Fama and French show that average stock returns on firms with small market capitalizations have been significantly higher than average returns for "large-cap" firms. What are the possible explanations for this result? Does the result disprove market efficiency? Explain briefly.

18. Column (A) in Table 11.1 shows the monthly return on the British FTSE 100 index from May 2007 through February 2009. Columns (B) and (C) show returns on the stocks of two firms—Executive Cheese and Paddington Beer. Both firms announced their earnings in February 2009. Calculate the average abnormal return of the two stocks during the month of the earnings announcement.

Visit us at
www.mhhe.com/bma

19. On May 15, 1997, the government of Kuwait offered to sell 170 million BP shares, worth about $2 billion. Goldman Sachs was contacted after the stock market closed in London and given one hour to decide whether to bid on the stock. They decided to offer 710.5 pence ($11.59) per share, and Kuwait accepted. Then Goldman Sachs went looking for buyers. They lined up 500 institutional and individual investors worldwide, and resold all the shares at 716 pence ($11.70). The resale was complete before the London Stock Exchange opened the next morning. Goldman Sachs made $15 million overnight.[36]

    What does this deal say about market efficiency? Discuss.

20. Explain how incentive and agency problems can contribute to mispricing of securities or to bubbles. Give examples.

21. Many commentators have blamed the subprime crisis on "irrational exuberance." What is your view? Explain briefly.

CHALLENGE

22. "The strong-form of the efficient-market hypothesis is nonsense. Look at mutual fund X; it has had superior performance for each of the last 10 years." Does the speaker have a point? Suppose that there is a 50% probability that X will obtain superior performance in any year simply by chance.

    a. If X is the only fund, calculate the probability that it will have achieved superior performance for each of the past 10 years.

    b. Now recognize that there are over 10,000 mutual funds in the United States. What is the probability that by chance there is at least 1 out of 10,000 funds that obtained 10 successive years of superior performance?

---

[36] "Goldman Sachs Earns a Quick $15 Million Sale of BP Shares," *The Wall Street Journal*, May 16, 1997, p. A4.

▶ **TABLE 11.1**

See Problem 18. Rates
of return in percent per
month.

Month	(A) Market Return	(B) Executive Cheese Return	(C) Paddington Beer Return
May 07	2.7	−3	1.6
Jun	−0.2	2.3	−0.8
Jul	−3.8	−5.1	0.3
Aug	−0.9	−0.7	−1.6
Sep	2.6	3.1	2.8
Oct	3.9	13	2.1
Nov	−4.3	−2.1	−6
Dec	0.4	6.2	−1.7
Jan 08	−8.9	−4	−5
Feb	0.1	0.4	−0.4
Mar	−3.1	−2.1	−2
Apr	6.8	4.6	3.2
May	−0.6	−0.3	0.4
Jun	−7.1	−12.7	−7.3
Jul	−3.8	1.1	−4.1
Aug	4.2	7.2	2.3
Sep	−13.0	−18.1	−8.7
Oct	−10.7	−6.2	−12
Nov	−2.0	0.5	−4.2
Dec	3.4	4.7	2.7
Jan 09	−6.4	−8.1	−0.4
Feb	−7.7	−2.1	−9.4

23. Some extreme bubbles are obvious with hindsight, *after* they burst. But how would you
define a bubble? There are many examples of good news and rising stock prices, followed
by bad news and falling stock prices. Can you set out rules and procedures to distinguish
bubbles from the normal ups and downs of stock prices?

● ● ● ● ●

**REAL-TIME
DATA ANALYSIS**

STANDARD
&POOR'S

Use either finance.yahoo.com **or the Market Insight database (**www.mhhe.com/
edumarketinsight**) to download daily prices for five U.S. stocks for a recent five-year period.**

For each stock, construct a scatter diagram of successive returns as in Figure 11.2. Calculate the
correlation among the returns on successive days. Do you find any consistent patterns?

Payout Policy

▶ **Corporations can return** cash to their shareholders by paying a dividend or by repurchasing shares. In this chapter we explain how financial managers decide on the amount and form of payout, and we discuss the controversial question of how payout policy affects shareholder value.

Suppose you own stock in a corporation that has $1 per share of unneeded cash. It can hold on to the cash or it can pay an extra cash dividend of $1 per share. Does the decision matter? Your first instinct should be to say no. The dividend puts $1 per share in your pocket but, at the same time, each share should be worth $1 less. Your wealth should be unaffected.

But corporations usually hold cash for a reason. What if that $1 per share is not redundant money? Suppose that it was set aside for capital investment. Then paying the extra dividend could mean cancelation of investment projects. The payout decision could also be an investment decision.

Suppose the firm pays out $1 per share, but replaces the cash by borrowing. Then the payout decision would also be a borrowing decision.

To fully understand payout policy, we must separate payout decisions from investment and borrowing decisions. If we hold investment and borrowing fixed, changes in cash dividends must be offset by issues or retirements of shares. For example, a company might pay generous cash dividends, knowing that it will have to schedule stock issues to raise cash for investment. Another company might pay no dividends, but instead use cash to repurchase shares.

Therefore we will take care to analyze the trade-off between higher or lower cash dividends and the issue or repurchase of common stock. The trade-off is more interesting than you might at first think, for at least three reasons. First, changes in dividends convey information about the firm's profitability to investors. Second, dividends are taxed at higher rates than capital gains. Third, investors worry that cash-cow corporations will run out of positive-NPV investments and waste cash on perks or poor projects. Generous cash payouts are one way of relieving such worries.

We start the chapter with facts about payout and a description of how dividends and repurchases happen.

●●●●●●

12-1 Facts about Payout

Corporations can pay out cash to their shareholders in two ways. They can pay a dividend or they can buy back some of the outstanding shares. In recent years dividend payments and stock repurchases have amounted to a high proportion of earnings.

Although dividends remain the principal channel for returning cash to shareholders, many corporations pay no dividends at all. In the U.S., the percentage of dividend-paying

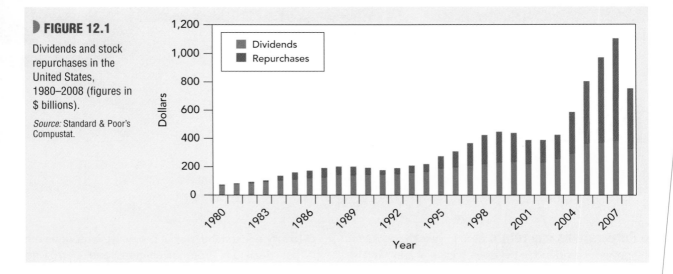

▶ **FIGURE 12.1**

Dividends and stock repurchases in the United States, 1980–2008 (figures in $ billions).

Source: Standard & Poor's Compustat.

firms fell from 64% in 1980 to 52% in 2007.[1] Some of the non–dividend payers did pay a dividend in the past but then fell on hard times and were forced to conserve cash. Further, a large number of new growth companies have gone public in recent years and do not pay a dividend. In the U.S. these include such household names as Sun Microsystems, Cisco, Amazon, and Google, as well as many small, rapidly growing firms that have not yet reached full profitability.

Figure 12.1 shows that before 1983 stock repurchases were fairly rare, but since then they have become increasingly common. In 2007, a record year for stock repurchases, 28 U.S. companies each bought back more than $5 billion of stock. Exxon Mobil bought back $31 billion, Microsoft bought back $28 billion, IBM $19 billion, and GE $14 billion.

12-2 How Firms Pay Dividends and Repurchase Stock

Before we look at the choice between dividends and stock repurchases, we need to review how these payments to shareholders take place.

A company's dividend is set by the board of directors. The announcement of the dividend states that the payment will be made to all stockholders who are registered on a particular *record date*. Then a week or so later dividend checks are mailed to stockholders. Stocks are normally bought or sold *with dividend* (or *cum dividend*) until two business days before the record date, and then they trade *ex dividend*. If you buy stock on the ex-dividend date, your purchase will not be entered on the company's books before the record date and you will not be entitled to the dividend.

Figure 12.2 illustrates this sequence of events. On April 15, 2009, Exxon Mobil declared a quarterly dividend of $.42 per share. The dividend was paid on June 10 to all shareholders who were registered on the company's books on May 13. Two days earlier on May 11 the shares began to trade ex dividend. Any investor who bought shares on that date would not have had his purchase registered by the record date and would not have been entitled to the dividend.

---

[1] The proportion of dividend payers among U.S. industrial companies is even lower. See E. Fama and K. French, "Disappearing Dividends: Changing Firm Characteristics or Lower Propensity to Pay?" *Journal of Financial Economics* 60 (2001), pp. 3–43. In Europe the decline in the proportion of dividend payers has been particularly marked in Germany. See D. J. Denis and I. Osobov, "Why Do Firms Pay Dividends? International Evidence on the Determinants of Dividend Policy," *Journal of Financial Economics* 89 (July 2008), pp. 62–82.

April 15, 2009	May 11, 2009	May 13, 2009	June 10, 2009
Exxon Mobil declares regular quarterly dividend of $.42 per share.	**Shares start to trade ex dividend.**	**Dividend will be paid to shareholders registered on this date.**	**Dividend checks are mailed to shareholders.**
Declaration date	Ex-dividend date	Record date	Payment date

▶ **FIGURE 12.2**

An illustration of how dividends are paid.

The company is not free to declare whatever dividend it chooses. In some countries, such as Brazil and Chile, companies are obliged by law to pay out a *minimum* proportion of their earnings. Conversely, some restrictions may be imposed by lenders, who are concerned that excessive dividend payments would not leave enough in the kitty to repay their loans. In the U.S., state law also helps to protect the firm's creditors against excessive dividend payments. For example, companies are not allowed to pay a dividend out of legal capital, which is generally defined as the par value of outstanding shares.[2]

Most U.S. companies pay a *regular* cash dividend each quarter, but occasionally this is supplemented by a one-off *extra* or *special dividend*. Many companies offer shareholders automatic dividend reinvestment plans (DRIPs). Often the new shares are issued at a 5% discount from the market price. Sometimes 10% or more of total dividends will be reinvested under such plans.[3]

Dividends are not always in the form of cash. Frequently companies also declare *stock dividends*. For example, if the firm pays a stock dividend of 5%, it sends each shareholder 5 extra shares for every 100 shares currently owned. A stock dividend is essentially the same as a stock split. Both increase the number of shares but do not affect the company's assets, profits, or total value. So both reduce value *per share*.[4] In this chapter we focus on *cash* dividends.

How Firms Repurchase Stock

Instead of paying a dividend to its stockholders, the firm can use the cash to repurchase stock. The reacquired shares are kept in the company's treasury and may be resold if the company needs money. There are four main ways to repurchase stock. By far the most common method is for the firm to announce that it plans to buy its stock in the open market, just like any other investor.[5] However, companies sometimes use a tender offer where they offer to buy back a stated number of shares at a fixed price, which is typically set at about 20% above the current market level. Shareholders can then choose whether to accept this offer. A third procedure is to employ a *Dutch auction*. In this case the firm states a series of

---

[2] Where there is no par value, legal capital is defined as part or all of the receipts from the issue of shares. Companies with wasting assets, such as mining companies, are sometimes permitted to pay out legal capital.

[3] Sometimes companies not only allow shareholders to reinvest dividends but also allow them to buy additional shares at a discount. For an amusing and true rags-to-riches story, see M. S. Scholes and M. A. Wolfson, "Decentralized Investment Banking: The Case of Dividend-Reinvestment and Stock-Purchase Plans," *Journal of Financial Economics* 24 (September 1989), pp. 7–36.

[4] The distinction between a stock dividend and a stock split is technical. A stock dividend is shown in the accounts as a transfer from retained earnings to equity capital. A split is shown as a reduction in the par value of each share.

[5] The U.S. Securities and Exchange Commission's rule 10b-18 protects repurchasing firms from accusations of share-price manipulation. Adoption of this rule was one reason why repurchases have grown so rapidly. Open-market repurchases are subject to several restrictions, however. For example, repurchases cannot exceed a small fraction of daily trading volume.

prices at which it is prepared to repurchase stock. Shareholders submit offers declaring how many shares they wish to sell at each price and the company calculates the lowest price at which it can buy the desired number of shares. Finally, repurchase sometimes takes place by direct negotiation with a major shareholder.

12-3 How Do Companies Decide on Payouts?

In 2004 a survey of senior executives asked about their firms' dividend policies.[6] Figure 12.3 paraphrases the executives' responses. Three features stand out:

1. Managers are reluctant to make dividend changes that may have to be reversed. They are particularly worried about having to rescind a dividend increase and, if necessary, would choose to raise new funds to maintain the payout.

2. To avoid the risk of a reduction in payout, managers "smooth" dividends. Consequently, dividend changes follow shifts in long-run sustainable earnings. Transitory earnings changes are unlikely to affect dividend payouts.

3. Managers focus more on dividend changes than on absolute levels. Thus paying a $2.00 dividend is an important financial decision if last year's dividend was $1.00, but no big deal if last year's dividend was $2.00.

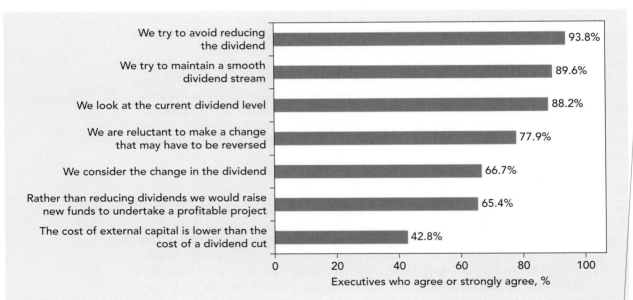

▶ **FIGURE 12.3**

A 2004 survey of financial executives suggested that their firms were reluctant to cut the dividend and tried to maintain a smooth series of payments.

Source: A. Brav, J. R. Graham, C. R. Harvey, and R. Michaely, "Payout Policy in the 21st Century," *Journal of Financial Economics* 77 (September 2005), pp. 483–527. © 2005 Elsevier Science, used with permission.

[6] See A. Brav, J. R. Graham, C. R. Harvey, and R. Michaely, "Payout Policy in the 21st Century," *Journal of Financial Economics* 77 (September 2005), pp. 483–527. This paper revisits an earlier classic series of interviews on dividend policy described in J. Lintner, "Distribution of Incomes of Corporations among Dividends, Retained Earnings, and Taxes," *American Economic Review* 46 (May 1956), pp. 97–113.

While stock repurchases are like bumper dividends, they do not typically *substitute* for dividends. Over two-thirds of the companies that paid a dividend in 2007 also repurchased stock. Firms are likely to buy back stock when they have accumulated a large amount of unwanted cash or wish to change their capital structure by replacing equity with debt.

Unlike a stock repurchase, dividends are not regarded as an appropriate way to pay out transitory earnings. Therefore, many firms that repurchase stock would not contemplate using the cash to raise the dividend and so incur a commitment to maintain the payout.[7]

Given these differences in the way that dividends and repurchases are used, it is not surprising to find that repurchases are much more volatile than dividends. Repurchases generally mushroom during boom times as firms accumulate excess cash but wither in recessions. You can see this from Figure 12.1, which shows that repurchases fell sharply during the early 1990s and then again between 2000 and 2002. In 2008, as the depth of the financial crisis became clear, repurchases were again cut back sharply. (Even Exxon Mobil, the all-time repurchase champion, announced in May 2009 that it was cutting back repurchases to $5 billion per quarter, down from $8 billion per quarter a year earlier.) Dividends were also reduced, but not by nearly as much.

Until recently many countries banned or severely restricted the use of stock repurchases. As a result, firms that had amassed large amounts of cash were tempted to invest it at very low rates of return rather than hand it back to shareholders, who could have reinvested it in firms that were short of cash. But many of these limitations have now been removed. For example, Japan permitted repurchases in 1995 and Sweden in 2000, while Germany relaxed its restrictions in 1998.[8] Many multinational giants now repurchase huge amounts of stock. For example, in 2007 the Spanish bank BBVA, BP, Royal Dutch Shell, and Glaxo Smith Kline all spent huge sums on buying back their stock.

12-4   The Information in Dividends and Stock Repurchases

In some countries you cannot rely on the information that companies provide. Passion for secrecy and a tendency to construct multilayered corporate organizations produce asset and earnings figures that are next to meaningless. Some people say that, thanks to creative accounting, the situation is little better for some companies in the U.S.

How does an investor in such a world separate marginally profitable firms from the real money makers? One clue is dividends. Investors can't read managers' minds, but they can learn from managers' actions. They know that a firm that reports good earnings and pays a generous dividend is putting its money where its mouth is. We can understand, therefore, why investors would value the *information content of dividends* and would refuse to believe a firm's reported earnings unless they were backed up by an appropriate dividend policy.

Of course, firms can cheat in the short run by overstating earnings and scraping up cash to pay a generous dividend. But it is hard to cheat in the long run, for a firm that is not making enough money will not have enough cash to pay out. If a firm chooses a high dividend payout without the cash flow to back it up, that firm will ultimately have to reduce its investment plans or turn to investors for additional debt or equity financing. All of these consequences are costly. Therefore, most managers don't increase dividends until they are confident that sufficient cash will flow in to pay them.

---

[7] See, for example, R. Dittmar and A. Dittmar, "Stock Repurchase Waves: An Examination of the Trends in Aggregate Corporate Payout Policy," working paper, University of Michigan at Ann Arbor, February 2004.

[8] For a survey of repurchase practices in different countries, see International Organization of Securities Commissions (IOSCO), "Report on Stock Repurchase Programs," February 2004, www.iosco.org.

Do dividend changes convey information about future as well as current profitability? The evidence is mixed. Several researchers find that dividend increases do not predict increased earnings growth. However, Healy and Palepu, who focus on companies that paid a dividend for the first time, find that on average earnings jumped 43% in the year a dividend was paid. If managers thought that this was a temporary windfall, they might have been cautious about committing themselves to paying out cash. But it looks as if these managers had good reason to be confident about prospects, for earnings continued to rise in the following years.[9]

Investors certainly appear to take comfort from an increase in dividends. When the increase is announced, analysts generally up their forecast of the current year's earnings.[10] It is no surprise, therefore, to find that a higher dividend prompts a rise in the stock price, whereas a dividend cut results in a fall in price. For example, in the case of the dividend initiations studied by Healy and Palepu, the dividend announcement resulted in a 4% stock-price increase on average.[11]

Notice that investors do not get excited about the *level* of a company's dividend; they worry about the *change*, which they view as an important indicator of the sustainability of earnings.

It seems that in some other countries investors are less preoccupied with dividend changes. For example, in Japan there is a much closer relationship between corporations and major stockholders, and therefore information may be more easily shared with investors. Consequently, Japanese corporations are more prone to cut their dividends when there is a drop in earnings, but investors do not mark the stocks down as sharply as in the U.S.[12]

Do not assume that all dividend cuts are bad news, however. The nearby box explains how investors endorsed a drastic dividend cut announced in 2009 by J.P. Morgan.

The Information Content of Share Repurchases

Share repurchases, like dividends, are a way to hand cash back to shareholders. But unlike dividends, share repurchases are frequently a one-off event. So a company that announces a repurchase program is not making a long-term commitment to distribute more cash. The information in the announcement of a share repurchase program is therefore different from the information in a dividend payment.

Corporations repurchase shares when they have accumulated excess cash or when they want to substitute debt for equity. Shareholders applaud payout of excess cash when they worry that the firm would otherwise fritter the money away on perks or unprofitable empire building. Shareholders also know that firms with large quantities of debt to service are less likely to squander cash. A study by Comment and Jarrell, who looked at the announcements of open-market repurchase programs, found that on average they resulted in an abnormal price rise of 2%.[13]

---

[9] P. Healy and K. Palepu, "Earnings Information Conveyed by Dividend Initiations and Omissions," *Journal of Financial Economics* 21 (1988), pp. 149–175. For an example of a study that finds no information in dividend changes, see G. Grullon, R. Michaely, and B. Swaminathan, "Are Dividend Changes a Sign of Firm Maturity?" *Journal of Business* 75 (July 2002), pp. 387–424.

[10] A. R. Ofer and D. R. Siegel, "Corporate Financial Policy, Information, and Market Expectations: An Empirical Investigation of Dividends," *Journal of Finance* 42 (September 1987), pp. 889–911.

[11] The 4% average return was adjusted for market returns. Healy and Palepu also looked at companies that *stopped* paying a dividend. In this case the stock price on average declined by 9.5% on the announcement and earnings fell over the next four quarters.

[12] The dividend policies of Japanese *keiretsus* are analyzed in K. L. Dewenter and V. A. Warther, "Dividends, Asymmetric Information, and Agency Conflicts: Evidence from a Comparison of the Dividend Policies of Japanese and U.S. Firms," *Journal of Finance* 53 (June 1998), pp. 879–904.

[13] R. Comment and G. Jarrell, "The Relative Signalling Power of Dutch-Auction and Fixed Price Self-Tender Offers and Open-Market Share Repurchases," *Journal of Finance* 46 (September 1991), pp. 1243–1271. There is also evidence of continuing superior performance during the years following a repurchase announcement. See D. Ikenberry, J. Lakonishok, and T. Vermaelen, "Market Underreaction to Open Market Share Repurchases," *Journal of Financial Economics* 39 (October 1995), pp. 181–208.

Good News: J.P. Morgan Cuts Its Dividend to a Nickel

▶ On February 23, 2009, J.P. Morgan cut its quarterly dividend from 38¢ to a nickel (5¢) per share. The cut was a surprise to investors, but the bank's share price *increased* by about 5%.

Usually dividend cuts or omissions are bad news, because investors infer trouble. Investors take the cut as a signal of a cash or earnings shortfall—and they are usually right. Managers know that cuts will be treated as bad news, so they usually put off cuts until enough bad news accumulates to force them to act. For example, General Motors, which lost $39 billion in 2007 and $31 billion in 2008, continued paying quarterly dividends of 25¢ per share until June 2008, when it cut its dividend to zero.

J.P. Morgan Chase, however, acted from a position of relative strength. It remained profitable when other large U.S. banks were announcing horrific losses. Its CEO James Dimon explained that the dividend cut would save $5 billion a year and prepare it for a worst-case recession. It would also "put the bank in a position to pay back more quickly the $25 billion that it took from the government under the Troubled Asset Relief Program." J.P. Morgan has said it was encouraged to take the money and didn't need it.

Thus investors interpreted the dividend cut as a signal of confidence, not of distress.

Source: R. Sidel and M. Rieker, "J.P. Morgan Makes 87% Cut in its Dividend to a Nickel," *The New York Times*, February 24, 2009, pp. C1, C3.

Stock repurchases may also be used to signal a manager's confidence in the future. Suppose that you, the manager, believe that your stock is substantially undervalued. You announce that the company is prepared to buy back a fifth of its stock at a price that is 20% above the current market price. But (you say) you are certainly not going to sell any of your own stock at that price. Investors jump to the obvious conclusion—you must believe that the stock is a good value even at 20% above the current price.

When companies offer to repurchase their stock at a premium, senior management and directors usually commit to hold on to their stock.[14] So it is not surprising that researchers have found that announcements of offers to buy back shares above the market price have prompted a larger rise in the stock price, averaging about 11%.[15]

12-5 The Payout Controversy

We have seen that a change in payout may provide information about management's confidence in the future and so affect the stock price. But eventually this change in the stock price would happen anyway as information seeps out through other channels. But does payout policy change the value of the firm's common stock, rather than just sending a signal about value?

One endearing feature of economics is its ability to accommodate not just two, but three, opposing points of view. And so it is with payout policy. On the right, a conservative

---

[14] Not only do managers hold on to their stock; on average they also add to their holdings *before* the announcement of a repurchase. See D. S. Lee, W. Mikkelson, and M. M. Partch, "Managers' Trading around Stock Repurchases," *Journal of Finance* 47 (December 1992), pp. 1947–1961.

[15] See R. Comment and G. Jarrell, see footnote 13.

group argues that investors prefer higher dividend payouts. On the left, another group argues that higher dividends decrease value, because dividends are taxed more heavily than capital gains. And in the center, there is a middle-of-the-road party that claims that payout policy makes no difference.

Dividend Policy Is Irrelevant in Perfect Capital Markets

The middle-of-the-road party was founded in 1961 by Miller and Modigliani (always referred to as "MM"), when they published a proof that dividend policy is irrelevant in a world without taxes, transaction costs, or other market imperfections.[16] MM argued as follows. Suppose your firm has settled on its investment program. You have a plan to finance the investments with cash on hand, additional borrowing, and reinvestment of future earnings. Any surplus cash is to be paid out as dividends.

Now think what happens if you want to increase the total payout by upping the dividend without also changing the investment and financing policy. The extra money must come from somewhere. If the firm fixes its borrowing, the only way it can finance the extra dividend is to print some more shares and sell them. The new stockholders are going to part with their money only if you can offer them shares that are worth as much as they cost. But how can the firm sell more shares when its assets, earnings, investment opportunities, and, therefore, market value are all unchanged? The answer is that there must be a *transfer of value* from the old to the new stockholders. The new ones get the newly printed shares, each one worth less than before the dividend change was announced, and the old ones suffer a capital loss on their shares. The capital loss borne by the old shareholders just offsets the extra cash dividend they receive.

Figure 12.4 shows how this transfer of value occurs. Our hypothetical company pays out a third of its total value as a dividend and it raises the money to do so by selling new shares.

► FIGURE 12.4

This firm pays out a third of its worth as a dividend and raises the money by selling new shares. The transfer of value to the new stockholders is equal to the dividend payment. The total value of the firm is unaffected.

---

[16] M. H. Miller and F. Modigliani, "Dividend Policy, Growth and the Valuation of Shares," *Journal of Business* 34 (October 1961), pp. 411–433. MM's arguments were anticipated in 1938 in J. B. Williams, *The Theory of Investment Value* (Cambridge, MA: Harvard University Press, 1938). Also, a proof similar to MM's was developed in J. Lintner, "Dividends, Earnings, Leverage and Stock Prices and the Supply of Capital to Corporations," *Review of Economics and Statistics* 44 (August 1962), pp. 243–269.

The capital loss suffered by the old stockholders is represented by the reduction in the size of the red boxes. But that capital loss is exactly offset by the fact that the new money raised (the black boxes) is paid over to them as dividends.

Does it make any difference to the old stockholders that they receive an extra dividend payment plus an offsetting capital loss? It might if that were the only way they could get their hands on cash. But as long as there are efficient capital markets, they can raise the cash by selling shares. Thus the old shareholders can cash in either by persuading the management to pay a higher dividend or by selling some of their shares. In either case there will be a transfer of value from old to new shareholders. The only difference is that in the former case this transfer is caused by a dilution in the value of each of the firm's shares, and in the latter case it is caused by a reduction in the number of shares held by the old shareholders. The two alternatives are compared in Figure 12.5.

Because investors do not need dividends to get their hands on cash, they will not pay higher prices for the shares of firms with high payouts. Therefore firms ought not to worry about dividend policy. They can let dividends fluctuate as a by-product of their investment and financing decisions.

Dividend Irrelevance—An Illustration

Consider the case of Rational Demiconductor, which at this moment has the following balance sheet:

Rational Demiconductor's Balance Sheet (Market Values)

Cash ($1,000 held for investment)	$ 1,000	$ 0	Debt
Fixed assets	9,000	10,000 + NPV	Equity
Investment opportunity ($1,000 investment required)	NPV		
Total asset value	$10,000 + NPV	$10,000 + NPV	Value of firm

Rational Demiconductor has $1,000 cash earmarked for a project requiring a $1,000 investment. We do not know how attractive the project is, and so we enter it at NPV; after the project is undertaken it will be worth $1,000 + NPV. Note that the balance sheet is

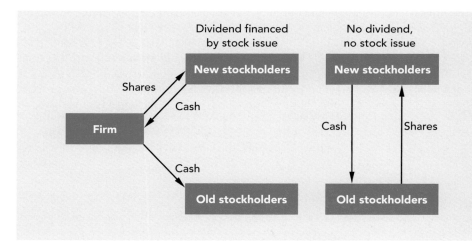

Dividend financed by stock issue

No dividend, no stock issue

▶ **FIGURE 12.5**

Two ways of raising cash for the firm's original shareholders. In each case the cash received is offset by a decline in the value of the old stockholders' claim on the firm. If the firm pays a dividend, each share is worth less because more shares have to be issued against the firm's assets. If the old stockholders sell some of their shares, each share is worth the same but the old stockholders have fewer shares.

constructed with market values; equity equals the market value of the firm's outstanding shares (price per share times number of shares outstanding). It is not necessarily equal to their book value.

Now Rational Demiconductor uses the cash to pay a $1,000 dividend to its stockholders. The benefit to them is obvious: $1,000 of spendable cash. It is also obvious that there must be a cost. The cash is not free.

Where does the money for the dividend come from? Of course, the immediate source of funds is Rational Demiconductor's cash account. But this cash was earmarked for the investment project. Since we want to isolate the effects of dividend policy on shareholders' wealth, we assume that the company *continues* with the investment project. That means that $1,000 in cash must be raised by new financing. This could consist of an issue of either debt or stock. Again, we just want to look at dividend policy for now, and we defer discussion of the debt–equity choice until Chapters 13 and 14. Thus Rational Demiconductor ends up financing the dividend with a $1,000 stock issue.

Now we examine the balance sheet after the dividend is paid, the new stock is sold, and the investment is undertaken. Because Rational Demiconductor's investment and borrowing policies are unaffected by the dividend payment, its *overall* market value must be unchanged at $10,000 + NPV.[17] We know also that if the new stockholders pay a fair price, their stock is worth $1,000. That leaves us with only one missing number—the value of the stock held by the original stockholders. It is easy to see that this must be

$$\text{Value of original stockholders' shares} = \text{value of company} - \text{value of new shares}$$
$$= (10{,}000 + \text{NPV}) - 1{,}000$$
$$= \$9{,}000 + \text{NPV}$$

The old shareholders have received a $1,000 cash dividend and incurred a $1,000 capital loss. Dividend policy doesn't matter.

By paying out $1,000 with one hand and taking it back with the other, Rational Demiconductor is recycling cash. To suggest that this makes shareholders better off is like advising a cook to cool the kitchen by leaving the refrigerator door open.

Of course, our proof ignores taxes, issue costs, and a variety of other complications. We turn to those items in a moment. The really crucial assumption in our proof is that the new shares are sold at a fair price. The shares sold to raise $1,000 must actually be *worth* $1,000.[18] In other words, we have assumed efficient capital markets.

Calculating Share Price

We have assumed that Rational Demiconductor's new shares can be sold at a fair price, but what is that price and how many new shares are issued?

Suppose that before this dividend payout the company had 1,000 shares outstanding and that the project had an NPV of $2,000. Then the old stock was worth in total $10,000 + NPV = $12,000, which works out at $12,000/1,000 = $12 per share. After the company has paid the dividend and completed the financing, this old stock is worth $9,000 + NPV = $11,000. That works out at $11,000/1,000 = $11 per share. In other words, the price of the old stock falls by the amount of the $1 per share dividend payment.

Now let us look at the new stock. Clearly, after the issue this must sell at the same price as the rest of the stock. In other words, it must be valued at $11. If the new stockholders

---

[17] All other factors that might affect Rational Demiconductor's value are assumed constant. This is not a necessary assumption, but it simplifies the proof of MM's theory.

[18] The "old" shareholders get all the benefit of the positive-NPV project. The new shareholders require only a fair rate of return. They are making a zero-NPV investment.

get fair value, the company must issue $1,000/$11 or 91 new shares in order to raise the $1,000 that it needs.

Stock Repurchase

We have seen that any increased cash dividend payment must be offset by a stock issue if the firm's investment and borrowing policies are held constant. In effect the stockholders finance the extra dividend by selling off part of their ownership of the firm. Consequently, the stock price falls by just enough to offset the extra dividend.

This process can also be run backward. With investment and borrowing policy given, any *reduction* in dividends must be balanced by a reduction in the number of shares issued or by repurchase of previously outstanding stock. But if the process has no effect on stockholders' wealth when run forward, it must likewise have no effect when run in reverse. We will confirm this by another numerical example.

Suppose that a technical discovery reveals that Rational Demiconductor's new project is not a positive-NPV venture but a sure loser. Management announces that the project is to be discarded and that the $1,000 earmarked for it will be paid out as an extra dividend of $1 per share. After the dividend payout, the balance sheet is

Rational Demiconductor's Balance Sheet (Market Values)

Cash	$ 0	$ 0	Debt
Existing fixed assets	9,000	9,000	Equity
New project	0		
Total asset value	$ 9,000	$ 9,000	Total firm value

Since there are 1,000 shares outstanding, the stock price is $10,000/1,000 = $10 before the dividend payment and $9,000/1,000 = $9 *after* the payment.

What if Rational Demiconductor uses the $1,000 to repurchase stock instead? As long as the company pays a fair price for the stock, the $1,000 buys $1,000/$10 = 100 shares. That leaves 900 shares worth 900 × $10 = $9,000.

As expected, we find that switching from cash dividends to share repurchase has no effect on shareholders' wealth. They forgo a $1 cash dividend but end up holding shares worth $10 instead of $9.

Note that when shares are repurchased the transfer of value is in favor of those stockholders who do not sell. They forgo any cash dividend but end up owning a larger slice of the firm. In effect they are using their share of Rational Demiconductor's $1,000 distribution to buy out some of their fellow shareholders.

Stock Repurchase and Valuation

Valuing the equity of a firm that repurchases its own stock can be confusing. Let's work through a simple example.

Company X has 100 shares outstanding. It earns $1,000 a year, all of which is paid out as a dividend. The dividend per share is, therefore, $1,000/100 = $10. Suppose that investors expect the dividend to be maintained indefinitely and that they require a return of 10%. In this case the value of each share is $PV_{share} = \$10/.10 = \$100$. Since there are 100 shares outstanding, the *total* market value of the equity is $PV_{equity} = 100 \times \$100 = \$10,000$. Note that we could reach the same conclusion by discounting the *total* dividend payments to shareholders ($PV_{equity} = \$1,000/.10 = \$10,000$).[19]

---

[19] When valuing the entire equity, remember that if the company is expected to issue additional shares in the future, we should include the dividend payments on these shares only if we also include the amount that investors pay for them. See Chapter 15.

Now suppose the company announces that instead of paying a cash dividend in year 1, it will spend the same money repurchasing its shares in the open market. The total expected cash flows to shareholders (dividends and cash from stock repurchase) are unchanged at $1,000. So the total value of the equity also remains at $1,000/.10 = $10,000. This is made up of the value of the $1,000 received from the stock repurchase in year 1 ($PV_{repurchase}$ = $1,000/1.1 = $909.1) and the value of the $1,000-a-year dividend starting in year 2 [$PV_{dividends}$ = $1,000/(.10 × 1.1) = $9,091]. Each share continues to be worth $10,000/100 = $100 just as before.

Think now about those shareholders who plan to sell their stock back to the company. They will demand a 10% return on their investment. So the expected price at which the firm buys back shares must be 10% higher than today's price, or $110. The company spends $1,000 buying back its stock, which is sufficient to buy $1,000/$110 = 9.09 shares.

The company starts with 100 shares, it buys back 9.09, and therefore 90.91 shares remain outstanding. Each of these shares can look forward to a dividend stream of $1,000/90.91 = $11 per share. So after the repurchase shareholders have 10% fewer shares, but earnings and dividends per share are 10% higher. An investor who owns one share today that is not repurchased will receive no dividends in year 1 but can look forward to $11 a year thereafter. The value of each share is therefore 11/(.1 × 1.1) = $100.

Our example illustrates several points. First, other things equal, company value is unaffected by the decision to repurchase stock rather than to pay a cash dividend. Second, when valuing the entire equity you need to include both the cash that is paid out as dividends and the cash that is used to repurchase stock. Third, when calculating the cash flow *per share*, it is double counting to include both the forecasted dividends per share *and* the cash received from repurchase (if you sell back your share, you don't get any subsequent dividends). Fourth, a firm that repurchases stock instead of paying dividends reduces the number of shares outstanding but produces an offsetting increase in subsequent earnings and dividends per share.

12-6 The Rightists

MM said that dividend policy is irrelevant because it does not affect shareholder value. MM did not say that payout should be random or erratic; for example, it may change over the life cycle of the firm. A young growth firm pays out little or nothing, to maximize the cash flow available for investment. As the firm matures, positive-NPV investment opportunities are harder to come by and growth slows down. There is cash available for payout to shareholders. At some point the firm commits to pay a regular dividend. It may also repurchase shares. In old age, profitable growth opportunities disappear, and payout may become much more generous.

Of course MM assumed absolutely perfect and efficient capital markets. In MM's world, everyone is a rational optimizer. The right-wing payout party points to real-world imperfections that could make high dividend payout ratios better than low ones. There is a natural clientele for high-payout stocks, for example. Some financial institutions are legally restricted from holding stocks lacking established dividend records.[20] Trusts and endowment funds may prefer high-dividend stocks because dividends are regarded as spendable "income," whereas capital gains are "additions to principal."

There is also a natural clientele of investors, such as the elderly, who look to their stock portfolios for a steady source of cash to live on.[21] In principle, this cash could be easily

---

[20] Most colleges and universities are legally free to spend capital gains from their endowments, but they usually restrict spending to a moderate percentage that can be covered by dividends and interest receipts.

[21] See, for example, J. R. Graham and A. Kumar, "Do Dividend Clienteles Exist? Evidence on Dividend Preferences of Retail Investors," *Journal of Finance* 61 (June 2006), pp. 1305–1336; and M. Baker, S. Nagel and J. Wurgler, "The Effect of Dividends on Consumption," *Brookings Papers on Economic Activity* (2007), pg 277–291.

Microsoft's Payout Bonanza

▶ There is a point at which hoarding money becomes embarrassing. . . . Microsoft, which grew into the world's largest software company . . . and which has been generating cash at the rate of $1 billion a month passed that point years ago. On July 20th, it finally addressed the issue.

Its solution was to give back to its shareholders, in various forms, an unprecedented $75 billion. One dollop, to the tune of $32 billion, will be a one-time dividend to be paid in December. Another will be share buybacks worth $30 billion over four years.

The third will be a doubling of Microsoft's ongoing dividend to 32 cents a share annually, payable in quarterly instalments. Not bad for a company that has not even turned 30 yet, and that only declared its first dividend in January 2003.

The decision is impressive for the mature analysis by Microsoft of its role in the industry and the prospects for the future that it implies.

Source: "An End to Growth?" *The Economist,* July 24, 2004, p. 61. © 2004 The Economist Newspaper Group, Inc. Reprinted with permission. Further reproduction prohibited (www.economist.com).

---

generated from stocks paying no dividends at all; the investor could just sell off a small fraction of his or her holdings from time to time. But it is simpler and cheaper for the company to send a quarterly check than for its shareholders to sell, say, one share every three months. Regular dividends relieve many of its shareholders of transaction costs and considerable inconvenience.[22]

Some observers have appealed to behavioral psychology to explain why we may prefer to receive those regular dividends rather than sell small amounts of stock.[23] We are all, they point out, liable to succumb to temptation. Some of us may hanker after fattening foods, while others may be dying for a drink. We could seek to control these cravings by willpower, but that can be a painful struggle. Instead, it may be easier to set simple rules for ourselves ("cut out chocolate," or "wine with meals only"). In just the same way, we may welcome the self-discipline that comes from spending only dividend income, and thereby sidestep the difficult decision of how much we should dip into capital.

Payout Policy, Investment Policy, and Management Incentives

Perhaps the most persuasive argument in favor of the rightist position is that paying out funds to shareholders prevents managers from misusing or wasting funds.[24] Suppose a company has plenty of free cash flow but few profitable investment opportunities. Shareholders may not trust the managers to spend retained earnings wisely and may fear that the money will be plowed back into building a larger empire rather than a more profitable one. In such cases investors may demand higher dividends or a stock repurchase not because these are valuable in themselves, but because they encourage a more careful, value-oriented investment policy.

---

[22] Those advocating generous dividends might go on to argue that a regular cash dividend relieves stockholders of the risk of having to sell shares at "temporarily depressed" prices. Of course, the firm will have to issue shares eventually to finance the dividend, but (the argument goes) the firm can pick the *right time* to sell. If firms really try to do this and if they are successful—two big *ifs*—then stockholders of high-payout firms might indeed get something for nothing.

[23] See H. Shefrin and M. Statman, "Explaining Investor Preference for Cash Dividends," *Journal of Financial Economics* 13 (June 1984), pp. 253–282.

[24] See M. Rozeff, "Growth, Beta and Agency Costs as Determinants of Dividend Payout Ratios," *Journal of Financial Research* 5 (1982), pp. 249–259; F. Easterbrook, "Two Agency Cost Explanations of Dividends," *American Economic Review* 74 (1984), pp. 650–659; and especially M. Jensen, "Agency Costs of Free Cash Flow, Corporate Finance, and Takeovers," *American Economic Review* 76 (May 1986), pp. 323–329.

The nearby box describes how Microsoft announced the largest cash distribution in corporate history. By 2004 the company's investment opportunities had diminished, and investors were, therefore, happy to see Microsoft distribute its cash mountain.

Microsoft paid out its gigantic special dividend willingly. Other cash-cow corporations may let go of cash grudgingly under pressure from investors. Stock price falls when investors sense excessive perks or empire building. The threat of a falling stock price is an excellent motivator, particularly for top managers holding valuable stock options.

The willingness of mature corporations to make generous payouts shows that corporate governance works in the U.S. and other developed economies. But governance is less effective in many emerging economies, and managers' and stockholders' interests are not as closely aligned. Payout ratios are smaller where governance is weak.[25]

12-7   Taxes and the Radical Left

The left-wing dividend creed is simple: Whenever dividends are taxed more heavily than capital gains, firms should pay the lowest cash dividend they can get away with. Available cash should be retained or used to repurchase shares.

By shifting their distribution policies in this way, corporations can transmute dividends into capital gains. If this financial alchemy results in lower taxes, it should be welcomed by any taxpaying investor. That is the basic point made by the leftist party when it argues for low-dividend payout.

If dividends are taxed more heavily than capital gains, investors should pay more for stocks with low dividend yields. In other words, they should accept a lower *pretax* rate of return from securities offering returns in the form of capital gains rather than dividends. Table 12.1 illustrates this. The stocks of firms A and B are equally risky. Investors expect A to be worth $112.50 per share next year. The share price of B is expected to be only $102.50, but a $10 dividend is also forecasted, and so the total pretax payoff is the same, $112.50.

	Firm A (No Dividend)	Firm B (High Dividend)
Next year's price	$112.50	$102.50
Dividend	$0	$10.00
Total pretax payoff	$112.50	$112.50
Today's stock price	$100	$97.78
Capital gain	$12.50	$4.72
Before-tax rate of return	$100 \times \left(\dfrac{12.5}{100}\right) = 12.5\%$	$100 \times \left(\dfrac{14.72}{97.78}\right) = 15.05\%$
Tax on dividend at 40%	$0	$.40 \times 10 = \$4.00$
Tax on capital gains at 20%	$.20 \times 12.50 = \$2.50$	$.20 \times 4.72 = \$.94$
Total after-tax income (dividends plus capital gains less taxes)	$(0 + 12.50) - 2.50 = \$10.00$	$(10.00 + 4.72) - (4.00 + .94) = \$9.78$
After-tax rate of return	$100 \times \left(\dfrac{10}{100}\right) = 10.0\%$	$100 \times \left(\dfrac{9.78}{97.78}\right) = 10.0\%$

▶ **TABLE 12.1**   Effects of a shift in dividend policy when dividends are taxed more heavily than capital gains. The high-payout stock (firm B) must sell at a lower price to provide the same after-tax return.

---

[25] See R. La Porta, F. Lopez-de-Silanes, A. Shleifer, and R. W. Vishny, "Agency Problems and Dividend Policies around the World," *Journal of Finance* 55 (February 2000), pp. 1–34.

Yet we find B's stock selling for less than A's and therefore offering a higher pretax rate of return. The reason is obvious: Investors prefer A because its return comes in the form of capital gains. Table 12.1 shows that A and B are equally attractive to investors who, we assume, pay a 40% tax on dividends and a 20% tax on capital gains. Each offers a 10% return after all taxes. The difference between the stock prices of A and B is exactly the present value of the extra taxes the investors face if they buy B.[26]

The management of B could save these extra taxes by eliminating the $10 dividend and using the released funds to repurchase stock instead. Its stock price should rise to $100 as soon as the new policy is announced.

Why Pay Any Dividends at All?

It is true that, when companies make very large one-off distributions of cash to shareholders, they generally choose to do so by share repurchase rather than by a large temporary hike in dividends. But if dividends attract more tax than capital gains, why should any firm ever pay a cash dividend? If cash is to be distributed to stockholders, isn't share repurchase always the best channel for doing so? The leftist position seems to call not just for low payouts but for *zero* payouts whenever capital gains have a tax advantage.

Few leftists would go quite that far. A firm that eliminates dividends and starts repurchasing stock on a regular basis may find that the Internal Revenue Service recognizes the repurchase program for what it really is and taxes the payments accordingly. That is why financial managers do not usually announce that they are repurchasing shares to save stockholders taxes; they give some other reason.[27]

The low-payout party has nevertheless maintained that the market rewards firms that have low-payout policies. They have claimed that firms that paid dividends and as a result had to issue shares from time to time were making a serious mistake. Any such firm was essentially financing its dividends by issuing stock; it should have cut its dividends at least to the point at which stock issues were unnecessary. This would not only have saved taxes for shareholders but it would also have avoided the transaction costs of the stock issues.[28]

Empirical Evidence on Dividends and Taxes

It is hard to deny that taxes are important to investors. You can see that in the bond market. Interest on municipal bonds is not taxed, and so municipals usually sell at low pretax yields. Interest on federal government bonds is taxed, and so these bonds sell at higher pretax yields. It does not seem likely that investors in bonds just forget about taxes when they enter the stock market.

There is some evidence that in the past taxes have affected U.S. investors' choice of stocks.[29] Lightly taxed institutional investors have tended to hold high-yield stocks and retail investors have preferred low-yield stocks. Moreover, this preference for low-yield stocks has been somewhat more marked for high-income individuals. Nevertheless, it seems that taxes have been only a secondary consideration with these investors, and have not deterred individuals in high-tax brackets from holding substantial amounts of dividend-paying stocks.

---

[26] Michael Brennan has modeled what happens when you introduce taxes into an otherwise perfect market. He found that the capital asset pricing model continues to hold, but on an *after-tax* basis. Thus, if A and B have the same beta, they should offer the same after-tax rate of return. The spread between pretax and post-tax returns is determined by a weighted average of investors' tax rates. See M. J. Brennan, "Taxes, Market Valuation and Corporate Financial Policy," *National Tax Journal* 23 (December 1970), pp. 417–427.

[27] They might say, "Our stock is a good investment," or, "We want to have the shares available to finance acquisitions of other companies." What do you think of these rationales?

[28] Costs of issuing common stock typically exceed 4%.

[29] See, for example, Y. Grinstein and R. Michaely, "Institutional Holdings and Payout Policy," *Journal of Finance* 60 (June 2005), pp. 1389–1426; and J. R. Graham and A. Kumar, "Do Dividend Clienteles Exist? Evidence on Dividend Preferences of Retail Investors," *Journal of Finance* 61 (June 2006), pp. 1305–1336.

If investors are concerned about taxes, we might also expect that, when the tax penalty on dividends is high, companies would think twice about increasing the payout. Only about a fifth of U.S. financial managers cite investor taxes as an important influence when the firm makes its dividend decision. On the other hand, firms have sometimes responded to major shifts in the way that investors are taxed. For example, when Australia introduced a tax change in 1987 that effectively eliminated the tax penalty on dividends for Australian investors, firms became more willing to increase their payout.[30]

If tax considerations are important, we would expect to find a historical tendency for high-dividend stocks to sell at lower prices and therefore to offer higher returns, just as in Table 12.1. Unfortunately, there are difficulties in measuring this effect. For example, suppose that stock A is priced at $100 and is expected to pay a $5 dividend. The *expected* yield is, therefore, 5/100 = .05, or 5%. The company now announces bumper earnings and a $10 dividend. Thus with the benefit of hindsight, A's *actual* dividend yield is 10/100 = .10, or 10%. If the unexpected increase in earnings causes a rise in A's stock price, we will observe that a high actual yield is accompanied by a high actual return. But that would not tell us anything about whether a high *expected* yield was accompanied by a high *expected* return. To measure the effect of dividend policy, we need to estimate the dividends that investors expected.

A second problem is that nobody is quite sure what is meant by high dividend yield. For example, utility stocks have generally offered high yields. But did they have a high yield all year, or only in months or on days that dividends were paid? Perhaps for most of the year, they had zero yields and were perfect holdings for the highly taxed individuals.[31] Of course, high-tax investors did not want to hold a stock on the days dividends were paid, but they could sell their stock temporarily to a security dealer. Dealers are taxed equally on dividends and capital gains and therefore should not have demanded any extra return for holding stocks over the dividend period.[32] If shareholders could pass stocks freely between each other at the time of the dividend payment, we should not observe any tax effects at all.

A number of researchers have attempted to tackle these problems and to measure whether investors demand a higher return from high-yielding stocks. Their findings offer some limited comfort to the dividends-are-bad school, for most of the researchers have suggested that high-yielding stocks have provided higher returns. However, the estimated tax rates differ substantially from one study to another. For example, while Litzenberger and Ramaswamy concluded that investors have priced stocks as if dividend income attracted an extra 14% to 23% rate of tax, Miller and Scholes used a different methodology and came up with a negligible 4% difference in the rate of tax.[33]

The Taxation of Dividends and Capital Gains

Many of these attempts to measure the effect of dividends are of more historical than current interest, for they look back at the years before 1986 when there was a dramatic

---

[30] K. Pattenden and G. Twite, "Taxes and Dividend Policy under Alternative Tax Regimes," *Journal of Corporate Finance* 14 (2008), pp. 1–16.

[31] Suppose there are 250 trading days in a year. Think of a stock paying quarterly dividends. We could say that the stock offers a high dividend yield on 4 days but a zero dividend yield on the remaining 246 days.

[32] The stock could also be sold to a corporation, which could "capture" the dividend and then resell the shares. Corporations are natural buyers of dividends, because they pay tax only on 30% of dividends received from other corporations. (We say more on the taxation of intercorporate dividends later in this section.)

[33] See R. H. Litzenberger and K. Ramaswamy, "The Effects of Dividends on Common Stock Prices: Tax Effects or Information Effects," *Journal of Finance* 37 (May 1982), pp. 429–443; and M. H. Miller and M. Scholes, "Dividends and Taxes: Some Empirical Evidence," *Journal of Political Economy* 90 (1982), pp. 1118–1141. Merton Miller provides a broad review of the empirical literature in "Behavioral Rationality in Finance: The Case of Dividends," *Journal of Business* 59 (October 1986), pp. S451–S468.

difference between the taxation of dividends and capital gains.[34] As we write this in 2009, the top rate of tax on both dividends and capital gains is 15%.[35]

There is, however, one way that tax law continues to favor capital gains. Taxes on dividends have to be paid immediately, but taxes on capital gains can be deferred until shares are sold and the capital gains are realized. Stockholders can choose when to sell their shares and thus when to pay the capital gains tax. The longer they wait, the less the present value of the capital gains tax liability.[36]

The distinction between dividends and capital gains is not important for many financial institutions, which operate free of all taxes and therefore have no reason to prefer capital gains to dividends or vice versa. For example, pension funds are untaxed. These funds hold roughly $3 trillion in common stocks, so they have enormous clout in the U.S. stock market. Only corporations have a tax reason to *prefer* dividends. They pay corporate income tax on only 30% of any dividends received. Thus the effective tax rate on dividends received by large corporations is 30% of 35% (the marginal corporate tax rate), or 10.5%. But they have to pay a 35% tax on the full amount of any realized capital gain.

The implications of these tax rules for dividend policy are pretty simple. Capital gains have advantages to many investors, but they are far less advantageous than they were 20 or 30 years ago.[37] Thus, the leftist case for minimizing cash dividends is weaker than it used to be.

Alternative Tax Systems

In the U.S. shareholders' returns are taxed twice. They are taxed at the corporate level (corporate tax) and in the hands of the shareholder (income tax or capital gains tax). These two tiers of tax are illustrated in Table 12.2, which shows the after-tax return to the shareholder if the company distributes all its income as dividends. We assume the company earns $100 a share before tax and therefore pays corporate tax of .35 × 100 = $35. This leaves $65

Operating income	100	
Corporate tax at 35%	35 ⟵	Corporate tax
After-tax income (paid out as dividends)	65	
Income tax paid by investor at 15%	9.75 ⟵	Second tax paid by investor
Net income to shareholder	55.25	

▶ **TABLE 12.2**   In the United States returns to shareholders are taxed twice. This example assumes that all income after corporate taxes is paid out as cash dividends to an investor in the top income tax bracket (figures in dollars per share).

---

[34] The Tax Reform Act of 1986 equalized the tax rates on dividends and capital gains. A gap began to open up again in 1992.

[35] These rates were established by the *Jobs and Growth Tax Relief Reconciliation Act* of 2003 and have been extended to 2010. Note that capital gains realized within a year of purchase and dividends on stocks held for less than 61 days are taxed as ordinary income.

[36] When securities are sold, capital gains tax is paid on the difference between the selling price and the initial purchase price or *basis*. Thus, shares purchased in 2004 for $20 (the basis) and sold for $30 in 2009 would generate $10 per share in capital gains and a tax of $1.50 at a 15% tax rate.

Suppose the investor now decides to defer sale for one year. Then, if the interest rate is 5%, the present value of the tax, viewed from 2009, falls to 1.50/1.05 = $1.43. That is, the *effective* capital gains rate is 14.3%. The longer sale is deferred, the lower the effective rate will be.

The effective rate falls to zero if the investor dies before selling, because the investor's heirs get to "step up" the basis without recognizing any taxable gain. Suppose the price is still $30 when the investor dies. The heirs could sell for $30 and pay no tax, because they could claim a $30 basis. The $10 capital gain would escape tax entirely.

[37] We described above how Microsoft in 2004 declared a special dividend of $32 billion. Would the company have done so if there had still been a substantial tax disadvantage to dividend payments? We doubt it.

a share to be paid out as a dividend, which is then subject to a second layer of tax. For example, a shareholder who is taxed at 15% pays tax on this dividend of .15 × 65 = $9.75. Only a tax-exempt pension fund or charity would retain the full $65.

Of course, dividends are regularly paid by companies that operate under very different tax systems. For example, Germany partly compensates for the corporate layer of tax by levying income tax on only half an individual's dividend income.

In some other countries, such as Australia and New Zealand, shareholders' returns are not taxed twice. For example, in Australia shareholders are taxed on dividends, but they may deduct from this tax bill their share of the corporate tax that the company has paid. This is known as an *imputation tax system*. Table 12.3 shows how the imputation system works. Suppose that an Australian company earns pretax profits of A$100 a share. After it pays corporate tax at 30%, the profit is A$70 a share. The company now declares a net dividend of A$70 and sends each shareholder a check for this amount. This dividend is accompanied by a tax credit saying that the company has already paid A$30 of tax on the shareholder's behalf. Thus shareholders are treated as if each received a total, or gross, dividend of 70 + 30 = A$100 and paid tax of A$30. If the shareholder's tax rate is 30%, there is no more tax to pay and the shareholder retains the net dividend of A$70. If the shareholder pays tax at the top personal rate of 45%, then he or she is required to pay an additional $15 of tax; if the tax rate is 15% (the rate at which Australian pension funds are taxed), then the shareholder receives a *refund* of 30 − 15 = A$15.[38]

Under an imputation tax system, millionaires have to cough up the extra personal tax on dividends. If this is more than the tax that they would pay on capital gains, then millionaires would prefer that the company does not distribute earnings. If it is the other way around, they would prefer dividends.[39] Investors with low tax rates have no doubts about the matter. If the company pays a dividend, these investors receive a check from the revenue service for the excess tax that the company has paid, and therefore they prefer high payout rates.

	Rate of Income Tax		
	15%	30%	45%
Operating income	100	100	100
Corporate tax (T_c = .30)	30	30	30
After-tax income	70	70	70
Grossed-up dividend	100	100	100
Income tax	15	30	45
Tax credit for corporate payment	−30	−30	−30
Tax due from shareholder	−15	0	15
Available to shareholder	85	70	55

▶ **TABLE 12.3**   Under imputation tax systems, such as that in Australia, shareholders receive a tax credit for the corporate tax that the firm has paid (figures in Australian dollars per share).

[38] In Australia, shareholders receive a credit for the full amount of corporate tax that has been paid on their behalf. In other countries the tax credit is less than the corporate tax rate. You can think of the tax system in these countries as lying between the Australian and U.S. systems.

[39] In the case of Australia the tax rate on capital gains is the same as the tax rate on dividends. However, for securities that are held for more than 12 months only half of the gain is taxed.

Look once again at Table 12.3 and think what would happen if the corporate tax rate were zero. The shareholder with a 15% tax rate would still end up with A$85, and the shareholder with the 45% rate would still receive A$55. Thus, under an imputation tax system, when a company pays out all its earnings, there is effectively only one layer of tax—the tax on the shareholder. The revenue service collects this tax through the company and then sends a demand to the shareholder for any excess tax or makes a refund for any overpayment.[40]

12-8 The Middle-of-the-Roaders

The middle-of-the-road party, which is principally represented by Miller, Black, and Scholes,[41] maintains that a company's value is not affected by its dividend policy. Unlike the other two parties, they emphasize that the supply of dividends is free to adjust to the demand. Therefore, if companies could increase their stock price by changing their dividend payout, they would surely have done so. Presumably, dividends are where they are because no company believes that it could add value simply by upping or reducing its dividend payout.

This "supply argument" is not inconsistent with the existence of a clientele of investors who prefer low-payout stocks. If necessary, these investors would be prepared to pay a premium for low-payout stocks. But perhaps they do not have to. Enough firms may have already noticed the existence of this clientele and switched to low-payout policies. If so, there is no incentive for *additional* firms to switch to low-payout policies. Similarly, there may well be some investors who prefer high dividends, but these investors too already have a wide choice of suitable stocks. A third group of investors, such as pension funds and other tax-exempt institutions, may have no reason to prefer dividends to capital gains. These investors will be happy to hold both low- and high-payout stocks, and the value that they place on each stock will be unaffected by the company's dividend policy. In that case we are back in an MM world where dividend policy does not affect value.[42]

The middle-of-the-roaders stress that companies would not supply such a large quantity of dividends unless they believed that this was what investors wanted. But that still leaves a puzzle. Even in the days when there was a large tax disadvantage to dividends, many investors were apparently happy to hold high-payout stocks. Why? The response of the middle-of-the-roaders has been to argue that there are always plenty of wrinkles in the tax system that shareholders can use to avoid paying taxes on dividends. For example, instead of investing directly in common stocks, they can do so through a pension fund or insurance company, which receives more favorable tax treatment. However, it is not clear that this is the whole story, for a high proportion of dividends is regularly paid out to wealthy individuals and included in their taxable income.[43]

---

[40] This is only true for earnings that are paid out as dividends. Retained earnings are subject to corporate tax. Shareholders get the benefit of retained earnings in the form of capital gains.

[41] F. Black and M. S. Scholes, "The Effects of Dividend Yield and Dividend Policy on Common Stock Prices and Returns," *Journal of Financial Economics* 1 (May 1974), pp. 1–22; M. H. Miller and M. S. Scholes, "Dividends and Taxes," *Journal of Financial Economics* 6 (December 1978), pp. 333–364; and M. H. Miller, "Behavioral Rationality in Finance: The Case of Dividends," *Journal of Business* 59 (October 1986), pp. S451–S468.

[42] Baker and Wurgler argue that the demand for dividends may change. When this is reflected in stock prices, firms adjust their dividend policy to cater for the shift in demand. Thus a shift in clienteles shows up in a change in firms' propensity to pay dividends. See M. Baker and J. Wurgler, "A Catering Theory of Dividends," *Journal of Finance* 59 (June 2004), pp. 1125–1165.

[43] See, for example, F. Allen and R. Michaely, "Payout Policy," in G. Constantinides, M. Harris, and R. Stulz, (eds.), *Handbook of the Economics of Finance: Corporate Finance* (Amsterdam: North-Holland, 2003).

There is another possible reason that U.S. companies may pay dividends even when these dividends result in higher tax bills. Companies that pay *low* dividends will be more attractive to highly taxed individuals; those that pay *high* dividends will have a greater proportion of pension funds or other tax-exempt institutions as their stockholders. These financial institutions are sophisticated investors; they monitor carefully the companies that they invest in and they bring pressure on poor managers to perform. Successful, well-managed companies are happy to have financial institutions as investors, but their poorly managed brethren would prefer unsophisticated and more docile stockholders.

You can probably see now where the argument is heading. Well-managed companies want to signal their worth. They can do so by having a high proportion of demanding institutions among their stockholders. How do they achieve this? By paying high dividends. Those shareholders who pay tax do not object to these high dividends as long as the effect is to encourage institutional investors who are prepared to put the time and effort into monitoring the management.[44]

Payout Policy and the Life Cycle of the Firm

MM said that dividend policy does not affect shareholder value. Shareholder value is driven by the firm's investment policy, including its future growth opportunities. Financing policy, including the choice between debt and equity, can also affect value, as we will see in Chapter 14.

In MM's analysis, payout is a residual, a by-product of other financial policies. The firm should make investment and financing decisions, and then pay out whatever cash is left over. Therefore payout should change over the life cycle of the firm.

MM assumed a perfect and rational world, but many of the complications discussed in this chapter actually reinforce the life cycle of payout. Let's review the life-cycle story.[45]

Young growth firms have plenty of profitable investment opportunities. During this time it is efficient to retain and reinvest all operating cash flow. Why pay out cash to investors if the firm then has to replace the cash by borrowing or issuing more shares? Retaining cash avoids costs of issuing securities and minimizes shareholders' taxes. Investors are not worried about wasteful overinvestment, because investment opportunities are good, and managers' compensation is tied to stock price.

As the firm matures, positive-NPV projects become scarcer relative to cash flow. The firm begins to accumulate cash. Now investors begin to worry about overinvestment or excessive perks. The investors pressure management to start paying out cash. Sooner or later, managers comply—otherwise stock price stagnates. The payout may come as share repurchases, but initiating a regular cash dividend sends a stronger and more reassuring signal of financial discipline. The commitment to financial discipline can outweigh the tax costs of dividends. (The middle-of-the-road party argues that the tax costs of paying cash dividends may not be that large, particularly in recent years, when U.S. personal tax rates on dividends and capital gains have been low.) Regular dividends may also be attractive to some types of investors, for example, retirees who depend on dividends for living expenses.

As the firm ages, more and more payout is called for. The payout may come as higher dividends or large repurchases. Sometimes the payout comes as the result of a takeover. Shareholders are bought out, and the firm's new owners generate cash by selling assets and restructuring operations.

---

[44] This signaling argument is developed in F. Allen, A. E. Bernardo, and I. Welch, "A Theory of Dividends Based on Tax Clienteles," *Journal of Finance* 55 (December 2000), pp. 2499–2536.

[45] Here we are following a life-cycle theory set out in H. DeAngelo, L. DeAngelo, and D. Skinner, "Corporate Payout Policy," *Foundations and Trends in Finance* 3 (2008), pp. 95–287.

When managers decide on the dividend, their primary concern seems to be to give shareholders a "fair" payment on their investment. However, most managers are very reluctant to reduce dividends and will not increase the payout unless they are confident it can be maintained.

As an alternative to dividend payments, the company can repurchase its own stock. In recent years companies have bought back their stock in large quantities, but repurchases do not generally substitute for dividends. Instead they are used to return unwanted cash to shareholders or to retire equity and replace it with debt.

If we hold the company's investment decision and capital structure constant, then payout policy is a trade-off between cash dividends and the issue or repurchase of common stock. Should firms retain whatever earnings are necessary to finance growth and pay out any residual as cash dividends? Or should they increase dividends and then (sooner or later) issue stock to make up the shortfall of equity capital? Or should they reduce dividends and use the released cash to repurchase stock?

If we lived in an ideally simple and perfect world, there would be no problem, for the choice would have no effect on market value. The controversy centers on the effects of dividend policy in our flawed world. Many investors believe that a high dividend payout enhances share price. Perhaps they welcome the self-discipline that comes from spending only dividend income rather than having to decide whether they should dip into capital. We suspect also that investors often pressure companies to increase dividends when they do not trust management to spend free cash flow wisely. In this case a dividend increase may lead to a rise in the stock price not because investors like dividends as such but because they want managers to run a tighter ship.

The most obvious and serious market imperfection has been the different tax treatment of dividends and capital gains. In the past, dividends in the United States have often been much more heavily taxed than capital gains. In 2003 the maximum tax rate was set at 15% on both dividends and gains, though capital gains continued to enjoy one advantage—the tax payment is not due until any gain was realized. If dividends are more heavily taxed, highly taxed investors should hold mostly low-payout stocks, and we would expect high-payout stocks to offer investors the compensation of greater pretax returns.

This view has a respectable theoretical basis. It is supported by some evidence that, when dividends were at a significant tax disadvantage in the U.S., gross returns did reflect the tax differential. The weak link is the theory's silence on the question of why companies continued to distribute such large dividends when they landed investors with such large tax bills.

The third view of dividend policy starts with the notion that the actions of companies do reflect investors' preferences; thus the fact that companies pay substantial dividends is the best evidence that investors want them. If the supply of dividends exactly meets the demand, no single company could improve its market value by changing its payout policy.

It is difficult to be dogmatic over these controversies. If investment policy and borrowing are held constant, then the arguments over payout policy are largely about shuffling money from one pocket to another. Unless there are substantial tax consequences to these shuffles, it is unlikely that firm value is greatly affected either by the total amount of the payout or the choice between dividends and repurchase. Investors' concern with payout decisions seems to stem mainly from the information that they read into managers' actions.

The bottom-line conclusion, if there is one, is that payout varies over the life cycle of the firm. Young growth firms pay no cash dividends and rarely repurchase stock. These firms have profitable investment opportunities. They finance these investments as much as possible from internally generated cash flow. As firms mature, profitable investment opportunities shrink relative to cash flow. The firm comes under pressure from investors, because investors worry that managers will overinvest if there is too much idle cash available. The threat of a lagging stock price pushes managers to distribute cash by repurchases or cash dividends. Committing to a regular cash dividend sends the more credible signal of financial discipline.

Visit us at www.mhhe.com/bma

● ● ● ● ●

**FURTHER
READING**

For comprehensive reviews of the literature on payout policy, see:

F. Allen and R. Michaely, "Payout Policy," in G. Constantinides, M. Harris, and R. Stulz, (eds.), *Handbook of the Economics of Finance: Corporate Finance* (Amsterdam: North-Holland, 2003).

H. DeAngelo, L. DeAngelo, and D. Skinner, "Corporate Payout Policy," *Foundations and Trends in Finance* 3 (2008), pp. 95–287.

For a recent survey of managers' attitudes to the payout decision, see:

A. Kalay and M. Lemmon, "Payout Policy," in B. E. Eckbo (ed.), *Handbook of Empirical Corporate Finance* (Amsterdam: Elsevier/North-Holland, 2007), Chapter 10.

A. Brav, J. R. Graham, C. R. Harvey, and R. Michaely, "Payout Policy in the 21st Century," *Journal of Financial Economics* 77 (September 2005), pp. 483–527.

● ● ● ● ●

PROBLEM SETS

BASIC

1. In 2009 J. M. Smucker paid a regular quarterly dividend of $.35 a share.
   a. Match each of the following sets of dates:

      (A1) 17 July 2009   (B1) Record date
      (A2) 11 August 2009   (B2) Payment date
      (A3) 12 August 2009   (B3) Ex-dividend date
      (A4) 14 August 2009   (B4) Last with-dividend date
      (A5) 1 September 2009   (B5) Declaration date

   b. On one of these dates the stock price is likely to fall by about the value of the dividend. Which date? Why?
   c. Smucker's stock price in August 2009 was $52. What was the dividend yield?
   d. If earnings per share for 2009 are $4.56, what is the percentage payout rate?
   e. Suppose that in 2009 the company paid a 10% stock dividend. What would be the expected fall in price?

2. Here are several "facts" about typical corporate dividend policies. Which are true and which false?
   a. Companies decide each year's dividend by looking at their capital expenditure requirements and then distributing whatever cash is left over.
   b. Managers and investors seem more concerned with dividend changes than with dividend levels.
   c. Managers often increase dividends temporarily when earnings are unexpectedly high for a year or two.
   d. Companies undertaking substantial share repurchases usually finance them with an offsetting reduction in cash dividends.

3. a. Wotan owns 1,000 shares of a firm that has just announced an increase in its dividend from $2.00 to $2.50 a share. The share price is currently $150. If Wotan does not wish to spend the extra cash, what should he do to offset the dividend increase?
   b. Brunhilde owns 1,000 shares of a firm that has just announced a dividend cut from $8.00 a share to $5.00. The share price is currently $200. If Brunhilde wishes to maintain her consumption, what should she do to offset the dividend cut?

4. Patriot Games has 5 million shares outstanding. The president has proposed that, given the firm's large cash holdings, the annual dividend should be increased from $6.00 a share to $8.00. If you agree with the president's plans for investment and capital structure, what else must the company do as a consequence of the dividend increase?

5. House of Haddock has 5,000 shares outstanding and the stock price is $140. The company is expected to pay a dividend of $20 per share next year and thereafter the dividend is expected to grow indefinitely by 5% a year. The president, George Mullet, now makes a surprise announcement: He says that the company will henceforth distribute half the cash in the form of dividends and the remainder will be used to repurchase stock.

   a. What is the total value of the company before and after the announcement? What is the value of one share?

   b. What is the expected stream of dividends per share for an investor who plans to retain his shares rather than sell them back to the company? Check your estimate of share value by discounting this stream of dividends per share.

6. Here are key financial data for House of Herring, Inc.:

Earnings per share for 2015	$5.50
Number of shares outstanding	40 million
Target payout ratio	50%
Planned dividend per share	$2.75
Stock price, year-end 2015	$130

   House of Herring plans to pay the entire dividend early in January 2016. All corporate and personal taxes were repealed in 2014.

   a. Other things equal, what will be House of Herring's stock price after the planned dividend payout?

   b. Suppose the company cancels the dividend and announces that it will use the money saved to repurchase shares. What happens to the stock price on the announcement date? Assume that investors learn nothing about the company's prospects from the announcement. How many shares will the company need to repurchase?

   c. Suppose the company increases dividends to $5.50 per share and then issues new shares to recoup the extra cash paid out as dividends. What happens to the with- and ex-dividend share prices? How many shares will need to be issued? Again, assume investors learn nothing from the announcement about House of Herring's prospects.

7. Answer the following questions twice, once assuming current tax law and once assuming zero tax on capital gains.

   Suppose all investments offered the same expected return *before* tax. Consider two equally risky shares, Hi and Lo. Hi shares pay a generous dividend and offer low expected capital gains. Lo shares pay low dividends and offer high expected capital gains. Which of the following investors would prefer the Lo shares? Which would prefer the Hi shares? Which should not care? (Assume that any stock purchased will be sold after one year.)

   a. A pension fund.

   b. An individual.

   c. A corporation.

   d. A charitable endowment.

   e. A security dealer.

INTERMEDIATE

8. Look in a recent issue of *The Wall Street Journal* at "Dividend News" and choose a company reporting a regular dividend.
   a. How frequently does the company pay a regular dividend?
   b. What is the amount of the dividend?
   c. By what date must your stock be registered for you to receive the dividend?
   d. How much later is the dividend paid?
   e. Look up the stock price and calculate the annual yield on the stock.

9. Which types of companies would you expect to distribute a relatively high or low proportion of current earnings? Which would you expect to have a relatively high or low price–earnings ratio?
   a. High-risk companies.
   b. Companies that have experienced an unexpected decline in profits.
   c. Companies that *expect* to experience a decline in profits.
   d. Growth companies with valuable future investment opportunities.

10. Little Oil has outstanding 1 million shares with a total market value of $20 million. The firm is expected to pay $1 million of dividends next year, and thereafter the amount paid out is expected to grow by 5% a year in perpetuity. Thus the expected dividend is $1.05 million in year 2, $1.105 million in year 3, and so on. However, the company has heard that the value of a share depends on the flow of dividends, and therefore it announces that next year's dividend will be increased to $2 million and that the extra cash will be raised immediately by an issue of shares. After that, the total amount paid out each year will be as previously forecasted, that is, $1.105 million in year 2 and increasing by 5% in each subsequent year.
   a. At what price will the new shares be issued in year 1?
   b. How many shares will the firm need to issue?
   c. What will be the expected dividend payments on these new shares, and what therefore will be paid out to the *old* shareholders after year 1?
   d. Show that the present value of the cash flows to current shareholders remains $20 million.

11. We stated in Section 12–5 that MM's proof of dividend irrelevance assumes that new shares are sold at a fair price. Look back at Problem 10. Assume that new shares are issued in year 1 at $10 a share. Show who gains and who loses. Is dividend policy still irrelevant? Why or why not?

12. Respond to the following comment: "It's all very well saying that I can sell shares to cover cash needs, but that may mean selling at the bottom of the market. If the company pays a regular cash dividend, investors avoid that risk."

13. Refer to the first balance sheet prepared for Rational Demiconductor in Section 12–5. Again it uses cash to pay a $1,000 cash dividend, planning to issue stock to recover the cash required for investment. But this time catastrophe hits before the stock can be issued. A new pollution control regulation increases manufacturing costs to the extent that the value of Rational Demiconductor's existing business is cut in half, to $4,500. The NPV of the new investment opportunity is unaffected, however. Show that dividend policy is still irrelevant.

14. "Many companies use stock repurchases to increase earnings per share. For example, suppose that a company is in the following position:

Net profit	$10 million
Number of shares before repurchase	1 million
Earnings per share	$10
Price–earnings ratio	20
Share price	$200

The company now repurchases 200,000 shares at $200 a share. The number of shares declines to 800,000 shares and earnings per share increase to $12.50. Assuming the price–earnings ratio stays at 20, the share price must rise to $250." Discuss.

15. Hors d'Age Cheeseworks has been paying a regular cash dividend of $4 per share each year for over a decade. The company is paying out all its earnings as dividends and is not expected to grow. There are 100,000 shares outstanding selling for $80 per share. The company has sufficient cash on hand to pay the next annual dividend.

    Suppose that Hors d'Age decides to cut its cash dividend to zero and announces that it will repurchase shares instead.

    a. What is the immediate stock price reaction? Ignore taxes, and assume that the repurchase program conveys no information about operating profitability or business risk.

    b. How many shares will Hors d'Age purchase?

    c. Project and compare future stock prices for the old and new policies. Do this for at least years 1, 2, and 3.

16. An article on stock repurchase in the *Los Angeles Times* noted: "An increasing number of companies are finding that the best investment they can make these days is in themselves." Discuss this view. How is the desirability of repurchase affected by company prospects and the price of its stock?

17. Comment briefly on each of the following statements:

    a. "Unlike American firms, which are always being pressured by their shareholders to increase dividends, Japanese companies pay out a much smaller proportion of earnings and so enjoy a lower cost of capital."

    b. "Unlike new capital, which needs a stream of new dividends to service it, retained earnings have zero cost."

    c. "If a company repurchases stock instead of paying a dividend, the number of shares falls and earnings per share rise. Thus stock repurchase must always be preferred to paying dividends."

18. Formaggio Vecchio has just announced its regular quarterly cash dividend of $1 per share.

    a. When will the stock price fall to reflect this dividend payment—on the record date, the ex-dividend date, or the payment date?

    b. Assume that there are no taxes. By how much is the stock price likely to fall?

    c. Now assume that *all* investors pay tax of 30% on dividends and nothing on capital gains. What is the likely fall in the stock price?

    d. Suppose, finally, that everything is the same as in part (c), except that security dealers pay tax on *both* dividends and capital gains. How would you expect your answer to (c) to change? Explain.

19. Refer back to Problem 18. Assume no taxes and a stock price immediately after the dividend announcement of $100.

    a. If you own 100 shares, what is the value of your investment? How does the dividend payment affect your wealth?

    b. Now suppose that Formaggio Vecchio cancels the dividend payment and announces that it will repurchase 1% of its stock at $100. Do you rejoice or yawn? Explain.

20. The shares of A and B both sell for $100 and offer a pretax return of 10%. However, in the case of company A the return is entirely in the form of dividend yield (the company pays a regular annual dividend of $10 a share), while in the case of B the return comes entirely as capital gain (the shares appreciate by 10% a year). Suppose that dividends and capital gains are both taxed at 30%. What is the after-tax return on share A? What is the after-tax return on share B to an investor who sells after two years? What about an investor who sells after 10 years?

21. a. The Horner Pie Company pays a quarterly dividend of $1. Suppose that the stock price is expected to fall on the ex-dividend date by $.90. Would you prefer to buy on the with-dividend date or the ex-dividend date if you were (i) a tax-free investor, (ii) an investor with a marginal tax rate of 40% on income and 16% on capital gains?

    b. In a study of ex-dividend behavior, Elton and Gruber[46] estimated that the stock price fell on the average by 85% of the dividend. Assuming that the tax rate on capital gains was 40% of the rate on income tax, what did Elton and Gruber's result imply about investors' marginal rate of income tax?

    c. Elton and Gruber also observed that the ex-dividend price fall was different for high-payout stocks and for low-payout stocks. Which group would you expect to show the larger price fall as a proportion of the dividend?

    d. Would the fact that investors can trade stocks freely around the ex-dividend date alter your interpretation of Elton and Gruber's study?

    e. Suppose Elton and Gruber repeated their tests for 2009, when the tax rate was the same on dividends and capital gains. How would you expect their results to have changed?

22. The middle-of-the-road party holds that dividend policy doesn't matter because the *supply* of high-, medium-, and low-payout stocks has already adjusted to satisfy investors' demands. Investors who like generous dividends hold stocks that give them all the dividends that they want. Investors who want capital gains see ample low-payout stocks to choose from. Thus, high-payout firms cannot gain by transforming to low-payout firms, or vice versa.

    Suppose the government reduces the tax rate on dividends but not on capital gains. Suppose that before this change the supply of dividends matched investor needs. How would you expect the tax change to affect the total cash dividends paid by U.S. corporations and the proportion of high- versus low-payout companies? Would dividend policy still be irrelevant after any dividend supply adjustments are completed? Explain.

CHALLENGE

23. Consider the following two statements: "Dividend policy is irrelevant," and "Stock price is the present value of expected future dividends." (See Chapter 4.) They *sound* contradictory. This question is designed to show that they are fully consistent.

    The current price of the shares of Charles River Mining Corporation is $50. Next year's earnings and dividends per share are $4 and $2, respectively. Investors expect perpetual growth at 8% per year. The expected rate of return demanded by investors is $r = 12\%$.

    We can use the perpetual-growth model to calculate stock price:

    $$P_0 = \frac{DIV}{r - g} = \frac{2}{.12 - .08} = 50$$

    Suppose that Charles River Mining announces that it will switch to a 100% payout policy, issuing shares as necessary to finance growth. Use the perpetual-growth model to show that current stock price is unchanged.

24. "If a company pays a dividend, the investor is liable for tax on the total value of the dividend. If instead the company distributes the cash by stock repurchase, the investor is liable for tax only on any capital gain rather than on the entire amount. Therefore, even if the tax rates on dividend income and capital gains are the same, stock repurchase is always preferable to a dividend payment." Explain with a simple example why this is not the case. (Ignore the fact that capital gains may be postponed.)

---

[46] E. J. Elton and M. J. Gruber, "Marginal Stockholders' Tax Rates and the Clientele Effect," *Review of Economics and Statistics* 52 (1970), pp. 68–74.

25. Adherents of the "dividends-are-good" school sometimes point to the fact that stocks with high yields tend to have above-average price–earnings multiples. Is this evidence convincing? Discuss.

26. Suppose that there are just three types of investors with the following tax rates:

	Individuals	Corporations	Institutions
Dividends	50%	5%	0%
Capital gains	15	35	0

Individuals invest a total of $80 billion in stock and corporations invest $10 billion. The remaining stock is held by the institutions. All three groups simply seek to maximize their after-tax income.

These investors can choose from three types of stock offering the following pretax payouts:

	Low Payout	Medium Payout	High Payout
Dividends	$5	$5	$30
Capital gains	15	5	0

These payoffs are expected to persist in perpetuity. The low-payout stocks have a total market value of $100 billion, the medium-payout stocks have a value of $50 billion, and the high-payout stocks have a value of $120 billion.

a. Who are the marginal investors that determine the prices of the stocks?

b. Suppose that this marginal group of investors requires a 12% after-tax return. What are the prices of the low-, medium-, and high-payout stocks?

c. Calculate the after-tax returns of the three types of stock for each investor group.

d. What are the dollar amounts of the three types of stock held by each investor group?

13 CHAPTER • • • • •

Does Debt Policy Matter?

▶ **A firm's basic** resource is the stream of cash flows produced by its assets. When the firm is financed entirely by common stock, all those cash flows belong to the stockholders. When it issues both debt and equity securities, it splits the cash flows into two streams, a relatively safe stream that goes to the debtholders and a riskier stream that goes to the stockholders.

The firm's mix of debt and equity financing is called its capital structure. Of course capital structure is not just "debt versus equity." There are many different flavors of debt, at least two flavors of equity (common versus preferred), plus hybrids such as convertible bonds. The firm can issue dozens of distinct securities in countless combinations. It attempts to find the particular combination that maximizes the overall market value of the firm.

Are such attempts worthwhile? We must consider the possibility that *no* combination has any greater appeal than any other. Perhaps the really important decisions concern the company's assets, and decisions about capital structure are mere details—matters to be attended to but not worried about.

Modigliani and Miller (MM), who showed that payout policy doesn't matter in perfect capital markets, also showed that financing decisions don't matter in perfect markets. Their famous "proposition 1" states that a firm cannot change the total value of its securities just by splitting its cash flows into different streams: The firm's value is determined by its real assets, not by the securities it issues. Thus capital structure is irrelevant as long as the firm's investment decisions are taken as given.

MM's proposition 1 allows complete separation of investment and financing decisions. It implies that any firm could use the capital budgeting procedures presented in Chapters 5 through 10 without worrying about where the money for capital expenditures comes from. In those chapters, we assumed all-equity financing without really thinking about it. If MM are right, that is exactly the right approach. If the firm uses a mix of debt and equity financing, its overall cost of capital will be exactly the same as its cost of equity with all-equity financing.

We believe that in practice capital structure does matter, but we nevertheless devote all of this chapter to MM's argument. If you don't fully understand the conditions under which MM's theory holds, you won't fully understand why one capital structure is better than another. The financial manager needs to know what kinds of market imperfection to look for.

For example, the firm may invent some new security that a particular clientele of investors is willing to buy at a premium price, thereby increasing the overall market value of the firm. (We argue, however, that such financial innovations are easily copied and that any gains in value will be confined to the first few issuers.)

In Chapter 14 we undertake a detailed analysis of the imperfections that are most likely to make a difference, including taxes, the costs of bankruptcy and financial distress, the costs of writing and enforcing complicated debt contracts, differences created by imperfect information, and the effects of debt on incentives for management. In Chapter 15 we show how such imperfections (especially taxes) affect the weighted-average cost of capital and the value of the firm.

• • • • •

13-1   The Effect of Financial Leverage in a Competitive Tax-free Economy

Financial managers try to find the combination of securities that has the greatest overall appeal to investors—the combination that maximizes the market value of the firm. Before tackling this problem, we should check whether a policy that maximizes the total value of the firm's securities also maximizes the wealth of the shareholders.

Let D and E denote the market values of the outstanding debt and equity of the Wapshot Mining Company. Wapshot's 1,000 shares sell for $50 apiece. Thus

$$E = 1,000 \times 50 = \$50,000$$

Wapshot has also borrowed $25,000, and so V, the aggregate market value of all Wapshot's outstanding securities, is

$$V = D + E = \$75,000$$

Wapshot's stock is known as *levered equity*. Its stockholders face the benefits and costs of **financial leverage,** or *gearing.* Suppose that Wapshot "levers up" still further by borrowing an additional $10,000 and paying the proceeds out to shareholders as a special dividend of $10 per share. This substitutes debt for equity capital with no impact on Wapshot's assets.

What will Wapshot's equity be worth after the special dividend is paid? We have two unknowns, E and V:

Old debt	$25,000 ⎫	
New debt	$10,000 ⎭	$35,000 = D
Equity		? = E
Firm value		? = V

If V is $75,000 as before, then E must be $V - D = 75,000 - 35,000 = \$40,000$. Stockholders have suffered a capital loss that exactly offsets the $10,000 special dividend. But if V *increases* to, say, $80,000 as a result of the change in capital structure, then $E = \$45,000$ and the stockholders are $5,000 ahead. In general, any increase or decrease in V caused by a shift in capital structure accrues to the firm's stockholders. We conclude that a policy that maximizes the market value of the firm is also best for the firm's stockholders.

This conclusion rests on two important assumptions: first, that Wapshot can ignore payout policy and, second, that after the change in capital structure the old and new debt are *worth* $35,000.

Payout policy may or may not be relevant, but there is no need to repeat the discussion of Chapter 12. We need only note that shifts in capital structure sometimes force important decisions about payout policy. Perhaps Wapshot's cash dividend has costs or benefits that should be considered in addition to any benefits achieved by its increased financial leverage.

Our second assumption that old and new debt ends up worth $35,000 seems innocuous. But it could be wrong. Perhaps the new borrowing has increased the risk of the old bonds. If the holders of old bonds cannot demand a higher rate of interest to compensate for the increased risk, the value of their investment is reduced. In this case Wapshot's stockholders gain at the expense of the holders of old bonds even though the overall value of the firm is unchanged.

But this anticipates issues better left to Chapter 14. In this chapter we assume that any new issue of debt has no effect on the market value of existing debt.

Enter Modigliani and Miller

Let us accept that the financial manager would like to find the combination of securities that maximizes the value of the firm. How is this done? MM's answer is that the financial manager should stop worrying: In a perfect market any combination of securities is as good as another. The value of the firm is unaffected by its choice of capital structure.[1]

You can see this by imagining two firms that generate the same stream of operating income and differ only in their capital structure. Firm U is unlevered. Therefore the total value of its equity E_U is the same as the total value of the firm V_U. Firm, L, on the other hand, is levered. The value of its stock is, therefore, equal to the value of the firm less the value of the debt: $E_L = V_L - D_L$.

Now think which of these firms you would prefer to invest in. If you don't want to take much risk, you can buy common stock in the unlevered firm U. For example, if you buy 1% of firm U's shares, your investment is $.01 V_U$ and you are entitled to 1% of the gross profits:

Dollar Investment	Dollar Return
$.01 V_U$	$.01 \times$ Profits

Now compare this with an alternative strategy. This is to purchase the same fraction of *both* the debt and the equity of firm L. Your investment and return would then be as follows:

	Dollar Investment	Dollar Return
Debt	$.01 D_L$	$.01 \times$ Interest
Equity	$.01 E_L$	$.01 \times$ (Profits − interest)
Total	$.01 (D_L + E_L)$	$.01 \times$ Profits
	$= .01 V_L$	

Both strategies offer the same payoff: 1% of the firm's profits. The law of one price tells us that in well-functioning markets two investments that offer the same payoff must have the same price. Therefore, $.01 V_U$ must equal $.01 V_L$: The value of the unlevered firm must equal the value of the levered firm.

Suppose that you are willing to run a little more risk. You decide to buy 1% of the outstanding shares in the *levered* firm. Your investment and return are now as follows:

Dollar Investment	Dollar Return
$.01 E_L$	$.01 \times$ (Profits − interest)
$= .01(V_L - D_L)$	

But there is an alternative strategy. This is to borrow $.01 D_L$ on your own account and purchase 1% of the stock of the *unlevered* firm. In this case, your borrowing gives you an immediate cash *inflow* of $.01 D_L$, but you have to pay interest on your loan equal to 1% of the interest that is paid by firm L. Your total investment and return are, therefore, as follows:

	Dollar Investment	Dollar Return
Borrowing	$-.01 D_L$	$-.01 \times$ Interest
Equity	$.01 V_U$	$.01 \times$ Profits
Total	$.01(V_U - D_L)$	$.01 \times$ (Profits − interest)

---

[1] F. Modigliani and M. H. Miller, "The Cost of Capital, Corporation Finance and the Theory of Investment," *American Economic Review* 48 (June 1958), pp. 261–297. MM's basic argument was anticipated in 1938 by J. B. Williams and to some extent by David Durand. See J. B. Williams, *The Theory of Investment Value* (Cambridge, MA: Harvard University Press, 1938) and D. Durand, "Cost of Debt and Equity Funds for Business: Trends and Problems of Measurement," *Conference on Research in Business Finance* (New York: National Bureau of Economic Research, 1952).

Again both strategies offer the same payoff: 1% of profits after interest. Therefore, both investments must have the same cost. The payoff $.01(V_U - D_L)$ must equal $.01(V_L - D_L)$ and V_U must equal V_L.

It does not matter whether the world is full of risk-averse chickens or venturesome lions. All would agree that the value of the unlevered firm U must be equal to the value of the levered firm L. As long as investors can borrow or lend on their own account on the same terms as the firm, they can "undo" the effect of any changes in the firm's capital structure. This is the basis for MM's famous proposition 1: "The market value of any firm is independent of its capital structure."

The Law of Conservation of Value

MM's argument that debt policy is irrelevant is an application of an astonishingly simple idea. If we have two streams of cash flow, A and B, then the present value of $A + B$ is equal to the present value of A plus the present value of B. We met this principle of *value additivity* in our discussion of capital budgeting, where we saw that the present value of two assets combined is equal to the sum of their present values considered separately.

In the present context we are not combining assets but splitting them up. But value additivity works just as well in reverse. We can slice a cash flow into as many parts as we like; the values of the parts will always sum back to the value of the unsliced stream. (Of course, we have to make sure that none of the stream is lost in the slicing. We cannot say, "The value of a pie is independent of how it is sliced," if the slicer is also a nibbler.)

This is really a *law of conservation of value.* The value of an asset is preserved regardless of the nature of the claims against it. Thus proposition 1: Firm value is determined on the *left-hand* side of the balance sheet by real assets—not by the proportions of debt and equity securities issued to buy the assets.

The simplest ideas often have the widest application. For example, we could apply the law of conservation of value to the choice between issuing preferred stock, common stock, or some combination. The law implies that the choice is irrelevant, assuming perfect capital markets and providing that the choice does not affect the firm's investment and operating policies. If the total value of the equity "pie" (preferred and common combined) is fixed, the firm's owners (its common stockholders) do not care how this pie is sliced.

The law also applies to the *mix* of debt securities issued by the firm. The choices of long-term versus short-term, secured versus unsecured, senior versus subordinated, and convertible versus nonconvertible debt all should have no effect on the overall value of the firm.

Combining assets and splitting them up will not affect values as long as they do not affect an investor's choice. When we showed that capital structure does not affect choice, we implicitly assumed that both companies and individuals can borrow and lend at the same risk-free rate of interest. As long as this is so, individuals can undo the effect of any changes in the firm's capital structure.

In practice corporate debt is not risk-free and firms cannot escape with rates of interest appropriate to a government security. Some people's initial reaction is that this alone invalidates MM's proposition. It is a natural mistake, but capital structure can be irrelevant even when debt is risky.

If a company borrows money, it does not *guarantee* repayment: It repays the debt in full only if its assets are worth more than the debt obligation. The shareholders in the company, therefore, have limited liability.

Many individuals would like to borrow with limited liability. They might, therefore, be prepared to pay a small premium for levered shares *if the supply of levered shares were insufficient to meet their needs.*[2] But there are literally thousands of common stocks of companies that borrow. Therefore it is unlikely that an issue of debt would induce them to pay a premium for *your* shares.[3]

An Example of Proposition 1

Macbeth Spot Removers is reviewing its capital structure. Table 13.1 shows its current position. The company has no leverage and all the operating income is paid as dividends to the common stockholders (we assume still that there are no taxes). The expected earnings and dividends per share are $1.50, but this figure is by no means certain—it could turn out to be more or less than $1.50. The price of each share is $10. Since the firm expects to produce a level stream of earnings in perpetuity, the expected return on the share is equal to the earnings–price ratio, 1.50/10.00 = .15, or 15%.

Ms. Macbeth, the firm's president, has come to the conclusion that shareholders would be better off if the company had equal proportions of debt and equity. She therefore proposes to issue $5,000 of debt at an interest rate of 10% and use the proceeds to repurchase 500 shares. To support her proposal, Ms. Macbeth has analyzed the situation under different assumptions about operating income. The results of her calculations are shown in Table 13.2.

To see more clearly how leverage would affect earnings per share, Ms. Macbeth has also produced Figure 13.1. The brown line shows how earnings per share would vary with operating income under the firm's current all-equity financing. It is, therefore, simply a plot of the data in Table 13.1. The green line shows how earnings per share would vary given equal proportions of debt and equity. It is, therefore, a plot of the data in Table 13.2.

Ms. Macbeth reasons as follows: "It is clear that the effect of leverage depends on the company's income. If income is greater than $1,000, the return to the equityholder is *increased* by leverage. If it is less than $1,000, the return is *reduced* by leverage. The return is unaffected when operating income is exactly $1,000. At this point the return on the market value of the assets is 10%, which is exactly equal to the interest rate on the debt. Our capital structure decision, therefore, boils down to what we think about income prospects. Since we expect operating income to be above the $1,000 break-even point, I believe we can best help our shareholders by going ahead with the $5,000 debt issue."

▶ TABLE 13.1
Macbeth Spot Removers is entirely equity-financed. Although it expects to have an income of $1,500 a year in perpetuity, this income is not certain. This table shows the return to the stockholder under different assumptions about operating income. We assume no taxes.

Data				
Number of shares	1,000			
Price per share	$10			
Market value of shares	$10,000			
Outcomes				
Operating income ($)	500	1,000	**1,500**	2,000
Earnings per share ($)	.50	1.00	**1.50**	2.00
Return on shares (%)	5	10	**15**	20
			Expected outcome	

---

[2] Of course, individuals could *create* limited liability if they chose. In other words, the lender could agree that borrowers need repay their debt in full only if the assets of company X are worth more than a certain amount. Presumably individuals don't enter into such arrangements because they can obtain limited liability more simply by investing in the stocks of levered companies.

[3] Capital structure is also irrelevant if each investor holds a fully diversified portfolio. In that case he or she owns *all* the risky securities offered by a company (both debt and equity). But anybody who owns *all* the risky securities doesn't care about how the cash flows are divided among different securities.

Data			
Number of shares	500		
Price per share	$10		
Market value of shares	$5,000		
Market value of debt	$5,000		
Interest at 10%	$500		

Outcomes			
Operating income ($)	500	1,000	**1,500**	2,000
Interest ($)	500	500	**500**	500
Equity earnings ($)	0	500	**1,000**	1,500
Earnings per share ($)	0	1	**2**	3
Return on shares (%)	0	10	**20**	30

**Expected
outcome**

▶ **TABLE 13.2**
Macbeth Spot Removers
is wondering whether
to issue $5,000 of debt
at an interest rate of
10% and repurchase
500 shares. This table
shows the return to the
shareholder under differ-
ent assumptions about
operating income.

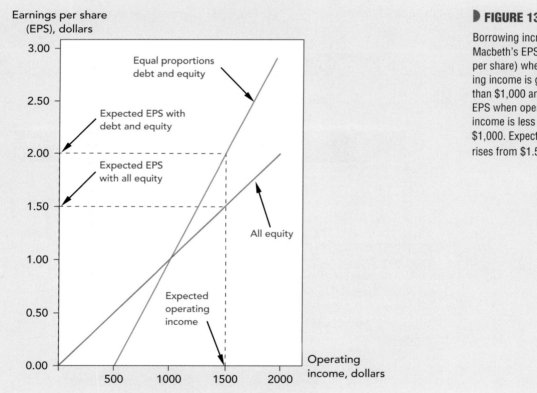

▶ **FIGURE 13.1**

Borrowing increases
Macbeth's EPS (earnings
per share) when operat-
ing income is greater
than $1,000 and reduces
EPS when operating
income is less than
$1,000. Expected EPS
rises from $1.50 to $2.

As financial manager of Macbeth Spot Removers, you reply as follows: "I agree that leverage will help the shareholder as long as our income is greater than $1,000. But your argument ignores the fact that Macbeth's shareholders have the alternative of borrowing on their own account. For example, suppose that an investor borrows $10 and then invests $20 in two unlevered Macbeth shares. This person has to put up only $10 of his or her own

▶ **TABLE 13.3**
Individual investors can replicate Macbeth's leverage.

	Operating Income ($)			
	500	**1,000**	**1,500**	**2,000**
Earnings on two shares ($)	1	2	3	4
Less interest at 10% ($)	1	1	1	1
Net earnings on investment ($)	0	1	2	3
Return on $10 investment (%)	0	10	20	30
			Expected outcome	

money. The payoff on the investment varies with Macbeth's operating income, as shown in Table 13.3. This is exactly the same set of payoffs as the investor would get by buying one share in the levered company. [Compare the last two lines of Tables 13.2 and 13.3.] Therefore, a share in the levered company must also sell for $10. If Macbeth goes ahead and borrows, it will not allow investors to do anything that they could not do already, and so it will not increase value."

The argument that you are using is exactly the same as the one MM used to prove proposition 1.

13-2 Financial Risk and Expected Returns

Consider now the implications of MM's proposition 1 for the expected returns on Macbeth stock:

	Current Structure: All Equity	Proposed Structure: Equal Debt and Equity
Expected earnings per share ($)	1.50	2.00
Price per share ($)	10	10
Expected return on share (%)	15	20

Leverage increases the expected stream of earnings per share but *not* the share price. The reason is that the change in the expected earnings stream is exactly offset by a change in the rate at which the earnings are discounted. The expected return on the share (which for a perpetuity is equal to the earnings–price ratio) increases from 15% to 20%. We now show how this comes about.

The expected return on Macbeth's assets r_A is equal to the expected operating income divided by the total market value of the firm's securities:

$$\text{Expected return on assets} = r_A = \frac{\text{expected operating income}}{\text{market value of all securities}}$$

We have seen that in perfect capital markets the company's borrowing decision does not affect *either* the firm's operating income *or* the total market value of its securities. Therefore the borrowing decision also does not affect the expected return on the firm's assets r_A.

Suppose that an investor holds all of a company's debt and all of its equity. This investor is entitled to all the firm's operating income; therefore, the expected return on the portfolio is just r_A.

The expected return on a portfolio is equal to a weighted average of the expected returns on the individual holdings. Therefore the expected return on a portfolio consisting of *all* the firm's securities is

Expected return on assets = (proportion in debt × expected return on debt)
+ (proportion in equity × expected return on equity)

$$r_A = \left(\frac{D}{D + E} \times r_D \right) + \left(\frac{E}{D + E} \times r_E \right)$$

This formula is of course an old friend from Chapter 9. The overall expected return r_A is called the *company cost of capital* or the *weighted-average cost of capital* (WACC).

We can turn the formula around to solve for r_E, the expected return to equity for a levered firm:

Expected return on equity = expected return on assets
+ (expected return on assets − expected return on debt)
× debt–equity ratio

$$r_E = r_A + (r_A - r_D)\frac{D}{E}$$

Proposition 2

This is MM's proposition 2: The expected rate of return on the common stock of a levered firm increases in proportion to the debt–equity ratio (*D/E*), expressed in market values; the rate of increase depends on the spread between r_A, the expected rate of return on a portfolio of all the firm's securities, and r_D, the expected return on the debt. Note that $r_E = r_A$ if the firm has no debt.

We can check out this formula for Macbeth Spot Removers. Before the decision to borrow

$$r_E = r_A = \frac{\text{expected operating income}}{\text{market value of all securities}}$$

$$= \frac{1,500}{10,000} = .15, \text{ or } 15\%$$

If the firm goes ahead with its plan to borrow, the expected return on assets r_A is still 15%. The expected return on equity is

$$r_E = r_A + (r_A - r_D)\frac{D}{E}$$

$$= .15 + (.15 - .10)\frac{5,000}{5,000} = .20, \text{ or } 20\%$$

When the firm was unlevered, equity investors demanded a return of r_A. When the firm is levered, they require a premium of $(r_A - r_D)D/E$ to compensate for the extra risk.

MM's proposition 1 says that financial leverage has no effect on shareholders' wealth. Proposition 2 says that the rate of return they can expect to receive on their shares increases as the firm's debt–equity ratio increases. How can shareholders be indifferent to increased leverage when it increases expected return? The answer is that any increase in expected return is exactly offset by an increase in risk and therefore in shareholders' *required* rate of return.

Look at what happens to the risk of Macbeth shares if it moves to equal debt–equity proportions. Table 13.4 shows how a shortfall in operating income affects the payoff to the shareholders.

If operating income falls from		$1,500	to	$500	Change
No debt:	Earnings per share	$1.50		$.50	−$1.00
	Return	15%		5%	−10%
50% debt:	Earnings per share	$2.00		0	−$2.00
	Return	20%		0	−20%

▶ **TABLE 13.4** Financial leverage increases the risk of Macbeth shares. A $1,000 drop in operating income reduces earnings per share by $1 with all-equity financing, but by $2 with 50% debt.

The debt–equity proportion does not affect the *dollar* risk borne by equityholders. Suppose operating income drops from $1,500 to $500. Under all-equity financing, equity earnings drop by $1 per share. There are 1,000 outstanding shares, and so *total* equity earnings fall by $1 × 1,000 = $1,000. With 50% debt, the same drop in operating income reduces earnings per share by $2. But there are only 500 shares outstanding, and so total equity income drops by $2 × 500 = $1,000, just as in the all-equity case.

However, the debt–equity choice does amplify the spread of *percentage* returns. If the firm is all-equity-financed, a decline of $1,000 in the operating income reduces the return on the shares by 10%. If the firm issues risk-free debt with a fixed interest payment of $500 a year, then a decline of $1,000 in the operating income reduces the return on the shares by 20%. In other words, the effect of the proposed leverage is to double the amplitude of the swings in Macbeth's shares. Whatever the beta of the firm's shares before the refinancing, it would be twice as high afterward.

Now you can see why investors require higher returns on levered equity. The required return simply rises to match the increased risk.

EXAMPLE 13.1 ● Leverage and the Cost of Equity

Let us revisit a numerical example from Chapter 9. We looked at a company with the following market-value balance sheet:

Asset value	100	Debt (D)	30	at r_D = 7.5%
		Equity (E)	70	at r_E = 15%
Asset value	100	Firm value (V)	100	

and an overall cost of capital of:

$$r_A = r_D \frac{D}{V} + r_E \frac{E}{V}$$

$$= \left(7.5 \times \frac{30}{100} \right) + \left(15 \times \frac{70}{100} \right) = 12.75\%$$

If the firm is contemplating investment in a project that has the same risk as the firm's existing business, the opportunity cost of capital for this project is the same as the firm's cost of capital; in other words, it is 12.75%.

What would happen if the firm issued an additional 10 of debt and used the cash to repurchase 10 of its equity? The revised market-value balance sheet is

Asset value	100	Debt (*D*)	40
		Equity (*E*)	60
Asset value	100	Firm value (*V*)	100

The change in financial structure does not affect the amount or risk of the cash flows on the total package of debt and equity. Therefore, if investors required a return of 12.75% on the total package before the refinancing, they must require a 12.75% return on the firm's assets afterward.

Although the required return on the *package* of debt and equity is unaffected, the change in financial structure does affect the required return on the individual securities. Since the company has more debt than before, the debtholders are likely to demand a higher interest rate. Suppose that the expected return on the debt rises to 7.875%. Now you can write down the basic equation for the return on assets

$$r_A = r_D \frac{D}{V} + r_E \frac{E}{V}$$

$$= \left(7.875 \times \frac{40}{100}\right) + \left(r_E \times \frac{60}{100}\right) = 12.75\%$$

and solve for the return on equity $r_E = 16.0\%$.

Increasing the amount of debt increased debtholder risk and led to a rise in the return that debtholders required (r_{debt} rose from 7.5 to 7.875%). The higher leverage also made the equity riskier and increased the return that shareholders required (r_E rose from 15% to 16%). The weighted-average return on debt and equity remained at 12.75%:

$$r_A = (r_D \times .4) + (r_E \times .6)$$

$$= (7.875 \times .4) + (16 \times 6) = 12.75\%$$

Suppose that the company decided instead to repay all its debt and to replace it with equity. In that case all the cash flows would go to the equityholders. The company cost of capital, r_A, would stay at 12.75%, and r_E would also be 12.75%.

•••••

How Changing Capital Structure Affects Beta

We have looked at how changes in financial structure affect expected return. Let us now look at the effect on beta.

The stockholders and debtholders both receive a share of the firm's cash flows, and both bear part of the risk. For example, if the firm's assets turn out to be worthless, there will be no cash to pay stockholders or debtholders. But debtholders usually bear much less risk than stockholders. Debt betas of large firms are typically in the range of .1 to .3.

If you owned a portfolio of all the firm's securities, you wouldn't share the cash flows with anyone. You wouldn't share the risks with anyone either; you would bear them all. Thus the firm's asset beta is equal to the beta of a portfolio of all the firm's debt and its equity.

The beta of this hypothetical portfolio is just a weighted average of the debt and equity betas:

$$\beta_A = \beta_{portfolio} = \beta_D \frac{D}{V} + \beta_E \frac{E}{V}$$

Think back to our example. If the debt before the refinancing has a beta of .1 and the equity has a beta of 1.1, then

$$\beta_A = \left(.1 \times \frac{30}{100}\right) + \left(1.1 \times \frac{70}{100}\right) = .8$$

What happens after the refinancing? The risk of the total package is unaffected, but both the debt and the equity are now more risky. Suppose that the debt beta increases to .2. We can work out the new equity beta:

$$\beta_A = \beta_{portfolio} = \beta_D\frac{D}{V} + \beta_E\frac{E}{V}$$

$$.8 = \left(.2 \times \frac{40}{100}\right) + \left(\beta_E \times \frac{60}{100}\right)$$

$$\beta_E = 1.2$$

Our example shows how borrowing creates financial leverage or gearing. Financial leverage does not affect the risk or the expected return on the firm's assets, but it does push up the risk of the common stock. Shareholders demand a correspondingly higher return because of this *financial risk*.

Now you can see how to *unlever* betas, that is, how to go from an observed β_E to β_A. You have the equity beta, say, 1.2. You also need the debt beta, say, .2, and the relative market values of debt (D/V) and equity (E/V). If debt accounts for 40% of overall value V, then the unlevered beta is

$$\beta_A = \left(.2 \times \frac{40}{100}\right) + \left(1.2 \times \frac{60}{100}\right) = .8$$

This runs the previous example in reverse. Just remember the basic relationship:

$$\beta_A = \beta_{portfolio} = \beta_D\left(\frac{D}{V}\right) + \beta_E\left(\frac{E}{V}\right)$$

MM's propositions warn us that higher leverage increases both expected equity returns and equity risk. It does *not* increase shareholder value. Having worked through the example of Macbeth, this much should now seem obvious. But watch out for hidden changes in leverage, such as a decision to lease new equipment or to underfund the pension scheme. Do not interpret any resultant increase in the expected equity return as creating additional shareholder value.

13-3 The Weighted-Average Cost of Capital

What did financial experts think about debt policy before MM? It is not easy to say because with hindsight we see that they did not think too clearly.[4] However, a "traditional" position emerged in response to MM. To understand it, we have to return to the weighted-average cost of capital.

Figure 13.2 sums up the implications of MM's propositions for the costs of debt and equity and the weighted-average cost of capital. The figure assumes that the firm's bonds are essentially risk-free at low debt levels. Thus r_D is independent of D/E, and r_E increases linearly as D/E increases. As the firm borrows more, the risk of default increases and the firm is required to pay higher rates of interest. Proposition 2 predicts that when this occurs

---

[4] Financial economists in 20 years may remark on Brealey, Myers, and Allen's blind spots and clumsy reasoning. On the other hand, they may not remember us at all.

MM's proposition 2. The expected return on equity r_E increases linearly with the debt–equity ratio so long as debt is risk-free. But if leverage increases the risk of the debt, debtholders demand a higher return on the debt. This causes the rate of increase in r_E to slow down.

the rate of increase in r_E slows down. This is also shown in Figure 13.2. The more debt the firm has, the less sensitive r_E is to further borrowing.

Why does the slope of the r_E line in Figure 13.2 taper off as D/E increases? Essentially because holders of risky debt bear some of the firm's business risk. As the firm borrows more, more of that risk is transferred from stockholders to bondholders.

Two Warnings

Sometimes the objective in financing decisions is stated not as "maximize overall market value" but as "minimize the weighted-average cost of capital." If MM's proposition 1 holds, then these are equivalent objectives. If MM's proposition 1 does *not* hold, then the capital structure that maximizes the value of the firm also minimizes the weighted-average cost of capital, *provided* that operating income is independent of capital structure. Remember that the weighted-average cost of capital is the expected rate of return on the market value of all of the firm's securities. Anything that increases the value of the firm reduces the weighted-average cost of capital if operating income is constant. But if operating income is varying too, all bets are off.

In Chapter 14 we show that financial leverage can affect operating income in several ways. Therefore maximizing the value of the firm is *not* always equivalent to minimizing the weighted-average cost of capital.

Warning 1   Shareholders want management to increase the firm's value. They are more interested in being rich than in owning a firm with a low weighted-average cost of capital.

Warning 2   Trying to minimize the weighted-average cost of capital seems to encourage logical short circuits like the following. Suppose that someone says, "Shareholders demand—and deserve—higher expected rates of return than bondholders do. Therefore debt is the cheaper capital source. We can reduce the weighted-average cost of capital by borrowing more." But this doesn't follow if the extra borrowing leads stockholders to demand a still higher expected rate of return. According to MM's proposition 2 the cost of equity capital r_E increases by just enough to keep the weighted-average cost of capital constant.

This is not the only logical short circuit you are likely to encounter. We have cited two more in Problem 15 at the end of this chapter.

Rates of Return on Levered Equity—The Traditional Position

You may ask why we have even mentioned the aim of minimizing the weighted-average cost of capital if it is often wrong or confusing. We had to because the traditionalists accept this objective and argue their case in terms of it.

The logical short circuit we just described rested on the assumption that r_E, the expected rate of return demanded by stockholders, does not rise, or rises very slowly, as the firm borrows more. Suppose, just for the sake of argument, that this is true. Then r_A, the weighted-average cost of capital, must decline as the debt–equity ratio rises.

The traditionalists' position is shown in Figure 13.3. They say that a moderate degree of financial leverage may increase the expected equity return r_E, but not as much as predicted by MM's proposition 2. But irresponsible firms that borrow *excessively* find r_E shooting up *faster* than MM predict. Therefore the weighted-average cost of capital declines at first, then rises. It reaches a minimum at some intermediate debt ratio. Remember that minimizing the weighted-average cost of capital is equivalent to maximizing firm value if operating income is not affected by borrowing.

Two arguments could be advanced in support of this position. First, perhaps investors do not notice or appreciate the financial risk created by moderate borrowing, although they wake up when debt is "excessive." If so, stockholders in moderately leveraged firms may accept a lower rate of return than they really should.

That seems naive.[5] The second argument is better. It accepts MM's reasoning as applied to perfect capital markets but holds that actual markets are imperfect. Because

▶ FIGURE 13.3

The dashed lines show MM's view of the effect of leverage on the expected return on equity r_E and the weighted-average cost of capital r_A. (See Figure 13.2.) The solid lines show the traditional view. Traditionalists say that borrowing at first increases r_E more slowly than MM predict but that r_E shoots up with excessive borrowing. If so, the weighted-average cost of capital can be minimized if you use just the right amount of debt.

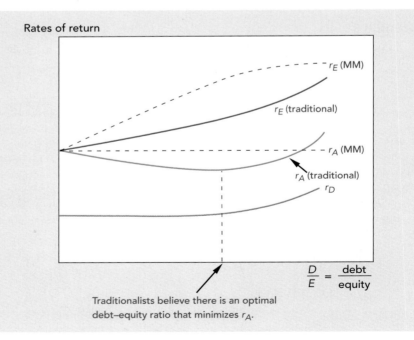

Rates of return

r_E (MM)

r_E (traditional)

r_A (MM)

r_A (traditional)

r_D

$\dfrac{D}{E} = \dfrac{\text{debt}}{\text{equity}}$

Traditionalists believe there is an optimal debt–equity ratio that minimizes r_A.

---

[5] This first argument may reflect a confusion between financial risk and the risk of default. Default is not a serious threat when borrowing is moderate; stockholders worry about it only when the firm goes "too far." But stockholders bear financial risk—in the form of increased volatility of rates of return and a higher beta—even when the chance of default is nil.

of these imperfections, firms that borrow may provide a valuable service for investors. If so, levered shares might trade at premium prices compared to their theoretical values in perfect markets.

Suppose that corporations can borrow more cheaply than individuals. Then it would pay investors who want to borrow to do so indirectly by holding the stock of levered firms. They would be willing to live with expected rates of return that do not fully compensate them for the business and financial risk they bear.

Is corporate borrowing really cheaper? It's hard to say. Interest rates on home mortgages are not too different from rates on high-grade corporate bonds.[6] Rates on margin debt (borrowing from a stockbroker with the investor's shares tendered as security) are not too different from the rates firms pay banks for short-term loans.

There are some individuals who face relatively high interest rates, largely because of the costs lenders incur in making and servicing small loans. There are economies of scale in borrowing. A group of small investors could do better by borrowing via a corporation, in effect pooling their loans and saving transaction costs.[7]

Suppose that this class of investors is large, both in number and in the aggregate wealth it brings to capital markets. That creates a clientele for whom corporate borrowing is better than personal borrowing. That clientele would, in principle, be willing to pay a premium for the shares of a levered firm.

But maybe it doesn't *have* to pay a premium. Perhaps smart financial managers long ago recognized this clientele and shifted the capital structures of their firms to meet its needs. The shifts would not have been difficult or costly. But if the clientele is now satisfied, it no longer needs to pay a premium for levered shares. Only the financial managers who *first* recognized the clientele extracted any advantage from it.

Maybe the market for corporate leverage is like the market for automobiles. Americans need millions of automobiles and are willing to pay thousands of dollars apiece for them. But that doesn't mean that you could strike it rich by going into the automobile business. You're at least 80 years too late.

Today's Unsatisfied Clienteles Are Probably Interested in Exotic Securities

So far we have made little progress in identifying cases where firm value might plausibly depend on financing. But our examples illustrate what smart financial managers look for. They look for an *unsatisfied* clientele, investors who want a particular kind of financial instrument but because of market imperfections can't get it or can't get it cheaply.

MM's proposition 1 is violated when the firm, by imaginative design of its capital structure, can offer some *financial service* that meets the needs of such a clientele. Either the service must be new and unique or the firm must find a way to provide some old service more cheaply than other firms or financial intermediaries can.

Now, is there an unsatisfied clientele for garden-variety debt or levered equity? We doubt it. But perhaps you can invent an exotic security and uncover a latent demand for it.

In the next several chapters we will encounter a number of new securities that have been invented by companies and advisers. These securities take the company's basic cash flows

[6] One of the authors once obtained a home mortgage at a rate 1/2 percentage point *less* than the contemporaneous yield on long-term AAA bonds.

[7] Even here there are alternatives to borrowing on personal account. Investors can draw down their savings accounts or sell a portion of their investment in bonds. The impact of reductions in lending on the investor's balance sheet and risk position is exactly the same as increases in borrowing.

and repackage them in ways that are thought to be more attractive to investors. However, while inventing these new securities is easy, it is more difficult to find investors who will rush to buy them.

Imperfections and Opportunities

The most serious capital market imperfections are often those created by government. An imperfection that supports a violation of MM's proposition 1 *also* creates a money-making opportunity. Firms and intermediaries will find some way to reach the clientele of investors frustrated by the imperfection.

For many years the U.S. government imposed a limit on the rate of interest that could be paid on savings accounts. It did so to protect savings institutions by limiting competition for their depositors' money. The fear was that depositors would run off in search of higher yields, causing a cash drain that savings institutions would not be able to meet.

These regulations created an opportunity for firms and financial institutions to design new savings schemes that were not subject to the interest-rate ceilings. One invention was the *floating-rate note,* first issued in 1974 by Citicorp, and with terms designed to appeal to individual investors. Floating-rate notes are medium-term debt securities whose interest payments "float" with short-term interest rates. On the Citicorp issue, for example, the coupon rate used to calculate each semiannual interest payment was set at 1 percentage point above the contemporaneous yield on Treasury bills. The holder of the Citicorp note was therefore protected against fluctuating interest rates, because Citicorp sent a larger check when interest rates rose (and, of course, a smaller check when rates fell).

Citicorp evidently found an untapped clientele of investors, for it was able to raise $650 million in the first offering. The success of the issue suggests that Citicorp was able to add value by changing its capital structure. However, other companies were quick to jump on Citicorp's bandwagon, and within five months an additional $650 million of floating-rate notes were issued by other companies. By the mid-1980s about $43 billion of floating-rate securities were outstanding, and now floating-rate debt securities seem ubiquitous.

Interest-rate regulation also provided financial institutions with an opportunity to create value by offering money-market funds. These are mutual funds invested in Treasury bills, commercial paper, and other high-grade, short-term debt instruments. Any saver with a few thousand dollars to invest can gain access to these instruments through a money-market fund and can withdraw money at any time by writing a check against his or her fund balance. Thus the fund resembles a checking or savings account that pays close to market interest rates. These money-market funds have become enormously popular. By 2009 their assets had risen to $3.7 trillion.[8]

Long before interest-rate ceilings were finally removed, most of the gains had gone out of issuing the new securities to individual investors. Once the clientele was finally satisfied, MM's proposition 1 was restored (until the government creates a new imperfection). The moral of the story is this: If you ever find an unsatisfied clientele, do something right away, or capital markets will evolve and steal it from you.

This is actually an encouraging message for the economy as a whole. If MM are right, investors' demands for different types of securities are satisfied at minimal cost. The cost

---

[8] Money-market funds are not totally safe. In 2008 the Reserve Primary Fund incurred heavy losses on its holdings of Lehman Brothers debt and became only the second money-market fund in history to "break the buck" by paying investors 97 cents to the dollar.

of capital will reflect only business risk. Capital will flow to companies with positive-NPV investments, regardless of the companies' capital structures. This is the efficient outcome.

13-4 A Final Word on the After-Tax Weighted-Average Cost of Capital

MM left us a simple message. When the firm changes its mix of debt and equity securities, the risk and expected returns of these securities change, but the company's overall cost of capital does not change.

Now if you think that message is too neat and simple, you're right. The complications are spelled out in the next two chapters. But we must note one complication here: Interest paid on a firm's borrowing can be deducted from taxable income. Thus the *after-tax* cost of debt is $r_D(1 - T_c)$, where T_c is the marginal corporate tax rate. So, when companies discount an average-risk project, they do not use the company cost of capital as we have just computed it. Instead they use the after-tax cost of debt to compute the after-tax weighted-average cost of capital or WACC:

$$\text{After-tax WACC} = r_D(1 - T_c)\frac{D}{V} + r_E\frac{E}{V}$$

We briefly introduced this formula in Chapter 9, where we used it to estimate the weighted-average cost of capital for Union Pacific. In 2009 Union Pacific's long-term borrowing rate was $r_D = 7.8\%$, and its estimated cost of equity was $r_E = 9.9\%$. With a 35% corporate tax rate, the after-tax cost of debt was $r_D(1 - T_c) = 7.8(1 - .35) = 5.1\%$. The ratio of debt to overall company value was $D/V = 31.5\%$. Therefore

$$\text{After-tax WACC} = r_D(1 - T_c)\frac{D}{V} + r_E\frac{E}{V}$$

$$= (1 - .35) \times 7.8 \times .315 + 9.9 \times .685 = 8.4\%$$

MM's proposition 2 states that *in the absence of taxes* the company cost of capital stays the same regardless of the amount of leverage. But, if companies receive a tax shield on their interest payments, then the after-tax WACC declines as debt increases. This is illustrated in Figure 13.4, which shows how Union Pacific's WACC changes as the debt–equity ratio changes.

▶ **FIGURE 13.4**

Estimated after-tax WACC for Union Pacific at different debt–equity ratios. The figure assumes $r_E = 9.9\%$ at a 31.5% debt ratio (equivalent to a 46% debt–equity ratio) and a borrowing rate of $r_D = 7.8\%$. Notice that the debt interest rate is assumed to increase with the debt–equity ratio.

• • • • •

SUMMARY

Think of the financial manager as taking all of the firm's real assets and selling them to investors as a package of securities. Some financial managers choose the simplest package possible: all-equity financing. Some end up issuing dozens of debt and equity securities. The problem is to find the particular combination that maximizes the market value of the firm.

Modigliani and Miller's (MM's) famous proposition 1 states that no combination is better than any other—that the firm's overall market value (the value of all its securities) is independent of capital structure. Firms that borrow do offer investors a more complex menu of securities, but investors yawn in response. The menu is redundant. Any shift in capital structure can be duplicated or "undone" by investors. Why should they pay extra for borrowing indirectly (by holding shares in a levered firm) when they can borrow just as easily and cheaply on their own accounts?

MM agree that borrowing raises the expected rate of return on shareholders' investments. But it also increases the risk of the firm's shares. MM show that the higher risk exactly offsets the increase in expected return, leaving stockholders no better or worse off.

Proposition 1 is an extremely general result. It applies not just to the debt–equity trade-off but to *any* choice of financing instruments. For example, MM would say that the choice between long-term and short-term debt has no effect on firm value.

The formal proofs of proposition 1 all depend on the assumption of perfect capital markets. MM's opponents, the "traditionalists," argue that market imperfections make personal borrowing excessively costly, risky, and inconvenient for some investors. This creates a natural clientele willing to pay a premium for shares of levered firms. The traditionalists say that firms should borrow to realize the premium.

But this argument is incomplete. There may be a clientele for levered equity, but that is not enough; the clientele has to be *unsatisfied*. There are already thousands of levered firms available for investment. Is there still an unsatiated clientele for garden-variety debt and equity? We doubt it.

Proposition 1 is violated when financial managers find an untapped demand and satisfy it by issuing something new and different. The argument between MM and the traditionalists finally boils down to whether this is difficult or easy. We lean toward MM's view: Finding unsatisfied clienteles and designing exotic securities to meet their needs is a game that's fun to play but hard to win.

If MM are right, the overall cost of capital—the expected rate of return on a portfolio of all the firm's outstanding securities—is the same regardless of the mix of securities issued to finance the firm. The overall cost of capital is usually called the company cost of capital or the weighted-average cost of capital (WACC). MM say that WACC doesn't depend on capital structure. But MM assume away lots of complications. The first complication is taxes. When we recognize that debt interest is tax-deductible, and compute WACC with the after-tax interest rate, WACC declines as the debt ratio increases. There is more—lots more—on taxes and other complications in the next two chapters.

• • • • •

FURTHER READING

The fall 1988 issue of the Journal of Economic Perspectives *contains a collection of articles, including one by Modigliani and Miller, which reviews and assesses the MM propositions. The summer 1989 issue of* Financial Management *contains three more articles under the heading "Reflections on the MM Propositions 30 Years Later."*

Two surveys of financial innovation include:

K. A. Karow, G. R. Erwin, and J. J. McConnell, "Survey of U.S. Corporate Financing Innovations: 1970–1997," *Journal of Applied Corporate Finance* 12 (Spring 1999), pp. 55–69.

P. Tufano, "Financial Innovation," in G. M. Constantinides, M. Harris, and R. Stulz (eds.), *Handbook of the Economics of Finance*, Vol. 1A (Amsterdam: Elsevier/North-Holland, 2003).

Miller reviews the MM propositions in:

M. H. Miller, "The Modigliani-Miller Propositions after Thirty Years," *Journal of Applied Corporate Finance* 2 (Spring 1989), pp. 6–18.

For a skeptic's view of MM's arguments see:

S. Titman, "The Modigliani-Miller Theorem and the Integration of Financial Markets," *Financial Management* 31 (Spring 2002), pp. 101–115.

● ● ● ● ●

BASIC

PROBLEM SETS

1. Ms. Kraft owns 50,000 shares of the common stock of Copperhead Corporation with a market value of $2 per share, or $100,000 overall. The company is currently financed as follows:

	Book Value
Common stock (8 million shares)	$2 million
Short-term loans	$2 million

   Copperhead now announces that it is replacing $1 million of short-term debt with an issue of common stock. What action can Ms. Kraft take to ensure that she is entitled to exactly the same proportion of profits as before?

2. Spam Corp. is financed entirely by common stock and has a beta of 1.0. The firm is expected to generate a level, perpetual stream of earnings and dividends. The stock has a price–earnings ratio of 8 and a cost of equity of 12.5%. The company's stock is selling for $50. Now the firm decides to repurchase half of its shares and substitute an equal value of debt. The debt is risk-free, with a 5% interest rate. The company is exempt from corporate income taxes. Assuming MM are correct, calculate the following items after the refinancing:
   a. The cost of equity.
   b. The overall cost of capital (WACC).
   c. The price–earnings ratio.
   d. The stock price.
   e. The stock's beta.

3. The common stock and debt of Northern Sludge are valued at $50 million and $30 million, respectively. Investors currently require a 16% return on the common stock and an 8% return on the debt. If Northern Sludge issues an additional $10 million of common stock and uses this money to retire debt, what happens to the expected return on the stock? Assume that the change in capital structure does not affect the risk of the debt and that there are no taxes.

4. Suppose that Macbeth Spot Removers issues only $2,500 of debt and uses the proceeds to repurchase 250 shares.
   a. Rework Table 13.2 to show how earnings per share and share return now vary with operating income.
   b. If the beta of Macbeth's assets is .8 and its debt is risk-free, what would be the beta of the equity after the debt issue?

5. True or false?

   a. MM's propositions assume perfect financial markets, with no distorting taxes or other imperfections.

   b. MM's proposition 1 says that corporate borrowing increases earnings per share but reduces the price–earnings ratio.

   c. MM's proposition 2 says that the cost of equity increases with borrowing and that the increase is proportional to D/V, the ratio of debt to firm value.

   d. MM's proposition 2 assumes that increased borrowing does not affect the interest rate on the firm's debt.

   e. Borrowing does not increase financial risk and the cost of equity if there is no risk of bankruptcy.

   f. Borrowing increases firm value if there is a clientele of investors with a reason to prefer debt.

6. Look back to Section 13–1. Suppose that Ms. Macbeth's investment bankers have informed her that since the new issue of debt is risky, debtholders will demand a return of 12.5%, which is 2.5% above the risk-free interest rate.

   a. What are r_A and r_E?

   b. Suppose that the beta of the unlevered stock was .6. What will β_A, β_E, and β_D be after the change to the capital structure?

7. Note the two blank graphs in Figure 13.5 below. On graph (*a*), assume MM are right, and plot the relationship between financial leverage (debt–equity ratio) and (i) the rates of return on debt and equity and (ii) the weighted-average cost of capital. Then fill in graph (*b*), assuming the traditionalists are right.

8. Gaucho Services starts life with all-equity financing and a cost of equity of 14%. Suppose it refinances to the following market-value capital structure:

Debt (*D*)	45%	at $r_D = 9.5\%$
Equity (*E*)	55%	

   Use MM's proposition 2 to calculate the new cost of equity. Gaucho pays taxes at a marginal rate of $T_c = 40\%$. Calculate Gaucho's after-tax weighted-average cost of capital.

INTERMEDIATE

9. Companies A and B differ only in their capital structure. A is financed by 30% debt and 70% equity; B is financed by 10% debt and 90% equity. The debt of both companies is risk-free.

   a. Rosencrantz owns 1% of the common stock of A. What other investment package would produce identical cash flows for Rosencrantz?

   b. Guildenstern owns 2% of the common stock of B. What other investment package would produce identical cash flows for Guildenstern?

▶ **FIGURE 13.5**

See Problem 7.

   c. Show that neither Rosencrantz nor Guildenstern would invest in the common stock of B if the *total* value of company A were less than that of B.

10. Here is a limerick:

There once was a man named Carruthers,
Who kept cows with miraculous udders.
He said, "Isn't this neat?
They give cream from one teat,
And skim milk from each of the others!"

What is the analogy between Mr. Carruthers's cows and firms' financing decisions? What would MM's proposition 1, suitably adapted, say about the value of Mr. Carruthers's cows? Explain.

11. Executive Chalk is financed solely by common stock and has outstanding 25 million shares with a market price of $10 a share. It now announces that it intends to issue $160 million of debt and to use the proceeds to buy back common stock.

   a. How is the market price of the stock affected by the announcement?

   b. How many shares can the company buy back with the $160 million of new debt that it issues?

   c. What is the market value of the firm (equity plus debt) after the change in capital structure?

   d. What is the debt ratio after the change in structure?

   e. Who (if anyone) gains or loses?

Now try the next question.

12. Executive Cheese has issued debt with a market value of $100 million and has outstanding 15 million shares with a market price of $10 a share. It now announces that it intends to issue a further $60 million of debt and to use the proceeds to buy back common stock. Debtholders, seeing the extra risk, mark the value of the existing debt down to $70 million.

   a. How is the market price of the stock affected by the announcement?

   b. How many shares can the company buy back with the $60 million of new debt that it issues?

   c. What is the market value of the firm (equity plus debt) after the change in capital structure?

   d. What is the debt ratio after the change in structure?

   e. Who (if anyone) gains or loses?

13. Hubbard's Pet Foods is financed 80% by common stock and 20% by bonds. The expected return on the common stock is 12% and the rate of interest on the bonds is 6%. Assuming that the bonds are default-risk-free, draw a graph that shows the expected return of Hubbard's common stock (r_E) and the expected return on the package of common stock and bonds (r_A) for different debt–equity ratios.

14. "MM totally ignore the fact that as you borrow more, you have to pay higher rates of interest." Explain carefully whether this is a valid objection.

15. Indicate what's wrong with the following arguments:

   a. "As the firm borrows more and debt becomes risky, both stockholders and bondholders demand higher rates of return. Thus by *reducing* the debt ratio we can reduce *both* the cost of debt and the cost of equity, making everybody better off."

   b. "Moderate borrowing doesn't significantly affect the probability of financial distress or bankruptcy. Consequently moderate borrowing won't increase the expected rate of return demanded by stockholders."

16. Each of the following statements is false or at least misleading. Explain why in each case.

    a. "A capital investment opportunity offering a 10% DCF rate of return is an attractive project if it can be 100% debt-financed at an 8% interest rate."

    b. "The more debt the firm issues, the higher the interest rate it must pay. That is one important reason why firms should operate at conservative debt levels."

17. Can you invent any new kinds of debt that might be attractive to investors? Why do you think they have not been issued?

18. Imagine a firm that is expected to produce a level stream of operating profits. As leverage is increased, what happens to:

    a. The ratio of the market value of the equity to income after interest?

    b. The ratio of the market value of the *firm* to income before interest if (i) MM are right and (ii) the traditionalists are right?

19. Archimedes Levers is financed by a mixture of debt and equity. You have the following information about its cost of capital:

$r_E = $ ___	$r_D = 12\%$	$r_A = $ ___
$\beta_E = 1.5$	$\beta_D = $ ___	$\beta_A = $ ___
$r_f = 10\%$	$r_m = 18\%$	$D/V = .5$

    Can you fill in the blanks?

20. Look back to Problem 19. Suppose now that Archimedes repurchases debt and issues equity so that $D/V = .3$. The reduced borrowing causes r_D to fall to 11%. How do the other variables change?

21. Omega Corporation has 10 million shares outstanding, now trading at $55 per share. The firm has estimated the expected rate of return to shareholders at about 12%. It has also issued long-term bonds at an interest rate of 7%. It pays tax at a marginal rate of 35%.

    a. What is Omega's after-tax WACC?

    b. How much higher would WACC be if Omega used no debt at all? (*Hint:* For this problem you can assume that the firm's overall beta [β_A] is not affected by its capital structure or the taxes saved because debt interest is tax-deductible.)

22. Gamma Airlines has an asset beta of 1.5. The risk-free interest rate is 6%, and the market risk premium is 8%. Assume the capital asset pricing model is correct. Gamma pays taxes at a marginal rate of 35%. Draw a graph plotting Gamma's cost of equity and after-tax WACC as a function of its debt-to-equity ratio D/E, from no debt to $D/E = 1.0$. Assume that Gamma's debt is risk-free up to $D/E = .25$. Then the interest rate increases to 6.5% at $D/E = .5$, 7% at $D/E = .8$, and 8% at $D/E = 1.0$. As in Problem 21, you can assume that the firm's overall beta (β_A) is not affected by its capital structure or the taxes saved because debt interest is tax-deductible.

CHALLENGE

23. Consider the following three tickets: Ticket A pays $10 if _____ is elected as president, ticket B pays $10 if _____ is elected, and ticket C pays $10 if neither is elected. (Fill in the blanks yourself.) Could the three tickets sell for less than the present value of $10? Could they sell for more? Try auctioning off the tickets. What are the implications for MM's proposition 1?

24. People often convey the idea behind MM's proposition 1 by various supermarket analogies, for example, "The value of a pie should not depend on how it is sliced," or, "The cost of a whole chicken should equal the cost of assembling one by buying two drumsticks, two wings, two breasts, and so on."

Actually proposition 1 doesn't work in the supermarket. You'll pay less for an uncut whole pie than for a pie assembled from pieces purchased separately. Supermarkets charge more for chickens after they are cut up. Why? What costs or imperfections cause proposition 1 to fail in the supermarket? Are these costs or imperfections likely to be important for corporations issuing securities on the U.S. or world capital markets? Explain.

25. Suppose that new security designs could be patented.[9] The patent holder could restrict use of the new design or charge other firms royalties for using it. What effect would such patents have on MM's capital-structure irrelevance theory?

---

[9] So far security designs cannot be patented, but other financial applications have received patent protection. See J. Lerner, "Where Does State Street Lead? A First Look at Finance Patents," *Journal of Finance* 57 (April 2002), pp. 901–930.

14

CHAPTER ● ● ● ● ●

PAYOUT POLICY AND CAPITAL STRUCTURE

How Much Should a Corporation Borrow?

▶ **In Chapter 13** we found that debt policy rarely matters in well-functioning capital markets with no frictions or imperfections. Few financial managers would accept that conclusion as a practical guideline. If debt policy doesn't matter, then they shouldn't worry about it—financing decisions could be routine or erratic—it wouldn't matter. Yet financial managers do worry about debt policy. This chapter explains why.

If debt policy were completely irrelevant, then actual debt ratios should vary randomly from firm to firm and industry to industry. Yet almost all airlines, utilities, banks, and real estate development companies rely heavily on debt. And so do many firms in capital-intensive industries such as steel, aluminum, chemicals, petroleum, and mining. On the other hand, it is rare to find a pharmaceutical company or advertising agency that is not predominantly equity-financed. Glamorous growth companies rarely use much debt despite rapid expansion and often heavy requirements for capital.

The explanation of these patterns lies partly in the things we left out of the last chapter. We mostly ignored taxes. We assumed bankruptcy was cheap, quick, and painless. It isn't, and there are costs associated with financial distress even if legal bankruptcy is ultimately avoided. We ignored potential conflicts of interest between the firm's security holders. For example, we did not consider what happens to the firm's "old" creditors when new debt is issued or when a shift in investment strategy takes the firm into a riskier business. We ignored the information problems that favor debt over equity when cash must be raised from new security issues. We ignored the incentive effects of financial leverage on management's investment and payout decisions.

Now we will put all these things back in: taxes first, then the costs of bankruptcy and financial distress. This will lead us to conflicts of interest and to information and incentive problems. In the end we will have to admit that debt policy does matter.

However, we will not throw away the MM theory we developed so carefully in Chapter 13. We're shooting for a theory combining MM's insights plus the effects of taxes, costs of bankruptcy and financial distress, and various other complications. We're not dropping back to a theory based on inefficiencies in the capital market. Instead, we want to see how well-functioning capital markets respond to taxes and the other things covered in this chapter.

● ● ● ● ●

14-1 Corporate Taxes

Debt financing has one important advantage under the corporate income tax system in the U.S. and many other countries. The interest that the company pays is a tax-deductible expense. Thus the return to bondholders escapes taxation at the corporate level.

Table 14.1 shows simple income statements for firm U, which has no debt, and firm L, which has borrowed $1,000 at 8%. L's tax bill is $28 less than U's. This is the *tax shield*

	Income Statement of Firm U	Income Statement of Firm L
Earnings before interest and taxes	$1,000	$1,000
Interest paid to bondholders	0	80
Pretax income	1,000	920
Tax at 35%	350	322
Net income to stockholders	$ 650	$ 598
Total income to both bondholders and stockholders	$0 + 650 = $650	$80 + 598 = $678
Interest tax shield (.35 × interest)	$0	$28

▶ **TABLE 14.1**   The tax deductibility of interest increases the total income that can be paid out to bondholders and stockholders.

provided by the debt of L. In effect the government pays 35% of the interest expense of L. The total income that L can pay out to its bondholders and stockholders increases by that amount.

Tax shields can be valuable assets. Suppose that the debt of L is fixed and permanent. (That is, the company commits to refinance its present debt obligations when they mature and to keep rolling over its debt obligations indefinitely.) Then L can look forward to a permanent stream of cash flows of $28 per year. The risk of these flows is likely to be less than the risk of the operating assets of L. The tax shields depend only on the corporate tax rate[1] and on the ability of L to earn enough to cover interest payments. The corporate tax rate has been pretty stable. And the ability of L to earn its interest payments must be reasonably sure; otherwise it could not have borrowed at 8%. Therefore we should discount the interest tax shields at a relatively low rate.

But what rate? One common assumption is that the risk of the tax shields is the same as that of the interest payments generating them. Thus we discount at 8%, the expected rate of return demanded by investors who are holding the firm's debt:

$$\text{PV(tax shield)} = \frac{28}{.08} = \$350$$

In effect the government assumes 35% of the $1,000 debt obligation of L.

Under these assumptions, the present value of the tax shield is independent of the return on the debt r_D. It equals the corporate tax rate T_c times the amount borrowed D:

$$\text{Interest payment} = \text{return on debt} \times \text{amount borrowed}$$
$$= r_D \times D$$

$$\text{PV(tax shield)} = \frac{\text{corporate tax rate} \times \text{interest payment}}{\text{expected return on debt}}$$
$$= \frac{T_c r_D D}{r_D} = T_c D$$

---

[1] Always use the marginal corporate tax rate, not the average rate. Average rates are often much lower than marginal rates because of accelerated depreciation and other tax adjustments. For large corporations, the marginal rate is usually taken as the statutory rate, which was 35% when this chapter was written (2009). However, effective marginal rates can be less than the statutory rate, especially for smaller, riskier companies that cannot be sure that they will earn taxable income in the future.

Of course, PV(tax shield) is less if the firm does not plan to borrow a permanent fixed amount,[2] or if it may not have enough taxable income to use the interest tax shields.[3]

How Do Interest Tax Shields Contribute to the Value of Stockholders' Equity?

MM's proposition 1 amounts to saying that the value of a pie does not depend on how it is sliced. The pie is the firm's assets, and the slices are the debt and equity claims. If we hold the pie constant, then a dollar more of debt means a dollar less of equity value.

But there is really a third slice, the government's. Look at Table 14.2. It shows an expanded balance sheet with *pretax* asset value on the left and the value of the government's tax claim recognized as a liability on the right. MM would still say that the value of the pie—in this case *pretax* asset value—is not changed by slicing. But anything the firm can do to reduce the size of the government's slice obviously makes stockholders better off. One thing it can do is borrow money, which reduces its tax bill and, as we saw in Table 14.1, increases the cash flows to debt and equity investors. The *after-tax* value of the firm (the sum of its debt and equity values as shown in a normal market-value balance sheet) goes up by PV(tax shield).

Recasting Merck's Capital Structure

Merck is a large, successful firm that uses relatively little long-term debt. Table 14.3(*a*) shows simplified book- and market-value balance sheets for Merck in December 2008.

Suppose that you were Merck's financial manager with complete responsibility for its capital structure. You decide to borrow an additional $1 billion on a permanent basis and use the proceeds to repurchase shares.

Table 14.3(*b*) shows the new balance sheets. The book version simply has $1,000 million more long-term debt and $1,000 million less equity. But we know that Merck's assets must be worth more because its tax bill has been reduced by 35% of the interest on the new

▶ **TABLE 14.2**

Normal and expanded market-value balance sheets. In a normal balance sheet, assets are valued after tax. In the expanded balance sheet, assets are valued pretax, and the value of the government's tax claim is recognized on the right-hand side. Interest tax shields are valuable because they reduce the government's claim.

Normal Balance Sheet (Market Values)

Asset value of (present value of after-tax cash flows)	Debt
	Equity
Total assets	Total value

Expanded Balance Sheet (Market Values)

Pretax asset value (present value of pretax cash flows)	Debt
	Government's claim (present value of future taxes)
	Equity
Total pretax assets	Total pretax value

---

[2] In this example, we assume that the amount of debt is fixed and stable over time. The natural alternative assumption is a fixed *ratio* of debt to firm value. If the ratio is fixed, then the level of debt and the amount of interest tax shields will fluctuate as firm value fluctuates. In that case projected interest tax shields can't be discounted at the cost of debt. We cover this point in detail in the next chapter.

[3] If the income of L does not cover interest in some future year, the tax shield is not necessarily lost. L can carry back the loss and receive a tax refund up to the amount of taxes paid in the previous two years. If L has a string of losses, and thus no prior tax payments that can be refunded, then losses can be carried forward and used to shield income in later years.

Book Values

Net working capital	$ 4,986.2	$ 3,943.3	Long-term debt
		10,175.4	Other long-term liabilities
Long-term assets	27,890.8	18,758.3	Equity
Total assets	$32,877.0	$32,877.0	Total value

Market Values

Net working capital	$ 4,986.2	$ 3,943.3	Long-term debt
PV interest tax shield	1,380.2	10,175.4	Other long-term liabilities
Long-term assets	72,680.6	64,928.3	Equity
Total assets	$79,047.0	$79,047.0	Total value

▶ **TABLE 14.3a** Simplified balance sheets for Merck, December 2008 (figures in millions).

Notes:
1. Market value is equal to book value for net working capital, long-term debt, and other long-term liabilities. Market value of equity = number of shares times closing price for December 2008. The difference between the market and book values of long-term assets is equal to the difference between the market and book values of equity.
2. PV interest tax shield assumes fixed, perpetual debt, with a 35% tax rate.

Book Values

Net working capital	$ 4,986.2	$ 4,943.3	Long-term debt
		10,175.4	Other long-term liabilities
Long-term assets	27,890.8	17,758.3	Equity
Total assets	$32,877.0	$32,877.0	Total value

Market Values

Net working capital	$ 4,986.2	$ 4,943.3	Long-term debt
PV interest tax shield	1,730.2	10,175.4	Other long-term liabilities
Long-term assets	72,680.6	64,278.3	Equity
Total assets	$79,397.0	$79,397.0	Total value

▶ **TABLE 14.3b** Balance sheets for Merck with additional $1 billion of long-term debt substituted for stockholders' equity (figures in millions).

debt. In other words, Merck has an increase in PV(interest tax shield), which is worth $T_cD = .35 \times \$1,000$ million $= \$350$ million. If the MM theory holds *except* for taxes, firm value must increase by $350 million to $79,397 million. Merck's equity ends up worth $64,278 million.

Now you have repurchased $1,000 million worth of shares, but Merck's equity value has dropped by only $650 million. Therefore Merck's stockholders must be $350 million ahead. Not a bad day's work.[4]

MM and Taxes

We have just developed a version of MM's proposition 1 as corrected by them to reflect corporate income taxes.[5] The new proposition is

$$\text{Value of firm} = \text{value if all-equity-financed} + \text{PV(tax shield)}$$

In the special case of permanent debt,

$$\text{Value of firm} = \text{value if all-equity-financed} + T_cD$$

---

[4] Notice that, as long as the bonds are sold at a fair price, all the benefits from the tax shield must go to the shareholders.

[5] Interest tax shields are recognized in MM's original article, F. Modigliani and M. H. Miller, "The Cost of Capital, Corporation Finance and the Theory of Investment," *American Economic Review* 48 (June 1958), pp. 261–296. The valuation procedure used in Table 14.3(*b*) is presented in their 1963 article, "Corporate Income Taxes and the Cost of Capital: A Correction," *American Economic Review* 53 (June 1963), pp. 433–443.

Our imaginary financial surgery on Merck provides the perfect illustration of the problems inherent in this "corrected" theory. That $350 million came too easily; it seems to violate the law that there is no such thing as a money machine. And if Merck's stockholders would be richer with $4,943 million of corporate debt, why not $5,943 or $15,943 million? At what debt level should Merck stop borrowing? Our formula implies that firm value and stockholders' wealth continue to go up as D increases. The optimal debt policy appears to be embarrassingly extreme. All firms should be 100% debt-financed.

MM were not that fanatical about it. No one would expect the formula to apply at extreme debt ratios. There are several reasons why our calculations overstate the value of interest tax shields. First, it's wrong to think of debt as fixed and perpetual; a firm's ability to carry debt changes over time as profits and firm value fluctuate. Second, many firms face marginal tax rates less than 35%. Third, you can't use interest tax shields unless there will be future profits to shield—and no firm can be absolutely sure of that.

But none of these qualifications explains why companies like Merck survive and thrive at low debt ratios. It's hard to believe that Merck's financial managers are simply missing the boat.

A conservative debt policy can of course be great comfort when a company suffers a sudden adverse shock. For Merck, that shock came in September 2004, when it became clear that its blockbuster painkiller Vioxx increased the risk of heart attacks in some patients. When Merck withdrew Vioxx from the market, it lost billions of dollars in future revenues and had to spend or set aside nearly $5 billion for legal costs and settlements. Yet the company's credit rating was not harmed, and it retained ample cash flow to fund all its investments, including research and development, and to maintain its regular dividend. But if Merck was that strong financially *after* the loss of Vioxx, was its debt policy before the loss excessively conservative? Why did it pass up the opportunity to borrow a few billion more (as in Table 14.3[b]), thus substituting tax-deductible interest for taxable income to shareholders?

We seem to have argued ourselves into a blind alley. But there may be two ways out:

1. Perhaps a fuller examination of the U.S. system of corporate *and personal* taxation will uncover a tax disadvantage of corporate borrowing, offsetting the present value of the interest tax shield.

2. Perhaps firms that borrow incur other costs—bankruptcy costs, for example.

We now explore these two escape routes.

14-2 Corporate and Personal Taxes

When personal taxes are introduced, the firm's objective is no longer to minimize the *corporate* tax bill; the firm should try to minimize the present value of *all* taxes paid on corporate income. "All taxes" include *personal* taxes paid by bondholders and stockholders.

Figure 14.1 illustrates how corporate and personal taxes are affected by leverage. Depending on the firm's capital structure, a dollar of operating income will accrue to investors either as debt interest or equity income (dividends or capital gains). That is, the dollar can go down either branch of Figure 14.1.

Notice that Figure 14.1 distinguishes between T_p, the personal tax rate on interest, and T_{pE}, the effective personal tax rate on equity income. This rate can be well below T_p, depending on the mix of dividends and capital gains realized by shareholders. The top marginal rate on dividends and capital gains is now (2009) only 15% while the top rate on

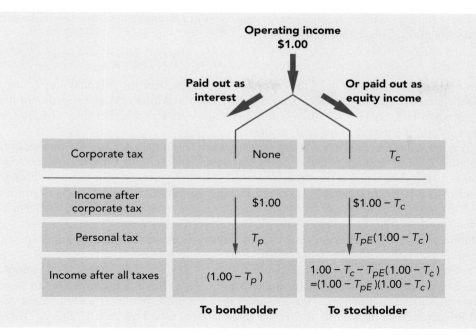

▶ FIGURE 14.1

The firm's capital structure determines whether operating income is paid out as interest or equity income. Interest is taxed only at the personal level. Equity income is taxed at both the corporate and the personal levels. However, T_{pE}, the personal tax rate on equity income, can be less than T_p, the personal tax rate on interest income.

other income, including interest income, is 35%. Also capital gains taxes can be deferred until shares are sold, so the top *effective* capital gains rate is usually less than 15%.

The firm's objective should be to arrange its capital structure to maximize after-tax income. You can see from Figure 14.1 that corporate borrowing is better if $(1 - T_p)$ is more than $(1 - T_{pE}) \times (1 - T_c)$; otherwise it is worse. The *relative tax* advantage of debt over equity is

$$\text{Relative tax advantage of debt} = \frac{1 - T_p}{(1 - T_{pE})(1 - T_c)}$$

This suggests two special cases. First, suppose that debt and equity income were taxed at the same effective personal rate. But with $T_{pE} = T_p$, the relative advantage depends only on the *corporate rate:*

$$\text{Relative advantage} = \frac{1 - T_p}{(1 - T_{pE})(1 - T_c)} = \frac{1}{1 - T_c}$$

In this case, we can forget about personal taxes. The tax advantage of corporate borrowing is exactly as MM calculated it.[6] They do not have to assume away personal taxes. Their theory of debt and taxes requires only that debt and equity be taxed at the same rate.

---

[6] Personal taxes reduce the dollar amount of corporate interest tax shields, but the appropriate discount rate for cash flows after personal tax is also lower. If investors are willing to lend at a prospective return *before* personal taxes of r_D, then they must also be willing to accept a return *after* personal taxes of $r_D(1 - T_p)$, where T_p is the marginal rate of personal tax. Thus we can compute the value after personal taxes of the tax shield on permanent debt:

$$\text{PV(tax shield)} = \frac{T_c \times r_D D \times (1 - T_p)}{r_D \times (1 - T_p)} = T_c D$$

This brings us back to our previous formula for firm value:

$$\text{Value of firm} = \text{value if all-equity-financed} + T_c D$$

The second special case occurs when corporate and personal taxes cancel to make debt policy irrelevant. This requires

$$1 - T_p = (1 - T_{pE})(1 - T_c)$$

This case can happen only if T_c, the corporate rate, is less than the personal rate T_p *and* if T_{pE}, the effective rate on equity income, is small. Merton Miller explored this situation at a time when U.S. tax rates on interest and dividends were much higher than now, but we won't go into the details of his analysis here.[7]

In any event we seem to have a simple, practical decision rule. Arrange the firm's capital structure to shunt operating income down that branch of Figure 14.1 where the tax is least. Unfortunately that is not as simple as it sounds. What's T_{pE}, for example? The shareholder roster of any large corporation is likely to include tax-exempt investors (such as pension funds or university endowments) as well as millionaires. All possible tax brackets will be mixed together. And it's the same with T_p, the personal tax rate on interest. The large corporation's "typical" bondholder might be a tax-exempt pension fund, but many taxpaying investors also hold corporate debt.

Some investors may be much happier to buy your debt than others. For example, you should have no problems inducing pension funds to lend; they don't have to worry about personal tax. But taxpaying investors may be more reluctant to hold debt and will be prepared to do so only if they are compensated by a high rate of interest. Investors paying tax on interest at the top rate of 35% may be particularly reluctant to hold debt. They will prefer to hold common stock or tax-exempt bonds issued by states and municipalities.

To determine the net tax advantage of debt, companies would need to know the tax rates faced by the *marginal* investor—that is, an investor who is equally happy to hold debt or equity. This makes it hard to put a precise figure on the tax benefit, but we can nevertheless provide a back-of-the-envelope calculation. Let's consider a large, dividend-paying company like Merck. Merck's dividend payout ratio has averaged about 65%, so for each $1.00 of income, $.65 is received as dividends and $.35 as capital gains. Suppose the marginal investor is in the top tax bracket, paying 35% on interest and 15% on dividends and capital gains. Let's assume that deferred realization of capital gains cuts the effective capital gains rate in half, to $15/2 = 7.5\%$. Therefore, if the investor invests in Merck common stock, the tax on each $1.00 of equity income is $T_{pE} = (.65 \times 15) + (.35 \times 7.5) = 12.4\%$.

Now we can calculate the effect of shunting a dollar of income down each of the two branches in Figure 14.1:

	Interest	Equity Income
Income before tax	$1.00	$1.00
Less corporate tax at $T_c = .35$	0	.35
Income after corporate tax	1.00	.65
Personal tax at $T_p = .35$ and $T_{pE} = .124$	.35	.081
Income after all taxes	$ .65	$ .569
	Advantage to debt = $.081	

The advantage to debt financing appears to be about $.08 on the dollar.

We should emphasize that our back-of-the-envelope calculation is just that. But it's interesting to see how debt's tax advantage shrinks when we account for the relatively low personal tax rate on equity income.

---

[7] M. H. Miller, "Debt and Taxes," *Journal of Finance* 32 (May 1977), pp. 261–276.

Most financial managers believe that there is a moderate tax advantage to corporate borrowing, at least for companies that are reasonably sure they can use the corporate tax shields. For companies that cannot benefit from corporate tax shields there is probably a moderate tax disadvantage.

Do companies make full use of interest tax shields? John Graham argues that they don't. His estimates suggest that a typical tax-paying corporation could add 7.5% to firm value by levering up to a still-conservative debt ratio.[8] This is hardly spare change. Therefore it still appears that financial managers have passed by some easy tax savings. Perhaps they saw some offsetting disadvantage to increased borrowing. We now explore this second escape route.

14-3 Costs of Financial Distress

Financial distress occurs when promises to creditors are broken or honored with difficulty. Sometimes financial distress leads to bankruptcy. Sometimes it only means skating on thin ice.

As we will see, financial distress is costly. Investors know that levered firms may fall into financial distress, and they worry about it. That worry is reflected in the current market value of the levered firm's securities. Thus, the value of the firm can be broken down into three parts:

$$\text{Value of firm} = \text{value if all-equity-finaced} + \text{PV(tax shield)} - \text{PV(costs of financial distress)}$$

The costs of financial distress depend on the probability of distress and the magnitude of costs encountered if distress occurs.

Figure 14.2 shows how the trade-off between the tax benefits and the costs of distress could determine optimal capital structure. PV(tax shield) initially increases as the firm

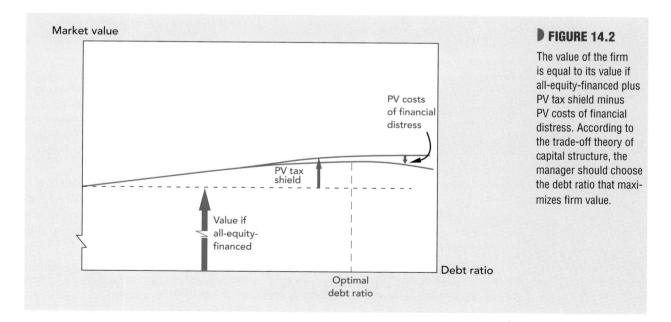

FIGURE 14.2

The value of the firm is equal to its value if all-equity-financed plus PV tax shield minus PV costs of financial distress. According to the trade-off theory of capital structure, the manager should choose the debt ratio that maximizes firm value.

[8] Graham's estimates for individual firms recognize both the uncertainty in future profits and the existence of noninterest tax shields. See J. R. Graham, "How Big Are the Tax Benefits of Debt?" *Journal of Finance* 55 (October 2000), pp. 1901–1941.

borrows more. At moderate debt levels the probability of financial distress is trivial, and so PV(cost of financial distress) is small and tax advantages dominate. But at some point the probability of financial distress increases rapidly with additional borrowing; the costs of distress begin to take a substantial bite out of firm value. Also, if the firm can't be sure of profiting from the corporate tax shield, the tax advantage of additional debt is likely to dwindle and eventually disappear. The theoretical optimum is reached when the present value of tax savings due to further borrowing is just offset by increases in the present value of costs of distress. This is called the *trade-off theory* of capital structure.

Costs of financial distress cover several specific items. Now we identify these costs and try to understand what causes them.

Bankruptcy Costs

You rarely hear anything nice said about corporate bankruptcy. But there is some good in almost everything. Corporate bankruptcies occur when stockholders exercise their *right to default*. That right is valuable; when a firm gets into trouble, limited liability allows stockholders simply to walk away from it, leaving all its troubles to its creditors. The former creditors become the new stockholders, and the old stockholders are left with nothing.

Stockholders in corporations automatically get *limited liability*. But suppose that this were not so. Suppose that there are two firms with identical assets and operations. Each firm has debt outstanding, and each has promised to repay $1,000 (principal and interest) next year. But only one of the firms, Ace Limited, enjoys limited liability. The other firm, Ace Unlimited, does not; its stockholders are personally liable for its debt.[9]

Figure 14.3 compares next year's possible payoffs to the creditors and stockholders of these two firms. The only differences occur when next year's asset value turns out to be less than $1,000. Suppose that next year the assets of each company are worth only $500. In this case Ace Limited defaults. Its stockholders walk away; their payoff is zero. Bondholders get the assets worth $500. But Ace Unlimited's stockholders can't walk away. They have to cough up $500, the difference between asset value and the bondholders' claim. The debt is paid whatever happens.

Suppose that Ace Limited does go bankrupt. Of course, its stockholders are disappointed that their firm is worth so little, but that is an operating problem having nothing to do with financing. Given poor operating performance, the right to go bankrupt—the right to default—is a valuable privilege. As Figure 14.3 shows, Ace Limited's stockholders are in better shape than Unlimited's are.

The example illuminates a mistake people often make in thinking about the costs of bankruptcy. Bankruptcies are thought of as corporate funerals. The mourners (creditors and especially shareholders) look at their firm's present sad state. They think of how valuable their securities used to be and how little is left. But they may also think of the lost value as a cost of bankruptcy. That is the mistake. The decline in the value of assets is what the mourning is really about. That has no necessary connection with financing. The bankruptcy is merely a legal mechanism for allowing creditors to take over when the decline in the value of assets triggers a default. Bankruptcy is not the *cause* of the decline in value. It is the result.

Be careful not to get cause and effect reversed. When a person dies, we do not cite the implementation of his or her will as the cause of death.

---

[9] Ace Unlimited could be a partnership or sole proprietorship, which do not provide limited liability.

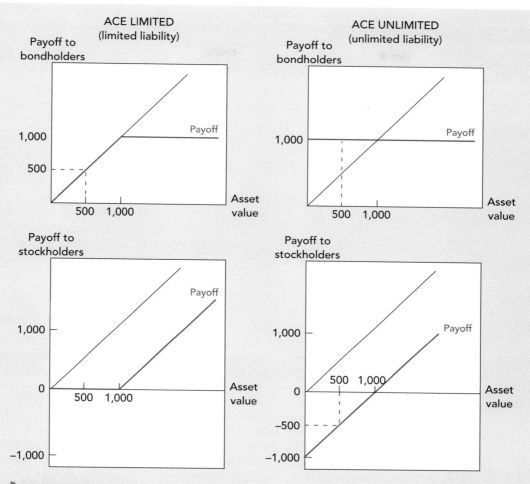

ACE LIMITED
(limited liability)

ACE UNLIMITED
(unlimited liability)

▶ **FIGURE 14.3**

Comparison of limited and unlimited liability for two otherwise identical firms. If the two firms' asset values are less than $1,000, Ace Limited stockholders default and its bondholders take over the assets. Ace Unlimited stockholders keep the assets, but they must reach into their own pockets to pay off its bondholders. The total payoff to both stockholders and bondholders is the same for the two firms.

We said that bankruptcy is a legal mechanism allowing creditors to take over when a firm defaults. *Bankruptcy costs* are the costs of using this mechanism. There are no bankruptcy costs at all shown in Figure 14.3. Note that only Ace Limited can default and go bankrupt. But, regardless of what happens to asset value, the *combined* payoff to the bondholders and stockholders of Ace Limited is always the same as the *combined* payoff to the bondholders and stockholders of Ace Unlimited. Thus the overall market values of the two firms now (this year) must be identical. Of course, Ace Limited's stock is worth more than Ace Unlimited's stock because of Ace Limited's right to default. Ace Limited's debt is worth correspondingly less.

Our example was not intended to be strictly realistic. Anything involving courts and lawyers cannot be free. Suppose that court and legal fees are $200 if Ace Limited defaults.

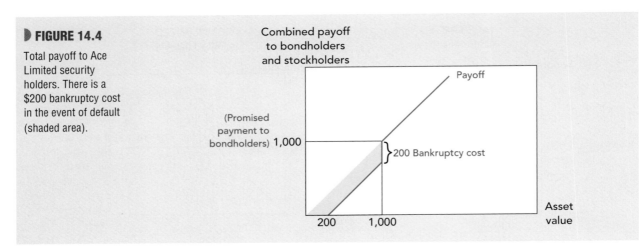

▶ **FIGURE 14.4**

Total payoff to Ace Limited security holders. There is a $200 bankruptcy cost in the event of default (shaded area).

The fees are paid out of the remaining value of Ace Limited's assets. Thus if asset value turns out to be $500, creditors end up with only $300. Figure 14.4 shows next year's *total* payoff to bondholders and stockholders net of this bankruptcy cost. Ace Limited, by issuing risky debt, has given lawyers and the court system a claim on the firm if it defaults. The market value of the firm is reduced by the present value of this claim.

It is easy to see how increased leverage affects the present value of the costs of financial distress. If Ace Limited borrows more, it increases the probability of default and the value of the lawyers' claim. It increases PV (costs of financial distress) and reduces Ace's present market value.

The costs of bankruptcy come out of stockholders' pockets. Creditors foresee the costs and foresee that *they* will pay them if default occurs. For this they demand compensation in advance in the form of higher payoffs when the firm does *not* default; that is, they demand a higher promised interest rate. This reduces the possible payoffs to stockholders and reduces the present market value of their shares.

Evidence on Bankruptcy Costs

Bankruptcy costs can add up fast. While United Airlines was in bankruptcy, it paid over $350 million to lawyers, accountants, and consultants.[10] Enron set a record with legal, accounting, and other professional costs of nearly $1 billion. Professional fees for another distressed energy company, Mirant Corp., were a bit more moderate. The "burn rate" of fees for the first year of Mirant's bankruptcy proceedings was $120 to $140 million.[11]

Daunting as such numbers may seem, they are not a large fraction of the companies' asset values. Lawrence Weiss, who studied 31 firms that went bankrupt between 1980 and 1986, found average costs of about 3% of total book assets and 20% of the market value of equity in the year prior to bankruptcy. A study by Andrade and Kaplan of a sample of troubled and highly leveraged firms estimated costs of financial distress amounting to 10% to 20% of predistress market value, although they found it hard to

---

[10] "Bankruptcy Lawyers Flying High; Airlines' Woes Mean Big Paydays for Consultants and Law Firms; Partner's $177,000 Bill for August," *The Wall Street Journal*, October 21, 2005, p. C1.

[11] "Enron Bankruptcy Specialist to File for Additional Payment; On Top of $63.4 Million, 'Success Fee' to Be Sought of Additional $25 Million," *The Wall Street Journal*, September 3, 2004, p. A2; and "Mirant Bankruptcy Legal Fees Seen Topping $120 Million," Reuters, January 20, 2004.

decide whether these costs were caused by financial distress or by the business setbacks that led to distress.[12]

Bankruptcy eats up a larger fraction of asset value for small companies than for large ones. There are significant economies of scale in going bankrupt. For example, a study of smaller U.K. bankruptcies by Franks and Sussman found that fees (legal and accounting) and other costs soaked up roughly 20% to 40% of the proceeds from liquidation of the companies.[13]

Direct versus Indirect Costs of Bankruptcy

So far we have discussed the *direct* (that is, legal and administrative) costs of bankruptcy. There are indirect costs too, which are nearly impossible to measure. But we have circumstantial evidence indicating their importance.

Managing a bankrupt firm is not easy. Consent of the bankruptcy court is required for many routine business decisions, such as the sale of assets or investment in new equipment. At best this involves time and effort; at worst proposals to reform and revive the firm are thwarted by impatient creditors, who stand first in line for cash from asset sales or liquidation of the entire firm.

Sometimes the problem is reversed: The bankruptcy court is so anxious to maintain the firm as a going concern that it allows the firm to engage in negative-NPV activities. When Eastern Airlines entered the "protection" of the bankruptcy court in 1989, it still had some valuable, profit-making routes and salable assets such as planes and terminal facilities. The creditors would have been best served by a prompt liquidation, which probably would have generated enough cash to pay off all debt and preferred stockholders. But the bankruptcy judge was keen to keep Eastern's planes flying at all costs, so he allowed the company to sell many of its assets to fund hefty operating losses. When Eastern finally closed down after two years, it was not just bankrupt, but *administratively* insolvent: There was almost nothing for creditors, and the company was running out of cash to pay legal expenses.[14]

We do not know what the sum of direct and indirect costs of bankruptcy amounts to. We suspect it is a significant number, particularly for large firms for which proceedings would be lengthy and complex. Perhaps the best evidence is the reluctance of creditors to force bankruptcy. In principle, they would be better off to end the agony and seize the assets as soon as possible. Instead, creditors often overlook defaults in the hope of nursing the firm over a difficult period. They do this in part to avoid costs of bankruptcy. There is an old financial saying, "Borrow $1,000 and you've got a banker. Borrow $10,000,000 and you've got a partner."

Creditors may also shy away from bankruptcy because they worry about violations of absolute priority. *Absolute priority* means that creditors are paid in full before stockholders receive a penny. But sometimes reorganizations provide something for everyone, including consolation prizes for stockholders. Sometimes other claimants move up in the queue. For

---

[12] The pioneering study of bankruptcy costs is J. B. Warner, "Bankruptcy Costs: Some Evidence," *Journal of Finance* 26 (May 1977), pp. 337–348. See also L. A. Weiss, "Bankruptcy Resolution: Direct Costs and Violation of Priority of Claims," *Journal of Financial Economics* 27 (October 1990), pp. 285–314; E. I. Altman, "A Further Investigation of the Bankruptcy Cost Question," *Journal of Finance* 39 (September 1984), pp. 1067–1089; and G. Andrade and S. N. Kaplan, "How Costly Is Financial (not Economic) Distress? Evidence from Highly Leveraged Transactions That Became Distressed," *Journal of Finance* 53 (October 1998), pp. 1443–1493.

[13] J. Franks and O. Sussman, "Financial Distress and Bank Restructuring of Small to Medium Size UK Companies," *Review of Finance* 9 (2005), pp. 65–96. Karin Thornburg found that the Swedish bankruptcy system is reasonably efficient for smaller firms, however. See "Bankruptcy Auctions: Costs, Debt Recovery and Firm Survival," *Journal of Financial Economics* 58 (December 2000), pp. 337–368.

[14] See L. A. Weiss and K. H. Wruck, "Information Problems, Conflicts of Interest, and Asset Stripping: Chapter 11's Failure in the Case of Eastern Airlines," *Journal of Financial Economics* 48 (1998), pp. 55–97.

example, after the Chrysler bankruptcy in 2009, the State of Indiana sued (unsuccessfully) on behalf of local pension funds that had invested in Chrysler bonds. The funds complained bitterly about the terms of sale of the bankrupt company's assets to Fiat, arguing that they would get only $.29 on the dollar, while other, more junior claimants fared better. The Chrysler bankruptcy was a special case, however. One of the key players in the proceedings was the U.S. government, which was anxious to protect tens of thousands of jobs in the middle of a severe recession.

Financial Distress without Bankruptcy

Not every firm that gets into trouble goes bankrupt. As long as the firm can scrape up enough cash to pay the interest on its debt, it may be able to postpone bankruptcy for many years. Eventually the firm may recover, pay off its debt, and escape bankruptcy altogether.

But the mere threat of financial distress can be costly to the threatened firm. Customers and suppliers are extra cautious about doing business with a firm that may not be around for long. Customers worry about resale value and the availability of service and replacement parts. (This was a serious drag on Chrysler's sales prebankruptcy, for example.) Suppliers are disinclined to put effort into servicing the distressed firm's account and may demand cash on the nail for their products. Potential employees are unwilling to sign on and existing staff keep slipping away from their desks for job interviews.

High debt, and thus high financial risk, also appear to reduce firms' appetites for business risk. For example, Luigi Zingales looked at the fortunes of U.S. trucking companies after the trucking industry was deregulated in the late 1970s.[15] The deregulation sparked a wave of competition and restructuring. Survival required new investment and improvements in operating efficiency. Zingales found that conservatively financed trucking companies were more likely to survive in the new competitive environment. High-debt firms were more likely to drop out of the game.

Debt and Incentives

When a firm is in trouble, both bondholders and stockholders want it to recover, but in other respects their interests may be in conflict. In times of financial distress the security holders are like many political parties—united on generalities but threatened by squabbling on any specific issue.

Financial distress is costly when these conflicts of interest get in the way of proper operating, investment, and financing decisions. Stockholders are tempted to forsake the usual objective of maximizing the overall market value of the firm and to pursue narrower self-interest instead. They are tempted to play games at the expense of their creditors. We now illustrate how such games can lead to costs of financial distress.

Here is the Circular File Company's book balance sheet:

Circular File Company (Book Values)

Net working capital	$ 20	$ 50	Bonds outstanding
Fixed assets	80	50	Common stock
Total assets	$100	$100	Total value

We will assume there is only one share and one bond outstanding. The stockholder is also the manager. The bondholder is somebody else.

---

[15] L. Zingales, "Survival of the Fittest or the Fattest? Exit and Financing in the Trucking Industry," *Journal of Finance* 53 (June 1998), pp. 905–938.

Here is its balance sheet in market values—a clear case of financial distress, since the face value of Circular's debt ($50) exceeds the firm's total market value ($30):

Circular File Company (Market Values)

Net working capital	$20	$25	Bonds outstanding
Fixed assets	10	5	Common stock
Total assets	$30	$30	Total value

If the debt matured today, Circular's owner would default, leaving the firm bankrupt. But suppose that the bond actually matures one year hence, that there is enough cash for Circular to limp along for one year, and that the bondholder cannot "call the question" and force bankruptcy before then.

The one-year grace period explains why the Circular share still has value. Its owner is betting on a stroke of luck that will rescue the firm, allowing it to pay off the debt with something left over. The bet is a long shot—the owner wins only if firm value increases from $30 to more than $50.[16] But the owner has a secret weapon: He controls investment and operating strategy.

Risk Shifting: The First Game

Suppose that Circular has $10 cash. The following investment opportunity comes up:

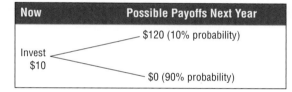

This is a wild gamble and probably a lousy project. But you can see why the owner would be tempted to take it anyway. Why not go for broke? Circular will probably go under anyway, so the owner is essentially betting with the bondholder's money. But the owner gets most of the loot if the project pays off.

Suppose that the project's NPV is −$2 but that it is undertaken anyway, thus depressing firm value by $2. Circular's new balance sheet might look like this:

Circular File Company (Market Values)

Net working capital	$10	$20	Bonds outstanding
Fixed assets	18	8	Common stock
Total assets	$28	$28	Total value

Firm value falls by $2, but the owner is $3 ahead because the bond's value has fallen by $5.[17] The $10 cash that used to stand behind the bond has been replaced by a very risky asset worth only $8.

Thus a game has been played at the expense of Circular's bondholder. The game illustrates the following general point: Stockholders of levered firms gain when business risk increases. Financial managers who act strictly in their shareholders' interests (and *against* the interests of creditors) will favor risky projects over safe ones. They may even take risky projects with negative NPVs.

---

[16] We are not concerned here with how to work out whether $5 is a fair price for stockholders to pay for the bet.

[17] We are not calculating this $5 drop. We are simply using it as a plausible assumption.

This warped strategy for capital budgeting clearly is costly to the firm and to the economy as a whole. Why do we associate the costs with financial distress? Because the temptation to play is strongest when the odds of default are high. A blue-chip company like Exxon Mobil would never invest in our negative-NPV gamble. Its creditors are not vulnerable to one risky project.

Refusing to Contribute Equity Capital: The Second Game

We have seen how stockholders, acting in their immediate, narrow self-interest, may take projects that reduce the overall market value of their firm. These are errors of commission. Conflicts of interest may also lead to errors of omission.

Assume that Circular cannot scrape up any cash, and therefore cannot take that wild gamble. Instead a *good* opportunity comes up: a relatively safe asset costing $10 with a present value of $15 and NPV = +$5.

This project will not in itself rescue Circular, but it is a step in the right direction. We might therefore expect Circular to issue $10 of new stock and to go ahead with the investment. Suppose that two new shares are issued to the original owner for $10 cash. The project is taken. The new balance sheet might look like this:

Circular File Company (Market Values)

Net working capital	$20	$33	Bonds outstanding
Fixed assets	25	12	Common stock
Total assets	$45	$45	Total value

The total value of the firm goes up by $15 ($10 of new capital and $5 NPV). Notice that the Circular bond is no longer worth $25, but $33. The bondholder receives a capital gain of $8 because the firm's assets include a new, safe asset worth $15. The probability of default is less, and the payoff to the bondholder if default occurs is larger.

The stockholder loses what the bondholder gains. Equity value goes up not by $15 but by $15 − $8 = $7. The owner puts in $10 of fresh equity capital but gains only $7 in market value. Going ahead is in the firm's interest but not the owner's.

Again, our example illustrates a general point. If we hold business risk constant, any increase in firm value is shared among bondholders and stockholders. The value of any investment opportunity to the firm's *stockholders* is reduced because project benefits must be shared with bondholders. Thus it may not be in the stockholders' self-interest to contribute fresh equity capital even if that means forgoing positive-NPV investment opportunities.

This problem theoretically affects all levered firms, but it is most serious when firms land in financial distress. The greater the probability of default, the more bondholders have to gain from investments that increase firm value.

And Three More Games, Briefly

As with other games, the temptation to play the next three games is particularly strong in financial distress.

Cash In and Run Stockholders may be reluctant to put money into a firm in financial distress, but they are happy to take the money out—in the form of a cash dividend, for example. The market value of the firm's stock goes down by less than the amount of the dividend paid, because the decline in *firm* value is shared with creditors. This game is just "refusing to contribute equity capital" run in reverse.[18]

---

[18] If stockholders or managers take money out of the firm in anticipation of financial distress or bankruptcy, the bankruptcy court can treat the payout as *fraudulent conveyance* and claw back the money to the firm and its creditors.

Playing for Time   When the firm is in financial distress, creditors would like to salvage what they can by forcing the firm to settle up. Naturally, stockholders want to delay this as long as they can. There are various devious ways of doing this, for example, through accounting changes designed to conceal the true extent of trouble, by encouraging false hopes of spontaneous recovery, or by cutting corners on maintenance, research and development, and so on, in order to make this year's operating performance look better.

Bait and Switch   This game is not always played in financial distress, but it is a quick way to get *into* distress. You start with a conservative policy, issuing a limited amount of relatively safe debt. Then you suddenly switch and issue a lot more. That makes all your debt risky, imposing a capital loss on the "old" bondholders. Their capital loss is the stockholders' gain.

A dramatic example of bait and switch occurred in October 1988, when the management of RJR Nabisco announced its intention to acquire the company in a *leveraged buy-out* (LBO). This put the company "in play" for a transaction in which existing shareholders would be bought out and the company would be "taken private." The cost of the buy-out would be almost entirely debt-financed. The new private company would start life with an extremely high debt ratio.

RJR Nabisco had debt outstanding with a market value of about $2.4 billion. The announcement of the coming LBO drove down this market value by $298 million.[19]

What the Games Cost

Why should anyone object to these games so long as they are played by consenting adults? Because playing them means poor decisions about investments and operations. These poor decisions are *agency costs* of borrowing.

The more the firm borrows, the greater is the temptation to play the games (assuming the financial manager acts in the stockholders' interest). The increased odds of poor decisions in the future prompt investors to mark down the present market value of the firm. The fall in value comes out of the shareholders' pockets. Therefore it is ultimately in their interest to avoid temptation. The easiest way to do this is to limit borrowing to levels at which the firm's debt is safe or close to it.

Banks and other corporate lenders are also not financial innocents. They realize that games may be played at their expense and so protect themselves by rationing the amount that they will lend or by imposing restrictions on the company's actions.

EXAMPLE 14.1   ● Ms. Ketchup Faces Credit Rationing

Consider the case of Henrietta Ketchup, a budding entrepreneur with two possible investment projects that offer the following payoffs:

	Investment	Payoff	Probability of Payoff
Project 1	−12	+15	1.0
Project 2	−12	+24	.5
		0	.5

---

[19] We thank Paul Asquith for these figures. RJR Nabisco was finally taken private not by its management but by another LBO partnership..

Project 1 is surefire and very profitable; project 2 is risky and a rotten project. Ms. Ketchup now approaches her bank and asks to borrow the present value of $10 (she will find the remaining money out of her own purse). The bank calculates that the payoff will be split as follows:

	Expected Payoff to Bank	Expected Payoff to Ms. Ketchup
Project 1	+10	+5
Project 2	(.5 × 10) + (.5 × 0) = +5	.5 × (24 − 10) = +7

If Ms. Ketchup accepts project 1, the bank's debt is certain to be paid in full; if she accepts project 2, there is only a 50% chance of payment and the expected payoff to the bank is only $5. Unfortunately, Ms. Ketchup will prefer to take project 2, for if things go well, she gets most of the profit, and if they go badly, the bank bears most of the loss. Unless Ms. Ketchup can convince the bank that she will not gamble with its money, the bank will limit the amount that it is prepared to lend.[20]

● ● ● ● ●

How can Ms. Ketchup in Example 14.1 reassure the bank of her intentions? The obvious answer is to give it veto power over potentially dangerous decisions. There we have the ultimate economic rationale for all that fine print backing up corporate debt. Debt contracts frequently limit dividends or equivalent transfers of wealth to stockholders; the firm may not be allowed to pay out more than it earns, for example. Additional borrowing is almost always limited. For example, many companies are prevented by existing bond indentures from issuing any additional long-term debt unless their ratio of earnings to interest charges exceeds 2.0.

Sometimes firms are restricted from selling assets or making major investment outlays except with the lenders' consent. The risks of playing for time are reduced by specifying accounting procedures and by giving lenders access to the firm's books and its financial forecasts.

Of course, fine print cannot be a complete solution for firms that insist on issuing risky debt. The fine print has its own costs; you have to spend money to save money. Obviously a complex debt contract costs more to negotiate than a simple one. Afterward it costs the lender more to monitor the firm's performance. Lenders anticipate monitoring costs and demand compensation in the form of higher interest rates; thus the monitoring costs—another agency cost of debt—are ultimately paid by stockholders.

Perhaps the most severe costs of the fine print stem from the constraints it places on operating and investment decisions. For example, an attempt to prevent the risk-shifting game may also prevent the firm from pursuing *good* investment opportunities. At the minimum there are delays in clearing major investments with lenders. In some cases lenders may veto high-risk investments even if net present value is positive. The lenders are tempted to play a game of their own, forcing the firm to stay in cash or low-risk assets even if good projects are forgone.

Debt contracts cannot cover every possible manifestation of the games we have just discussed. Any attempt to do so would be hopelessly expensive and doomed to failure in any event. Human imagination is insufficient to conceive of all the possible things that could go wrong. Therefore contracts are always *incomplete*. We will always find surprises coming at us on dimensions we never thought to think about.

---

[20] You might think that, if the bank suspects Ms. Ketchup will undertake project 2, it should just raise the interest rate on its loan. In this case Ms. Ketchup will not want to take on project 2 (they can't both be happy with a lousy project). But Ms. Ketchup also would not want to pay a high rate of interest if she is going to take on project 1 (she would do better to borrow less money at the risk-free rate). So simply raising the interest rate is not the answer.

We hope we have not left the impression that managers and stockholders always succumb to temptation unless restrained. Usually they refrain voluntarily, not only from a sense of fair play but also on pragmatic grounds: A firm or individual that makes a killing today at the expense of a creditor will be coldly received when the time comes to borrow again. Aggressive game playing is done only by out-and-out crooks and by firms in extreme financial distress. Firms limit borrowing precisely because they don't wish to land in distress and be exposed to the temptation to play.

Costs of Distress Vary with Type of Asset

Suppose your firm's only asset is a large downtown hotel, mortgaged to the hilt. The recession hits, occupancy rates fall, and the mortgage payments cannot be met. The lender takes over and sells the hotel to a new owner and operator. You use your firm's stock certificates for wallpaper.

What is the cost of bankruptcy? In this example, probably very little. The value of the hotel is, of course, much less than you hoped, but that is due to the lack of guests, not to the bankruptcy. Bankruptcy doesn't damage the hotel itself. The direct bankruptcy costs are restricted to items such as legal and court fees, real estate commissions, and the time the lender spends sorting things out.

Suppose we repeat the story of Heartbreak Hotel for Fledgling Electronics. Everything is the same, except for the underlying real assets—not real estate but a high-tech going concern, a growth company whose most valuable assets are technology, investment opportunities, and its employees' human capital.

If Fledgling gets into trouble, the stockholders may be reluctant to put up money to cash in on its growth opportunities. Failure to invest is likely to be much more serious for Fledgling than for the Heartbreak Hotel.

If Fledgling finally defaults on its debt, the lender will find it much more difficult to cash in by selling off the assets. Many of them are intangibles that have value only as a part of a going concern.

Could Fledgling be kept as a going concern through default and reorganization? It may not be as hopeless as putting a wedding cake through a car wash, but there are a number of serious difficulties. First, the odds of defections by key employees are higher than they would be if the firm had never gotten into financial trouble. Special guarantees may have to be given to customers who have doubts about whether the firm will be around to service its products. Aggressive investment in new products and technology will be difficult; each class of creditors will have to be convinced that it is in its interest for the firm to invest new money in risky ventures.

Some assets, like good commercial real estate, can pass through bankruptcy and reorganization largely unscathed;[21] the values of other assets are likely to be considerably diminished. The losses are greatest for the intangible assets that are linked to the health of the firm as a going concern—for example, technology, human capital, and brand image. That may be why debt ratios are low in the pharmaceutical industry, where value depends on continued success in research and development, and in many service industries where value depends on human capital. We can also understand why highly profitable growth companies, such as Microsoft or Google, use mostly equity finance.

---

[21] In 1989 the Rockefeller family sold 80% of Rockefeller Center—several acres of extremely valuable Manhattan real estate—to Mitsubishi Estate Company for $1.4 billion. A REIT, Rockefeller Center Properties, held a $1.3 billion mortgage loan (the REIT's only asset) secured by this real estate. But rents and occupancy rates did not meet forecasts, and by 1995 Mitsubishi had incurred losses of about $600 million. Then Mitsubishi quit, and Rockefeller Center was bankrupt. That triggered a complicated series of maneuvers and negotiations. But did this damage the value of the Rockefeller Center properties? Was Radio City Music Hall, one of the properties, any less valuable because of the bankruptcy? We doubt it.

The moral of these examples is this: *Do not think only about the probability that borrowing will bring trouble. Think also of the value that may be lost if trouble comes.*

Heartbreak Hotel for Enron?   Enron was one of the most glamorous, fast-growing, and (apparently) profitable companies of the 1990s. It played a lead role in the deregulation of electric power markets, both in the United States and internationally. It invested in electric power generation and distribution, gas pipelines, telecommunications networks, and various other ventures. It also built up an active energy trading business. At its peak the aggregate market value of Enron's common stock exceeded $60 billion. By the end of 2001, Enron was in bankruptcy and its shares were worthless.

With hindsight we see that Enron was playing many of the games that we described earlier in this section. It was borrowing aggressively and hiding the debt in "special purpose entities" (SPEs). The SPEs also allowed it to pump up its reported earnings, playing for time while making more and more risky investments. When the bubble burst, there was hardly any value left.

The collapse of Enron didn't really destroy $60 billion in value, because that $60 billion wasn't there in the first place. But there were genuine costs of financial distress. Let's focus on Enron's energy trading business. That business was not as profitable as it appeared, but it was nevertheless a valuable asset. It provided an important service for wholesale energy customers and suppliers who wanted to buy or sell contracts that locked in the future prices and quantities of electricity, natural gas, and other commodities.

What happened to this business when it became clear that Enron was in financial distress and probably headed for bankruptcy? It disappeared. Trading volume went to zero immediately. None of its customers were willing to make a new trade with Enron, because it was far from clear that Enron would be around to honor its side of the bargain. With no trading volume, there was no trading business. As it turned out, Enron's trading business more resembled Fledgling Electronics than a tangible asset like Heartbreak Hotel.

The value of Enron's trading business depended on Enron's creditworthiness. The value should have been protected by conservative financing. Most of the lost value can be traced back to Enron's aggressive borrowing. This loss of value was therefore a cost of financial distress.

The Trade-off Theory of Capital Structure

Financial managers often think of the firm's debt–equity decision as a trade-off between interest tax shields and the costs of financial distress. Of course, there is controversy about how valuable interest tax shields are and what kinds of financial trouble are most threatening, but these disagreements are only variations on a theme. Thus, Figure 14.2 illustrates the debt–equity trade-off.

This *trade-off theory* of capital structure recognizes that target debt ratios may vary from firm to firm. Companies with safe, tangible assets and plenty of taxable income to shield ought to have high target ratios. Unprofitable companies with risky, intangible assets ought to rely primarily on equity financing.

If there were no costs of adjusting capital structure, then each firm should always be at its target debt ratio. However, there are costs, and therefore delays, in adjusting to the optimum. Firms cannot immediately offset the random events that bump them away from their capital structure targets, so we should see random differences in actual debt ratios among firms having the same target debt ratio.

All in all, this trade-off theory of capital structure choice tells a comforting story. Unlike MM's theory, which seemed to say that firms should take on as much debt as possible, it avoids extreme predictions and rationalizes moderate debt ratios. Also, if you ask financial managers whether their firms have target debt ratios, they will usually say yes—although the target is often specified not as a debt ratio but as a debt rating. For example, the firm might manage its capital structure to maintain a single-A bond rating. Ratio or rating, a target is consistent with the trade-off theory.[22]

But what are the facts? Can the trade-off theory of capital structure explain how companies actually behave?

The answer is "yes and no." On the "yes" side, the trade-off theory successfully explains many industry differences in capital structure. High-tech growth companies, whose assets are risky and mostly intangible, normally use relatively little debt. Airlines can and do borrow heavily because their assets are tangible and relatively safe.[23]

On the "no" side, there are some things the trade-off theory cannot explain. It cannot explain why some of the most successful companies thrive with little debt. Think of Merck, which as Table 14.3 (*a*) shows is basically all-equity-financed. Granted, Merck's most valuable assets are intangible, the fruits of its pharmaceutical research and development. We know that intangible assets and conservative capital structures go together. But Merck also has a very large corporate income tax bill (about $2 billion in 2008) and the highest possible credit rating. It could borrow enough to save tens of millions of dollars without raising a whisker of concern about possible financial distress.

Merck illustrates an odd fact about real-life capital structures: The most profitable companies commonly borrow the least.[24] Here the trade-off theory fails, for it predicts exactly the reverse. Under the trade-off theory, high profits should mean more debt-servicing capacity and more taxable income to shield and so should give a *higher* target debt ratio.[25]

In general it appears that public companies rarely make major shifts in capital structure just because of taxes,[26] and it is hard to detect the present value of interest tax shields in firms' market values.[27] Also, there are large, long-lived differences between debt ratios of firms in the same industry, even after controlling for attributes that the trade-off theory says should be important.[28]

A final point on the "no" side for the trade-off theory: Debt ratios today are no higher than they were in the early 1900s, when income tax rates were low (or zero). Debt ratios in other industrialized countries are equal to or higher than those in the U.S. Many of these countries have imputation tax systems, which should eliminate the value of the interest tax shields.[29]

---

[22] See J. Graham and C. Harvey, "The Theory and Practice of Corporate Finance: Evidence from the Field," *Journal of Financial Economics* 60 (May/June 2001), pp. 187–244.

[23] We are not suggesting that all airline companies are safe; many are not. But air*craft* can support debt where air*lines* cannot. If Fly-by-Night Airlines fails, its planes retain their value in another airline's operations. There's a good secondary market in used aircraft, so a loan secured by aircraft can be well protected even if made to an airline flying on thin ice (and in the dark).

[24] For example, in an international comparison Wald found that profitability was the single largest determinant of firm capital structure. See J. K. Wald, "How Firm Characteristics Affect Capital Structure: An International Comparison," *Journal of Financial Research* 22 (Summer 1999), pp. 161–187.

[25] Here we mean debt as a fraction of the book or replacement value of the company's assets. Profitable companies might not borrow a greater fraction of their market value. Higher profits imply higher market value as well as stronger incentives to borrow.

[26] Mackie-Mason found that taxpaying companies are more likely to issue debt (vs. equity) than nontaxpaying companies. This shows that taxes do affect financing choices. However, it is not necessarily evidence for the trade-off theory. Look back to Section 14–2, and note the special case where corporate and personal taxes cancel to make debt policy irrelevant. In that case, taxpaying firms would see no net tax advantage to debt: Corporate interest tax shields would be offset by the taxes paid by investors in the firm's debt. But the balance would tip in favor of equity for a firm that was losing money and reaping no benefits from interest tax shields. See J. Mackie-Mason, "Do Taxes Affect Corporate Financing Decisions?" *Journal of Finance* 45 (December 1990), pp. 1471–1493.

[27] A study by E. F. Fama and K. R. French, covering over 2,000 firms from 1965 to 1992, failed to find any evidence that interest tax shields contributed to firm value. See "Taxes, Financing Decisions and Firm Value," *Journal of Finance* 53 (June 1998), pp. 819–843.

[28] M. L. Lemmon, M. R. Roberts, and J. F. Zender, "Back to the Beginning: Persistence and the Cross-Section of Corporate Capital Structure," *Journal of Finance* 63 (August 2008), pp. 1575–1608.

[29] We described the Australian imputation tax system in Section 12–7. Look again at Table 12.3, supposing that an Australian corporation pays A$10 of interest. This reduces the corporate tax by A$3.00; it also reduces the tax credit taken by the shareholders by A$3.00. The final tax does not depend on whether the corporation or the shareholder borrows.

You can check this by redrawing Figure 14.1 for the Australian system. The corporate tax rate T_c will cancel out. Since income after all taxes depends only on investors' tax rates, there is no special advantage to corporate borrowing.

None of this disproves the trade-off theory. As George Stigler emphasized, theories are not rejected by circumstantial evidence; it takes a theory to beat a theory. So we now turn to a completely different theory of financing.

14-4 The Pecking Order of Financing Choices

The pecking-order theory starts with *asymmetric information*—a fancy term indicating that managers know more about their companies' prospects, risks, and values than do outside investors.

Managers obviously know more than investors. We can prove that by observing stock price changes caused by announcements by managers. For example, when a company announces an increased regular dividend, stock price typically rises, because investors interpret the increase as a sign of management's confidence in future earnings. In other words, the dividend increase transfers information from managers to investors. This can happen only if managers know more in the first place.

Asymmetric information affects the choice between internal and external financing and between new issues of debt and equity securities. This leads to a *pecking order*, in which investment is financed first with internal funds, reinvested earnings primarily; then by new issues of debt; and finally with new issues of equity. New equity issues are a last resort when the company runs out of debt capacity, that is, when the threat of costs of financial distress brings regular insomnia to existing creditors and to the financial manager.

We will take a closer look at the pecking order in a moment. First, you must appreciate how asymmetric information can force the financial manager to issue debt rather than common stock.

Debt and Equity Issues with Asymmetric Information

To the outside world Smith & Company and Jones, Inc., our two example companies, are identical. Each runs a successful business with good growth opportunities. The two businesses are risky, however, and investors have learned from experience that current expectations are frequently bettered or disappointed. Current expectations price each company's stock at $100 per share, but the true values could be higher or lower:

	Smith & Co.	Jones, Inc.
True value could be higher, say	$120	$120
Best current estimate	100	100
True value could be lower, say	80	80

Now suppose that both companies need to raise new money from investors to fund capital investment. They can do this either by issuing bonds or by issuing new shares of common stock. How would the choice be made? One financial manager—we will not tell you which one—might reason as follows:

> Sell stock for $100 per share? Ridiculous! It's worth at least $120. A stock issue now would hand a free gift to new investors. I just wish those skeptical shareholders would appreciate the true value of this company. Our new factories will make us the world's lowest-cost producer. We've painted a rosy picture for the press and security analysts, but it just doesn't seem to be working. Oh well, the decision is obvious: We'll issue debt, not underpriced equity. A debt issue will save underwriting fees too.

The other financial manager is in a different mood:

> Beefalo burgers were a hit for a while, but it looks like the fad is fading. The fast-food division's gotta find some good new products or it's all downhill from here. Export markets are OK for now, but how are we going to compete with those new Siberian ranches? Fortunately the stock price has held up pretty well—we've had some good short-run news

for the press and security analysts. Now's the time to issue stock. We have major investments under way, and why add increased debt service to my other worries?

Of course, outside investors can't read the financial managers' minds. If they could, one stock might trade at $120 and the other at $80.

Why doesn't the optimistic financial manager simply educate investors? Then the company could sell stock on fair terms, and there would be no reason to favor debt over equity or vice versa.

This is not so easy. (Note that both companies are issuing upbeat press releases.) Investors can't be told what to think; they have to be convinced. That takes a detailed layout of the company's plans and prospects, including the inside scoop on new technology, product design, marketing plans, and so on. Getting this across is expensive for the company and also valuable to its competitors. Why go to the trouble? Investors will learn soon enough, as revenues and earnings evolve. In the meantime the optimistic financial manager can finance growth by issuing debt.

Now suppose there are two press releases:

Jones, Inc., will issue $120 million of five-year senior notes.

Smith & Co. announced plans today to issue 1.2 million new shares of common stock. The company expects to raise $120 million.

As a rational investor, you immediately learn two things. First, Jones's financial manager is optimistic and Smith's is pessimistic. Second, Smith's financial manager is also naive to think that investors would pay $100 per share. The *attempt* to sell stock shows that it must be worth less. Smith might sell stock at $80 per share, but certainly not at $100.[30]

Smart financial managers think this through ahead of time. The end result? Both Smith and Jones end up issuing debt. Jones, Inc., issues debt because its financial manager is optimistic and doesn't want to issue undervalued equity. A smart, but pessimistic, financial manager at Smith issues debt because an attempt to issue equity would force the stock price down and eliminate any advantage from doing so. (Issuing equity also reveals the manager's pessimism immediately. Most managers prefer to wait. A debt issue lets bad news come out later through other channels.)

The story of Smith and Jones illustrates how asymmetric information favors debt issues over equity issues. If managers are better informed than investors and both groups are rational, then any company that can borrow will do so rather than issuing fresh equity. In other words, debt issues will be higher in the pecking order.

Taken literally this reasoning seems to rule out any issue of equity. That's not right, because asymmetric information is not always important and there are other forces at work. For example, if Smith had already borrowed heavily, and would risk financial distress by borrowing more, then it would have a good reason to issue common stock. In this case announcement of a stock issue would not be entirely bad news. The announcement would still depress the stock price—it would highlight managers' concerns about financial distress— but the fall in price would not necessarily make the issue unwise or infeasible.

High-tech, high-growth companies can also be credible issuers of common stock. Such companies' assets are mostly intangible, and bankruptcy or financial distress would be especially costly. This calls for conservative financing. The only way to grow rapidly and keep a conservative debt ratio is to issue equity. If investors see equity issued for these reasons, problems of the sort encountered by Smith's financial manager become much less serious.

With such exceptions noted, asymmetric information can explain the dominance of debt financing over new equity issues, at least for mature public corporations. Debt issues are frequent; equity issues, rare. The bulk of external financing comes from debt, even in

---

[30] A Smith stock issue might not succeed even at $80. Persistence in trying to sell at $80 could convince investors that the stock is worth even less!

the United States, where equity markets are highly information-efficient. Equity issues are even more difficult in countries with less well developed stock markets.

None of this says that firms ought to strive for high debt ratios—just that it's better to raise equity by plowing back earnings than issuing stock. In fact, a firm with ample internally generated funds doesn't have to sell any kind of security and thus avoids issue costs and information problems completely.

Implications of the Pecking Order

The *pecking-order theory* of corporate financing goes like this.

1. Firms prefer internal finance.
2. They adapt their target dividend payout ratios to their investment opportunities, while trying to avoid sudden changes in dividends.
3. Sticky dividend policies, plus unpredictable fluctuations in profitability and investment opportunities, mean that internally generated cash flow is sometimes more than capital expenditures and other times less. If it is more, the firm pays off debt or invests in marketable securities. If it is less, the firm first draws down its cash balance or sells its marketable securities.
4. If external finance is required, firms issue the safest security first. That is, they start with debt, then possibly hybrid securities such as convertible bonds, then perhaps equity as a last resort.

In this theory, there is no well-defined target debt–equity mix, because there are two kinds of equity, internal and external, one at the top of the pecking order and one at the bottom. Each firm's observed debt ratio reflects its cumulative requirements for external finance.

The pecking order explains why the most profitable firms generally borrow less—not because they have low target debt ratios but because they don't need outside money. Less profitable firms issue debt because they do not have internal funds sufficient for their capital investment programs and because debt financing is first on the pecking order of *external* financing.

In the pecking-order theory, the attraction of interest tax shields is assumed to be second-order. Debt ratios change when there is an imbalance of internal cash flow, net of dividends, and real investment opportunities. Highly profitable firms with limited investment opportunities work down to low debt ratios. Firms whose investment opportunities outrun internally generated funds are driven to borrow more and more.

This theory explains the inverse intraindustry relationship between profitability and financial leverage. Suppose firms generally invest to keep up with the growth of their industries. Then rates of investment will be similar within an industry. Given sticky dividend payouts, the least profitable firms will have less internal funds and will end up borrowing more.

The Trade-off Theory vs. the Pecking-Order Theory—Some Recent Tests

In 1995 Rajan and Zingales published a study of debt versus equity choices by large firms in Canada, France, Germany, Italy, Japan, the U.K., and the U.S. Rajan and Zingales found that the debt ratios of individual companies seemed to depend on four main factors:[31]

1. *Size.* Large firms tend to have higher debt ratios.
2. *Tangible assets.* Firms with high ratios of fixed assets to total assets have higher debt ratios.
3. *Profitability.* More profitable firms have lower debt ratios.
4. *Market to book.* Firms with higher ratios of market-to-book value have lower debt ratios.

---

[31] R. G. Rajan and L. Zingales, "What Do We Know about Capital Structure? Some Evidence from International Data," *Journal of Finance* 50 (December 1995), pp. 1421–1460. The same four factors seem to work in developing economies. See L. Booth, V. Aivazian, A. Demirguc-Kunt, and V. Maksimovic, "Capital Structure in Developing Countries," *Journal of Finance* 56 (February 2001), pp. 87–130.

These results convey good news for both the trade-off and pecking-order theories. Trade-off enthusiasts note that large companies with tangible assets are less exposed to costs of financial distress and would be expected to borrow more. They interpret the market-to-book ratio as a measure of growth opportunities and argue that growth companies could face high costs of financial distress and would be expected to borrow less. Pecking-order advocates stress the importance of profitability, arguing that profitable firms use less debt because they can rely on internal financing. They interpret the market-to-book ratio as just another measure of profitability.

It seems that we have two competing theories, and they're both right! That's not a comfortable conclusion. So recent research has tried to run horse races between the two theories in order to find the circumstances in which one or the other wins. It seems that the pecking order works best for large, mature firms that have access to public bond markets. These firms rarely issue equity. They prefer internal financing, but turn to debt markets if needed to finance investment. Smaller, younger, growth firms are more likely to rely on equity issues when external financing is required.[32]

There is also some evidence that debt ratios incorporate the cumulative effects of *market timing*.[33] Market timing is an example of behavioral corporate finance. Suppose that investors are sometimes irrationally exuberant (as in the late 1990s) and sometimes irrationally despondent. If the financial manager's views are more stable than investors', then he or she can take advantage by issuing shares when the stock price is too high and switching to debt when the price is too low. Thus lucky companies with a history of buoyant stock prices will issue less debt and more shares, ending up with low debt ratios. Unfortunate and unpopular companies will avoid share issues and end up with high debt ratios.

Market timing could explain why companies tend to issue shares after run-ups in stock prices and also why aggregate stock issues are concentrated in bull markets and fall sharply in bear markets.

There are other behavioral explanations for corporate financing policies. For example, Bertrand and Schoar tracked the careers of individual CEOs, CFOs, and other top managers. Their individual "styles" persisted as they moved from firm to firm.[34] For example, older CEOs tended to be more conservative and pushed their firms to lower debt. CEOs with MBA degrees tended to be more aggressive. In general, financial decisions depended not just on the nature of the firm and its economic environment, but also on the personalities of the firm's top management.

The Bright Side and the Dark Side of Financial Slack

Other things equal, it's better to be at the top of the pecking order than at the bottom. Firms that have worked down the pecking order and need external equity may end up living with excessive debt or passing by good investments because shares can't be sold at what managers consider a fair price.

In other words, *financial slack* is valuable. Having financial slack means having cash, marketable securities, readily salable real assets, and ready access to debt markets or to bank financing. Ready access basically requires conservative financing so that potential lenders see the company's debt as a safe investment.

---

[32] L. Shyam-Sunder and S. C. Myers found that the pecking-order hypothesis outperformed the trade-off hypothesis for a sample of large companies in the 1980s. See "Testing Static Trade-off against Pecking-Order Theories of Capital Structure," *Journal of Financial Economics* 51 (February 1999), pp. 219–244. M. Frank and V. Goyal found that the performance of the pecking-order hypothesis deteriorated in the 1990s, especially for small growth firms. See "Testing the Pecking Order Theory of Capital Structure," *Journal of Financial Economics* 67 (February 2003), pp. 217–248. See also E. Fama and K. French, "Testing Trade-off and Pecking Order Predictions about Dividends and Debt," *Review of Financial Studies* 15 (Spring 2002), pp. 1–33; and M. L. Lemmon and J. F. Zender, "Debt Capacity and Tests of Capital Structure Theories," *Journal of Financial and Quantitative Analysis,* forthcoming.

[33] M. Baker and J. Wurgler, "Market Timing and Capital Structure," *Journal of Finance* 57 (February 2002), pp. 1–32.

[34] M. Bertrand and A. Schoar, "Managing with Style: The Effect of Managers on Firm Policies," *Quarterly Journal of Economics* 118 (November 2003), pp. 1169–1208.

Ford Cashes in All of its Financial Slack

▶ In 2006, Ford Motor Company brought in a new CEO, Alan Mulally, who launched a thorough restructuring of the company. The company had to cut costs, improve efficiency, and renew its products. This was a massive investment, but debt financing was available. The company decided to borrow as much as it could, to maximize the amount of cash on hand to pay for the restructuring.

In December 2006, Ford issued $5 billion of senior convertible notes. It also arranged a $7 billion, seven-year term loan and an $11.5 billion, five-year revolving credit facility. The total was $23.5 billion.

Ford was able to get this money by pledging almost all of its assets as collateral, including its U.S. property, plant, and equipment; its equity investments in Ford Credit and Ford's foreign subsidiaries; and its trademarks, including the Ford brand name and logo.

Why did Ford decide to use up all of its financial slack in one gigantic gulp? First, debt financing was available on relatively easy terms in 2006. Second, Mulally must have been aware of the history of restructuring programs in the U.S. auto industry. Some of these initiatives were failures, some partial successes, but none solved Ford, GM, or Chrysler's competitive problems. The companies shrank but did not improve significantly.

So Mulally was in effect sending a wake-up call to Ford's managers and employees: "We've raised all the cash that we can get. This is our last chance to reform the company. If we don't make it, Ford is gone."

As we write in 2009 Ford has *not* followed GM and Chrysler into bankruptcy. It's losing money in a severe recession, but still launching new models. It looks like Ford is a survivor.

In the long run, a company's value rests more on its capital investment and operating decisions than on financing. Therefore, you want to make sure your firm has sufficient financial slack so that financing is quickly available for good investments. Financial slack is most valuable to firms with plenty of positive-NPV growth opportunities. That is another reason why growth companies usually aspire to conservative capital structures.

Of course financial slack is only valuable if you're willing to use it. Take a look at the nearby box, which describes how Ford used up all of its financial slack in one enormous debt issue.

There is also a dark side to financial slack. Too much of it may encourage managers to take it easy, expand their perks, or empire-build with cash that should be paid back to stockholders. In other words, slack can make agency problems worse.

Michael Jensen has stressed the tendency of managers with ample free cash flow (or unnecessary financial slack) to plow too much cash into mature businesses or ill-advised acquisitions. "The problem," Jensen says, "is how to motivate managers to disgorge the cash rather than investing it below the cost of capital or wasting it in organizational inefficiencies."[35]

If that's the problem, then maybe debt is an answer. Scheduled interest and principal payments are contractual obligations of the firm. Debt forces the firm to pay out cash. Perhaps the best debt level would leave just enough cash in the bank, after debt service, to finance all positive-NPV projects, with not a penny left over.

We do not recommend this degree of fine-tuning, but the idea is valid and important. Debt can discipline managers who are tempted to invest too much. It can also provide the pressure to force improvements in operating efficiency.

---

[35] M. C. Jensen, "Agency Costs of Free Cash Flow, Corporate Finance and Takeovers," *American Economic Review* 26 (May 1986), pp. 323–329.

Is There a Theory of Optimal Capital Structure?

No. That is, there is no *one* theory that can capture everything that drives thousands of corporations' debt vs. equity choices. Instead there are several theories, each more or less helpful, depending on each particular corporation's assets, operations, and circumstances.

In other words, *relax:* Don't waste time searching for a magic formula for the optimal debt ratio. Remember too that most value comes from the left side of the balance sheet, that is, from the firm's operations, assets, and growth opportunities. Financing is less important. Of course, financing can subtract value rapidly if you screw it up, but you won't do that.

In practice, financing choices depend on the relative importance of the factors discussed in this chapter. In some cases, reducing taxes will be the primary objective. Thus high debt ratios are found in the lease-financing business. Long-term leases are often tax-driven transactions. High debt ratios are also found in developed commercial real estate. For example, modern downtown office buildings can be safe, cash-cow assets if the office space is rented to creditworthy tenants. Bankruptcy costs are small, so it makes sense to lever up and save taxes.

For smaller growth companies, interest tax shields are less important than preserving financial slack. Profitable growth opportunities are valuable only if financing is available when it comes time to invest. Costs of financial distress are high, so it's no surprise that growth companies try to use mostly equity financing.

Mature public corporations often end up following the pecking order. Information problems deter large equity issues, so such firms prefer to finance investment with retained earnings. They issue more debt when investments outrun retained earnings, and pay down debt when earnings outpace investment.

Sooner or later a corporation's operations age to the point where growth opportunities evaporate. In that case, the firm may issue large amounts of debt and retire equity, to constrain investment and force payout of cash to investors. The higher debt ratio may come voluntarily or be forced by a takeover.

These examples are not exhaustive, but they give some flavor of how a thoughtful CEO can set financing strategy.

Our task in this chapter was to show why capital structure matters. We did not throw away MM's proposition that capital structure is irrelevant; we added to it. However, we did not arrive at any simple, universal theory of optimal capital structure.

SUMMARY

The trade-off theory emphasizes interest tax shields and the costs of financial distress. The value of the firm is broken down as

$$\text{Value if all-equity-financed} + PV(\text{tax shield}) - PV(\text{costs of financial distress})$$

According to this theory, the firm should increase debt until the value from PV(tax shield) is just offset, at the margin, by increases in PV(costs of financial distress).

The costs of financial distress are:

1. Bankruptcy costs
   a. Direct costs such as legal and accounting fees.
   b. Indirect costs reflecting the difficulty of managing a company undergoing liquidation or reorganization.
2. Costs of financial distress short of bankruptcy
   a. Doubts about a firm's creditworthiness can hobble its operations. Customers and suppliers will be reluctant to deal with a firm that may not be around next year. Key employees will be tempted to leave. Highly leveraged firms seem to be less vigorous product-market competitors.

b. Conflicts of interest between bondholders and stockholders of firms in financial distress may lead to poor operating and investment decisions. Stockholders acting in their narrow self-interest can gain at the expense of creditors by playing "games" that reduce the overall value of the firm.

c. The fine print in debt contracts is designed to prevent these games. But fine print increases the costs of writing, monitoring, and enforcing the debt contract.

The value of the interest tax shield would be easy to compute if we had only corporate taxes to worry about. In that case the net tax saving from borrowing would be just the marginal corporate tax rate T_c times $r_D D$, the interest payment. If debt is fixed, the tax shield can be valued by discounting at the borrowing rate r_D. In the special case of fixed, permanent debt

$$\text{PV(tax shield)} = \frac{T_c r_D D}{r_D} = T_c D$$

However, corporate taxes are only part of the story. If investors pay higher taxes on interest income than on equity income (dividends and capital gains), then interest tax shields to the corporation will be partly offset by higher taxes paid by investors. The low (15% maximum) U.S. tax rates on dividends and capital gains have reduced the tax advantage to corporate borrowing.

The trade-off theory balances the tax advantages of borrowing against the costs of financial distress. Corporations are supposed to pick a target capital structure that maximizes firm value. Firms with safe, tangible assets and plenty of taxable income to shield ought to have high targets. Unprofitable companies with risky, intangible assets ought to rely more on equity financing.

This theory of capital structure successfully explains many industry differences in capital structure, but it does not explain why the most profitable firms *within* an industry generally have the most conservative capital structures. Under the trade-off theory, high profitability should mean high debt capacity *and* a strong tax incentive to use that capacity.

There is a competing, pecking-order theory, which states that firms use internal financing when available and choose debt over equity when external financing is required. This explains why the less profitable firms in an industry borrow more—not because they have higher target debt ratios but because they need more external financing and because debt is next on the pecking order when internal funds are exhausted.

The pecking order is a consequence of asymmetric information. Managers know more about their firms than outside investors do, and they are reluctant to issue stock when they believe the price is too low. They try to time issues when shares are fairly priced or overpriced. Investors understand this, and interpret a decision to issue shares as bad news. That explains why stock price usually falls when a stock issue is announced.

Debt is better than equity when these information problems are important. Optimistic managers will prefer debt to undervalued equity, and pessimistic managers will be pressed to follow suit. The pecking-order theory says that equity will be issued only when debt capacity is running out and financial distress threatens.

The pecking-order theory stresses the value of financial slack. Without sufficient slack, the firm may be caught at the bottom of the pecking order and be forced to choose between issuing undervalued shares, borrowing and risking financial distress, or passing up positive-NPV investment opportunities.

There is, however, a dark side to financial slack. Surplus cash or credit tempts managers to overinvest or to indulge an easy and glamorous corporate lifestyle. When temptation wins, or threatens to win, a high debt ratio can help: It forces the company to disgorge cash and prods managers and organizations to try harder to be more efficient.

Visit us at www.mhhe.com/bma

●　●　●　●　●

FURTHER READING

The research literature on capital structure is enormous. We cite only a few of the most important and interesting articles. The following review articles give broader surveys.

M. Harris and A. Raviv, "The Theory of Capital Structure," *Journal of Finance* 46 (March 1991), pp. 297–355.

S. C. Myers, "Financing of Corporations," in G. M. Constantinides, M. Harris, and R. Stulz (eds.), *Handbook of the Economics of Finance* (Amsterdam: Elsevier North-Holland, 2003).

The Winter 2005 issue of the Journal of Applied Corporate Finance *contains several articles on capital structure decisions in practice.*

The following paper surveys chief financial officers' views about capital structure:

J. Graham and C. Harvey, "How Do CFOs Make Capital Budgeting and Capital Structure Decisions?" *Journal of Applied Corporate Finance* 15 (Spring 2002), pp. 8–23.

BASIC

PROBLEM SETS

1. The present value of interest tax shields is often written as $T_c D$, where D is the amount of debt and T_c is the marginal corporate tax rate. Under what assumptions is this present value correct?

2. Here are book- and market-value balance sheets of the United Frypan Company (UF):

Book				Market		
Net working capital	$ 20	$ 40	Debt	Net working capital	$ 20	$ 40	Debt
Long-term assets	80	60	Equity	Long-term assets	140	120	Equity
	$100	$100			$160	$160	

Assume that MM's theory holds with taxes. There is no growth, and the $40 of debt is expected to be permanent. Assume a 40% corporate tax rate.

   a. How much of the firm's value is accounted for by the debt-generated tax shield?

   b. How much better off will UF's shareholders be if the firm borrows $20 more and uses it to repurchase stock?

3. What is the relative tax advantage of corporate debt if the corporate tax rate is $T_c = .35$, the personal tax rate is $T_p = .35$, but all equity income is received as capital gains and escapes tax entirely ($T_{pE} = 0$)? How does the relative tax advantage change if the company decides to pay out all equity income as cash dividends that are taxed at 15%?

4. "The firm can't use interest tax shields unless it has (taxable) income to shield." What does this statement imply for debt policy? Explain briefly.

5. This question tests your understanding of financial distress.

   a. What are the costs of going bankrupt? Define these costs carefully.

   b. "A company can incur costs of financial distress without ever going bankrupt." Explain how this can happen.

   c. Explain how conflicts of interest between bondholders and stockholders can lead to costs of financial distress.

6. On February 29, 2009, when PDQ Computers announced bankruptcy, its share price fell from $3.00 to $.50 per share. There were 10 million shares outstanding. Does that imply bankruptcy costs of 10 × (3.00 − .50) = $25 million? Explain.

7. The traditional theory of optimal capital structure states that firms trade off corporate interest tax shields against the possible costs of financial distress due to borrowing. What does this theory predict about the relationship between book profitability and target book debt ratios? Is the theory's prediction consistent with the facts?

8. Rajan and Zingales identified four variables that seemed to explain differences in debt ratios in several countries. What are the four variables?

9. Why does asymmetric information push companies to raise external funds by borrowing rather than by issuing common stock?

10. Fill in the blanks: According to the pecking-order theory,

   a. The firm's debt ratio is determined by _____.

   b. Debt ratios depend on past profitability, because _____.

11. For what kinds of companies is financial slack most valuable? Are there situations in which financial slack should be reduced by borrowing and paying out the proceeds to the stockholders? Explain.

INTERMEDIATE

12. Compute the present value of interest tax shields generated by these three debt issues. Consider corporate taxes only. The marginal tax rate is $T_c = .35$.

   a. A $1,000, one-year loan at 8%.

   b. A five-year loan of $1,000 at 8%. Assume no principal is repaid until maturity.

   c. A $1,000 perpetuity at 7%.

13. Suppose that, in an effort to reduce the federal deficit, Congress increases the top personal tax rate on interest and dividends to 35% but retains a 15% tax rate on realized capital gains. The corporate tax rate stays at 35%. Compute the total corporate plus personal taxes paid on debt versus equity income if (a) all capital gains are realized immediately and (b) capital gains are deferred forever. Assume capital gains are half of equity income.

14. "The trouble with MM's argument is that it ignores the fact that individuals can deduct interest for personal income tax." Show why this is not an objection if personal tax rates on interest and equity income are the same.

15. Look back at the Merck example in Section 14–1. Suppose Merck increases its long-term debt to $10 billion. It uses the additional debt to repurchase shares. Reconstruct Table 14.3(*b*) with the new capital structure. How much additional value is added for Merck shareholders if the table's assumptions are correct?

16. In Section 14–3, we briefly referred to three games: cash in and run, playing for time, and bait and switch.

   For each game, construct a simple numerical example (like the example for the risk-shifting game) showing how shareholders can gain at the expense of creditors. Then explain how the temptation to play these games could lead to costs of financial distress.

17. Look at some real companies with different types of assets. What operating problems would each encounter in the event of financial distress? How well would the assets keep their value?

18. Let us go back to Circular File's market-value balance sheet:

Net working capital	$20	$25	Bonds outstanding
Fixed assets	10	5	Common stock
Total assets	$30	$30	Total value

Who gains and who loses from the following maneuvers?

   a. Circular scrapes up $5 in cash and pays a cash dividend.

   b. Circular halts operations, sells its fixed assets, and converts net working capital into $20 cash. Unfortunately the fixed assets fetch only $6 on the secondhand market. The $26 cash is invested in Treasury bills.

   c. Circular encounters an acceptable investment opportunity, NPV = 0, requiring an investment of $10. The firm borrows to finance the project. The new debt has the same security, seniority, etc., as the old.

d. Suppose that the new project has NPV = +$2 and is financed by an issue of preferred stock.

e. The lenders agree to extend the maturity of their loan from one year to two in order to give Circular a chance to recover.

19. The Salad Oil Storage (SOS) Company has financed a large part of its facilities with long-term debt. There is a significant risk of default, but the company is not on the ropes yet. Explain:

a. Why SOS stockholders could lose by investing in a positive-NPV project financed by an equity issue.

b. Why SOS stockholders could gain by investing in a negative-NPV project financed by cash.

c. Why SOS stockholders could gain from paying out a large cash dividend.

20. a. Who benefits from the fine print in bond contracts when the firm gets into financial trouble? Give a one-sentence answer.

b. Who benefits from the fine print when the bonds are issued? Suppose the firm is offered the choice of issuing (i) a bond with standard restrictions on dividend payout, additional borrowing, etc., and (ii) a bond with minimal restrictions but a much higher interest rate? Suppose the interest rates on both (i) and (ii) are fair from the viewpoint of lenders. Which bond would you expect the firm to issue? Why?

21. "I was amazed to find that the announcement of a stock issue drives down the value of the issuing firm by 30%, on average, of the proceeds of the issue. That issue cost dwarfs the underwriter's spread and the administrative costs of the issue. It makes common stock issues prohibitively expensive."

a. You are contemplating a $100 million stock issue. On past evidence, you anticipate that announcement of this issue will drive down stock price by 3% and that the market value of your firm will fall by 30% of the amount to be raised. On the other hand, additional equity financing is required to fund an investment project that you believe has a positive NPV of $40 million. Should you proceed with the issue?

b. Is the fall in market value on announcement of a stock issue an *issue cost* in the same sense as an underwriter's spread? Respond to the quote that begins this question.

Use your answer to (a) as a numerical example to explain your response to (b).

22. Ronald Masulis analyzed the stock price impact of *exchange offers* of debt for equity or vice versa.[36] In an exchange offer, the firm offers to trade freshly issued securities for seasoned securities in the hands of investors. Thus, a firm that wanted to move to a higher debt ratio could offer to trade new debt for outstanding shares. A firm that wanted to move to a more conservative capital structure could offer to trade new shares for outstanding debt securities.

Masulis found that debt for equity exchanges were good news (stock price increased on announcement) and equity for debt exchanges were bad news.

a. Are these results consistent with the trade-off theory of capital structure?

b. Are the results consistent with the evidence that investors regard announcements of (i) stock issues as bad news, (ii) stock repurchases as good news, and (iii) debt issues as no news, or at most trifling disappointments?

c. How could Masulis's results be explained?

23. The possible payoffs from Ms. Ketchup's projects (see Example 14.1, pages 361–362) have not changed but there is now a 40% chance that project 2 will pay off $24 and a 60% chance that it will pay off $0.

---

[36] R. W. Masulis, "The Effects of Capital Structure Change on Security Prices: A Study of Exchange Offers," *Journal of Financial Economics* 8 (June 1980), pp. 139–177, and "The Impact of Capital Structure Change on Firm Value," *Journal of Finance* 38 (March 1983), pp. 107–126.

a. Recalculate the expected payoffs to the bank and Ms. Ketchup if the bank lends the present value of $10. Which project would Ms. Ketchup undertake?

b. What is the maximum amount the bank could lend that would induce Ms. Ketchup to take project 1?

24. Some corporations' debt–equity targets are expressed not as a debt ratio but as a target debt rating on the firm's outstanding bonds. What are the pros and cons of setting a target rating rather than a target ratio?

CHALLENGE

25. Most financial managers measure debt ratios from their companies' book balance sheets. Many financial economists emphasize ratios from market-value balance sheets. Which is the right measure in principle? Does the trade-off theory propose to explain book or market leverage? How about the pecking-order theory?

26. The trade-off theory relies on the threat of financial distress. But why should a public corporation ever have to land in financial distress? According to the theory, the firm should operate at the top of the curve in Figure 14.2. Of course market movements or business setbacks could bump it up to a higher debt ratio and put it on the declining, right-hand side of the curve. But in that case, why doesn't the firm just issue equity, retire debt, and move to back up to the optimal debt ratio?

What are the reasons why companies don't issue stock—or enough stock—quickly enough to avoid financial distress?

● ● ● ● ●

You can download data for the following questions from Standard & Poor's Market Insight Web site (www.mhhe.com/edumarketinsight).

REAL-TIME DATA ANALYSIS

STANDARD &POOR'S

STANDARD &POOR'S

STANDARD &POOR'S

1. Look up Merck on the Market Insight database.
   a. Recalculate book- and market-value balance sheets using the most recent available financial information. Use the same format as for Table 14.3.
   b. Track Merck's long-term debt and debt ratio over the last five years. How have they changed? Does it appear that Merck has a stable target debt ratio? Do you see any evidence of pecking-order financing?
   c. How much has Merck spent to repurchase its own shares? Would the trade-off theory predict share repurchases for a conservatively financed company like Merck?

2. Select three or four companies from the Market Insight database. Estimate how much more these companies could borrow before they would exhaust taxable profits.

3. The Market Insight database gives access to dozens of industry surveys. Check out the financial tables at the end of these surveys for several different industries. We suggest that you start with Autos and Auto Parts, Broadcasting and Cable TV, Department Stores and Trucking, plus a couple more industries that interest you. Write down the debt-to-capital ratios for a few of the largest companies in each industry, and average within the industry. Can you explain the differences between these industry-average ratios?

Financing and Valuation

▶ **In Chapters 5** and 6 we showed how to value a capital investment project by a four-step procedure:

1. Forecast after-tax cash flows, assuming all-equity financing.
2. Assess the project's risk.
3. Estimate the opportunity cost of capital.
4. Calculate NPV, using the opportunity cost of capital as the discount rate.

There's nothing wrong with this procedure, but now we're going to extend it to include value contributed by financing decisions. There are two ways to do this:

1. *Adjust the discount rate.* The adjustment is typically downward, to account for the value of interest tax shields. This is the most common approach, which is usually implemented via the after-tax weighted-average cost of capital (WACC). We introduced the after-tax WACC in Chapters 9 and 13, but here we provide a lot more guidance on how it is calculated and used.

2. *Adjust the present value.* That is, start by estimating the firm or project's base-case value, assuming it is all-equity-financed, and then adjust this base-case value to account for financing.

Adjusted present value (APV)
= base-case value + value of financing side effects

Once you identify and value the financing side effects, calculating APV is no more than addition or subtraction.

This is a how-to-do-it chapter. In the first section, we explain and derive the after-tax WACC and use it to value a project and business. Then in Section 15–2 we work through a more complex and realistic valuation problem. Section 15–3 covers some tricks of the trade: helpful hints on how to estimate inputs and on how to adjust WACC when business risk or capital structure changes. Section 15–4 turns to the APV method. The idea behind APV is simple enough, but tracing through all the financing side effects can be tricky. We conclude the chapter with a question-and-answer section designed to clarify points that managers and students often find confusing. The Appendix covers an important special case, namely, the after-tax valuation of safe cash flows.

•••••

15-1 The After-Tax Weighted-Average Cost of Capital

We first addressed problems of valuation and capital budgeting in Chapters 2 to 6. In those early chapters we said hardly a word about financing decisions. In fact we proceeded under the simplest possible financing assumption, namely, all-equity financing. We were really assuming a Modigliani–Miller (MM) world in which all financing decisions are irrelevant. In a strict MM world, firms can analyze real investments as if they are all-equity-financed; the actual financing plan is a mere detail to be worked out later.

Under MM assumptions, decisions to spend money can be separated from decisions to raise money. Now we reconsider the capital budgeting decision when investment and financing decisions interact and cannot be wholly separated.

One reason that financing and investment decisions interact is taxes. Interest is a tax-deductible expense. Think back to Chapters 9 and 13 where we introduced the *after-tax* weighted-average cost of capital:

$$\text{WACC} = r_D(1 - T_c)\frac{D}{V} + r_E\frac{E}{V}$$

Here D and E are the market values of the firm's debt and equity, $V = D + E$ is the total market value of the firm, r_D and r_E are the costs of debt and equity, and T_c is the marginal corporate tax rate.

Notice that the WACC formula uses the *after-tax* cost of debt $r_D (1 - T_c)$. That is how the after-tax WACC captures the value of interest tax shields. Notice too that all the variables in the WACC formula refer to the firm as a whole. As a result, the formula gives the right discount rate only for projects that are just like the firm undertaking them. The formula works for the "average" project. It is incorrect for projects that are safer or riskier than the average of the firm's existing assets. It is incorrect for projects whose acceptance would lead to an increase or decrease in the firm's target debt ratio.

The WACC is based on the firm's *current* characteristics, but managers use it to discount *future* cash flows. That's fine as long as the firm's business risk and debt ratio are expected to remain constant, but when the business risk and debt ratio are expected to change, discounting cash flows by the WACC is only approximately correct.

EXAMPLE 15.1 • Calculating Sangria's WACC

Sangria is a U.S.-based company whose products aim to promote happy, low-stress lifestyles. Let's calculate Sangria's WACC. Its book- and market-value balance sheets are:

Sangria Corporation (Book Values, $ millions)

Asset value	$1,000	$ 500	Debt
		500	Equity
	$1,000	$1,000	

Sangria Corporation (Market Values, $ millions)

Asset value	$1,250	$ 500	Debt
		750	Equity
	$1,250	$1,250	

We calculated the market value of equity on Sangria's balance sheet by multiplying its current stock price ($7.50) by 100 million, the number of its outstanding shares. The company's future prospects are good, so the stock is trading above book value ($7.50 vs. $5.00 per share). However, interest rates have been stable since the firm's debt was issued and the book and market values of debt are in this case equal.

Sangria's cost of debt (the market interest rate on its existing debt and on any new borrowing[1]) is 6%. Its cost of equity (the expected rate of return demanded by investors in Sangria's stock) is 12.4%.

---

[1] Always use an up-to-date interest rate (yield to maturity), not the interest rate when the firm's debt was first issued and not the coupon rate on the debt's book value.

The market-value balance sheet shows assets worth $1,250 million. Of course we can't observe this value directly, because the assets themselves are not traded. But we know what they are worth to debt and equity investors ($500 + 750 = $1,250 million). This value is entered on the left of the market-value balance sheet.

Why did we show the book balance sheet? Only so you could draw a big X through it. Do so now.

When estimating the weighted-average cost of capital, you are not interested in past investments but in current values and expectations for the future. Sangria's true debt ratio is not 50%, the book ratio, but 40%, because its assets are worth $1,250 million. The cost of equity, $r_E = .124$, is the expected rate of return from purchase of stock at $7.50 per share, the current market price. It is not the return on book value per share. You can't buy shares in Sangria for $5 anymore.

Sangria is consistently profitable and pays taxes at the marginal rate of 35%. This tax rate is the final input for Sangria's WACC. The inputs are summarized here:

Cost of debt (r_D)	.06
Cost of equity (r_E)	.124
Marginal tax rate (T_c)	.35
Debt ratio (D/V)	500/1,250 = .4
Equity ratio (E/V)	750/1,250 = .6

The company's after-tax WACC is:

$$\text{WACC} = .06 \times (1 - .35) \times .4 + .124 \times .6 = .090, \text{ or } 9.0\%$$

● ● ● ● ●

That's how you calculate the weighted-average cost of capital. Now let's see how Sangria would *use* it.

EXAMPLE 15.2 ● Using Sangria's WACC to Value a Project

Sangria's enologists have proposed investing $12.5 million in the construction of a perpetual crushing machine, which (conveniently for us) never depreciates and generates a perpetual stream of earnings and cash flow of $1.731 million per year pretax. The project is average risk, so we can use WACC. The after-tax cash flow is:

Pretax cash flow	$1.731 million
Tax at 35%	.606
After-tax cash flow	$C = \$1.125$ million

Notice: This after-tax cash flow takes no account of interest tax shields on debt supported by the perpetual crusher project. As we explained in Chapter 6, standard capital budgeting practice calculates after-tax cash flows as if the project were all-equity-financed. However, the interest tax shields will not be ignored: We are about to discount the project's cash flows by Sangria's WACC, in which the cost of debt is entered after tax. The value of interest tax shields is picked up not as higher after-tax cash flows, but in a lower discount rate.

The crusher generates a perpetual after-tax cash flow of $C = \$1.125$ million, so NPV is:

$$\text{NPV} = -12.5 + \frac{1.125}{0.09} = 0$$

NPV = 0 means a barely acceptable investment. The annual cash flow of $1.125 million per year amounts to a 9% rate of return on investment (1.125/12.5 = .09), exactly equal to Sangria's WACC.

If project NPV is exactly zero, the return to equity investors must exactly equal the cost of equity, 12.4%. Let's confirm that Sangria shareholders can actually look forward to a 12.4% return on their investment in the perpetual crusher project.

Suppose Sangria sets up this project as a mini-firm. Its market-value balance sheet looks like this:

Perpetual Crusher (Market Values, $ millions)

Asset value	$ 12.5	$ 5.0	Debt
		7.5	Equity
	$ 12.5	$ 12.5	

Calculate the expected dollar return to shareholders:

$$\text{After-tax interest} = r_D(1 - T_c)D = .06 \times (1 - .35) \times 5 = .195$$
$$\text{Expected equity income} = C - r_D(1 - T_c)D = 1.125 - .195 = .93$$

The project's earnings are level and perpetual, so the expected rate of return on equity is equal to the expected equity income divided by the equity value:

$$\text{Expected equity return} = r_E = \frac{\text{expected equity income}}{\text{equity value}}$$

$$= \frac{.93}{7.5} = .124, \text{ or } 12.4\%$$

The expected return on equity equals the cost of equity, so it makes sense that the project's NPV is zero.

● ● ● ● ●

Review of Assumptions

When discounting the perpetual crusher's cash flows at Sangria's WACC, we assume that:

- The project's business risks are the same as those of Sangria's other assets and remain so for the life of the project.
- The project supports the same fraction of debt to value as in Sangria's overall capital structure, which remains constant for the life of the project.

You can see the importance of these two assumptions: If the perpetual crusher had greater business risk than Sangria's other assets, or if the acceptance of the project would lead to a permanent, material change in Sangria's debt ratio,[2] then Sangria's shareholders would not be content with a 12.4% expected return on their equity investment in the project.

We have illustrated the WACC formula only for a project offering perpetual cash flows. But the formula works for any cash-flow pattern if the firm adjusts its borrowing

---

[2] Users of WACC need not worry about small or temporary fluctuations in debt-to-value ratios. Suppose that Sangria management decides for convenience to borrow $12.5 million to allow immediate construction of the crusher. This does not necessarily change Sangria's long-term financing policy. If the crusher supports only $5.0 million of debt, Sangria would have to pay down debt to restore its overall debt ratio to 40%. For example, it could fund later projects with less debt and more equity.

to maintain a constant debt ratio over time.[3] When the firm departs from this borrowing policy, WACC is only approximately correct.

15-2   Valuing Businesses

On most workdays the financial manager concentrates on valuing projects, arranging financing, and helping run the firm more effectively. The valuation of the business as a whole is left to investors and financial markets. But on some days the financial manager has to take a stand on what an entire business is worth. When this happens, a *big* decision is typically in the offing. For example:

· If firm A is about to make a takeover offer for firm B, then A's financial managers have to decide how much the combined business A + B is worth under A's management. This task is particularly difficult if B is a private company with no observable share price.

· If firm C is considering the sale of one of its divisions, it has to decide what the division is worth in order to negotiate with potential buyers.

· When a firm goes public, the investment bank must evaluate how much the firm is worth in order to set the issue price.

In addition, thousands of analysts in stockbrokers' offices and investment firms spend every workday burrowing away in the hope of finding undervalued firms. Many of these analysts use the valuation tools we are about to cover.

In Chapter 4 we took a first pass at valuing an entire business. We assumed then that the business was financed solely by equity. Now we will show how WACC can be used to value a company that is financed by a mixture of debt and equity as long as the debt ratio is expected to remain approximately constant. You just treat the company as if it were one big project. You forecast the company's cash flows (the hardest part of the

---

[3] We can prove this statement as follows. Denote expected after-tax cash flows (assuming all-equity financing) as $C_1, C_2, \ldots, C_T$. With all-equity financing, these flows would be discounted at the opportunity cost of capital r. But we need to value the cash flows for a firm that is financed partly with debt.

Start with value in the next to last period: $V_{T-1} = D_{T-1} + E_{T-1}$. The total cash payoff to debt and equity investors is the cash flow plus the interest tax shield. The expected total return to debt and equity investors is:

$$\text{Expected cash payoff in } T = C_T + T_c r_D D_{T-1} \tag{1}$$

$$= V_{T-1}\left(1 + r_D \frac{D_{T-1}}{V_{T-1}} + r_E \frac{E_{T-1}}{V_{T-1}}\right) \tag{2}$$

Assume the debt ratio is constant at $L = D/V$. Equate (1) and (2) and solve for V_{T-1}:

$$V_{T-1} = \frac{C_T}{1 + (1 - T_c)r_D L + r_E(1 - L)} = \frac{C_T}{1 + \text{WACC}}$$

The logic repeats for V_{T-2}. Note that the next period's payoff includes V_{T-1}:

$$\text{Expected cash payoff in } T - 1 = C_{T-1} + T_c r_D D_{T-2} + V_{T-1}$$

$$= V_{T-2}\left(1 + r_D \frac{D_{T-2}}{V_{T-2}} + r_E \frac{E_{T-2}}{V_{T-2}}\right)$$

$$V_{T-2} = \frac{C_{T-1} + V_{T-1}}{1 + (1 - T_c)r_D L + r_E(1 - L)} = \frac{C_{T-1} + V_{T-1}}{1 + \text{WACC}} = \frac{C_{T-1}}{1 + \text{WACC}} + \frac{C_T}{(1 + \text{WACC})^2}$$

We can continue all the way back to date 0:

$$V_0 = \sum_{t=1}^{T} \frac{C_t}{(1 + \text{WACC})^t}$$

exercise) and discount back to present value. But be sure to remember three important points:

1. If you discount at WACC, cash flows have to be projected just as you would for a capital investment project. Do not deduct interest. Calculate taxes as if the company were all-equity-financed. (The value of interest tax shields is not ignored, because the after-tax cost of debt is used in the WACC formula.)

2. Unlike most projects, companies are potentially immortal. But that does not mean that you need to forecast every year's cash flow from now to eternity. Financial managers usually forecast to a medium-term horizon and add a terminal value to the cash flows in the horizon year. The terminal value is the present value at the horizon of all subsequent cash flows. Estimating the terminal value requires careful attention because it often accounts for the majority of the company's value.

3. Discounting at WACC values the assets and operations of the company. If the object is to value the company's equity, that is, its common stock, don't forget to subtract the value of the company's outstanding debt.

Here's an example.

Valuing Rio Corporation

Sangria is tempted to acquire the Rio Corporation, which is also in the business of promoting relaxed, happy lifestyles. Rio has developed a special weight-loss program called the Brazil Diet, based on barbecues, red wine, and sunshine. The firm guarantees that within three months you will have a figure that will allow you to fit right in at Ipanema or Copacabana beach in Rio de Janeiro. But before you head for the beach, you've got the job of working out how much Sangria should pay for Rio.

Rio is a U.S. company. It is privately held, so Sangria has no stock-market price to rely on. Rio has 1.5 million shares outstanding and debt with a market and book value of $36 million. Rio is in the same line of business as Sangria, so we will assume that it has the same business risk as Sangria and can support the same proportion of debt. Therefore we can use Sangria's WACC.

Your first task is to forecast Rio's *free cash flow* (FCF). Free cash flow is the amount of cash that the firm can pay out to investors after making all investments necessary for growth. Free cash flow is calculated assuming the firm is all-equity-financed. Discounting the free cash flows at the after-tax WACC gives the total value of Rio (debt *plus* equity). To find the value of its equity, you will need to subtract the $36 million of debt.

We will forecast each year's free cash flow out to a *valuation horizon* (H) and predict the business's value at that horizon (PV_H). The cash flows and horizon value are then discounted back to the present:

$$PV = \underbrace{\frac{FCF_1}{1 + WACC} + \frac{FCF_2}{(1 + WACC)^2} + \cdots + \frac{FCF_H}{(1 + WACC)^H}}_{\text{PV (free cash flow)}} + \underbrace{\frac{PV_H}{(1 + WACC)^H}}_{\text{PV (horizon value)}}$$

Of course, the business will continue after the horizon, but it's not practical to forecast free cash flow year by year to infinity. PV_H stands in for the value in year H of free cash flow in periods $H + 1$, $H + 2$, etc.

Free cash flow and net income are not the same. They differ in several important ways:

· Income is the return to shareholders, calculated after interest expense. Free cash flow is calculated before interest.

· Income is calculated after various noncash expenses, including depreciation. Therefore we will add back depreciation when we calculate free cash flow.

· Capital expenditures and investments in working capital do not appear as expenses on the income statement, but they do reduce free cash flow.

Free cash flow can be negative for rapidly growing firms, even if the firms are profitable, because investment exceeds cash flow from operations. Negative free cash flow is normally temporary, fortunately for the firm and its stockholders. Free cash flow turns positive as growth slows down and the payoffs from prior investments start to roll in.

Table 15.1 sets out the information that you need to forecast Rio's free cash flows. We will follow common practice and start with a projection of sales. In the year just ended Rio had sales of $83.6 million. In recent years sales have grown by between 5% and 8% a year. You forecast that sales will grow by about 7% a year for the next three years. Growth will then slow to 4% for years 4 to 6 and to 3% starting in year 7.

The other components of cash flow in Table 15.1 are driven by these sales forecasts. For example, you can see that costs are forecasted at 74% of sales in the first year with a gradual increase to 76% of sales in later years, reflecting increased marketing costs as Rio's competitors gradually catch up.

Increasing sales are likely to require further investment in fixed assets and working capital. Rio's net fixed assets are currently about $.79 for each dollar of sales. Unless Rio has surplus capacity or can squeeze more output from its existing plant and equipment, its investment in fixed assets will need to grow along with sales. Therefore we assume that

	Latest Year 0	Forecast 1	2	3	4	5	6	7
1 Sales	83.6	89.5	95.8	102.5	106.6	110.8	115.2	118.7
2 Cost of goods sold	63.1	66.2	71.3	76.3	79.9	83.1	87.0	90.2
3 EBITDA (1 − 2)	20.5	23.3	24.4	26.1	26.6	27.7	28.2	28.5
4 Depreciation	3.3	9.9	10.6	11.3	11.8	12.3	12.7	13.1
5 Profit before tax (EBIT) (3 − 4)	17.2	13.4	13.8	14.8	14.9	15.4	15.5	15.4
6 Tax	6.0	4.7	4.8	5.2	5.2	5.4	5.4	5.4
7 Profit after tax (5 − 6)	11.2	8.7	9.0	9.6	9.7	10.0	10.1	10.0
8 Investment in fixed assets	11.0	14.6	15.5	16.6	15.0	15.6	16.2	15.9
9 Investment in working capital	1.0	0.5	0.8	0.9	0.5	0.6	0.6	0.4
10 Free cash flow (7 + 4 − 8 − 9)	2.5	3.5	3.2	3.4	5.9	6.1	6.0	6.8
PV free cash flow, years 1–6	20.3							
PV horizon value	67.6			(Horizon value in year 6)			113.4	
PV of company	87.9							
Assumptions:								
Sales growth, %	6.7	7.0	7.0	7.0	4.0	4.0	4.0	3.0
Costs (percent of sales)	75.5	74.0	74.5	74.5	75.0	75.0	75.5	76.0
Working capital (percent of sales)	13.3	13.0	13.0	13.0	13.0	13.0	13.0	13.0
Net fixed assets (percent of sales)	79.2	79.0	79.0	79.0	79.0	79.0	79.0	79.0
Depreciation (percent of net fixed assets)	5.0	14.0	14.0	14.0	14.0	14.0	14.0	14.0
Tax rate, %	35.0							
WACC, %	9.0							
Long-term growth forecast, %	3.0							
Fixed assets and working capital								
Gross fixed assets	95.0	109.6	125.1	141.8	156.8	172.4	188.6	204.5
Less accumulated depreciation	29.0	38.9	49.5	60.8	72.6	84.9	97.6	110.7
Net fixed assets	66.0	70.7	75.6	80.9	84.2	87.5	91.0	93.8
Net working capital	11.1	11.6	12.4	13.3	13.9	14.4	15.0	15.4

▶ **TABLE 15.1** Free-cash-flow projections and company value for Rio Corporation ($ millions).

Visit us at
www.mhhe.com/bma

every dollar of sales growth requires an increase of $.79 in net fixed assets. We also assume that working capital grows in proportion to sales.

Rio's free cash flow is calculated in Table 15.1 as profit after tax, plus depreciation, minus investment. Investment is the change in the stock of (gross) fixed assets and working capital from the previous year. For example, in year 1:

$$\text{Free cash flow} = \text{Profit after tax} + \text{depreciation} - \text{investment in fixed assets}$$
$$- \text{investment in working capital}$$
$$= 8.7 + 9.9 - (109.6 - 95.0) - (11.6 - 11.1) = \$3.5 \text{ million}$$

Estimating Horizon Value

We will forecast cash flows for each of the first six years. After that, Rio's sales are expected to settle down to stable, long-term growth starting in year 7. To find the present value of the cash flows in years 1 to 6, we discount at the 9% WACC:

$$PV = \frac{3.5}{1.09} + \frac{3.2}{1.09^2} + \frac{3.4}{1.09^3} + \frac{5.9}{1.09^4} + \frac{6.1}{1.09^5} + \frac{6.0}{1.09^6} = \$20.3 \text{ million}$$

Now we need to find the value of the cash flows from year 7 onward. In Chapter 4 we looked at several ways to estimate horizon value. Here we will use the constant-growth DCF formula. This requires a forecast of the free cash flow for year 7, which we have worked out in the final column of Table 15.1, assuming a long-run growth rate of 3% per year.[4] The free cash flow is $6.8 million, so

$$PV_H = \frac{FCF_{H+1}}{\text{WACC} - g} = \frac{6.8}{.09 - .03} = \$113.4 \text{ million}$$

$$PV \text{ at year } 0 = \frac{1}{1.09^6} \times 113.4 = \$67.6 \text{ million}$$

We now have all we need to value the business:

$$PV(\text{company}) = PV(\text{cash flow years 1–6}) + PV(\text{horizon value})$$
$$= \$20.3 + 67.6 = \$87.9 \text{ million}$$

This is the total value of Rio. To find the value of the equity, we simply subtract the value of the debt:

$$\text{Total value of equity} = \$87.9 - 36.0 = \$51.9 \text{ million}$$

And to find the value per share, we divide by the total number of shares outstanding:

$$\text{Value per share} = 51.9/1.5 = \$34.60$$

Thus Sangria could afford to pay up to $34.60 per share for Rio.

You now have an estimate of the value of Rio Corporation. But how confident can you be in this figure? Notice that less than a quarter of Rio's value comes from cash flows in the first six years. The rest comes from the horizon value. Moreover, this horizon value can change in response to only minor changes in assumptions. For example, if the long-run growth rate is 4% rather than 3%, Rio needs to invest more to support this higher growth, but firm value increases from $87.9 million to $89.9 million.

In Chapter 4 we stressed that wise managers won't stop at this point. They will check their calculations by identifying comparable companies and comparing their price–earnings multiples and ratios of market to book value.[5]

---

[4] Notice that expected free cash flow increases by about 14% from year 6 to year 7 because the transition from 4% to 3% sales growth reduces required investment. But sales, investment, and free cash flow will all increase at 3% once the company settles into stable growth. Recall that the first cash flow in the constant-growth DCF formula occurs in the next year, year 7 in this case. Growth progresses at a steady-state 3% from year 7 onward. Therefore it's OK to use the 3% growth rate in the horizon-value formula.

[5] See Section 4–5.

When you forecast cash flows, it is easy to become mesmerized by the numbers and just do it mechanically. It is important to take a strategic view. Are the revenue figures consistent with what you expect your competitors to do? Are the costs you have predicted realistic? Probe the assumptions behind the numbers to make sure they are sensible. Be particularly careful about the growth rates and profitability assumptions that drive horizon values. Don't assume that the business you are valuing will grow and earn more than the cost of capital in perpetuity.[6] This would be a nice outcome for the business, but not an outcome that competition will tolerate.

You should also check whether the business is worth more dead than alive. Sometimes a company's *liquidation value* exceeds its value as a going concern. Smart financial analysts sometimes ferret out idle or underexploited assets that would be worth much more if sold to someone else. You may end up counting these assets at their likely sale price and valuing the rest of the business without them.

WACC vs. the Flow-to-Equity Method

When valuing Rio we forecast the cash flows assuming all-equity financing and we used the WACC to discount these cash flows. The WACC formula picked up the value of the interest tax shields. Then to find equity value, we subtracted the value of debt from the total value of the firm.

If our task is to value a firm's equity, there's an obvious alternative to discounting company cash flows at the firm's WACC: Discount cash flows to *equity,* after interest and after taxes, at the cost of equity capital. This is called the *flow-to-equity* method. If the company's debt ratio is constant over time, the flow-to equity method should give the same answer as discounting cash flows at the WACC and then subtracting debt.

The flow-to-equity method seems simple, and it is simple if the proportions of debt and equity financing stay reasonably close to constant for the life of the company. But the cost of equity depends on financial leverage; in other words, it depends on financial risk as well as business risk. If financial leverage is expected to change significantly, discounting flows to equity at today's cost of equity will not give the right answer.

15-3 Using WACC In Practice

Some Tricks of the Trade

Sangria had just one asset and two sources of financing. A real company's market-value balance sheet has many more entries, for example:[7]

---

[6] Table 15.1 is too optimistic in this respect, because the horizon value increases with the assumed long-run growth rate. This implies that Rio has valuable growth opportunities (PVGO) even after the horizon in year 6. A more sophisticated spreadsheet would add an intermediate growth stage, say from years 7 through 10, and gradually reduce profitability to competitive levels. See Problem 26 at the end of this chapter.

[7] This balance sheet is for exposition and should not be confused with a real company's books. It includes the value of growth opportunities, which accountants do not recognize, though investors do. It excludes certain accounting entries, for example, deferred taxes.

Deferred taxes arise when a company uses faster depreciation for tax purposes than it uses in reports to investors. That means the company reports more in taxes than it pays. The difference is accumulated as a liability for deferred taxes. In a sense there is a liability, because the Internal Revenue Service "catches up," collecting extra taxes, as assets age. But this is irrelevant in capital investment analysis, which focuses on actual after-tax cash flows and uses accelerated tax depreciation.

Deferred taxes should not be regarded as a source of financing or an element of the weighted-average cost of capital formula. The liability for deferred taxes is not a security held by investors. It is a balance sheet entry created for accounting purposes.

Deferred taxes can be important in regulated industries, however. Regulators take deferred taxes into account in calculating allowed rates of return and the time patterns of revenues and consumer prices.

Current assets, including cash, inventory, and accounts receivable	Current liabilities, including accounts payable and short-term debt
Property, plant, and equipment	Long-term debt (D)
	Preferred stock (P)
Growth opportunities	Equity (E)
Total assets	Total liabilities plus equity

Several questions immediately arise:

How does the formula change when there are more than two sources of financing? Easy: There is one cost for each element. The weight for each element is proportional to its market value. For example, if the capital structure includes both preferred and common shares,

$$\text{WACC} = r_D(1 - T_c)\frac{D}{V} + r_P\frac{P}{V} + r_E\frac{E}{V}$$

where r_P is investors' expected rate of return on the preferred stock, P is the amount of preferred stock outstanding, and $V = D + P + E$.

What about short-term debt? Many companies consider only long-term financing when calculating WACC. They leave out the cost of short-term debt. In principle this is incorrect. The lenders who hold short-term debt are investors who can claim their share of operating earnings. A company that ignores this claim will misstate the required return on capital investments.

But "zeroing out" short-term debt is not a serious error if the debt is only temporary, seasonal, or incidental financing or if it is offset by holdings of cash and marketable securities. Suppose, for example, that one of your foreign subsidiaries takes out a six-month loan to finance its inventory and accounts receivable. The dollar equivalent of this loan will show up as a short-term debt. At the same time headquarters may be lending money by investing surplus dollars in short-term securities. If this lending and borrowing offset, there is no point in including the cost of short-term debt in the weighted-average cost of capital, because the company is not a *net* short-term borrower.

What about other current liabilities? Current liabilities are usually "netted out" by subtracting them from current assets. The difference is entered as net working capital on the left-hand side of the balance sheet. The sum of long-term financing on the right is called *total capitalization.*

Net working capital = current assets − current liabilities	Long-term debt (D)
Property, plant, and equipment	Preferred stock (P)
Growth opportunities	Equity (E)
	Total capitalization (V)

When net working capital is treated as an asset, forecasts of cash flows for capital investment projects must treat increases in net working capital as a cash outflow and decreases as an inflow. This is standard practice, which we followed in Section 6–2. We also did so when we estimated the future investments that Rio would need to make in working capital.

Since current liabilities include short-term debt, netting them out against current assets excludes the cost of short-term debt from the weighted-average cost of capital. We have just explained why this can be an acceptable approximation. But when short-term debt is an important, permanent source of financing—as is common for small firms, and firms outside the United States—it should be shown explicitly on the right-hand side of the balance sheet, not netted out against current assets.[8] The interest cost of short-term debt is then one element of the weighted-average cost of capital.

How are the costs of financing calculated? You can often use stock market data to get an estimate of r_E, the expected rate of return demanded by investors in the company's stock. With that estimate, WACC is not too hard to calculate, because the borrowing rate r_D and the debt and equity ratios D/V and E/V can be directly observed or estimated without too much trouble.[9] Estimating the value and required return for preferred shares is likewise usually not too complicated.

Estimating the required return on other security types can be troublesome. Convertible debt, where the investors' return comes partly from an option to exchange the debt for the company's stock, is one example.

Junk debt, where the risk of default is high, is likewise difficult. The higher the odds of default, the lower the market price of the debt, and the higher the *promised* rate of interest. But the weighted-average cost of capital is an *expected*, that is average, rate of return, not a promised one. For example, in July 2009, MGM Mirage bonds maturing in 2015 sold at only 66% of face value and offered a 15% promised yield, nearly 13 percentage points above yields on the highest-quality debt issues maturing at the same time. The price and yield on the MGM bond demonstrated investors' concern about the company's chronic financial ill-health. But the 15% yield was not an expected return, because it did not average in the losses to be incurred if MGM were to default. Including 15% as a "cost of debt" in a calculation of WACC would therefore have overstated MGM's true cost of capital.

This is bad news: There is no easy or tractable way of estimating the expected rate of return on most junk debt issues.[10] The good news is that for most debt the odds of default are small. That means the promised and expected rates of return are close, and the promised rate can be used as an approximation in the weighted-average cost of capital.

Company vs. Industry WACCs   Of course you want to know what your company's WACC is. Yet industry WACCs are sometimes more useful. Here's an example. Kansas City Southern used to be a portfolio of (1) the Kansas City Southern Railroad, with operations running from the U.S. Midwest south to Texas and Mexico, and (2) Stillwell Financial, an investment-management business that included the Janus mutual funds. It's hard to think of two more dissimilar businesses. Kansas City Southern's overall WACC was not right for either of them. The company would have been well advised to use a railroad industry WACC for its railroad operations and an investment management WACC for Stillwell.

KCS spun off Stillwell in 2000 and is now a pure-play railroad. But even now the company would be wise to check its WACC against a railroad industry WACC. Industry WACCs are less exposed to random noise and estimation errors. Fortunately for Kansas City Southern, there are several large, pure-play U.S. railroads from which a railroad industry WACC can be estimated.[11] Of course, use of an industry WACC for a particular company's investments assumes that the company and industry have approximately the same business risk and financing.

---

[8] Financial practitioners have rules of thumb for deciding whether short-term debt is worth including in WACC. One rule checks whether short-term debt is at least 10% of total liabilities and net working capital is negative. If so, then short-term debt is almost surely being used to finance long-term assets and is explicitly included in WACC.

[9] Most corporate debt is not actively traded, so its market value cannot be observed directly. But you can usually value a nontraded debt security by looking to securities that *are* traded and that have approximately the same default risk and maturity.

For healthy firms the market value of debt is usually not too far from book value, so many managers and analysts use book value for D in the weighted-average cost of capital formula. However, be sure to use *market*, not book, values for E.

[10] When betas can be estimated for the junk issue or for a sample of similar issues, the expected return can be calculated from the capital asset pricing model. Otherwise the yield should be adjusted for the probability of default.

[11] See Tables 4.4 and 9.1.

Mistakes People Make in Using the Weighted-Average Formula

The weighted-average formula is very useful but also dangerous. It tempts people to make logical errors. For example, manager Q, who is campaigning for a pet project, might look at the formula

$$\text{WACC} = r_D(1 - T_c)\frac{D}{V} + r_E\frac{E}{V}$$

and think, "Aha! My firm has a good credit rating. It could borrow, say, 90% of the project's cost if it likes. That means $D/V = .9$ and $E/V = .1$. My firm's borrowing rate r_D is 8%, and the required return on equity, r_E, is 15%. Therefore

$$\text{WACC} = .08(1 - .35)(.9) + .15(.1) = .062$$

or 6.2%. When I discount at that rate, my project looks great."

Manager Q is wrong on several counts. First, the weighted-average formula works only for projects that are carbon copies of the firm. The firm isn't 90% debt-financed.

Second, the immediate source of funds for a project has no necessary connection with the hurdle rate for the project. What matters is the project's overall contribution to the firm's borrowing power. A dollar invested in Q's pet project will not increase the firm's debt capacity by $.90. If the firm borrows 90% of the project's cost, it is really borrowing in part against its *existing* assets. Any advantage from financing the new project with more debt than normal should be attributed to the old projects, not to the new one.

Third, even if the firm were willing and able to lever up to 90% debt, its cost of capital would not decline to 6.2% (as Q's naive calculation predicts). You cannot increase the debt ratio without creating financial risk for stockholders and thereby increasing r_E, the expected rate of return they demand from the firm's common stock. Going to 90% debt would certainly increase the borrowing rate, too.

Adjusting WACC When Debt Ratios and Business Risks Differ

The WACC formula assumes that the project or business to be valued will be financed in the same debt–equity proportions as the company (or industry) as a whole. What if that is not true? For example, what if Sangria's perpetual crusher project supports only 20% debt, versus 40% for Sangria overall?

Moving from 40% to 20% debt may change all the inputs to the WACC formula.[12] Obviously the financing weights change. But the cost of equity r_E is less, because financial risk is reduced. The cost of debt may be lower too.

Take another look at Figure 13.4 on page 339, which plots WACC and the costs of debt and equity as a function of the debt–equity ratio. The flat line is r, the opportunity cost of capital. Remember, this is the expected rate of return that investors would want from the project if it were all-equity-financed. The opportunity cost of capital depends only on business risk and is the natural reference point.

Suppose Sangria or the perpetual crusher project were all-equity-financed ($D/V = 0$). At that point WACC equals cost of equity, and both equal the opportunity cost of capital. Start from that point in Figure 15.1. As the debt ratio increases, the cost of equity increases, because of financial risk, but notice that WACC declines. The decline is *not* caused by use of "cheap" debt in place of "expensive" equity. It falls because of the tax shields on debt interest payments. If there were no corporate income taxes, the weighted-average cost of

---

[12] Even the tax rate could change. For example, Sangria might have enough taxable income to cover interest payments at 20% debt but not at 40% debt. In that case the effective marginal tax rate would be higher at 20% than at 40% debt.

FIGURE 15.1

This plot shows WACC for Sangria Corporation at debt-to-equity ratios of 25% and 67%. The corresponding debt-to-value ratios are 20% and 40%.

eXcel

Visit us at
www.mhhe.com/bma

capital would be constant, and equal to the opportunity cost of capital, at all debt ratios. We showed this in Chapter 13.

Figure 15.1 shows the *shape* of the relationship between financing and WACC, but initially we have numbers only for Sangria's current 40% debt ratio. We want to recalculate WACC at a 20% ratio.

Here is the simplest way to do it. There are three steps.

Step 1 Calculate the opportunity cost of capital. In other words, calculate WACC and the cost of equity at zero debt. This step is called *unlevering* the WACC. The simplest unlevering formula is

$$\text{Opportunity cost of capital} = r = r_D D/V + r_E E/V$$

This formula comes directly from Modigliani and Miller's proposition 1 (see Section 13–1). If taxes are left out, the weighted-average cost of capital equals the opportunity cost of capital and is independent of leverage.

Step 2 Estimate the cost of debt, r_D, at the new debt ratio, and calculate the new cost of equity.

$$r_E = r + (r - r_D)D/E$$

This formula is Modigliani and Miller's proposition 2 (see Section 13–2). It calls for D/E, the ratio of debt to *equity*, not debt to value.

Step 3 Recalculate the weighted-average cost of capital at the new financing weights.
Let's do the numbers for Sangria at $D/V = .20$, or 20%.
Step 1. Sangria's current debt ratio is $D/V = .4$. So

$$r = .06(.4) + .124(.6) = .0984, \text{ or } 9.84\%$$

Step 2. We will assume that the debt cost stays at 6% when the debt ratio is 20%. Then

$$r_E = .0984 + (.0984 - .06)(.25) = .108, \text{ or } 10.8\%$$

Note that the debt–*equity* ratio is $.2/.8 = .25$.

Step 3. Recalculate WACC.

$$\text{WACC} = .06(1 - .35)(.2) + .108(.8) = .0942, \text{ or } 9.42\%$$

Figure 15.1 enters these numbers on the plot of WACC versus the debt–equity ratio.

Unlevering and Relevering Betas

Our three-step procedure (1) unlevers and then (2) relevers the cost of equity. Some financial managers find it convenient to (1) unlever and then (2) relever the equity beta. Given the beta of equity at the new debt ratio, the cost of equity is determined from the capital asset pricing model. Then WACC is recalculated.

The formula for unlevering beta was given in Section 13–2.

$$\beta_A = \beta_D (D/V) + \beta_E (E/V)$$

This equation says that the beta of a firm's assets is revealed by the beta of a portfolio of all of the firm's outstanding debt and equity securities. An investor who bought such a portfolio would own the assets free and clear and absorb only business risks.

The formula for relevering beta closely resembles MM's proposition 2, except that betas are substituted for rates of return:

$$\beta_E = \beta_A + (\beta_A - \beta_D)D/E$$

Use this formula to recalculate β_E when D/E changes.

The Importance of Rebalancing

The formulas for WACC and for unlevering and relevering expected returns are simple, but we must be careful to remember underlying assumptions. The most important point is *rebalancing*.

Calculating WACC for a company at its existing capital structure requires that the capital structure *not* change; in other words, the company must rebalance its capital structure to maintain the same market-value debt ratio for the relevant future. Take Sangria Corporation as an example. It starts with a debt-to-value ratio of 40% and a market value of $1,250 million. Suppose that Sangria's products do unexpectedly well in the marketplace and that market value increases to $1,500 million. Rebalancing means that it will then increase debt to $.4 \times 1,500 = \$600$ million,[13] thus regaining a 40% ratio. If market value instead falls, Sangria would have to pay down debt proportionally.

Of course real companies do not rebalance capital structure in such a mechanical and compulsive way. For practical purposes, it's sufficient to assume gradual but steady adjustment toward a long-run target. But if the firm plans significant changes in capital structure (for example, if it plans to pay off its debt), the WACC formula won't work. In such cases, you should turn to the APV method, which we describe in the next section.

---

[13] The proceeds of the additional borrowing would be paid out to shareholders or used, along with additional equity investment, to finance Sangria's growth.

Our three-step procedure for recalculating WACC makes a similar rebalancing assumption.[14] Whatever the starting debt ratio, the firm is assumed to rebalance to maintain that ratio in the future.[15]

The Modigliani–Miller Formula, Plus Some Final Advice

What if the firm does not rebalance to keep its debt ratio constant? In this case the only general approach is adjusted present value, which we cover in the next section. But sometimes financial managers turn to other discount-rate formulas, including one derived by Modigliani and Miller (MM). MM considered a company or project generating a level, perpetual stream of cash flows financed with fixed, perpetual debt, and derived a simple after-tax discount rate:[16]

$$r_{MM} = r(1 - T_c D/V)$$

---

[14] Similar, but not identical. The basic WACC formula is correct whether rebalancing occurs at the end of each period or continuously. The unlevering and relevering formulas used in steps 1 and 2 of our three-step procedure are exact only if rebalancing is continuous so that the debt ratio stays constant day-to-day and week-to-week. However, the errors introduced from annual rebalancing are very small and can be ignored for practical purposes.

[15] Here's why the formulas work with continuous rebalancing. Think of a market-value balance sheet with assets and interest tax shields on the left and debt and equity on the right, with $D + E = $ PV(assets) + PV(tax shield). The total risk (beta) of the firm's debt and equity equals the blended risk of PV(assets) and PV(tax shield)

$$\beta_D \frac{D}{V} + \beta_E \frac{E}{V} = \alpha\beta_A + (1 - \alpha)\beta_{tax\ shield} \tag{1}$$

where α is the proportion of the total firm value from its assets and $1 - \alpha$ is the proportion from interest tax shields. If the firm readjusts its capital structure to keep D/V constant, then the beta of the tax shield must be the same as the beta of the assets. With rebalancing, an x% change in firm value V changes debt D by x%. So the interest tax shield $T_c r_D D$ will change by x% as well. Thus the risk of the tax shield must be the same as the risk of the firm as a whole:

$$\beta_{tax\ shield} = \beta_A = \beta_D \frac{D}{V} + \beta_E \frac{E}{V} \tag{2}$$

This is our unlevering formula expressed in terms of beta. Since expected returns depend on beta:

$$r_A = r_D \frac{D}{V} + r_E \frac{E}{V} \tag{3}$$

Rearrange formulas (2) and (3) to get the relevering formulas for β_E and r_E.

$$\beta_E = \beta_A + (\beta_A - \beta_D)D/E$$
$$r_E = r_A + (r_A - r_D)D/E$$

All this assumes continuous rebalancing. Suppose instead that the firm rebalances once a year, so that the next year's interest tax shield, which depends on this year's debt, is known. Then you can use a formula developed by Miles and Ezzell:

$$r_{Miles-Ezzell} = r_A - (D/V)r_D T_c \left(\frac{1 + r_A}{1 + r_D}\right)$$

See J. Miles and J. Ezzell, "The Weighted Average Cost of Capital, Perfect Capital Markets, and Project Life: A Clarification," *Journal of Financial and Quantitative Analysis* 15 (September 1980), pp. 719–730.

[16] The formula first appeared in F. Modigliani and M. H. Miller, "Corporate Income Taxes and the Cost of Capital: A Correction," *American Economic Review* 53 (June 1963), pp. 433–443. It is explained more fully in M. H. Miller and F. Modigliani: "Some Estimates of the Cost of Capital to the Electric Utility Industry: 1954–1957," *American Economic Review* 56 (June 1966), pp. 333–391.

Given perpetual fixed debt,

$$V = \frac{C}{r} + T_c D$$

$$V = \frac{C}{r(1 - T_c D/V)} = \frac{C}{r_{MM}}$$

Here it's easy to unlever: Just set the debt-capacity parameter (D/V) equal to zero.[17]

MM's formula is still used in practice, but the formula is exact only in the special case where there is a level, perpetual stream of cash flows and fixed, perpetual debt. However, the formula is not a bad approximation for shorter-lived projects when debt is issued in a fixed amount.[18]

So which team do you want to play with, the fixed-debt team or the rebalancers? If you join the fixed-debt team you will be outnumbered. Most financial managers use the plain, after-tax WACC, which assumes constant market-value debt ratios and therefore assumes rebalancing. That makes sense, because the debt *capacity* of a firm or project must depend on its future value, which will fluctuate.

At the same time, we must admit that the typical financial manager doesn't care much if his or her firm's debt ratio drifts up or down within a reasonable range of moderate financial leverage. The typical financial manager acts as if a plot of WACC against the debt ratio is "flat" (constant) over this range. This too makes sense, if we just remember that interest tax shields are the *only* reason why the after-tax WACC declines in Figure 13.4 or 15.1. The WACC formula doesn't explicitly capture costs of financial distress or any of the other nontax complications discussed in Chapter 14.[19] All these complications may roughly cancel the value added by interest tax shields (within a range of moderate leverage). If so, the financial manager is wise to focus on the firm's operating and investment decisions, rather than on fine-tuning its debt ratio.

15-4 Adjusted Present Value

The idea behind **adjusted present value (APV)** is to divide and conquer. APV does not attempt to capture taxes or other effects of financing in a WACC or adjusted discount rate. A series of present value calculations is made instead. The first establishes a base-case value for the project or firm: its value as a separate, all-equity-financed venture. The discount rate for the base-case value is just the opportunity cost of capital. Once the base-case value is set, then each financing side effect is traced out, and the present value of its cost or benefit to the firm is calculated. Finally, all the present values are added together to estimate the project's total contribution to the value of the firm:

$$APV = \text{base-case NPV} + \text{sum of PVs of financing side effects}[20]$$

---

[17] In this case the relevering formula for the cost of equity is:

$$r_E = r_A + (1 - T_c)(r_A - r_D)D/E$$

The unlevering and relevering formulas for betas are

$$\beta_A = \frac{\beta_D(1 - T_c)D/E + \beta_E}{1 + (1 - T_c)D/E}$$

and

$$\beta_E = \beta_A + (1 - T_c)(\beta_A - \beta_D)D/E$$

See R. Hamada: "The Effect of a Firm's Capital Structure on the Systematic Risk of Common Stocks," *Journal of Finance* 27 (May 1972), pp. 435–452.

[18] See S. C. Myers, "Interactions of Corporate Financing and Investment Decisions—Implications for Capital Budgeting," *Journal of Finance* 29 (March 1974), pp. 1–25.

[19] Costs of financial distress can show up as rapidly increasing costs of debt and equity, especially at high debt ratios. The costs of financial distress could "flatten out" the WACC curve in Figures 13.4 and 15.1, and finally increase WACC as leverage climbs. Thus some practitioners calculate an industry WACC and take it as constant, at least within the range of debt ratios observed for healthy companies in the industry.

Personal taxes could also generate a flatter curve for after-tax WACC as a function of leverage. See Section 14–2.

[20] "The adjusted-present-value rule was developed in S. C. Myers, "Interactions of Corporate Financing and Investment Decisions—Implications for Capital Budgeting," *Journal of Finance* 29 (March 1974), pp. 1–25.

The most important financing side effect is the interest tax shield on the debt supported by the project (a plus). Other possible side effects are the issue costs of securities (a minus) or financing packages subsidized by a supplier or government (a plus).

APV gives the financial manager an explicit view of the factors that are adding or sub-tracting value. APV can prompt the manager to ask the right follow-up questions. For example, suppose that base-case NPV is positive but less than the costs of issuing shares to finance the project. That should prompt the manager to look around to see if the project can be rescued by an alternative financing plan.

APV for the Perpetual Crusher

APV is easiest to understand in simple numerical examples. Let's apply it to Sangria's perpetual crusher project. We start by showing that APV is equivalent to discounting at WACC if we make the same assumptions about debt policy.

We used Sangria's WACC (9%) as the discount rate for the crusher's projected cash flows. The WACC calculation assumed that debt will be maintained at a constant 40% of the future value of the project or firm. In this case, the risk of interest tax shields is the same as the risk of the project.[21] Therefore we will discount the tax shields at the opportunity cost of capital (r). We calculated the opportunity cost of capital in the last section by unlevering Sangria's WACC to obtain $r = 9.84\%$.

The first step is to calculate base-case NPV. We discount after-tax project cash flows of $1.125 million at the opportunity cost of capital of 9.84% and subtract the $12.5 million outlay. The cash flows are perpetual, so:

$$\text{Base-case NPV} = -12.5 + \frac{1.125}{.0984} = -\$1.067 \text{ million}$$

Thus the project would not be worthwhile with all-equity financing. But it actually sup-ports debt of $5 million. At a 6% borrowing rate ($r_D = .06$) and a 35% tax rate ($T_c = .35$), annual tax shields are $.35 \times .06 \times 5 = .105$, or $105,000.

What are those tax shields worth? If the firm is constantly rebalancing its debt, we dis-count at $r = 9.84\%$:

$$\text{PV(interest tax shields, debt rebalanced)} = \frac{105,000}{.0984} = \$1.067 \text{ million}$$

APV is the sum of base-case value and PV(interest tax shields)

$$\text{APV} = -1.067 \text{ million} + 1.067 \text{ million} = 0$$

This is exactly the same as we obtained by one-step discounting with WACC. The per-petual crusher is a break-even project by either valuation method.

But with APV, we don't have to hold debt at a constant proportion of value. Suppose Sangria plans to keep project debt fixed at $5 million. In this case we assume the risk of the tax shields is the same as the risk of the debt and we discount at the 6% rate on debt:

$$\text{PV(tax shields, debt fixed)} = \frac{105,000}{.06} = \$1.75 \text{ million}$$

$$\text{APV} = -1.067 + 1.75 = \$.683 \text{ million}$$

Now the project is more attractive. With fixed debt, the interest tax shields are safe and therefore worth more. (Whether the fixed debt is safer for Sangria is another matter. If the perpetual crusher project fails, the $5 million of fixed debt may end up as a burden on Sangria's other assets.)

---

[21] That is, $\beta_A = \beta_{\text{tax shields}}$. See footnote 15 above.

Other Financing Side Effects

Suppose Sangria has to finance the perpetual crusher by issuing debt and equity. It issues $7.5 million of equity with issue costs of 7% ($525,000) and $5 million of debt with issue costs of 2% ($100,000). Assume the debt is fixed once issued, so that interest tax shields are worth $1.75 million. Now we can recalculate APV, taking care to subtract the issue costs:

$$APV = -1.067 + 1.75 - .525 - .100 = .058 \text{ million, or } \$58,000$$

The issue costs would reduce APV to nearly zero.

Sometimes there are favorable financing side effects that have nothing to do with taxes. For example, suppose that a potential manufacturer of crusher machinery offers to sweeten the deal by leasing it to Sangria on favorable terms. Then you could calculate APV as the sum of base-case NPV plus the NPV of the lease. Or suppose that a local government offers to lend Sangria $5 million at a very low interest rate if the crusher is built and operated locally. The NPV of the subsidized loan could be added in to APV. (We cover subsidized loans in the Appendix to this chapter.)

APV for Businesses

APV can also be used to value businesses. Let's take another look at the valuation of Rio. In Table 15.1, we assumed a constant 40% debt ratio and discounted free cash flow at Sangria's WACC. Table 15.2 runs the same analysis, but with a fixed debt schedule.

We'll suppose that Sangria has decided to make an offer for Rio. If successful, it plans to finance the purchase with $51 million of debt. It intends to pay down the debt to $45 million in year 6. Recall Rio's horizon value of $113.4 million, which is calculated in Table 15.1 and shown again in Table 15.2. The debt ratio at the horizon is therefore projected at 45/113.4 = .397, about 40%. Thus Sangria plans to take Rio back to a normal 40% debt ratio at the horizon.[22] But Rio will be carrying a heavier debt load before the horizon. For example, the $51 million of initial debt is about 58% of company value as calculated in Table 15.1.

Let's see how Rio's APV is affected by this more aggressive borrowing schedule. Table 15.2 shows projections of free cash flows from Table 15.1.[23] Now we need Rio's base-case value, so we discount these flows at the opportunity cost of capital (9.84%), not at WACC. The resulting base-case value for Rio is $84.3 million. Table 15.2 also projects debt levels, interest, and interest tax shields. If the debt levels are taken as fixed, then the tax shields should be discounted back at the 6% borrowing rate. The resulting PV of interest tax shields is $5.0 million. Thus,

$$APV = \text{base-case NPV} + \text{PV(interest tax shields)}$$
$$= \$84.3 + 5.0 = \$89.3 \text{ million}$$

an increase of $1.4 million from NPV in Table 15.1. The increase can be traced to the higher early debt levels and to the assumption that the debt levels and interest tax shields are fixed and relatively safe.[24]

Now a difference of $1.4 million is not a big deal, considering all the lurking risks and pitfalls in forecasting Rio's free cash flows. But you can see the advantage of the flexibility that APV provides. The APV spreadsheet allows you to explore the implications of different

---

[22] Therefore we still calculate the horizon value in year 6 by discounting subsequent free cash flows at WACC. The horizon value in year 6 is discounted back to year 0 at the opportunity cost of capital, however.

[23] Many of the assumptions and calculations in Table 15.1 have been hidden in Table 15.2. The hidden rows can be recalled in the "live" version of Table 15.2, which is available on this book's Web site (www.mhhe.com/bma).

[24] But will Rio really *support* debt at the levels shown in Table 15.2? If not, then the debt must be partly supported by Sangria's other assets, and only part of the $5 million in PV(interest tax shields) can be attributed to Rio itself.

	Latest							
	Year	Forecast						
	0	**1**	**2**	**3**	**4**	**5**	**6**	**7**
Free cash flow	2.5	3.5	3.2	3.4	5.9	6.1	6.0	6.8
PV free cash flow, years 1–6	**19.7**							
PV horizon value	**64.6**			(Horizon value in year 6)			113.4	
Base-case PV of company	**84.3**							
Debt	51.0	50.0	49.0	48.0	47.0	46.0	45.0	
Interest		3.06	3.00	2.94	2.88	2.82	2.76	
Interest tax shield		1.07	1.05	1.03	1.01	0.99	0.97	
PV Interest tax shields	**5.0**							
APV	**89.3**							
Tax rate, %	35.0							
Opportunity cost of capital, %	9.84							
WACC, % (to discount horizon value to year 6)	9.0							
Long-term growth forecast, %	3.0							
Interest rate, % (years 1–6)	6.0							
After-tax debt service		2.99	2.95	2.91	2.87	2.83	2.79	

▶ **TABLE 15.2**   APV valuation of Rio Corporation ($ millions).

e**X**cel

Visit us at
www.mhhe.com/bma

financing strategies without locking into a fixed debt ratio or having to calculate a new WACC for every scenario.

APV is particularly useful when the debt for a project or business is tied to book value or has to be repaid on a fixed schedule. For example, Kaplan and Ruback used APV to analyze the prices paid for a sample of leveraged buyouts (LBOs). LBOs are takeovers, typically of mature companies, financed almost entirely with debt. However, the new debt is not intended to be permanent. LBO business plans call for generating extra cash by selling assets, shaving costs, and improving profit margins. The extra cash is used to pay down the LBO debt. Therefore you can't use WACC as a discount rate to evaluate an LBO because its debt ratio will not be constant.

APV works fine for LBOs. The company is first evaluated as if it were all-equity-financed. That means that cash flows are projected after tax, but without any interest tax shields generated by the LBO's debt. The tax shields are then valued separately and added to the all-equity value. Any other financing side effects are added also. The result is an APV valuation for the company.[25] Kaplan and Ruback found that APV did a pretty good job explaining prices paid in these hotly contested takeovers, considering that not all the information available to bidders had percolated into the public domain. Kaplan and Ruback were restricted to publicly available data.

APV for International Investments

APV is most useful when financing side effects are numerous and important. This is frequently the case for large international investments, which may have custom-tailored *project*

---

[25] Kaplan and Ruback actually used "compressed" APV, in which all cash flows, including interest tax shields, are discounted at the opportunity cost of capital. S. N. Kaplan and R. S. Ruback, "The Valuation of Cash Flow Forecasts: An Empirical Analysis," *Journal of Finance* 50 (September 1995), pp. 1059–1093.

financing and special contracts with suppliers, customers, and governments. Here are a few examples of financing side effects encountered in international finance.

Major international projects often involve special financing deals. Project finance in such cases typically means very high debt ratios to start, with most or all of a project's early cash flows committed to debt service. Equity investors have to wait. Since the debt ratio will not be constant, you have to turn to APV.

Project financing may include debt available at favorable interest rates. Most governments subsidize exports by making special financing packages available, and manufacturers of industrial equipment may stand ready to lend money to help close a sale. Suppose, for example, that your project requires construction of an on-site electricity generating plant. You solicit bids from suppliers in various countries. Don't be surprised if the competing suppliers sweeten their bids with offers of low interest rate project loans or if they offer to lease the plant on favorable terms. You should then calculate the NPVs of these loans or leases and include them in your project analysis.

Sometimes international projects are supported by contracts with suppliers or customers. Suppose a manufacturer wants to line up a reliable supply of a crucial raw material—powdered magnoosium, say. The manufacturer could subsidize a new magnoosium smelter by agreeing to buy 75% of production and guaranteeing a minimum purchase price. The guarantee is clearly a valuable addition to project APV: If the world price of powdered magnoosium falls below the minimum, the project doesn't suffer. You would calculate the value of this guarantee and add it to APV.

Sometimes local governments impose costs or restrictions on investment or disinvestment. For example, Chile, in an attempt to slow down a flood of short-term capital inflows in the 1990s, required investors to "park" part of their incoming money in non-interest-bearing accounts for a period of two years. An investor in Chile during this period would calculate the cost of this requirement and subtract it from APV.

15-5 Your Questions Answered

Question: All these cost of capital formulas—which ones do financial managers actually use?

Answer: The after-tax weighted-average cost of capital, most of the time. WACC is estimated for the company, or sometimes for an industry. We recommend industry WACCs when data are available for firms with similar assets, operations, business risks, and growth opportunities.

Of course, conglomerate companies, with divisions operating in two or more unrelated industries, should not use a single company or industry WACC. Such firms should try to estimate a different industry WACC for each operating division.

Question: But WACC is the correct discount rate only for "average" projects. What if the project's financing differs from the company's or industry's?

Answer: Remember, investment projects are usually not separately financed. Even when they are, you should focus on the project's contribution to the firm's overall debt capacity, not on its immediate financing. (Suppose it's convenient to raise all the money for a particular project with a bank loan. That doesn't mean the project itself supports 100% debt financing. The company is borrowing against its existing assets as well as the project.)

But if the project's debt capacity is materially different from the company's existing assets, or if the company's overall debt policy changes, WACC should be adjusted. The adjustment can be done by the three-step procedure explained in Section 15–3.

Question: Could we do one more numerical example?

Answer: Sure. Suppose that WACC has been estimated as follows at a 30% debt ratio:

$$\text{WACC} = r_D(1 - T_c)\frac{D}{V} + r_E\frac{E}{V}$$

$$= .09(1 - .35)(.3) + .15(.7) = .1226, \text{ or } 12.26\%$$

What is the correct discount rate at a 50% debt ratio?

Step 1. Calculate the opportunity cost of capital.

$$r = r_D D/V + r_E E/V$$
$$= .09(.3) + .15(.7) = .132, \text{ or } 13.2\%$$

Step 2. Calculate the new costs of debt and equity. The cost of debt will be higher at 50% debt than 30%. Say it is $r_D = .095$. The new cost of equity is:

$$r_E = r + (r - r_D)D/E$$
$$= .132 + (.132 - .095)50/50$$
$$= .169, \text{ or } 16.9\%$$

Step 3. Recalculate WACC.

$$\text{WACC} = r_D(1 - T_c)D/V + r_E E/V$$
$$= .095(1 - .35)(.5) + .169(.5) = .1154, \text{ or about } 11.5\%$$

Question: How do I use the capital asset pricing model to calculate the after-tax weighted-average cost of capital?

Answer: First plug the equity beta into the capital asset pricing formula to calculate r_E, the expected return to equity. Then use this calculation, along with the after-tax cost of debt and the debt-to-value and equity-to-value ratios, in the WACC formula.

Of course the CAPM is not the only way to estimate the cost of equity. For example, you might be able to use the dividend-discount model (see Section 4–3).

Question: But suppose I do use the CAPM? What if I have to recalculate the equity beta for a different debt ratio?

Answer: The formula for the equity beta is:

$$\beta_E = \beta_A + (\beta_A - \beta_D)D/E$$

where β_E is the equity beta, β_A is the asset beta, and β_D is the beta of the company's debt. The asset beta is a weighted average of the debt and equity betas:

$$\beta_A = \beta_D (D/V) + \beta_E (E/V)$$

Suppose you needed the opportunity cost of capital r. You could calculate β_A and then r from the capital asset pricing model.

Question: I think I understand how to adjust for differences in debt capacity or debt policy. How about differences in business risk?

Answer: If business risk is different, then r, the opportunity cost of capital, is different.

Figuring out the right r for an unusually safe or risky project is never easy. Sometimes the financial manager can use estimates of risk and expected return for companies similar to the project. Suppose, for example, that a traditional pharmaceutical company is considering a major commitment to biotech research. The financial manager could pick a sample of biotech companies, estimate their average beta and cost of capital, and use these estimates as benchmarks for the biotech investment.

But in many cases it's difficult to find a good sample of matching companies for an unusually safe or risky project. Then the financial manager has to adjust the opportunity cost of capital by judgment. Section 9–3 may be helpful in such cases.

Question: When do I need adjusted present value (APV)?

Answer: The WACC formula picks up only one financing side effect: the value of interest tax shields on debt supported by a project. If there are other side effects—subsidized financing tied to a project, for example—you should use APV.

You can also use APV to break out the value of interest tax shields:

$$\text{APV} = \text{base-case NPV} + \text{PV(tax shield)}$$

Suppose, for example, that you are analyzing a company just after a leveraged buyout. The company has a very high initial debt level but plans to pay down the debt as rapidly as possible. APV could be used to obtain an accurate valuation.

Question: When should personal taxes be incorporated into the analysis?

Answer: Always use T_c, the marginal corporate tax rate, when calculating WACC as a weighted average of the costs of debt and equity. The discount rate is adjusted *only* for corporate taxes.

In principle, APV can be adjusted for personal taxes by replacing the marginal corporate rate T_c with an effective tax rate that combines corporate and personal taxes and reflects the net tax advantage per dollar of interest paid by the firm. We provided back-of-the-envelope calculations of this advantage in Section 14–2. The effective tax rate is almost surely less than T_c, but it is very difficult to pin down the numerical difference. Therefore, in practice T_c is almost always used as an approximation.

Question: Are taxes really that important? Do financial managers really fine-tune the debt ratio to minimize WACC?

Answer: As we saw in Chapter 14, financing decisions reflect many forces beyond taxes, including costs of financial distress, differences in information, and incentives for managers. There may not be a sharply defined optimal capital structure. Therefore most financial managers don't fine-tune their companies' debt ratios, and they don't rebalance financing to keep debt ratios strictly constant. In effect they assume that a plot of WACC for different debt ratios is "flat" over a reasonable range of moderate leverage.

• • • • •

SUMMARY

In this chapter we considered how financing can be incorporated into the valuation of projects and ongoing businesses. There are two ways to take financing into account. The first is to calculate NPV by discounting at an adjusted discount rate, usually the after-tax weighted-average cost of capital (WACC). The second approach discounts at the opportunity cost of capital and then adds or subtracts the present values of financing side effects. The second approach is called adjusted present value, or APV.

The formula for the after-tax WACC is:

$$\text{WACC} = r_D(1 - T_c)\frac{D}{V} + r_E\frac{E}{V}$$

where r_D and r_E are the expected rates of return demanded by investors in the firm's debt and equity securities, D and E are the current *market values* of debt and equity, and V is the total market value of the firm ($V = D + E$). Of course, the WACC formula expands if there are other sources of financing, for example, preferred stock.

Strictly speaking, discounting at WACC works only for projects that are carbon copies of the existing firm—projects with the same business risk that will be financed to maintain the firm's current, market debt ratio. But firms can use WACC as a benchmark rate to be adjusted for differences in business risk or financing. We gave a three-step procedure for adjusting WACC for different debt ratios.

Discounting cash flows at the WACC assumes that debt is rebalanced to keep a constant ratio of debt to market value. The amount of debt supported by a project is assumed to rise or fall with the project's after-the-fact success or failure. The WACC formula also assumes that financing matters *only* because of interest tax shields. When this or other assumptions are violated, only APV will give an absolutely correct answer.

APV is, in concept at least, simple. First calculate the base-case NPV of the project or business on the assumption that financing *doesn't* matter. (The discount rate is not WACC, but the opportunity cost of capital.) Then calculate the present values of any relevant financing side effects and add or subtract from base-case value. A capital investment project is worthwhile if

$$\text{APV} = \text{base-case NPV} + \text{PV(financing side effects)}$$

is positive. Common financing side effects include interest tax shields, issue costs, and special financing packages offered by suppliers or governments.

For firms or going-concern businesses, value depends on free cash flow. Free cash flow is the amount of cash that can be paid out to all investors, debt as well as equity, after deducting cash needed for new investment or increases in working capital. Free cash flow does not include the value of interest tax shields, however. The WACC formula accounts for interest tax shields by using the after-tax cost of debt. APV adds PV(interest tax shields) to base-case value.

Businesses are usually valued in two steps. First free cash flow is forecasted out to a valuation horizon and discounted back to present value. Then a horizon value is calculated and also discounted back. The horizon value is usually estimated by using the perpetual-growth DCF formula or by multiplying forecasted EBIT or EBITDA[26] by multiples observed for similar firms. Be particularly careful to avoid unrealistically high horizon values. By the time the horizon arrives, competitors will have had several years to catch up. Also, when you are done valuing the business, don't forget to subtract its debt to get the value of the firm's equity.

All of this chapter's examples reflect assumptions about the amount of debt supported by a project or business. Remember not to confuse "supported by" with the immediate source of funds for investment. For example, a firm might, as a matter of convenience, borrow $1 million for a $1 million research program. But the research is unlikely to contribute $1 million in debt capacity; a large part of the $1 million new debt would be supported by the firm's other assets.

Also remember that *debt capacity* is not meant to imply an absolute limit on how much the firm *can* borrow. The phrase refers to how much it *chooses* to borrow against a project or ongoing business.

• • • • •

FURTHER READING

The Harvard Business Review *has published a popular account of APV:*

T. A. Luehrman, "Using APV: A Better Tool for Valuing Operations," *Harvard Business Review* 75 (May–June 1997), pp. 145–154.

There have been dozens of articles on the weighted-average cost of capital and other issues discussed in this chapter. Here are three:

J. Miles and R. Ezzell, "The Weighted Average Cost of Capital, Perfect Capital Markets, and Project Life: A Clarification," *Journal of Financial and Quantitative Analysis* 15 (September 1980), pp. 719–730.

R. S. Ruback, "Capital Cash Flows: A Simple Approach to Valuing Risky Cash Flows," *Financial Management* 31 (Summer 2002), pp. 85–103.

R. A. Taggart, Jr., "Consistent Valuation and Cost of Capital Expressions with Corporate and Personal Taxes," *Financial Management* 20 (Autumn 1991), pp. 8–20.

Two books that provide detailed explanations of how to value companies are:

T. Koller, M. Goedhart, and D. Wessels, *Valuation: Measuring and Managing the Value of Companies,* 4th ed. (New York: Wiley, 2005).

S. P. Pratt and A.V. Niculita, *Valuing a Business: The Analysis and Appraisal of Closely Held Companies,* 5th ed. (New York: McGraw-Hill, 2007).

The valuation rule for safe, nominal cash flows is developed in:

R. S. Ruback, "Calculating the Market Value of Risk-Free Cash Flows," *Journal of Financial Economics* 15 (March 1986), pp. 323–339.

---

[26] Recall that EBIT = earnings before interest and taxes and EBITDA = EBIT plus depreciation and amortization.

●●●●●

BASIC

1. Calculate the weighted-average cost of capital (WACC) for Federated Junkyards of America, using the following information:
   - Debt: $75,000,000 book value outstanding. The debt is trading at 90% of book value. The yield to maturity is 9%.
   - Equity: 2,500,000 shares selling at $42 per share. Assume the expected rate of return on Federated's stock is 18%.
   - Taxes: Federated's marginal tax rate is $T_c = .35$.

2. Suppose Federated Junkyards decides to move to a more conservative debt policy. A year later its debt ratio is down to 15% ($D/V = .15$). The interest rate has dropped to 8.6%. Recalculate Federated's WACC under these new assumptions. The company's business risk, opportunity cost of capital, and tax rate have not changed. Use the three-step procedure explained in Section 15–3.

3. True or false? Use of the WACC formula assumes
   a. A project supports a fixed amount of debt over the project's economic life.
   b. The *ratio* of the debt supported by a project to project value is constant over the project's economic life.
   c. The firm rebalances debt each period, keeping the debt-to-value ratio constant.

4. What is meant by the flow-to-equity valuation method? What discount rate is used in this method? What assumptions are necessary for this method to give an accurate valuation?

5. True or false? The APV method
   a. Starts with a base-case value for the project.
   b. Calculates the base-case value by discounting project cash flows, forecasted assuming all-equity financing, at the WACC for the project.
   c. Is especially useful when debt is to be paid down on a fixed schedule.

6. A project costs $1 million and has a base-case NPV of exactly zero (NPV = 0). What is the project's APV in the following cases?
   a. If the firm invests, it has to raise $500,000 by a stock issue. Issue costs are 15% of *net* proceeds.
   b. If the firm invests, its debt capacity increases by $500,000. The present value of interest tax shields on this debt is $76,000.

7. Whispering Pines, Inc., is all-equity-financed. The expected rate of return on the company's shares is 12%.
   a. What is the opportunity cost of capital for an average-risk Whispering Pines investment?
   b. Suppose the company issues debt, repurchases shares, and moves to a 30% debt-to-value ratio ($D/V = .30$). What will the company's weighted-average cost of capital be at the new capital structure? The borrowing rate is 7.5% and the tax rate is 35%.

8. Consider a project lasting one year only. The initial outlay is $1,000 and the expected inflow is $1,200. The opportunity cost of capital is $r = .20$. The borrowing rate is $r_D = .10$, and the tax shield per dollar of interest is $T_c = .35$.
   a. What is the project's base-case NPV?
   b. What is its APV if the firm borrows 30% of the project's required investment?

9. The WACC formula seems to imply that debt is "cheaper" than equity—that is, that a firm with more debt could use a lower discount rate. Does this make sense? Explain briefly.

10. Suppose KCS Corp. buys out Patagonia Trucking, a privately owned business, for $50 million. KCS has only $5 million cash in hand, so it arranges a $45 million bank loan. A normal debt-to-value ratio for a trucking company would be 50% at most, but the bank is satisfied with KCS's credit rating.

    Suppose you were valuing Patagonia by APV in the same format as Table 15.2. How much debt would you include? Explain briefly.

INTERMEDIATE

11. Table 15.3 shows a *book* balance sheet for the Wishing Well Motel chain. The company's long-term debt is secured by its real estate assets, but it also uses short-term bank financing. It pays 10% interest on the bank debt and 9% interest on the secured debt. Wishing Well has 10 million shares of stock outstanding, trading at $90 per share. The expected return on Wishing Well's common stock is 18%.

    Calculate Wishing Well's WACC. Assume that the book and market values of Wishing Well's debt are the same. The marginal tax rate is 35%.

12. Suppose Wishing Well is evaluating a new motel and resort on a romantic site in Madison County, Wisconsin. Explain how you would forecast the after-tax cash flows for this project. (*Hints:* How would you treat taxes? Interest expense? Changes in working capital?)

13. To finance the Madison County project, Wishing Well will have to arrange an additional $80 million of long-term debt and make a $20 million equity issue. Underwriting fees, spreads, and other costs of this financing will total $4 million. How would you take this into account in valuing the proposed investment?

14. Table 15.4 shows a simplified balance sheet for Rensselaer Felt. Calculate this company's weighted-average cost of capital. The debt has just been refinanced at an interest rate of 6% (short term) and 8% (long term). The expected rate of return on the company's shares is 15%. There are 7.46 million shares outstanding, and the shares are trading at $46. The tax rate is 35%.

15. How will Rensselaer Felt's WACC and cost of equity change if it issues $50 million in new equity and uses the proceeds to retire long-term debt? Assume the company's borrowing rates are unchanged. Use the three-step procedure from Section 15–3.

16. Digital Organics (DO) has the opportunity to invest $1 million now ($t = 0$) and expects after-tax returns of $600,000 in $t = 1$ and $700,000 in $t = 2$. The project will last for two years only. The appropriate cost of capital is 12% with all-equity financing, the

Cash and marketable securities	100	Bank loan	280
Accounts receivable	200	Accounts payable	120
Inventory	50	Current liabilities	400
Current assets	350		
Real estate	2,100	Long-term debt	1,800
Other assets	150	Equity	400
Total	2,600	Total	2,600

▶ **TABLE 15.3**
Balance sheet for Wishing Well, Inc. (figures in $ millions).

Cash and marketable securities	1,500	Short-term debt	75,600
Accounts receivable	120,000	Accounts payable	62,000
Inventories	125,000	Current liabilities	137,600
Current assets	246,500		
Property, plant, and equipment	302,000	Long-term debt	208,600
		Deferred taxes	45,000
Other assets	89,000	Shareholders' equity	246,300
Total	637,500	Total	637,500

▶ **TABLE 15.4**
Simplified book balance sheet for Rensselaer Felt (figures in $ thousands).

borrowing rate is 8%, and DO will borrow $300,000 against the project. This debt must be repaid in two equal installments. Assume debt tax shields have a net value of $.30 per dollar of interest paid. Calculate the project's APV using the procedure followed in Table 15.2.

17. Consider another perpetual project like the crusher described in Section 15–1. Its initial investment is $1,000,000, and the expected cash inflow is $95,000 a year in perpetuity. The opportunity cost of capital with all-equity financing is 10%, and the project allows the firm to borrow at 7%. The tax rate is 35%.

    Use APV to calculate this project's value.

    a. Assume first that the project will be partly financed with $400,000 of debt and that the debt amount is to be fixed and perpetual.

    b. Then assume that the initial borrowing will be increased or reduced in proportion to changes in the market value of this project.

    Explain the difference between your answers to (a) and (b).

18. Suppose the project described in Problem 17 is to be undertaken by a university. Funds for the project will be withdrawn from the university's endowment, which is invested in a widely diversified portfolio of stocks and bonds. However, the university can also borrow at 7%. The university is tax exempt.

    The university treasurer proposes to finance the project by issuing $400,000 of perpetual bonds at 7% and by selling $600,000 worth of common stocks from the endowment. The expected return on the common stocks is 10%. He therefore proposes to evaluate the project by discounting at a weighted-average cost of capital, calculated as:

$$r = r_D \frac{D}{V} + r_E \frac{E}{V}$$

$$= .07\left(\frac{400,000}{1,000,000}\right) + .10\left(\frac{600,000}{1,000,000}\right)$$

$$= .088, \text{ or } 8.8$$

What's right or wrong with the treasurer's approach? Should the university invest? Should it borrow? Would the project's value to the university change if the treasurer financed the project entirely by selling common stocks from the endowment?

19. Consider a project to produce solar water heaters. It requires a $10 million investment and offers a level after-tax cash flow of $1.75 million per year for 10 years. The opportunity cost of capital is 12%, which reflects the project's business risk.

    a. Suppose the project is financed with $5 million of debt and $5 million of equity. The interest rate is 8% and the marginal tax rate is 35%. The debt will be paid off in equal annual installments over the project's 10-year life. Calculate APV.

    b. How does APV change if the firm incurs issue costs of $400,000 to raise the $5 million of required equity?

20. Take another look at the valuations of Rio in Tables 15.1 and 15.2. Now use the live spreadsheets on this book's Web site (**www.mhhe.com/bma**) to show how the valuations depend on:

    a. The forecasted long-term growth rate.

    b. The required amounts of investment in fixed assets and working capital.

    c. The opportunity cost of capital. Note you can also vary the opportunity cost of capital in Table 15.1.

    d. Profitability, that is, cost of goods sold as a percentage of sales.

    e. The assumed amount of debt financing.

Visit us at
www.mhhe.com/bma

21. The Bunsen Chemical Company is currently at its target debt ratio of 40%. It is contemplating a $1 million expansion of its existing business. This expansion is expected to produce a cash inflow of $130,000 a year in perpetuity.

The company is uncertain whether to undertake this expansion and how to finance it. The two options are a $1 million issue of common stock or a $1 million issue of 20-year debt. The flotation costs of a stock issue would be around 5% of the amount raised, and the flotation costs of a debt issue would be around 1½%.

Bunsen's financial manager, Ms. Polly Ethylene, estimates that the required return on the company's equity is 14%, but she argues that the flotation costs increase the cost of new equity to 19%. On this basis, the project does not appear viable.

On the other hand, she points out that the company can raise new debt on a 7% yield, which would make the cost of new debt 8½%. She therefore recommends that Bunsen should go ahead with the project and finance it with an issue of long-term debt.

Is Ms. Ethylene right? How would you evaluate the project?

22. Nevada Hydro is 40% debt-financed and has a weighted-average cost of capital of 9.7%:

$$\text{WACC} = (1 - T_c)r_D\frac{D}{V} + r_E\frac{E}{V}$$

$$= (1 - .35)(.085)(.40) + .125(.60) = .097$$

Goldensacks Company is advising Nevada Hydro to issue $75 million of preferred stock at a dividend yield of 9%. The proceeds would be used to repurchase and retire common stock. The preferred issue would account for 10% of the preissue market value of the firm.

Goldensacks argues that these transactions would reduce Nevada Hydro's WACC to 9.4%:

$$\text{WACC} = (1 - .35)(.085)(.40) + .09(.10) + .125(.50)$$
$$= .094, \text{ or } 9.4\%$$

Do you agree with this calculation? Explain..

23. Chiara Company's management has made the projections shown in Table 15.5. Use this Excel spreadsheet as a starting point to value the company as a whole. The WACC for

Visit us at
www.mhhe.com/bma

	Year:	Historical			Forecast				
		−2	−1	0	1	2	3	4	5
1. Sales		35,348	39,357	40,123	36,351	30,155	28,345	29,982	30,450
2. Cost of goods sold		17,834	18,564	22,879	21,678	17,560	16,459	15,631	14,987
3. Other costs		6,968	7,645	8,025	6,797	5,078	4,678	4,987	5,134
4. EBITDA (1 − 2 − 3)		10,546	13,148	9,219	7,876	7,517	7,208	9,364	10,329
5. Depreciation		5,671	5,745	5,678	5,890	5,670	5,908	6,107	5,908
6. EBIT (Pretax profit) (4 − 5)		4,875	7,403	3,541	1,986	1,847	1,300	3,257	4,421
7. Tax at 35%		1,706	2,591	1,239	695	646	455	1,140	1,547
8. Profit after tax (6 − 7)		3,169	4,812	2,302	1,291	1,201	845	2,117	2,874
9. Change in working capital		325	566	784	−54	−342	−245	127	235
10. Investment (change in gross fixed assets)		5,235	6,467	6,547	7,345	5,398	5,470	6,420	6,598

▶ **TABLE 15.5** Cash flow projections for Chiara Corp. ($ thousands).

Chiara is 12% and the long-run growth rate after year 5 is 4%. The company has $5 million debt and 865,000 shares outstanding. What is the value per share?

CHALLENGE

24. In Footnote 15 we referred to the Miles–Ezzell discount rate formula, which assumes that debt is not rebalanced continuously, but at one-year intervals. Derive this formula. Then use it to unlever Sangria's WACC and calculate Sangria's opportunity cost of capital. Your answer will be slightly different from the opportunity cost that we calculated in Section 15–3. Can you explain why?

25. The WACC formula assumes that debt is rebalanced to maintain a constant debt ratio D/V. Rebalancing ties the level of future interest tax shields to the future value of the company. This makes the tax shields risky. Does that mean that fixed debt levels (no rebalancing) are better for stockholders?

26. Modify Table 15.1 on the assumption that competition eliminates any opportunities to earn more than WACC on new investment after year 7 (PVGO = 0). How does the valuation of Rio change?

• • • • •

REAL-TIME DATA ANALYSIS

Table 15.6 is a simplified book balance sheet for Apache Corp. at year-end 2008. Here is some further information:

Number of outstanding shares (N)	335.75 million
Price per share (P)	$74.0
Beta	1.21
Treasury bill rate	.11%
20-year Treasury bond rate	2.25%
Cost of debt (r_D)	7.50
Marginal tax rate	35%

a. Calculate Apache's WACC. Use the capital asset pricing model and the additional information given above. Make additional assumptions and approximations as necessary.

b. What is Apache's opportunity cost of capital?

c. Finally, go to the Standard & Poor's Market Insight Web site (**www.mhhe.com/ edumarketinsight**) and update your answers to questions (a) and (b).

STANDARD &POOR'S

▶ **TABLE 15.6**
Simplified book balance sheet for Apache, year-end 2008 (figures in $ millions).

Current assets	4,451	Current liabilities		2,615
Net property, plant, and equipment	23,959	Long-term debt		4,816
Investments and other assets	7,776	Other liabilities		5,246
		Shareholders' equity		16,509
Total	29,186	Total		29,186

APPENDIX • • • • •

Discounting Safe, Nominal Cash Flows

Suppose you're considering purchase of a $100,000 machine. The manufacturer sweetens the deal by offering to finance the purchase by lending you $100,000 for five years, with annual interest payments of 5%. You would have to pay 13% to borrow from a bank. Your marginal tax rate is 35% ($T_c = .35$).

How much is this loan worth? If you take it, the cash flows, in thousands of dollars, are:

	Period					
	0	**1**	**2**	**3**	**4**	**5**
Cash flow	+100	−5	−5	−5	−5	−105
Tax shield		+1.75	+1.75	+1.75	+1.75	+1.75
After-tax cash flow	+100	−3.25	−3.25	−3.25	−3.25	−103.25

What is the right discount rate?

Here you are discounting *safe, nominal* cash flows—safe because your company must commit to pay if it takes the loan,[27] and nominal because the payments would be fixed regardless of future inflation. Now, the correct discount rate for safe, nominal cash flows is your company's *after-tax*, unsubsidized borrowing rate,[28] which is $r_D(1 - T_c) = .13(1 - .35) = .0845$. Therefore,

$$\text{NPV} = +100 - \frac{3.25}{1.0845} - \frac{3.25}{(1.0845)^2} - \frac{3.25}{(1.0845)^3} - \frac{3.25}{(1.0845)^4} - \frac{103.25}{(1.0845)^5}$$

$$= +20.52, \text{ or } \$20,520$$

The manufacturer has effectively cut the machine's purchase price from $100,000 to $100,000 − $20,520 = $79,480. You can now go back and recalculate the machine's NPV using this fire-sale price, or you can use the NPV of the subsidized loan as one element of the machine's adjusted present value.

A General Rule   Clearly, we owe an explanation of why $r_D(1 - T_c)$ is the right discount rate for safe, nominal cash flows. It's no surprise that the rate depends on r_D, the unsubsidized borrowing rate, for that is investors' opportunity cost of capital, the rate they would demand from your company's debt. But why should r_D be converted to an *after-tax* figure?

Let's simplify by taking a *one-year* subsidized loan of $100,000 at 5%. The cash flows, in thousands of dollars, are:

	Period 0	Period 1
Cash flow	+100	−105
Tax shield		+1.75
After-tax cash flow	+100	−103.25

Now ask, What is the maximum amount X that could be borrowed for one year through regular channels if $103,250 is set aside to service the loan?

"Regular channels" means borrowing at 13% pretax and 8.45% after tax. Therefore you will need 108.45% of the amount borrowed to pay back principal plus after-tax interest charges. If $1.0845X = 103,250$, then $X = 95,205$. Now if you can borrow $100,000 by a subsidized loan, but only $95,205 through normal channels, the difference ($4,795) is money in the bank. Therefore, it must also be the NPV of this one-period subsidized loan.

When you discount a safe, nominal cash flow at an after-tax borrowing rate, you are implicitly calculating the *equivalent loan,* the amount you could borrow through normal channels, using the cash flow as debt service. Note that:

$$\text{Equivalent loan} = \text{PV(cash flow available for debt service)} = \frac{103,250}{1.0845} = 95,205$$

---

[27] In theory, *safe* means literally "risk-free," like the cash returns on a Treasury bond. In practice, it means that the risk of not paying or receiving a cash flow is small.

[28] In Section 11–1 we calculated the NPV of subsidized financing using the *pretax* borrowing rate. Now you can see that was a mistake. Using the pretax rate implicitly defines the loan in terms of its pretax cash flows, violating a rule promulgated way back in Section 6–1: *Always* estimate cash flows on an after-tax basis.

In some cases, it may be easier to think of taking the lender's side of the equivalent loan rather than the borrower's. For example, you could ask, How much would my company have to invest today to cover next year's debt service on the subsidized loan? The answer is $95,205: If you lend that amount at 13%, you will earn 8.45% after tax, and therefore have 95,205(1.0845) = $103,250. By this transaction, you can in effect cancel, or "zero out," the future obligation. If you can borrow $100,000 and then set aside only $95,205 to cover all the required debt service, you clearly have $4,795 to spend as you please. That amount is the NPV of the subsidized loan.

Therefore, regardless of whether it's easier to think of borrowing or lending, the correct discount rate for safe, nominal cash flows is an after-tax interest rate.[29]

In some ways, this is an obvious result once you think about it. Companies are free to borrow or lend money. If they *lend,* they receive the after-tax interest rate on their investment; if they *borrow* in the capital market, they pay the after-tax interest rate. Thus, the opportunity cost to companies of investing in debt-equivalent cash flows is the after-tax interest rate. This is the adjusted cost of capital for debt-equivalent cash flows.[30]

Some Further Examples   Here are some further examples of debt-equivalent cash flows.

Payout Fixed by Contract   Suppose you sign a maintenance contract with a truck leasing firm, which agrees to keep your leased trucks in good working order for the next two years in exchange for 24 fixed monthly payments. These payments are debt-equivalent flows.

Depreciation Tax Shields   Capital projects are normally valued by discounting the total after-tax cash flows they are expected to generate. Depreciation tax shields contribute to project cash flow, but they are not valued separately; they are just folded into project cash flows along with dozens, or hundreds, of other specific inflows and outflows. The project's opportunity cost of capital reflects the average risk of the resulting aggregate.

However, suppose we ask what depreciation tax shields are worth *by themselves.* For a firm that's sure to pay taxes, depreciation tax shields are a safe, nominal flow. Therefore, they should be discounted at the firm's after-tax borrowing rate.

Suppose we buy an asset with a depreciable basis of $200,000, which can be depreciated by the five-year tax depreciation schedule (see Table 6.4). The resulting tax shields are:

			Period			
	1	**2**	**3**	**4**	**5**	**6**
Percentage deductions	20	32	19.2	11.5	11.5	5.8
Dollar deductions (thousands)	$40	$64	$38.4	$23	$23	$11.6
Tax shields at T_c = .35 (thousands)	$14	$22.4	$13.4	$8.1	$8.1	$4.0

The after-tax discount rate is $r_D(1 - T_c) = .13(1 - .35) = .0845$. (We continue to assume a 13% pretax borrowing rate and a 35% marginal tax rate.) The present value of these shields is:

$$\text{PV} = \frac{14}{1.0845} + \frac{22.4}{(1.0845)^2} + \frac{13.4}{(1.0845)^3} + \frac{8.1}{(1.0845)^4} + \frac{8.1}{(1.0845)^5} + \frac{4.0}{(1.0845)^6}$$

$$= +56.2, \text{ or } \$56,200$$

---

[29] Borrowing and lending rates should not differ by much if the cash flows are truly safe, that is, if the chance of default is small. Usually your decision will not hinge on the rate used. If it does, ask which offsetting transaction—borrowing or lending—seems most natural and reasonable for the problem at hand. Then use the corresponding interest rate.

[30] All the examples in this section are forward-looking; they call for the value today of a stream of future debt-equivalent cash flows. But similar issues arise in legal and contractual disputes when a *past* cash flow has to be brought forward in time to a present value today. Suppose it's determined that company A should have paid B $1 million 10 years ago. B clearly deserves more than $1 million today, because it has lost the time value of money. The time value of money should be expressed as an after-tax borrowing or lending rate or, if no risk enters, as the after-tax risk-free rate. The time value of money is *not* equal to B's overall cost of capital. Allowing B to "earn" its overall cost of capital on the payment allows it to earn a risk premium without bearing risk. For a broader discussion of these issues, see F. Fisher and C. Romaine, "Janis Joplin's Yearbook and Theory of Damages," *Journal of Accounting, Auditing & Finance* 5 (Winter/Spring 1990), pp. 145–157.

A Consistency Check You may have wondered whether our procedure for valuing debt-equivalent cash flows is consistent with the WACC and APV approaches presented earlier in this chapter. Yes, it is consistent, as we will now illustrate.

Let's look at another very simple numerical example. You are asked to value a $1 million payment to be received from a blue-chip company one year hence. After taxes at 35%, the cash inflow is $650,000. The payment is fixed by contract.

Since the contract generates a debt-equivalent flow, the opportunity cost of capital is the rate investors would demand on a one-year note issued by the blue-chip company, which happens to be 8%. For simplicity, we'll assume this is your company's borrowing rate too. Our valuation rule for debt-equivalent flows is therefore to discount at $r_D(1 - T_c) = .08(1 - .35) = .052$:

$$PV = \frac{650,000}{1.052} = \$617,900$$

What is the *debt capacity* of this $650,000 payment? Exactly $617,900. Your company could borrow that amount and pay off the loan completely—principal and after-tax interest—with the $650,000 cash inflow. The debt capacity is 100% of the PV of the debt-equivalent cash flow.

If you think of it that way, our discount rate $r_D(1 - T_c)$ is just a special case of WACC with a 100% debt ratio ($D/V = 1$).

$$WACC = r_D(1 - T_c)D/V + r_E E/V$$
$$= r_D(1 - T_c) \text{ if } D/V = 1 \text{ and } E/V = 0$$

Now let's try an APV calculation. This is a two-part valuation. First, the $650,000 inflow is discounted at the opportunity cost of capital, 8%. Second, we add the present value of interest tax shields on debt supported by the project. Since the firm can borrow 100% of the cash flow's value, the tax shield is $r_D T_c$ APV, and APV is:

$$APV = \frac{650,000}{1.08} + \frac{.08(.35)APV}{1.08}$$

Solving for APV, we get $617,900, the same answer we obtained by discounting at the after-tax borrowing rate. Thus our valuation rule for debt-equivalent flows is a special case of APV.

QUESTIONS

1. The U.S. government has settled a dispute with your company for $16 million. It is committed to pay this amount in exactly 12 months. However, your company will have to pay tax on the award at a marginal tax rate of 35%. What is the award worth? The one-year Treasury rate is 5.5%.

2. You are considering a five-year lease of office space for R&D personnel. Once signed, the lease cannot be canceled. It would commit your firm to six annual $100,000 payments, with the first payment due immediately. What is the present value of the lease if your company's borrowing rate is 9% and its tax rate is 35%? (*Note:* The lease payments would be tax-deductible.)

Understanding Options

▶ **Pop quiz: What** do the following events have in common?

- The coffee roaster, Green Mountain, buys options that put a ceiling on the price that it will pay for its future purchases of beans.

- Flatiron offers its president a bonus if the company's stock price exceeds $120.

- Blitzen Computer dips a toe in the water and enters a new market.

- Malted Herring postpones investment in a positive-NPV plant.

- Hewlett-Packard exports partially assembled printers even though it would be cheaper to ship the finished product.

- Dominion installs a dual-fired unit at its Possum Point power station that can use either fuel oil or natural gas.

- In 2004 Air France acquires the Dutch airline, KLM, in exchange for a package of Air France shares and warrants. The warrants entitle KLM's shareholders to buy additional Air France shares for €20 each within the next 3.5 years.

- In February 2008 Chiquita Brands issues $200 million of 4.25% convertible bonds maturing in 2016. Each bond can be exchanged for 44.55 shares at any time before maturity.

Answers: (1) Each of these events involves an option, and (2) they illustrate why the financial manager of an industrial company needs to understand options.

Companies regularly use commodity, currency, and interest-rate options to reduce risk. For example, a meatpacking company that wishes to put a ceiling on the cost of beef might take out an option to buy live cattle at a fixed price. A company that wishes to limit its future borrowing costs might take out an option to sell long-term bonds at a fixed price. And so on.

Many capital investments include an embedded option to expand in the future. For instance, the company may invest in a patent that allows it to exploit a new technology or it may purchase adjoining land that gives it the option in the future to increase capacity. In each case the company is paying money today for the opportunity to make a further investment. To put it another way, the company is acquiring *growth opportunities.*

Here is another disguised option to invest: You are considering the purchase of a tract of desert land that is known to contain gold deposits. Unfortunately, the cost of extraction is higher than the current price of gold. Does this mean the land is almost worthless? Not at all. You are not obliged to mine the gold, but ownership of the land gives you the option to do so. Of course, if you know that the gold price will remain below the extraction cost, then the option is worthless. But if there is uncertainty about future gold prices, you could be lucky and make a killing.

If the option to expand has value, what about the option to bail out? Projects don't usually go on until the equipment disintegrates. The decision to terminate a project is usually taken by management, not by nature. Once the project is no longer profitable, the company will cut its losses and exercise its option to abandon the project. Some projects have higher abandonment value than others. Those that use standardized equipment may offer a valuable abandonment option. Others may actually cost money to discontinue. For example, it is very costly to decommission an offshore oil platform.

The other important reason why financial managers need to understand options is that they are often tacked on to an issue of corporate securities and so provide the investor or the company with the flexibility to change the terms of the issue. For example, warrants or convertibles give their holders an option to buy common stock in exchange for cash or bonds.

In fact, whenever a company borrows, it gains an option to walk away from its debts and surrender its assets to the bondholders. If the value of the company's assets is less than the amount of the debt, the company will choose to default on the payment and the bondholders will get to keep the company's assets. Thus, when the firm borrows, the lender effectively acquires the company and the shareholders obtain the option to buy it back by paying off the debt. This is an extremely important insight. It means that anything that

we can learn about traded options applies equally to corporate liabilities.

In this chapter we use traded stock options to explain how options work, but we hope that our brief survey has convinced you that the interest of financial managers in options goes far beyond traded stock options. That is why we are asking you to invest here to acquire several important ideas for use later.

If you are unfamiliar with the wonderful world of options, it may seem baffling on first encounter. We therefore divide this chapter into three bite-sized pieces. Our first task is to introduce you to call and put options and to show you how the payoff on these options depends on the price of the underlying asset. We then show how financial alchemists can combine options to produce a variety of interesting strategies.

We conclude the chapter by identifying the variables that determine option values. There you encounter some surprising and counterintuitive effects. For example, investors are used to thinking that increased risk reduces present value. But for options it is the other way around.

• • • • •

16-1 Calls, Puts, and Shares

Investors regularly trade options on common stocks.[1] For example, Table 16.1 reproduces quotes for options on the stock of Google. You can see that there are two types of option—calls and puts. We explain each in turn.

Call Options and Position Diagrams

A **call option** gives its owner the right to buy stock at a specified *exercise* or *strike price* on or before a specified maturity date. If the option can be exercised only at maturity, it is conventionally known as a *European call;* in other cases (such as the Google options shown in Table 16.1), the option can be exercised on or at any time before maturity, and it is then known as an *American call.*

The third column of Table 16.1 sets out the prices of Google call options with different exercise prices and exercise dates. Look at the quotes for options maturing in December 2008. The first entry says that for $78.90 you could acquire an option to buy one share[2] of Google stock for $370 on or before December 2008. Moving down to the

---

[1] The two principal options exchanges in the United States are the International Securities Exchange (ISE) and the Chicago Board Options Exchange (CBOE).

[2] You can't actually buy an option on a single share. Trades are in multiples of 100. The minimum order would be for 100 options on 100 Google shares.

▶ **TABLE 16.1**

Selected prices of
put and call options
on Google stock in
September 2008, when
the closing stock price
was $430.

* Long-term options are
called "LEAPS."

Source: Yahoo! Finance,
http://finance.yahoo.com.
Reproduced with permission
of Yahoo! Inc. © 2008 by
Yahoo! Inc. Yahoo! and
the Yahoo! logo are
trademarks of Yahoo! Inc.

Maturity Date	Exercise Price	Price of Call Option	Price of Put Option
December 2008	$370	$ 78.90	$16.45
	400	58.65	26.10
	430	41.75	38.90
	460	28.05	55.45
	490	17.85	75.45
March 2009	$370	$ 90.20	$25.05
	400	70.80	35.65
	430	**54.35**	**48.55**
	460	39.85	64.10
	490	28.75	83.20
January 2010*	$370	$116.90	$42.55
	400	100.00	54.75
	430	85.05	69.85
	460	71.60	86.00
	490	59.90	103.70

next row, you can see that an option to buy for $30 more ($400 vs. $370) costs $20.25 less, that is $58.65. In general, the value of a call option goes down as the exercise price goes up.

Now look at the quotes for options maturing in March 2009 and January 2010. Notice how the option price increases as option maturity is extended. For example, at an exercise price of $430, the December 2008 call option costs $41.75, the March 2009 option costs $54.35, and the January 2010 option costs $85.05.

In Chapter 11 we met Louis Bachelier, who in 1900 first suggested that security prices follow a random walk. Bachelier also devised a very convenient shorthand to illustrate the effects of investing in different options. We use this shorthand to compare a call option and a put option on Google stock.

The *position diagram* in Figure 16.1(*a*) shows the possible consequences of investing in Google March 2009 call options with an exercise price of $430 (boldfaced in Table 16.1). The outcome from investing in Google calls depends on what happens to the stock price. If the stock price at the end of this six-month period turns out to be less than the $430 exercise price, nobody will pay $430 to obtain the share via the call option. Your call will in that case be valueless, and you will throw it away. On the other hand, if the stock price turns out to be greater than $430, it will pay to exercise your option to buy the share. In this case, when the call expires, it will be worth the market price of the share minus the $430 that you must pay to acquire it. For example, suppose that the price of Google stock rises to $500. Your call will then be worth $500 − $430 = $70. That is your payoff, but of course it is not all profit. Table 16.1 shows that you had to pay $54.35 to buy the call.

Put Options

Now let us look at the Google **put options** in the right-hand column of Table 16.1. Whereas a call option gives you the right to *buy* a share for a specified exercise price, a put gives you

▶ FIGURE 16.1

Position diagrams show how payoffs to owners of Google calls and puts (shown by the colored lines) depend on the share price. (*a*) Result of buying Google call exercisable at $430. (*b*) Result of buying Google put exercisable at $430.

the right to *sell* the share. For example, the boldfaced entry in the right-hand column of Table 16.1 shows that for $48.55 you could acquire an option to sell Google stock for a price of $430 anytime before March 2009. The circumstances in which the put turns out to be profitable are just the opposite of those in which the call is profitable. You can see this from the position diagram in Figure 16.1(*b*). If Google's share price immediately before expiration turns out to be *greater* than $430, you won't want to sell stock at that price. You would do better to sell the share in the market, and your put option will be worthless. Conversely, if the share price turns out to be *less* than $430, it will pay to buy stock at the low price and then take advantage of the option to sell it for $430. In this case, the value of the put option on the exercise date is the difference between the $430 proceeds of the sale and the market price of the share. For example, if the share is worth $340, the put is worth $90:

$$\text{Value of put option at expiration} = \text{exercise price} - \text{market price of the share}$$
$$= \$430 - \$340 = \$90$$

Selling Calls, Puts, and Shares

Let us now look at the position of an investor who *sells* these investments. If you sell, or "write," a call, you promise to deliver shares if asked to do so by the call buyer. In other words, the buyer's asset is the seller's liability. If the share price is below the exercise price when the option matures, the buyer will not exercise the call and the seller's liability will be zero. If it rises above the exercise price, the buyer will exercise and the seller must give up the shares. The seller loses the difference between the share price and the exercise price received from the buyer. Notice that it is the buyer who always has the option to exercise; option sellers simply do as they are told.

Suppose that the price of Google stock turns out to be $500, which is above the option's exercise price of $430. In this case the buyer will exercise the call. The seller is forced to sell

▶ FIGURE 16.2

Payoffs to *sellers* of Google calls and puts (shown by the colored lines) depend on the share price. (*a*) Result of selling Google call exercisable at $430. (*b*) Result of selling Google put exercisable at $430.

stock worth $500 for only $430 and so has a payoff of −$70.[3] Of course, that $70 loss is the buyer's gain. Figure 16.2(*a*) shows how the payoffs to the seller of the Google call option vary with the stock price. Notice that for every dollar the buyer makes, the seller loses a dollar. Figure 16.2(*a*) is just Figure 16.1(*a*) drawn upside down.

In just the same way we can depict the position of an investor who sells, or writes, a put by standing Figure 16.1(*b*) on its head. The seller of the put has agreed to pay $430 for the share if the buyer of the put should request it. Clearly the seller will be safe as long as the share price remains above $430 but will lose money if the share price falls below this figure. The worst thing that can happen is that the stock becomes worthless. The seller would then be obliged to pay $430 for a stock worth $0. The payoff to the option position would be −$430.

Position Diagrams Are Not Profit Diagrams

Position diagrams show *only* the payoffs at option exercise; they do not account for the initial cost of buying the option or the initial proceeds from selling it.

This is a common point of confusion. For example, the position diagram in Figure 16.1(*a*) makes purchase of a call *look* like a sure thing—the payoff is at worst zero, with plenty of upside if Google's stock price goes above $430 by March 2009. But compare the *profit diagram* in Figure 16.3(*a*), which subtracts the $54.35 *cost* of the call in September 2008 from the payoff at maturity. The call buyer loses money at all share prices less than $430 + 54.35 = $484.35. Take another example: The position diagram in Figure 16.2(*b*) makes selling a put *look* like a sure loss—the *best* payoff is zero. But the profit diagram in Figure 16.3(*b*), which recognizes the $48.55 received by the seller, shows that the seller gains at all prices above $430 − 48.55 = $381.45.[4]

---

[3] The seller has some consolation, for he or she was paid $54.35 in September for selling the call.

[4] The fact that you have made a profit on your position is not necessarily a cause for rejoicing. The profit needs to compensate you for the time value of money and the risk that you took.

(a) Profit to call buyer

$430

Share price

0

−$54.35

Breakeven is $484.35

(b) Profit to put seller

$48.55

0

$430

Share price

Breakeven is $381.45

▶ **FIGURE 16.3**

Profit diagrams incorporate the costs of buying an option or the proceeds from selling one. In panel (a), we subtract the $54.35 cost of the Google call from the payoffs plotted in Figure 16.1(a). In panel (b), we add the $48.55 proceeds from selling the Google put to the payoffs in Figure 16.2(b).

Profit diagrams like those in Figure 16.3 may be helpful to the options beginner, but options experts rarely draw them.[5] Now that you've graduated from the first options class we won't draw them either. We stick to position diagrams, because you have to focus on payoffs at exercise to understand options and to value them properly.

16-2 Financial Alchemy with Options

Look now at Figure 16.4(a), which shows the payoff if you buy Google stock at $430. You gain dollar-for-dollar if the stock price goes up and you lose dollar-for-dollar if it falls. That's trite; it doesn't take a genius to draw a 45-degree line.

Look now at panel (b), which shows the payoffs from an investment strategy that retains the upside potential of Google stock but gives complete downside protection. In this case your payoff stays at $430 even if the Google stock price falls to $400, $100, or zero. Panel (b)'s payoffs are clearly better than panel (a)'s. If a financial alchemist could turn panel (a) into panel (b), you'd be willing to pay for the service.

Of course alchemy has its dark side. Panel (c) shows an investment strategy for masochists. You lose if the stock price falls, but you give up any chance of profiting from a rise in the stock price. If you *like* to lose, or if someone pays you enough to take the strategy on, this is the investment for you.

Now, as you have probably suspected, all this financial alchemy is for real. You can do both the transmutations shown in Figure 16.4. You do them with options, and we will show you how.

Consider first the strategy for masochists. The first diagram in Figure 16.5 shows the payoffs from buying a share of Google stock, while the second shows the payoffs from *selling* a call option with a $430 exercise price. The third diagram shows what happens if you combine these two positions. The result is the no-win strategy that we depicted in panel

---

[5] Profit diagrams such as Figure 16.3 deduct the initial cost of the option from the final payoff. They therefore ignore the first lesson of finance—"A dollar today is worth more than a dollar in the future."

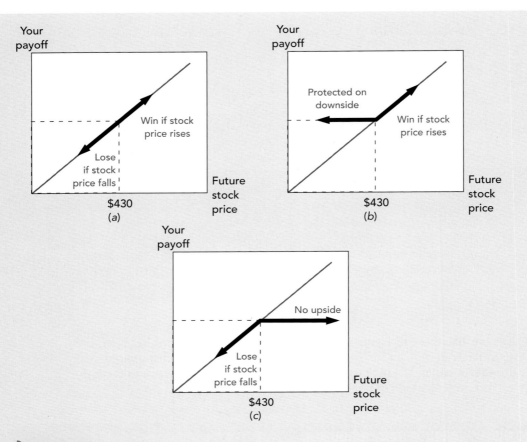

▶ FIGURE 16.4

Payoffs at the end of six months to three investment strategies for Google stock. (*a*) You buy one share for $430. (*b*) No downside. If stock price falls, your payoff stays at $430. (*c*) A strategy for masochists? You lose if stock price falls, but you don't gain if it rises.

(*c*) of Figure 16.4. You lose if the stock price declines below $430, but, if the stock price rises above $430, the owner of the call will demand that you hand over your stock for the $430 exercise price. So you lose on the downside and give up any chance of a profit. That's the bad news. The good news is that you get paid for taking on this liability. In September 2008 you would have been paid $54.35, the price of a six-month call option.

Now, we'll create the downside protection shown in Figure 16.4(*b*). Look at row 1 of Figure 16.6. The first diagram again shows the payoff from buying a share of Google stock, while the next diagram in row 1 shows the payoffs from buying a Google put option with an exercise price of $430. The third diagram shows the effect of combining these two positions. You can see that, if Google's stock price rises above $430, your put option is valueless, so you simply receive the gains from your investment in the share. However, if the stock price falls below $430, you can exercise your put option and sell your stock for $430. Thus, by adding a put option to your investment in the stock, you have protected yourself against loss.[6] This is the strategy that we depicted in panel (*b*) of Figure 16.4. Of course, there is no

---

[6] This combination of a stock and a put option is known as a *protective put*.

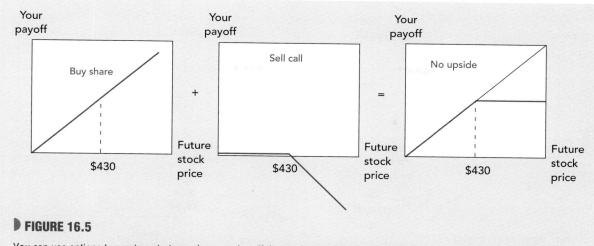

▶ **FIGURE 16.5**

You can use options to create a strategy where you lose if the stock price falls but do not gain if it rises (strategy [c] in Figure 16.4).

gain without pain. The *cost* of insuring yourself against loss is the amount that you pay for a six-month put option on Google stock with an exercise price of $430. In September 2008 the price of this put was $48.55. This was the going rate for financial alchemists.

We have just seen how put options can be used to provide downside protection. We now show you how call options can be used to get the same result. This is illustrated in row 2 of Figure 16.6. The first diagram shows the payoff from placing the present value of $430 in a bank deposit. Regardless of what happens to the price of Google stock, your bank deposit will pay off $430. The second diagram in row 2 shows the payoff from a call option on Google stock with an exercise price of $430, and the third diagram shows the effect of combining these two positions. Notice that, if the price of Google stock falls, your call is worthless, but you still have your $430 in the bank. For every dollar that Google stock price rises above $430, your investment in the call option pays off an extra dollar. For example, if the stock price rises to $500, you will have $430 in the bank and a call worth $70. Thus you participate fully in any rise in the price of the stock, while being fully protected against any fall. So we have just found another way to provide the downside protection depicted in panel (*b*) of Figure 16.4.

These two rows of Figure 16.6 tell us something about the relationship between a call option and a put option. Regardless of the future stock price, both investment strategies provide identical payoffs. In other words, if you buy the share and a put option to sell it for $430, you receive the same payoff as from buying a call option and setting enough money aside to pay the $430 exercise price. Therefore, if you are committed to holding the two packages until the options expire, the two packages should sell for the same price today. This gives us a fundamental relationship for European options:

> Value of call + present value of exercise price = value of put + share price

To repeat, this relationship holds because the payoff of

> Buy call, invest present value of exercise price in safe asset[7]

is identical to the payoff from

> Buy put, buy share

---

[7] The present value is calculated at the *risk-free* rate of interest. It is the amount that you would have to invest today in a bank deposit or Treasury bills to realize the exercise price on the option's expiration date.

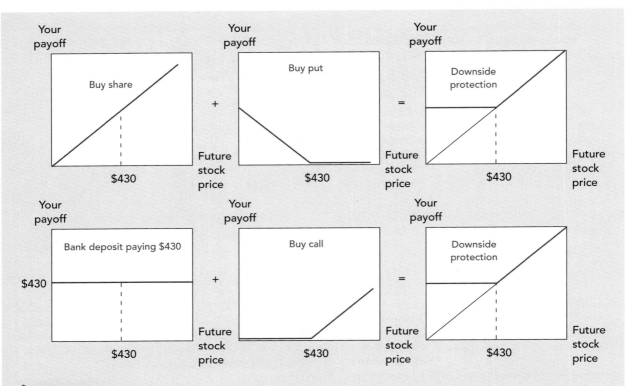

> **FIGURE 16.6**

Each row in the figure shows a different way to create a strategy where you gain if the stock price rises but are protected on the downside (strategy [b] in Figure 16.4).

This basic relationship among share price, call and put values, and the present value of the exercise price is called **put–call parity.**[8]

Put–call parity can be expressed in several ways. Each expression implies two investment strategies that give identical results. For example, suppose that you want to solve for the value of a put. You simply need to twist the put–call parity formula around to give

Value of put = value of call + present value of exercise price − share price

From this expression you can deduce that

Buy put

is identical to

Buy call, invest present value of exercise price in safe asset, sell share

In other words, if puts are not available, you can get exactly the same payoff by buying calls, putting cash in the bank, and selling shares.

---

[8] Put–call parity holds only if you are committed to holding the options until the final exercise date. It therefore does not hold for American options, which you can exercise *before* the final date. We discuss possible reasons for early exercise in Chapter 17. Also if the stock makes a dividend payment before the final exercise date, you need to recognize that the investor who buys the call misses out on this dividend. In this case the relationship is

Value of call + present value of exercise price = value of put + share price − present value of dividend

▶ **FIGURE 16.7**

A strategy of buying a call, depositing the present value of the exercise price in the bank, and selling the stock is equivalent to buying a put.

If you find this difficult to believe, look at Figure 16.7, which shows the possible payoffs from each position. The diagram on the left shows the payoffs from a call option on Google stock with an exercise price of $430. The second diagram shows the payoffs from placing the present value of $430 in the bank. Regardless of what happens to the share price, this investment will pay off $430. The third diagram shows the payoffs from selling Google stock. When you sell a share that you don't own, you have a liability—you must sometime buy it back. As they say on Wall Street:

> He who sells what isn't his'n
> Buys it back or goes to pris'n

Therefore the best that can happen to you is that the share price falls to zero. In that case it costs you nothing to buy the share back. But for every extra dollar on the future share price, you will need to spend an extra dollar to buy the share. The final diagram in Figure 16.7 shows that the *total* payoff from these three positions is the same as if you had bought a put option. For example, suppose that when the option matures the stock price is $400. Your call will be worthless, your bank deposit will be worth $430, and it will cost you $400 to repurchase the share. Your total payoff is $0 + 430 − 400 = 30, exactly the same as the payoff from the put.

If two investments offer identical payoffs, then they should sell for the same price today. If the law of one price is violated, you have a potential arbitrage opportunity. So let's check whether there are any arbitrage profits to be made from our Google calls and puts. In September 2008 the price of a six-month call with a $430 exercise price was $54.35, the interest rate was about 3%, and the price of Google stock was $430. Therefore the cost of a homemade put was:

Buy call + present value of exercise price − share price = cost of homemade put

$$54.35 \quad + \quad 430/1.03^{.5} \quad - \quad 430 \quad = \quad 48.04$$

This is almost exactly the same as it would have cost you to buy a put directly.

▶ **FIGURE 16.8**

The payoff from one of Ms. Higden's "tickets" depends on Flatiron's stock price.

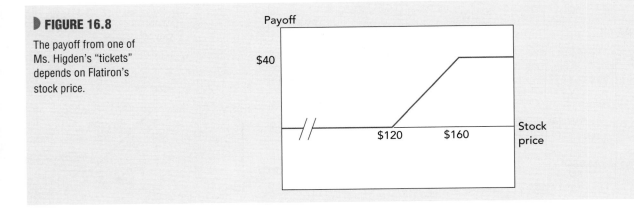

▶ **FIGURE 16.9**

The solid black line shows the payoff from buying a call with an exercise price of $120. The dotted line shows the sale of a call with an exercise price of $160. The combined purchase and sale (shown by the colored line) is identical to one of Ms. Higden's "tickets."

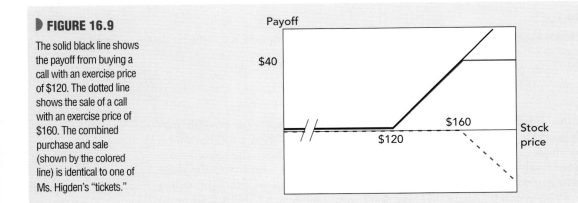

Spotting the Option

Options rarely come with a large label attached. Often the trickiest part of the problem is to identify the option. When you are not sure whether you are dealing with a put or a call or a complicated blend of the two, it is a good precaution to draw a position diagram. Here is an example.

The Flatiron and Mangle Corporation has offered its president, Ms. Higden, the following incentive scheme: At the end of the year Ms. Higden will be paid a bonus of $50,000 for every dollar that the price of Flatiron stock exceeds its current figure of $120. However, the maximum bonus that she can receive is set at $2 million.

You can think of Ms. Higden as owning 50,000 tickets, each of which pays nothing if the stock price fails to beat $120. The value of each ticket then rises by $1 for each dollar rise in the stock price up to the maximum of $2,000,000/50,000 = $40. Figure 16.8 shows the payoffs from just one of these tickets. The payoffs are not the same as those of the simple put and call options that we drew in Figure 16.1, but it is possible to find a combination of options that exactly replicates Figure 16.8. Before going on to read the answer, see if you can spot it yourself. (If you are someone who enjoys puzzles of the make-a-triangle-from-just-two-matchsticks type, this one should be a walkover.)

The answer is in Figure 16.9. The solid black line represents the purchase of a call option with an exercise price of $120, and the dotted line shows the sale of another call option with an exercise price of $160. The colored line shows the payoffs from a combination of the purchase and the sale—exactly the same as the payoffs from one of Ms. Higden's tickets.

Thus, if we wish to know how much the incentive scheme is costing the company, we need to calculate the difference between the value of 50,000 call options with an exercise price of $120 and the value of 50,000 calls with an exercise price of $160.

We could have made the incentive scheme depend in a much more complicated way on the stock price. For example, the bonus could peak at $2 million and then fall steadily back to zero as the stock price climbs above $160.[9] You could still have represented this scheme as a combination of options. In fact, we can state a general theorem:

> Any set of contingent payoffs—that is, payoffs that depend on the value of some other asset—can be constructed with a mixture of simple options on that asset.

In other words, you can create any position diagram—with as many ups and downs or peaks and valleys as your imagination allows—by buying or selling the right combinations of puts and calls with different exercise prices.[10]

Finance pros often talk about **financial engineering,** which is the practice of packaging different investments to create new tailor-made instruments. Perhaps a German company would like to set a minimum and maximum cost at which it can buy dollars in six months' time. Or perhaps an oil company would like to pay a lower rate of interest on its debt if the price of oil falls. Options provide the building blocks that financial engineers use to create these interesting payoff structures.

16-3 What Determines Option Values?

So far we have said nothing about how the market value of an option is determined. We do know what an option is worth when it matures, however. Consider, for instance, our earlier example of an option to buy Google stock at $430. If Google's stock price is below $430 on the exercise date, the call will be worthless; if the stock price is above $430, the call will be worth $430 less than the value of the stock. This relationship is depicted by the heavy, lower line in Figure 16.10.

Even before maturity the price of the option can never remain *below* the heavy, lower-bound line in Figure 16.10. For example, if our option were priced at $10 and the stock were priced at $460, it would pay any investor to sell the stock and then buy it back by purchasing the option and exercising it for an additional $430. That would give an arbitrage opportunity with a profit of $20. The demand for options from investors seeking to exploit this opportunity would quickly force the option price up, at least to the heavy line in the figure. For options that still have some time to run, the heavy line is therefore a *lower bound* on the market price of the option. Option geeks express the same idea more concisely when they write Lower Bound = Max(stock price − exercise price, 0).

The diagonal line in Figure 16.10 is the *upper bound* to the option price. Why? Because the option cannot give a higher ultimate payoff than the stock. If at the option's expiration the stock price ends up *above* the exercise price, the option is worth the stock price *less* the exercise price.

---

[9] This is not as nutty a bonus scheme as it may sound. Maybe Ms. Higden's hard work can lift the value of the stock by so much and the only way she can hope to increase it further is by taking on extra risk. You can deter her from doing this by making her bonus start to decline beyond some point. Too bad that the bonus schemes for some bank CEOs did not contain this feature.

[10] In some cases you may also have to borrow or lend money to generate a position diagram with your desired pattern. Lending raises the payoff line in position diagrams, as in the bottom row of Figure 16.6. Borrowing lowers the payoff line.

▶ **FIGURE 16.10**

Value of a call before its expiration date (dashed line). The value depends on the stock price. It is always worth more than its value if exercised now (heavy line). It is never worth more than the stock price itself.

If the stock price ends up *below* the exercise price, the option is worthless, but the stock's owner still has a valuable security. For example, if the option's exercise price is $430, then the extra dollar returns realized by stockholders are shown in the following table:

	Stock Payoff	Option Payoff	Extra Payoff from Holding Stock Instead of Option
Option exercised (stock price greater than $430)	Stock price	Stock price − 430	$430
Option expires unexercised (stock price less than or equal to $430)	Stock price	0	Stock price

If the stock and the option have the same price, everyone will rush to sell the option and buy the stock. Therefore, the option price must be somewhere in the shaded region of Figure 16.10. In fact, it will lie on a curved, upward-sloping line like the dashed curve shown in the figure. This line begins its travels where the upper and lower bounds meet (at zero). Then it rises, gradually becoming parallel to the upward-sloping part of the lower bound.

But let us look more carefully at the shape and location of the dashed line. Three points, *A, B,* and *C,* are marked on the dashed line. As we explain each point you will see why the option price has to behave as the dashed line predicts.

Point A   *When the stock is worthless, the option is worthless.* A stock price of zero means that there is no possibility the stock will ever have any future value.[11] If so, the option is sure to expire unexercised and worthless, and it is worthless today.

That brings us to our first important point about option value:

The value of an option increases as stock price increases, if the exercise price is held constant.

That should be no surprise. Owners of call options clearly hope for the stock price to rise and are happy when it does.

Point B   *When the stock price becomes large, the option price approaches the stock price less the present value of the exercise price.* Notice that the dashed line representing the option price

---

[11] If a stock *can* be worth something in the future, then investors will pay *something* for it today, although possibly a very small amount.

in Figure 16.10 eventually becomes parallel to the ascending heavy line representing the lower bound on the option price. The reason is as follows: The higher the stock price, the higher is the probability that the option will eventually be exercised. If the stock price is high enough, exercise becomes a virtual certainty; the probability that the stock price will fall below the exercise price before the option expires becomes trivially small.

If you own an option that you *know* will be exchanged for a share of stock, you effectively own the stock now. The only difference is that you don't have to pay for the stock (by handing over the exercise price) until later, when formal exercise occurs. In these circumstances, buying the call is equivalent to buying the stock but financing part of the purchase by borrowing. The amount implicitly borrowed is the present value of the exercise price. The value of the call is therefore equal to the stock price less the present value of the exercise price.

This brings us to another important point about options. Investors who acquire stock by way of a call option are buying on credit. They pay the purchase price of the option today, but they do not pay the exercise price until they actually take up the option. The delay in payment is particularly valuable if interest rates are high and the option has a long maturity.

Thus, the value of an option increases with both the rate of interest and the time to maturity.

Point C *The option price always exceeds its minimum value* (except when stock price is zero). We have seen that the dashed and heavy lines in Figure 16.10 coincide when stock price is zero (point *A*), but elsewhere the lines diverge; that is, the option price must exceed the minimum value given by the heavy line. The reason for this can be understood by examining point *C*.

At point *C*, the stock price exactly equals the exercise price. The option is therefore worthless if exercised today. However, suppose that the option will not expire until three months hence. Of course we do not know what the stock price will be at the expiration date. There is roughly a 50% chance that it will be higher than the exercise price and a 50% chance that it will be lower. The possible payoffs to the option are therefore:

Outcome	Payoff
Stock price rises (50% probability)	Stock price less exercise price (option is exercised)
Stock price falls (50% probability)	Zero (option expires worthless)

If there is a positive probability of a positive payoff, and if the worst payoff is zero, then the option must be valuable. That means the option price at point *C* exceeds its lower bound, which at point *C* is zero. In general, the option prices will exceed their lower-bound values as long as there is time left before expiration.

One of the most important determinants of the *height* of the dashed curve (i.e., of the difference between actual and lower-bound value) is the likelihood of substantial movements in the stock price. An option on a stock whose price is unlikely to change by more than 1% or 2% is not worth much; an option on a stock whose price may halve or double is very valuable.

As an option holder, you gain from volatility because the payoffs are not symmetric. If the stock price falls *below* the exercise price, your call option will be worthless, regardless of whether the shortfall is a few cents or many dollars. On the other hand, for every dollar that the stock price rises *above* the exercise price, your call will be worth an extra dollar. Therefore, the option holder gains from the increased volatility on the upside, but does not lose on the downside.

A simple example may help to illustrate the point. Consider two stocks, X and Y, each of which is priced at $100. The only difference is that the outlook for Y is much less easy

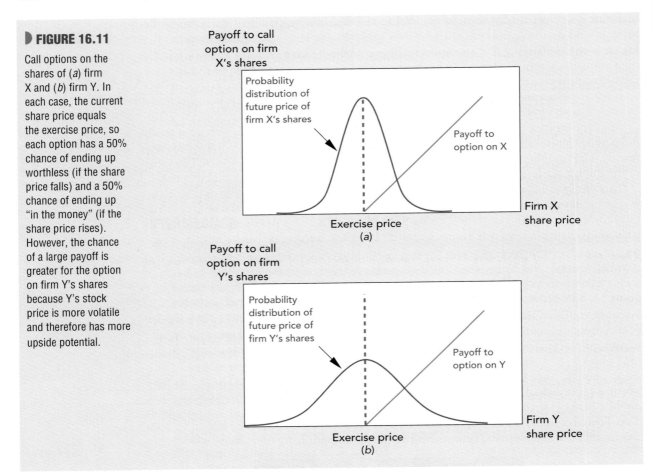

▶ **FIGURE 16.11**

Call options on the shares of (*a*) firm X and (*b*) firm Y. In each case, the current share price equals the exercise price, so each option has a 50% chance of ending up worthless (if the share price falls) and a 50% chance of ending up "in the money" (if the share price rises). However, the chance of a large payoff is greater for the option on firm Y's shares because Y's stock price is more volatile and therefore has more upside potential.

to predict. There is a 50% chance that the price of Y will rise to $150 and a similar chance that it will fall to $70. By contrast, there is a 50-50 chance that the price of X will either rise to $130 or fall to $90.

Suppose that you are offered a call option on each of these stocks with an exercise price of $100. The following table compares the possible payoffs from these options:

	Stock Price Falls	Stock Price Rises
Payoff from option on X	$0	$130 − $100 = $30
Payoff from option on Y	$0	$150 − $100 = $50

In both cases there is a 50% chance that the stock price will decline and make the option worthless but, if the stock price rises, the option on Y will give the larger payoff. Since the chance of a zero payoff is the same, the option on Y is worth more than the option on X.

Of course, in practice future stock prices may take on a range of different values. We have recognized this in Figure 16.11, where the uncertain outlook for Y's stock price shows up in the wider probability distribution of future prices.[12] The greater spread of outcomes

---

[12] Figure 16.11 continues to assume that the exercise price on both options is equal to the current stock price. This is not a necessary assumption. Also in drawing Figure 16.11 we have assumed that the distribution of stock prices is symmetric. This also is not a necessary assumption, and we will look more carefully at the distribution of stock prices in the next chapter.

Values of Google call option

FIGURE 16.12

How the value of the Google call option increases with the volatility of the stock price. Each of the curved lines shows the value of the option for different initial stock prices. The only difference is that the upper line assumes a much higher level of uncertainty about Google's future stock price.

e**X**cel

Visit us at
www.mhhe.com/bma

for stock Y again provides more upside potential and therefore increases the chance of a large payoff on the option.

Figure 16.12 shows how volatility affects the value of an option. The upper curved line depicts the value of the Google call option assuming that Google's stock price, like that of stock Y, is highly variable. The lower curved line assumes a lower (and more realistic) degree of volatility.[13]

The probability of large stock price changes during the remaining life of an option depends on two things: (1) the variance (i.e., volatility) of the stock price *per period* and (2) the number of periods until the option expires. If there are t remaining periods, and the variance per period is σ^2, the value of the option should depend on cumulative variability $\sigma^2 t$.[14] Other things equal, you would like to hold an option on a volatile stock (high σ^2). Given volatility, you would like to hold an option with a long life ahead of it (large t).

Thus the value of an option increases with both the volatility of the share price and the time to maturity.

It's a rare person who can keep all these properties straight at first reading. Therefore, we have summed them up in Table 16.2.

Risk and Option Values

In most financial settings, risk is a bad thing; you have to be paid to bear it. Investors in risky (high-beta) stocks demand higher expected rates of return. High-risk capital investment projects have correspondingly high costs of capital and have to beat higher hurdle rates to achieve positive NPV.

---

[13] The option values shown in Figure 16.12 were calculated by using the Black–Scholes option-valuation model. We explain this model in Chapter 17 and use it to value the Google option.

[14] Here is an intuitive explanation: If the stock price follows a random walk (see Section 11–2), successive price changes are statistically independent. The cumulative price change before expiration is the sum of t random variables. The variance of a sum of independent random variables is the sum of the variances of those variables. Thus, if σ^2 is the variance of the daily price change, and there are t days until expiration, the variance of the cumulative price change is $\sigma^2 t$.

> **TABLE 16.2**

What the price of a call option depends on.

* The direct effect of increases in r_f or σ on option price, *given* the stock price. There may also be *indirect* effects. For example, an increase in r_f could reduce stock price P. This in turn could affect option price.

1. If there is an *increase* in:	The change in the call option price is:
Stock price (P)	Positive
Exercise price (EX)	Negative
Interest rate (r_f)	Positive*
Time to expiration (t)	Positive
Volatility of stock price (σ)	Positive*

2. Other properties of call options:

   a. *Upper bound.* The option price is always less than the stock price.

   b. *Lower bound.* The call price never falls below the payoff to immediate exercise ($P - EX$ or zero, whichever is larger).

   c. If the stock is worthless, the call is worthless.

   d. As the stock price becomes very large, the call price approaches the stock price less the present value of the exercise price.

> **TABLE 16.3**

Which package of executive stock options would you choose? The package offered by Digital Organics is more valuable, because the volatility of that company's stock is higher.

	Establishment Industries	Digital Organics
Number of options	100,000	100,000
Exercise price	$25	$25
Maturity	5 years	5 years
Current stock price	$22	$22
Stock price volatility (standard deviation of return)	24%	36%

For options it's the other way around. As we have just seen, options written on volatile assets are worth *more* than options written on safe assets. If you can understand and remember that one fact about options, you've come a long way.

EXAMPLE 16.1 ● Volatility and Executive Stock Options

Suppose you have to choose between two job offers, as CFO of either Establishment Industries or Digital Organics. Establishment Industries' compensation package includes a grant of the stock options described on the left side of Table 16.3. You demand a similar package from Digital Organics, and it complies. In fact it matches the Establishment Industries options in every respect, as you can see on the right side of Table 16.3. (The two companies' current stock prices just happen to be the same.) The only difference is that Digital Organics' stock is 50% more volatile than Establishment Industries' stock (36% annual standard deviation vs. 24% for Establishment Industries).

If your job choice hinges on the value of the executive stock options, you should take the Digital Organics offer. The Digital Organics options are written on the more volatile asset and therefore are worth more.

We value the two stock-option packages in the next chapter.

● ● ● ● ●

If you have managed to reach this point, you are probably in need of a rest and a stiff gin and tonic. So we will summarize what we have learned so far and take up the subject of options again in the next chapter when you are rested (or drunk).

There are two types of option. An American call is an option to buy an asset at a specified exercise price on or before a specified maturity date. Similarly, an American put is an option to sell the asset at a specified price on or before a specified date. European calls and puts are exactly the same except that they cannot be exercised before the specified maturity date. Calls and puts are the basic building blocks that can be combined to give any pattern of payoffs.

What determines the value of a call option? Common sense tells us that it ought to depend on three things:

1. To exercise an option you have to pay the exercise price. Other things being equal, the less you are obliged to pay, the better. Therefore, the value of a call option increases with the ratio of the asset price to the exercise price.

2. You do not have to pay the exercise price until you decide to exercise the option. Therefore, a call option gives you a free loan. The higher the rate of interest and the longer the time to maturity, the more this free loan is worth. So the value of a call option increases with the interest rate and time to maturity.

3. If the price of the asset falls short of the exercise price, you won't exercise the call option. You will, therefore, lose 100% of your investment in the option no matter how far the asset depreciates below the exercise price. On the other hand, the more the price rises *above* the exercise price, the more profit you will make. Therefore the option holder does not lose from increased volatility if things go wrong, but gains if they go right. The value of an option increases with the variance per period of the stock return multiplied by the number of periods to maturity.

Always remember that an option written on a risky (high-variance) asset is worth more than an option on a safe asset. It's easy to forget, because in most other financial contexts increases in risk reduce present value.

See Further Reading for Chapter 17.

BASIC

1. Complete the following passage:

   A _____ option gives its owner the opportunity to buy a stock at a specified price that is generally called the _____ price. A _____ option gives its owner the opportunity to sell stock at a specified price. Options that can be exercised only at maturity are called _____ options.

2. Note Figure 16.13 on the next page. Match each diagram, (*a*) and (*b*), with one of the following positions:

   - Call buyer
   - Call seller
   - Put buyer
   - Put seller

3. Suppose that you hold a share of stock and a put option on that share. What is the payoff when the option expires if (a) the stock price is below the exercise price? (b) the stock price is above the exercise price?

4. What is put–call parity and why does it hold? Could you apply the parity formula to a call and put with different exercise prices?

5. There is another strategy involving calls and borrowing or lending that gives the same payoffs as the strategy described in Problem 3. What is the alternative strategy?

6. Dr. Livingstone I. Presume holds £600,000 in East African gold stocks. Bullish as he is on gold mining, he requires absolute assurance that at least £500,000 will be available in six months to fund an expedition. Describe two ways for Dr. Presume to achieve this goal. There is an active market for puts and calls on East African gold stocks, and the rate of interest is 6% per year.

7. Suppose you buy a one-year European call option on Wombat stock with an exercise price of $100 and sell a one-year European put option with the same exercise price. The current stock price is $100, and the interest rate is 10%.

    a. Draw a position diagram showing the payoffs from your investments.

    b. How much will the combined position cost you? Explain.

8. Look again at Figure 16.13. It appears that the investor in panel (*b*) can't lose and the investor in panel (*a*) can't win. Is that correct? Explain. (*Hint:* Draw a profit diagram for each panel.)

9. What is a call option worth if (a) the stock price is zero? (b) the stock price is extremely high relative to the exercise price?

10. How does the price of a call option respond to the following changes, other things equal? Does the call price go up or down?

    a. Stock price increases.

    b. Exercise price is increased.

    c. Risk-free rate increases.

    d. Expiration date of the option is extended.

    e. Volatility of the stock price falls.

    f. Time passes, so the option's expiration date comes closer.

11. Respond to the following statements.

    a. "I'm a conservative investor. I'd much rather hold a call option on a safe stock like Exxon Mobil than a volatile stock like Google."

▶ FIGURE 16.13

See Problem 2.

b. "I bought an American call option on Fava Farms stock, with an exercise price of $45 per share and three more months to maturity. Fava Farms' stock has skyrocketed from $35 to $55 per share, but I'm afraid it will fall back below $45. I'm going to lock in my gain and exercise my call right now."

INTERMEDIATE

12. Discuss briefly the risks and payoffs of the following positions:
    a. Buy stock and a put option on the stock.
    b. Buy stock.
    c. Buy call.
    d. Buy stock and sell call option on the stock.
    e. Buy bond.
    f. Buy stock, buy put, and sell call.
    g. Sell put.

13. "The buyer of the call and the seller of the put both hope that the stock price will rise. Therefore the two positions are identical." Is the speaker correct? Illustrate with a position diagram.

14. Pintail's stock price is currently $200. A one-year *American* call option has an exercise price of $50 and is priced at $75. How would you take advantage of this great opportunity? Now suppose the option is a *European* call. What would you do?

15. It is possible to buy three-month call options and three-month puts on stock Q. Both options have an exercise price of $60 and both are worth $10. If the interest rate is 5% a year, what is the stock price? (*Hint:* Use put–call parity.)

16. In January 2009, a one-year call on the stock of Amazon.com, with an exercise price of $45.00, sold for $19.55. The stock price was $55. The risk-free interest rate was 2.5%. How much would you be willing to pay for a put on Amazon stock with the same maturity and exercise price? Assume that the Amazon options are European options. (*Note:* Amazon does not pay a dividend.)

17. FX Bank has succeeded in hiring ace foreign exchange trader Lucinda Cable. Her remuneration package reportedly includes an annual bonus of 20% of the profits that she generates in excess of $100 million. Does Ms. Cable have an option? Does it provide her with the appropriate incentives?

18. Suppose that Mr. Colleoni borrows the present value of $100, buys a six-month put option on stock Y with an exercise price of $150, and sells a six-month put option on Y with an exercise price of $50.
    a. Draw a position diagram showing the payoffs when the options expire.
    b. Suggest two other combinations of loans, options, and the underlying stock that would give Mr. Colleoni the same payoffs.

19. Which *one* of the following statements is correct?
    a. Value of put + present value of exercise price = value of call + share price.
    b. Value of put + share price = value of call + present value of exercise price.
    c. Value of put − share price = present value of exercise price − value of call.
    d. Value of put + value of call = share price − present value of exercise price.

    The correct statement equates the value of two investment strategies. Plot the payoffs to each strategy as a function of the stock price. Show that the two strategies give identical payoffs.

20. Test the formula linking put and call prices by using it to explain the relative prices of actual traded puts and calls. (*Note:* The formula is exact only for European options. Most traded puts and calls are American.)

21. a. If you can't sell a share short, you can achieve exactly the same final payoff by a combination of options and borrowing or lending. What is this combination?

    b. Now work out the mixture of stock and options that gives the same final payoff as investment in a risk-free loan.

22. The common stock of Triangular File Company is selling at $90. A 26-week call option written on Triangular File's stock is selling for $8. The call's exercise price is $100. The risk-free interest rate is 10% per year.

    a. Suppose that puts on Triangular stock are not traded, but you want to buy one. How would you do it?

    b. Suppose that puts *are* traded. What should a 26-week put with an exercise price of $100 sell for?

23. Ms. Higden has been offered yet another incentive scheme (see Section 16–2). She will receive a bonus of $500,000 if the stock price at the end of the year is $120 or more; otherwise she will receive nothing. (Don't ask why anyone should want to offer such an arrangement. Maybe there's some tax angle.)

    a. Draw a position diagram illustrating the payoffs from such a scheme.

    b. What combination of options would provide these payoffs? (*Hint:* You need to buy a large number of options with one exercise price and sell a similar number with a different exercise price.)

24. Option traders often refer to "straddles" and "butterflies." Here is an example of each:

    • *Straddle:* Buy call with exercise price of $100 and simultaneously buy put with exercise price of $100.

    • *Butterfly:* Simultaneously buy one call with exercise price of $100, sell two calls with exercise price of $110, and buy one call with exercise price of $120.

    Draw position diagrams for the straddle and butterfly, showing the payoffs from the investor's net position. Each strategy is a bet on variability. Explain briefly the nature of each bet.

25. Look at actual trading prices of call options on stocks to check whether they behave as the theory presented in this chapter predicts. For example,

    a. Follow several options as they approach maturity. How would you expect their prices to behave? Do they actually behave that way?

    b. Compare two call options written on the same stock with the same maturity but different exercise prices.

    c. Compare two call options written on the same stock with the same exercise price but different maturities.

26. Is it more valuable to own an option to buy a portfolio of stocks or to own a portfolio of options to buy each of the individual stocks? Say briefly why.

27. Table 16.4 lists some prices of options on common stocks (prices are quoted to the nearest dollar). The interest rate is 10% a year. Can you spot any mispricing? What would you do to take advantage of it?

▷ **TABLE 16.4**

Prices of options on common stocks (in dollars). See Problem 27.

Stock	Time to Exercise (months)	Exercise Price	Stock Price	Put Price	Call Price
Drongo Corp.	6	$ 50	$80	$20	$52
Ragwort, Inc.	6	100	80	10	15
Wombat Corp.	3	40	50	7	18
	6	40	50	5	17
	6	50	50	8	10

28. You've just completed a month-long study of energy markets and conclude that energy prices will be *much* more volatile in the next year than historically. Assuming you're right, what types of option strategies should you undertake? (*Note:* You can buy or sell options on oil-company stocks or on the price of future deliveries of crude oil, natural gas, fuel oil, etc.)

CHALLENGE

29. Figure 16.14 below shows some complicated position diagrams. Work out the combination of stocks, bonds, and options that produces each of these positions.

30. Some years ago the Australian firm Bond Corporation sold a share in some land that it owned near Rome for $110 million and as a result boosted its annual earnings by $74 million. A television program subsequently revealed that the buyer was given a put option to sell its share in the land back to Bond for $110 million and that Bond had paid $20 million for a call option to repurchase the share in the land for the same price.

   a. What happens if the land is worth more than $110 million when the options expire? What if it is worth less than $110 million?

   b. Use position diagrams to show the net effect of the land sale and the option transactions.

   c. Assume a one-year maturity on the options. Can you deduce the interest rate?

   d. The television program argued that it was misleading to record a profit on the sale of land. What do you think?

31. Three six-month call options are traded on Hogswill stock:

Exercise Price	Call Option Price
$ 90	$ 5
100	11
110	15

How would you make money by trading in Hogswill options? (*Hint:* Draw a graph with the option price on the vertical axis and the ratio of stock price to exercise price on the horizontal axis. Plot the three Hogswill options on your graph. Does this fit with what you know about how option prices should vary with the ratio of stock price to exercise price?) Now look in the newspaper at options with the same maturity but different exercise prices. Can you find any money-making opportunities?

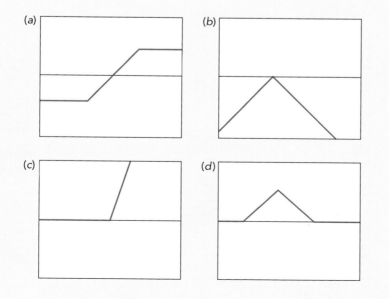

▶ **FIGURE 16.14**

Some complicated position diagrams. See Problem 29.

32. Digital Organics has 10 million outstanding shares trading at $25 per share. It also has a large amount of debt outstanding, all coming due in one year. The debt pays interest at 8%. It has a par (face) value of $350 million, but is trading at a market value of only $280 million. The one-year risk-free interest rate is 6%.

   a. Write out the put–call parity formula for Digital Organics' stock, debt, and assets.

   b. What is the value of the company's option to default on its debt?

● ● ● ● ●

**REAL-TIME
DATA ANALYSIS**

Go to **finance.yahoo.com**. Check out the delayed quotes for Google for different exercise prices and maturities.

   a. Confirm that higher exercise prices mean lower call prices and higher put prices.

   b. Confirm that longer maturity means higher prices for both puts and calls.

   c. Choose a Google put and call with the same exercise price and maturity. Confirm that put–call parity holds (approximately). (*Note:* You will have to use an up-to-date risk-free interest rate.)

OPTIONS

Valuing Options

▶ **In the last** chapter we introduced you to call and put options. Call options give the owner the right to buy an asset at a specified exercise price; put options give the right to sell. We also took the first step toward understanding how options are valued. The value of a call option depends on five variables:

1. The higher the price of the asset, the more valuable an option to buy it.

2. The lower the price that you must pay to exercise the call, the more valuable the option.

3. You do not need to pay the exercise price until the option expires. This delay is most valuable when the interest rate is high.

4. If the stock price is below the exercise price at maturity, the call is valueless regardless of whether the price is $1 below or $100 below. However, for every dollar that the stock price rises above the exercise price, the option holder gains an additional dollar. Thus, the value of the call option increases with the volatility of the stock price.

5. Finally, a long-term option is more valuable than a short-term option. A distant maturity delays the point at which the holder needs to pay the exercise price

and increases the chance of a large jump in the stock price before the option matures.

In this chapter we show how these variables can be combined into an exact option-valuation model— a formula we can plug numbers into to get a definite answer. We first describe a simple way to value options, known as the binomial model. We then introduce the Black–Scholes formula for valuing options. Finally, we provide a checklist showing how these two methods can be used to solve a number of practical option problems.

The most efficient way to value most options is to use a computer. But in this chapter we will work through some simple examples by hand. We do so because unless you understand the basic principles behind option valuation, you are likely to make mistakes in setting up an option problem and you won't know how to interpret the computer's answer and explain it to others.

In the last chapter we looked at the put and call options on Google stock. In this chapter we stick with that example and show you how to value the Google options. But remember *why* you need to understand option valuation. It is not to make a quick buck trading on an options exchange. It is because many capital budgeting and financing decisions have options embedded in them.

● ● ● ● ●

17-1 A Simple Option-Valuation Model

Why Discounted Cash Flow Won't Work for Options

For many years economists searched for a practical formula to value options until Fischer Black and Myron Scholes finally hit upon the solution. Later we will show you what they found, but first we should explain why the search was so difficult.

Our standard procedure for valuing an asset is to (1) figure out expected cash flows and (2) discount them at the opportunity cost of capital. Unfortunately, this is not practical for options. The first step is messy but feasible, but finding *the* opportunity cost of capital is impossible, because the risk of an option changes every time the stock price moves.

When you buy a call, you are taking a position in the stock but putting up less of your own money than if you had bought the stock directly. Thus, an option is always riskier than the underlying stock. It has a higher beta and a higher standard deviation of return.

How much riskier the option is depends on the stock price relative to the exercise price. A call option that is in the money (stock price greater than exercise price) is safer than one that is out of the money (stock price less than exercise price). Thus a stock price increase raises the option's price *and* reduces its risk. When the stock price falls, the option's price falls *and* its risk increases. That is why the expected rate of return investors demand from an option changes day by day, or hour by hour, every time the stock price moves.

We repeat the general rule: The higher the stock price is relative to the exercise price, the safer the call option is, although the option is always riskier than the stock. The option's risk changes every time the stock price changes.

Constructing Option Equivalents from Common Stocks and Borrowing

If you've digested what we've said so far, you can appreciate why options are hard to value by standard discounted-cash-flow formulas and why a rigorous option-valuation technique eluded economists for many years. The breakthrough came when Black and Scholes exclaimed, "Eureka! We have found it![1] The trick is to set up an *option equivalent* by combining common stock investment and borrowing. The net cost of buying the option equivalent must equal the value of the option."

We'll show you how this works with a simple numerical example. We'll travel back to September 2008 and consider a six-month call option on Google stock with an exercise price of $430. We'll pick a day when Google stock was also trading at $430, so that this option is *at the money*. The short-term, risk-free interest rate was 3% per year, or about 1.5% for six months.

To keep the example as simple as possible, we assume that Google stock can do only two things over the option's six-month life: Either the price will fall by a quarter to $322.5 or rise by one-third to $573.33.

If Google's stock price falls to $322.50, the call option will be worthless, but if the price rises to $573.33, the option will be worth 573.33 − 430 = $143.33. The possible payoffs to the option are therefore:

	Stock Price = $322.50	Stock Price = $573.33
1 call option	$0	$143.33

Now compare these payoffs with what you would get if you bought 4/7 Google shares and borrowed $181.56 from the bank:[2]

	Stock Price = $322.50	Stock Price = $573.33
4/7 shares	$184.29	$327.62
Repayment of loan + interest	−184.29	−184.29
Total payoff	$ 0	$143.33

---

[1] We do not know whether Black and Scholes, like Archimedes, were sitting in bathtubs at the time.

[2] The amount that you need to borrow from the bank is simply the present value of the difference between the payoffs from the option and the payoffs from 4/7 shares. In our example, amount borrowed = ((4/7) × 322.50 − 0)/1.015 = ((4/7) × 573.33 − 143.33)/1.015 = $181.56.

Notice that the payoffs from the levered investment in the stock are identical to the payoffs from the call option. Therefore, the law of one price tells us that both investments must have the same value:

$$\text{Value of call} = \text{value of } (4/7) \text{ shares} - \$181.56 \text{ bank loan}$$
$$= 430 \times (4/7) - 181.56 = 64.15$$

Presto! You've valued a call option.

To value the Google option, we borrowed money and bought stock in such a way that we exactly replicated the payoff from a call option. This is called a **replicating portfolio.** The number of shares needed to replicate one call is called the **hedge ratio** or **option delta.** In our Google example one call is replicated by a levered position in 4/7 shares. The option delta is, therefore, 4/7, or about .571.

How did we know that Google's call option was equivalent to a levered position in 4/7 shares? We used a simple formula that says:

$$\text{Option delta} = \frac{\text{spread of possible option prices}}{\text{spread of possible share prices}} = \frac{143.33 - 0}{573.33 - 322.50} = \frac{143.33}{250.83} = \frac{4}{7}$$

You have learned not only to value a simple option but also that you can replicate an investment in the option by a levered investment in the underlying asset. Thus, if you can't buy or sell a call option on an asset, you can create a homemade option by a replicating strategy—that is, you buy or sell delta shares and borrow or lend the balance.

Risk-Neutral Valuation Notice why the Google call option should sell for $64.15. If the option price is higher than $64.15, you could make a certain profit by buying 4/7 shares of stock, selling a call option, and borrowing $181.56. Similarly, if the option price is less than $64.15, you could make an equally certain profit by selling 4/7 shares, buying a call, and lending the balance. In either case there would be an arbitrage opportunity.[3]

If there's a possible arbitrage profit, everyone scurries to take advantage of it. So when we said that the option price had to be $64.15 or there would be an arbitrage opportunity, we did not have to know anything about investor attitudes to risk. The option price cannot depend on whether investors detest risk or do not care a jot.

This suggests an alternative way to value the option. We can *pretend* that all investors are *indifferent* about risk, work out the expected future value of the option in such a world, and discount it back at the risk-free interest rate to give the current value. Let us check that this method gives the same answer.

If investors are indifferent to risk, the expected return on the stock must be equal to the risk-free rate of interest:

$$\text{Expected return on Google stock} = 1.5\% \text{ per six months}$$

We know that Google stock can either rise by 33.3% to $573.33 or fall by 25% to $322.50. We can, therefore, calculate the probability of a price rise in our hypothetical risk-neutral world:

$$\text{Expected return} = [\text{probability of rise} \times 33.3]$$
$$+ [(1 - \text{probability of rise}) \times (-25)]$$
$$= 1.5\%$$

Therefore,

$$\text{Probability of rise} = .4543, \text{ or } 45.43\%$$

---

[3] Of course, you don't get seriously rich by dealing in 4/7 shares. But if you multiply each of our transactions by a million, it begins to look like real money.

Notice that this is *not* the *true* probability that Google stock will rise. Since investors dislike risk, they will almost surely require a higher expected return than the risk-free interest rate from Google stock. Therefore the true probability is greater than .4543.

The general formula for calculating the risk-neutral probability of a rise in value is:

$$p = \frac{\text{interest rate} - \text{downside change}}{\text{upside change} - \text{downside change}}$$

In the case of Google stock:

$$p = \frac{.015 - (-.25)}{.333 - (-.25)} = .4543$$

We know that if the stock price rises, the call option will be worth $143.33; if it falls, the call will be worth nothing. Therefore, if investors are risk-neutral, the expected value of the call option is:

$$[\text{Probability of rise} \times 143.33] + [(1 - \text{probability of rise}) \times 0]$$
$$= (.4543 \times 143.33) + (.5457 \times 0)$$
$$= \$65.11$$

And the *current* value of the call is:

$$\frac{\text{Expected future value}}{1 + \text{interest rate}} = \frac{65.11}{1.015} = \$64.15$$

Exactly the same answer that we got earlier!

We now have two ways to calculate the value of an option:

1. Find the combination of stock and loan that replicates an investment in the option. Since the two strategies give identical payoffs in the future, they must sell for the same price today.

2. Pretend that investors do not care about risk, so that the expected return on the stock is equal to the interest rate. Calculate the expected future value of the option in this hypothetical *risk-neutral* world and discount it at the risk-free interest rate. This idea may seem familiar to you. In Chapter 9 we showed how you can value an investment either by discounting the expected cash flows at a risk-adjusted discount rate or by adjusting the expected cash flows for risk and then discounting these *certainty-equivalent* flows at the risk-free interest rate. We have just used this second method to value the Google option. The certainty-equivalent cash flows on the stock and option are the cash flows that would be expected in a risk-neutral world.

Valuing the Google Put Option

Valuing the Google call option may well have seemed like pulling a rabbit out of a hat. To give you a second chance to watch how it is done, we will use the same method to value another option—this time, the six-month Google put option with a $430 exercise price.[4] We continue to assume that the stock price will either rise to $573.33 or fall to $322.50.

If Google's stock price rises to $573.33, the option to sell for $430 will be worthless. If the price falls to $322.50, the put option will be worth $430 - 322.50 = $107.50. Thus the payoffs to the put are:

	Stock Price = $322.50	Stock Price = $573.33
1 put option	$107.50	$0

---

[4] When valuing *American* put options, you need to recognize the possibility that it will pay to exercise early. We discuss this complication later in the chapter, but it is unimportant for valuing the Google put and we ignore it here.

We start by calculating the option delta using the formula that we presented above:[5]

$$\text{Option delta} = \frac{\text{spread of possible option prices}}{\text{spread of possible stock prices}} = \frac{0 - 107.50}{573.33 - 322.50}$$

$$= -\frac{3}{7} \text{ or about } -.429$$

Notice that the delta of a put option is always negative; that is, you need to *sell* delta shares of stock to replicate the put. In the case of the Google put you can replicate the option payoffs by *selling* 3/7 Google shares and *lending* $242.09. Since you have sold the share short, you will need to lay out money at the end of six months to buy it back, but you will have money coming in from the loan. Your net payoffs are exactly the same as the payoffs you would get if you bought the put option:

	Stock Price = $322.50	Stock Price = $573.33
Sale of 3/7 shares	− $138.22	− $245.72
Repayment of loan + interest	+245.72	+245.72
Total payoff	$107.50	$ 0

Since the two investments have the same payoffs, they must have the same value:

$$\text{Value of put} = -(3/7) \text{ shares} + \$242.09 \text{ bank loan}$$
$$= -(3/7) \times 430 + \$242.09 = \$57.82$$

Valuing the Put Option by the Risk-Neutral Method   Valuing the Google put option with the risk-neutral method is a cinch. We already know that the probability of a rise in the stock price is .4543. Therefore the expected value of the put option in a risk-neutral world is:

$$[\text{Probability of rise} \times 0] + [(1 - \text{probability of rise}) \times 107.50]$$
$$= (.4543 \times 0) + (.5457 \times 107.50)$$
$$= \$58.66$$

And therefore the *current* value of the put is:

$$\frac{\text{Expected future value}}{1 + \text{interest rate}} = \frac{58.66}{1.015} = \$57.80$$

The Relationship between Call and Put Prices   We pointed out earlier that for European options there is a simple relationship between the value of the call and that of the put.[6]

$$\text{Value of put} = \text{value of call} + \text{present value of exercise price} - \text{share price}$$

Since we had already calculated the value of the Google call, we could also have used this relationship to find the value of the put:

$$\text{Value of put} = 64.15 + \frac{430}{1.015} - 430 = \$57.80$$

Everything checks.

---

[5] The delta of a put option is always equal to the delta of a call option with the same exercise price minus one. In our example, delta of put = (4/7) − 1 = − 3/7.

[6] *Reminder:* This formula applies only when the two options have the same exercise price and exercise date.

17-2 The Binomial Method for Valuing Options

The essential trick in pricing any option is to set up a package of investments in the stock and the loan that will exactly replicate the payoffs from the option. If we can price the stock and the loan, then we can also price the option. Equivalently, we can pretend that investors are risk-neutral, calculate the expected payoff on the option in this fictitious risk-neutral world, and discount by the rate of interest to find the option's present value.

These *concepts* are completely general, but there are several ways to find the replicating package of investments. The example in the last section used a simplified version of what is known as the **binomial method.** The method starts by reducing the possible changes in next period's stock price to two, an "up" move and a "down" move. This assumption that there are just two possible prices for Google stock at the end of six months is clearly fanciful.

We could make the Google problem a trifle more realistic by assuming that there are two possible price changes in each three-month period. This would give a wider variety of six-month prices. And there is no reason to stop at three-month periods. We could go on to take shorter and shorter intervals, with each interval showing two possible changes in Google's stock price and giving an even wider selection of six-month prices.

This is illustrated in Figure 17.1. The top diagram shows our starting assumption: just two possible prices at the end of six months. Moving down, you can see what happens when there are two possible price changes every three months. This gives three possible stock prices when the option matures. In Figure 17.1(*c*) we have gone on to divide the six-month period into 26 weekly periods, in each of which the price can make one of two small moves. The distribution of prices at the end of six months is now looking much more realistic.

We could continue in this way to chop the period into shorter and shorter intervals, until eventually we would reach a situation in which the stock price is changing continuously and there is a continuum of possible future stock prices.

Example: The Two-Stage Binomial Method

Dividing the period into shorter intervals doesn't alter the basic method for valuing a call option. We can still replicate the call by a levered investment in the stock, but we need to adjust the degree of leverage at each stage. We demonstrate first with our simple two-stage case in Figure 17.1(*b*). Then we work up to the situation where the stock price is changing continuously.

Figure 17.2 is taken from Figure 17.1(*b*) and shows the possible prices of Google stock, assuming that in each three-month period the price will either rise by 22.56% or fall by 18.41%.[7] We show in parentheses the possible values at maturity of a six-month call option with an exercise price of $430. For example, if Google's stock price turns out to be $286.27 in month 6, the call option will be worthless; at the other extreme, if the stock value is $645.90, the call will be worth $645.90 − $430 = $215.90. We haven't worked out yet what the option will be worth *before* maturity, so we just put question marks there for now.

Option Value in Month 3 To find the value of Google's option today, we start by working out its possible values in month 3 and then work back to the present. Suppose that at the end of three months the stock price is $527.00. In this case investors know that, when the option finally matures in month 6, the stock price will be either $430 or

---

[7] We explain shortly why we picked these figures.

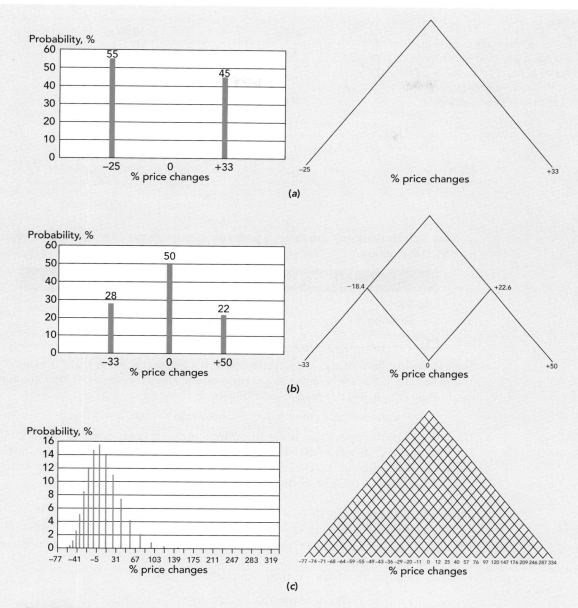

▶ **FIGURE 17.1**

This figure shows the possible six-month price changes for Google stock assuming that the stock makes a single up or down move each six months (Fig. 17.1[a]), 2 moves, one every three months (Fig. 17.1[b]), or 26 moves, one every week (Fig. 17.1[c]). Beside each tree we show a histogram of the possible six-month price changes, assuming investors are risk-neutral.

$645.89, and the corresponding option price will be $0 or $215.89. We can therefore use our simple formula to find how many shares we need to buy in month 3 to replicate the option:

$$\text{Option delta} = \frac{\text{spread of possible option prices}}{\text{spread of possible stock prices}} = \frac{215.89 - 0}{645.89 - 430} = 1.0$$

▶ FIGURE 17.2

Present and possible future prices of Google stock assuming that in each three-month period the price will either rise by 22.6% or fall by 18.4%. Figures in parentheses show the corresponding values of a six-month call option with an exercise price of $430.

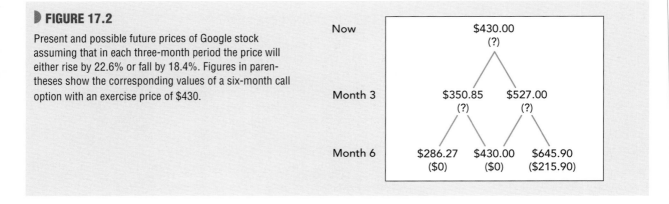

Now we can construct a leveraged position in delta shares that would give identical payoffs to the option:

	Month 6 Stock Price = $430	Month 6 Stock Price = $645.90
Buy 1.0 shares	$430	$645.90
Borrow PV(430)	−430	−430
Total payoff	$ 0	$215.90

Since this portfolio provides identical payoffs to the option, we know that the value of the option in month 3 must be equal to the price of one share less the $430 loan discounted for three months at 3% per year, about .75% for three months:

$$\text{Value of call in month 3} = \$527.00 - \$430/1.0075 = \$100.20$$

Therefore, if the share price rises in the first three months, the option will be worth $100.20. But what if the share price falls to $350.85? In that case the most that you can hope for is that the share price will recover to $430. Therefore the option is bound to be worthless when it matures and must be worthless at month 3.

Option Value Today We can now get rid of two of the question marks in Figure 17.2. Figure 17.3 shows that if the stock price in month 3 is $527.00, the option value is $100.20, and if the stock price is $350.85, the option value is zero. It only remains to work back to the option value today.

We again begin by calculating the option delta:

$$\text{Option delta} = \frac{\text{spread of possible option prices}}{\text{spread of possible stock prices}} = \frac{100.20 - 0}{527.00 - 350.85} = .5688$$

We can now find the leveraged position in delta shares that would give identical payoffs to the option:

	Month 3 Stock Price = $350.85	Month 3 Stock Price = $527.00
Buy .5688 shares	$199.56	$299.76
Borrow PV(199.56)	−199.56	−199.56
Total payoff	$ 0	$100.20

The value of the Google option today is equal to the value of this leveraged position:

$$\text{PV option} = .5688 \times \text{share price} - \text{PV}(\$199.56)$$
$$= .5688 \times \$430 - \$199.56/1.0075 = \$46.51$$

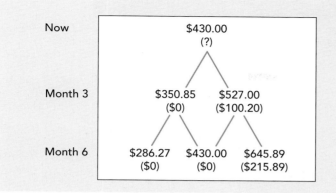

Now $430.00 (?)

Month 3 $350.85 ($0) $527.00 ($100.20)

Month 6 $286.27 ($0) $430.00 ($0) $645.89 ($215.89)

▶ **FIGURE 17.3**

Present and possible future prices of Google stock. Figures in parentheses show the corresponding values of a six-month call option with an exercise price of $430.

The General Binomial Method

Moving to two steps when valuing the Google call probably added extra realism. But there is no reason to stop there. We could go on, as in Figure 17.1, to chop the period into smaller and smaller intervals. We could still use the binomial method to work back from the final date to the present. Of course, it would be tedious to do the calculations by hand, but simple to do so with a computer.

Since a stock can usually take on an almost limitless number of future values, the binomial method gives a more realistic and accurate measure of the option's value if we work with a large number of subperiods. But that raises an important question. How do we pick sensible figures for the up and down changes in value? For example, why did we pick figures of +22.6% and −18.4% when we revalued Google's option with two subperiods? Fortunately, there is a neat little formula that relates the up and down changes to the standard deviation of stock returns:

$$1 + \text{upside change} = u = e^{\sigma\sqrt{h}}$$
$$1 + \text{downside change} = d = 1/u$$

where,

e = base for natural logarithms = 2.718
σ = standard deviation of (continuously compounded) stock returns
h = interval as fraction of a year

When we said that Google's stock price could either rise by 33.3% or fall by 25% over six months ($h = .5$), our figures were consistent with a figure of 40.68% for the standard deviation of annual returns:[8]

$$1 + \text{upside change(6-month interval)} = u = e^{.4068\sqrt{.5}} = 1.333$$
$$1 + \text{downside change} = d = 1/u = 1/1.333 = .75$$

To work out the equivalent upside and downside changes when we divide the period into two three-month intervals ($h = .25$), we use the same formula:

$$1 + \text{upside change(3-month interval)} = u = e^{.4068\sqrt{.25}} = 1.226$$
$$1 + \text{downside change} = d = 1/u = 1/1.226 = .816$$

---

[8] To find the standard deviation given u, we turn the formula around:

$$\sigma = \log(u)/\sqrt{h}$$

where log = natural logarithm. In our example:

$$\sigma = \log(1.333)/\sqrt{.5} = .2877/\sqrt{.5} = .4068$$

TABLE 17.1 As the number of steps is increased, you must adjust the range of possible changes in the value of the asset to keep the same standard deviation. But you will get increasingly close to the Black–Scholes value of the Google call option.

(*Note:* The standard deviation is $\sigma = .4068$)

	Change per Interval (%)		
Number of Steps	**Upside**	**Downside**	**Estimated Option Value**
1	+33.3	−25.0	$64.15
2	+22.6	−18.4	46.49
6	+12.5	−11.1	50.05
26	+5.8	−5.5	51.57
		Black–Scholes value =	52.04

The center columns in Table 17.1 show the equivalent up and down moves in the value of the firm if we chop the period into six monthly or 26 weekly periods, and the final column shows the effect on the estimated option value. (We explain the Black–Scholes value shortly.)

The Binomial Method and Decision Trees

Calculating option values by the binomial method is basically a process of solving decision trees. You start at some future date and work back through the tree to the present. Eventually the possible cash flows generated by future events and actions are folded back to a present value.

Is the binomial method *merely* another application of decision trees, a tool of analysis that you learned about in Chapter 10? The answer is no, for at least two reasons. First, option pricing theory is absolutely essential for discounting within decision trees. Discounting expected cash flows doesn't work within decision trees for the same reason that it doesn't work for puts and calls. As we pointed out in Section 17–1, there is no single, constant discount rate for options because the risk of the option changes as time and the price of the underlying asset change. There is no single discount rate inside a decision tree, because if the tree contains meaningful future decisions, it also contains options. The market value of the future cash flows described by the decision tree has to be calculated by option pricing methods.

Second, option theory gives a simple, powerful framework for describing complex decision trees. For example, suppose that you have the option to abandon an investment. The complete decision tree would overflow the largest classroom chalkboard. But now that you know about options, the opportunity to abandon can be summarized as "an American put." Of course, not all real problems have such easy option analogies, but we can often approximate complex decision trees by some simple package of assets and options. A custom decision tree may get closer to reality, but the time and expense may not be worth it. Most men buy their suits off the rack even though a custom-made Armani suit would fit better and look nicer.

17-3 The Black–Scholes Formula

Look back at Figure 17.1, which showed what happens to the distribution of possible Google stock price changes as we divide the option's life into a larger and larger number of increasingly small subperiods. You can see that the distribution of price changes becomes increasingly smooth.

▶ **FIGURE 17.4**

As the option's life is divided into more and more subperiods, the distribution of possible stock price changes approaches a lognormal distribution.

Percent price changes

If we continued to chop up the option's life in this way, we would eventually reach the situation shown in Figure 17.4, where there is a continuum of possible stock price changes at maturity. Figure 17.4 is an example of a lognormal distribution. The lognormal distribution is often used to summarize the probability of different stock price changes.[9] It has a number of good commonsense features. For example, it recognizes the fact that the stock price can never fall by more than 100%, but that there is some, perhaps small, chance that it could rise by much more than 100%.

Subdividing the option life into indefinitely small slices does not affect the principle of option valuation. We could still replicate the call option by a levered investment in the stock, but we would need to adjust the degree of leverage continuously as time went by. Calculating option value when there is an infinite number of subperiods may sound a hopeless task. Fortunately, Black and Scholes derived a formula that does the trick.[10] It is an unpleasant-looking formula, but on closer acquaintance you will find it exceptionally elegant and useful. The formula is:

$$\text{Value of call option} = [\text{delta} \times \text{share price}] - [\text{bank loan}]$$

$$[N(d_1) \times P] - [N(d_2) \times \text{PV(EX)}]$$

where,

$$d_1 = \frac{\log[P/\text{PV(EX)}]}{\sigma \sqrt{t}} + \frac{\sigma \sqrt{t}}{2}$$

$$d_2 = d_1 - \sigma \sqrt{t}$$

$N(d)$ = cumulative normal probability density function[11]

EX = exercise price of option; PV(EX) is calculated by discounting at the risk-free interest rate r_f

[9] When we first looked at the distribution of stock price changes in Chapter 8, we depicted these changes as normally distributed. We pointed out at the time that this is an acceptable approximation for very short intervals, but the distribution of changes over longer intervals is better approximated by the lognormal.

[10] The pioneering articles on options are F. Black and M. Scholes, "The Pricing of Options and Corporate Liabilities," *Journal of Political Economy* 81 (May–June 1973), pp. 637–654; and R. C. Merton, "Theory of Rational Option Pricing," *Bell Journal of Economics and Management Science* 4 (Spring 1973), pp. 141–183.

[11] That is, $N(d)$ is the probability that a normally distributed random variable $\tilde{x}$ will be less than or equal to d. $N(d_1)$ in the Black–Scholes formula is the option delta. Thus the formula tells us that the value of a call is equal to an investment of $N(d_1)$ in the common stock less borrowing of $N(d_2) \times \text{PV(EX)}$.

t = number of periods to exercise date

P = price of stock now

σ = standard deviation per period of (continuously compounded) rate of return on stock

Notice that the value of the call in the Black–Scholes formula has the same properties that we identified earlier. It increases with the level of the stock price P and decreases with the present value of the exercise price PV(EX), which in turn depends on the interest rate and time to maturity. It also increases with the time to maturity and the stock's variability ($\sigma \sqrt{t}$).

To derive their formula Black and Scholes assumed that there is a continuum of stock prices, and therefore to replicate an option investors must continuously adjust their holding in the stock.[12] Of course this is not literally possible, but even so the formula performs remarkably well in the real world, where stocks trade only intermittently and prices jump from one level to another. The Black–Scholes model has also proved very flexible; it can be adapted to value options on a variety of assets such as foreign currencies, bonds, and commodities. It is not surprising, therefore, that it has been extremely influential and has become the standard model for valuing options. Every day dealers on the options exchanges use this formula to make huge trades. These dealers are not for the most part trained in the formula's mathematical derivation; they just use a computer or a specially programmed calculator to find the value of the option.

Using the Black–Scholes Formula

The Black–Scholes formula may look difficult, but it is very straightforward to apply. Let us practice using it to value the Google call.

Here are the data that you need:

- Price of stock now = P = 430
- Exercise price = EX = 430
- Standard deviation of continuously compounded annual returns = σ = .4068
- Years to maturity = t = .5
- Interest rate per annum = r_f = 3% (or about 1.5% for six months)[13]

Remember that the Black–Scholes formula for the value of a call is

$$[N(d_1) \times P] - [N(d_2) \times \text{PV(EX)}]$$

where,

$$d_1 = \log[P/\text{PV(EX)}]/\sigma \sqrt{t} + \sigma \sqrt{t}/2$$
$$d_2 = d_1 - \sigma \sqrt{t}$$
$$N(d) = \text{cumulative normal probability function}$$

There are three steps to using the formula to value the Google call:

---

[12] The important assumptions of the Black–Scholes formula are that (a) the price of the underlying asset follows a lognormal random walk, (b) investors can adjust their hedge continuously and costlessly, (c) the risk-free rate is known, and (d) the underlying asset does not pay dividends.

[13] More precisely, an annually compounded interest rate of 3% is equivalent to a six-month rate of $1.03^{.5} - 1 = .014889$, or 1.4889%. Thus PV(EX) = 430/1.014889 = $423.69.

When valuing options, it is more common to use continuously compounded rates (see Section 2–4). If the annually compounded rate is 3%, the equivalent continuously compounded rate is 2.956%. (The natural log of 1.03 is .02956 and $e^{.02956} = 1.03$.) Using continuous compounding, PV(EX) = $430 \times e^{-.5 \times .02956}$ = $423.69.

If both methods give the same answer, why do we bother to mention the subject here? It is simply because most computer programs for valuing options call for a continuously compounded rate. If you enter an annually compounded rate by mistake, the error will usually be small, but you can waste a lot of time trying to trace it.

Step 1 Calculate d_1 and d_2. This is just a matter of plugging numbers into the formula (noting that "log" means *natural* log):

$$d_1 = \log[P/PV(EX)]/\sigma\sqrt{t} + \sigma\sqrt{t}/2$$
$$= \log[430/(430/1.015)]/(.4068 \times \sqrt{.5}) + .4068 \times \sqrt{.5}/2$$
$$= .1956$$
$$d_2 = d_1 - \sigma\sqrt{t} = .1956 - .4068 \times \sqrt{.5} = -.0921$$

Step 2 Find $N(d_1)$ and $N(d_2)$. $N(d_1)$ is the probability that a normally distributed variable will be less than d_1 standard deviations above the mean. If d_1 is large, $N(d_1)$ is close to 1.0 (i.e., you can be almost certain that the variable will be less than d_1 standard deviations above the mean). If d_1 is zero, $N(d_1)$ is .5 (i.e., there is a 50% chance that a normally distributed variable will be below the average).

The simplest way to find $N(d_1)$ is to use the Excel function NORMSDIST. For example, if you enter NORMSDIST(.1956) into an Excel spreadsheet, you will see that there is a .5775 probability that a normally distributed variable will be less than .1956 standard deviations above the mean. Alternatively, you can use a set of normal probability tables such as the present value tables (Appendix Table 6) located on the book Web site at **www.mhhe. com/bma**.

Again you can use the Excel function to find $N(d_2)$. If you enter NORMSDIST(−.0921) into an Excel spreadsheet, you should get the answer .4633. In other words, there is a probability of .4633 that a normally distributed variable will be less than .0921 standard deviations *below* the mean. Alternatively, if you use Appendix Table 6 (again located at **www. mhhe.com/bma** under the Present Value Tables heading), you need to look up the value for +.0921 and subtract it from 1.0:

$$N(d_2) = N(-.0921) = 1 - N(+.0921)$$
$$= 1 - .5367 = .4633$$

Step 3 Plug these numbers into the Black–Scholes formula. You can now calculate the value of the Google call:

$$[\text{Delta} \times \text{price}] - [\text{bank loan}]$$
$$= [N(d_1) \times P] - [N(d_2) \times PV(EX)]$$
$$= [.5775 \times 430] - [.4633 \times 430/1.015] = 248.32 - 196.29 = 52.04$$

In other words, you can replicate the Google call option by investing $248.32 in the company's stock and borrowing $196.29. Subsequently, as time passes and the stock price changes, you may need to borrow a little more to invest in the stock or you may need to sell some of your stock to reduce your borrowing.

The Risk of an Option

How risky is the Google call option? We have seen that you can exactly replicate a call by a combination of risk-free borrowing and an investment in the stock. So the risk of the option must be the same as the risk of this replicating portfolio. We know that the beta of any port-folio is simply a weighted average of the betas of the separate holdings. So the risk of the option is just a weighted average of the betas of the investments in the loan and the stock.

On past evidence the beta of Google stock is $\beta_{\text{stock}} = 1.27$; the beta of a risk-free loan is $\beta_{\text{loan}} = 0$. You are investing $248.32 in the stock and −$196.29 in the loan. (Notice that the investment in the loan is negative—you are *borrowing* money.) Therefore the beta of the option is $\beta_{\text{option}} = (-196.29 \times 0 + 248.32 \times 1.27)/(-196.29 + 248.32) = 6.07$. Notice that, because a call option is equivalent to a levered position in the stock, it is always riskier

FIGURE 17.5

The curved line shows how the value of the Google call option changes as the price of Google stock changes.

Visit us at
www.mhhe.com/bma

than the stock itself. In Google's case the option is nearly five times as risky as the stock. As time passes and the price of Google stock changes, the risk of the option will also change.

Some More Practice Suppose you repeat the calculations for the Google call for a wide range of stock prices. The result is shown in Figure 17.5. You can see that the option values lie along an upward-sloping curve that starts its travels in the bottom left-hand corner of the diagram. As the stock price increases, the option value rises and gradually becomes parallel to the lower bound for the option value. This is exactly the shape we deduced in Chapter 16 (see Figure 16.10).

The height of this curve of course depends on risk and time to maturity. For example, if the risk of Google stock had suddenly decreased, the curve shown in Figure 17.5 would drop at every possible stock price.

The Black–Scholes Formula and the Binomial Method

Look back at Table 17.1 where we used the binomial method to calculate the value of the Google call. Notice that, as the number of intervals is increased, the values that you obtain from the binomial method begin to snuggle up to the Black–Scholes value of $52.04.

The Black–Scholes formula recognizes a continuum of possible outcomes. This is usually more realistic than the limited number of outcomes assumed in the binomial method. The formula is also more accurate and quicker to use than the binomial method. So why use the binomial method at all? The answer is that there are many circumstances in which you cannot use the Black–Scholes formula but the binomial method will still give you a good measure of the option's value. We will look at several such cases in Section 17-5.

17-4 Black–Scholes in Action

To illustrate the principles of option valuation, we focused on the example of Google's options. But financial managers turn to the Black–Scholes model to estimate the value of a variety of different options. Here are five examples.

Executive Stock Options

The 2007 winner in *Forbes*'s annual list of the most highly paid executives was Larry Ellison, the CEO of Oracle Corporation. His salary was just $1 million, but he also pocketed another $182 million from the exercise of stock options.

The example highlights that executive stock options are often an important part of compensation. For many years companies were able to avoid reporting the cost of these options in their annual statements. However, they must now treat options as an expense just like salaries and wages, so they need to estimate the value of all new options that they have granted. For example, Oracle's financial statements show that in fiscal 2008 the company issued a total of 69 million options with an average life of five years and an exercise price of $20.49. Oracle calculated that the average value of these options was $7.53. How did it come up with this figure? It just used the Black–Scholes model assuming a standard deviation of 29% and an interest rate of 4.6%.[14]

Some companies have disguised how much their management is paid by backdating the grant of an option. Suppose, for example, that a firm's stock price has risen from $20 to $40. At that point the firm awards its CEO options exercisable at $20. That is generous but not illegal. However, if the firm pretends that the options were *actually* awarded when the stock price was $20 and values them on that basis, it will substantially understate the CEO's compensation.[15] The nearby box discusses the backdating scandal.

Speaking of executive stock options, we can now use the Black–Scholes formula to value the option packages you were offered in Section 16–3 (see Table 16.3). Table 17.2 calculates the value of the options from the safe-and-stodgy Establishment Industries at $5.26 each. The options from risky-and-glamorous Digital Organics are worth $7.40 each. Congratulations.

Warrants

When Owens Corning emerged from bankruptcy in 2006, the debtholders became the sole owners of the company. But the old stockholders were not left entirely empty-handed. They were given warrants to buy the new common stock at any point in the next seven

	Establishment Industries	Digital Organics
Stock price (P)	$22	$22
Exercise price (EX)	$25	$25
Interest rate (r_f)	.04	.04
Maturity in years (t)	5	5
Standard deviation (σ)	.24	.36
$d_1 = \log[P/PV(EX)]/\sigma\sqrt{t} + \sigma\sqrt{t}/2$	0.3955	0.4873
$d_2 = d_1 - \sigma\sqrt{t}$	−0.1411	−0.3177
Call value = $[N(d_1) \times P] - [N(d_2) \times PV(EX)]$	$5.26	$7.40

▶ **TABLE 17.2**

Using the Black–Scholes formula to value the executive stock options for Establishment Industries and Digital Organics (see Table 16.3).

Visit us at www.mhhe.com/bma

---

[14] Many of the recipients of these options may not have agreed with Oracle's valuation. First, the options were less valuable to their owners if they created substantial undiversifiable risk. Second, if the holders planned to quit the company in the next few years, they were liable to forfeit the options. For a discussion of these issues see J. I. Bulow and J. B. Shoven, "Accounting for Stock Options," *Journal of Economic Perspectives* 19 (Fall 2005), pp. 115–134.

[15] Until 2005 companies were obliged to record as an expense any difference between the stock price when the options were granted and the exercise price. Thus, as long as the options were granted at-the-money (exercise price equals stock price), the company was not obliged to show any expense.

The Perfect Payday[*]

On an October day in 1999 the shares of the giant insurer United Health Group sank to their lowest level of the year. That may have been bad news for investors but it was good news for William McGuire, the chief executive, for the company granted him options to buy the stock in the future at that low price. If the options had been dated a month later when the stock price was 40% higher, those options would have been far less valuable. Lucky coincidence? Possibly, but the following year also Mr. McGuire was granted options on the day that the stock price hit the year's low. And in 2001 the grant came near the bottom of a sharp dip in the stock price.

Over the following years evidence began to accumulate that in other companies too executives were being granted options at unusually favorable prices. It seemed that these firms were using hindsight to choose the date on which the options were granted. Such backdating is not necessarily illegal, but most options are granted under a shareholder-approved plan that typically requires the exercise price to be equal to the fair market value of the company's stock

at the time of the grant. Also backdating may result in an underestimate of the amount of compensation paid and therefore to a misstatement of earnings and an underpayment of taxes.

Investigations by the SEC and prosecutions by disgruntled shareholders led to the resignation of a number of directors and officers of major corporations that were found to have backdated options. William McGuire was among those who fell on their sword. He subsequently agreed to pay $39 million and forfeit another 3.7 million compensatory stock options to settle a class-action suit headed by the California Public Employee Retirement System (Calpers).

---

[*]"The Perfect Payday" is the title of an article in *The Wall Street Journal* that drew attention to the practice of backdating. See C. Forelle and J. Bandler, "The Perfect Payday; Some CEOs Reap Millions by Landing Stock Options When They Are Most Valuable; Luck—or Something Else?" *The Wall Street Journal*, March 18, 2006, p. A1. Earlier evidence of backdating appeared in D. Yermack, "Good Timing: CEO Stock Option Awards and Company News Announcements," *Journal of Finance* 52 (1997), pp. 449–476; and in E. Lie, "On the Timing of CEO Stock Option Awards," *Management Science* 51 (2005), pp. 802–812.

---

years for $45.25 a share. Because the stock in the restructured firm was worth about $30 a share, the stock needed to appreciate by 50% before the warrants would be worth exercising. However, this option to buy Owens Corning stock was clearly valuable and shortly after the warrants started trading they were selling for $6 each. You can be sure that before shareholders were handed this bone, all the parties calculated the value of the warrants under different assumptions about the stock's volatility. The Black–Scholes model is tailor-made for this purpose.

Portfolio Insurance

Your company's pension fund owns an $800 million diversified portfolio of common stocks that moves closely in line with the market index. The pension fund is currently fully funded, but you are concerned that if it falls by more than 20% it will start to be underfunded. Suppose that your bank offers to insure you for one year against this possibility. What would you be prepared to pay for this insurance? Think back to Section 16–2 (Figure 16.6), where we showed that you can shield against a fall in asset prices by buying a protective put option. In the present case the bank would be selling you a one-year put option on U.S. stock prices with an exercise price 20% below their current level. You can get the value of that option in two steps. First use the Black–Scholes formula to value a call with the same exercise price and maturity. Then back out the put value from put–call parity. (You will have to adjust for dividends, but we'll leave that to the next section.)

The Fear Index[*]

▶ The Market Volatility Index or VIX measures the volatility that is implied by near-term Standard & Poor's 500 Index options and is therefore an estimate of expected *future* market volatility over the next 30 calendar days. Implied market volatilities have been calculated by the Chicago Board Options Exchange (CBOE) since January 1986, though in its current form the VIX dates back only to 2003.

Investors regularly trade volatility. They do so by buying or selling VIX futures and options contracts. Since these were introduced by the Chicago Board Options Exchange, combined trading activity in the two contracts has grown to more than 100,000 contracts per day, making them two of the most successful innovations ever introduced by the exchange.

Because VIX measures investor uncertainty, it has been dubbed the "fear index." The market for index options tends to be dominated by equity investors who buy index puts when they are concerned about a potential drop in the stock market. Any subsequent decline in the value of their portfolio is then offset by the increase in the value of the put option. The more

that investors demand such insurance, the higher the price of index put options. Thus VIX is an indicator that reflects the price of portfolio insurance.

Between January 1986 and April 2009 the VIX has averaged 20.5%, almost identical to the long-term level of market volatility that we cited in Chapter 7. The high point for the index was in October 1987 when the VIX closed the month at 61%,[**] but there have been several other short-lived spikes, for example, at the time of Iraq's invasion of Kuwait and the subsequent response by U.N. forces.

Although the VIX is the most widely quoted measure of volatility, volatility measures are also available for several other U.S. and overseas stock market indexes (such as the FTSE 100 Index in the U.K. and the CAC 40 in France), as well as for gold, oil, and the euro.

---

[*]For a review of the VIX index see R. E. Whaley, "Understanding the VIX," *Journal of Portfolio Management* 35 (Spring 2009), pp. 98–105.

[**]On October 19, 1987 (Black Monday), the VIX closed at 150. Fortunately, the market volatility returned fairly rapidly to less exciting levels.

Calculating Implied Volatilities

So far we have used our option pricing model to calculate the value of an option given the standard deviation of the asset's returns. Sometimes it is useful to turn the problem around and ask what the option price is telling us about the asset's volatility. For example, the Chicago Board Options Exchange trades options on several market indexes. As we write this, the Standard and Poor's 500 index is 890, while a nine-month at-the-money call on the index is priced at 120. If the Black–Scholes formula is correct, then an option value of 120 makes sense only if investors believe that the standard deviation of index returns is about 40% a year.[16]

The Chicago Board Options Exchange regularly publishes the implied volatility on the Standard and Poor's index, which it terms the VIX (see the nearby box). There is an active market in the VIX. For example, suppose you feel that the implied volatility is implausibly low. Then you can "buy" the VIX at the current low price and hope to "sell" it at a profit when implied volatility has increased.

You may be interested to compare the current implied volatility that we calculated earlier with Figure 17.6, which shows past measures of implied volatility for the Standard and Poor's index and for the Nasdaq index (VXN). Notice the sharp increase in investor uncertainty at the height of the credit crunch in 2008. This uncertainty showed up in the price that investors were prepared to pay for options.

---

[16] In calculating the implied volatility we need to allow for the dividends paid on the shares. We explain how to take these into account in the next section.

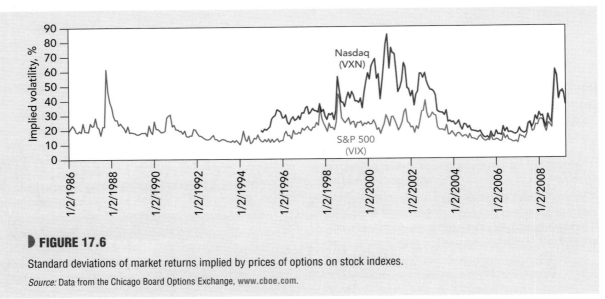

▶ FIGURE 17.6

Standard deviations of market returns implied by prices of options on stock indexes.

Source: Data from the Chicago Board Options Exchange, **www.cboe.com**.

Valuing an Option to Expand

Real options, such as the option to expand or abandon a project, are often complex and can absorb a lot of analytical and computational horsepower. But to give you some feel for how option techniques can be used to evaluate these real options, we will take a step back in time and come to the aid of the chief financial officer (CFO) of Blitzen Computers.

It is 1982. You are assistant to the CFO of Blitzen Computers, an established computer manufacturer casting a profit-hungry eye on the rapidly developing personal computer market. You are helping the CFO evaluate the proposed introduction of the Blitzen Mark I Micro.

The Mark I would involve an investment of $450 million. Unfortunately it can't meet Blitzen's customary 20% hurdle rate and has a $46.5 million negative NPV, contrary to top management's strong gut feeling that Blitzen ought to be in the personal computer market.

The CFO has called you in to discuss the project:

"The Mark I just can't make it on financial grounds," the CFO says. "But we've got to do it for strategic reasons. I'm recommending we go ahead."

"But you're missing the all-important financial advantage, Chief," you reply.

"Don't call me 'Chief.' What financial advantage?"

"If we don't launch the Mark I, it will probably be too expensive to enter the micro market later, when Apple, IBM, and others are firmly established. If we go ahead, we have the opportunity to make follow-on investments that could be extremely profitable. The Mark I provides not only its own cash flows but also a call option to go on with a Mark II micro. That call option is the real source of strategic value."

"So it's strategic value by another name. That doesn't tell me what the Mark II investment's worth. The Mark II could be a great investment or a lousy one—we haven't got a clue."

"That's exactly when a call option is worth the most," you point out perceptively. "The call lets us invest in the Mark II if it's great and walk away from it if it's lousy."

"So what's it worth?"

"Hard to say precisely, but I've done a back-of-the-envelope calculation, which suggests that the value of the option to invest in the Mark II could more than offset the Mark I's $46 million negative NPV. If, as I estimate, the option to invest is worth $55 million, the total value of the Mark I is its own NPV, −$46 million, plus the $55 million option attached to it, or +$9 million."

"You're just overestimating the Mark II," the CFO says gruffly. "It's easy to be optimistic when an investment is three years away."

"No, no," you reply patiently. "The Mark II is expected to be no more profitable than the Mark I—just twice as big and therefore twice as bad in terms of discounted cash flow. I'm forecasting it to have a negative NPV of nearly $100 million. But there's a chance the Mark II could be extremely valuable. The call option allows Blitzen to cash in on those upside outcomes. The chance to cash in could be worth $55 million.

"Of course, the $55 million is only a trial calculation, but it illustrates how valuable follow-on investment opportunities can be, especially when uncertainty is high and the product market is growing rapidly. Moreover, the Mark II will give us a call on the Mark III, the Mark III on the Mark IV, and so on. My calculations don't take subsequent calls into account."

"I think I'm beginning to understand a little bit of corporate strategy," mumbles the CFO.

Tables 17.3 and 17.4 show how you arrived at your estimate of the value of the option to develop the Mark II. Table 17.3 shows that the project involves an initial outlay of $900 million in 1985. The cash inflows start in the following year and have a present value of $807 million in 1985, equivalent to $467 million in 1982. So the real option to invest in the Mark II amounts to a three-year call on an underlying asset worth $467 million, with a $900 million exercise price.

Table 17.4 uses the Black–Scholes model to value this call. The option to invest in the Mark II is "out-of-the-money" because the Mark II's value is far less than the required investment. Nevertheless, the option is worth +$55 million. It is especially valuable because the Mark II is a risky project with lots of upside potential. Of course, it also has lots of downside potential, but this is irrelevant because Blitzen won't invest unless the Mark II's value turns out to be higher than the $900 million investment.

	Year						
	1982	**1985**	**1986**	**1987**	**1988**	**1989**	**1990**
After-tax operating cash flow			+220	+318	+590	+370	0
Increase in working capital			100	200	200	−250	−250
Net cash flow			+120	+118	+390	+620	+250
Present value at 20%	+467	◄———— +807					
		+900					
Forecasted NPV in 1985		−93					

▶ **TABLE 17.3**

Cash flows of the Mark II microcomputer as forecasted from 1982 ($ millions). The Mark II requires double the investment of the Mark I and it is forecasted to be twice as unprofitable with an NPV of −$93 million vs. an NPV of −$46.5 for the Mark I.

Assumptions

1. The decision to invest in the Mark II must be made after 3 years, in 1985.

2. The investment required for the Mark II is $900 million (the exercise price), which is taken as fixed.

3. Forecasted cash inflows of the Mark II have a present value of $807 million in 1985 and $807/(1.2)^2 = $467 million in 1982. With traded call options, you can see the value of the *underlying asset* that the call is written on. Here the option is to buy a nontraded real asset, the Mark II. We can't observe the Mark II's value; we have to use DCF to compute it.

4. The future value of the Mark II's cash flows is highly uncertain. This value evolves as a stock price does with a standard deviation of 35% per year. (Many high-technology stocks have standard deviations higher than 35%.)

5. The annual interest rate is 10%.

Interpretation

The opportunity to invest in the Mark II is a three-year call option ($t = 3$) on an asset worth $467 million ($P = 467$) with an exercise price of $900 million (EX = 900).

Valuation

$$PV(\text{exercise price}) = \frac{900}{(1.1)^3} = 676$$

$$\text{Call value} = [N(d_1) \times P] - [N(d_2) \times PV(EX)]$$

$$d_1 = \log[P/PV(EX)]/\sigma\sqrt{t} + (\sigma\sqrt{t})/2$$

$$= \log[.691]/.606 + .606/2 = -.3075$$

$$d_2 = d_1 - \sigma\sqrt{t} = -.3075 - .606 = -.9317$$

$$N(d_1) = .3792, N(d_2) = .1804$$

$$\text{Call value} = [.3792 \times 467] - [.1804 \times 676] = \$55.1 \text{ million}$$

17-5 Option Values at a Glance

So far our discussion of option values has assumed that investors hold the option until maturity. That is certainly the case with European options that *cannot* be exercised before maturity but may not be the case with American options that can be exercised at any time. Also, when we valued the Google call, we could ignore dividends, because Google did not pay any. Can the same valuation methods be extended to American options and to stocks that pay dividends?

Another question concerns dilution. When investors buy and then exercise traded options, there is no effect on the number of shares issued by the company. But sometimes the company itself may give options to key employees or sell them to investors. When these options are exercised, the number of outstanding shares *does* increase, and therefore the stake of existing stockholders is diluted. Can standard option-valuation models cope with the effect of dilution?

In this section we look at how the possibility of early exercise and dividends affect option value. We hold over the problem of dilution to the Appendix to this chapter.

American Calls—No Dividends   Unlike European options, American options can be exercised anytime. However, we know that in the absence of dividends the value of a call option increases with time to maturity. So, if you exercised an American call option early, you would needlessly reduce its value. Since an American call should not be exercised before maturity, its value is the same as that of a European call, and the Black–Scholes model applies to both options.

European Puts—No Dividends   If we wish to value a European put, we can use the put–call parity formula from Chapter 16:

$$\text{Value of put} = \text{value of call} - \text{value of stock} + PV(\text{exercise price})$$

American Puts—No Dividends   It can sometimes pay to exercise an American put before maturity in order to reinvest the exercise price. For example, suppose that immediately after you buy an American put, the stock price falls to zero. In this case there is no advantage to holding onto the option since it *cannot* become more valuable. It is better to exercise the put and invest the exercise money. Thus an American put is always more valuable than a European put. In our extreme example, the difference is equal to the present value of the interest that you could earn on the exercise price. In all other cases the difference is less.

Because the Black–Scholes formula does not allow for early exercise, it cannot be used to value an American put exactly. But you can use the step-by-step binomial method as long as you check at each point whether the option is worth more dead than alive and then use the higher of the two values.

European Calls and Puts on Dividend-Paying Stocks   Part of the share value comprises the present value of dividends. The option holder is not entitled to dividends. Therefore, when using the Black–Scholes model to value a European option on a dividend-paying stock, you should reduce the price of the stock by the present value of the dividends to be paid before the option's maturity.

Dividends don't always come with a big label attached, so look out for instances where the asset holder gets a benefit and the option holder does not. For example, when you buy foreign currency, you can invest it to earn interest; but if you own an option to buy foreign currency, you miss out on this income. Therefore, when valuing an option to buy foreign currency, you need to deduct the present value of this foreign interest from the current price of the currency.[17]

American Calls on Dividend-Paying Stocks   We have seen that, when the stock does not pay dividends, an American call option is *always* worth more alive than dead. By holding onto the option, you not only keep your option open but also earn interest on the exercise money. Even when there are dividends, you should never exercise early if the dividend you gain is less than the interest you lose by having to pay the exercise price early. However, if the dividend is sufficiently large, you might want to capture it by exercising the option just before the ex-dividend date.

The only general method for valuing an American call on a dividend-paying stock is to use the step-by-step binomial method. In this case you must check at each stage to see whether the option is more valuable if exercised just before the ex-dividend date than if held for at least one more period.

17-6 The Option Menagerie

Our focus in the past two chapters has been on plain-vanilla puts and calls or combinations of them. An understanding of these options and how they are valued will allow you to handle most of the option problems that you are likely to encounter in corporate finance. However, you may occasionally encounter some more unusual options. We are not going to be looking at them in this book, but just for fun and to help you hold your own in

---

[17] For example, suppose that it currently costs $2 to buy £1 and that this pound can be invested to earn interest of 5%. The option holder misses out on interest of .05 × $2 = $.10. So, before using the Black–Scholes formula to value an option to buy sterling, you must adjust the current price of sterling:

$$\text{Adjusted price of sterling} = \text{current price} - \text{PV(interest)}$$
$$= \$2 - .10/1.05 = \$1.905$$

conversations with your investment banker friends, here is a crib sheet that summarizes a few of these exotic options:

Asian (or average) option	The exercise price is equal to the *average* of the asset's price during the life of the option.
Barrier option	Option where the payoff depends on whether the asset price reaches a specified level. A knock-in option (up-and-in call or down-and-in put) comes into existence only when the underlying asset reaches the barrier. Knock-out options (down-and-out call or up-and-out put) *cease* to exist if the asset price reaches the barrier.
Bermuda option	The option is exercisable on discrete dates before maturity.
Caput option	Call option on a put option.
Chooser (as-you-like-it) option	The holder must decide before maturity whether the option is a call or a put.
Compound option	An option on an option.
Digital (binary or cash-or-nothing) option	The option payoff is zero if the asset price is the wrong side of the exercise price and otherwise is a fixed sum.
Lookback option	The option holder chooses as the exercise price any of the asset prices that occurred before the final date.
Rainbow option	Call (put) option on the best (worst) of a basket of assets.

• • • • •

SUMMARY

In this chapter we introduced the basic principles of option valuation by considering a call option on a stock that could take on one of two possible values at the option's maturity. We showed that it is possible to construct a package of the stock and a loan that would provide exactly the same payoff as the option *regardless* of whether the stock price rises or falls. Therefore the value of the option must be the same as the value of this replicating portfolio.

We arrived at the same answer by pretending that investors are risk-neutral, so that the expected return on every asset is equal to the interest rate. We calculated the expected future value of the option in this imaginary risk-neutral world and then discounted this figure at the interest rate to find the option's present value.

The general binomial method adds realism by dividing the option's life into a number of subperiods in each of which the stock price can make one of two possible moves. Chopping the period into these shorter intervals doesn't alter the basic method for valuing a call option. We can still replicate the call by a package of the stock and a loan, but the package changes at each stage.

Finally, we introduced the Black–Scholes formula. This calculates the option's value when the stock price is constantly changing and takes on a continuum of possible future values.

An option can be replicated by a package of the underlying asset and a risk-free loan. Therefore, we can measure the risk of any option by calculating the risk of this portfolio. Naked options are often substantially more risky than the asset itself.

When valuing options in practical situations there are a number of features to look out for. For example, you may need to recognize that the option value is reduced by the fact that the holder is not entitled to any dividends.

• • • • •

FURTHER READING

Three readable articles about the Black–Scholes model are:

F. Black, "How We Came up with the Option Formula," *Journal of Portfolio Management* 15 (1989), pp. 4–8.

F. Black, "The Holes in Black–Scholes," *RISK Magazine* 1 (1988), pp. 27–29.

F. Black, "How to use the Holes in Black–Scholes," *Journal of Applied Corporate Finance* 1 (Winter 1989), pp. 67–73.

There are a number of good books on option valuation. They include:

J. Hull, *Options, Futures and Other Derivatives,* 7th ed. (Englewood Cliffs, NJ: Prentice-Hall, Inc., 2008).

R. L. McDonald, *Derivatives Markets,* 2nd ed. (Reading, MA: Pearson Addison Wesley, 2005).

P. Wilmott, *Paul Wilmott on Quantitative Finance,* 2nd ed. (New York: John Wiley & Sons, 2006).

● ● ● ● ●

BASIC

PROBLEM SETS

1. The stock price of Heavy Metal (HM) changes only once a month: Either it goes up by 20% or it falls by 16.7%. Its price now is $40. The interest rate is 12.7% per year, or about 1% per month.

   a. What is the value of a one-month call option with an exercise price of $40?

   b. What is the option delta?

   c. Show how the payoffs of this call option can be replicated by buying HM's stock and borrowing.

   d. What is the value of a two-month call option with an exercise price of $40?

   e. What is the option delta of the two-month call over the first one-month period?

2. a. Can the delta of a call option be greater than 1.0? Explain.

   b. Can it be less than zero?

   c. How does the delta of a call change if the stock price rises?

   d. How does it change if the risk of the stock increases?

3. Take another look at our two-step binomial trees for Google, for example, in Figure 17.2. Use the replicating-portfolio or risk-neutral method to value six-month call and put options with an exercise price of $400. Assume the Google stock price is $430.

4. Imagine that Google's stock price will either rise by 25% or fall by 20% over the next six months (see Section 17–1). Recalculate the value of the call option (exercise price = $430) using (a) the replicating-portfolio method and (b) the risk-neutral method. Explain intuitively why the option value falls from the value computed in Section 17–1.

5. Over the coming year Ragwort's stock price will halve to $50 from its current level of $100 or it will rise to $200. The one-year interest rate is 10%.

   a. What is the delta of a one-year call option on Ragwort stock with an exercise price of $100?

   b. Use the replicating-portfolio method to value this call.

   c. In a risk-neutral world what is the probability that Ragwort stock will rise in price?

   d. Use the risk-neutral method to check your valuation of the Ragwort option.

   e. If someone told you that in reality there is a 60% chance that Ragwort's stock price will rise to $200, would you change your view about the value of the option? Explain.

6. Use the Black–Scholes formula to value the following options:

   a. A call option written on a stock selling for $60 per share with a $60 exercise price. The stock's standard deviation is 6% per month. The option matures in three months. The risk-free interest rate is 1% per month.

   b. A put option written on the same stock at the same time, with the same exercise price and expiration date.

Now for each of these options find the combination of stock and risk-free asset that would replicate the option.

7. "An option is always riskier than the stock it is written on." True or false? How does the risk of an option change when the stock price changes?

8. For which of the following options *might* it be rational to exercise before maturity? Explain briefly why or why not.

   a. American put on a non-dividend-paying stock.

   b. American call—the dividend payment is $5 per annum, the exercise price is $100, and the interest rate is 10%.

   c. American call—the interest rate is 10%, and the dividend payment is 5% of future stock price. (*Hint:* The dividend depends on the stock price, which could either rise or fall.)

INTERMEDIATE

9. Johnny Jones's high school derivatives homework asks for a binomial valuation of a 12-month call option on the common stock of the Overland Railroad. The stock is now selling for $45 per share and has an annual standard deviation of 24%. Johnny first constructs a binomial tree like Figure 17.2, in which stock price moves up or down every six months. Then he constructs a more realistic tree, assuming that the stock price moves up or down once every three months, or four times per year.

   a. Construct these two binomial trees.

   b. How would these trees change if Overland's standard deviation were 30%? (*Hint:* Make sure to specify the right up and down percentage changes.)

10. Suppose a stock price can go up by 15% or down by 13% over the next year. You own a one-year put on the stock. The interest rate is 10%, and the current stock price is $60.

    a. What exercise price leaves you indifferent between holding the put or exercising it now?

    b. How does this break-even exercise price change if the interest rate is increased?

11. The price of Moria Mining stock is $100. During each of the next two six-month periods the price may either rise by 25% or fall by 20% (equivalent to a standard deviation of 31.5% a year). At month 6 the company will pay a dividend of $20. The interest rate is 10% per six-month period. What is the value of a one-year American call option with an exercise price of $80? Now recalculate the option value, assuming that the dividend is equal to 20% of the with-dividend stock price.

12. Buffelhead's stock price is $220 and could halve or double in each six-month period (equivalent to a standard deviation of 98%). A one-year call option on Buffelhead has an exercise price of $165. The interest rate is 21% a year.

    a. What is the value of the Buffelhead call?

    b. Now calculate the option delta for the second six months if (i) the stock price rises to $440 and (ii) the stock price falls to $110.

    c. How does the call option delta vary with the level of the stock price? Explain intuitively why.

    d. Suppose that in month 6 the Buffelhead stock price is $110. How at that point could you replicate an investment in the stock by a combination of call options and risk-free lending? Show that your strategy does indeed produce the same returns as those from an investment in the stock.

13. Suppose that you own an American put option on Buffelhead stock (see Problem 12) with an exercise price of $220.

    a. Would you ever want to exercise the put early?

    b. Calculate the value of the put.

    c. Now compare the value with that of an equivalent European put option.

14. Recalculate the value of the Buffelhead call option (see Problem 12), assuming that the option is American and that at the end of the first six months the company pays a dividend of $25. (Thus the price at the end of the year is either double or half the *ex*-dividend price in month 6.) How would your answer change if the option were European?

15. Suppose that you have an option that allows you to sell Buffelhead stock (see Problem 12) in month 6 for $165 *or* to buy it in month 12 for $165. What is the value of this unusual option?

16. The current price of the stock of Mont Tremblant Air is C$100. During each six-month period it will either rise by 11.1% or fall by 10% (equivalent to an annual standard deviation of 14.9%). The interest rate is 5% per six-month period.

    a. Calculate the value of a one-year European put option on Mont Tremblant's stock with an exercise price of C$102.

    b. Recalculate the value of the Mont Tremblant put option, assuming that it is an American option.

17. The current price of United Carbon (UC) stock is $200. The standard deviation is 22.3% a year, and the interest rate is 21% a year. A one-year call option on UC has an exercise price of $180.

    a. Use the Black–Scholes model to value the call option on UC. You may find it helpful to use the "live" spreadsheet in Table 17.2 on the book's Web site, **www.mhhe.com/ bma**.

    b. Use the formula given in Section 17–2 to calculate the up and down moves that you would use if you valued the UC option with the one-period binomial method. Now value the option by using that method.

    c. Recalculate the up and down moves and revalue the option by using the two-period binomial method.

    d. Use your answer to part (c) to calculate the option delta (i) today; (ii) next period if the stock price rises; and (iii) next period if the stock price falls. Show at each point how you would replicate a call option with a levered investment in the company's stock.

18. Suppose you construct an option hedge by buying a levered position in delta shares of stock and selling one call option. As the share price changes, the option delta changes, and you will need to adjust your hedge. You can minimize the cost of adjustments if changes in the stock price have only a small effect on the option delta. Construct an example to show whether the option delta is likely to vary more if you hedge with an in-the-money option, an at-the-money option, or an out-of-the-money option.

19. a. In Section 17–3 we calculated the risk (beta) of a six-month call option on Google stock with an exercise price of $430. Now repeat the exercise for a similar option with an exercise price of $400. Does the risk rise or fall as the exercise price is reduced?

    b. Now calculate the risk of a one-year call on Google stock with an exercise price of $430. Does the risk rise or fall as the maturity of the option lengthens?

20. Other things equal, which of these American options are you most likely to want to exercise early?

    a. A put option on a stock with a large dividend or a call on the same stock.

    b. A put option on a stock that is selling below exercise price or a call on the same stock.

    c. A put option when the interest rate is high or the same put option when the interest rate is low.

    Illustrate your answer with examples.

21. Is it better to exercise a call option on the with-dividend date or on the ex-dividend date? How about a put option? Explain.

22. Use the "live" Black–Scholes program on this book's Web site, **www.mhhe.com/bma,** to value the Owens Corning warrants described in Section 17–4. The standard deviation of

Owens Corning stock was 41% a year and the interest rate when the warrants were issued was 5%. Owens Corning did not pay a dividend. Ignore the problem of dilution.

23. Use the "live" Black–Scholes program at **www.mhhe.com/bma** to estimate how much you should be prepared to pay to insure the value of your pension fund portfolio for the coming year. Make reasonable assumptions about the volatility of the market and use current interest rates. Remember to subtract the present value of likely dividend payments from the current level of the market index.

CHALLENGE

24. Use the formula that relates the value of the call and the put (see Section 16–2) and the one-period binomial model to show that the option delta for a put option is equal to the option delta for a call option minus 1.

25. Show how the option delta changes as the stock price rises relative to the exercise price. Explain intuitively why this is the case. (What happens to the option delta if the exercise price of an option is zero? What happens if the exercise price becomes indefinitely large?)

26. Your company has just awarded you a generous stock option scheme. You suspect that the board will either decide to increase the dividend or announce a stock repurchase program. Which do you secretly hope they will decide? Explain. (You may find it helpful to refer back to Chapter 12.)

27. Calculate and compare the risk (betas) of the following investments: (a) a share of Google stock; (b) a one-year call option on Google; (c) a one-year put option; (d) a portfolio consisting of a share of Google stock and a one-year put option; (e) a portfolio consisting of a share of Google stock, a one-year put option, and the sale of a one-year call. In each case assume that the exercise price of the option is $430, which is also the current price of Google stock.

28. Some corporations have issued *perpetual* warrants. Warrants are call options issued by a firm, allowing the warrant holder to buy the firm's stock.

    a. What does the Black–Scholes formula predict for the value of an infinite-lived call option on a non-dividend-paying stock? Explain the value you obtain. (*Hint:* What happens to the present value of the exercise price of a long-maturity option?)

    b. Do you think this prediction is realistic? If not, explain carefully why. (*Hints:* What about dividends? What about bankruptcy?)

● ● ● ● ●

**REAL-TIME
DATA ANALYSIS**

Look back at the stocks listed in Table 7.3. Pick at least three stocks and find call option prices for each of them on **finance.yahoo.com**. Now find monthly adjusted prices and calculate the standard deviation from the monthly returns using the Excel function STDEV. Convert the standard deviation from monthly to annual units by multiplying by the square root of 12.

a. For each stock pick a traded option with a maturity of about six months and an exercise price equal to the current stock price. Use the Black–Scholes formula and your estimate of standard deviation to value each option. If the stock pays dividends, remember to subtract from the stock price the present value of any dividends that the option holder will miss out on. How close is your calculated value to the traded price of the option?

b. Your answer to part (a) will not exactly match the traded price. Experiment with different values for the standard deviation until your calculated values match the prices of the traded options as closely as possible. What are these implied volatilities? What do the implied volatilities say about investors' forecasts of future volatility?

MINI-CASE • • • • •

Bruce Honiball's Invention

It was another disappointing year for Bruce Honiball, the manager of retail services at Gibb River Bank. Sure, the retail side of Gibb River was making money, but it didn't grow at all in 2009. Gibb River had plenty of loyal depositors, but few new ones. Bruce had to figure out some new product or financial service—something that would generate some excitement and attention.

Bruce had been musing on one idea for some time. How about making it easy *and safe* for Gibb River's customers to put money in the stock market? How about giving them the upside of investing in equities—at least *some* of the upside—but none of the downside?

Bruce could see the advertisements now:

How would you like to invest in Australian stocks completely risk-free? You can with the new Gibb River Bank *Equity-Linked Deposit*. You share in the good years; we take care of the bad ones.

Here's how it works. Deposit A$100 with us for one year. At the end of that period you get back your A$100 *plus* A$5 for every 10% rise in the value of the Australian All Ordinaries stock index. But, if the market index falls during this period, the Bank will still refund your A$100 deposit in full.

There's no risk of loss. Gibb River Bank is your safety net.

Bruce had floated the idea before and encountered immediate skepticism, even derision: "Heads they win, tails we lose—is that what you're proposing, Mr. Honiball?" Bruce had no ready answer. Could the bank really afford to make such an attractive offer? How should it invest the money that would come in from customers? The bank had no appetite for major new risks.

Bruce has puzzled over these questions for the past two weeks but has been unable to come up with a satisfactory answer. He believes that the Australian equity market is currently fully valued, but he realizes that some of his colleagues are more bullish than he is about equity prices.

Fortunately, the bank had just recruited a smart new MBA graduate, Sheila Liu. Sheila was sure that she could find the answers to Bruce Honiball's questions. First she collected data on the Australian market to get a preliminary idea of whether equity-linked deposits could work. These data are shown in Table 17.5. She was just about to undertake some quick calculations when she received the following further memo from Bruce:

Sheila, I've got another idea. A lot of our customers probably share my view that the market is overvalued. Why don't we also give them a chance to make some money by offering a "bear

Year	Interest Rate	Market Return	Year-End Dividend Yield	Year	Interest Rate	Market Return	Year-End Dividend Yield
1989	17.3%	17.4%	5.7%	1999	4.9%	16.1%	3.2%
1990	15.9	−17.5	6.8	2000	4.9	5.2	3.4
1991	11.1	34.2	3.8	2001	4.8	10.4	3.3
1992	6.8	−2.3	3.8	2002	4.8	−8.8	4.0
1993	5.3	45.4	3.0	2003	4.8	14.6	3.9
1994	5.4	−8.7	4.0	2004	5.4	28.0	3.5
1995	8.0	20.2	4.0	2005	5.6	22.8	3.7
1996	7.4	14.6	3.6	2006	5.9	24.2	3.7
1997	5.5	12.2	3.9	2007	6.4	11.8	3.7
1998	5.0	11.6	3.5	2008	7.16	−40.38	6.8

▶ **TABLE 17.5**
Australian interest rates and equity returns, 1989–2008.

market deposit"? If the market goes up, they would just get back their A$100 deposit. If it goes down, they get their A$100 back plus $5 for each 10% that the market falls. Can you figure out whether we could do something like this? —Bruce

QUESTION

1. What kinds of options is Bruce proposing? How much would the options be worth? Would the equity-linked and bear-market deposits generate positive NPV for Gibb River Bank?

APPENDIX • • • • •

How Dilution Affects Option Value

If you buy a call option on an options exchange and then exercise it, you have no effect on the number of outstanding shares. The investor who sold the call simply hands over to you his or her shares. However, sometimes the company itself may issue options to buy its own shares. For example, we saw in Section 17–4 that in 2008 Oracle Corporation issued a total of 69 million executive stock options.

Companies also issue convertible bonds, which give investors the option to exchange their bonds in the future for common stock. Therefore, a convertible bond resembles a package of a straight bond and an option to buy the stock. Alternatively, the company may sell a package of bonds and warrants. These warrants are long-term call options to buy the company's stock. Presumably the company hopes that the warrants will serve as a "sweetener," so that by including options in the package investors will be induced to pay a much higher price. If the holders of the convertible bonds or the warrants decide to exercise their option, the company must issue the additional shares to them.

Options that are issued by the company are somewhat trickier to value than exchange-traded options. When these options are exercised, the firm's assets and profits are spread over a larger number of shares. Sometimes this dilution is negligible and can safely be ignored. But, if the number of shares can increase substantially, you need to take it into account when valuing the options. To illustrate how you can do so, we will work through the example of United Glue's warrants.

Example: Valuing United Glue's Warrants   United Glue has just issued a $2 million package of debt and warrants. Here are some basic data that we can use to value the warrants:

Number of shares outstanding (N)	1 million
Current stock price (P)	$12
Number of warrants issued per share outstanding (q)	.10
Total number of warrants issued (Nq)	100,000
Exercise price of warrants (EX)	$10
Time to expiration of warrants (t)	4 years
Annual standard deviation of stock price changes (σ)	.40
Rate of interest (r)	10%
United stock pays no dividends	

Before the Issue

Existing assets	$16	$ 4	Existing loans
		12	Common stock
			(1 million shares at
			$12 a share)
Total	$16	$16	Total

After the Issue

Existing assets	$16	$ 4	Existing loans
New assets financed		1.5	New loan without warrants
by debt and warrants	2	5.5	Total debt
		.5	Warrants
		12	Common stock
		12.5	Total equity
Total	$18	$18.0	Total

▶ **TABLE 17A.1**
United Glue's market-value balance sheet (in $ millions).

Suppose that without the warrants the debt is worth $1.5 million. Then investors must be paying $.5 million for the warrants:

$$\text{Cost of warrants} = \text{total amount of financing} - \text{value of loan without warrants}$$
$$\$500{,}000 \quad = \quad \$2{,}000{,}000 \quad - \quad \$1{,}500{,}000$$

$$\text{Each warrant costs investors } \frac{500{,}000}{100{,}000} = \$5$$

Table 17A.1 shows the market value of United's assets and liabilities both before and after the issue.

Now let us take a stab at checking whether the warrants are really worth the $500,000 that investors are paying for them. Since the warrant is a call option to buy the United stock, we can use the Black–Scholes formula to value the warrant. It turns out that a four-year call to buy United stock at $10 is worth $6.15.[18] Thus the warrant issue looks like a good deal for investors and a bad deal for United. Investors are paying $5 a share for warrants that are worth $6.15.

How the Value of United Warrants Is Affected by Dilution Unfortunately, our calculations for United warrants do not tell the whole story. Remember that when investors exercise a traded call or put option, there is no change in either the company's assets or the number of shares outstanding. But, if United's warrants are exercised, the number of shares outstanding will increase by $Nq = 100{,}000$. Also the assets will increase by the amount of the exercise money ($Nq \times \text{EX} = 100{,}000 \times \$10 = \$1$ million). In other words, there will be dilution. We need to allow for this dilution when we value the warrants.

Let us call the value of United's equity V:

$$\text{Value of equity} = V = \text{value of United's total assets} - \text{value of debt}$$

If the warrants are exercised, equity value will increase by the amount of the exercise money to $V + Nq\text{EX}$. At the same time the number of shares will increase to $N + Nq$. So the share price after the warrants are exercised will be:

$$\text{Share price after exercise} = \frac{V + Nq\text{EX}}{N + Nq}$$

---

[18] Plugging the data for United into the Black–Scholes formula gives

$$d_1 = \log[12/(10/1.1^4)]/(.40 \times \sqrt{4}) + (.40 \times \sqrt{4})/2 = 1.104 \text{ and } d_2 = 1.104 - .40 \times \sqrt{4} = .304$$

The Excel NORMSDIST function tells us that $N(d_1) = .865$, and $N(d_2) = .620$.
Therefore, estimated warrant value $= .865 \times 12 - .620 \times (10/1.1^4) = \$6.15$.

Visit us at www.mhhe.com/bma

At maturity the warrant holder can choose to let the warrants lapse or to exercise them and receive the share price less the exercise price. Thus the value of the warrants will be the share price minus the exercise price or zero, whichever is the higher. Another way to write this is:

$$\text{Warrant value at maturity} = \text{maximum}(\text{share price} - \text{exercise price}, \text{zero})$$

$$= \text{maximum}\left(\frac{V + Nq\text{EX}}{N + Nq} - \text{EX}, 0\right)$$

$$= \text{maximum}\left(\frac{V/N - \text{EX}}{1 + q}, 0\right)$$

$$= \frac{1}{1 + q}\text{maximum}\left(\frac{V}{N} - \text{EX}, 0\right)$$

This tells us the effect of dilution on the value of United's warrants. The warrant value is the value of $1/(1 + q)$ call options written on the stock of an alternative firm with the same total equity value V, *but with no outstanding warrants.* The alternative firm's stock price would be equal to V/N—that is, the total value of United's equity (V) divided by the number of shares outstanding (N). The stock price of this alternative firm is more variable than United's stock price. So when we value the call option on the alternative firm, we must remember to use the standard deviation of the changes in V/N.

Now we can recalculate the value of United's warrants allowing for dilution. First we find the stock price of the alternative firm:

$$\text{Current equity value of alternative firm} = V = \text{value of United's total assets} - \text{value of loans}$$

$$= 18 - 5.5 = \$12.5 \text{ millon}$$

$$\text{Current share price of alternative firm} = \frac{V}{N} = \frac{12.5 \text{ millon}}{1 \text{ millon}} = \$12.50$$

Also, suppose the standard deviation of the share price changes of this alternative firm is $\sigma^* = .41$.[19]

The Black–Scholes formula gives a value of $6.64 for a call option on a stock with a price of $12.50 and a standard deviation of .41. The value of United warrants is equal to the value of $1/(1 + q)$ call options on the stock of this alternative firm. Thus warrant value is:

$$\frac{1}{1 + q} \times \text{value of call on alternative firm} = \frac{1}{1.1} \times 6.64 = \$6.04$$

---

[19] How in practice could we compute σ^*? It would be easy if we could wait until the warrants had been trading for some time. In that case σ^* could be computed from the returns on a package of *all* the company's shares and warrants. In the present case we need to value the warrants *before* they start trading. We argue as follows: The standard deviation of the *assets* before the issue is equal to the standard deviation of a package of the common stock and the existing loans. For example, suppose that the company's debt is risk-free and that the standard deviation of stock returns *before* the bond-warrant issue is 38%. Then we calculate the standard deviation of the initial assets as follows:

$$\begin{array}{c}\text{Standard deviation} \\ \text{of initial assets}\end{array} = \begin{array}{c}\text{proportion in} \\ \text{common stock}\end{array} \times \begin{array}{c}\text{standard deviation} \\ \text{of common stock}\end{array}$$

$$= \frac{12}{16} \times 38 = 28.5\%$$

Now suppose that the assets after the issue are equally risky. Then,

$$\begin{array}{c}\text{Standard deviation} \\ \text{of assets after issue}\end{array} = \begin{array}{c}\text{proportion of equity} \\ \text{after issue}\end{array} \times \begin{array}{c}\text{standard deviation} \\ \text{of equity}(\sigma^*)\end{array}$$

$$28.5 = \frac{12.5}{18} \times \text{standard deviation of equity}(\sigma^*)$$

$$\text{Standard deviation of equity } (\sigma^*) = 41\%$$

Notice that in our example the standard deviation of the stock returns *before* the warrant issue was slightly lower than the standard deviation of the package of stock and warrants. However, the warrant holders bear proportionately more of this risk than do the stockholders; so the bond-warrant package could either increase or reduce the risk of the stock.

This is a somewhat lower value than the one we computed when we ignored dilution but still a bad deal for United.

It may sound from all this as if you need to know the value of United warrants to compute their value. This is not so. The formula does not call for warrant value but for V, the value of United's equity (that is, the shares *plus* warrants). Given equity value, the formula calculates how the overall value of equity should be split up between stock and warrants. Thus, suppose that United's underwriter advises that $500,000 extra can be raised by issuing a package of bonds and warrants rather than bonds alone. Is this a fair price? You can check using the Black–Scholes formula with the adjustment for dilution.

Finally, notice that these modifications are necessary to apply the Black–Scholes formula to value a warrant. They are not needed by the warrant holder, who must decide whether to exercise at maturity. If at maturity the price of the stock exceeds the exercise price of the warrant, the warrant holder will of course exercise.

QUESTION

1. Here is a question about dilution. The Electric Bassoon Company has outstanding 2,000 shares with a total market value of $20,000 *plus* 1,000 warrants with a total market value of $5,000. Each warrant gives its holder the option to buy one share at $20.

   a. To value the warrants, you first need to value a call option on an alternative share. How might you calculate its standard deviation?

   b. Suppose that the value of a call option on this alternative share was $6. Calculate whether the Electric Bassoon warrants were undervalued or overvalued.

PART 7

18

CHAPTER ●●●●●

Financial Analysis

▶ **Good financial managers** plan for the future. They check that they will have enough cash to pay the upcoming tax bill or dividend payment. They think about how much investment the firm will need to make over the next few years and about how they might finance that investment. They reflect on whether they are well placed to ride out an unexpected downturn in demand or an increase in the cost of materials.

In Chapter 19 we will describe how the financial manager develops both short- and long-term financial plans. But knowing where you stand today is a necessary prelude to contemplating where you might be in the future. Therefore, in this chapter we show how the firm's financial statements help you to understand the firm's overall performance and how some key financial ratios may alert senior management to potential problem

areas. For example, when the firm needs a loan from the bank, the financial manager can expect some searching questions about the firm's debt ratio and the proportion of profits that is absorbed by interest. Likewise, if a division is earning a low return on its capital or its profit margins are under pressure, you can be sure that management will demand an explanation.

You have probably heard stories of whizzes who can take a company's accounts apart in minutes, calculate some financial ratios, and divine the company's future. Such people are like abominable snowmen: often spoken of but never truly seen. Financial ratios are no substitute for a crystal ball. They are just a convenient way to summarize large quantities of financial data and to compare firms' performance. The ratios help you to ask the right questions; they seldom answer them.

●●●●●

18-1 Financial Statements

Public companies have a variety of stakeholders, such as shareholders, bondholders, bankers, suppliers, employees, and management. All these stakeholders need to monitor the firm and to ensure that their interests are being served. They rely on the company's financial statements to provide the necessary information. Public companies report to their shareholders quarterly and annually. The annual financial statements are filed with the SEC on form 10-K and the quarterly statements are filed on form 10-Q. Therefore you often hear financial analysts refer loosely to the company's "10-K" or its "10-Q."

When reviewing a company's financial statements, it is important to remember that accountants still have a fair degree of leeway in reporting earnings and book values. For example, they have discretion in the choice of depreciation method and the speed at which the firm's assets are written off.

Although accountants around the world are working toward common practices, there are still considerable variations in the accounting rules of different countries. In Anglo-Saxon

Speaking in Tongues

▶ Forget Esperanto. Too straightforward. The *lingua franca* that is increasingly spanning the globe is a tongue-twisting accounting-speak that is forcing even Americans to rethink some precious notions of financial sovereignty.

International Financial Reporting Standards (IFRS), which aim to harmonize financial reporting in a world of cross-border trade and investment, have made great strides since they were adopted by 7,000 or so listed companies in the European Union. To date, over 100 countries from Canada to China have adopted the rules or say they plan to adopt them. The London-based International Accounting Standards Board (IASB) expects that to swell to 150 in the next four years.

Even America, no ardent internationalist, is working with the IASB to narrow the gap between its own accounting standards and IFRS, which rules foreign companies listed in America could choose by 2009 or possibly sooner. Today such companies must "reconcile" their accounts with American rules—a costly exercise that some believe is driving foreign listings away from the United States.

In 2007 America's Securities and Exchange Commission (SEC) unexpectedly floated the idea of giving American, and not just foreign, companies the choice of using IFRS. Critics of the idea claim that this will give companies the option of shopping around for whichever regime best suits their business. Inevitably, however, by opening the door (if only a crack), America's own accounting regime would be in jeopardy.

Whether pure IFRS or not, all countries are prone to interpret the rules in ways that reflect their old accounting standards. Regulators are working through IOSCO, an international body of securities regulators, to attempt to whittle down these differences. The task is further complicated by the fact that international accounting rules tend to be "principles based," which means there are no hard-and-fast codes to follow. This is different from America, where accounting principles are accompanied by thousands of pages of prescriptive regulatory guidance and interpretations from auditors and accounting groups, some of it gleaned from SEC speeches. IFRS have no such baggage, leaving more room for judgment.

Source: Adapted from "Speaking in Tongues," *The Economist,* May 19, 2007, p. 83.

---

countries such as the U.S. or the U.K., which have large and active equity markets, the rules have been designed largely with the shareholder in mind. By contrast, in Germany the focus of accounting standards is to verify that the creditors are properly protected.

Another difference is the way that taxes are shown in the income statement. For example, in Germany taxes are paid on the published profits, and the depreciation method must therefore be approved by the revenue service. That is not the case in Anglo-Saxon countries, where the numbers shown in the published accounts are generally *not* the basis for calculating the company's tax payments. For instance, the depreciation method used to calculate the published profits usually differs from the depreciation method used by the tax authorities.

For investors and multinational companies these variations in accounting rules can be irksome. Accounting bodies have therefore been getting together to see whether they can iron out some of the differences. It is not a simple task, as the nearby box illustrates.

18-2 Lowe's Financial Statements

Your task is to assess the financial standing of Lowe's, the home improvement retailer. Perhaps you are a mutual fund manager trying to decide whether to allocate $25 million of new money to Lowe's stock. Perhaps you are a major shareholder pondering a sellout.

You could be an investment banker seeking business from the company or a bondholder concerned with its credit standing. You could be the financial manager of Lowe's or of one of its competitors.

In each case your first step is to assess the company's *current* condition. You have before you the latest balance sheet and income statement.

The Balance Sheet

Table 18.1 sets out a simplified balance sheet for Lowe's Companies for its fiscal year 2008. It provides a snapshot of the company's assets at the end of that year and the sources of the money that was used to buy those assets.

The assets are listed in declining order of liquidity. For example, the accountant lists first those assets that are most likely to be turned into cash in the near future. They include cash itself, marketable securities and receivables (that is, bills to be paid by the firm's customers), and inventories of raw materials, work in process, and finished goods. These assets are all known as *current assets*.

▶ **TABLE 18.1**

Balance sheet of Lowe's Companies, fiscal 2007 and 2008 (figures in $ millions).

Visit us at
www.mhhe.com/bma

	2008	2007
Assets		
Current assets:		
Cash and marketable securities	661	530
Accounts receivable	166	247
Inventories	8,209	7,611
Other current assets	215	298
Total current assets	9,251	8,686
Fixed assets:		
Tangible fixed assets		
Property, plant, and equipment	31,477	28,836
Less accumulated depreciation	8,755	7,475
Net tangible fixed assets	22,722	21,361
Long-term investments	253	509
Other long-term assets	460	313
Total assets	32,686	30,869
Liabilities and Shareholders' Equity		
Current liabilities:		
Debt due for repayment	1,021	1,104
Accounts payable	4,543	4,137
Other current liabilities	2,458	2,510
Total current liabilities	8,022	7,751
Long-term debt	5,039	5,576
Deferred income taxes	660	670
Other long-term liabilities	910	774
Total liabilities	14,631	14,771
Common stock and other paid-in capital	735	729
Retained earnings and capital surplus	17,320	15,369
Total shareholders' equity	18,055	16,098
Total liabilities and shareholders' equity	32,686	30,869

The remaining assets on the balance sheet consist of long-term, usually illiquid, assets such as warehouses, stores, fixtures, and vehicles. The balance sheet does not show up-to-date market values of these long-term assets. Instead, the accountant records the amount that each asset originally cost and deducts a fixed annual amount for depreciation of buildings, plant, and equipment. The balance sheet does not include all the company's assets. Some of the most valuable ones are intangible, such as reputation, skilled management, and a well-trained labor force. Accountants are generally reluctant to record these assets in the balance sheet unless they can be readily identified and valued.

Now look at the right-hand portion of Lowe's balance sheet, which shows where the money to buy the assets came from.[1] The accountant starts by looking at the liabilities, that is, the money owed by the company. First come those liabilities that need to be paid off in the near future. These *current liabilities* include debts that are due to be repaid within the next year and payables (that is, amounts owed by the company to its suppliers).

The difference between the current assets and current liabilities is known as the *net current assets* or *net working capital*. It roughly measures the company's potential reservoir of cash. For Lowe's in 2008

$$\text{Net working capital} = \text{current assets} - \text{current liabilities}$$
$$= 9{,}251 - 8{,}022 = \$1{,}229 \text{ million}$$

The bottom portion of the balance sheet shows the sources of the cash that were used to acquire the net working capital and fixed assets. Some of the cash has come from the issue of bonds and leases that will not be repaid for many years. After all these long-term liabilities have been paid off, the remaining assets belong to the common stockholders. The company's equity is simply the total value of the net working capital and fixed assets less the long-term liabilities. Part of this equity has come from the sale of shares to investors, and the remainder has come from earnings that the company has retained and invested on behalf of the shareholders.

The Income Statement

If Lowe's balance sheet resembles a snapshot of the firm at a particular point in time, its income statement is like a video. It shows how profitable the firm has been over the past year.

Look at the summary income statement in Table 18.2. You can see that during 2008 Lowe's sold goods worth $48,230 million. The total cost of purchasing and selling these

	$ millions
Net sales	48,230
Cost of goods sold	31,729
Selling, general, and administrative expenses	11,158
Depreciation	1,539
Earnings before interest and taxes (EBIT)	3,804
Interest expense	298
Taxable income	3,506
Tax	1,311
Net income	2,195
Dividends	491
Addition to retained earnings	1,704

TABLE 18.2

Income statement of Lowe's Companies, 2008 (figures in $ millions).

Visit us at
www.mhhe.com/bma

---

[1] The British and Americans can never agree whether to keep to the left or the right. British accountants list liabilities on the left and assets on the right. (The right-hand side is actually plotted below in Table 18.1.)

goods was $31,729 + $11,158 = $42,887 million.[2] In addition to these out-of-pocket expenses, Lowe's also deducted depreciation of $1,539 million for the value of the fixed assets used up in producing the goods. Thus Lowe's earnings before interest and taxes (EBIT) were

$$EBIT = \text{total revenues} - \text{costs} - \text{depreciation}$$
$$= 48,230 - 42,887 - 1,539$$
$$= \$3,804 \text{ million}$$

Of this sum $298 million went to pay the interest on the short- and long-term debt (remember debt interest is paid out of pretax income) and a further $1,311 million went to the government in the form of taxes. The $2,195 million that was left over belonged to the shareholders. Lowe's paid out $491 million as dividends and reinvested the remainder in the business.

18-3   Measuring Lowe's Performance

You want to use Lowe's financial statements to assess its financial performance and current standing. Where do you start?

At the close of fiscal 2008 Lowe's common stock was priced at $18.19 per share.[3] There were 1,470 million shares outstanding, so total **market capitalization** was 1,470 × $18.19 = $26,739 million. This is a big number, of course, but Lowe's is a sizeable company. Its shareholders have, over the years, invested billions in the company. Therefore, you decide to compare Lowe's market capitalization with the book value of its equity. The book value measures shareholders' cumulative investment in the company.

At the end of fiscal 2008 the book value of Lowe's equity was $18,055 million. Therefore, the **market value added,** the difference between the market value of the firm's shares and the amount of money that shareholders have invested in the firm, was $26,739 − $18,055 = $8,684 million. In other words, Lowe's shareholders have contributed about $18 billion and ended up with shares worth about $27 billion. They have accumulated about $9 billion in market value added.

The consultancy firm, EVA Dimensions, calculates market value added for a large sample of U.S. companies. Table 18.3 shows a few of the firms from EVA Dimension's list. Exxon Mobil heads the group. It has created $154 billion of wealth for its shareholders. AT&T is near the bottom of the class: The market value of AT&T's shares is $49 billion *less* than the amount of shareholders' money invested in the firm.

Exxon Mobil is a large firm. Its managers have lots of assets to work with. A small firm could not hope to create so much extra value. Therefore, financial managers and analysts also like to calculate how much value has been added *for each dollar that shareholders have invested.* To do this, they compute the *ratio* of market value to book value. For example, Lowe's **market-to-book ratio** is[4]

$$\text{Market-to-book ratio} = \text{market value of equity/book value of equity}$$
$$= 26,739/18,055 = 1.5$$

In other words, Lowe's has multiplied the value of its shareholders' investment 1.5 times.

---

[2] For simplicity we have deducted $18 million of interest income from the selling, general, and administrative expenses.

[3] Lowe's 2008 fiscal year ended on January 30, 2009.

[4] The market-to-book ratio can also be calculated by dividing stock price by book value per share.

	Market Value Added	Market-to-Book Ratio		Market Value Added	Market-to-Book Ratio
Exxon Mobil	$154,397	1.69	FedEx	−$1,538	.96
Wal-Mart	128,159	2.02	J.C. Penney	−3,777	.69
Coca-Cola	106,957	3.46	Xerox	−9,981	.37
Google	96,880	6.82	Dow Chemical	−17,823	.55
Johnson & Johnson	67,645	1.80	AT&T	−49,052	.85

▷ **TABLE 18.3** Stock market measures of company performance, 2008 (dollar values in millions). Companies are ranked by market value added.

Source: We are grateful to EVA Dimensions for providing these statistics.

Table 18.3 also shows market-to-book ratios for our sample U.S. companies. Notice that Google has a much higher market-to-book ratio than Exxon Mobil. But Exxon Mobil's market value added is higher because of its larger scale.

The market-value performance measures in Table 18.3 have two drawbacks. First, the market value of the company's shares reflects investors' expectations about *future* performance. Investors pay attention to current profits and investment, of course, but market-value measures can nevertheless be noisy measures of current performance.

Second, you can't look up the market value of privately owned companies whose shares are not traded. Nor can you observe the market value of divisions or plants that are parts of larger companies. You may use market values to satisfy yourself that Lowe's as a whole has performed well, but you can't use them to drill down to look at the performance of, say, its overseas stores or particular U.S. stores. To do this, you need accounting measures of profitability. We start with economic value added (EVA).

Economic Value Added (EVA)

When accountants draw up an income statement, they start with revenues and then deduct operating and other costs. But one important cost is *not* included: the cost of the capital that the company has raised from investors. Therefore, to see whether the firm has truly created value, we need to measure whether it has earned a profit after deducting *all* costs, including its cost of capital.

The cost of capital is the minimum acceptable rate of return on capital investment. It is an *opportunity* cost of capital, because it equals the expected rate of return on investment opportunities open to investors in financial markets. The firm creates value for investors only if it can earn more than its cost of capital, that is, more than its investors can earn by investing on their own.

The profit after deducting all costs, *including the cost of capital,* is called the company's **economic value added** or **EVA**. Let's calculate EVA for Lowe's.

Total long-term capital, sometimes called *total capitalization,* is the sum of long-term debt and shareholders' equity. At the end of 2007 Lowe's total capitalization amounted to $21,674 million, which was made up of $5,576 million of long-term debt and $16,098 million of shareholders' equity. This was the cumulative amount that had been invested in the past by the debt and equityholders. Lowe's weighted-average cost of capital was about 7.4%. Therefore, investors who provided the $21,674 million required the company in 2008 to earn at least .074 × 21,674 = $1,604 million for its debt and equityholders.

In 2008 Lowe's after-tax interest and net income totaled $(1 - .35) \times 298 + 2,195 = \$2,389$ million (we assume a 35% tax rate). If you deduct the total cost of Lowe's capital from this figure, you can see that the company earned $\$2,389 - 1,604 = \$785$ million *more* than investors required. This was Lowe's residual income, or EVA:

$$\text{EVA} = (\text{after-tax interest} + \text{net income}) - (\text{cost of capital} \times \text{capital})$$
$$= 2,389 - 1,604 = \$785 \text{ million}$$

Sometimes it is helpful to re-express EVA as follows:

$$\text{EVA} = \left(\frac{\text{after-tax interest} + \text{net income}}{\text{total capital}} - \text{cost of capital} \right) \times \text{total capital}$$
$$= (\text{return on capital} - \text{cost of capital}) \times \text{total capital}$$

The **return on capital** (or **ROC**) is equal to the total profits that the company has earned for its debt and equityholders, divided by the amount of money that they have contributed. If the company earns a higher return on its capital than investors require, EVA is positive. In the case of Lowe's, the return on capital was

$$\frac{\text{after-tax interest} + \text{net income}}{\text{total capital}} = \frac{(1 - .35) \times 298 + 2,195}{21,674} = .1102, \text{ about } 11\%$$

Lowe's cost of capital was about 7.4%. So,

$$\text{EVA} = (\text{return on capital} - \text{cost of capital}) \times \text{total capital}$$
$$= (.1102 - .074) \times 21,674 = \$785 \text{ million}$$

The first four columns of Table 18.4 show measures of EVA for our sample of large companies. Exxon Mobil again heads the list. In 2008 it earned $33 billion more than was needed to satisfy investors. By contrast, AT&T was a laggard. Although it earned an accounting profit of nearly $16 billion, this figure was calculated before deducting the cost of the capital that was employed. After deducting the cost of the capital, AT&T made an EVA *loss* of $11.8 billion.

	1. After-tax interest + net income	2. Cost of Capital (WACC), %	3. Total Long-term Capital	4. EVA = $(1 - 2) \times 3$	5. Return on Capital (ROC), % $(1 \div 3)$
Exxon Mobil	$46,378	6.0	$224,051	$33,006	20.7
Wal-Mart	14,169	5.7	125,059	7,286	11.3
Johnson & Johnson	11,964	7.5	84,848	5,529	14.1
Google	5,128	12.3	16,644	3,143	30.8
Coca-Cola	4,900	5.8	33,246	3,031	14.7
J.C. Penney	553	7.0	12,191	−302	4.5
FedEx	1,898	6.7	37,067	−583	5.1
Dow Chemical	1,420	6.1	39,458	−1,004	3.6
Xerox	583	9.9	15,876	−1,047	3.7
AT&T	15,745	8.6	321,320	−11,779	4.9

▶ **TABLE 18.4**   Accounting measures of company performance, 2008 (dollar values in millions). Companies are ranked by economic value added (EVA).

Note: EVAs do not compute exactly because of rounding in column 2.
Source: We are grateful to EVA Dimensions for providing these statistics.

Accounting Rates of Return

EVA measures how many dollars a business is earning after deducting the cost of capital. Other things equal, the more assets the manager has to work with, the greater the opportunity to generate a large EVA. The manager of a small division may be highly competent, but if that division has few assets, she is unlikely to rank high in the EVA stakes. Therefore, when comparing managers, it can also be helpful to measure the firm's return *per dollar of investment*.

Three common return measures are the return on capital (ROC), the return on equity (ROE), and the return on assets (ROA). All are based on accounting information and are therefore known as *book rates of return*.

Return on Capital (ROC)[5]   We have already calculated Lowe's return on capital in 2008:

$$\text{ROC} = \frac{\text{after-tax interest} + \text{net income}}{\text{total capital}} = \frac{(1 - .35) \times 298 + 2,195}{21,674} = .11, \text{ or } 11.0\%$$

You will encounter a variety of alternative ways to calculate any book rate of return. For example, a company may have issued new capital during the year and invested the proceeds. If that is the case, it may be better to use the average of the capital at the beginning and end of the year.[6] If we do so, Lowe's ROC changes to

$$\text{ROC} = \frac{\text{after-tax interest} + \text{net income}}{\text{average total capital}} = \frac{(1 - .35) \times 298 + 2,195}{(21,674 + 23,094)/2} = .107, \text{ or } 10.7\%$$

Here is another technical point. When we calculated Lowe's return on capital we summed the company's *after-tax* interest and net income.[7] The reason that we subtracted the tax shield on debt interest was that we wished to calculate the income that the company would have earned with all-equity financing. The tax advantages of debt financing are picked up when we compare the company's return on capital with its weighted-average cost of capital (WACC).[8] WACC already includes an adjustment for the interest tax shield.[9] More often than not, financial analysts ignore this refinement and use the gross interest payment to calculate ROC. It is only approximately correct to compare this measure with the weighted-average cost of capital.

The last column in Table 18.4 shows the return on capital for our sample of well-known companies. Notice that Google's return on capital was 30.8%, over 18 percentage points above its cost of capital. Although Google had a higher return on capital than Exxon Mobil, it had a lower EVA. This was partly because Google was more risky than Exxon Mobil, and so had a higher cost of capital, but also because it had far fewer dollars invested than Exxon.

---

[5] The expression, *return on capital,* is commonly used when calculating the profitability of an entire firm. When measuring the profitability of an individual plant, the equivalent measure is generally called *return on investment* (or *ROI*).

[6] Averages are used when a flow figure (in this case, income) that builds up over the course of the year is compared with a snapshot figure of assets or liabilities (in this case, capital). Sometimes it's convenient to use a snapshot figure at the end of the year, although this procedure is not strictly correct.

[7] This figure is called the company's Net Operating Profit After Tax or NOPAT:

$$\text{NOPAT} = \text{after-tax interest} + \text{net income}$$

In the case of Lowe's

$$\text{NOPAT} = (1 - .35) \times 298 + 2,195 = \$2,389 \text{ million}$$

[8] For the same reason we used the after-tax interest payment when we calculated Lowe's EVA.

[9] Remember WACC is a weighted average of the *after-tax* rate of interest and the cost of equity.

Return on Equity (ROE)   We measure the **return on equity (ROE)** as the income to shareholders per dollar invested. Lowe's had net income of $2,195 million in 2008 and stockholders' equity of $16,098 million at the start of the year. So its return on equity was

$$\text{ROE} = \frac{\text{net income}}{\text{equity}} = \frac{2{,}195}{16{,}098} = .136, \text{ or } 13.6\%$$

If we recalculate ROE using average equity, then the return was

$$\text{ROE} = \frac{\text{net income}}{\text{average equity}} = \frac{2{,}195}{(16{,}098 + 18{,}055)/2} = .129, \text{ or } 12.9\%$$

Has Lowe's provided an adequate return for shareholders? To answer that question, we need to compare it with the company's cost of equity. Lowe's cost of equity capital in 2008 was about 8.7%, so its return on equity was about 4 percentage points higher than its cost of equity.

Return on Assets (ROA)   **Return on assets** measures the income available to debt and equity investors per dollar of the firm's *total* assets. Total assets (which equal total liabilities plus shareholders' equity) are greater than total capital because total capital does not include current liabilities. For Lowe's, return on assets was

$$\text{ROA} = \frac{(\text{after-tax interest} + \text{net income})}{\text{total assets}} = \frac{(1 - .35) \times 298 + 2{,}195}{30{,}869} = .077, \text{ or } 7.7\%$$

When we subtract the tax shield on Lowe's interest payments, we are asking how much the company would have earned if all-equity-financed. This adjustment is helpful when comparing the profitability of firms with very different capital structures. Again, this refinement is ignored more often than not, and ROA is calculated using the gross interest payment.[10] Sometimes analysts take no account of interest payments and measure ROA as the income for equityholders divided by total assets. This measure ignores entirely the income that the assets have generated for debtholders.

We see shortly how Lowe's return on assets is determined by the sales that these assets generate and the profit margin that the company earns on its sales.

Problems with EVA and Accounting Rates of Return

Rate of return and economic value added have some obvious attractions as measures of performance. Unlike market-value-based measures, they show current performance and are not affected by the expectations about future events that are reflected in today's stock market prices. Rate of return and economic value added can also be calculated for an entire company or for a particular plant or division. However, remember that both measures are based on book (balance sheet) values for assets. Debt and equity are also book values. Accountants do not show every asset on the balance sheet, yet our calculations take accounting data at face value. For example, we ignored the fact that Lowe's has invested large sums in marketing to establish its brand name. This brand name is an important asset, but its value is not shown on the balance sheet. If it were shown, the book values of assets, capital, and equity would increase, and Lowe's would not appear to earn such high returns.

EVA Dimensions, which produced the data in Tables 18.3 and 18.4, does make a number of adjustments to the accounting data. However, it is impossible to include the value of all assets or to judge how rapidly they depreciate. For example, did Google really earn a return of 30.8% and add $3.1 billion of economic value? It's difficult to say, because its investment over the years in search engines and other software is not shown on the balance sheet and cannot be measured exactly.

---

[10] Again, when calculating ROA, financial analysts sometimes use an average of the assets at the start and end of the year.

Remember also that the balance sheet does not show the current market values of the firm's assets. The assets in a company's books are valued at their original cost less any depreciation. Older assets may be grossly undervalued in today's market conditions and prices. So a high return on assets indicates that the business has performed well by making profitable investments in the past, but it does not necessarily mean that you could buy the same assets today at their reported book values. Conversely a low return suggests some poor decisions in the past, but it does not always mean that today the assets could be employed better elsewhere.

18-4 Measuring Efficiency

We began our analysis of Lowe's by calculating how much value the company has added for its shareholders and how much profit it is earning after deducting the cost of the capital that it employs. We examined Lowe's rates of return on capital, equity, and total assets and found that its return has been higher than the cost of capital. Our next task is to probe a little deeper to understand the reasons for the company's success. What factors contribute to a firm's overall profitability? One factor clearly must be the efficiency with which it uses its many types of assets.

Asset Turnover Ratio The asset turnover, or sales-to-assets, ratio shows how much sales are generated by each dollar of total assets, and therefore it measures how hard the firm's assets are working. For Lowe's, each dollar of assets produced $1.56 of sales:

$$\text{Asset turnover} = \frac{\text{sales}}{\text{total assets at start of year}} = \frac{48,230}{30,869} = 1.56$$

Like some of our profitability ratios, the sales-to-assets ratio compares a flow measure (sales over the entire year) to a snapshot measure (assets on one day). Therefore, financial managers and analysts often calculate the ratio of sales over the entire year to the *average* level of assets over the same period. In this case,

$$\text{Asset turnover} = \frac{\text{sales}}{\text{average total assets}} = \frac{48,230}{(30,869 + 32,686)/2} = 1.52$$

The asset turnover ratio measures how efficiently the business is using its entire asset base. But you also might be interested in how hard *particular types* of assets are being put to use. Below are a couple of examples.

Inventory Turnover Efficient firms don't tie up more capital than they need in raw materials and finished goods. They hold only a relatively small level of inventories of raw materials and finished goods, and they turn over those inventories rapidly. The balance sheet shows the cost of inventories rather than the amount that the finished goods will eventually sell for. So it is usual to compare the average level of inventories with the cost of goods sold rather than with sales. In Lowe's case,

$$\text{Inventory turnover} = \frac{\text{cost of goods sold}}{\text{inventory at start of year}} = \frac{31,729}{7,611} = 4.2$$

Another way to express this measure is to look at how many days of output are represented by inventories. This is equal to the level of inventories divided by the daily cost of goods sold:

$$\text{Average days in inventory} = \frac{\text{inventory at start of year}}{\text{daily cost of goods sold}} = \frac{7,611}{31,729/365} = 88 \text{ days}$$

Receivables Turnover   Receivables are sales for which the company has not yet been paid. The receivables turnover ratio measures the firm's sales as a proportion of its receivables. For Lowe's,

$$\text{Receivables turnover} = \frac{\text{sales}}{\text{receivables at start of year}} = \frac{48,230}{247} = 195.3$$

If customers are quick to pay, unpaid bills will be a relatively small proportion of sales and the receivables turnover will be high. Therefore, a comparatively high ratio often indicates an efficient credit department that is quick to follow up on late payers. Sometimes, however, a high ratio indicates that the firm has an unduly restrictive credit policy and offers credit only to customers who can be relied on to pay promptly.[11]

Another way to measure the efficiency of the credit operation is by calculating the average length of time for customers to pay their bills. The faster the firm turns over its receivables, the shorter the collection period. Lowe's customers pay their bills in about 1.9 days:

$$\text{Average collection period} = \frac{\text{receivables at start of year}}{\text{average daily sales}} = \frac{247}{48,230/365} = 1.9 \text{ days}$$

If you are thinking that this is a remarkably short time to wait before Lowe's customers pay, you are right. There are two reasons for the unusually short collection period. First, only a small proportion of Lowe's sales are made on credit. Second, the notes to Lowe's financial statements reveal that the company finances most of its unpaid bills by selling them to GE at a discount. This prompts us to warn you not to mindlessly compute financial ratios without checking whether there are good reasons for an unusually high or low figure. The notes to the financial statements often provide that reason.

The receivables turnover ratio and the inventory turnover ratio may help to highlight particular areas of inefficiency, but they are not the only possible indicators. For example, Lowe's might compare its sales per square foot with those of its competitors, a steel producer might calculate the cost per ton of steel produced, an airline might look at revenues per passenger-mile, and a law firm might look at revenues per partner. A little thought and common sense should suggest which measures are likely to produce the most helpful insights into your company's efficiency.

18-5 Analyzing the Return on Assets: The Du Pont System

We have seen that every dollar of Lowe's assets generates $1.56 of sales. But a company's success depends not only on the volume of its sales but also on how profitable those sales are. This is measured by the profit margin.

Profit Margin   The profit margin measures the proportion of sales that finds its way into profits. It is sometimes defined as

$$\text{Profit margin} = \frac{\text{net income}}{\text{sales}} = \frac{2,195}{48,230} = .0455, \text{ or } 4.55\%$$

This definition can be misleading. When companies are partly financed by debt, a portion of the profits from the sales must be paid as interest to the firm's lenders. We would not want to say that a firm is less profitable than its rivals simply because it employs debt finance and pays out part of its profits as interest. Therefore, when we are calculating the

---

[11] Where possible, it makes sense to look only at *credit* sales. Otherwise a high ratio might simply indicate that a small proportion of sales is made on credit.

profit margin, it is useful to add back the debt interest to net income. This gives an alternative measure of profit margin, which is called the **operating profit margin:**[12]

$$\text{Operating profit margin} = \frac{\text{after-tax interest} + \text{net income}}{\text{sales}}$$

$$= \frac{(1 - .35) \times 298 + 2,195}{48,230}$$

$$= .0495, \text{ or } 4.95\%$$

The Du Pont System

We calculated earlier that Lowe's has earned a return of 7.7% on its assets. The following equation shows that this return depends on two factors—the sales that the company generates from its assets (asset turnover) and the profit that it earns on each dollar of sales (operating profit margin):

$$\text{Return on assets} = \frac{\text{after-tax interest} + \text{net income}}{\text{assets}} = \underset{\underset{\text{asset turnover}}{\uparrow}}{\frac{\text{sales}}{\text{assets}}} \times \underset{\underset{\text{operating profit margin}}{\uparrow}}{\frac{\text{after-tax interest} + \text{net income}}{\text{sales}}}$$

This breakdown of ROA into the product of turnover and margin is often called the **Du Pont formula,** after the chemical company that popularized the procedure. In Lowe's case the formula gives the following breakdown of ROA:

$$\text{ROA} = \text{asset turnover} \times \text{operating profit margin} = 1.56 \times .0495 = .077$$

All firms would like to earn a higher return on their assets, but their ability to do so is limited by competition. The Du Pont formula helps to identify the constraints that firms face. Fast-food chains, which have high asset turnover, tend to operate on low margins. Classy hotels have relatively low turnover ratios but tend to compensate with higher margins.

Firms often seek to improve their profit margins by acquiring a supplier. The idea is to capture the supplier's profit as well as their own. Unfortunately, unless they have some special skill in running the new business, they are likely to find that any gain in profit margin is offset by a decline in asset turnover.

A few numbers may help to illustrate this point. Table 18.5 shows the sales, profits, and assets of Admiral Motors and its components supplier, Diana Corporation. Both earn a 10% return on assets, though Admiral has a lower operating profit margin (20% versus Diana's 25%). Since all of Diana's output goes to Admiral, Admiral's management reasons that it would be better to merge the two companies. That way, the merged company would capture the profit margin on both the auto components and the assembled car.

	Sales	Profits	Assets	Asset Turnover	Profit Margin	ROA
Admiral Motors	$20	$4	$40	.50	20%	10%
Diana Corporation	8	2	20	.40	25	10
Diana Motors (the merged firm)	20	6	60	.33	30	10

▶ **TABLE 18.5**
Merging with suppliers or customers generally increases the profit margin, but this increase is offset by a reduction in asset turnover.

---

[12] If a firm pays out most of its profits as interest, it will pay less tax and have a higher operating profit margin than one that is financed solely by equity. To obtain a measure of the profit margin that is unaffected by the firm's financial structure, we need to subtract the tax savings on the interest.

The bottom row of Table 18.5 shows the effect of the merger. The merged firm does indeed earn the combined profits. Total sales remain at $20 million, however, because all the components produced by Diana are used within the company. With higher profits and unchanged sales, the profit margin increases. Unfortunately, the asset turnover is *reduced* by the merger since the merged firm has more assets. This exactly offsets the benefit of the higher profit margin. The return on assets is unchanged.

18-6 Measuring Leverage

When a firm borrows money, it promises to make a series of interest payments and then to repay the amount that it has borrowed. If profits rise, the debtholders continue to receive only the fixed interest payment, so all the gains go to the shareholders. Of course, the reverse happens if profits fall. In this case shareholders bear the greater part of the pain. If times are sufficiently hard, a firm that has borrowed heavily may not be able to pay its debts. The firm is then bankrupt, and shareholders lose most or all of their investment.

Because debt increases the returns to shareholders in good times and reduces them in bad times, it is said to create *financial leverage*. Leverage ratios measure how much financial leverage the firm has taken on. CFOs keep an eye on leverage ratios to ensure that lenders are happy to continue to take on the firm's debt.

Debt Ratio   Financial leverage is usually measured by the ratio of long-term debt to total long-term capital. (Here "long-term debt" should include not just bonds or other borrowing but also financing from long-term leases.)[13] For Lowe's,

$$\text{Long-term debt ratio} = \frac{\text{long-term debt}}{\text{long-term debt} + \text{equity}} = \frac{5,039}{5,039 + 18,055} = .22, \text{ or } 22\%$$

This means that 22 cents of every dollar of long-term capital is in the form of debt.

Leverage is also measured by the debt–equity ratio. For Lowe's,

$$\text{Long-term debt–equity ratio} = \frac{\text{long-term debt}}{\text{equity}} = \frac{5,039}{18,055} = .28, \text{ or } 28\%$$

Lowe's long-term debt ratio is fairly typical of U.S. nonfinancial companies, but some companies deliberately operate at much higher debt levels. For example, firms that are acquired in a leveraged buyout usually issue large amounts of debt. When LBOs first became popular in the 1990s, these companies had average debt ratios of about 90%. Many of them flourished and paid back their debtholders in full; others were not so fortunate.

Notice that debt ratios make use of book (i.e., accounting) values rather than market values.[14] The market value of the company finally determines whether the debtholders get their money back, so you might expect analysts to look at the face amount of the debt as a proportion of the total market value of debt and equity. On the other hand, the market value includes the value of intangible assets generated by research and development, advertising, staff training, and so on. These assets are not readily salable and, if the company falls

---

[13] A finance lease is a long-term rental agreement that commits the firm to make regular payments. This commitment is just like the obligation to make payments on an outstanding loan.

[14] In the case of leased assets, accountants estimate the value of the lease commitments. In the case of long-term debt, they simply show the face value, which can be very different from market value. For example, the present value of low-coupon debt may be only a fraction of its face value. The difference between the book value of equity and its market value can be even more dramatic.

on hard times, their value may disappear altogether. For some purposes, it may be just as good to follow the accountant and ignore these intangible assets. This is what lenders do when they insist that the borrower should not allow the book debt ratio to exceed a specified limit.

Notice also that these measures of leverage ignore short-term debt. That probably makes sense if the short-term debt is temporary or is matched by similar holdings of cash, but if the company is a regular short-term borrower, it may be preferable to widen the definition of debt to include all liabilities. In this case,

$$\text{Total debt ratio} = \frac{\text{total liabilities}}{\text{total assets}} = \frac{14{,}631}{32{,}686} = .45, \text{ or } 45\%$$

Therefore, Lowe's is financed 45% with long- and short-term debt and 55% with equity.[15] We could also say that its ratio of total debt to equity is $14{,}631/18{,}055 = .81$.

Managers sometimes refer loosely to a company's debt ratio, but we have just seen that the debt ratio may be measured in several different ways. For example, Lowe's has a debt ratio of .28 (the long-term debt ratio) and also .45 (the total debt ratio). This is not the first time we have come across several ways to define a financial ratio. There is no law stating how a ratio should be defined. So be warned: Do not use a ratio without understanding how it has been calculated.

Times-Interest-Earned Ratio   Another measure of financial leverage is the extent to which interest obligations are covered by earnings. Banks prefer to lend to firms whose earnings cover interest payments with room to spare. *Interest coverage* is measured by the ratio of earnings before interest and taxes (EBIT) to interest payments. For Lowe's,[16]

$$\text{Times-interest-earned} = \frac{\text{EBIT}}{\text{interest payments}} = \frac{3{,}804}{298} = 12.8$$

Lowe's enjoys a comfortable interest coverage or *times-interest-earned* ratio. Sometimes lenders are content with coverage ratios as low as 2 or 3.

The regular interest payment is a hurdle that companies must keep jumping if they are to avoid default. Times-interest-earned measures how much clear air there is between hurdle and hurdler. The ratio is only part of the story, however. For example, it doesn't tell us whether Lowe's is generating enough cash to repay its debt as it comes due.

Cash Coverage Ratio   In earlier chapters, we pointed out that depreciation is deducted when calculating the firm's earnings, even though no cash goes out the door. Suppose we add back depreciation to EBIT to calculate operating cash flow. We can then calculate a *cash* coverage ratio. For Lowe's,

$$\text{Cash coverage} = \frac{\text{EBIT + depreciation}}{\text{interest payments}} = \frac{3{,}804 + 1{,}539}{298} = 17.9$$

Leverage and the Return on Equity

When the firm raises cash by borrowing, it must make interest payments to its lenders. This reduces net profits. On the other hand, if a firm borrows instead of issuing equity, it has fewer equityholders to share the remaining profits. Which effect dominates? An extended

---

[15] In this case, the debt consists of all liabilities, including current liabilities.

[16] The numerator of times-interest-earned can be defined in several ways. Sometimes depreciation is excluded. Sometimes it is just earnings plus interest, that is, earnings before interest but *after* tax. This last definition seems nutty to us, because the point of times-interest-earned is to assess the risk that the firm won't have enough money to pay interest. If EBIT falls below interest obligations, the firm won't have to worry about taxes. Interest is paid before the firm pays taxes.

version of the Du Pont formula helps us answer this question. It breaks down the return on equity (ROE) into four parts:

$$\text{ROE} = \frac{\text{net income}}{\text{equity}}$$

$$= \underset{\substack{\uparrow \\ \text{leverage} \\ \text{ratio}}}{\frac{\text{assets}}{\text{equity}}} \times \underset{\substack{\uparrow \\ \text{asset} \\ \text{turnover}}}{\frac{\text{sales}}{\text{assets}}} \times \underset{\substack{\uparrow \\ \text{operating profit} \\ \text{margin}}}{\frac{\text{after-tax interest} + \text{net income}}{\text{sales}}} \times \underset{\substack{\uparrow \\ \text{``debt} \\ \text{burden''}}}{\frac{\text{net income}}{\text{after-tax interest} + \text{net income}}}$$

Notice that the product of the two middle terms is the return on assets. It depends on the firm's production and marketing skills and is unaffected by the firm's financing mix. However, the first and fourth terms do depend on the debt–equity mix. The first term, assets/equity, which we call the *leverage ratio,* can be expressed as (equity + liabilities)/equity, which equals 1 + total-debt-to-equity ratio. The last term, which we call the "debt burden," measures the proportion by which interest expense reduces net income.

Suppose that the firm is financed entirely by equity. In this case, both the leverage ratio and the debt burden are equal to 1, and the return on equity is identical to the return on assets. If the firm borrows, however, the leverage ratio is greater than 1 (assets are greater than equity) and the debt burden is less than 1 (part of the profits is absorbed by interest). Thus leverage can either increase or reduce return on equity.

18-7 Measuring Liquidity

If you are extending credit to a customer or making a short-term bank loan, you are interested in more than the company's leverage. You want to know whether the company can lay its hands on the cash to repay you. That is why credit analysts and bankers look at several measures of **liquidity.** Liquid assets can be converted into cash quickly and cheaply.

Think, for example, what you would do to meet a large unexpected bill. You might have some money in the bank or some investments that are easily sold, but you would not find it so easy to turn your old sweaters into cash. Companies, likewise, own assets with different degrees of liquidity. For example, accounts receivable and inventories of finished goods are generally quite liquid. As inventories are sold off and customers pay their bills, money flows into the firm. At the other extreme, real estate may be very *illiquid.* It can be hard to find a buyer, negotiate a fair price, and close a deal on short notice.

Managers have another reason to focus on liquid assets: Their book (balance sheet) values are usually reliable. The book value of a catalytic cracker may be a poor guide to its true value, but at least you know what cash in the bank is worth. Liquidity ratios also have some *less* desirable characteristics. Because short-term assets and liabilities are easily changed, measures of liquidity can rapidly become outdated. You might not know what the catalytic cracker is worth, but you can be fairly sure that it won't disappear overnight. Cash in the bank can disappear in seconds.

Also, assets that seem liquid sometimes have a nasty habit of becoming illiquid. This happened during the subprime mortgage crisis in 2007. Some financial institutions had set up funds known as *structured investment vehicles (SIVs)* that issued short-term debt backed by residential mortgages. As mortgage default rates began to climb, the market in this debt dried up and dealers became very reluctant to quote a price. Investors, who were forced to sell, found that the prices that they received were less than half the debt's estimated value.

Bankers and other short-term lenders applaud firms that have plenty of liquid assets. They know that when they are due to be repaid, the firm will be able to get its hands on the cash. But more liquidity is not always a good thing. For example, efficient firms do not leave excess cash in their bank accounts. They don't allow customers to postpone paying their bills, and they don't leave stocks of raw materials and finished goods littering the warehouse floor. In other words, high levels of liquidity may indicate sloppy use of capital. Here, EVA can help, because it penalizes managers who keep more liquid assets than they really need.

Net-Working-Capital-to-Total-Assets Ratio Current assets include cash, marketable securities, inventories, and accounts receivable. Current assets are mostly liquid. The difference between current assets and current liabilities is known as *net working capital.* Since current assets usually exceed current liabilities, net working capital is generally positive. For Lowe's,

$$\text{Net working capital} = 9,251 - 8,022 = \$1,229 \text{ million}$$

Net working capital was 3.8% of total assets:

$$\frac{\text{Net working capital}}{\text{total assets}} = \frac{1,229}{32,686} = .038, \text{ or } 3.8\%$$

Current Ratio The current ratio is just the ratio of current assets to current liabilities:

$$\text{Current ratio} = \frac{\text{current assets}}{\text{current liabilities}} = \frac{9,251}{8,022} = 1.15$$

Lowe's has $1.15 in current assets for every dollar in current liabilities.

Changes in the current ratio can be misleading. For example, suppose that a company borrows a large sum from the bank and invests it in marketable securities. Current liabilities rise and so do current assets. If nothing else changes, net working capital is unaffected but the current ratio changes. For this reason it is sometimes preferable to compare net short-term investments against short-term debt when calculating the current ratio.

Quick (Acid-Test) Ratio Some current assets are closer to cash than others. If trouble comes, inventory may not sell at anything above fire-sale prices. (Trouble typically comes *because* the firm can't sell its inventory of finished products for more than production cost.) Thus managers often exclude inventories and other less liquid components of current assets when comparing current assets to current liabilities. They focus instead on cash, marketable securities, and bills that customers have not yet paid. This results in the quick ratio:

$$\text{Quick ratio} = \frac{\text{cash} + \text{marketable securities} + \text{receivables}}{\text{current liabilities}} = \frac{661 + 166}{8,022} = .103$$

Cash Ratio A company's most liquid assets are its holdings of cash and marketable securities. That is why analysts also look at the cash ratio:

$$\text{Cash ratio} = \frac{\text{cash} + \text{marketable securities}}{\text{current liabilities}} = \frac{661}{8,022} = .082$$

A low cash ratio may not matter if the firm can borrow on short notice. Who cares whether the firm has actually borrowed from the bank or whether it has a guaranteed line of credit so it can borrow whenever it chooses? None of the standard measures of liquidity takes the firm's "reserve borrowing power" into account.

18-8 Interpreting Financial Ratios

We have shown how to calculate some common summary measures of Lowe's performance and financial condition. These are summarized in Table 18.6.[17] Now that you have calculated these measures, you need some way to judge whether they are high or low. In some cases there may be a natural benchmark. For example, if a firm has negative economic value added or a return on capital less than the cost of that capital, it is not creating wealth for its shareholders.

But what about some of our other measures? There is no right level for, say, the asset turnover or profit margin, and if there were, it would almost certainly vary from industry to industry and company to company. For example, you would not expect a soft-drink manufacturer to have the same profit margin as a jeweler or the same leverage as a finance company.

The alternative is to confine your comparison to companies that are in a similar business. A good starting point is to prepare *common-size financial statements* for each of these firms. In this case all items in the balance sheet are expressed as a percentage of total assets and all items in the income statement are expressed as a percentage of revenues.

We have not calculated here common-size statements for Lowe's, but Tables 18.7 and 18.8 provide summary common-size statements for a sample of U.S. industries. Notice the large variations. For example, retail firms have a major investment in inventory; software companies have almost none. High-tech businesses, such as semiconductors, hold huge amounts of cash; utilities hold very little. Oil companies and utilities invest principally in fixed assets; software companies and computer manufacturers have mainly current assets.

> **TABLE 18.6**
> Summary of Lowe's financial ratios.
>
>
>
> Visit us at
> www.mhhe.com/bma

Performance Measures:		
Market value added ($ millions)	market value of equity − book value of equity	8,684
Market-to-book ratio	market value of equity/book value of equity	1.5
EVA ($ millions)	(after-tax interest + net income) − (cost of capital × capital)	785
Return on capital (ROC)	(after-tax interest + net income)/total capital	11.0%
Return on equity (ROE)	net income/equity	13.6%
Return on assets (ROA)	(after-tax interest + net income)/total assets	7.7%
Efficiency Measures:		
Asset turnover	sales/total assets at start of year	1.56
Inventory turnover	cost of goods sold/inventory at start of year	4.17
Days in inventory	inventory at start of year/daily cost of goods sold	87.6
Receivables turnover	sales/receivables at start of year	195.3
Average collection period (days)	receivables at start of year/average daily sales	1.9
Profit margin (%)	net income/sales	4.55
Operating profit margin (%)	(after-tax interest + net income)/sales	4.95
Leverage Measures:		
Long-term debt ratio	long-term debt/(long-term debt + equity)	.22
Long-term debt–equity ratio	long-term debt/equity	.28
Total debt ratio	total liabilities/total assets	.45
Times-interest-earned	EBIT/interest payments	12.8
Cash coverage ratio	(EBIT + depreciation)/interest payments	17.9
Liquidity Measures:		
Net-working-capital-to-total-assets	net working capital/total assets	.038
Current ratio	current assets/current liabilities	1.15
Quick ratio	(cash + marketable securities + receivables)/current liabilities	.103
Cash ratio	(cash + marketable securities)/current liabilities	.082

---

[17]If you would like to see how we calculated these ratios or to calculate your own, you can use the "live" Excel spreadsheet available on our Web site at **www.mhhe.com/bma**.

	Industrials	Paper	Oil	Chemicals	Metals	Machinery	Pharmaceuticals	Computers	Software	Semiconductors	Telecoms	Utilities	Food	Retail
Assets:														
Cash & securities	11	4	6	5	7	13	19	35	21	31	31	2	3	6
Receivables	12	13	11	13	12	16	10	13	12	7	14	6	11	4
Inventories	9	11	5	11	15	15	9	4	1	6	7	3	12	26
Other current assets	4	3	2	2	3	5	5	7	12	5	3	4	4	3
Total current assets	36	30	24	31	37	49	44	58	46	49	55	15	30	38
Fixed assets	57	77	104	111	61	38	35	18	20	60	21	94	61	81
Depreciation	26	42	42	69	31	21	16	10	12	31	13	32	33	30
Net fixed assets	31	35	62	42	30	17	19	8	8	29	8	62	28	51
Other long-term assets	33	35	14	26	33	34	37	34	46	22	37	23	43	11
Total assets	100	100	100	100	100	100	100	100	100	100	100	100	100	100
Liabilities:														
Short-term debt	4	4	1	5	3	5	5	0	1	2	2	5	8	3
Payables	8	7	13	7	7	6	4	10	3	4	5	4	9	14
Other current liabilities	12	10	8	10	10	13	12	20	29	10	12	7	11	12
Total current liabilities	24	21	22	22	20	23	21	30	32	16	18	16	28	28
Long-term debt	23	31	12	25	22	15	18	9	20	27	19	33	34	22
Other long-term liabilities	15	16	20	23	18	10	10	10	12	8	8	27	15	9
Total liabilities	62	69	54	71	61	48	49	49	65	51	46	75	77	60
Stockholders' equity	37	30	45	28	38	52	51	51	34	49	54	24	23	40
Total liabilities and equity	100	100	100	100	100	100	100	100	100	100	100	100	100	100

▶ TABLE 18.7 Common-size balance sheets for U.S. companies in Standard & Poor's Composite Index, 2008. Entries for each company are expressed as a percentage of total assets and averaged by industry.

Note: Some columns do not add up because of rounding.
Source: Wharton Research Data Services (WRDS), http://wrds.wharton.upenn.edu.

Visit us at
www.mhhe.com/bma

	Industrials	Paper	Oil	Chemicals	Metals	Machinery	Pharmaceuticals	Computers	Software	Semiconductors	Telecoms	Utilities	Food	Retail
Sales	100.0	100.0	100.0	100.0	100.0	100.0	100.0	100.0	100.0	100.0	100.0	100.0	100.0	100.0
Costs	80.8	86.4	85.8	84.7	84.6	80.9	69.2	87.2	74.9	75.0	87.5	72.7	86.7	93.1
Depreciation	5.5	4.6	3.4	5.0	3.1	4.2	6.3	4.0	5.7	11.9	4.9	9.2	2.7	2.6
EBIT	13.6	9.1	10.8	10.3	12.3	14.9	24.5	8.8	19.4	13.1	7.6	18.1	10.6	4.3
Interest	1.8	2.2	0.4	1.7	1.3	1.2	1.6	0.3	1.9	1.8	1.0	7.1	2.1	0.8
Other items	0.0	0.6	1.7	0.8	0.2	0.5	2.4	1.8	1.0	0.4	0.5	2.1	0.3	0.0
Pretax income	11.8	6.2	8.6	7.8	10.8	13.2	20.6	6.7	16.5	11.0	6.1	8.9	8.2	3.5
Tax	7.0	1.7	5.3	1.8	3.2	3.9	5.7	3.9	4.7	2.2	2.0	3.7	2.2	1.1
Net income	4.8	4.5	3.4	6.0	7.6	9.4	14.9	2.7	11.8	8.8	4.0	5.2	6.1	2.3

▶ **TABLE 18.8** Common-size income statements for U.S. companies in Standard & Poor's Composite Index, 2008. Entries for each company are expressed as a percentage of revenues and averaged by industry.

Note: Some columns do not add up because of rounding.
Source: Wharton Research Data Services (WRDS), http://wrds.wharton.upenn.edu.

eXcel

Visit us at
www.mhhe.com/bma

	Industrials	Paper	Oil	Chemicals	Metals	Machinery	Pharmaceuticals	Computers	Software	Semiconductors	Telecoms	Utilities	Food	Retail
Return on equity, %*	12.8	15.2	7.4	21.6	20.5	17.9	29.2	5.4	34.4	18.9	7.4	21.3	26.9	5.8
Return on assets, %*	5.9	5.9	7.9	7.4	10.1	8.6	10.1	2.7	9.7	7.3	3.3	4.1	10.5	6.4
Sales-to-assets ratio*	.98	.98	2.19	1.04	1.19	.85	.63	.92	.75	.74	.71	.42	1.4	2.2
Operating profit margin, %	6.0	6.0	3.6	7.1	8.5	10.1	15.9	2.9	13.1	9.9	4.7	9.8	7.4	2.9
Sales to net working capital*	8.0	11.2	137.7	11.6	7.2	3.2	2.7	3.3	5.4	2.3	1.9	**	104.4	23.3
Receivables turnover*	8.5	7.7	20.3	8.1	10.0	5.1	6.2	7.1	6.4	10.5	5.2	7.4	12.9	63.2
Inventory turnover*	6.4	66.6	15.1	6.6	5.1	3.8	3.2	15.4	6.4	6.4	8.3	20.8	5.6	2.7
Long-term debt ratio, %	37.9	51.1	21.0	47.6	37.6	22.1	25.8	14.8	64.0	36.9	26.1	57.0	60.4	35.2
Current ratio	1.5	1.4	1.1	1.4	1.8	2.1	2.1	1.9	1.4	3.0	3.0	0.9	1.0	1.3
Quick ratio	1.0	0.8	0.7	0.8	0.9	1.3	1.4	1.6	1.0	2.3	2.5	0.5	0.5	0.3
Cash ratio	.5	.6	.5	.6	.6	.7	.5	.4	.4	.4	.8	.4	.4	.1

▶ **TABLE 18.9** Financial ratios for U.S. companies in Standard & Poor's Composite Index, 2008.

* Computed using year-end balance sheet data (see footnote 6).
**Negative working capital.
Source: Wharton Research Data Services (WRDS), http://wrds.wharton.upenn.edu.

eXcel

Visit us at
www.mhhe.com/bma

Table 18.9 lists some financial ratios for these companies. The variation between industries also shows up in many of the ratios. The differences arise partly from chance; sometimes the sun shines more kindly on some industries than on others. But the differences also reflect some fundamental industry factors. For example, notice the high debt ratios of utilities. By contrast, computer companies scarcely borrow at all. We pointed out earlier that some businesses are able to generate a high level of sales from relatively few assets. For example, you can see that the sales-to-assets ratio for retailers is more than three times that for pharmaceutical companies. But competition ensures that retailers earn a correspondingly lower margin on their sales. In the recession of 2008 retailers earned a lower return on assets than pharmaceutical firms.

When comparing Lowe's financial position, it makes sense to limit your comparison to the firm's main competitors. Table 18.10 sets out some key performance measures for Lowe's and The Home Depot. The Home Depot is a larger company and this extra scale allowed it to add more economic value. But in many other respects the two companies are similar. They generated a similar level of sales per dollar of assets, but Lowe's was able to realize a higher profit margin on these sales. As a result, Lowe's had a somewhat higher return on assets. Lowe's was also somewhat more conservatively financed than The Home Depot and had a higher cash ratio.

	Lowe's	The Home Depot
Performance Measures:		
Market value added ($ millions)	8,684	17,856
Market-to-book ratio	1.5	2.0
EVA ($ millions)	785	1,882
Return on capital (ROC) (%)	11.0	9.3
Return on equity (ROE) (%)	13.6	13.1
Return on assets (ROA) (%)	7.7	6.1
Efficiency Measures:		
Asset turnover	1.56	1.61
Inventory turnover	4.2	4.0
Days in inventory	87.6	90.5
Receivables turnover *	195.3	56.5
Average collection period (days) *	1.9	6.5
Profit margin (%)	4.55	3.2
Operating profit margin (%)	4.95	3.82
Leverage Measures:		
Long-term debt ratio	.22	.35
Total debt ratio	.45	.57
Times-interest-earned	12.8	6.8
Cash coverage ratio	17.9	9.6
Liquidity Measures:		
Net-working-capital-to-total-assets ratio	.038	.054
Current ratio	1.15	1.20
Quick ratio	.103	.134
Cash ratio	.082	.047

▶ **TABLE 18.10**
Selected financial ratios for Lowe's and The Home Depot, 2008.

* Both companies sell most of their receivables to a third party.

It may also be helpful to compare Lowe's financial ratios in 2008 with the equivalent figures in earlier years. For example, you can see in Figure 18.1 that, until 2006, Lowe's had been successful in increasing its return on assets. What accounts for this improvement? We know that ROA = asset turnover × operating profit margin. The figure shows that the improvement in ROA came from an increase in the profit margin. The sales that the company generated per dollar of assets declined. Here is where it may be useful to look at any changes in the makeup of the business.

▶ **FIGURE 18.1**

Lowe's financial ratios, 1996–2008

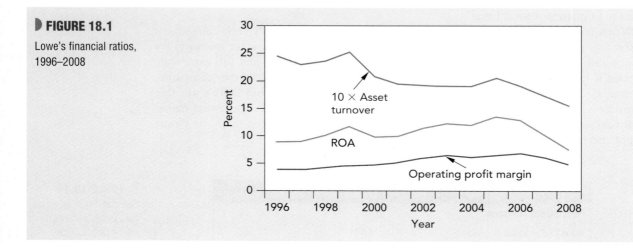

● ● ● ● ●

SUMMARY

Managers use financial statements to monitor their own company's performance, to help understand the policies of a competitor, and to check on the financial health of customers. But there is a danger of being overwhelmed by the sheer volume of data in the company's annual report.[18] That is why managers use a few salient ratios to summarize the firm's market valuation, profitability, efficiency, capital structure, and liquidity. We have described some of the more popular financial ratios.

We offer the following general advice to users of these ratios:

1. Financial ratios seldom provide answers, but they do help you to ask the right questions.
2. There is no international standard for financial ratios. A little thought and common sense are worth far more than blind application of formulas.
3. You need a benchmark for assessing a company's financial position. It is generally useful to compare the company's current financial ratios with the equivalent ratios in the past and with the ratios of other firms in the same business.

● ● ● ● ●

FURTHER READING

There are some good general texts on financial statement analysis. See, for example:

K. G. Palepu, V. L. Bernard, and P. M. Healy, *Business Analysis and Valuation*, 4th ed. (Cincinnati, OH: South-Western Publishing, 2008).

---

[18] HSBC's 2007 *Annual Report* totaled 454 pages. The *Financial Times* reported that Britain's postal service was obliged to limit the number that its postal carriers carried in order to prevent back injuries.

L. Revsine, D. Collins, B. Johnson, and F. Mittelstaedt, *Financial Reporting and Analysis,* 4th ed. (New York: McGraw-Hill/Irwin, 2008).

S. Penman, *Financial Statement Analysis and Security Valuation,* 4th ed. (New York: McGraw-Hill/Irwin, 2009).

BASIC

1. Construct a balance sheet for Galactic Enterprises given the following data:

Cash balances	$25,000
Inventories	$30,000
Net plant and equipment	$140,000
Accounts receivable	$35,000
Accounts payable	$24,000
Long-term debt	$130,000

   What is shareholders' equity?

2. Table 18.11 gives abbreviated balance sheets and income statements for Estée Lauder Companies. Calculate the following ratios:

   a. Return on assets.

   b. Operating profit margin.

   c. Sales-to-assets ratio.

   d. Inventory turnover.

   e. Debt–equity ratio.

   f. Current ratio.

   g. Quick ratio

3. Look again at Table 18.11. Calculate a common-size balance sheet and income statement for Estée Lauder.

4. Look again at Table 18.11. At the end of fiscal 2008 Estée Lauder had 195 million shares outstanding[19] with a share price of $45.50. The company's weighted-average cost of capital was about 10%. Calculate

   a. Market value added.

   b. Market-to-book ratio.

   c. Economic value added.

   d. Return on capital.

5. There are no universally accepted definitions of financial ratios, but five of the following ratios are clearly incorrect. Substitute the correct definitions.

   a. Debt–equity ratio = (long-term debt + value of leases)/(long-term debt + value of leases + equity)

   b. Return on equity = (EBIT − tax)/average equity

---

[19] The shares outstanding include a relatively small number of class B shares.

TABLE 18.11

Balance sheets and income statement for Estée Lauder Companies, fiscal 2008 (figures in $ millions).

Visit us at
www.mhhe.com/bma

	End of Year	Start of Year
Balance Sheet		
Assets		
Current assets:		
Cash and marketable securities	402	254
Accounts receivable	1,039	861
Inventories	987	856
Other current assets	360	269
Total current assets	2,787	2,239
Fixed assets:		
Tangible fixed assets		
Property, plant, and equipment	2,394	2,113
Less accumulated depreciation	1,351	1,232
Net tangible fixed assets	1,043	881
Long-term investments	24	22
Other long-term assets	1,157	984
Total assets	5,011	4,126
Liabilities and Shareholders' Equity		
Current liabilities:		
Debt due for repayment	119	60
Accounts payable	1,581	1,440
Total current liabilities	1,699	1,501
Long-term debt	1,078	1,028
Other long-term liabilities	581	398
Total liabilities	3,358	2,927
Total shareholders' equity	1,653	1,199
Total liabilities and shareholders' equity	5,011	4,126
Income Statement		
Net sales	7,911	
Cost of goods sold	1,997	
Selling, general, and administrative expenses	4,852	
Depreciation	251	
Earnings before interest and taxes (EBIT)	811	
Interest expense	67	
Taxable income	744	
Tax	260	
Minority interest	10	
Net income	474	
Dividends	107	
Addition to retained earnings	367	

    c. Profit margin = net income/sales

    d. Days in inventory = sales/(inventory/365)

    e. Current ratio = current liabilities/current assets

    f. Sales-to-net-working-capital = average sales/average net working capital

    g. Quick ratio = (current assets − inventories)/current liabilities

    h. Times-interest-earned = interest earned × long-term debt

6. True or false?

    a. A company's debt–equity ratio is always less than 1.

    b. The quick ratio is always less than the current ratio.

    c. The return on equity is always less than the return on assets.

7. Keller Cosmetics maintains an operating profit margin of 8% and a sales-to-assets ratio of 3. It has assets of $500,000 and equity of $300,000. Interest payments are $30,000 and the tax rate is 35%.

   a. What is the return on assets?

   b. What is the return on equity?

8. A firm has a long-term debt–equity ratio of .4. Shareholders' equity is $1 million. Current assets are $200,000, and total assets are $1.5 million. If the current ratio is 2.0, what is the ratio of debt to total long-term capital?

9. Magic Flutes has total receivables of $3,000, which represent 20 days' sales. Total assets are $75,000. The firm's operating profit margin is 5%. Find the firm's sales-to-assets ratio and return on assets.

10. Consider this simplified balance sheet for Geomorph Trading:

Current assets	$100	$ 60	Current liabilities
Long-term assets	500	280	Long-term debt
		70	Other liabilities
		190	Equity
	$600	$600	

   a. Calculate the ratio of debt to equity.

   b. What are Geomorph's net working capital and total long-term capital? Calculate the ratio of debt to total long-term capital.

11. Look again at the balance sheet for Geomorph in Problem 10. Suppose that at year-end Geomorph had $30 in cash and marketable securities. Immediately after the year-end it used a line of credit to borrow $20 for one year, which it invested in additional marketable securities. Would the company appear to be (a) more or less liquid, (b) more or less highly leveraged? Make any additional assumptions that you need.

12. Airlux Antarctica has current assets of $300 million, current liabilities of $200 million, and a crash—sorry—*cash* ratio of .05. How much cash and marketable securities does it hold?

13. On average, it takes Microlimp's customers 60 days to pay their bills. If Microlimp has annual sales of $500 million, what is the average value of unpaid bills?

INTERMEDIATE

14. This question reviews some of the difficulties encountered in interpreting accounting numbers.

   a. Give four examples of important assets, liabilities, or transactions that may not be shown on the company's books.

   b. How does investment in intangible assets, such as research and development, distort accounting ratios? Give at least two examples.

15. Describe some alternative measures of a firm's overall performance. What are their advantages and disadvantages? In each case discuss what benchmarks you might use to judge whether performance is satisfactory.

16. Discuss alternative measures of financial leverage. Should the market value of equity be used or the book value? Is it better to use the market value of debt, the book value, or the book value discounted at the risk-free interest rate? How should you treat off-balance-sheet obligations such as pension liabilities? How would you treat preferred stock?

17. Suppose that a firm has both fixed-rate and floating-rate debt outstanding. What effect will a decline in interest rates have on the firm's times-interest-earned ratio? What about the ratio of the market value of debt to that of equity? Would you judge that leverage has increased or decreased?

18. How would the following actions affect a firm's current ratio?

    a. Inventory is sold.

    b. The firm takes out a bank loan to pay its suppliers.

    c. The firm arranges a line of credit with a bank that allows it to borrow at any time to pay its suppliers.

    d. A customer pays its overdue bills.

    e. The firm uses cash to purchase additional inventories.

19. Sara Togas sells all its output to Federal Stores. The following table shows selected financial data, in millions, for the two firms:

	Sales	Interest Payment	Net Income	Assets at Start of Year
Federal Stores	$100	$4	$10	$50
Sara Togas	20	1	4	20

   Calculate the sales-to-assets ratio, the operating profit margin, and the return on assets for the two firms. Now assume that the two companies merge. If Federal continues to sell goods worth $100 million, how will the three ratios change?

Visit us at
www.mhhe.com/bma

20. As you can see, someone has spilled ink over some of the entries in the balance sheet and income statement of Transylvania Railroad (Table 18.12). Can you use the following information to work out the missing entries?

    • Debt ratio: .4.

    • Times-interest-earned: 6.25.

    • Current ratio: 1.4.

    • Quick ratio: 1.0.

    • Cash ratio: .2.

    • Return on equity: 24%.

    • Inventory turnover: 5.0.

    • Receivables collection period: 71.2 days.

21. Here are some data for five companies in the same industry:

	Company Code				
	A	B	C	D	E
EBIT	10	30	100	−3	80
Interest expense	5	15	50	2	1

   You have been asked to calculate a measure of times-interest-earned for the industry. Discuss the possible ways that you might calculate such a measure. Does changing the method of calculation make a significant difference to the end result?

22. How would rapid inflation affect the accuracy and relevance of a manufacturing company's balance sheet and income statement? Does your answer depend on how much debt the firm has issued?

23. Suppose that you wish to use financial ratios to estimate the risk of a company's stock. Which of those that we have described in this chapter are likely to be helpful? Can you think of other accounting measures of risk?

24. Look up some firms that have been in trouble. Plot the changes over the preceding years in the principal financial ratios. Are there any patterns?

Visit us at www.mhhe.com/bma

	December 2009	December 2008
Balance Sheet		
Cash	✦✦✦	20
Accounts receivable	✦✦✦	34
Inventory	✦✦✦	26
Total current assets	✦✦✦	80
Fixed assets, net	✦✦✦	110
Total	✦✦✦	190
Notes payable	30	20
Accounts payable	25	15
Total current liabilities	✦✦✦	35
Long-term debt	✦✦✦	55
Equity	✦✦✦	100
Total	235	190
Income Statement		
Sales	✦✦✦	
Cost of goods sold	✦✦✦	
Selling, general, and administrative expenses	10	
Depreciation	20	
EBIT	✦✦✦	
Interest	✦✦✦	
Earnings before tax	✦✦✦	
Tax	✦✦✦	
Earnings available for common stock	✦✦✦	

▶ **TABLE 18.12**
Balance sheet and income statement of Transylvania Railroad (figures in $ millions).

CHALLENGE

25. We noted that, when calculating EVA, you should calculate income as the sum of the after-tax interest payment and net income. Why do you need to deduct the tax shield? Would an alternative be to use a different measure of the cost of capital? Or would you get the same result if you simply deducted the cost of equity from net income (as is often done)?

26. Sometimes analysts use the average of capital at the start and end of the year to calculate return on capital. Provide some examples to illustrate when this does and does not make sense. (*Hint:* Start by assuming that capital increases solely as a result of retained earnings.)

27. Take another look at Geomorph Trading's balance sheet in Problem 10 and consider the following additional information:

Current Assets		Current Liabilities		Other Liabilities	
Cash	$ 15	Payables	$35	Deferred tax	$32
Inventories	35	Taxes due	10	Unfunded pensions	22
Receivables	50	Bank loan	15	R&R reserve	16
	$100		$60		$70

The "R&R reserve" covers the future costs of removal of an oil pipeline and environmental restoration of the pipeline route.

There are many ways to calculate a debt ratio for Geomorph. Suppose you are evaluating the safety of Geomorph's debt and want a debt ratio for comparison with the ratios of other companies in the same industry. Would you calculate the ratio in terms of total liabilities or total capitalization? What would you include in debt—the bank loan, the deferred tax account, the R&R reserve, the unfunded pension liability? Explain the pros and cons of these choices.

● ● ● ● ●

REAL-TIME DATA ANALYSIS

STANDARD &POOR'S

STANDARD &POOR'S

STANDARD &POOR'S

STANDARD &POOR'S

Use data from the Standard & Poor's Market Insight Database (www.mhhe.com/edumarketinsight) or Yahoo! Finance (http://finance.yahoo.com) to answer the following questions.

1. Find financial ratios for five different industries. Can you account for some of the differences between industries?

2. Select two companies that are in a similar line of business and find their simplified balance sheets and income statements. Then draw up common-size statements for each company and compute the principal financial ratios. Compare and contrast the companies based on these data.

3. Look up the latest financial statements for a company of your choice and calculate the following ratios for the latest year:
   a. Return on capital.
   b. Return on equity.
   c. Operating profit margin.
   d. Days in inventory.
   e. Debt ratio.
   f. Times-interest-earned.
   g. Current ratio.
   h. Quick ratio.

4. Select five companies and, using their financial statements, compare the days in inventory and average collection period for receivables. Can you explain the differences between the companies?

FINANCIAL PLANNING AND
WORKING CAPITAL MANAGEMENT

Financial Planning

▶ **This chapter is** concerned with financial planning. We look first at short-term planning where the focus is on ensuring that the firm does not run out of cash. Short-term planning is, therefore, often termed *cash budgeting.* In the second half of the chapter we look at how firms also use financial planning models to develop a coherent *long-term* strategy.

In the last chapter we introduced you to the principal short-term assets—inventory, accounts receivable, cash, and marketable securities. Decisions on these assets cannot be made in isolation. For example, suppose that the marketing manager wishes to give customers more time to pay for their purchases. This reduces the firm's future cash balances. Or perhaps the production manager adopts a just-in-time system for ordering from suppliers. That allows the firm to get by on smaller inventories and frees up cash.

Managers concerned with short-term financial decisions can avoid many of the difficult conceptual issues encountered elsewhere in this book. In that respect short-term decisions are easier than long-term decisions, but they are not less important. A firm can identify extremely valuable capital investment opportunities, find the precise

optimal debt ratio, follow the perfect dividend policy, and yet founder because no one bothers to raise the cash to pay this year's bills. Hence the need for short-term planning.

Companies that need to borrow to fund a short-term deficit may either take out a loan from a bank or issue their own short-term loans. Those that are in the happier position of having a short-term cash surplus can invest it in the money market. In the Appendix to this chapter we describe these short-term sources and uses of cash.

Short-term planning rarely looks further ahead than the next 12 months. It seeks to ensure that the firm has enough cash to pay its bills and makes sensible short-term borrowing and lending decisions. But the financial manager also needs to think about the investments that will be needed to meet the firm's *long-term* goals and the financing that must be arranged. Long-term financial planning focuses on the implications of alternative financial strategies. It allows managers to avoid some surprises and consider how they should react to surprises that *cannot* be avoided. And it helps to establish goals for the firm and to provide standards for measuring performance.

● ● ● ● ●

19-1 Links between Short-Term and Long-Term Financing Decisions

Short-term financial decisions differ in two ways from long-term decisions such as the purchase of plant and equipment or the choice of capital structure. First, they generally involve short-lived assets and liabilities, and, second, they are usually easily reversed. Compare, for example, a 60-day bank loan with an issue of 20-year bonds. The bank loan is clearly a short-term decision. The firm can repay it two months later and be right back where it started. A firm might conceivably issue a 20-year bond in January and retire it in March, but it would be extremely inconvenient and expensive to do so. In practice, the bond issue is a long-term decision, not only because of the bond's 20-year maturity but also because the decision to issue it cannot be reversed on short notice.

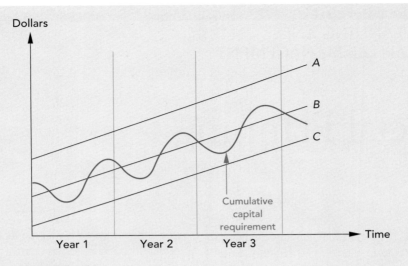

FIGURE 19.1

The firm's cumulative capital requirement (red line) is the cumulative investment in all the assets needed for the business. This figure shows that the requirement grows year by year, but there is some seasonal fluctuation within each year. The requirement for short-term financing is the difference between long-term financing (lines *A*, *B*, and *C*) and the cumulative capital requirement. If long-term financing follows line *C*, the firm always needs short-term financing. At line *B*, the need is seasonal. At line *A*, the firm never needs short-term financing. There is always extra cash to invest.

Short-term financing needs are nevertheless tied to the firm's long-term decisions. All businesses require capital—that is, money invested in plant, machinery, inventories, accounts receivable, and all the other assets it takes to run a business. These assets can be financed by either long-term or short-term sources of capital.

Let us call the total investment the firm's *cumulative capital requirement*. For most firms the cumulative capital requirement grows irregularly, like the wavy line in Figure 19.1. This line shows a clear upward trend as the firm's business grows. But the figure also shows seasonal variation around the trend, with the capital requirement peaking late in each year. In addition, there would be unpredictable week-to-week and month-to-month fluctuations, but we have not attempted to show these in Figure 19.1.

When long-term financing does not cover the cumulative capital requirement, the firm must raise short-term capital to make up the difference. When long-term financing *more* than covers the cumulative capital requirement, the firm has surplus cash available. Thus the amount of long-term financing raised, given the capital requirement, determines whether the firm is a short-term borrower or lender.

Lines *A*, *B*, and *C* in Figure 19.1 illustrate this. Each depicts a different long-term financing strategy. Strategy *A* implies a permanent cash surplus, which can be invested in short-term securities. Strategy *C* implies a permanent need for short-term borrowing. Under *B*, which is probably the most common strategy, the firm is a short-term lender during part of the year and a borrower during the rest.

What is the *best* level of long-term financing relative to the cumulative capital requirement? It is hard to say. There is no convincing theoretical analysis of this question. We can make practical observations, however. First, most financial managers attempt to "match maturities" of assets and liabilities.[1] That is, they largely finance long-lived assets like plant and machinery with long-term borrowing and equity. Second, most firms make a permanent investment in net working capital (current assets less current liabilities). This investment is financed from long-term sources.

Current assets can be converted into cash more easily than long-term assets. So firms with large holdings of current assets enjoy greater liquidity. Of course, some of these assets are more liquid than others. Inventories are converted into cash only when the goods are produced, sold, and paid for. Receivables are more liquid; they become cash as customers pay their outstanding bills. Short-term securities can generally be sold if the firm needs cash on short notice and are therefore more liquid still.

Some firms choose to hold more liquidity than others. For example, many high-tech companies, such as Intel and Cisco, hold huge amounts of short-term securities. On the other hand, firms in old-line manufacturing industries—such as chemicals, paper, or steel—manage with a far smaller reserve of liquidity. Why is this? One reason is that companies with rapidly growing profits may generate cash faster than they can redeploy it in new positive-NPV investments. This produces a surplus of cash that can be invested in short-term securities. Of course, companies faced with a growing mountain of cash may eventually respond by adjusting their payout policies. In Chapter 12 we saw how Microsoft reduced its cash mountain by paying a special dividend and repurchasing its stock.

There are some advantages to holding a large reservoir of cash, particularly for smaller firms that face relatively high costs to raising funds on short notice. For example, biotech firms require large amounts of cash to develop new drugs. Therefore, these firms generally have substantial cash holdings to fund their R&D programs. If these precautionary reasons for holding liquid assets are important, we should find that small companies in relatively high-risk industries are more likely to hold large cash surpluses. A study by Tim Opler and others confirms that this is in fact the case.[2]

Financial managers of firms with a surplus of long-term financing and with cash in the bank don't have to worry about finding the money to pay next month's bills. The cash can help to protect the firm against a rainy day and give it the breathing space to make changes to operations. However, there are also drawbacks to surplus cash. Holdings of marketable securities are at best a zero-NPV investment for a taxpaying firm.[3] Also managers of firms with large cash surpluses may be tempted to run a less tight ship and may simply allow the cash to seep away in a succession of operating losses. For example, at the end of 2007 General Motors held $27 billion in cash and short-term investments. But shareholders valued GM stock at less than $14 billion. It seemed that shareholders realized that the cash would be used to support ongoing losses and to service GM's huge debts.

Pinkowitz and Williamson looked at the value that investors place on a firm's cash and found that on average shareholders valued a dollar of cash at $1.20.[4] They placed a particularly high value on liquidity in the case of firms with plenty of growth opportunities. At the

[1] A survey by Graham and Harvey found that managers considered that the desire to match the maturity of the debt with that of the assets was the single most important factor in their choice between short- and long-term debt. See J. R. Graham and C. R. Harvey, "The Theory and Practice of Finance: Evidence from the Field," *Journal of Financial Economics* 61 (May 2001), pp. 187–243. Stohs and Mauer confirm that firms with a preponderance of short-term assets do indeed tend to issue short-term debt. See M. H. Stohs and D. C. Mauer, "The Determinants of Corporate Debt Maturity Structure," *Journal of Business* 69 (July 1996), pp. 279–312.

[2] T. Opler, L. Pinkowitz, R. Stulz, and R. Williamson, "The Determinants and Implications of Corporate Cash Holdings," *Journal of Financial Economics* 52 (April 1999), pp. 3–46.

[3] If, as most people believe, there is a tax advantage to borrowing there must be a corresponding tax disadvantage to lending, since the firm must pay tax at the corporate rate on the interest that it receives from Treasury bills. In this case investment in Treasury bills has a negative NPV. See Section 14–1.

[4] L. Pinkowitz and R. Williamson. "The Market Value of Cash," *Journal of Applied Corporate Finance* 19 (2007), pp. 74–81.

other extreme, they found that, when a firm was likely to face financial distress, a dollar of cash within the firm was often worth less than a dollar to the shareholders.[5]

19-2 Tracing Changes in Cash

Table 19.1 shows the 2009 income statement for Dynamic Mattress Company, and Table 19.2 compares the firm's 2008 and 2009 year-end balance sheets. You can see that in 2009 Dynamic's cash balance increased from $20 million to $25 million.

What caused this increase? Did the extra cash come from Dynamic's issue of long-term debt, from reinvested earnings, from cash released by reducing inventory, or from extra credit extended by Dynamic's suppliers? (Note the increase in accounts payable.) The answer is provided in the company's cash flow statement shown in Table 19.3.

Cash flow statements classify cash flows into those from operating activities, investing activities, and financing activities. Sources of cash are shown as positive numbers; uses of

▶ **TABLE 19.1**

Income statement for Dynamic Mattress Company, 2009 (figures in $ millions).

Visit us at
www.mhhe.com/bma

1	Sales	2,200
2	Cost of goods sold	1,644
3	Other expenses	411
4	Depreciation	20
5	EBIT (1−2−3−4)	125
6	Interest	5
7	Pretax income (5−6)	120
8	Tax at 50%	60
9	Net income (7−8)	60
	Dividend	30
	Earnings retained in the business	30

▶ **TABLE 19.2**

Year-end balance sheets for 2009 and 2008 for Dynamic Mattress Company (figures in $ millions).

Visit us at
www.mhhe.com/bma

	2009	2008
Current assets:		
Cash	25	20
Marketable securities	25	0
Accounts receivable	150	125
Inventory	125	130
Total current assets	325	275
Fixed assets:		
Gross investment	350	320
Less depreciation	100	80
Net fixed assets	250	240
Total assets	575	515
Current liabilities:		
Bank loans	0	25
Accounts payable	135	110
Total current liabilities	135	135
Long-term debt	90	60
Net worth (equity and retained earnings)	350	320
Total liabilities and net worth	575	515

---

[5] The apparent implication is that the firm should distribute the cash to shareholders. However, debtholders may place restrictions on dividend payments to the shareholders.

Cash flows from operating activities:	
Net income	60
Depreciation	20
Decrease (increase) in accounts receivable	−25
Decrease (increase) in inventories	5
Increase (decrease) in accounts payable	25
Net cash flow from operating activities	85
Cash flows from investing activities:	
Investment in fixed assets	−30
Cash flows from financing activities:	
Dividends	−30
Sale (purchase) of marketable securities	−25
Increase (decrease) in long-term debt	30
Increase (decrease) in short-term debt	−25
Net cash flow from financing activities	−50
Increase (decrease) in cash balance	5

▶ **TABLE 19.3**

Statement of cash flows for Dynamic Mattress Company, 2009 (figures in $ millions).

Visit us at
www.mhhe.com/bma

cash are shown as negative numbers. Dynamic's cash flow statement shows that Dynamic *generated* cash from the following sources:

1. It earned $60 million of net income (*operating activity*).
2. It set aside $20 million as depreciation. Remember that depreciation is *not* a cash outlay. Thus, it must be added back to obtain Dynamic's cash flow (*operating activity*).
3. It reduced inventory, releasing $5 million (*operating activity*).
4. It increased its accounts payable, in effect borrowing an additional $25 million from its suppliers (*operating activity*).
5. It issued $30 million of long-term debt (*financing activity*).

Dynamic's cash flow statement shows that it *used* cash for the following purposes:

1. It allowed accounts receivable to expand by $25 million (*operating activity*). In effect, it lent this additional amount to its customers.
2. It invested $30 million (*investing activity*). This shows up as the increase in gross fixed assets in Table 19.2.
3. It paid a $30 million dividend (*financing activity*). (*Note:* The $30 million increase in Dynamic's equity in Table 19.2 is due to retained earnings—$60 million of equity income, less the $30 million dividend.)
4. It purchased $25 million of marketable securities (*financing activity*).
5. It repaid $25 million of short-term bank debt (*financing activity*).[6]

Look again at Table 19.3. Notice that to calculate cash flows from operating activities, we start with net income and then make two adjustments. First, since depreciation is *not* a cash outlay, we must add it back to net income.[7] Second, we need to recognize the fact

---

[6] This is principal repayment, not interest. Sometimes interest payments are explicitly recognized as a use of funds. If so, cash flow from operations would be defined *before* interest, that is, as net income plus interest plus depreciation.

[7] There is a potential complication here, for the depreciation figure shown in the company's report to shareholders is rarely the same as the depreciation figure used to calculate tax. The reason is that firms can minimize their current tax payments by using *accelerated* depreciation when computing their taxable income. As a result, the shareholder books (which generally use straight-line depreciation) overstate the firm's current tax liability. Accelerated depreciation does not eliminate taxes; it only delays them. Since the ultimate liability has to be recognized, the additional taxes that will need to be paid are shown on the balance sheet as a deferred tax liability. In the statement of cash flows any increase in deferred taxes is treated as a source of funds. In the Dynamic Mattress example we ignore deferred taxes.

that the income statement shows sales and expenditures when they are made, rather than when cash changes hands. For example, think of what happens when Dynamic sells goods on credit. The company records a profit at the time of sale, but there is no cash inflow until the bills are paid. Since there is no cash inflow, there is no change in the company's cash balance, although there is an increase in working capital in the form of an increase in accounts receivable. No net addition to cash would be shown in a cash flow statement like Table 19.3. The increase in cash from operations would be offset by an increase in accounts receivable. Later, when the bills are paid, there is an increase in the cash balance. However, there is no further profit at this point and no increase in working capital. The increase in the cash balance is exactly matched by a decrease in accounts receivable.

Table 19.3 adjusts the cash flow from operating activities *downward* by $25 million to reflect the additional credit that Dynamic has extended to its customers. On the other hand, in 2009 Dynamic reduced its inventories and increased the amount that is owed to its suppliers. The cash flow from operating activities is adjusted *upward* to reflect these changes.

That brings up an interesting characteristic of working capital. Imagine a company that conducts a very simple business. It buys raw materials for cash, processes them into finished goods, and then sells these goods on credit. The whole cycle of operations looks like this:

If you draw up a balance sheet at the beginning of the process, you see cash. If you delay a little, you find the cash replaced by inventories of raw materials and, still later, by inventories of finished goods. When the goods are sold, the inventories give way to accounts receivable, and, finally, when the customers pay their bills, the firm draws out its profit and replenishes the cash balance.

There is only one constant in this process, namely, working capital. That is one reason why (net) working capital is a useful summary measure of current assets and liabilities. The strength of the working-capital measure is that it is unaffected by seasonal or other temporary movements between different current assets or liabilities. But the strength is also its weakness, for the working-capital figure hides a lot of interesting information. In our example cash was transformed into inventory, then into receivables, and back into cash again. But these assets have different degrees of risk and liquidity. You can't pay bills with inventory or with receivables, you must pay with cash.

The Cash Cycle

In Chapter 18 we showed how to calculate the average time that materials remain in inventory and the average time that it takes for customers to pay their bills. In the case of Dynamic:

$$\text{Average days in inventory} = \frac{\text{inventory at start of year}}{\text{daily cost of goods sold}} = \frac{130}{1,644/365} = 29 \text{ days}$$

$$\text{Average collection period} = \frac{\text{receivables at start of year}}{\text{average daily sales}} = \frac{125}{2,200/365} = 21 \text{ days}$$

We can also calculate the average time that it takes *Dynamic* to pay its bills:[8]

$$\text{Average payment period} = \frac{\text{payables at start of year}}{\text{daily cost of goods sold}} = \frac{110}{1,644/365} = 24 \text{ days}$$

Think what this implies for the financing that is needed to maintain regular operations. Suppose that Dynamic purchases materials on day 0. It pays for these materials on day 24 (average payment period = 24 days). By day 29 Dynamic has converted the raw materials into finished mattresses that are then sold (days in inventory = 29). Twenty-one days later on day 50 Dynamic's customers pay for their purchases (collection period = 21). Thus, cash went out the door on day 24; it did not come back in again until day 50. This 26-day interval is called the *cash cycle* or *cash conversion period:*[9]

Cash cycle (days)	=	average days in inventory	+	average collection period	−	average payment period
26	=	29	+	21	−	24

The cash cycle affects the amount of working capital that the firm needs. For example, major machinery manufacturers typically hold large inventories and offer long payment periods. Their cash cycle is nearly six months and they need to make a substantial investment in net working capital. By contrast, utilities with their low investment in inventory have a cash cycle of only about one and a half months. Utilities often have negative working capital.

19-3 Cash Budgeting

The past is interesting for what one can learn from it. The financial manager's problem is to forecast *future* sources and uses of cash. These forecasts serve two purposes. First, they provide a standard, or budget, against which subsequent performance can be judged. Second, they alert the manager to future cash-flow needs. Cash, as we all know, has a habit of disappearing fast.

Preparing the Cash Budget: Inflows

We illustrate the preparation of the capital budget by continuing the example of Dynamic Mattress.

Most of Dynamic's cash inflow comes from the sale of mattresses. We therefore start with a sales forecast by quarter for 2010:[10]

	First Quarter	Second Quarter	Third Quarter	Fourth Quarter
Sales ($ millions)	560	502	742	836

But sales become accounts receivable before they become cash. Cash flow comes from *collections* on accounts receivable.

Most firms keep track of the average time it takes customers to pay their bills. From this they can forecast what proportion of a quarter's sales is likely to be converted into cash in that quarter and what proportion is likely to be carried over to the next quarter as accounts receivable. Suppose that 70% of sales are "cashed in" in the immediate quarter and 30% are cashed

---

[8] Since the balance sheet shows the cost of materials rather than the amount that the finished goods will eventually sell for, it makes sense to compare the level of inventories and payables with the cost of goods sold rather than with sales.

[9] The total length of time from the purchase of raw materials until the final payment by the customer is termed the *operating cycle.*

[10] Most firms would forecast by month instead of by quarter. Sometimes weekly or even daily forecasts are made. But presenting a monthly forecast would triple the number of entries in Table 19.4 and subsequent tables. We wanted to keep the examples as simple as possible.

in the following quarter. Table 19.4 shows forecasted collections under this assumption. For example, you can see that in the first quarter collections from current sales are 70% of $560, or $392 million. But the firm also collects 30% of the previous quarter's sales, or .3($397) = $119 million. Therefore total collections are $392 + $119 = $511 million.

Dynamic started the first quarter with $150 million of accounts receivable. The quarter's sales of $560 million were *added* to accounts receivable, but collections of $511 million were *subtracted*. Therefore, Table 19.4 shows that Dynamic ended the quarter with accounts receivable of $150 + 560 − 511 = $199 million. The general formula is

$$\text{Ending accounts receivable} = \text{beginning accounts receivable} + \text{sales} - \text{collections}$$

The top section of Table 19.5 shows forecasted sources of cash for Dynamic Mattress. Collection of receivables is the main source, but it is not the only one. Perhaps the firm plans to dispose of some land or expects a tax refund or payment of an insurance claim. All such items are included as "other" sources. It is also possible that you may raise additional capital by borrowing or selling stock, but we don't want to prejudge that question. Therefore, for the moment we just assume that Dynamic will not raise further long-term finance.

Preparing the Cash Budget: Outflows

So much for the incoming cash. Now for the outgoing. There always seem to be many more uses for cash than there are sources. For simplicity, we have condensed the uses into five categories in Table 19.5.

1. *Payments on accounts payable.* The firm has to pay its bills for raw materials, parts, electricity, etc. The cash-flow forecast assumes all these bills are paid on time, although Dynamic could probably delay payment to some extent. Delaying payment is sometimes called *stretching payables*. Stretching is one source of short-term financing, but for most firms it is an expensive source, because by stretching they lose discounts given to firms that pay promptly.

2. *Increase in inventories.* The expected increase in sales in 2010 requires additional investment in inventories.

3. *Labor, administrative, and other expenses.* This category includes all other regular business expenses.

4. *Capital expenditures.* Note that Dynamic Mattress plans a major capital outlay in the first quarter.

		First Quarter	Second Quarter	Third Quarter	Fourth Quarter
1	Receivables at start of period	150	199	181.6	253.6
2	Sales	560	502	742	836
	Collections:				
	Sales in current period (70%)	392	351.4	519.4	585.2
	Sales in last period (30%)	119*	168	150.6	222.6
3	Total collections	511	519.4	670	807.8
4	Receivables at end of period 1+2−3	199	181.6	253.6	281.8

▶ **TABLE 19.4**

To forecast Dynamic Mattress's collections on accounts receivable, you have to forecast sales and collection rates in 2010 (figures in $ millions).

Visit us at
www.mhhe.com/bma

*We assume that sales in the last quarter of the previous year were $397 million.

	First Quarter	Second Quarter	Third Quarter	Fourth Quarter
Sources of cash:				
Collections on accounts receivable	511	519.4	670	807.8
Other	0	0	77	0
Total sources	511	519.4	747	807.8
Uses of cash:				
Payments on accounts payable	250	250	267	261
Increase in inventory	150	150	170	180
Labor and other expenses	136	136	136	136
Capital expenditures	70	10	8	14.5
Taxes, interest, and dividends	46	46	46	46
Total uses	652	592	627	637.5
Sources minus uses	−141	−72.6	120	170.3
Calculation of short-term borrowing requirement:				
Cash at start of period	25	−116	−188.6	−68.6
Change in cash balance	−141	−72.6	120	170.3
Cash at end of period	−116	−188.6	−68.6	101.7
Minimum operating balance	25	25	25	25
Cumulative financing required	141	213.6	93.6	−76.7

▶ **TABLE 19.5**

Dynamic Mattress's cash budget for 2010 (figures in $ millions)

e**X**cel

Visit us at
www.mhhe.com/bma

5. *Taxes, interest, and dividend payments.* This includes interest on presently outstanding long-term debt but does not include interest on any additional borrowing to meet cash requirements in 2010. At this stage in the analysis, Dynamic does not know how much it will have to borrow, or whether it will have to borrow at all.

The forecasted net inflow of cash (sources *minus* uses) is shown by the shaded line in Table 19.5. Note the large negative figure for the first quarter: a $141 million forecasted *outflow*. There is a smaller forecasted outflow in the second quarter, and then substantial cash inflows in the third and fourth quarters.

The bottom part of Table 19.5 calculates how much financing Dynamic will have to raise if its cash-flow forecasts are right. It starts the year with $25 million in cash. There is a $141 million cash outflow in the first quarter, and so Dynamic will have to obtain at least $141 − 25 = $116 million of additional financing. This would leave the firm with a forecasted cash balance of exactly zero at the start of the second quarter.

Most financial managers regard a planned cash balance of zero as driving too close to the edge of the cliff. They establish a *minimum operating cash balance* to absorb unexpected cash inflows and outflows. We assume that Dynamic's minimum operating cash balance is $25 million. This means it will have to raise the full $141 million in the first quarter and $72.6 million more in the second quarter. Thus its *cumulative* financing requirement is $213.6 million by the second quarter. Fortunately, this is the peak: The cumulative requirement declines in the third quarter by $120 million to $93.6 million. In the final quarter Dynamic is out of the woods: Its cash balance is $101.7 million, well clear of its minimum operating balance.

The next step is to develop a *short-term financing plan* that covers the forecasted requirements in the most economical way. We move on to that topic after two general observations:

1. The large cash outflows in the first two quarters do not necessarily spell trouble for Dynamic Mattress. In part, they reflect the capital investment made in the first quarter: Dynamic is spending $70 million, but it should be acquiring an asset worth that much or more. In part, the cash outflows reflect low sales in the first half of the year; sales recover in the second half.[11] If this is a predictable seasonal pattern, the firm should have no trouble borrowing to tide it over the slow months.

2. Table 19.5 is only a best guess about future cash flows. It is a good idea to think about the *uncertainty* in your estimates. For example, you could undertake a sensitivity analysis, in which you inspect how Dynamic's cash requirements would be affected by a shortfall in sales or by a delay in collections. The trouble with such sensitivity analyses is that you are changing only one item at a time, whereas in practice a downturn in the economy might affect, say, sales levels *and* collection rates. An alternative but more complicated solution is to build a model of the cash budget and then to simulate possible alternative cash requirements. If cash requirements are difficult to predict, you may wish to hold additional cash or marketable securities to cover a possible unexpected cash outflow.

19-4 The Short-Term Financing Plan

Dynamic's cash budget defines its problem: Its financial manager must find short-term financing to cover the firm's forecasted cash requirements. There are dozens of sources of short-term financing, but for simplicity we assume that Dynamic has just two options.

Options for Short-Term Financing

1. *Bank loan:* Dynamic has an existing arrangement with its bank allowing it to borrow up to $100 million at an interest cost of 10% a year or 2.5% per quarter. The firm can borrow and repay whenever it wants to do so, as long as it does not exceed its credit limit.

2. *Stretching payables:* Dynamic can also raise capital by putting off paying its bills. The financial manager believes that Dynamic can defer up to $100 million of payables each quarter. Thus, $100 million can be saved in the first quarter by *not* paying bills in that quarter. (Note that the cash-flow forecasts in Table 19.5 assumed that these bills *will* be paid in the first quarter.) If deferred, these payments *must* be made in the second quarter, but a further $100 million of the second-quarter bills can be deferred to the third quarter, and so on.

Stretching payables is often costly, even if no ill will is incurred. The reason is that suppliers may offer discounts for prompt payment. Dynamic loses this discount if it pays late. In this example we assume the lost discount is 5% of the amount deferred. In other words, if a $100 payment is delayed, the firm must pay $105 in the next quarter.

Dynamic's Financing Plan

With these two options, the short-term financing strategy is obvious. Use the bank loan first, if necessary up to the $100 million limit. If there is still a shortage of cash, stretch payables.

Table 19.6 shows the resulting plan. In the first quarter the plan calls for borrowing the full amount from the bank ($100 million) and stretching $16 million of payables (see lines 1 and 2 in the table). In addition the company sells the $25 million of marketable securities

---

[11] Maybe people buy more mattresses late in the year when the nights are longer.

		First Quarter	Second Quarter	Third Quarter	Fourth Quarter
	New borrowing:				
1	Bank loan	100.0	0.0	0.0	0.0
2	Stretching payables	16.0	92.4	0.0	0.0
3	Total	116.0	92.4	0.0	0.0
	Repayments:				
4	Bank loan	0.0	0.0	20.0	80.0
5	Stretching payables	0.0	16.0	92.4	0.0
6	Total	0.0	16.0	112.4	80.0
7	Net new borrowing	116.0	76.4	−112.4	−80.0
8	Plus securities sold	25.0	0.0	0.0	0.0
9	Less securities bought	0.0	0.0	0.0	87.8
10	Total cash raised	141.0	76.4	−112.4	−167.8
	Note: Cumulative borrowing and security sales				
	Bank loan	*100.0*	*100.0*	*80.0*	*0.0*
	Stretching payables	*16.0*	*92.4*	*0.0*	*0.0*
	Net securities sold	*25.0*	*25.0*	*25.0*	*−62.8*
	Interest payments:				
11	Bank loan	0.0	2.5	2.5	2.0
12	Stretching payables	0.0	0.8	4.6	0.0
13	Interest on securities sold	0.0	0.5	0.5	0.5
14	Net interest paid	0.0	3.8	7.6	2.5
15	Cash required for operations	141.0	72.6	−120.0	−170.3
16	Total cash required	141.0	76.4	−112.4	−167.8

▶ **TABLE 19.6**

Dynamic Mattress's financing plan (figures in $ millions).

Visit us at
www.mhhe.com/bma

it held at the end of 2009 (line 8). Thus it raises 100 + 16 + 25 = $141 million of cash in the first quarter (line 10).

In the second quarter, the plan calls for Dynamic to continue to borrow $100 million from the bank and to stretch $92.4 million of payables. This raises $76.4 million after paying off the $16 million of bills deferred from the first quarter.

Why raise $76.4 million when Dynamic needs only an additional $72.6 million to finance its operations? The answer is that the company must pay interest on the borrowings that it undertook in the first quarter and it forgoes interest on the marketable securities that were sold.[12]

In the third and fourth quarters the plan calls for Dynamic to pay off its debt and to make a purchase of marketable securities.

Evaluating the Plan

Does the plan shown in Table 19.6 solve Dynamic's short-term financing problem? No: The plan is feasible, but Dynamic can probably do better. The most glaring weakness is its reliance on stretching payables, an extremely expensive financing device. Remember that it costs Dynamic 5% *per quarter* to delay paying bills—an effective interest rate of over 20% per year. The first plan would merely stimulate the financial manager to search for cheaper sources of short-term borrowing.

---

[12] The bank loan calls for quarterly interest of .025 × 100 = $2.5 million; the lost discount on the payables amounts to .05 × 16 = $.8 million, and the interest lost on the marketable securities is .02 × 25 = $.5 million.

The financial manager would ask several other questions as well. For example:

1. Does the plan yield satisfactory current and quick ratios?[13] Its bankers may be worried if these ratios deteriorate.[14]

2. Are there intangible costs of stretching payables? Will suppliers begin to doubt Dynamic's creditworthiness?

3. Does the plan for 2010 leave Dynamic in good financial shape for 2011? (Here the answer is yes, since Dynamic will have paid off its short-term borrowing by the end of the year.)

4. Should Dynamic try to arrange long-term financing for the major capital expenditure in the first quarter? This seems sensible, following the rule of thumb that long-term assets deserve long-term financing. It would also reduce the need for short-term borrowing dramatically. A counterargument is that Dynamic is financing the capital investment only temporarily by short-term borrowing. By year-end, the investment is paid for by cash from operations. Thus Dynamic's initial decision not to seek immediate long-term financing may reflect a preference for ultimately financing the investment with retained earnings.

5. Is it possible to adjust the firm's operating and investment plans to make the short-term financing problem easier. Perhaps there is a way to defer the first quarter's large cash outflow? For example, suppose that the large capital investment in the first quarter is for new mattress-stuffing machines to be delivered and installed in the first half of the year. The new machines are not scheduled to be ready for full-scale use until August. Perhaps the machine manufacturer could be persuaded to accept 60% of the purchase price on delivery and 40% when the machines are installed and operating satisfactorily.

6. Should Dynamic release cash by reducing the level of other current assets? For example, it could reduce receivables by getting tough with customers who are late paying their bills. (The cost is that in the future these customers may take their business elsewhere.) Or it may be able to get by with lower inventories of mattresses. (The cost is that it may lose business if there is a rush of orders that it cannot supply.)

Short-term financing plans are developed by trial and error. You lay out one plan, think about it, and then try again with different assumptions on financing and investment alternatives. You continue until you can think of no further improvements.

Trial and error is important because it helps you understand the real nature of the problem the firm faces. Here we can draw a useful analogy between the *process* of planning and Chapter 10, "Project Analysis." In Chapter 10 we described sensitivity analysis and other tools used by firms to find out what makes capital investment projects tick and what can go wrong with them. Dynamic's financial manager faces the same kind of task here: not just to choose a plan but to understand what can go wrong and what will be done if conditions change unexpectedly.[15]

A Note on Short-Term Financial Planning Models

Working out a consistent short-term plan requires burdensome calculations.[16] Fortunately much of the arithmetic can be delegated to a computer. Many large firms have

---

[13] These ratios were discussed in Chapter 18.

[14] We have not worked out these ratios explicitly, but you can infer from Table 19.6 that they would be fine at the end of the year but relatively low midyear, when Dynamic's borrowing is high.

[15] This point is even more important in *long-term* financial planning.

[16] If you doubt that, look again at Table 19.6. Notice that the cash requirements in each quarter depend on borrowing in the previous quarter, because borrowing creates an obligation to pay interest. Moreover, the problem's complexity would have been tripled had we not simplified by forecasting per quarter rather than by month.

built *short-term financial planning models* to do this. Smaller companies do not face so much detail and complexity and find it easier to work with a spreadsheet program on a personal computer. In either case the financial manager specifies forecasted cash requirements or surpluses, interest rates, credit limits, etc., and the model grinds out a plan like the one shown in Table 19.6.

The computer also produces balance sheets, income statements, and whatever special reports the financial manager may require. Smaller firms that do not want custom-built models can rent general-purpose models offered by banks, accounting firms, management consultants, or specialized computer software firms.

Most of these models simply work out the consequences of the assumptions and policies specified by the financial manager. *Optimization* models for short-term financial planning are also available. These models are usually linear programming models. They search for the *best* plan from a range of alternative policies identified by the financial manager. Optimization helps when the firm faces complex problems where trial and error might never identify the *best* combination of alternatives.

Of course the best plan for one set of assumptions may prove disastrous if the assumptions are wrong. Thus the financial manager has to explore the implications of alternative assumptions about future cash flows, interest rates, and so on.

19-5 Long-Term Financial Planning

It's been said that a camel looks like a horse designed by a committee. If a firm made every decision piecemeal, it would end up with a financial camel. That is why smart financial managers also need to plan for the long term and to consider the financial actions that will be needed to support the company's long-term growth. Here is where finance and strategy come together. A coherent long-term plan demands an understanding of how the firm can generate superior returns by its choice of industry and by the way that it positions itself within that industry.

Long-term planning involves capital budgeting on a grand scale. It focuses on the investment by each line of business and avoids getting bogged down in details. Of course, some individual projects may be large enough to have significant individual impact. For example, the telecom giant Verizon recently began implementing a project to spend billions of dollars to deploy fiber-optic-based broadband technology to its residential customers. You can bet that this project was explicitly analyzed as part of its long-range financial plan. Normally, however, planners do not work on a project-by-project basis. Instead, they are content with rules of thumb that relate average levels of fixed and short-term assets to annual sales, and do not worry so much about seasonal variations in these relationships. In such cases, the likelihood that accounts receivable may rise as sales peak in the holiday season would be a needless detail that would distract from more important strategic decisions.

Why Build Financial Plans?

Firms spend considerable time and resources in long-term planning. What do they get for this investment?

Contingency Planning   Planning is not just forecasting. Forecasting concentrates on the most likely outcomes, but planners worry about unlikely events as well as likely ones. If you think ahead about what could go wrong, then you are less likely to ignore the danger signals and you can respond faster to trouble.

Companies have developed a number of ways of asking "what if" questions about both individual projects and the overall firm. For example, managers often work through the consequences of their decisions under different scenarios. One scenario might envisage high interest rates contributing to a slowdown in world economic growth and lower commodity prices. A second scenario might involve a buoyant domestic economy, high inflation, and a weak currency. The idea is to formulate responses to inevitable surprises. What will you do, for example, if sales in the first year turn out to be 10% below forecast? A good financial plan should help you adapt as events unfold.

Considering Options   Planners need to think whether there are opportunities for the company to exploit its existing strengths by moving into a wholly new area. Often they may recommend entering a market for "strategic" reasons—that is, not because the immediate investment has a positive net present value but because it establishes the firm in a new market and creates options for possibly valuable follow-on investments.

For example, Verizon's costly fiber-optic initiative gives the company the *real option* to offer additional services that may be highly valuable in the future, such as the rapid delivery of an array of home entertainment services. The justification for the huge investment lies in these potential growth options.

Forcing Consistency   Financial plans draw out the connections between the firm's plans for growth and the financing requirements. For example, a forecast of 25% growth might require the firm to issue securities to pay for necessary capital expenditures, while a 5% growth rate might enable the firm to finance these expenditures by using only reinvested profits.

Financial plans should help to ensure that the firm's goals are mutually consistent. For example, the chief executive might say that she is shooting for a profit margin of 10% and sales growth of 20%, but financial planners need to think about whether the higher sales growth may require price cuts that will reduce profit margin.

Moreover, a goal that is stated in terms of accounting ratios is not operational unless it is translated back into what that means for business decisions. For example, a higher profit margin can result from higher prices, lower costs, or a move into new, high-margin products. Why then do managers define objectives in this way? In part, such goals may be a code to communicate real concerns. For example, a target profit margin may be a way of saying that, in pursuing sales growth, the firm has allowed costs to get out of control. The danger is that everyone may forget the code and the accounting targets may be seen as goals in themselves. No one should be surprised when lower-level managers focus on the goals for which they are rewarded. For example, when Volkswagen set a goal of a 6.5% profit margin, some VW groups responded by developing and promoting expensive, high-margin cars. Less attention was paid to marketing cheaper models, which had lower profit margins but higher sales volume. As soon as this became apparent, Volkswagen announced that it would de-emphasize its profit margin goal and would instead focus on return on investment. It hoped that this would encourage managers to get the most profit out of every dollar of invested capital.

A Long-Term Financial Planning Model for Dynamic Mattress

Financial planners often use a financial planning model to help them explore the consequences of alternative strategies. We will drop in again on the financial manager of Dynamic Mattress to see how he uses a simple spreadsheet program to draw up the firm's long-term plan.

Long-term planning is concerned with the big picture. Therefore, when constructing long-term planning models it is generally acceptable to collapse all current assets and liabilities into a single figure for net working capital. Table 19.7 replaces Dynamic's latest balance sheets with condensed versions that report only net working capital rather than individual current assets or liabilities.

	2009	2008
Net working capital	190	140
Fixed assets:		
Gross investment	350	320
Less depreciation	100	80
Net fixed assests	250	240
Total net assets	440	380
Long-term debt	90	60
Net worth (equity and retained earnings)	350	320
Long-term liabilities and net worth*	440	380

▶ **TABLE 19.7**

Condensed year-end balance sheets for 2009 and 2008 for Dynamic Mattress Company (figures in $ millions).

*When only net working capital appears on a firm's balance sheet, this figure (the sum of long-term liabilities and net worth) is often referred to as *total capitalization.*

Visit us at
www.mhhe.com/bma

Suppose that Dynamic's analysis of the industry leads it to forecast a 20% annual growth in the company's sales and profits over the next five years. Can the company realistically expect to finance this out of retained earnings and borrowing, or should it plan for an issue of equity? Spreadsheet programs are tailor-made for such questions. Let's investigate.

The basic sources and uses relationship tells us that

$$\text{External capital required} = \text{investment in net working capital} + \text{investment in fixed assets}$$
$$+ \text{dividends} - \text{cash flow from operations}$$

Thus there are three steps to finding how much extra capital Dynamic will need and the implications for its debt ratio.

Step 1   Project next year's net income plus depreciation, assuming the planned 20% increase in revenues. The first column of Table 19.8 shows this figure for Dynamic in the latest year (2009) and is taken from Table 19.1. The remaining columns show the forecasted values for the following five years.

Step 2   Project what additional investment in net working capital and fixed assets will be needed to support this increased activity and how much of the net income will be paid out as dividends. The sum of these expenditures gives you the total *uses* of capital. If the total uses of capital exceed the cash flow generated by operations, Dynamic will need to raise additional long-term capital. The first column of Table 19.9 shows that in 2009 Dynamic needed to raise $30 million of new capital. The remaining columns forecast its capital needs for the following five years. For example, you can see that Dynamic will need to issue $144.5 million of debt in 2010 if it is to expand at the planned rate and not sell more shares.

Step 3   Finally, construct a forecast, or pro forma, balance sheet that incorporates the additional assets and the new levels of debt and equity. For example, the first column in Table 19.10 shows the latest condensed balance sheet for Dynamic Mattress. The remaining columns show that the company's equity grows by the additional retained earnings (net income less dividends), while long-term debt increases steadily to $691 million.

Over the five-year period Dynamic Mattress is forecasted to borrow an additional $601 million, and by year 2014 its debt ratio will have risen from 20% to 54%. The interest payments would still be comfortably covered by earnings and most financial managers could just about live with this amount of debt. However, the company could not continue to borrow at that rate beyond five years, and the debt ratio might be close to the limit set by the company's banks and bondholders.

An obvious alternative is for Dynamic to issue a mix of debt and equity, but there are other possibilities that the financial manager may want to explore. One option may be to hold back dividends during this period of rapid growth. An alternative might be to

		2009	2010	2011	2012	2013	2014
1	Revenues	2,200.0	2,640.0	3,168.0	3,801.6	4,561.9	5,474.3
2	Costs (92% of revenues)	2,055.0	2,428.8	2,914.6	3,497.5	4,197.0	5,036.4
3	Depreciation (9% of net fixed assets at start of year)	20.0	22.5	29.7	35.6	42.8	51.3
4	EBIT $(1-2-3)$	125.0	188.7	223.7	268.5	322.2	386.6
5	Interest (10% of long-term debt at start of year)	5.0	9.0	23.4	31.8	42.0	54.3
6	Tax at 50%	60.0	89.8	100.1	118.3	140.1	166.2
7	Net income $(4-5-6)$	60.0	89.8	100.1	118.3	140.1	166.2
8	Operating cash flow $(3+7)$	80.0	112.4	129.8	154.0	182.9	217.5

▶ **TABLE 19.8**

Actual (2009) and forecasted operating cash flows for Dynamic Mattress Company (figures in $ millions).

		2009	2010	2011	2012	2013	2014
	Sources of capital:						
1	Net income plus depreciation	80.0	112.4	129.8	154.0	182.9	217.5
	Uses of capital:						
2	Increase in net working capital (NWC) assuming NWC = 11% of revenues	50.0	100.4	58.1	69.7	83.6	100.4
3	Investment in fixed assets (FA) assuming net FA = 12.5% of revenues	30.0	102.5	95.7	114.8	137.8	165.4
4	Dividend (60% of net income)	30.0	53.9	60.1	71.0	84.1	99.7
5	Total uses of funds $(2+3+4)$	110.0	256.8	213.9	255.5	305.5	365.4
6	External capital required $(1-5)$	30.0	144.5	84.0	101.6	122.6	147.9

▶ **TABLE 19.9**

Actual (2009) and forecasted amounts of external capital required for Dynamic Mattress Company (figures in $ millions).

	2009	2010	2011	2012	2013	2014
Net working capital	190	290.4	348.5	418.2	501.8	602.2
Net fixed assets	250	330.0	396.0	475.2	570.2	684.3
Total net assets	440	620.4	744.5	893.4	1072.1	1286.5
Long-term debt	90	234.5	318.5	420.0	542.7	690.6
Equity	350	385.9	426.0	473.3	529.4	595.8
Total long-term liabilities and equity	440	620.4	744.5	893.4	1072.1	1286.5

▶ **TABLE 19.10**

Actual (2009) and pro forma balance sheets for Dynamic Mattress Company (figures in $ millions).

investigate whether the company could cut back on net working capital. For example, it may be able to economize on inventories or speed up the collection of receivables. The model makes it easy to examine these alternatives.

We stated earlier that financial planning is not just about exploring how to cope with the most likely outcomes. It also needs to ensure that the firm is prepared for unlikely or unexpected ones. For example, management would certainly wish to check that Dynamic

Mattress could cope with a cyclical decline in sales and profit margins. Sensitivity analysis or scenario analysis can help to do this.

Pitfalls in Model Design

The Dynamic Mattress model that we have developed is too simple for practical application. You probably have already thought of several ways to improve it—by keeping track of the outstanding shares, for example, and printing out earnings and dividends per share. Or you might want to distinguish between short-term lending and borrowing opportunities, now buried in working capital.

The model that we developed for Dynamic Mattress is known as a *percentage of sales model*. Almost all the forecasts for the company are proportional to the forecasted level of sales. However, in reality many variables will *not* be proportional to sales. For example, important components of working capital such as inventory and cash balances will generally rise less rapidly than sales. In addition, fixed assets such as plant and equipment are not usually added in small increments as sales increase. The Dynamic Mattress plant may well be operating at less than full capacity, so that the company can initially increase output without *any* additions to capacity. Eventually, however, if sales continue to increase, the firm may need to make a large new investment in plant and equipment.

But beware of adding too much complexity: There is always the temptation to make a model bigger and more detailed. You may end up with an exhaustive model that is too cumbersome for routine use. The fascination of detail, if you give in to it, distracts attention from crucial decisions like stock issues and payout policy.

Choosing a Plan

Financial planning models help the manager to develop consistent forecasts of crucial financial variables. For example, if you wish to value Dynamic Mattress, you need forecasts of future free cash flows. These are easily derived up to the end of the planning period from our financial planning model.[17] However, a planning model does not tell you whether the plan is optimal. It does not even tell you which alternatives are worth examining. For example, we saw that Dynamic Mattress is planning for a rapid growth in sales and earnings per share. But is that good news for the shareholders? Well, not necessarily; it depends on the opportunity cost of the capital that Dynamic Mattress needs to invest. If the new investment earns more than the cost of capital, it will have a positive NPV and add to shareholder wealth. If the investment earns less than the cost of capital, shareholders will be worse off, even though the company expects steady growth in earnings.

The capital that Dynamic Mattress needs to raise depends on its decision to pay out 60% of its earnings as a dividend. But the financial planning model does not tell us whether this dividend payment makes sense or what mixture of equity or debt the company should issue. In the end the management has to decide. We would like to tell you exactly how to make the choice, but we can't. There is no model that encompasses all the complexities encountered in financial planning and decision making.

As a matter of fact, there never will be one. This bold statement is based on Brealey, Myers, and Allen's Third Law:[18]

Axiom: The number of unsolved problems is infinite.

Axiom: The number of unsolved problems that humans can hold in their minds is at any time limited to 10.

---

[17] Look back at Table 15.1, where we set out the free cash flows for Rio Corporation. A financial planning model would be a natural tool for deriving these figures.

[18] The Second Law is presented in Section 10–1.

Law: Therefore in any field there will always be 10 problems that can be addressed but that have no formal solution.

BMA's Third Law implies that no model can find the best of all financial strategies.[19]

19-6 Growth and External Financing

We started this chapter by noting that financial plans force managers to be consistent in their goals for growth, investment, and financing. Before leaving the topic of financial planning, we should look at some general relationships between a firm's growth objectives and its financing needs.

Recall that Dynamic Mattress ended 2009 with fixed assets and net working capital of $440 million. In 2010 it plans to plow back retained earnings of $35.9 million, so net assets will increase by 35.9/440, or 8.16%. Thus Dynamic Mattress can grow by 8.16% without needing to raise additional capital. The maximum growth rate that a company can achieve without external funds is known as the **internal growth rate.** For Dynamic Mattress

$$\text{Internal growth rate} = \frac{\text{retained earnings}}{\text{net assets}} = 8.16\%$$

We can gain more insight into what determines this growth rate by multiplying the top and bottom of the expression for internal growth rate by *net income* and *equity* as follows:

$$\text{Internal growth rate} = \frac{\text{retained earnings}}{\text{net income}} \times \frac{\text{net income}}{\text{equity}} \times \frac{\text{equity}}{\text{net assets}}$$

In 2010 Dynamic Mattress expects to plow back 40% of net income and to earn a return of 25.66% on the equity with which it began the year. At the start of the year equity finances 79.55% of Dynamic Mattress's net assets. Therefore

$$\text{Internal growth rate} = .40 \times .2566 \times .7955 = .0816 \text{ or } 8.16\%$$

Notice that if Dynamic Mattress wishes to grow faster than this without raising equity capital, it would need to (1) plow back a higher proportion of its earnings, (2) earn a higher return on equity (ROE), or (3) have a lower debt-to-equity ratio.[20]

Instead of focusing on how rapidly the company can grow without *any* external financing, Dynamic Mattress's financial manager may be interested in the growth rate that can be sustained without additional *equity* issues. Of course, if the firm is able to raise enough debt, virtually any growth rate can be financed. It makes more sense to assume that the firm has settled on an optimal capital structure that it will maintain as equity is increased by the retained earnings. Thus the firm issues only enough debt to keep the debt–equity ratio constant. The **sustainable growth rate** is the highest growth rate the firm can maintain without increasing its financial leverage. It turns out that the sustainable growth rate depends only on the plowback rate and the return on equity:

$$\text{Sustainable growth rate} = \text{plowback ratio} \times \text{return on equity}$$

For Dynamic Mattress,

$$\text{Sustainable growth rate} = .40 \times .2566 = .1026, \text{ or } 10.26\%$$

---

[19] It is possible to build linear programming models that help search for the best strategy subject to specified assumptions and conditions. These models can be more effective in screening alternative financial strategies.

[20] Notice, however, that if assets grow by only 8.16%, either the sales-to-assets ratio or the profit margin must increase to maintain a 25.66% return on equity.

We first encountered this formula in Chapter 4, where we used it to value common stocks.

These simple formulas remind us that firms may grow rapidly in the short term by relying on debt finance, but such growth can rarely be maintained without incurring excessive debt levels.

SUMMARY

Short-term financial planning is concerned with the management of the firm's short-term, or current, assets and liabilities. The most important current assets are cash, marketable securities, accounts receivable, and inventory. The most important current liabilities are short-term loans and accounts payable. The difference between current assets and current liabilities is called (net) working capital.

The nature of the firm's short-term financial planning problem is determined by the amount of long-term capital it raises. A firm that issues large amounts of long-term debt or common stock, or that retains a large part of its earnings, may find it has permanent excess cash. In such cases there is never any problem paying bills, and short-term financial planning consists of managing the firm's portfolio of marketable securities. A firm holding a reserve of cash is able to buy itself time to react to a short-term crisis. This may be important for growth firms that find it difficult to raise cash on short notice. However, large cash holdings can lead to complacency. We suggest that firms with permanent cash surpluses ought to consider returning the excess cash to their stockholders.

Other firms raise relatively little long-term capital and end up as permanent short-term debtors. Most firms attempt to find a golden mean by financing all fixed assets and part of current assets with equity and long-term debt. Such firms may invest cash surpluses during part of the year and borrow during the rest of the year.

The starting point for short-term financial planning is an understanding of sources and uses of cash. Firms forecast their net cash requirements by estimating collections on accounts receivable, adding other cash inflows, and subtracting all cash outlays. If the forecasted cash balance is insufficient to cover day-to-day operations and to provide a buffer against contingencies, the company will need to find additional finance. The search for the best short-term financial plan inevitably proceeds by trial and error. The financial manager must explore the consequences of different assumptions about cash requirements, interest rates, sources of finance, and so on. Firms use computerized financial models to help in this process. These models range from simple spreadsheet programs that merely help with the arithmetic to linear programming models that search for the best financial plan.

Short-term financial planning focuses on the firm's cash flow over the coming year. But the financial manager also needs to consider what financial actions will be needed to support the firm's plans for growth over the next 5 or 10 years. Most firms, therefore, prepare a long-term financial plan that describes the firm's strategy and projects its financial consequences. The plan establishes financial goals and is a benchmark for evaluating subsequent performance.

The process that produces this plan is valuable in its own right. First, planning forces the financial manager to consider the combined effects of all the firm's investment and financing decisions. This is important because these decisions interact and should not be made independently. Second, planning requires the manager to consider events that could upset the firm's progress and to devise strategies to be held in reserve for counterattack when unhappy surprises occur.

There is no theory or model that leads straight to *the* optimal financial strategy. As in the case of short-term planning, many different strategies may be projected under a range of assumptions about the future. The dozens of separate projections that may need to be made generate a heavy load of arithmetic. We showed how you can use a simple spreadsheet model to analyze Dynamic Mattress's long-term strategy.

Visit us at www.mhhe.com/bma

● ● ● ● ●

FURTHER READING

The following text is concerned with liquidity management and short-term planning:

J. G. Kallberg and K. Parkinson, *Corporate Liquidity Management and Measurement*, (Burr Ridge, IL: Irwin/McGraw-Hill, 1996).

Long-term financial models are discussed in:

J. R. Morris and J. P Daley, *Introduction to Financial Models for Management and Planning* (Boca Raton, FL: Chapman & Hall/CRC Finance Series, 2009).

● ● ● ● ●

PROBLEM SETS

BASIC

1. Listed below are six transactions that Dynamic Mattress might make. Indicate how each transaction would affect (a) cash and (b) working capital.

   The transactions are

   i. Pay out an extra $10 million cash dividend.

   ii. Receive $2,500 from a customer who pays a bill resulting from a previous sale.

   iii. Pay $50,000 previously owed to one of its suppliers.

   iv. Borrow $10 million long term and invest the proceeds in inventory.

   v. Borrow $10 million short term and invest the proceeds in inventory.

   vi. Sell $5 million of marketable securities for cash.

2. State how each of the following events would affect the firm's balance sheet. State whether each change is a source or use of cash.

   a. An automobile manufacturer increases production in response to a forecasted increase in demand. Unfortunately, the demand does not increase.

   b. Competition forces the firm to give customers more time to pay for their purchases.

   c. Rising commodity prices increase the value of raw material inventories by 20%.

   d. The firm sells a parcel of land for $100,000. The land was purchased five years earlier for $200,000.

   e. The firm repurchases its own common stock.

   f. The firm doubles its quarterly dividend.

   g. The firm issues $1 million of long-term debt and uses the proceeds to repay a short-term bank loan.

3. Here is a forecast of sales by National Bromide for the first four months of 2010 (figures in $ thousands):

	Month 1	Month 2	Month 3	Month 4
Cash sales	15	24	18	14
Sales on credit	100	120	90	70

On the average 50% of credit sales are paid for in the current month, 30% are paid in the next month, and the remainder are paid in the month after that. What is the expected cash inflow from operations in months 3 and 4?

4. Dynamic Futon forecasts the following purchases from suppliers:

	Jan.	Feb.	Mar.	Apr.	May	Jun.
Value of goods ($ millions)	32	28	25	22	20	20

   a. Forty percent of goods are supplied cash-on-delivery. The remainder are paid with an average delay of one month. If Dynamic Futon starts the year with payables of $22 million, what is the forecasted level of payables for each month?

   b. Suppose that from the start of the year the company stretches payables by paying 40% after one month and 20% after two months. (The remainder continue to be paid cash on delivery.) Recalculate payables for each month assuming that there are no cash penalties for late payment.

5. Each of the following events affects one or more tables in Sections 19–2 to 19–3. Show the effects of each event by adjusting the tables listed in parentheses:

   a. Dynamic repays only $10 million of short-term debt in 2009. (Tables 19.2 and 19.3)

   b. Dynamic issues an additional $40 million of long-term debt in 2009 and invests $25 million in a new warehouse. (Tables 19.1–19.3)

   c. In 2009 Dynamic reduces the quantity of stuffing in each mattress. Customers don't notice, but operating costs fall by 10%. (Tables 19.1–19.3)

   d. Starting in the third quarter of 2010, Dynamic employs new staff members who prove very effective in persuading customers to pay more promptly. As a result, 90% of sales are paid for immediately and 10% are paid in the following quarter. (Tables 19.4 and 19.5)

   e. Starting in the first quarter of 2010, Dynamic cuts wages by $20 million a quarter. (Table 19.5)

   f. In the second quarter of 2010 a disused warehouse catches fire mysteriously. Dynamic receives a $50 million check from the insurance company. (Table 19.5)

   g. Dynamic's treasurer decides he can scrape by on a $10 million operating cash balance. (Table 19.5)

6. True or false?

   a. Financial planning should attempt to minimize risk.

   b. The primary aim of financial planning is to obtain better forecasts of future cash flows and earnings.

   c. Financial planning is necessary because financing and investment decisions interact and should not be made independently.

   d. Firms' planning horizons rarely exceed three years.

   e. Financial planning requires accurate forecasting.

   f. Financial planning models should include as much detail as possible.

7. Table 19.11 summarizes the 2011 income statement and year-end balance sheet of Drake's Bowling Alleys. Drake's financial manager forecasts a 10% increase in sales and costs in 2009. The ratio of sales to *average* assets is expected to remain at .40. Interest is forecasted at 5% of debt at the start of the year.

   a. What is the implied level of assets at the end of 2012?

   b. If the company pays out 50% of net income as dividends, how much cash will Drake need to raise in the capital markets in 2012?

   c. If Drake is unwilling to make an equity issue, what will be the debt ratio at the end of 2012?

8. Abbreviated financial statements for Archimedes Levers are shown in Table 19.12. If sales increase by 10% in 2011 and all other items, including debt, increase correspondingly, what must be the balancing item? What will be its value?

▶ **TABLE 19.11**

Financial statements for Drake's Bowling Alleys, 2011 (figures in thousands). See Problem 7.

*Assets at the end of 2010 were $2,400,000.

**Debt at the end of 2010 was $500,000.

Income Statement		
Sales	$1,000	(40% of average assets)*
Costs	750	(75% of sales)
Interest	25	(5% of debt at start of year)**
Pretax profit	225	
Tax	90	(40% of pretax profit)
Net income	$135	

Balance Sheet			
Assets	$2,600	Debt	$500
		Equity	2,100
Total	$2,600	Total	$2,600

▶ **TABLE 19.12**

Financial statements for Archimedes Levers, 2010. See Problems 8 and 9.

Income Statement	
Sales	$4,000
Costs, including interest	3,500
Net income	$500

Balance Sheet, Year-End					
	2010	**2009**		**2010**	**2009**
Assets	$3,200	$2,700	Debt	$1,200	$1,033
			Equity	2,000	1,667
Total	$3,200	$2,700	Total	$3,200	$2,700

9. What is the maximum possible growth rate for Archimedes (see Problem 8) if the payout ratio is set at 50% and (a) no external debt or equity is to be issued? (b) the firm maintains a fixed debt ratio but issues no equity?

INTERMEDIATE

10. Table 19.13 lists data from the budget of Ritewell Publishers. Half the company's sales are for cash on the nail; the other half are paid for with a one-month delay. The company pays all its credit purchases with a one-month delay. Credit purchases in January were $30, and total sales in January were $180. Complete the cash budget in Table 19.14 on page 511.

11. If a firm pays its bills with a 30-day delay, what fraction of its purchases will be paid in the current quarter? In the following quarter? What if the delay is 60 days?

12. Which items in Table 19.6 would be affected by the following events?

    a. There is a rise in interest rates.

    b. Suppliers demand interest for late payment.

    c. Dynamic receives an unexpected bill in the third quarter from the Internal Revenue Service for underpayment of taxes in previous years.

13. Table 19.15 on page 512 shows Dynamic Mattress's year-end 2007 balance sheet, and Table 19.16 on page 512 shows its income statement for 2008. Work out the statement of cash flows for 2008. Group these items into sources of cash and uses of cash.

14. Work out a short-term financing plan for Dynamic Mattress Company, assuming the limit on the line of credit is raised from $100 million to $120 million. Otherwise keep to the assumptions used in developing Table 19.6 on page 512.

	February	March	April
Total sales	$200	$220	$180
Purchases of materials			
For cash	70	80	60
For credit	40	30	40
Other expenses	30	30	30
Taxes, interest, and dividends	10	10	10
Capital investment	100	0	0

TABLE 19.13
Selected budget data for Ritewell Publishers. See Problem 10.

	February	March	April
Sources of cash:			
Collections on cash sales			
Collections on accounts receivables			
Total sources of cash			
Uses of cash:			
Payments of accounts payable			
Cash purchases of materials			
Other expenses			
Capital expenditures			
Taxes, interest, and dividends			
Total uses of cash			
Net cash inflow			
Cash at start of period	100		
+ Net cash inflow			
= Cash at end of period			
+ Minimum operating cash balance	100	100	100
= Cumulative short-term financing required			

TABLE 19.14
Cash budget for Ritewell Publishers. See Problem 10.

Current Assets:		Current Liabilities:	
Cash	$ 20	Bank loans	$ 20
Marketable securities	10	Accounts payable	75
Accounts receivable	110	Total current liabilities	95
Inventory	100		
Total current assets	240	Long-term debt	25
		Net worth (equity and retained earnings)	300
Fixed assets:			
Gross investment	250		
Less depreciation	70		
Net fixed assets	180		
Total assets	420	Total liabilities and net worth	420

TABLE 19.15
Year-end balance sheet for Dynamic Mattress for 2007 (figures in $ millions). See Problem 13.

▷ **TABLE 19.16**

Income statement for Dynamic Mattress for 2008 (figures in $ millions).

Note: Dividend = $30.
Retained earnings = $10.

Visit us at
www.mhhe.com/bma

Sales	$1,500
Operating costs	1,405
	95
Depreciation	10
	85
Interest	5
Pretax income	80
Tax at 50%	40
Net income	40

15. Dynamic Mattress decides to lease its new mattress-stuffing machines rather than buy them. As a result, capital expenditure in the first quarter is reduced by $50 million, but the company must make lease payments of $2.5 million for each of the four quarters. Assume that the lease has no effect on tax payments until after the fourth quarter. Construct two tables like Tables 19.5 and 19.6 showing Dynamic's cumulative financing requirement and a new financing plan. Check your answer using the "live" spreadsheet on the book's Web site, **www.mhhe.com/bma**.

16. Our long-term planning model of Dynamic Mattress is an example of a top-down planning model. Some firms use a bottom-up financial planning model, which incorporates forecasts of revenues and costs for particular products, advertising plans, major investment projects, and so on. What sort of firms would you expect to use each type, and what would they use them for?

17. Corporate financial plans are often used as a basis for judging subsequent performance. What do you think can be learned from such comparisons? What problems are likely to arise, and how might you cope with these problems?

18. The balancing item in the Dynamic long-term planning model is borrowing. What is meant by *balancing item?* How would the model change if dividends were made the balancing item instead? In that case how would you suggest that planned borrowing be determined?

19. Construct a new model for Dynamic Mattress based on your answer to Problem 18. Does your model generate a feasible financial plan for 2010? (*Hint:* If it doesn't, you may have to allow the firm to issue stock.)

20. a. Use the Dynamic Mattress model (Tables 19.8–19.10) and the "live" spreadsheets on the book's Web site at **www.mhhe.com/bma** to produce pro forma income statements, balance sheets, and statements of cash flows for 2010 and 2011. Assume business as usual except that now sales and costs are planned to expand by 30% per year, as are fixed assets and net working capital. The interest rate is forecasted to remain at 10% and stock issues are ruled out. Dynamic also sticks to its 60% dividend payout ratio.

   b. What are the firm's debt ratio and interest coverage under this plan?

   c. Can the company continue to finance expansion by borrowing?

21. The financial statements of Eagle Sport Supply are shown in Table 19.17. For simplicity, "Costs" include interest. Assume that Eagle's assets are proportional to its sales.

   a. Find Eagle's required external funds if it maintains a dividend payout ratio of 60% and plans a growth rate of 15% in 2012.

   b. If Eagle chooses not to issue new shares of stock, what variable must be the balancing item? What will its value be?

   c. Now suppose that the firm plans instead to increase long-term debt only to $1,100 and does not wish to issue any new shares of stock. Why must the dividend payment now be the balancing item? What will its value be?

22. a. What is the internal growth rate of Eagle Sport (see Problem 21) if the dividend payout ratio is fixed at 60% and the equity-to-asset ratio is fixed at two-thirds?

   b. What is the sustainable growth rate?

23. Bio-Plasma Corp. is growing at 30% per year. It is all-equity-financed and has total assets of $1 million. Its return on equity is 20%. Its plowback ratio is 40%.

   a. What is the internal growth rate?

   b. What is the firm's need for external financing this year?

Income Statement	
Sales	$950
Costs	250
Pretax income	700
Taxes (at 28.6%)	200
Net income	$500

Balance Sheet, Year-End					
	2011	**2010**		**2011**	**2010**
Assets	$3,000	$2,700	Debt	$1,000	$ 900
			Equity	2,000	1,800
Total	$3,000	$2,700	Total	$3,000	$2,700

▶ **TABLE 19.17**
Financial statements for Eagle Sport Supply, 2011. See Problem 21.

c. By how much would the firm increase its internal growth rate if it reduced its payout rate to zero?

d. By how much would such a move reduce the need for external financing? What do you conclude about the relationship between dividend policy and requirements for external financing?

CHALLENGE

24. Table 19.18 shows the 2010 financial statements for the Executive Cheese Company. Annual depreciation is 10% of fixed assets at the beginning of the year, plus 10% of new investment. The company plans to invest a further $200,000 per year in fixed assets for the next five years and net working capital is expected to remain a constant proportion of fixed

Income Statement	
Revenue	$1,785
Fixed costs	53
Variable costs (80% of revenue)	1,428
Depreciation	80
Interest (at 11.8%)	24
Taxes (at 40%)	80
Net income	$ 120

Balance Sheet, Year-End		
	2010	**2009**
Assets:		
Net working capital	$ 400	$ 340
Fixed assets	800	680
Total assets	$1,200	$1,020
Liabilities:		
Debt	$ 240	$ 204
Book equity	960	816
Total liabilities	$1,200	$1,020

▶ **TABLE 19.18**
Financial statements for Executive Cheese Company, 2010 (figures in thousands).

(*continued on next page*)

▶ **TABLE 19.18**
(*continued*)
Financial statements for
Executive Cheese Com-
pany, 2010 (figures
in thousands).

Sources and Uses	
Sources:	
Net income	$120
Depreciation	80
Borrowing	36
Stock issues	104
Total sources	$340
Uses:	
Increase in net working capital	$ 60
Investment	200
Dividends	80
Total uses	$340

assets. The company forecasts that the ratio of revenues to total assets at the start of each
year will remain at 1.75. Fixed costs are expected to remain at $53,000, and variable costs at
80% of revenue. The company's policy is to pay out two-thirds of net income as dividends
and to maintain a book debt ratio of 20%.

a. Construct a model for Executive Cheese like the one in Tables 19.8–19.10.

b. Use your model to produce a set of financial statements for 2011.

● ● ● ● ●

**REAL-TIME
DATA ANALYSIS**

**STANDARD
&POOR'S**

Look up the financial statements for any company either on **http://finance.yahoo.com** or on
the Market Insight Database (**www.mhhe.com/edumarketinsight**). Make some plausible forecasts for future growth and the asset base needed to support that growth. Then use a spreadsheet program to develop a five-year financial plan. What financing is needed to support the
planned growth? How vulnerable is the company to an error in your forecasts?

APPENDIX ● ● ● ● ●

Earlier in the chapter we saw how Dynamic Mattress needed to borrow initially to resolve a cash
deficiency and how later in the year it had excess cash which it invested in marketable securities.
In this Appendix, we briefly review the main sources of short- and medium-term debt and the
securities that firms use to park any excess cash.

A19-1 Sources of Short-Term Borrowing

If like Dynamic, your firm has a short-term cash shortage, it will probably need to take out a
short-term loan. Banks are the principal supplier of these loans, but finance companies are also
a major source of cash, particularly for financing receivables and inventories.[21] In addition to

---

[21] *Finance companies* are firms that specialize in lending to businesses or individuals. They include independent firms.

borrowing from an intermediary such as a bank or finance company, firms also sell short-term commercial paper or medium-term notes directly to investors.

Bank Loans

Bank loans come in a variety of flavors. Here are a few of the ways that they differ.

Commitment Companies sometimes wait until they need the money before they apply for a bank loan, but about 90% of commercial loans by U.S. banks are made under commitment. In this case the company establishes a line of credit that allows it to borrow up to an established limit from the bank. This line of credit may be an **evergreen credit** with no fixed maturity, but more commonly it is a **revolving credit** (*revolver*) with a fixed maturity. For example, one common arrangement is a 364-day facility that allows the company over the next year to borrow, repay, and re-borrow as its need for cash varies.

Credit lines are relatively expensive; in addition to paying interest on any borrowings, the company must pay a commitment fee of around .25% on the unused amount. In exchange for this extra cost, the firm receives a valuable option: It has guaranteed access to the bank's money at a fixed spread over the general level of interest rates.

The growth in the use of credit lines has changed the role of banks. They are no longer simply lenders; they are also in the business of providing companies with liquidity insurance. Many companies discovered the value of this insurance in 1998, when Russia stopped payments on part of its debt and created turmoil in the world's debt markets. Companies in the United States suddenly found it much more expensive to issue their own debt to investors. Those who had arranged lines of credit with their banks rushed to take advantage of them. As a result, new debt issues languished, while bank lending boomed.

Maturity Many bank loans are for only a few months. For example, a company may need a short-term **bridge loan** to finance the purchase of new equipment or the acquisition of another firm. In this case the loan serves as interim financing until the purchase is completed and long-term financing arranged. Often a short-term loan is needed to finance a temporary increase in inventory. Such a loan is described as **self-liquidating;** in other words, the sale of goods provides the cash to repay the loan.

Banks also provide longer-maturity loans, known as **term loans.** A term loan typically has a maturity of four to five years. Usually the loan is repaid in level amounts over this period, though there is sometimes a large final *balloon* payment or just a single *bullet* payment at maturity. Banks can accommodate the repayment pattern to the anticipated cash flows of the borrower. For example, the first repayment might be delayed a year until the new factory is completed. Term loans are often renegotiated before maturity. Banks are willing to do this if the borrower is an established customer, remains creditworthy, and has a sound business reason for making the change.[22]

Rate of Interest Most short-term bank loans are made at a fixed rate of interest, which is often quoted as a discount. For example, if the interest rate on a one-year loan is stated as a discount of 5%, the borrower receives $100 - $5 = $95 and undertakes to pay $100 at the end of the year. The return on such a loan is not 5%, but 5/95 = .0526, or 5.26%.

For longer-term bank loans the interest rate is usually linked to the general level of interest rates. The most common benchmarks are the London Interbank Offered Rate (LIBOR), the federal funds rate,[23] or the bank's prime rate. Thus, if the rate is set at "1% over LIBOR," the borrower may pay 5% in the first three months when LIBOR is 4%, 6% in the next three months when LIBOR is 5%, and so on.

---

[22] One study of private debt agreements found that over 90% are renegotiated before maturity. In most cases this is not because of financial distress. See M. R. Roberts and A. Sufi, "Renegotiation of Financial Contracts: Evidence from Private Credit Agreements," *Journal of Financial Economics,* forthcoming.

[23] The federal funds rate is the rate at which banks lend excess reserves to each other.

Syndicated Loans Some bank loans and credit lines are too large for a single lender. In these cases the borrower may pay an arrangement fee to one or more lead banks, which then parcel out the loan or credit line among a syndicate of banks.[24] For example, in 2008 the chemical company Ashland needed to borrow $1.65 billion to finance its purchase of Hercules. It did so by means of a package of term loans and a revolving credit facility. The package was arranged by BankAmerica and the Bank of Nova Scotia, and other members of the syndicate reportedly included Citibank, SunTrust Banks, Wells Fargo Bank, US Bank, and Fifth Third Bank. The loans had a maturity of around five years and were priced at between 2.75% and 4% above LIBOR. In addition, Ashland was required to pay a commitment fee of .5% on any unused portion of the revolving credit.

The syndicate arranger serves as underwriter to the loan. It prices the loan, markets it to other banks, and may also guarantee to take on any unsold portion. The arranger's first step is to prepare an *information memo* that provides potential lenders with information on the loan. The syndicate desk will then try to sound out the level of interest in the deal before the loan is finally priced and marketed to interested buyers. If the borrower has good credit or if the arranging bank has a particularly good reputation, the majority of the loan is likely to be syndicated. In other cases the arranging bank may need to demonstrate its faith in the deal by keeping a high proportion of the loan on its own books.[25]

Loan Sales and Collateralized Debt Obligations Bank loans used to be illiquid; once the bank had made a loan, it was stuck with it. This is no longer the case, so that banks with an excess demand for loans may solve the problem by selling a portion of their existing loans to other institutions. For example, about 20% of syndicated loans are subsequently resold, and these sales are reported weekly in *The Wall Street Journal.*

Loan sales generally take one of two forms: *assignments* or *participations.* In the former case a portion of the loan is transferred with the agreement of the borrower. In the second case the lead bank maintains its relationship with the borrower but agrees to pay over to the buyer a portion of the cash flows that it receives.

Loan sales often involve a single loan, but sometimes they can be huge deals involving a portfolio of several hundred loans. The buyer is then entitled to a share of the cash flows on this portfolio. In the early years of the century many banks repackaged the cash flows from a portfolio of loans and sold off separate slices (or *tranches*) known as *collateralized debt obligations* (or *CDOs*).[26] The senior tranches had first claim on the cash flows and therefore proved attractive to conservative investors such as insurance companies or pension funds. The riskiest (or *equity*) tranche was retained by the bank or bought by hedge funds or mutual funds that specialized in low-quality debt.[27]

By 2007 over half of the new issues of CDOs involved exposure to subprime mortgages. Because the mortgages were packaged together, investors in these CDOs were protected against the risk of default on an individual mortgage. However, even the senior tranches were exposed

---

[24] For a standard loan to a blue-chip company the fee for arranging a syndicated loan may be as low as 10 basis points, while a complex deal with a highly leveraged firm may carry a fee of up to 250 basis points. For good reviews of the syndicated loan market see S. C. Miller, "A Guide to the Syndicated Loan Market," Standard & Poor's, September 2005 (www.standardandpoors.com); and B. Gadanecz, "The Syndicated Loan Market: Structure, Development and Implications," *BIS Quarterly Review,* December 2004, pp. 75–89 (www.bis.org).

[25] See A. Sufi, "Information Asymmetry and Financing Arrangements: Evidence from Syndicated Loans," *Journal of Finance* 62 (April 2007), pp. 629–668.

[26] CDOs comprise collateralized loan obligations (CLOs), together with collateralized bond obligations (CBOs) and collateralized mortgage obligations (CMOs).

[27] Rather than backing the CLO with a package of risky loans, banks often created *synthetic CLOs.* In this case the bank kept the loans on its books. The cash flows on the CLO came from the purchase of high-grade bonds and the sale of a default swap on a package of the bank's loans. If none of the bank loans defaults, the CLO receives a series of fixed cash flows. If there is a default, the seller of the default swap must compensate the buyer for the amount of the loss. This loss would be borne first by the equity tranche of the CLO.

to the risk of an economy-wide slump in the housing market. For this reason the debt has been termed "economic catastrophe debt."[28]

Economic catastrophe struck in the summer of 2007, when the investment bank, Bear Stearns, revealed that two of its hedge funds had invested heavily in nearly worthless CDOs. Bear Stearns was rescued with help from the Federal Reserve, but it signalled the start of the credit crunch and the collapse of the CDO market. In 2008 issues of CDOs fell by nearly 90%.[29]

Security If a bank is concerned about a firm's credit risk, it will ask the firm to provide security for the loan. This is most common for longer-term bank loans, over half of which are secured.[30] The collateral usually consists of liquid assets such as receivables, inventories, or securities. Sometimes the bank will take a *floating charge*. This gives it a general claim if the firm defaults. However, it does not specify the assets in detail, and it sets few restrictions on what the company can do with the assets.

More commonly, banks require specific collateral. For example, suppose that there is a significant delay between the time that you ship your goods and when your customers pay you. If you need the money up front, you can borrow by using these receivables as collateral. First, you must send the bank a copy of each invoice and provide it with a claim against the money that you receive from your customers. The bank will then lend up to 80% of the value of the receivables.

Each day, as you make more sales, your collateral increases and you can borrow more money. Each day also some customers pay their bills. This money is placed in a special collateral account under the bank's control and is periodically used to reduce the size of the loan. Therefore, as the firm's business fluctuates, so does the amount of the collateral and the size of the loan.

You can also use inventories as security for a loan. For example, if your goods are stored in a warehouse, you need to arrange for an independent warehouse company to provide the bank with a receipt showing that the goods are held on the bank's behalf. The bank will generally be prepared to lend up to 50% of the value of the inventories. When the loan is repaid, the bank returns the warehouse receipt and you are free to remove the goods.[31]

Banks are naturally choosey about the security that they will accept. They want to make sure that they can identify and sell the collateral if you default. They may be happy to lend against a warehouse full of a standard nonperishable commodity, but they would turn up their nose at a warehouse of ripe Camemberts.

Banks also need to ensure that the collateral is safe and the borrower doesn't sell the assets and run off with the money. This is what happened in the great salad oil swindle. Fifty-one banks and companies made loans of nearly $200 million to the Allied Crude Vegetable Oil Refining Corporation. In return the company agreed to provide security in the form of storage tanks full of valuable salad oil. Unfortunately, cursory inspections failed to notice that the tanks contained seawater and sludge. When the fraud was discovered, the president of Allied went to jail and the 51 lenders were left out in the cold, looking for their $200 million.

Commercial Paper

Banks borrow money from one group of firms or individuals and relend the money to another group. They make their profit by charging the borrowers a higher rate of interest than they offer the lender.

---

[28] J. D. Coval, J. Jurek, and E. Stafford, "Economic Catastrophe Bonds," *American Economic Review* 3 (June 2009), pp. 628–666.

[29] www.sifma.org.

[30] The results of a survey of the terms of business lending by banks in the United States are published quarterly in the *Federal Reserve Bulletin* (see www.federalreserve.gov/releases/E2).

[31] It is not always practicable to keep inventory in a warehouse. For example, automobile dealers need to display their cars in a showroom. One solution is to enter into a floor-planning arrangement in which the finance company buys the cars and the dealer holds them in trust. When the cars are sold, the proceeds are used to redeem the cars from the finance company. The interest or "flooring charge" depends on how long the cars have been in the showroom.

Sometimes it is convenient to have a bank in the middle. It saves the lenders the trouble of looking for borrowers and assessing their creditworthiness, and it saves the borrowers the trouble of looking for lenders. Depositors do not care to whom the bank lends: They need only satisfy themselves that the bank as a whole is safe.

There are also occasions on which it is *not* worth paying an intermediary to perform these functions. Large well-known companies can bypass the banking system by issuing their own short-term unsecured notes. These notes are known as **commercial paper (CP).** Financial institutions, such as bank holding companies and finance companies,[32] also issue commercial paper, sometimes in very large quantities. For example, at one point GE Capital Corporation had over $100 billion of commercial paper in issue.[33] The major issuers of commercial paper have set up their own marketing departments and sell their paper directly to investors, often using the Web to do so. Smaller companies sell through dealers who receive a fee for marketing the issue.

Commercial paper in the United States has a maximum maturity of nine months, though most paper is for 60 days or less. Buyers of commercial paper generally hold it to maturity, but the company or dealer that sells the paper is usually prepared to repurchase it earlier.

The majority of commercial paper is issued by high-grade, nationally known companies.[34] Issuers generally support their commercial paper by arranging a backup line of credit with a bank, which guarantees that they can find the money to repay the paper.[35] The risk of default is, therefore, small.

Because investors are reluctant to buy commercial paper that does not have the highest credit rating, companies cannot rely on the commercial paper market to provide them always with the short-term capital that they need. For example, when the rating services downgraded the commercial paper of Ford and General Motors, both companies were forced to reduce sharply their sales of paper. Ford Credit had $45 billion of unsecured commercial paper outstanding at the end of 2000; five years later it had cut the amount to $1.0 billion.

Recent years have not been kind to the commercial paper market. In addition to Ford and GM, a number of other major companies have had their commercial paper downgraded. An even bigger shock occurred in 2007, when Lehman Brothers defaulted on its commercial paper. This led to a sharp fall in the volume of issues until the Fed announced plans to buy large volumes of high-grade paper.

In addition to unsecured commercial paper, there is also a market for *asset-backed commercial paper*. In this case the company sells its assets to a special-purpose vehicle that then issues the paper. For example, as the auto companies reduced their sales of unsecured commercial paper, they increasingly relied on asset-backed paper secured by the firm's receivables. As the customers paid their bills, the cash was passed through to the holders of this paper.

Weaknesses in this market surfaced when a number of banks set up structured investment vehicles (SIVs) that invested in mortgage-backed securities financed by asset-backed paper. Because the buyers of the commercial paper bore the credit risk, the banks had less incentive to worry about the quality of the underlying mortgages. Many of the SIVs found it impossible to refinance the maturing paper and went into default.

Medium-Term Notes

New issues of securities do not need to be registered with the SEC as long as they mature within 270 days. So by limiting the maturity of commercial paper issues, companies can avoid the delays and expense of registration. However, large blue-chip companies also make regular issues of unsecured **medium-term notes (MTNs).**

---

[32] A *bank holding company* is a firm that owns both a bank and nonbanking subsidiaries.

[33] GE reduced its reliance on commercial paper in 2008.

[34] Moody's, Standard and Poor's, and Fitch publish quality ratings for commercial paper. For example, Moody's provides three ratings, from P-1 (that is, Prime 1, the highest-grade paper) to P-3. Most investors are reluctant to buy low-rated paper. For example, money-market funds are largely limited to holding P-1 paper.

[35] For top-tier issuers the credit line is generally 75% of the amount of paper; for lower-grade issuers it is 100%. The company may not be able to draw on this line of credit if it does not satisfy bank covenants. Therefore, lower-rated companies may need to back their paper with an irrevocable line of credit.

You can think of MTNs as a hybrid between corporate bonds and commercial paper. Like bonds they are relatively long-term instruments; their maturity is never less than 270 days, though it is typically less than 10 years.[36] On the other hand, like commercial paper, MTNs are not underwritten but are sold on a regular basis either through dealers or, occasionally, directly to investors. Dealers support a secondary market in these MTNs and are prepared to buy the notes back before maturity.

Borrowers such as finance companies, which always need cash, welcome the flexibility of MTNs. For example, a company may tell its dealers the amount of money that it needs to raise that week, the range of maturities that it can offer, and the maximum interest that it is prepared to pay. It is then up to the dealers to find the buyers. Investors may also suggest their own terms to one of the dealers, and, if these terms are acceptable, the deal is done.

A19-2 Marketable Securities

In June 2008 Microsoft was sitting on a $24.3 billion mountain of cash and fixed income investments, amounting to a third of the company's total assets.[37] The company kept $3.3 billion in the bank to support day-to-day operations and invested the surplus as follows:

Fixed Income Investments	Value at Cost ($ millions)
Mutual funds	$ 1,044
Commercial paper	787
Certificates of deposit	1,580
U.S. government and agency securities	4,200
Foreign government bonds	3,466
Mortgage-backed securities	3,628
Corporate notes and bonds	5,013
Municipal securities	761
Other investments	520
Total	$20,999

Most companies do not have the luxury of such huge cash surpluses, but they also park any cash that is not immediately needed in short-term investments. The market for these investments is known as the **money market.** The money market has no physical marketplace. It consists of a loose collection of banks and dealers linked together by telephones or through the Web. But a huge volume of securities is regularly traded on the money market, and competition is vigorous.

Most large corporations manage their own money-market investments, but small companies sometimes find it more convenient to hire a professional investment management firm or to put their cash into a money-market fund. This is a mutual fund that invests only in low-risk, short-term securities.[38] Despite its large cash surplus, Microsoft invested a small proportion of its money in money-market funds.

The relative safety of money-market funds has made them particularly popular at times of financial stress. During the credit crunch of 2008 fund assets mushroomed as investors fled from plunging stock markets. Then it was revealed that one fund, the Reserve Primary Fund, had incurred heavy losses on its holdings of Lehman Brothers' commercial paper. The fund became only the second money-market fund in history to "break the buck," by offering just 97 cents

---

[36] Occasionally, an MTN registration may be used to issue much longer term bonds. For example, Disney has even used its MTN program to issue a 100-year bond.

[37] We described in Chapter 12 how Microsoft decided in July 2004 to pay out a large part of its surplus cash to shareholders.

[38] We discussed money-market funds in Section 13–3.

on the dollar to investors who cashed in their holdings. That week investors pulled nearly $200 billion out of money-market funds, prompting the government to offer emergency insurance to investors.

Calculating the Yield on Money-Market Investments

Many money-market investments are pure discount securities. This means that they don't pay interest. The return consists of the difference between the amount you pay and the amount you receive at maturity. Unfortunately, it is no good trying to persuade the Internal Revenue Service that this difference represents capital gain. The IRS is wise to that one and will tax your return as ordinary income.

Interest rates on money-market investments are often quoted on a discount basis. For example, suppose that three-month bills are issued at a discount of 5%. This is a rather complicated way of saying that the price of a three-month bill is $100 - (3/12) \times 5 = 98.75$. Therefore, for every $98.75 that you invest today, you receive $100 at the end of three months. The return over three months is $1.25/98.75 = .0127$, or 1.27%. This is equivalent to an annual yield of 5.18%. Note that the return is always higher than the discount. When you read that an investment is selling at a discount of 5%, it is very easy to slip into the mistake of thinking that this is its return.[39]

Yields on Money-Market Investments

When we value long-term debt, it is important to take account of default risk. Almost anything may happen in 30 years, and even today's most respectable company may get into trouble eventually. Therefore, corporate bonds offer higher yields than Treasury bonds.

Short-term debt is not risk-free either. When California was mired in the energy crisis of 2001, Southern California Edison and Pacific Gas and Electric were forced to suspend payments on nearly $1 billion of maturing commercial paper. However, such examples are exceptions; in general, the danger of default is less for money-market securities issued by corporations than for corporate bonds. There are two reasons for this. First, the range of possible outcomes is smaller for short-term investments. Even though the distant future may be clouded, you can usually be confident that a particular company will survive for at least the next month. Second, for the most part only well-established companies can borrow in the money market. If you are going to lend money for just a few days, you can't afford to spend too much time in evaluating the loan. Thus, you will consider only blue-chip borrowers.

Despite the high quality of money-market investments, there are often significant differences in yield between corporate and U.S. government securities. Why is this? One answer is the risk of default. Another is that the investments have different degrees of liquidity or "moneyness." Investors like Treasury bills because they are easily turned into cash on short notice. Securities that cannot be converted so quickly and cheaply into cash need to offer relatively high yields. During times of market turmoil investors may place a particularly high value on having ready access to cash. On these occasions the yield on illiquid securities can increase dramatically.

The International Money Market

In addition to the domestic money market, there is also an international market for short-term dollar investments, which is known as the *eurodollar* market. Eurodollars have nothing to do with the euro, the currency of the European Monetary Union (EMU). They are simply dollars deposited in a bank in Europe. For example, suppose that an American oil company buys crude oil from an Arab sheik and pays for it with a $1 million check drawn on JP Morgan Chase. The sheik then deposits the check with his account at Barclays Bank in London. As a result, Barclays

---

[39] To confuse things even more, dealers in the money market often quote rates as if there were only 360 days in a year. So a discount of 5% on a bill maturing in 91 days translates into a price of $100 - 5 \times (91/360) = 98.74\%$.

has an asset in the form of a $1 million credit in its account with JP Morgan Chase. It also has an offsetting liability in the form of a dollar deposit. Since that dollar deposit is placed in Europe, it is called a eurodollar deposit.[40]

Just as there is both a domestic U.S. money market and a eurodollar market, so there is both a domestic Japanese money market and a market in London for euroyen. So, if a U.S. corporation wishes to make a short-term investment in yen, it can deposit the yen with a bank in Tokyo or it can make a euroyen deposit in London. Similarly, there is both a domestic money market in the euro area as well as a money market for euros in London.[41] And so on.

Major international banks in London lend dollars to one another at the *London interbank offered rate* (LIBOR). Similarly, they lend yen to each other at the yen LIBOR interest rate, and they lend euros at the **euro interbank offered rate,** or **Euribor.** These interest rates are used as a benchmark for pricing many types of short-term loans in the United States and in other countries. For example, a corporation in the United States may issue a floating-rate note with interest payments tied to dollar LIBOR.

If we lived in a world without regulation and taxes, the interest rate on a eurodollar loan would have to be the same as the rate on an equivalent domestic dollar loan. However, the international debt markets thrive because governments attempt to regulate domestic bank lending. When the U.S. government limited the rate of interest that banks in the United States could pay on domestic deposits, companies could earn a higher rate of interest by keeping their dollars on deposit in Europe. As these restrictions have been removed, differences in interest rates have largely disappeared.

In the late 1970s the U.S. government was concerned that its regulations were driving business overseas to foreign banks and the overseas branches of American banks. To attract some of this business back to the States, the government in 1981 allowed U.S. and foreign banks to establish **international banking facilities (IBFs).** An IBF is the financial equivalent of a free-trade zone; it is physically located in the United States, but it is not required to maintain reserves with the Federal Reserve, and depositors are not subject to any U.S. tax.[42] However, there are tight restrictions on what business an IBF can conduct. In particular, it cannot accept deposits from domestic U.S. corporations or make loans to them.

Money-Market Instruments

The principal money-market instruments are summarized in Table A19.1. We describe each in turn.

U.S. Treasury Bills The first item in Table A19.1 is U.S. Treasury bills. These are usually issued weekly and mature in four weeks, three months, six months, or one year.[43] Sales are by a uniform-price auction. This means that all successful bidders are allotted bills at the same price.[44] You don't have to participate in the auction to invest in Treasury bills. There is also an excellent secondary market in which billions of dollars of bills are bought and sold every week.

Federal Agency Securities "Agency securities" is a general term used to describe issues by government agencies and government sponsored enterprises (GSEs). Although most of this debt

---

[40] The sheik could equally well deposit the check with the London branch of a U.S. bank or a Japanese bank. He would still have made a eurodollar deposit.

[41] Occasionally (but only occasionally) referred to as "euroeuros."

[42] For these reasons dollars held on deposit in an IBF are classed as eurodollars.

[43] Three-month bills actually mature 91 days after issue, six-month bills mature in 182 days, and one-year bills mature in 364 days. For information on bill auctions, see **www.publicdebt.treas.gov**.

[44] A small proportion of bills is sold to *noncompetitive* bidders. Noncompetitive bids are filled at the same price as the successful competitive bids.

Investment	Borrower	Maturities When Issued	Marketability	Basis for Calculating Interest	Comments
Treasury bills	U.S. government	4 weeks, 3 months, 6 months, or 1 year	Excellent secondary market	Discount	Auctioned weekly
Federal agency benchmark bills and discount notes	FHLB, "Fannie Mae," "Sallie Mae," "Freddie Mac," etc.	Overnight to 360 days	Very good secondary market	Discount	Benchmark bills by regular auction; discount notes sold through dealers
Tax-exempt municipal notes	Municipalities, states, school districts, etc.	3 months to 1 year	Good secondary market	Usually interest-bearing with interest at maturity	Tax-anticipation notes (TANs), revenue anticipation notes (RANs), bond anticipation notes (BANs), etc.
Tax-exempt variable-rate demand notes (VRDNs)	Municipalities, states, state universities, etc.	10 to 40 years	Good secondary market	Variable interest rate	Long-term bonds with put options to demand repayment
Nonnegotiable time deposits and negotiable certificates of deposit (CDs)	Commercial banks, savings and loans	Usually 1 to 3 months; also longer-maturity variable-rate CDs	Fair secondary market for negotiable CDs	Interest-bearing with interest at maturity	Receipt for time deposit
Commercial paper (CP)	Industrial firms, finance companies, and bank holding companies; also municipalities	Maximum 270 days; usually 60 days or less	Dealers or issuer will repurchase paper	Usually discount	Unsecured promissory note; may be placed through dealer or directly with investor
Medium-term notes (MTNs)	Largely finance companies and banks; also industrial firms	Minimum 270 days; usually less than 10 years	Dealers will repurchase notes	Interest-bearing; usually fixed rate	Unsecured promissory note placed through dealer
Bankers' acceptances (BAs)	Major commercial banks	1 to 6 months	Fair secondary market	Discount	Demand to pay that has been accepted by a bank
Repurchase agreements (repos)	Dealers in U.S. government securities	Overnight to about 3 months; also open repos (continuing contracts)	No secondary market	Repurchase price set higher than selling price; difference quoted as repo interest rate	Sales of government securities by dealer with simultaneous agreement to repurchase

▶ **TABLE A19.1** Money-market investments in the United States.

is not guaranteed by the U.S. government,[45] investors have generally assumed that the government would step in to prevent a default. That view was reinforced in 2008, when the two giant mortgage companies, the Federal National Mortgage Association (Fannie Mae) and the Federal Home Loan Mortgage Corporation (Freddie Mac) ran into trouble and were taken into government ownership.

Agencies and GSEs borrow both short and long term. The short-term debt consists of discount notes, which are similar to Treasury bills. They are very actively traded and often held

---

[45] Exceptions are the Government National Mortgage Association (Ginnie Mae), the Small Business Administration, the General Services Administration (GSA), the Financial Assistance Corporation, the Agency for International Development, and the Private Export Funding Corporation. Their debts are backed by the "full faith and credit" of the U.S. government.

by corporations. These notes have traditionally offered somewhat higher yields than U.S. Treasuries. One reason is that agency debt is not quite as marketable as Treasury issues. In addition, unless the debt has an explicit government guarantee, investors have demanded an extra return to compensate for the (small?) possibility that the government would allow the agency to default.

Short-Term Tax-Exempts Short-term notes are also issued by states, municipalities, and agencies such as state universities and school districts.[46] These have one particular attraction—the interest is not subject to federal tax.[47] Of course, this tax advantage of municipal debt is recognized in its price. Typically, triple-A municipal debt has yielded 10% to 30% less than equivalent Treasury debt.

Most tax-exempt debt is relatively low risk, and is often backed by an insurance policy, which promises to pay out if the municipality is about to default.[48] However, in the turbulent markets of 2008 even the backing of an insurance company did little to reassure investors, who worried that the insurers themselves could be in trouble. The tax advantage of "munis" no longer seemed quite so important and their yields climbed above those on Treasuries.

Variable-Rate Demand Notes There is no law preventing firms from making short-term investments in long-term securities. If a firm has $1 million set aside for an income tax payment, it could buy a long-term bond on January 1 and sell it on April 15, when the taxes must be paid. However, the danger with this strategy is obvious. What happens if bond prices fall by 10% between January and April? There you are with a $1 million liability to the Internal Revenue Service, bonds worth only $900,000, and a very red face. Of course, bond prices could also go up, but why take the chance? Corporate treasurers entrusted with excess funds for short-term investments are naturally averse to the price volatility of long-term bonds.

One solution is to buy municipal variable-rate demand notes (VRDNs). These are long-term securities, whose interest payments are linked to the level of short-term interest rates. Whenever the interest rate is reset, investors have the right to sell the notes back to the issuer for their face value.[49] This ensures that on these reset dates the price of the notes cannot be less than their face value. Therefore, although VRDNs are long-term loans, their prices are very stable. In addition, the interest on municipal debt has the advantage of being tax-exempt. So a municipal variable-rate demand note offers a relatively safe, tax-free, short-term haven for your $1 million of cash.

Bank Time Deposits and Certificates of Deposit If you make a time deposit with a bank, you are lending money to the bank for a fixed period. If you need the money before maturity, the bank usually allows you to withdraw it but exacts a penalty in the form of a reduced rate of interest.

In the 1960s banks introduced the **negotiable certificate of deposit (CD)** for time deposits of $1 million or more. In this case, when a bank borrows, it issues a certificate of deposit, which is simply evidence of a time deposit with that bank. If a lender needs the money before maturity, it can sell the CD to another investor. When the loan matures, the new owner of the CD presents it to the bank and receives payment.[50]

Commercial Paper and Medium-Term Notes These consist of unsecured, short- and medium-term debt issued by companies on a fairly regular basis.

---

[46] Some of these notes are *general obligations* of the issuer; others are *revenue securities*, and in these cases payments are made from rent receipts or other user charges.

[47] This advantage is partly offset by the fact that Treasury securities are free of state and local taxes.

[48] Defaults on tax-exempts have been rare and for the most part have involved not-for-profit hospitals. However, there have been two major defaults of tax-exempt debt. In 1983 Washington Public Power Supply System (unfortunately known as WPPSS or "WOOPS") defaulted on $2.25 billion of bonds. In 1994 Orange County in California also defaulted after losing $1.7 billion on its investment portfolio.

[49] The tendered bonds are then resold to new investors.

[50] Some CDs are not negotiable and are simply identical to time deposits. For example, banks may sell low-value nonnegotiable CDs to individuals.

Bankers' Acceptances   Bankers' acceptances (BAs) may be used to finance exports or imports. An acceptance begins life as a written demand for the bank to pay a given sum at a future date. Once the bank accepts this demand, it becomes a negotiable security that can be bought or sold through money-market dealers. Acceptances by the large U.S. banks generally mature in one to six months and involve very low credit risk.

Repurchase Agreements   **Repurchase agreements,** or *repos,* are effectively secured loans that are typically made to a government security dealer. They work as follows: The investor buys part of the dealer's holding of Treasury securities and simultaneously arranges to sell them back again at a later date at a specified higher price.[51] The borrower (the dealer) is said to have entered into a *repo;* the lender (who buys the securities) is said to have a *reverse repo.*

Repos sometimes run for several months, but more frequently they are just overnight (24-hour) agreements. No other domestic money-market investment offers such liquidity. Corporations can treat overnight repos almost as if they were interest-bearing demand deposits.

Suppose that you decide to invest cash in repos for several days or weeks. You don't want to keep renegotiating agreements every day. One solution is to enter into an *open repo* with a security dealer. In this case there is no fixed maturity to the agreement; either side is free to withdraw at one day's notice. Alternatively, you may arrange with your bank to transfer any excess cash automatically into repos.

Floating-Rate Preferred Stock   Common stock and preferred stock have an interesting tax advantage for corporations, since firms pay tax on only 30% of the dividends that they receive. So, for each $1 of dividends received, the firm gets to keep $1 - (.30 \times .35) = \$.895$. Thus the effective tax rate is only 10.5%. This is higher than the zero tax rate on the interest from municipal debt but much lower than the rate that the company pays on other debt interest.

Suppose that you consider investing your firm's spare cash in some other corporation's preferred stock. The 10.5% tax rate is very tempting. On the other hand, you worry that the price of the preferred shares may change if long-term interest rates change. You can reduce that worry by investing in preferred shares whose dividend payments are linked to the general level of interest rates.[52]

Varying the dividend payment doesn't quite do the trick, for the price of the preferred stock could still fall if the risk increases. So a number of companies added another wrinkle to floating-rate preferred. Instead of being tied rigidly to interest rates, the dividend can be reset periodically by means of an auction that is open to all investors. Investors can state the yield at which they are prepared to buy the stock. Existing shareholders who require a higher yield simply sell their stock to the new investors at its face value. The idea is similar to the variable-rate demand note. As long as auction-rate preferred stock can be resold at regular intervals for its face value, its price should not wander far in the interim.[53]

In 2007 disaster hit the auction-rate preferred market, when investors found that no one turned up at the auction for their stock. Holders claimed that banks had fraudulently marketed the issues as equivalent to cash, and many of the banks that originally handled the issues agreed to buy them back. Auction-rate preferred stock no longer seemed such a safe haven for cash.

---

[51] To reduce the risk of repos, it is common to value the security at less than its market value. This difference is known as a *haircut.*

[52] The company *issuing* preferred stock must pay dividends out of after-tax income. So most tax-paying firms would prefer to issue debt rather than floating-rate preferred. However, there are plenty of firms that are not paying taxes and cannot make use of the interest tax shield. Moreover, they have been able to issue floating-rate preferred at yields *lower* than they would have to pay on a debt issue. The corporations buying the preferreds are happy with these lower yields because 70% of the dividends they receive escape tax.

[53] Most auction-rate preferred stock was issued by closed-end mutual funds.

Answers to Select Basic Problems

CHAPTER 1

1. (a) Real; (b) executive airplanes; (c) brand names; (d) financial; (e) bonds; (f) investment; (g) capital budgeting; (h) financing.
3. a. Financial assets, such as stocks or bank loans, are claims held by investors. Corporations sell financial assets to raise the cash to invest in real assets such as plant and equipment. Some real assets are intangible.
   b. Capital budgeting means investment in real assets. Financing means raising the cash for this investment.
   c. The shares of public corporations are traded on stock exchanges and can be purchased by a wide range of investors. The shares of closely held corporations are not traded and are not generally available to investors.
   d. Unlimited liability: Investors are responsible for all the firm's debts. A sole proprietor has unlimited liability. Investors in corporations have limited liability. They can lose their investment, but no more.
5. *b, c.*

CHAPTER 2

1. $1.00.
3. $374/(1.09)^9 = $172.
5. $100 \times (1.15)^8 = $305.90.
7. $PV = 4/(.14 - .04) = $40.
9. a. $10,000/1.05^5 = $7,840.
   b. You need to set aside ($12,000 \times$ 6-year annuity factor) = $12,000 \times 4.623 = $55,476.
   c. At the end of 6 years you would have $1.08^6 \times (60,476 - 55,476) = $7,934.
11. (a) $12.625 million; (b) $12.705 million; (c) $12.712 million.

CHAPTER 3

1. (a) Does not change; (b) price falls; (c) yield rises.
3. The yield over 6 months is $3.965/2 = 1.79825\%$. Therefore, $PV = 3/1.0179825 + 3/1.0179825^2 + \ldots + 103/1.0179825^{34} = 130.37$.
5. a. Fall (e.g., 1-year 10% bond is worth $110/1.1 = 100$ if $r = 10\%$ and is worth $110/1.15 = 95.65$ if $r = 15\%$).

b. Less [e.g., see 5(a)].
   c. Less (e.g., with $r = 5\%$, 1-year 10% bond is worth $110/1.05 = 104.76$).
   d. Higher (e.g., if $r = 10\%$, 1-year 10% bond is worth $110/1.1 = 100$, while 1-year 8% bond is worth $108/1.1 = 98.18$).
   e. No, low-coupon bonds have longer durations (unless there is only one period to maturity) and are therefore more volatile (e.g., if r falls from 10% to 5%, the value of a 2-year 10% bond rises from 100 to 109.3 (a rise of 9.3%). The value of a 2-year 5% bond rises from 91.3 to 100 (a rise of 9.5%).
7. (a) 4%; (b) $PV = $1,075.44.
9. a. $r_1 = 100/99.423 - 1 = .58\%$; $r_2 = (100/97.546)^{.5} - 1 = 1.25\%$; $r_3 = (100/94.510)^{.33} - .1 = 1.90\%$; $r_4 = (100/90.524)^{.25} - 1 = 2.52\%$.
   b. Upward-sloping.
   c. Lower. (The yield on the bond is a complicated average of the separate spot rates.)
11. a. False. Duration depends on the coupon as well as the maturity.
   b. False. Given the yield to maturity, volatility is proportional to duration.
   c. True. A lower coupon rate means longer duration and therefore higher volatility.
   d. False. A higher interest rate reduces the relative present value of (distant) principal repayments.
13. 7.01%. (The extra return that you earn for investing for 2 years rather than 1 is $1.06^2/1.05 - 1 = .0701$.)

CHAPTER 4

1. (a) True; (b) true.
3. $P_0 = (5 + 110)/1.08 = 106.48
5. $P_0 = 10/(.08 - .05) = 333.33
7. $15/.08 + PVGO = 333.33$; therefore $PVGO = 145.83.
9. (a) False; (b) true.
11. Free cash flow is the amount of cash thrown off by a business after all investments necessary for growth. In our simple examples, free cash flow equals operating cash flow minus capital expenditure. Free cash flow can be negative if investments are large.
13. If $PVGO = 0$ at the horizon date H, horizon value = earnings forecasted for $H + 1$ divided by r.

CHAPTER 5

1. (a) A = 3 years, B = 2 years, C = 3 years; (b) B;
   (c) A, B, and C; (d) B and C (NPV $_B$ = $3,378;
   NPV $_C$ = $2,405); (e) true; (f) It will accept no
   negative-NPV projects but will turn down some
   with positive NPVs. A project can have positive
   NPV if all future cash flows are considered but
   still do not meet the stated cutoff period.

3. (a) $15,750; $4,250; $0; (b) 100%.

5. (a) Two; (b) − 50% and +50%; (c) yes, NPV = +14.6.

7. 1, 2, 4, and 6.

CHAPTER 6

1. *a, b, d, g, h.*

3. (a) False; (b) false; (c) false; (d) false.

5.

	2010	2011	2012	2013	2014
Working capital	50,000	230,000	305,000	250,000	0
Cash flows	+50,000	+180,000	+75,000	−55,000	−250,000

7. PV cost = 1.5 + .2 × 14.09 = $4.319 million.
   Equivalent annual cost = 4.319/14.09 = .306, or
   $306,000.

9. Replace at end of 5 years ($80,000 > $72,376).

CHAPTER 7

1. Expected payoff is $100 and expected return is
   zero. Variance is 20,000 (% squared) and standard
   deviation is 141%.

3. Ms. Sauros had a slightly higher average return
   (14.6% vs. 14.4% for the market). However, the fund
   also had a higher standard deviation (13.6% vs. 9.4%
   for the market).

5. *d*

7. (a) 26%; (b) zero; (c) .75; (d) less than 1.0 (the
   portfolio's risk is the same as the market, but some of
   this risk is unique risk).

9. A, 1.0; B, 2.0; C, 1.5; D, 0; E, −1.0.

CHAPTER 8

1. (a) 7%; (b) 27% with perfect positive correlation; 1%
   with perfect negative correlation; 19.1% with no
   correlation; (c) See Figure 1; (d) No, measure risk
   by beta, not by standard deviation.

3. Sharpe ratio = 7.1/20.2 = .351.

5. (a) See Figure 2; (b) A, D, G; (c) F; (d) 15% in C.
   (e) Put 25/32 of your money in F and lend 7/32 at
   12%: Expected return = 7/32 × 12 + (25/32) ×
   18 = 16.7%; standard deviation = 7/32 × 0 +
   (25/32) × 32 = 25%. If you could borrow without limit, you would achieve as high an expected
   return as you'd like, with correspondingly high
   risk, of course.

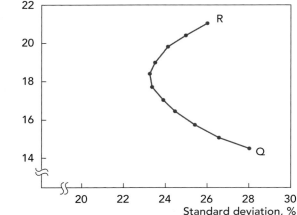

▶ **FIGURE 1**   Chapter 8, Problem 1(c).

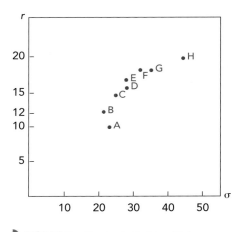

▶ **FIGURE 2**   Chapter 8, Problem 5(a).

7. (a) True; (b) false (it offers twice the market *risk premium*); (c) false.

CHAPTER 9

1. Overestimate.

3. .297, or 29.7% of variation, was due to market movements; .703, or 70.3% of the variation, was diversifiable. Diversifiable risk shows up in the scatter about the fitted line. The standard error of the estimated beta was unusually high at .436. If you said that the true beta was $2 \times .436 = .872$ either side of your estimate, you would have a 95% chance of being right.

5. Beta of assets $= .5 \times .15 + .5 \times 1.25 = .7$.

7. Suppose that the expected cash flow in year 1 is 100, but the project proposer provides an estimate of $100 \times 115/108 = 106.5$. Discounting this figure at 15% gives the same result as discounting the true expected cash flow at 8%. Adjusting the discount rate, therefore, works for the first cash flow but it does not do so for later cash flows (e.g., discounting a 2-year cash flow of 106.5 by 15% is *not* equivalent to discounting a 2-year flow of 100 by 8%).

9. (a) False; (b) false; (c) true.

CHAPTER 10

1. (a) False; (b) true; (c) true.

3. a. Analysis of how project profitability and NPV change if different assumptions are made about sales, cost, and other key variables.

b. Project NPV is recalculated by changing several inputs to new, but consistent, values.

c. Determines the level of future sales at which project profitability or NPV equals zero.

d. An extension of sensitivity analysis that explores all possible outcomes and weights each by its probability.

e. A graphical technique for displaying possible future events and decisions taken in response to those events.

f. Option to modify a project at a future date.

g. The additional present value created by the option to bail out of a project, and recover part of the initial investment, if the project performs poorly.

h. The additional present value created by the option to invest more and expand output, if a project performs well.

5. a. Describe how project cash flow depends on the underlying variables.

b. Specify probability distributions for forecast errors for these cash flows.

c. Draw from the probability distributions to simulate the cash flows.

7. Adding a fudge factor to the discount rate pushes project analysts to submit more optimistic forecasts.

CHAPTER 11

1. *c*

3. (a) False; (b) false; (c) true; (d) false; (e) false; (f) true.

5. $6 - (-.2 + 1.45 \times 5) = -1.05\%$.

7. Decrease. The stock price already reflects an expected 25% increase. The 20% increase conveys bad news relative to expectations.

9. a. Evidence that two securities with identical cash flows (e.g., Royal Dutch Shell and Shell Transport & Trading) can sell at different prices.

b. Small-cap stocks and high book-to-market stocks appear to have given above-average returns for their level of risk.

c. IPOs provide relatively low returns after their first few days of trading.

d. Stocks of firms that announce unexpectedly good earnings perform well over the coming months.

In each case there appear to have been opportunities for earning superior profits.

CHAPTER 12

1. a. A1, B5; A2, B4; A3, B3; A4, B1; A5, B2;

b. On August 12, the ex-dividend date;

c. $(.35 \times 4)/52 = .027$, or 2.7%;

d. $(.35 \times 4)/4.56 = .31$, or 3.1%;

e. The price would fall to $52/1.10 = \$47.27$.

3. a. Reinvest $1,000 \times \$.50 = \$500$ in the stock. If the ex-dividend price is $\$150 - \$2.50$, this should involve the purchase of 500/147.50, or about 3.4 shares.

b. Sell shares worth $1,000 \times \$3 = \$3,000$. If the ex-dividend price is $\$200 - \$5$, this should involve the sale of 3,000/195, or about 15 shares.

5. a. Company value is unchanged at $5,000 \times 140 = \$700,000$. Share price stays at $140.

b. The discount rate $r = (DIV_1/P_0) + g = (20/140) + .05 = .193$. The price at which shares are repurchased in year 1 is $140 \times (1 + r) = 140 \times 1.193 = \$167$. Therefore the firm repurchases $50,000/167 = 299$ shares. Total dividend payments in year 1 fall to $5,000 \times 10 = \$50,000$, which is equivalent to $50,000/(5000 - 299) = \$10.64$ a share. Similarly, in year 2 the firm repurchases 281 shares at $186.52 and the dividend per share increases by 11.7% to $11.88. In each subsequent year, total dividends increase by 5%, the number of shares declines by 6% and, therefore, dividends per share increase by 11.7%. The constant-growth model gives PV share = 10.64/(.193 − .117) = $140.

7. *Current tax law (assuming gains tax cannot be deferred):* All investors should be indifferent except the corporation which prefers Hi.
Zero tax on capital gains: As under the current tax law except that individuals now prefer Lo. (*Note:* Corporations and security dealers treat capital gains as income).

CHAPTER 13

1. Note the market value of Copperhead is far in excess of its book value:

	Market Value
Common stock (8 million shares at $2)	$16,000,000
Short-term loans	$ 2,000,000

Ms. Kraft owns .625% of the firm, which proposes to increase common stock to $17 million and cut short-term debt. Ms. Kraft can offset this by (*a*) borrowing .00625 × 1,000,000 = $6,250, and (*b*) buying that much more Copperhead stock.

3. Expected return on assets is
$r_A = .08 \times 30/80 + .16 \times 50/80 = .13$.
The new return on equity will be
$r_E = .13 + (20/60) \times (.13 − .08) = .147$.

5. a. True;
   b. True (as long as the return earned by the company is greater than the interest payment, earnings per share increase, but the P/E falls to reflect the higher risk);
   c. False (the cost of equity increases with the ratio D/E);
   d. False (the formula $r_E = r_A + (D/E)(r_A − r_D)$ does not require r_D to be constant);
   e. False (debt amplifies variations in equity income);
   f. False (value increases only if clientele is not satisfied).

7. See Figure 13.3.

CHAPTER 14

1. The calculation assumes that the tax rate is fixed, that debt is fixed and perpetual, and that investors' personal tax rates on interest and equity income are the same.

3. Relative advantage of debt = $\dfrac{1 − T_p}{(1 − T_{pE})(1 − T_c)}$

   $= \dfrac{.65}{(1)(.65)} = 1.00$

   Relative advantage = $\dfrac{.65}{(.85)(.65)} = 1.18$

5. a. Direct costs of financial distress are the legal and administrative costs of bankruptcy. Indirect costs include possible delays in liquidation (Eastern Airlines) or poor investment or operating decisions while bankruptcy is being resolved. Also the *threat* of bankruptcy can lead to costs.
   b. If financial distress increases odds of default, managers' and shareholders' incentives change. This can lead to poor investment or financing decisions.
   c. See the answer to 5(*b*). Examples are the "games" described in Section 14–3.

7. More profitable firms have more taxable income to shield and are less likely to incur the costs of distress. Therefore the trade-off theory predicts high (book) debt ratios. In practice the more profitable companies borrow least.

9. When a company issues securities, outside investors worry that management may have unfavorable information. If so the securities can be overpriced. This worry is much less with debt than equity. Debt securities are safer than equity, and their price is less affected if unfavorable news comes out later.
   A company that can borrow (without incurring substantial costs of financial distress) usually does so. An issue of equity would be read as "bad news" by investors, and the new stock could be sold only at a discount to the previous market price.

11. Financial slack is most valuable to growth companies with good but uncertain investment opportunities. Slack means that financing can be raised quickly for positive-NPV investments. But too much financial slack can tempt mature companies to overinvest. Increased borrowing can force such firms to pay out cash to investors.

CHAPTER 15

1. Market values of debt and equity
   are $D = .9 \times 75 = 67.5 million
   and $E = 42 \times 2.5 = 105 million. $D/V = .39$.
   WACC $= .09(1 − .35).39 + .18(.61) = .1325$, or 13.25%.

3. (a) False; (b) true; (c) true.

5. (a) True; (b) false, if interest tax shields are valued separately; (c) true.

7. a. 12%, of course.
   b. $r_E = .12 + (.12 − .075)$
      $(30/70) = .139$; WACC $= .075(1 − .35)(.30) + .139(.70) = .112$, or 11.2%.

9. No. The more debt you use, the higher rate of return equity investors will require. (Lenders may demand

more also.) Thus there is a hidden cost of the "cheap" debt: It makes equity more expensive.

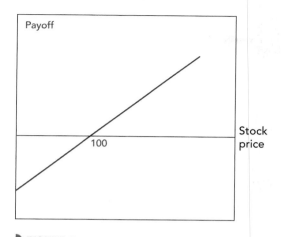

▶ **FIGURE 3**   Chapter 16, Problem 7(a).

CHAPTER 16

1. Call; exercise; put; European.

3. a. The exercise price of the put option (i.e., you'd sell stock for the exercise price).
   b. The value of the stock (i.e., you would throw away the put and keep the stock).

5. Buy a call and lend the present value of the exercise price.

7. (a) See Figure 3; (b) stock price − PV(EX) = 100 − 100/1.1 = $9.09.

9. (a) Zero; (b) stock price less the present value of the exercise price.

11. a. All investors, however risk-averse, should value more highly an option on a volatile stock. For both Exxon Mobil and Google the option is valueless if the final stock price is below the exercise price, but the option on Google has more upside potential.
    b. Other things equal, stockholders lose and debtholders gain if the company shifts to safer assets. When the assets are risky, the option to default is more valuable. Debtholders bear much of the losses if asset value declines, but shareholders get the gains if asset value increases.

CHAPTER 17

1. a. Using risk-neutral method,
   $(p \times 20) + (1 - p)(-16.7) = 1, p = .48.$

   $$\text{Value of call} = \frac{(.48 \times 8) + (.52 \times 0)}{1.01} = 3.8$$

b. $\text{Delta} = \dfrac{\text{spread of option prices}}{\text{spread of stock prices}}$

   $$= \frac{8}{14.7} = .544.$$

c.

	Current Cash Flow	Possible Future Cash Flows	
Buy call equals	−3.8	0	+8.0
Buy .544 shares	−21.8	−18.2	+26.2
Borrow 18.0	+18.0	−18.2	−18.2
	−3.8	0	+8.0

d. Possible stock prices with call option prices in parentheses:

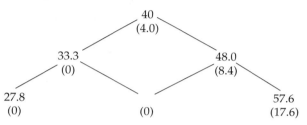

Option prices were calculated as follows:

Month 1: (i) $\dfrac{(.48 \times 0) + (.52 \times 0)}{1.01} = 0$

(ii) $\dfrac{(.48 \times 17.6) + (.52 \times 0)}{1.01} = 8.4$

Month 0: $= \dfrac{(.48 \times 8.4) + (.52 \times 0)}{1.01} = 4.0$

e. $\text{Delta} = \dfrac{\text{spread of option prices}}{\text{spread of stock prices}} = \dfrac{8.4}{14.7} = .57$

3. Using the replicating-portfolio method:
   a. If month 3 stock price = 350.85, delta = (30 − 0)/ (430 − 286.27) = .209
      To replicate call, buy .209 shares, and borrow PV(59.752)
      Option value = .209 × 350.85 − 59.752/1.0075 = 13.93
   b. If month 3 stock price = 527, delta = (245.90 − 30)/ (645.90 − 430) = 1
      To replicate call, buy 1 share, and borrow PV(527)
      Option value = 1 × 527 − 400/1.0075 = 129.98
   c. At month 0 delta = (129.98 − 13.93)/ (527 − 350.85) = .659
      To replicate call, buy .659 shares, and borrow PV(217.29)
      Option value = .659 × 430 − 217.29/1.0075 = 67.7
   Using the risk-neutral method:
   p × .2269 + (1 − p) × .184 = 0.0075: p = .4671
   a. If month 3 stock price = 350.85, option value = (.4671 × 30 + .5329 × 0)/1.0075 =13.93

b. If month 3 stock price = 527, option value = $(.4671 \times 245.90 + .5329 \times 30)/1.0075 = 129.99$

c. At month 0 option value = $(.4671 \times 129.99 + .5329 \times 13.93)/1.0075 = 67.7$

The put option can be valued using put-call parity:

Value of put = $67.7 + 400/1.0075 - 430 = 34.72$

5. a. Delta = $100/(200 - 50) = .667$.

b.

	Current Cash Flow	Possible Future Cash Flows	
Buy call equals	−36.36	0	+100
Buy .667 shares	−66.67	+33.33	+133.33
Borrow 30.30	+30.30	−33.33	−33.33
	−36.36	0	+100

c. $(p \times 100) + (1 - p)(-50) = 10, p = .4$.

d. Value of call = $\dfrac{(.4 \times 100) + (.6 \times 0)}{1.10} = 36.36$.

e. No. The true probability of a price rise is almost certainly higher than the risk-neutral probability, but it does not help to value the option.

7. True; as the stock price rises, the risk of the option falls.

CHAPTER 18

1.

$ Thousands		$ Thousands	
Cash	$25	$ 24	Accounts payable
Accounts receivable	35	24	Total current liabilities
Inventories	30	130	Long-term debt
Total current assets	90	76	Equity
Net plant & equipment	140		
Total assets	230	230	Total liabilities & equity

3.

Common-Size Balance Sheet, 2008

	%		%
Cash & marketable securities	8.0	Debt due for repayment	2.4
Accounts receivable	20.6	Accounts payable	31.6
Inventories	19.7	Total current liabilities	33.9
Other current assets	7.2	Long-term debt	21.5
Total current assets	55.6	Other long-term liabilities	11.6
Tangible fixed assets	47.8	Total liabilities	67.0
Less accumulated depreciation	27.0	Total shareholders' equity	33.0
Net tangible fixed assets	20.8		
Long-term investments	.5		
Other long-term assets	23.1		
Total assets	100	Total liabilities & shareholders' equity	100

Common-Size Income Statement, 2008

Sales	100%
Cost of goods sold	25.2
Selling, general, and administrative expenses	61.3
Depreciation	3.2
Earnings before interest & taxes	10.3
Interest expense	.9
Taxable income	9.4
Tax	3.3
Net income	6.0

5. The illogical ratios are $a, b, c, f,$ and i. The correct definitions are

$$\text{Debt-equity ratio} = \frac{\text{long-term debt} + \text{value of leases}}{\text{equity}}$$

$$\text{Return on equity} = \frac{\text{net income}}{\text{equity at start of year}}$$

$$\text{Payout ratio} = \frac{\text{dividend per share}}{\text{earnings per share}}$$

$$\text{Current ratio} = \frac{\text{current assets}}{\text{current liabilities}}$$

$$\text{Average collection period} = \frac{\text{receivables at start of year}}{\text{daily sales}}$$

7. a. Sales = $3 \times 500,000 = 1,500,000$; after-tax interest + net income = $.08 \times 1,500,000 = 120,000$; ROA = $120,000/500,000 = 24\%$;

b. Net income = $.08 \times 3 \times 500,000 - (1 - .35) \times 30,000 = 100,500$. ROE = net income/equity = $100,500/300,000 = .34$.

9. .73.; 3.65%

11. Assume that new debt is a current liability.

a. Current ratio goes from $100/60 = 1.67$ to $120/80 = 1.50$; cash ratio goes from $30/60 = .5$ to $50/80 = .63$;

b. Long-term debt ratio is unchanged; total liabilities/total assets goes from $410/600 = .6833$ to $430/620 = .6935$.

13. $82 million.

CHAPTER 19

1.

Cash	Working Capital
1. $2 million decline	$2 million decline
2. $2,500 increase	Unchanged
3. $50,000 decline	Unchanged
4. Unchanged	$10 million increase
5. Unchanged	Unchanged
6. $5 million increase	Unchanged

3. Month 3: $18 + (.5 \times 90) + (.3 \times 120) + (.2 \times 100) = \$119,000$.

Month 4: $14 + (.5 \times 70) + (.3 \times 90) + (.2 \times 120) = \$100,000$.

5. a. Table 19.2: Cash = 40, Total current assets = 340; Bank loans = 15; Current liabilities = 150; and Total assets = Total liabilities and net worth = 590.

Table 19.3: Increase (decrease) in short-term debt = −10; Net cash flow from financing activities = −35; Increase in cash balance = 20.

b. Table 19.2: Long-term debt = 130; Gross investment = 375; Net fixed assets = 275; Cash = 40; Current assets = 340; and Total assets = Total liabilities and net worth = 615.

Table 19.3: Increase (decrease) in long-term debt = 30 + 40 = 70; Net cash flow from financing activities = −50 + 40 = −10; Investment in fixed assets = −(25 + 30) = −55; Increase in cash balance = 20.

c. Table 19.1: Operating cost (cost of goods sold + other expenses) = $(1{,}644 + 411) \times .9 = 1{,}850$; Pretax income = $2{,}200 − 1{,}850 − 20 − 5 = 325$; Net income = $325 \times .5 = 162.5$. If dividend is unchanged, earnings retained in the business = $162.5 − 30 = 132.5$.

Table 19.2: Assuming inventories are unchanged, Cash = $25 + 132.5 − 30 = 127.5$; Current assets = 427.5; Net worth = 452.5; Total assets = Total liabilities and net worth = 677.5.

Table 19.3: Net income = 162.5; Net cash flow from operating activities = $85 + 102.5 = 187.5$; Increase (decrease) in cash balance = 107.5.

d. Table 19.4 changes as follows:

	Q3	Q4
Receivables at start	181.6	105.2
Sales	742	836
Collections:		
Current sales	667.8	752.4
Last period sales	150.6	74.2
Total collections	818.4	826.6
Receivables at end	105.2	114.6

Table 19.5 changes as follows:

	Q3	Q4
Collections on accounts receivable	818.4	826.6
Total sources	895.4	826.6
Sources minus uses	268.4	189.1
Cash at start	−188.6	79.8
Change in cash balance	268.4	189.1
Cash at end	79.8	268.9
Cumulative financing required	−54.8	243.9

e. Table 19.5 changes as follows:

	Q1	Q2	Q3	Q4
Labor and other expenses	116	116	116	116
Total sources	531	539.4	767	827.8
Sources minus uses	121	−52.6	140	190.3
Short-term borrowing requirement:				
Cash at start	25	−96	−148.6	−8.6
Change in cash balance	−121	−52.6	140	190.3
Cash at end	−96	−148.6	−8.6	181.7
Cumulative financing required	121	173.6	33.6	−156.7

f. Table 19.5 changes as follows:

	Q2	Q3	Q4
Other	50	77	
Total sources	569.4	747	807.8
Sources minus uses	−22.6	120	170.3
Short-term borrowing requirement:			
Cash at start	−116	−138.6	−18.6
Change in cash balance	−22.6	120	170.3
Cash at end	−138.6	−18.6	151.7
Cumulative financing required	163.6	43.6	−126.7

g. Table 19.5 changes as follows:

	Q1	Q2	Q3	Q4
Minimum operating balance	10	10	10	10
Cumulative financing required	126	198.6	78.6	−91.7

7. (a) \$2,900,000; (b) \$225,000; (c) .25.

9. (a) 8.6%; (b) 13.75%.

Glossary

Note:
1. *Italicized* words are listed elsewhere in the glossary.
2. A number of Web sites contain comprehensive financial glossaries. See, for example, **www.finance-glossary.com** and **www.duke.edu/~ charvey/Classes/wpg/glossary.htm**.

A

Abnormal return Part of return that is not due to marketwide price movements.

Absolute priority Rule in bankruptcy proceedings whereby senior creditors are required to be paid in full before junior creditors receive any payment.

Accelerated depreciation Any *depreciation* method that produces larger deductions for depreciation in the early years of a project's life.

Accounts payable (payables, trade debt) Money owed to suppliers.

Accounts receivable (receivables, trade credit) Money owed by customers.

Accrued interest Interest that has been earned but not yet paid.

ACH *Automated Clearing House.*

Acid-test ratio *Quick ratio.*

Adjusted present value (APV) *Net present value* of an asset if financed solely by equity plus the *present value* of any financing side effects.

ADR *American depository receipt.*

Adverse selection A situation in which a pricing policy causes only the less desirable customers to do business, e.g., a rise in insurance prices that leads only the worst risks to buy insurance.

Affirmative covenant Loan *covenant* specifying certain actions that the borrower must take.

Agency costs Losses that arise when an agent (e.g., a manager) does not act solely in the interests of the principal (e.g., the shareholder).

Agency theory Theory of the relationship between a principal, e.g., a shareholder, and an agent of the principal, e.g., the company's manager.

Aging schedule Summary of age of *receivables* that are outstanding from each customer.

AIBD Association of International Bond Dealers.

All-or-none underwriting An arrangement whereby a security issue is canceled if the *underwriter* is unable to resell the entire issue.

Alpha Measure of portfolio return adjusted for effect of market.

Alternative minimum tax (AMT) A separately calculated minimum amount of tax that must be paid by corporations or individuals.

American depository receipt (ADR) A certificate issued in the United States to represent shares of a foreign company.

American option *Option* that can be exercised any time before the final exercise date (cf. *European option*).

Amex American Stock Exchange.

Amortization (1) Repayment of a loan by installments; (2) allowance for *depreciation.*

AMT *Alternative minimum tax.*

Angel investor Wealthy individual who provides capital for small start-up businesses.

Annual percentage rate (APR) The interest rate per period (e.g., per month) multiplied by the number of periods in a year.

Annuity Investment that produces a level stream of cash flows for a limited number of periods.

Annuity due *Annuity* whose payments occur at the start of each period.

Annuity factor *Present value* of $1 paid for each of *t* periods.

Anticipation Arrangement whereby customers who pay before the final date may be entitled to deduct a normal rate of interest.

Appraisal rights A right of shareholders in a *merger* to demand the payment of a fair price for their shares, as determined independently.

Appropriation request Formal request for funds for a capital investment project.

APR *Annual percentage rate.*

APT *Arbitrage pricing theory.*

APV *Adjusted present value.*

Arbitrage Purchase of one security and simultaneous sale of another to give a risk-free profit.

"Arbitrage" or "risk arbitrage"   Often used loosely to describe the taking of offsetting positions in related securities, e.g., at the time of a takeover bid.

Arbitrage pricing theory (APT)   Model in which expected returns increase linearly with an asset's sensitivity to a small number of pervasive factors.

Arranger   Lead *underwriter* to a *syndicated loan*.

Articles of incorporation   Legal document establishing a corporation and its structure and purpose.

Asian currency units   Dollar deposits held in Singapore or other Asian centers.

Asian option   *Option* based on the average price of the asset during the life of the option.

Asked price (offer price)   Price at which a dealer is willing to sell (cf. *bid price*).

Asset-backed securities   Securities issued by a special-purpose company that holds a package of assets whose cash flows are sufficient to service the *bonds*.

Asset stripper   Acquirer who takes over firms in order to sell off a large part of their assets.

Asymmetric information   Difference in information available to two parties, e.g., a manager and investors.

At-the-money option   Option whose exercise price equals the current asset price (cf. *in-the-money option, out-of-the-money option*).

Auction market   Securities exchange in which prices are determined by an auction process, e.g., *NYSE* (cf. *dealer market*).

Auction-rate preferred   A variant of *floating-rate preferred* stock where the dividend is reset every 49 days by auction.

Authorized share capital   Maximum number of shares that a company can issue, as specified in the firm's *articles of incorporation*.

Automated Clearing House (ACH)   Private electronic system run by banks for high-volume, low-value payments.

Automatic debit   *Direct payment*.

Availability float   Checks deposited by a company that have not yet been cleared.

Aval   Bank guarantee for debt purchased by *forfaiter*.

B

BA   *Banker's acceptance*.

Backdating   Discredited practice of using hindsight to select a grant date for at-the-money executive stock *options* when the stock price (and therefore *exercise price*) were unusually low.

Backwardation   Condition in which *spot price* of commodity exceeds price of *future* (cf. *contango*).

Balloon payment   Large final payment (e.g., when a loan is repaid in installments).

Bank discount   Interest deducted from the initial amount of a loan.

Banker's acceptance (BA)   Written demand that has been accepted by a bank to pay a given sum at a future date (cf. *trade acceptance*).

Barrier option   *Option* whose existence depends on asset price hitting some specified barrier (cf. *down-and-out option, down-and-in option*).

Basel Accord   International agreement on the amount of capital to be maintained by large banks to support their risky loans.

Basis point (BP)   .01%.

Basis risk   Residual risk that results when the two sides of a hedge do not move exactly together.

Bearer security   Security for which primary evidence of ownership is possession of the certificate (cf. *registered security*).

Bear market   Widespread decline in security prices (cf. *bull market*).

Behavioral finance   Branch of finance that stresses aspects of investor irrationality.

Benchmark maturity   Maturity of a newly issued Treasury bond.

Benefit–cost ratio   One plus *profitability index*.

Bermuda option   *Option* that is exercisable on discrete dates before maturity.

Best-efforts underwriting   An arrangement whereby *underwriters* do not commit themselves to selling a security issue but promise only to use best efforts.

Beta   Measure of *market risk*.

Bid price   Price at which a dealer is willing to buy (cf. *asked price*).

Big Board   Colloquial term for the New York Stock Exchange.

Bill of exchange   General term for a document demanding payment.

Bill of lading   Document establishing ownership of goods in transit.

Binomial method   Method for valuing *options* that assumes there are only two possible changes in the asset price in any one period.

Blue-chip company   Large and creditworthy company.

Blue-sky laws   State laws covering the issue and trading of securities.

Boilerplate   Standard terms and conditions, e.g., in a debt contract.

Bond   Long-term debt.

Bond rating   Rating of the likelihood of bond's default.

Bookbuilding   The procedure whereby *underwriters* gather nonbinding indications of demand for a new issue.

Book entry   Registered ownership of stock without issue of stock certificate.

Book runner   The managing *underwriter* for a new issue. The book runner maintains the book of securities sold.

Bought deal   Security issue where one or two *underwriters* buy the entire issue.

BP   *Basis point.*

Bracket   A term signifying the extent of an *underwriter's* commitment in a new issue, e.g., major bracket, minor bracket.

Break-even analysis   Analysis of the level of sales at which a project would just break even.

Bridge loan   Short-term loan to provide temporary financing until more permanent financing is arranged.

Bull–bear bond   *Bond* whose *principal* repayment is linked to the price of another security. The bonds are issued in two *tranches:* In the first the repayment increases with the price of the other security; in the second the repayment decreases with the price of the other security.

Bulldog bond   *Foreign bond* issue made in London.

Bullet payment   Single final payment, e.g., of a loan (in contrast to payment in installments).

Bull market   Widespread rise in security prices (cf. *bear market*).

Bund   Long-term German government *bond*.

Butterfly spread   The purchase of two *call options* with different *exercise prices* and simultaneous sale of two calls exercisable at the average of these two exercise prices. Provides a bet that the share price will stay within a narrow range.

Buyback   *Repurchase agreement.*

C

Cable   The exchange rate between U.S. dollars and sterling.

Call option   Option to buy an asset at a specified exercise price on or before a specified exercise date (cf. *put option*).

Call premium   (1) Difference between the price at which a company can call its *bonds* and their *face value;* (2) price of a call *option.*

Call provision   Provision that allows an issuer to buy back the *bond* issue at a stated price.

Cap   An upper limit on the interest rate on a *floating-rate note.*

CAPEX   Capital expenditure.

Capital asset pricing model (CAPM)   Model in which expected returns increase linearly with an asset's *beta.*

Capital budget   List of planned investment projects, usually prepared annually.

Capitalization   Long-term debt plus *preferred stock* plus *net worth.*

Capital lease   *Financial lease.*

Capital market   Financial market (particularly the market for long-term securities).

Capital market line   A plot of the set of portfolios with the highest *Sharpe ratio*. The line passes through the risk-free interest rate and the *tangent efficient portfolio* of risky assets.

Capital rationing   Shortage of funds that forces a company to choose between worthwhile projects.

Capital structure   Mix of different securities issued by a firm.

CAPM   *Capital asset pricing model.*

Captive finance company   Subsidiary whose function is to provide finance for purchases from the parent company.

Caput option   *Call option* on a *put option.*

CAR   Cumulative *abnormal return.*

CARDs (Certificates for Amortizing Revolving Debt)   *Pass-through securities* backed by credit card *receivables.*

Carried interest   A proportion of the profits to which *private equity* partnerships, etc., are entitled.

Carry trade   Borrowing in country with low interest rate to relend in another country with a higher rate.

CARs (Certificates of Automobile Receivables)   *Pass-through securities* backed by automobile *receivables.*

Carve-out   Public offering of shares in a subsidiary.

Cascade   Rational herding in which each individual deduces that previous decisions by others may have been based on extra information.

Cash and carry   Purchase of a security and simultaneous sale of a *future,* with the balance being financed with a loan or *repo.*

Cash budget   Forecast of sources and uses of cash.

Cash cow   Mature company producing a large *free cash flow.*

Cash cycle The time from a firm's payment for raw materials until the payment for the finished product from the customer.

Cash-deficiency arrangement Arrangement whereby a project's shareholders agree to provide the operating company with sufficient *net working capital*.

Catastrophe bond (CAT bond) *Bond* whose payoffs are linked to a measure of catastrophe losses such as insurance claims.

CAT bond *Catastrophe bond*.

CBD Cash before delivery.

CD *Certificate of deposit*.

CDS *Credit default swap*.

CEO Chief executive officer.

Certainty equivalent A certain cash flow that has the same present value as a specified risky cash flow.

Certificate of deposit (CD) A certificate providing evidence of a bank time deposit.

CFTC Commodity Futures Trading Commission.

CFO Chief financial officer.

Chaebol A Korean conglomerate.

Chapter 7 Bankruptcy procedure whereby a debtor's assets are sold and the proceeds are used to repay creditors.

Chapter 11 Bankruptcy procedure designed to reorganize and rehabilitate defaulting firm.

Check conversion When customer writes a check, information is automatically captured and his or her bank account immediately debited.

Check 21 Check Clearing for the 21st Century Act allows banks to process checks electronically.

CHIPS *Clearinghouse Interbank Payments System*.

Chooser option Holder decides whether it is a *call option* or *put option*.

Clean price (flat price) *Bond* price excluding *accrued interest* (cf. *dirty price*).

Clearinghouse Interbank Payments System (CHIPS) An international wire transfer system operated by a group of major banks for high-value dollar payments.

CLO *Collateralized loan obligation*. Also CDO (collateralized debt obligation) and CMOs (collateralized mortgage obligations).

Closed-end fund Company whose assets consist of investments in a number of industrial and commercial companies.

Closed-end mortgage Mortgage against which no additional debt may be issued (cf. *open-end mortgage*).

CMOs *Collateralized mortgage obligations*.

COD Cash on delivery.

Collar An upper and lower limit on the interest rate on a *floating-rate note*.

Collateral Assets that are given as security for a loan.

Collateralized loan obligation (CLO) A security backed by a pool of loans and issued in *tranches* with different levels of seniority.

Collateralized mortgage obligations (CMOs) A variation on the mortgage *pass-through security* in which the cash flows from a pool of mortgages are repackaged into several *tranches* of *bonds* with different maturities.

Collateral trust bonds *Bonds* secured by *common stocks* or other securities that are owned by the borrower.

Collection float Customer-written checks that have not been received, deposited, and added to the company's available balance (cf. *payment float*).

Commercial draft (bill of exchange) Demand for payment.

Commercial paper Unsecured *notes* issued by companies and maturing within nine months.

Commitment fee Fee charged by bank on an unused *line of credit*.

Common-size financial statements Balance sheet where entries are expressed as proportion of total assets and income statement where entries are expressed as a proportion of revenues.

Common stock Security representing ownership of a *corporation*.

Company cost of capital The expected return on a portfolio of all the firm's securities.

Compensating balance Non-interest-bearing demand deposits to compensate banks for bank loans or services.

Competitive bidding Means by which public utility *holding companies* are required to choose their *underwriter* (cf. *negotiated underwriting*).

Completion bonding Insurance that a construction contract will be successfully completed.

Composition Voluntary agreement to reduce payments on a firm's debt.

Compound interest Reinvestment of each interest payment on money invested to earn more interest (cf. *simple interest*).

Compound option Option on an *option*.

Concentration banking System whereby customers make payments to a regional collection center. The collection center pays the funds into a regional bank account and surplus money is transferred to the company's principal bank.

Conditional sale   Sale in which ownership does not pass to the buyer until payment is completed.

Conglomerate merger   *Merger* between two companies in unrelated businesses (cf. *horizontal merger, vertical merger*).

Consol   Name of a perpetual *bond* issued by the British government. Sometimes used as a general term for *perpetuity*.

Contango   Condition in which spot price of a commodity is below that of the *future* (cf. *backwardation*).

Contingent claim   Claim whose value depends on the value of another asset.

Contingent project   Project that cannot be undertaken unless another project is also undertaken.

Continuous compounding   Interest compounded continuously rather than at fixed intervals.

Controller   Officer responsible for budgeting, accounting, and auditing in a firm (cf. *treasurer*).

Convenience yield   The extra advantage that firms derive from holding the commodity rather than the *future*.

Conversion price   *Par value* of a *convertible bond* divided by the number of shares into which it may be exchanged.

Conversion ratio   Number of shares for which a *convertible bond* may be exchanged.

Convertible bond   *Bond* that may be converted into another security at the holder's option. Similarly convertible *preferred stock*.

Convexity   In a plot of a *bond*'s price against the interest rate, convexity measures the curvature of the line.

Corporate venturing   Practice by which a large manufacturer provides financial support to new companies.

Corporation   A business that is legally separate from its owners.

Correlation coefficient   Measure of the closeness of the relationship between two variables.

Cost company arrangement   Arrangement whereby the shareholders of a project receive output free of charge but agree to pay all operating and financing charges of the project.

Cost of (equity) capital   *Opportunity cost of capital.*

Counterparty   Party on the other side of a *derivative* contract.

Coupon   (1) Specifically, an attachment to the certificate of a *bearer security* that must be surrendered to collect interest payment; (2) more generally, interest payment on debt.

Covariance   Measure of the co-movement between two variables.

Covenant   Clause in a loan agreement.

Covered option   *Option* position with an offsetting position in the underlying asset.

Cramdown   Action by a bankruptcy court to enforce a plan of reorganization.

Credit default swap (CDS)   *Credit derivative* in which one party makes fixed payments while the payments by the other party depend on the occurrence of a loan default.

Credit derivative   Contract for *hedging* against loan default or changes in credit risk (e.g., *credit default swap*).

Credit rating   Debt rating assigned by a rating agency such as Moody's or Standard & Poor's.

Credit scoring   A procedure for assigning scores to borrowers on the basis of the risk of default.

Cross-default clause   Clause in a loan agreement stating that the company is in default if it fails to meet its obligation on any other debt issue.

Cum dividend   *With dividend.*

Cum rights   *With rights.*

Cumulative preferred stock   Stock that takes priority over *common stock* in regard to dividend payments. Dividends may not be paid on the common stock until all past *dividends* on the *preferred stock* have been paid.

Cumulative voting   Voting system under which a stockholder may cast all of his or her votes for one candidate for the board of directors (cf. *majority voting*).

Current asset   Asset that will normally be turned into cash within a year.

Current liability   Liability that will normally be repaid within a year.

Current ratio   *Current assets* divided by *current liabilities*—a measure of liquidity.

Current yield   *Bond coupon* divided by price.

D

Data mining (data snooping)   Excessive search to find interesting (but probably coincidental) behavior in a body of data.

DCF   *Discounted cash flow.*

DDM   *Dividend discount model.*

Dealer market   Securities exchange in which dealers post offers to buy or sell, e.g., *Nasdaq* (cf. *auction market*).

Dealer paper   *Commercial paper* sold through a dealer rather than directly by the company.

Death spiral convertible   *Convertible bond* exchangeable for shares with a specified market value.

Debenture Unsecured *bond*.

Debtor-in–possession financing (DIP financing) Debt issued by a company in *Chapter 11* bankruptcy.

Decision tree Method of representing alternative sequential decisions and the possible outcomes from these decisions.

Defeasance Practice whereby the borrower sets aside cash or *bonds* sufficient to service the borrower's debt. Both the borrower's debt and the offsetting cash or bonds are removed from the balance sheet.

Degree of operating leverage (DOL) The percentage change in profits for a 1% change in sales.

Delta *Hedge ratio*.

Depository transfer check (DTC) Check made out directly by a local bank to a particular company.

Depreciation (1) Reduction in the book or market value of an asset; (2) portion of an investment that can be deducted from taxable income.

Derivative Asset whose value derives from that of some other asset (e.g., a *future* or an *option*).

Designated market maker Member of *NYSE* responsible for market in specified securities (formerly called "specialist").

Diff *Differential swap*.

Differential swap (diff, quanto swap) Swap between two *LIBOR* rates of interest, e.g., yen LIBOR for dollar LIBOR. Payments are in one currency.

Digital option *Option* paying fixed sum if asset price is the right side of *exercise price*, otherwise zero.

Dilution Diminution in the proportion of income to which each share is entitled.

DIP financing *Debtor-in–possession financing*.

Direct debit *Direct payment*.

Direct deposit The firm authorizes its bank to deposit money in the accounts of its employees or shareholders.

Direct lease *Lease* in which the *lessor* purchases new equipment from the manufacturer and leases it to the *lessee* (cf. *sale and lease-back*).

Direct payment (automatic debit, direct debit) The firm's customers authorize it to debit their bank accounts for the amounts due (cf. *direct deposit*).

Direct quote For foreign exchange, the number of U.S. dollars needed to buy one unit of a foreign currency (cf. *indirect quote*).

Dirty price *Bond* price including *accrued interest*, i.e., the price paid by the bond buyer (cf. *clean price*).

Discount bond Debt sold for less than its *principal* value. If a discount bond pays no interest, it is called a "pure" discount, or *zero-coupon, bond*.

Discounted cash flow (DCF) Future cash flows multiplied by *discount factors* to obtain *present value*.

Discounted payback rule Requirement that discounted values of cash flows should be sufficient to pay back initial investment within a specified time.

Discount factor *Present value* of $1 received at a stated future date.

Discount rate Rate used to calculate the *present value* of future cash flows.

Discriminatory price auction Auction in which successful bidders pay the price that they bid (cf. *uniform price auction*).

Disintermediation Withdrawal of funds from a financial institution in order to invest them directly (cf. *intermediation*).

Dividend Payment by a company to its stockholders.

Dividend discount model Model showing that the value of a share is equal to the discounted value of future *dividends*.

Dividend reinvestment plan (DRIP) Plan that allows shareholders to reinvest dividends automatically.

Dividend yield Annual *dividend* divided by share price.

DOL *Degree of operating leverage*.

Double-declining-balance depreciation Method of *accelerated depreciation*.

Double-tax agreement Agreement between two countries that taxes paid abroad can be offset against domestic taxes levied on foreign *dividends*.

Down-and-in option *Barrier option* that comes into existence if asset price hits a barrier.

Down-and-out option *Barrier option* that expires if asset price hits a barrier.

DRIP *Dividend reinvestment plan*.

Drop lock An arrangement whereby the interest rate on a *floating-rate note* or *preferred stock* becomes fixed if it falls to a specified level.

DTC *Depository transfer check*.

Dual-class equity Shares with different voting rights.

Dual-currency bond *Bond* with interest paid in one currency and *principal* paid in another.

Du Pont formula Formula expressing relationship between return on assets, sales-to-assets, profit margin, and measures of leverage.

Duration The average number of years to an asset's *discounted cash flows*.

Dutch auction In a Dutch auction investors submit the prices at which they are prepared to buy (or sell) the security. The purchase price is the lowest price that allows the firm to sell (or buy) the specified amount of the security.

E

EBIT Earnings before interest and taxes.

EBITDA Earnings before interest, taxes, depreciation, and *amortization*.

EBPP *Electronic bill presentment and payment.*

Economic depreciation Decline in *present value* of an asset.

Economic exposure Risk that arises from changes in real exchange rates (cf. *transaction exposure, translation exposure*).

Economic income Cash flow plus change in *present value*.

Economic rents Profits in excess of the competitive level.

Economic value added (EVA) A measure of *residual income* implemented by the consulting firm Stern Stewart.

Efficient market Market in which security prices reflect information instantaneously.

Efficient portfolio Portfolio that offers the lowest risk (*standard deviation*) for its *expected return* and the highest expected return for its level of risk.

EFT *Electronic funds transfer.*

Electronic bill presentment and payment (EBPP) Allows companies to bill customers and receive payments via the Internet.

Electronic funds transfer (EFT) Transfer of money electronically (e.g., by *Fedwire*).

Employee stock ownership plan (ESOP) A company contributes to a trust fund that buys stock on behalf of employees.

Entrenching investment An investment that makes particular use of the skills of existing management.

EPS Earnings per share.

Equipment trust certificate Form of *secured debt* generally used to finance railroad equipment. The trustee retains ownership of the equipment until the debt is repaid.

Equity (1) *Common stock* and *preferred stock*. Often used to refer to common stock only. (2) *Net worth*.

Equity-linked bond *Bond* whose payments are linked to a stock market index.

Equivalent annual cash flow (or cost) *Annuity* with the same *present value* as the company's proposed investment.

ESOP *Employee stock ownership plan.*

ETF *Exchange-traded fund.*

Euribor *Euro interbank offered rate.*

Eurobond *Bond* that is marketed internationally.

Euro interbank offered rate (Euribor) The interest rate at which major international banks in Europe lend euros to each other.

Eurocurrency Deposit held outside the currency's issuing country (e.g., euroyen, or *eurodollar deposit*)

Eurodollar deposit Dollar deposit with a bank outside the United States.

European option *Option* that can be exercised only on final exercise date (cf. *American option*).

EVA *Economic value added.*

Event risk The risk that an unanticipated event (e.g., a takeover) will lead to a debt default.

Evergreen credit *Revolving credit* without maturity.

Exchange of assets Acquisition of another company by purchase of its assets in exchange for cash or shares.

Exchange of stock Acquisition of another company by purchase of its stock in exchange for cash or shares.

Exchange-traded fund (ETF) A stock designed to track a stock market index.

Ex dividend Purchase of shares in which the buyer is not entitled to the forthcoming *dividend* (cf. *with dividend, cum dividend*).

Exercise price (strike price) Price at which a *call option* or *put option* may be exercised.

Expectations theory Theory that *forward interest rate* (*forward exchange rate*) equals expected *spot rate*.

Expected return Average of possible returns weighted by their probabilities.

Ex rights Purchase of shares that do not entitle the owner to buy shares in the company's *rights issue* (cf. *with rights, cum rights, rights on*).

Extendable bond *Bond* whose maturity can be extended at the option of the lender (or issuer).

External finance Finance that is not generated by the firm: new borrowing or an issue of stock (cf. *internal finance*).

Extra dividend *Dividend* that may or may not be repeated (cf. *regular dividend*).

F

Face value *Par value.*

Factoring Arrangement whereby a financial institution buys a company's *accounts receivable* and collects the debt.

Fair price provision *Appraisal rights.*

Fallen angel *Junk bond* that was formerly an *investment-grade bond*.

FASB Financial Accounting Standards Board.

FCIA Foreign Credit Insurance Association.

FDIC   Federal Deposit Insurance Corporation.

Federal funds   Non-interest-bearing deposits by banks at the Federal Reserve. Excess reserves are lent by banks to each other.

Fedwire   A wire transfer system for high-value payments operated by the Federal Reserve System (cf. *CHIPS*).

Field warehouse   Warehouse rented by a warehouse company on another firm's premises (cf. *public warehouse*).

Financial assets   Claims on *real assets*.

Financial engineering   Combining or dividing existing instruments to create new financial products.

Financial lease (capital lease, full-payout lease)   Long-term, noncancelable lease (cf. *operating lease*).

Financial leverage (gearing)   Use of debt to increase the *expected return* on *equity*. Financial leverage is measured by the ratio of debt to debt plus equity (cf. *operating leverage*).

Firm commitment   Arrangement whereby the *underwriter* guarantees to sell the entire issue.

Fiscal agency agreement   An alternative to a bond *trust deed*. Unlike the trustee, the fiscal agent acts as an agent of the borrower.

Flat price   *Clean price.*

Flipping   Buying shares in an *IPO* and selling immediately.

Float   *See availability float, collection float, payment float.*

Floating lien   General *lien* against a company's assets or against a particular class of assets.

Floating-price convertible   *Death spiral convertible.*

Floating-rate note (FRN)   *Note* whose interest payment varies with the short-term interest rate.

Floating-rate preferred   *Preferred stock* paying dividends that vary with short-term interest rates.

Floor planning   Arrangement used to finance inventory. A finance company buys the inventory, which is then held in trust by the user.

Flow-to-equity method   Discounted value of cash flows to equityholders.

Foreign bond   A *bond* issued on the domestic *capital market* of another country.

Forex   Foreign exchange.

Forfaiter   Purchaser of promises to pay (e.g., *bills of exchange* or *promissory notes*) issued by importers.

Forward cover   Purchase or sale of forward foreign currency in order to offset a known future cash flow.

Forward exchange rate   Exchange rate fixed today for exchanging currency at some future date (cf. *spot exchange rate*).

Forward interest rate   Interest rate fixed today on a loan to be made at some future date (cf. *spot interest rate*).

Forward rate agreement (FRA)   Agreement to borrow or lend at a specified future date at an interest rate that is fixed today.

FRA   *Forward rate agreement.*

Free cash flow   Cash not required for operations or for reinvestment.

Free-rider problem   The temptation not to incur the costs of participating in a decision when one's influence on that decision is small.

FRN   *Floating-rate note.*

Full-payout lease   *Financial lease.*

Full-service lease (rental lease)   *Lease* in which the *lessor* promises to maintain and insure the equipment (cf. *net lease*).

Fundamental analysis   Security analysis that seeks to detect misvalued securities by an analysis of the firm's business prospects (cf. *technical analysis*).

Funded debt   Debt maturing after more than one year (cf. *unfunded debt*).

Futures contract   A contract to buy a commodity or security on a future date at a price that is fixed today. Unlike forward contracts, futures are traded on organized exchanges and are *marked to market* daily.

G

GAAP   Generally accepted accounting principles.

Gamma   A measure of how the *option delta* changes as the asset price changes.

Gearing   *Financial leverage.*

General cash offer   Issue of securities offered to all investors (cf. *rights issue*).

Gilt   A British government *bond*.

Golden parachute   A large termination payment due to a company's officers if they lose their jobs as a result of a *merger*.

Goodwill   The difference between the amount paid for a firm in a *merger* and its book value.

Governance   The oversight of a firm's management.

Gray market   Purchases and sales of securities that occur before the issue price is set.

Greenmail   Situation in which a large block of stock is held by an unfriendly company, forcing the target company to repurchase the stock at a substantial premium to prevent a takeover.

Greenshoe option   *Option* that allows the *underwriter* for a new issue to buy and resell additional shares.

Growth stock   *Common stock* of a company that has an opportunity to invest money to earn more than the *opportunity cost of capital* (cf. *income stock*).

H

Haircut   An additional margin of *collateral* for a loan.

Hedge fund   An investment fund charging a performance fee and open to a limited range of investors. Funds often follow complex strategies including *short sales*.

Hedge ratio (delta, option delta)   The number of shares to buy for each *option* sold to create a safe position; more generally, the number of units of an asset that should be bought to hedge one unit of a liability.

Hedging   Buying one security and selling another to reduce risk. A perfect hedge produces a riskless portfolio.

Hell-or-high-water clause   Clause in a *lease* agreement that obligates the *lessee* to make payments regardless of what happens to the *lessor* or the equipment.

Highly leveraged transaction (HLT)   Bank loan to a highly leveraged firm (formerly needed to be separately reported to the Federal Reserve Board).

High-yield bond   *Junk bond*.

HLT   *Highly leveraged transaction*.

Holding company   Company whose sole function is to hold stock in the firm's subsidiaries.

Horizontal merger   *Merger* between two companies that manufacture similar products (cf. *vertical merger, conglomerate merger*).

Horizontal spread   The simultaneous purchase and sale of two *options* that differ only in their exercise date (cf. *vertical spread*).

Hurdle rate   Minimum acceptable rate of return on a project.

I

IBF   *International banking facility*.

IMM   *International Monetary Market*.

Immunization   The construction of an asset and a liability that have offsetting changes in value.

Implied volatility   The volatility implied by *option* prices.

Imputation tax system   Arrangement by which investors who receive a *dividend* also receive a tax credit for corporate taxes that the firm has paid.

Income bond   *Bond* on which interest is payable only if earned.

Income stock   *Common stock* with high *dividend yield* and few profitable investment opportunities (cf. *growth stock*).

Indenture   Formal agreement, e.g., establishing the terms of a *bond* issue.

Indexed bond   *Bond* whose payments are linked to an index, e.g., a consumer price index (see *TIPS*).

Index fund   Investment fund designed to match the returns on a stock market index.

Indirect quote   For foreign exchange, the number of units of a foreign currency needed to buy one U.S. dollar (cf. *direct quote*).

Industrial revenue bond (IRB)   Bond issued by local government agencies on behalf of *corporations*.

Initial public offering (IPO)   A company's first public issue of *common stock*.

Inside director   Director who is also employed by the company.

In-substance defeasance   *Defeasance* whereby debt is removed from the balance sheet but not canceled (cf. *novation*).

Intangible asset   Nonmaterial asset, such as technical expertise, a trademark, or a patent (cf. *tangible asset*).

Integer programming   Variant of *linear programming* whereby the solution values must be integers.

Interest cover   *Times-interest-earned*.

Interest rate parity   Theory that the differential between the *forward exchange rate* and the *spot exchange rate* is equal to the differential between the foreign and domestic interest rates.

Intermediation   Investment through a financial institution (cf. *disintermediation*).

Internal finance   Finance generated within a firm by *retained earnings* and *depreciation* (cf. *external finance*).

Internal growth rate   The maximum rate of firm growth without *external finance* (cf. *sustainable growth rate*).

Internal rate of return (IRR)   *Discount rate* at which investment has zero *net present value*.

International banking facility (IBF)   A branch that an American bank establishes in the United States to do eurocurrency business.

International Monetary Market (IMM)   The financial futures market within the Chicago Mercantile Exchange.

Interval measure   The number of days that a firm can finance operations without additional cash income.

In-the-money option   An *option* that would be worth exercising if it expired immediately (cf. *out-of-the-money option*).

Investment-grade bond   *Bond* rated at least Baa by Moody's, or BBB by Standard and Poor's or Fitch.

IOSCO   International Organization of Securities Commissions.

IPO   *Initial public offering.*

IRB   *Industrial revenue bond.*

IRR   *Internal rate of return.*

IRS   Internal Revenue Service.

ISDA   International Swap and Derivatives Association.

ISMA   International Securities Market Association.

Issued share capital   Total amount of shares that are in issue (cf. *outstanding share capital*).

J

Junior debt   *Subordinated debt.*

Junk bond (high-yield bond)   Debt that is rated below an *investment-grade bond.*

Just-in-time   System of inventory management that requires minimum inventories of materials and very frequent deliveries by suppliers.

K

Keiretsu   A network of Japanese companies organized around a major bank.

L

LBO   *Leveraged buyout.*

Lease   Long-term rental agreement.

Legal capital   Value at which a company's shares are recorded in its books.

Legal defeasance   *Novation.*

Lessee   User of a leased asset (cf. *lessor*).

Lessor   Owner of a leased asset (cf. *lessee*).

Letter of credit   Letter from a bank stating that it has established a credit in the company's favor.

Letter stock   Privately placed *common stock*, so called because the *SEC* requires a letter from the purchaser that the stock is not intended for resale.

Leverage   See *financial leverage, operating leverage.*

Leveraged buyout (LBO)   Acquisition in which (1) a large part of the purchase price is debt-financed and (2) the remaining *equity* is privately held by a small group of investors.

Leveraged lease   *Lease* in which the *lessor* finances part of the cost of the asset by an issue of debt secured by the asset and the lease payments.

Liabilities, total liabilities   Total value of financial claims on a firm's assets. Equals (1) total assets or (2) total assets minus *net worth.*

LIBOR   *London interbank offered rate.*

Lien   Lender's claims on specified assets.

Limited liability   Limitation of a shareholder's losses to the amount invested.

Limited partnership   *Partnership* in which some partners have *limited liability* and general partners have unlimited liability.

Limit order   Order to buy (sell) securities within a maximum (minimum) price (cf. *market order*).

Linear programming (LP)   Technique for finding the maximum value of some objective function subject to stated linear constraints.

Line of credit   Agreement by a bank that a company may borrow at any time up to an established limit.

Liquid asset   Asset that is easily and cheaply turned into cash—notably cash itself and short-term securities.

Liquidating dividend   *Dividend* that represents a return of capital.

Liquidator   Person appointed by unsecured creditors in the United Kingdom to oversee the sale of an insolvent firm's assets and the repayment of debts.

Liquidity-preference theory   Theory that investors demand a higher yield to compensate for the extra risk of long-term *bonds.*

Liquidity premium   (1) Additional return for investing in a security that cannot easily be turned into cash; (2) difference between the *forward interest rate* and the expected *spot interest rate.*

Liquid yield option note (LYON)   *Zero-coupon*, callable, puttable, *convertible bond.*

Loan origination fee   Up-front fee charged by the lending bank.

Lockbox system   Form of *concentration banking.* Customers send payments to a post office box. A local bank collects and processes the checks and transfers surplus funds to the company's principal bank.

London interbank offered rate (LIBOR)   The interest rate at which major international banks in London lend to each other. (LIBID is London interbank bid rate; LIMEAN is mean of bid and offered rate.)

Longevity bonds   *Bonds* that pay a higher rate of interest if a high proportion of the population survives to a particular age.

Long hedge   Purchase of a *hedging* instrument (e.g., a *future*) to hedge a short position in the underlying asset (cf. *short hedge*).

Lookback option   *Option* whose payoff depends on the highest asset price recorded over the life of the option.

LP   *Linear programming.*

LYON   *Liquid yield option note.*

M

MACRS   *Modified accelerated cost recovery system.*

Maintenance margin   Minimum margin that must be maintained on a *futures contract.*

Majority voting   Voting system under which each director is voted upon separately (cf. *cumulative voting*).

Management buyout (MBO)   *Leveraged buyout* whereby the acquiring group is led by the firm's management.

Mandatory convertible   *Bond* automatically convertible into equity, usually with a limit on the value of stock received.

Margin   Cash or securities set aside by an investor as evidence that he or she can honor a commitment.

Marked to market   An arrangement whereby the profits or losses on a *futures contract* are settled up each day.

Market capitalization   Market value of *outstanding share capital.*

Market capitalization rate   *Expected return* on a security.

Market model   Model suggesting a linear relationship between actual returns on a stock and on the market portfolio.

Market order   Order to buy or sell securities at the prevailing market price (cf. *limit order*).

Market risk (systematic risk)   Risk that cannot be diversified away.

Market-to-book ratio   Ratio of market value to book value of firm's *equity.*

Market value added   Difference between market value and book value of firm's *equity.*

Maturity factoring   *Factoring* arrangement that provides collection and insurance of *accounts receivable.*

MBO   *Management buyout.*

MDA   *Multiple-discriminant analysis.*

Medium-term note (MTN)   Debt with a typical maturity of 1 to 10 years offered regularly by a company using the same procedure as *commercial paper.*

Merger   (1) Acquisition in which all assets and liabilities are absorbed by the buyer (cf. *exchange of assets, exchange of stock*); (2) more generally, any combination of two companies.

MIP (Monthly income preferred security)   *Preferred stock* issued by a subsidiary located in a tax haven. The subsidiary relends the money to the parent.

Mismatch bond   *Floating-rate note* whose interest rate is reset at more frequent intervals than the rollover period (e.g., a note whose payments are set quarterly on the basis of the one-year interest rate).

Modified accelerated cost recovery system (MACRS)   Schedule of *depreciation* deductions allowed for tax purposes.

Modified IRR   *Internal rate of return* calculated by first discounting later cash flows back to earlier periods so that there remains only one change in the sign of the cash flows.

Momentum   Characteristic of stocks showing persistent recent high returns.

Money center bank   A major U.S. bank that undertakes a wide range of banking activities.

Money market   Market for short-term safe investments.

Money-market deposit account (MMDA)   A bank account paying *money-market* interest rate.

Money-market fund   *Mutual fund* that invests solely in short-term safe securities.

Monoline   Insurance company that insures debtholders against the risk of default.

Monte Carlo simulation   Method for calculating the probability distribution of possible outcomes, e.g., from a project.

Moral hazard   The risk that the existence of a contract will change the behavior of one or both parties to the contract; e.g., an insured firm may take fewer fire precautions.

Mortality bonds   *Bonds* that pay a higher rate of interest if there is a sharp rise in the death rate.

Mortgage bond   *Bond* secured against plant and equipment.

MTN   *Medium-term note.*

Multiple-discriminant analysis (MDA)   Statistical technique for distinguishing between two groups on the basis of their observed characteristics.

Mutual fund   Managed investment fund whose shares are sold to investors.

Mutually exclusive projects   Two projects that cannot both be undertaken.

N

Naked option   *Option* held on its own, i.e., not used for *hedging* a holding in the asset or other options.

Nasdaq   National Association of Security Dealers Automated Quote System. A U.S. stock exchange whose dealers tend to specialize in high-tech stocks.

Negative pledge clause Clause under which the borrower agrees not to permit an exclusive *lien* on any of its assets.

Negotiated underwriting Method of choosing an *underwriter*. Most firms may choose their *underwriter* by negotiation (cf. *competitive bidding*).

Net lease *Lease* in which the *lessee* promises to maintain and insure the equipment (cf. *full-service lease*).

Net present value (NPV) A project's net contribution to wealth—*present value* minus initial investment.

Net working capital *Current assets* minus *current liabilities*.

Net worth Book value of a company's *common stock*, surplus, and *retained earnings*.

Nominal interest rate Interest rate expressed in money terms (cf. *real interest rate*).

Nonrefundable debt Debt that may not be called in order to replace it with another issue at a lower interest cost.

NOPAT Net operating profit after tax.

Normal distribution Symmetric bell-shaped distribution that can be completely defined by its mean and *standard deviation*.

Note Unsecured debt with a maturity of up to 10 years.

Novation (legal defeasance) *Defeasance* whereby the firm's debt is canceled (cf. *in-substance defeasance*).

NPV *Net present value.*

NYSE New York Stock Exchange.

O

OAT (Obligation assimilable du Trésor) French government *bond*.

Odd lot A trade of less than 100 shares (cf. *round lot*).

Off-balance-sheet financing Financing that is not shown as a liability in a company's balance sheet.

Offer price *Asked price.*

OID debt *Original issue discount debt.*

Old-line factoring *Factoring* arrangement that provides collection, insurance, and finance for *accounts receivable.*

On the run The most recently issued (and, therefore, typically the most liquid) government *bond* in a particular maturity range.

Open account Arrangement whereby sales are made with no formal debt contract. The buyer signs a receipt, and the seller records the sale in the sales ledger.

Open-end mortgage Mortgage against which additional debt may be issued (cf. *closed-end mortgage*).

Open interest The number of currently outstanding *futures contracts.*

Operating cycle The time from a firm's initial purchase of raw materials until the payment from the customer for the finished product.

Operating lease Short-term, cancelable *lease* (cf. *financial lease*).

Operating leverage Fixed operating costs, so called because they accentuate variations in profits (cf. *financial leverage*).

Opportunity cost of capital (hurdle rate, cost of capital) *Expected return* that is foregone by investing in a project rather than in comparable financial securities.

Option See *call option, put option.*

Option delta *Hedge ratio.*

Original issue discount debt (OID debt) Debt that is initially offered at a price below *face value.*

OTC *Over-the-counter.*

Out-of-the-money option An *option* that would not be worth exercising if it matured immediately (cf. *in-the-money option*).

Outstanding share capital *Issued share capital* less the *par value* of shares that are held in the company's treasury.

Oversubscription privilege In a *rights issue*, arrangement by which shareholders are given the right to apply for any shares that are not taken up.

Over-the-counter (OTC) Informal market that does not involve a securities exchange.

P

Partnership Joint ownership of business whereby general partners have unlimited liability.

Par value (face value) Value of a security shown on the certificate.

Pass-through securities *Notes* or *bonds* backed by a package of assets (e.g., mortgage pass-throughs, *CARs, CARDs*).

Path-dependent option *Option* whose value depends on the sequence of prices of the underlying asset rather than just the final price of the asset.

Payables *Accounts payable.*

Payback rule Requirement that project should recover its initial investment within a specified time.

Pay-in-kind bond (PIK) *Bond* that allows the issuer to choose to make interest payments in the form of additional bonds.

Payment float Company-written checks that have not yet cleared (cf. *availability float*).

Payout ratio   *Dividend* as a proportion of earnings per share.

PBGC   Pension Benefit Guarantee Corporation.

P/E ratio   Share price divided by earnings per share.

PERC (Preferred equity redemption cumulative stock)   *Preferred stock* that converts automatically into equity at a stated date. A limit is placed on the value of the shares that the investor receives.

Perpetuity   Investment offering a level stream of cash flows in perpetuity (cf. *consol*).

PIK   *Pay-in-kind bond.*

PN   *Project note.*

Poison pill   Includes a variety of takeover defenses, notably the right of existing shareholders to acquire stock at a discount if a bidder acquires a minimum number of shares.

Poison put   A *covenant* allowing the *bond*holder to demand repayment in the event of a hostile *merger*.

Pooling of interest   Method of accounting for *mergers* (no longer available in the USA). The consolidated balance sheet of the merged firm is obtained by combining the balance sheets of the separate firms (cf. *purchase accounting*).

Position diagram   Diagram showing the possible payoffs from a *derivative* investment.

Postaudit   Evaluation of an investment project after it has been undertaken.

Praecipium   Arrangement fee for *syndicated loan*.

Preemptive right   Common stockholder's right to anything of value distributed by the company.

Preferred stock   Stock that takes priority over common stock in regard to *dividends*. Dividends may not be paid on *common stock* unless the dividend is paid on all preferred stock (cf. *cumulative preferred stock*). The dividend rate on preferred is usually fixed at time of issue.

Prenegotiated bankruptcy   *Chapter 11* bankruptcy where only principal creditors have agreed to the reorganization plan before filing (cf. *prepackaged bankruptcy*).

Prepack   *Prepackaged bankruptcy.*

Prepackaged bankruptcy (prepack)   Bankruptcy proceedings intended to confirm a reorganization plan that has already been agreed to informally.

Present value   Discounted value of future cash flows.

Present value of growth opportunities (PVGO)   *Net present value* of investments the firm is expected to make in the future.

PRIDE   Similar to a *PERC* except that as the equity price rises beyond a specified point, the investor shares in the stock appreciation.

Primary issue   Issue of new securities by a firm (cf. *secondary issue*).

Prime rate   Benchmark lending rate set by U.S. banks.

Principal   Amount of debt that must be repaid.

Principal–agent problem   Problem faced by a principal (e.g., shareholder) in ensuring that an agent (e.g., manager) acts on his or her behalf.

Private equity   *Equity* that is not publicly traded and that is used to finance business start-ups, *leveraged buyouts*, etc.

Private placement   Issue of *bonds* or *stock* that is placed privately with a few investors and is not then publicly traded.

Privileged subscription issue   *Rights issue.*

Production payment   Loan in the form of advance payment for future delivery of a product.

Profitability index   Ratio of a project's *NPV* to the initial investment.

Pro forma   Projected.

Project finance   Debt that is largely a claim against the cash flows from a particular project rather than against the firm as a whole.

Project note (PN)   *Note* issued by public housing or urban renewal agencies.

Promissory note   Promise to pay.

Prospect theory   A theory of asset pricing suggested by the observation of behavioral psychologists that investors have a particular aversion to losses even if very small.

Prospectus   Summary of the *registration* statement providing information on an issue of securities.

Protective put   *Put option* that is combined with holding in the underlying asset.

Proxy vote   Vote cast by one person on behalf of another.

Public warehouse (terminal warehouse)   Warehouse operated by an independent warehouse company on its own premises (cf. *field warehouse*).

Purchase accounting   Method of accounting for *mergers*. The assets of the acquired firm are shown at market value on the balance sheet of the acquirer (cf. *pooling of interest*).

Purchase fund   Resembles a *sinking fund* except that money is used only to purchase bonds if they are selling below their *par value*.

Put–call parity   The relationship between the prices of European *put* and *call options*.

Put option   *Option* to sell an asset at a specified *exercise price* on or before a specified exercise date (cf. *call option*).

PVGO   *Present value of growth opportunities.*

Pyramid   Created by forming a *holding company* whose only asset is a controlling interest in a second holding company, which in turn has a controlling interest in an operating company.

Q

q   Ratio of the market value of an asset to its replacement cost.

QIBs   *Qualified institutional buyers.*

Quadratic programming   Variant of *linear programming* whereby the equations are quadratic rather than linear.

Qualified Institutional buyers (QIBs)   Institutions that are allowed to trade unregistered stock among themselves.

Quanto swap   *Differential swap.*

Quick ratio (acid-test ratio)   Measure of liquidity: (cash + marketable securities + *receivables*) divided by *current liabilities*.

R

Range forward   A *forward exchange rate* contract that places upper and lower bounds on the cost of foreign exchange.

Ratchet bonds   Floating-rate *bonds* whose coupon can only be reset downward.

Rate-sensitive bonds   *Bonds* whose coupon rate changes as issuer's credit rating changes.

Real assets   *Tangible assets* and *intangible assets* used to carry on business (cf. *financial assets*).

Real estate investment trust (REIT)   Trust company formed to invest in real estate.

Real interest rate   Interest rate expressed in terms of real goods, i.e., *nominal interest rate* adjusted for inflation.

Real option   The flexibility to modify, postpone, expand, or abandon a project.

Receivables   *Accounts receivable.*

Receiver   A bankruptcy practitioner appointed by secured creditors in the United Kingdom to oversee the repayment of debts.

Record date   Date set by directors when making dividend payment. *Dividends* are sent to stockholders who are registered on the record date.

Recourse   Term describing a type of loan. If a loan is with recourse, the lender has a general claim against the parent company if the *collateral* is insufficient to repay the debt.

Red herring   Preliminary *prospectus*.

Refunding   Replacement of existing debt with a new issue of debt.

Registered security   Security whose ownership is recorded by the company's *registrar* (cf. *bearer security*).

Registrar   Financial institution appointed to record issue and ownership of company securities.

Registration   Process of obtaining *SEC* approval for a public issue of securities.

Regression analysis   In statistics, a technique for finding the line of best fit.

Regular dividend   *Dividend* that the company expects to maintain in the future.

Regulation A issue   Small security issues that are partially exempt from *SEC registration* requirements.

REIT   *Real estate investment trust.*

Rental lease   *Full-service lease.*

Replicating portfolio   Package of assets whose returns exactly replicate those of an *option*.

Repo   *Repurchase agreement.*

Repurchase agreement (RP, repo, buyback)   Purchase of Treasury securities from a securities dealer with an agreement that the dealer will repurchase them at a specified price.

Residual income   After-tax profit less the *opportunity cost of capital* employed by the business (cf. *economic value added*).

Residual risk   *Specific risk.*

Retained earnings   Earnings not paid out as *dividends*.

Return on equity   Usually, equity earnings as a proportion of the book value of equity.

Return on investment (ROI)   Generally, book income as a proportion of net book value.

Revenue bond   Municipal *bond* that is serviced out of the revenues from a particular project.

Reverse convertible   *Bond* that gives the issuer the right to convert it into *common stock*.

Reverse FRN (yield curve note)   *Floating-rate note* whose payments rise as the general level of interest rates falls and vice versa.

Reverse split   Action by the company to reduce the number of outstanding shares by replacing two or more of its shares with a single, more valuable share.

Revolving credit   Legally assured *line of credit* with a bank.

Rights issue (privileged subscription issue)   Issue of securities offered to current stockholders (cf. *general cash offer*).

Rights on   *With rights.*

Risk premium   Expected additional return for making a risky investment rather than a safe one.

Road show   Series of meetings between a company and potential investors before the company decides on the terms of a new issue.

ROI   *Return on investment.*

Roll-over CD   A package of successive *certificates of deposit.*

Round lot   A trade of 100 shares (cf. *odd lot*).

RP   *Repurchase agreement.*

R squared (R^2)   Square of the *correlation coefficient*—the proportion of the variability in one series that can be explained by the variability of one or more other series.

Rule 144a   *SEC* rule allowing *qualified institutional buyers* to buy and trade unregistered securities.

S

Sale and lease-back   Sale of an existing asset to a financial institution that then *leases* it back to the user (cf. *direct lease*).

Salvage value   Scrap or resale value of plant and equipment.

Samurai bond   A yen *bond* issued in Tokyo by a non-Japanese borrower (cf. *bulldog bond, Yankee bond*).

SBIC   Small Business Investment Company.

Scenario analysis   Analysis of the profitability of a project under alternative economic scenarios.

Season datings   Extended credit for customers who order goods out of the peak season.

Seasoned issue   Issue of a security for which there is an existing market (cf. *unseasoned issue*).

SEC   Securities and Exchange Commission.

Secondary issue   (1) Procedure for selling blocks of *seasoned issues* of stock; (2) more generally, sale of already issued stock.

Secondary market   Market in which one can buy or sell *seasoned issues* of securities.

Secured debt   Debt that, in the event of default, has first claim on specified assets.

Securitization   Substitution of tradable securities for privately negotiated instruments.

Security market line   Line representing the relationship between *expected return* and *market risk*.

Self-liquidating loan   Loan to finance *current assets*. The sale of the current assets provides the cash to repay the loan.

Self-selection   Consequence of a contract that induces only one group (e.g., low-risk individuals) to participate.

Semistrong-form efficient market   Market in which security prices reflect all publicly available information (cf. *weak-form efficient market* and *strong-form efficient market*).

Senior debt   Debt that, in the event of bankruptcy, must be repaid before *subordinated debt* receives any payment.

Sensitivity analysis   Analysis of the effect on project profitability of possible changes in sales, costs, and so on.

Serial bonds   Package of *bonds* that mature in successive years.

Series bond   *Bond* that may be issued in several series under the same *indenture.*

Shark repellant   Amendment to company charter intended to protect against takeover.

Sharpe ratio   Ratio of portfolio's *risk premium* to its risk (*standard deviation*).

Shelf registration   A procedure that allows firms to file one *registration* statement covering several issues of the same security.

Shogun bond   Dollar *bond* issued in Japan by a nonresident.

Short hedge   Sale of a *hedging* instrument (e.g., a *future*) to hedge a long position in the underlying asset (cf. *long hedge*).

Short sale   Sale of a security the investor does not own.

Sight draft   Demand for immediate payment (cf. *time draft*).

Signal   Action that demonstrates an individual's unobservable characteristics (because it would be unduly costly for someone without those characteristics to take the action).

Simple interest   Interest calculated only on the initial investment (cf. *compound interest*).

Simulation   *Monte Carlo simulation.*

Sinker   *Sinking fund.*

Sinking fund (sinker)   Fund established by a company to retire debt before maturity.

SIV (structured investment vehicle)   A fund that typically invested in mortgage-backed securities, which it financed by issuing senior and junior *tranches* of *asset-backed commercial paper* and longer-term *notes.*

Skewed distribution   Probability distribution in which an unequal number of observations lie below and above the mean.

SPE   *Special-purpose entity.*

Special dividend (extra dividend)   *Dividend* that is unlikely to be repeated.

Specialist   *Designated market maker.*

Special-purpose entity   *Partnerships* established by companies to hold certain assets and obtain funding. May be used to obtain off-balance-sheet debt for the parent.

Specific risk (residual risk, unique risk, unsystematic risk)   Risk that can be eliminated by diversification.

Spinning The *underwriter* of an *IPO* unethically allots a portion of offering to senior management of a client company.

Spin-off Distribution of shares in a subsidiary to the company's shareholders so that they hold shares separately in the two firms.

Spot exchange rate Exchange rate on currency for immediate delivery (cf. *forward exchange rate*).

Spot price Price of asset for immediate delivery (in contrast to forward or futures price).

Spot rate Interest rate fixed today on a loan that is made today (cf. *forward interest rate*).

Spread Difference between the price at which an *underwriter* buys an issue from a firm and the price at which the underwriter sells it to the public.

Staggered board Board whose directors are elected periodically, instead of at one time.

Standard deviation Square root of the *variance*—a measure of variability.

Standard error In statistics, a measure of the possible error in an estimate.

Standby agreement In a *rights issue*, agreement that the *underwriter* will purchase any stock not purchased by investors.

Step-up bond *Bond* whose *coupon* is stepped up over time (also step-down bond).

Stock dividend *Dividend* in the form of stock rather than cash.

Stock split "Free" issue of shares to existing shareholders.

Straddle The combination of a *put option* and a *call option* with the same *exercise price*.

Straight-line depreciation An equal dollar amount of *depreciation* in each period.

Strike price *Exercise price* of an *option*.

Stripped bond (strip) *Bond* that is subdivided into a series of *zero-coupon bonds*.

Strong-form efficient market Market in which security prices reflect instantaneously all information available to investors (cf. *weak-form efficient market* and *semistrong-form efficient market*).

Structured debt Debt that has been customized for the buyer, often by incorporating unusual *options*.

Subordinated debt (junior debt) Debt over which *senior debt* takes priority. In the event of bankruptcy, subordinated debtholders receive payment only after senior debt is paid off in full.

Subprime loans The most risky category of loans.

Sum-of-the-years'-digits depreciation Method of *accelerated depreciation*.

Sunk costs Costs that have been incurred and cannot be reversed.

Supermajority Provision in a company's charter requiring a majority of, say, 80% of shareholders to approve certain changes, such as a *merger*.

Sushi bond A *eurobond* issued by a Japanese corporation.

Sustainable growth rate Maximum rate of firm growth without increasing financial leverage (cf. *internal growth rate*).

Swap An arrangement whereby two companies lend to each other on different terms, e.g., in different currencies, or one at a fixed rate and the other at a floating rate.

Swaption *Option* on a *swap*.

Sweep program Arrangement whereby bank invests a company's available cash at the end of each day.

Swingline facility Bank borrowing facility to provide finance while the firm replaces U.S. *commercial paper* with eurocommercial paper.

Syndicated loan A large loan provided by a group of banks.

Systematic risk *Market risk*.

T

Take-or-pay In *project finance*, arrangement where parent company agrees to pay for output of project even if it chooses not to take delivery.

Take-up fee Fee paid to *underwriters* of a *rights issue* on any stock they are obliged to purchase.

Tangent efficient portfolio The portfolio of risky assets offering the highest risk premium per unit of risk (*standard deviation*).

Tangible asset Physical asset, such as plant, machinery, and offices (cf. *intangible asset*).

Tax-anticipation bill Short-term bill issued by the U.S. Treasury that can be surrendered at *face value* in payment of taxes.

T-bill *Treasury bill*.

Technical analysis Security analysis that seeks to detect and interpret patterns in past security prices (cf. *fundamental analysis*).

TED spread Difference between *LIBOR* and U.S. *Treasury bill* rate.

Tender offer General offer made directly to a firm's shareholders to buy their stock.

10-K Annual financial statements as filed with the *SEC*.

Tenor Maturity of a loan.

10-Q   Quarterly financial statements as filed with the *SEC*.

Terminal warehouse   *Public warehouse.*

Term loan   Medium-term, privately placed loan, usually made by a bank.

Term structure of interest rates   Relationship between interest rates on loans of different maturities (cf. *yield curve*).

Throughput arrangement   Arrangement by which shareholders of a pipeline company agree to make sufficient use of pipeline to enable the pipeline company to service its debt.

Tick   Minimum amount the price of a security may change.

Time draft   Demand for payment at a stated future date (cf. *sight draft*).

Times-interest-earned (interest cover)   Earnings before interest and tax, divided by interest payments.

TIPS (Treasury Inflation Protected Securities)   U.S. Treasury *bonds* whose *coupon* and *principal* payments are linked to the Consumer Price Index.

Toehold   Small investment by a company in the shares of a potential takeover target.

Tolling contract   In *project finance*, arrangement whereby parent company promises to deliver materials to project for processing and then to repurchase them.

Tombstone   Advertisement listing the *underwriters* to a security issue.

Trade acceptance   Written demand that has been accepted by an industrial company to pay a given sum at a future date (cf. *banker's acceptance*).

Trade credit   *Accounts receivable.*

Trade debt   *Accounts payable.*

Tranche   Portion of a new issue sold at a point in time different from the remainder or that has different terms.

Transaction exposure   Risk to a firm with known future cash flows in a foreign currency that arises from possible changes in the exchange rate (cf. *economic exposure, translation exposure*).

Transfer agent   Individual or institution appointed by a company to look after the transfer of securities.

Translation exposure   Risk of adverse effects on a firm's financial statements that may arise from changes in exchange rates (cf. *economic exposure, transaction exposure*).

Treasurer   Principal financial manager (cf. *controller*).

Treasury bill (T-bill)   Short-term discount debt maturing in less than one year, issued regularly by the government.

Treasury stock   *Common stock* that has been repurchased by the company and held in the company's treasury.

Trust deed   Agreement between trustee and borrower setting out terms of a *bond*.

Trust receipt   Receipt for goods that are to be held in trust for the lender.

Tunneling   Actions by a controlling shareholder to transfer wealth out of the firm (e.g., by supplying goods at an inflated price).

U

Underpricing   Issue of securities below their market value.

Underwriter   Firm that buys an issue of securities from a company and resells it to investors.

Unfunded debt   Debt maturing within one year (cf. *funded debt*).

Uniform price auction   Auction in which all successful bidders pay the same price (cf. *discriminatory price auction*).

Unique risk   *Specific risk.*

Unseasoned issue   Issue of a security for which there is no existing market (cf. *seasoned issue*).

Unsystematic risk   *Specific risk.*

V

Value additivity   Rule that the value of the whole must equal the sum of the values of the parts.

Value at risk (VAR)   The probability of portfolio losses exceeding some specified proportion.

Value stock   A stock that is expected to provide steady income but relatively low growth (often refers to stocks with a low ratio of market-to-book value).

Vanilla issue   Issue without unusual features.

VAR   *Value at risk.*

Variable-rate demand bond (VRDB)   Floating-rate *bond* that can be sold back periodically to the issuer.

Variance   Mean squared deviation from the expected value; a measure of variability.

Variation margin   The daily gains or losses on a *futures contract* credited to the investor's margin account.

Vega   A measure of how the *option* price changes as the asset's volatility changes.

Venture capital   Capital to finance a new firm.

Vertical merger   *Merger* between a supplier and its customer (cf. *horizontal merger, conglomerate merger*).

Vertical spread   Simultaneous purchase and sale of two options that differ only in their *exercise price* (cf. *horizontal spread*).

VIX   A measure of the *implied volatility* of stocks in the S&P 500 Index.

VRDB   *Variable-rate demand bond.*

W

WACC   *Weighted-average cost of capital.*

Warehouse receipt   Evidence that a firm owns goods stored in a warehouse.

Warrant   Long-term *call option* issued by a company.

Weak-form efficient market   Market in which security prices instantaneously reflect the information in the history of security prices. In such a market security prices follow a random walk (cf. *semistrong-form efficient market* and *strong-form efficient market*).

Weighted-average cost of capital (WACC)   *Expected return* on a portfolio of all the firm's securities. Used as *hurdle rate* for capital investment.

White knight   A friendly potential acquirer sought out by a target company threatened by a less welcome suitor.

Wi.   When issued.

Winner's curse   Problem faced by uninformed bidders. For example, in an *initial public offering* uninformed participants are likely to receive larger allotments of issues that informed participants know are overpriced.

With dividend (cum dividend)   Purchase of shares in which the buyer is entitled to the forthcoming *dividend* (cf. *ex dividend*).

Withholding tax   Tax levied on *dividends* paid abroad.

With rights (cum rights, rights on)   Purchase of shares in which the buyer is entitled to the rights to buy shares in the company's *rights issue* (cf. *ex rights*).

Working capital   *Current assets* and *current liabilities*. The term is commonly used as synonymous with *net working capital*.

Workout   Informal arrangement between a borrower and creditors.

Writer   *Option* seller.

X

xd   *Ex dividend.*

xr   *Ex rights.*

Y

Yankee bond   A dollar *bond* issued in the United States by a non-U.S. borrower (cf. *bulldog bond, Samurai bond*).

Yield curve   *Term structure of interest rates.*

Yield curve note   *Reverse FRN.*

Yield to maturity   *Internal rate of return* on a bond.

Z

Zero-coupon bond   *Discount bond* making no *coupon* payments.

Z-score   Measure of the likelihood of bankruptcy.

Index

SOME USEFUL FORMULAS

(The section number indicates the principal reference in the text.)

Perpetuity (2-2)

The value of a perpetuity of $1 per year is:

$$PV = \frac{1}{r}$$

Annuity (2-2)

The value of an annuity of $1 per period for t years (t-year annuity factor) is:

$$PV = \frac{1}{r} - \frac{1}{r(1 + r)^t}$$

A Growing Perpetuity (the "Gordon" model) (2-3)

If the first period's cash flow is $1 at year 1 and if cash flows thereafter grow at a constant rate of g in perpetuity,

$$PV = \frac{1}{r - g}$$

A Growing Annuity (2-3)

If the first period's cash flow is $1 at year 1 and if the cash flow grows at a constant rate of g for t years,

$$PV = \frac{1}{r - g} - \frac{1}{r - g} \times \frac{(1 + g)^t}{(1 + r)^t}$$

Continuous Compounding (2-4)

If r is the continuously compounded rate of interest, the present value of $1 received in year t is:

$$PV = \frac{1}{e^{rt}}$$

Bond Duration and Volatility (3-2)

$$\text{Duration of T-period bond} = \frac{\sum_{t=1}^{T} t \times C_t/(1 + y)^t}{\sum_{t=1}^{T} C_t/(1 + y)^t}$$

$$\text{Volatility (modified duration)} = \text{Duration}/(1 + y)$$

Equivalent Annual Cost (6-4)

If an asset has a life of t years, the equivalent annual cost is:

$$\frac{PV \text{ (costs)}}{t\text{-year annuity factor}}$$

Measures of Risk (7-2 to 7-4)

$$\text{Variance of returns} = \sigma^2 = \text{expected value of } (\tilde{r} - r)^2$$

$$\text{Standard deviation of returns} = \sqrt{\text{variance}} = \sigma$$

Covariance between returns of stocks 1 and 2

$$= \sigma_{12} = \text{expected value of } [(\tilde{r}_1 - r_1)(\tilde{r}_2 - r_2)]$$

Correlation between returns of stocks 1 and 2:

$$\rho_{12} = \frac{\sigma_{12}}{\sigma_1 \sigma_2}$$

$$\text{Beta of stock } i = \beta_i = \frac{\sigma_{im}}{\sigma_m^2}$$

The variance of returns on a portfolio with proportion x_i invested in stock i is:

$$\sum_{i=1}^{N} \sum_{j=1}^{N} x_i x_j \sigma_{ij}$$